ORACLE DATAI

ORACLE DATABASE 12c
Hands-on SQL and PL/SQL

SECOND EDITION

SATISH ASNANI

Senior Manager
Informatics Division
ITS (Information Technology Services)
BHEL, Piplani
Bhopal

PHI Learning Private Limited

Delhi-110092
2016

₹ 425.00

ORACLE DATABASE 12c: Hands-on SQL and PL/SQL, Second Edition
Satish Asnani

ISBN-978-81-203-5151-6

The export rights of this book are vested solely with the publisher.

Second Printing (Second Edition)   …   …   …   **November, 2015**

Published by Asoke K. Ghosh, PHI Learning Private Limited, Rimjhim House, 111, Patparganj Industrial Estate, Delhi-110092 and Printed by Raj Press, New Delhi-110012.

Contents

20 STORED FUNCTIONS

21 STORED PROCEDURES

Preface

Oracle database is one of the most popular relational database systems being used worldwide and can be used to develop applications ranging from small single user systems to applications supporting thousands of concurrent users. I have been an Oracle admirer from the early versions like 7.3, 8.0, 9i, 10g, 11g and now 12c.

Oracle database 12c is a cloud oriented technology and introduces a new concept of pluggable databases. This new edition of the book covers the detailed introspection of pluggable databases and explains practically the various new features incorporated in the new 12c version. With each new release, Oracle has come out with several new features which have enhanced the database management systems applicability in different scenarios.

I have been developing applications using Oracle database for more than eight years now, and it took me several years for exploring the various functionalities/features incorporated by Oracle Corporation with each new release. I have read numerous books on Oracle database, but I could not figure out a single book which could teach Oracle right from the very basic concepts to the advanced techniques in a practical way. The books are either too complicated for the beginners or too simplified from the professional programmer's perspective. This inspired me to produce a book which will begin teaching from a beginner perspective to the expert level for professionals working on real business applications. It will help an individual to migrate from novice to expert level in a short span of time. Each and every command has been explicitly displayed in boxes, and the results too have been shown so as to foster clear and precise understanding of the topics. The examples have been drawn from the long experience of designing, developing and implementing business applications using Oracle Database.

The book is distinctively different from the other books available in the market in following respects:

1. **Based on latest Oracle Database 12c:**   This new edition of the book explains the various features introduced with the new Oracle Database 12c software.

2. **Hands-on methodology:**   The basic objective has been to impart practical skills using hands-on methodology. All commands have been clearly placed in boxes along with the results. Emphasis is on learning by doing.

3. **Elaborate Practical Examples:**   Each topic begins with appropriate theory and concept followed by relevant examples for better understanding of the concepts. The individual will gain requisite knowledge and skills by following the practical examples.

4. **The examples have been drawn from the long-term experience** in designing, developing and implementing business applications using Oracle Database. "The most complicated theoretical concepts can be easily understood by simplest examples" has been the philosophy of the book.

5. **Commands tested and executed on Oracle Database software:**   All the programming examples have been tested on actual Oracle Database software, and the results have also been shown so as to foster clear and precise understanding of the concepts.

Feedback/suggestions are welcome and you can reach me at asnanisatish@gmail.com.

At the end of the book, an individual will possess sufficient knowledge and skills to develop various commercial applications using Oracle Database.

Intended Audience

The book is intended for beginning, intermediate and advanced oracle application developers. Topics begin from very basic concepts to advanced programming techniques in a practical way.

The students of BE/BTech/MCA/MSc/PGDCA/DCA will find it very useful for doing practical assignments based on RDBMS package like Oracle and will be able to develop professional applications after reading the book. Many of the universities have incorporated lab assignments on Oracle Database as part of their curriculum, and the book imparts all the requisite skills for practical Database application development.

The book can be used as a reference by professionals already working on business applications. The lecturers and professors in the field of DBMS and RDBMS can teach practical aspects of Database programming with precise and thorough understanding of theoretical concepts along with examples. Individuals aspiring for Oracle Certified Courses will find it a valuable resource for achieving the certification.

Satish Asnani

Acknowledgements

I would like to acknowledge each and every individual who has contributed in producing the book. It had been a pleasure working with PHI Learning who gave me the opportunity of sharing the knowledge and expertise that I have gained through the years of my working on professional business applications. I would like to thank the PHI team Babita Mishra, Pushpita Ghosh, Shivani and Laxmi, who consistently worked along with me to produce an excellent book. The book has been a result of the relentless hours of working, and I do hope that you will find this book extremely useful.

My family had been the source of inspiration and it was because of their encouragement and support that I have been able to complete this book. Their invaluable feedback and suggestions were the foundation stones for my work.

Bharat Heavy Electricals Limited (BHEL)—a Navratna company has given me a platform for understanding the various business requirements and has provided me several opportunities for developing and enhancing my skills. I would like to convey my regards to my seniors who always had faith and confidence in me and gave me challenging jobs. Thanks to my colleagues who used to refer typical programming problems/challenges and helped me in further enhancing my knowledge and skills.

This book represents many hours of work on the part of several people and we hope that you will enjoy reading this book and that it will help you in mastering Oracle database.

Satish Asnani

1

Introduction to DBMS and RDBMS

1.1 WHAT IS DATABASE?

A database is a collection of related information that is organized so that it can easily be accessed, managed, and updated. The most suitable example is the telephone directory. The entire telephone directory may be considered as a single FILE containing list of all citizens having telephone numbers. This FILE contains various information about each registered number like Name, Address and Telephone Number as shown in Table 1.1.

TABLE 1.1 Telephone directory (FILE as database)

Name	Address	Telephone no.
Anil Mehra	243, 9-B, Saket Nagar, Bhopal, MP	4289528
Rishi Arora	16-C, Sagar Avenue, Bhopal	3423456
Satish Asnani	28, 9-B, Kotra, Bhopal	5673455

1.2 PHYSICAL FILE AS DATABASE

- A field is a single piece of information (e.g. name, address, telephone no.).
- A record is one complete set of fields (each record represents a registered telephone no.).
- A file is a collection of records.

Synonyms

In database terminologies certain words are used interchangeably as indicated in Table 1.2.

TABLE 1.2   Synonyms in database terminology

Name	Alternative names
Table	Relation
Field	Column, Attribute, Characteristic
Record	Row, Tuple, Entity

1.3   DRAWBACKS OF PHYSICALLY MAINTAINED DATABASE (TELEPHONE DIRECTORY)

- **Searching is difficult and limited in scope:**   The problem with Printed Directory is that searching is quite difficult and reverse searching is not possible, i.e. is we cannot find the name and address for a known telephone no. It is a one-way organization wherein we can only search the telephone number in the order of Name and Address. What if we want to know all individuals who reside in a particular colony, say "Saket"? It is just not possible through the Printed Directory.

- **Dynamic updation of changes not possible:**   New telephones get registered and old ones disconnected every few days. It is not possible to present the day-to-day changes in the already distributed hardbound telephone directories.

- **Sharing of information:**   The same telephone directory cannot be accessed simultaneously by more than one individual.

- **Chances of errors:**   Files as database are prone to typing errors. The same telephone number may be assigned to more than one individual due to typographic or human errors.

- **Security of data:**   As far as telephone directory is concerned, it is meant for public use and may not require much of security. But databases like bank, hospital, insurance, e-mail accounts require a very secure environment demanding complicated authorization mechanisms as to "who can access what". Providing requisite information to the intended user depending on authorization level is something which is not feasible through files.

1.4   DATABASE MANAGEMENT SYSTEM: (DBMS)

Database Management System may be defined as a computerized record-keeping system— one which provides facility for creating new records, modifying and deleting the existing records. **DBMS is a collection of interrelated data and set of programs to access this data.** Access means **storing, retrieving and manipulating data in the form of tables.** A table may be defined as a collection of rows, columns and each intersection of a row and column contains the specific data. For example, a Student table will contain related data like Roll no., Name, Address, Marks, etc. In this table each record will represent a student. Each student is known as an ENTITY as it has physical existence.

1.4.1   Advantages of DBMS

Ease of searching

Finding records by desired criteria like name or address or may be just a few words of the name/address is possible with minimal effort.

Manageability

The various changes like registration of new telephone numbers, cancellation of existing numbers and change in name or address can be easily accomplished using the DBMS software.

Sharing of information

The same data can be shared simultaneously between several users with a single copy of the entire database file.

Data integrity and redundancy

In manual system it is quite possible that the same information is typed twice. Say, a single telephone number may get recorded twice. This is called redundancy and duplication of information. By using the capabilities of DBMS we can restrict such errors so that the information is correct and accurate to the greatest possible extent.

Security of data

The basic advantage of using DBMS is the security of information. Many of us use e-mail services which require us to enter e-mail id and password. This mechanism helps in securing our personal mails from other people. DBMS provide greater control on what others can see or change in our information.

Data independence

One of the major advantages of DBMS is that the actual data (in the form of tables) are separated from the programs which operate on that data. This provides the flexibility of using any of the known languages (SQL, C, C++ and Java) for storing, retrieving and manipulating data.

1.4.2   Popular DBMS Applications

The most popular DBMS applications are:

1. Railway Reservation System
2. Library Management System
3. Hospital Management System

1.5   RELATIONAL DATABASE MANAGEMENT SYSTEMS (RDBMS)

DBMS store data in the form of tables. RDBMS are a type of DBMS which store data in the form of tables and relationship can be established between different tables in the form of tables only. Moreover, they are capable of storing information about the tables like number of columns, data type of columns in the form of tables.

1.5.1   Differences between DBMS and RDBMS

The differences between DBMS and RDBMS are enumerated in Table 1.3.

TABLE 1.3   DBMS versus RDBMS

Concept	DBMS	RDBMS
Relation between tables	Maintained programmatically.	Relation between tables is stored in database itself in the form of tables only.
Multi-user	Generally do not support multiple users simultaneously accessing the same files.	RDBMS are multi-user systems.
Security of data	Not supported.	Multiple levels of security.
Table storage	Each table is stored as a single file with predefined extension.	All tables may be of different users are stored in single or multiple database files.
Access to database files	Users can directly access the stored files.	Users have no access to low-level database files.
Distributed database	Not supported.	Supported.
Abstract view	Generally do not support abstract views derived from base tables.	Abstract views are supported.
Codd's 12 rules	Satisfy less than 8 of Codd's 12 rules.	Satisfy 8 or more of Codd's 12 rules.

1.5.2   E.F. Codd's 12 Rules for RDBMS

E.F. Codd suggested 12 rules as the basis for determining whether a DBMS could be classified as Relational. Table 1.4 contains the list of 12 rules.

Information: Edgar Frank "Ted" Codd (August 23, 1923–April 18, 2003) was a British computer scientist who, while working for IBM, invented the relational model for database management, the theoretical basis for relational databases. He made other valuable contributions to computer science, but the relational model, a very influential general theory of data management, remains his most memorable achievement.

E.F. Codd 12 Rules are as follows:

TABLE 1.4   E.F. Codd's 12 rules for an RDBMS

Codd's rule	Rule name	Description	Oracle complies or not
1	The Information Rule	All data should be presented in the form of table (as collection of rows and columns with cells containing the specified data).	Yes
2	Guaranteed Access Rule	Each data must be accessible by combination of table name, primary key of row and column name.	Yes

(Contd.)

TABLE 1.4 E.F. Codd's 12 rules for an RDBMS *(Contd.)*

Codd's rule	Rule name	Description	Oracle complies or not
3	**Systematic Treatment of NULL Values**	A fully relational database system must offer a systematic way to handle missing information. Null is always treated as unknown. Null means no value or the absence of a value. Null is not the same as an empty string or 0. Each value, Null included, compared with Null, is Null.	**Yes**
4	**Dynamic On-line Catalog based on the Relational Model**	In addition to user-defined data, a relational database also contains data about itself. So there are two kinds of tables, namely user-defined and system-defined. Metadata is the data which describe the structure of the database, its objects and how they are related and stored in the system-defined tables. This catalog is an integral part of the database and can be queried by authorized users just like any other table. Another name for this online catalog is system catalog or data dictionary.	**Yes**
5	**Comprehensive Data Sublanguage Rule**	RDBMS may support many languages and modes of use, but there must be at least ONE language whose statements can express ALL of the following: Data Definition, View Definition, Data Manipulation, Integrity Constraints, Authorization and Transaction Boundaries.	**Yes**
6	**View Updating**	When presenting data to the user, a relational database should not be limited to tables. Views are 'virtual tables' or abstractions of the source tables. They react like tables with the one exception that they are dynamically created when the query is executed. Defining a view does not duplicate data. They are current at runtime. All theoretically updateable views should be updateable by the system. If data is changed in a view, it should also be changed in the underlying table. Updateable views are not always possible.	**Partially (Not supported by any RDBMS)**
7	**High-level insert, Update and Delete**	Capability of handling a base table or view as a single operand applies not only to data retrieval but also to insert, update and delete operations.	**Yes**

(Contd.)

TABLE 1.4   E.F. Codd's 12 rules for an RDBMS *(Contd.)*

Codd's rule	Rule name	Description	Oracle complies or not
8	**Physical Data Independence**	A DBMS is architecturally organized at 4 layers, namely physical, logical, user and abstract. The user is isolated from the physical method of storing and retrieving information from the database and interacts with the logical layer only. Rule 8 implies the changes can be made to the underlying architecture (hardware, disk storage methods) without affecting how the user accesses it.	**Partially**
9	**Logical Data Independence**	Users and applications are to a certain degree independent of the logical structure of a database. The logical structure can be modified without redeveloping the database and/or the application.	**Yes**
10	**Integrity Independence**	To be viewed as a relational database the RDBMS must implement data integrity as an internal part of the database. This is not the job of the application. Data integrity enforces consistence and correctness of the data in the database. Changes to integrity constraints should not have an affect on applications, in other words, constraints should not be applied through application but rather stored directly into the database engine itself. This simplifies applications, but is not always possible.	**Yes**
11	**Distribution Independence**	A user should be totally unaware of whether or not the database is distributed (whether parts of the database exist in multiple locations).	**Partially**
12	**Non-subversion Rule**	If the RDBMS supports a low-level (single record at a time) language, this low-level language should not be used to bypass and/or subvert data integrity that are expressed in the high-level (multiple records at a time) relational language.	**Yes**

Codd's 12 rules are very difficult to implement by any DBMS and therefore experts prefer to call any DBMS as RDBMS software if it satisfies 8 or more of the Codd's Rules. Oracle is one of the most popular RDBMS which complies with 9 of the above 12 rules and partially satisfies the remaining 3. Rule 6 is not satisfied by any available RDBMS, whereas Oracle has provided INSTEAD OF triggers for handling the same. Moreover, Oracle supports Rule 9 to a great extent by providing a feature called synonyms.

1.5.3 Popular RDBMS Available in Market

The most popular RDBMS available in the market are the following:

1. Oracle Database from Oracle Corporation
2. SQL Server from Microsoft
3. DB2 from IBM
4. Sybase
5. Ingress
6. MS Access
7. MySQL
8. PostgreSQL

REVIEW QUESTIONS

1. What is database? Explain the use of database.
2. What are the distinguishing features of a DBMS? List out the differences between DBMS and RDBMS.
3. What are Codd's Rules? What significance do these rules have in the relational model concept?
4. Define the following terms in brief
   (a) Table
   (b) Entity
   (c) Attribute

Installation of Oracle 10*g* XE (Express Edition)

The Oracle database 10g XE (Express Edition) for Windows can be downloaded from the Oracle website

http://www.oracle.com/technology/software/products/database/xe/index.html

2.1 PRE-REQUISITES FOR INSTALLATION OF ORACLE XE DATABASE

The minimum hardware and Operating System requirements are specified in Table 2.1.

TABLE 2.1 Pre-requisites for installing Oracle XE

Requirement	Value
System architecture	Intel (x86)
Operating system	One of the following 32-bit Windows operating systems: ● Windows 2000 Service Pack 4 or later ● Windows Server 2003 ● Windows XP Professional Service Pack 1 or later
Disk space	1.6 GB minimum
RAM	256 MB minimum, 512 MB recommended

Information: The Oracle database 10g Express Edition (Oracle Database XE) is a no-frills edition of the proven Oracle Database 10g product. It is completely free of charge, and may be installed on any size machine, supporting up to 4 GB of user data and running on a single processor, using a maximum of 1GB memory. Database administration is done via browser interface and applications can be developed using standard interfaces such as SQL, JDBC, ODP.NET, or using Oracle's unique Application Express feature.

2.2   INSTALLING ORACLE DATABASE 10g EXPRESS EDITION

Double click "OracleXE.exe" and "Installation Wizard" of Figure 2.1 will appear on the screen.

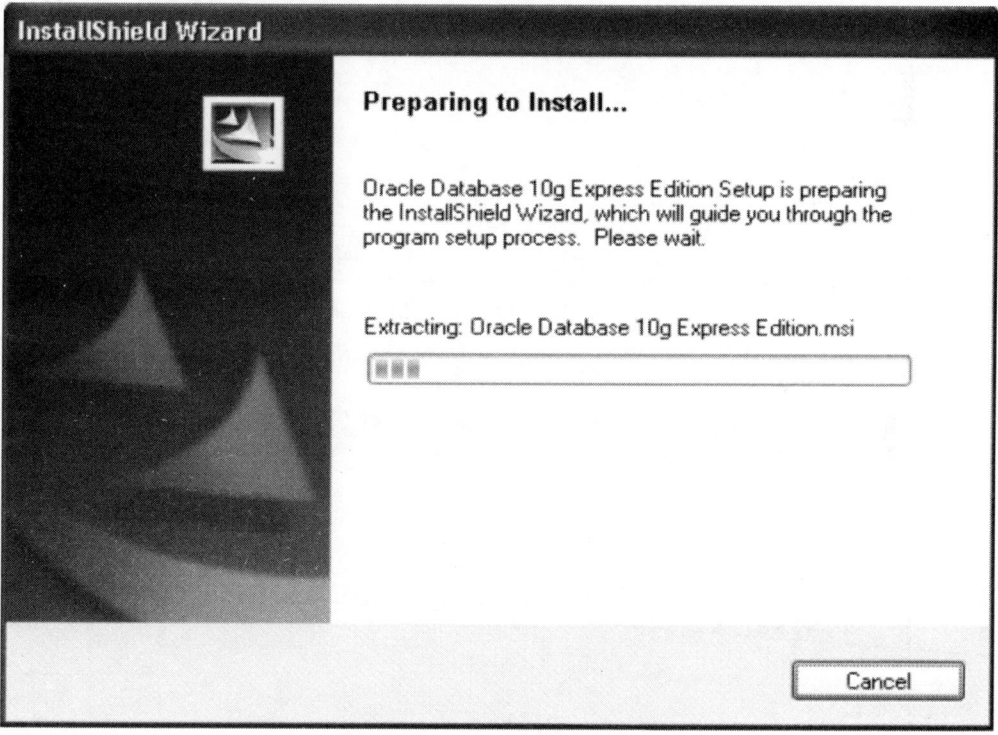

Figure 2.1   Installation Wizard.

After a few seconds Figure 2.2 will appear on the screen. Click "Next".

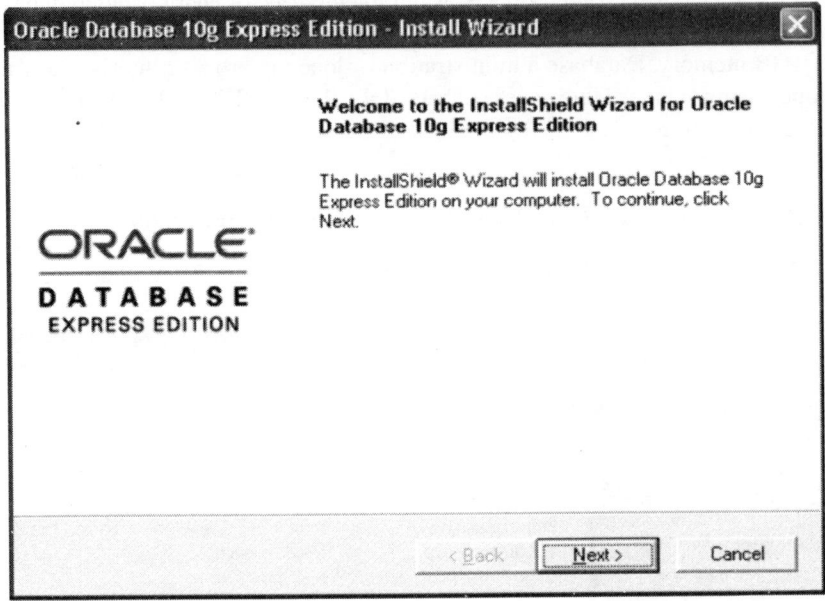

Figure 2.2 Continue installation.

Accept the Terms and Conditions as shown in Figure 2.3 and click "Next".

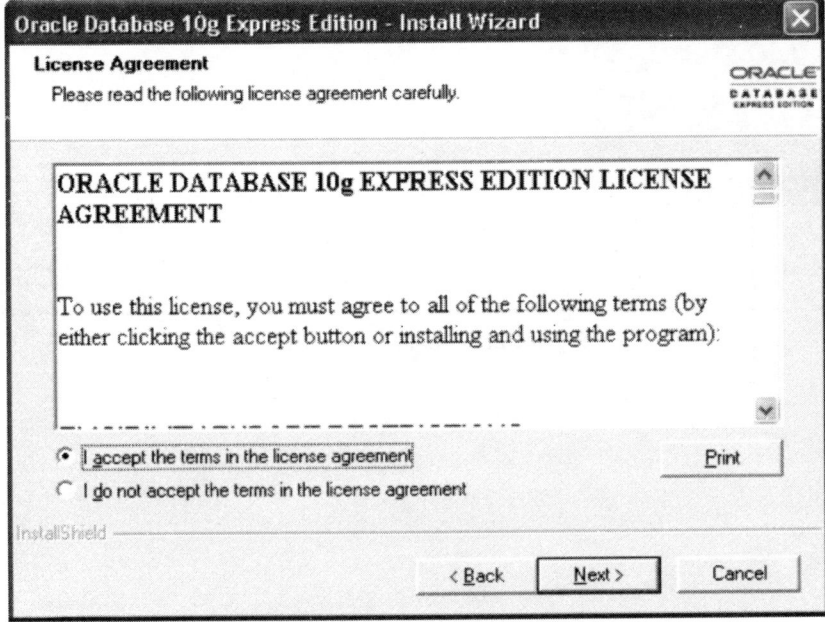

Figure 2.3 License agreement.

The Oracle10g Express Edition is by default installed in c:\oraclexe folder. You can specify any other location and click "Next" as indicated in Figure 2.4.

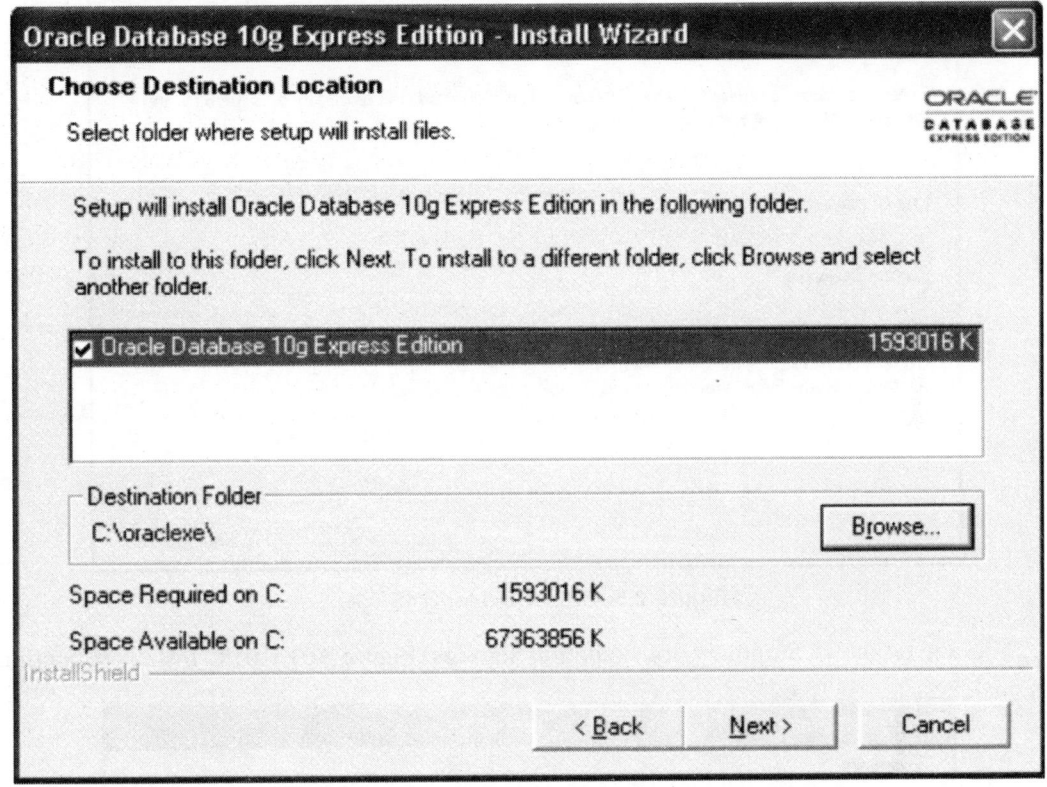

Figure 2.4   Destination folder for installation.

2.2.1   Assigning a Password to the "sys" User

Next you will be prompted for password for "sys" Oracle user as shown in Figure 2.5. Enter "sys" as the password and click "Next". You may specify any password of your choice but remember the password as we will be using it extensively in the subsequent chapters.

Caution: Remember the password. It is extremely difficult to recover the lost password and you may have to reinstall the Oracle database software.

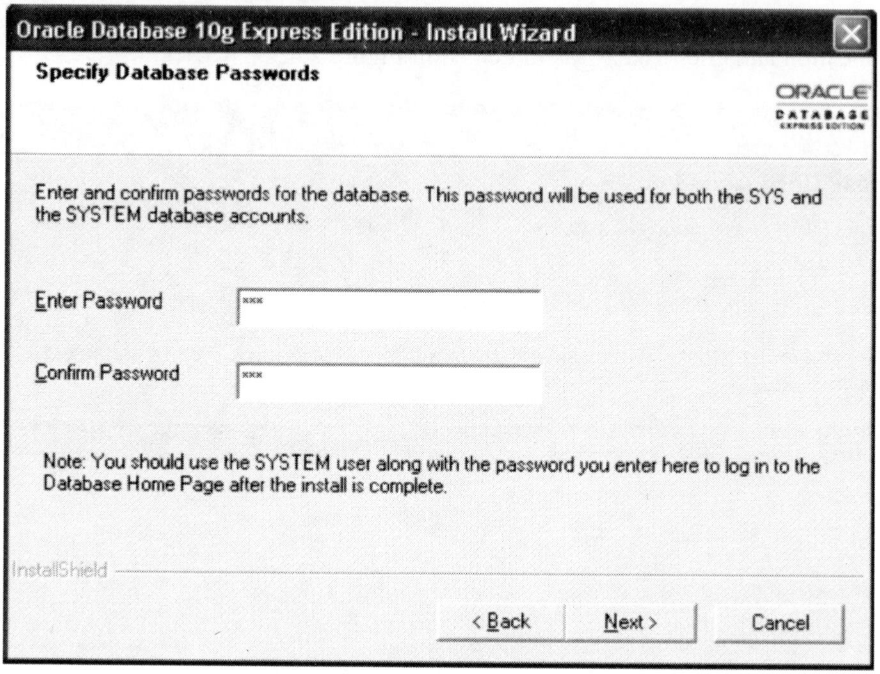

Figure 2.5   Password for SYS user.

You will be shown Summary of Installation Settings (Figure 2.6). Click "Install" to continue.

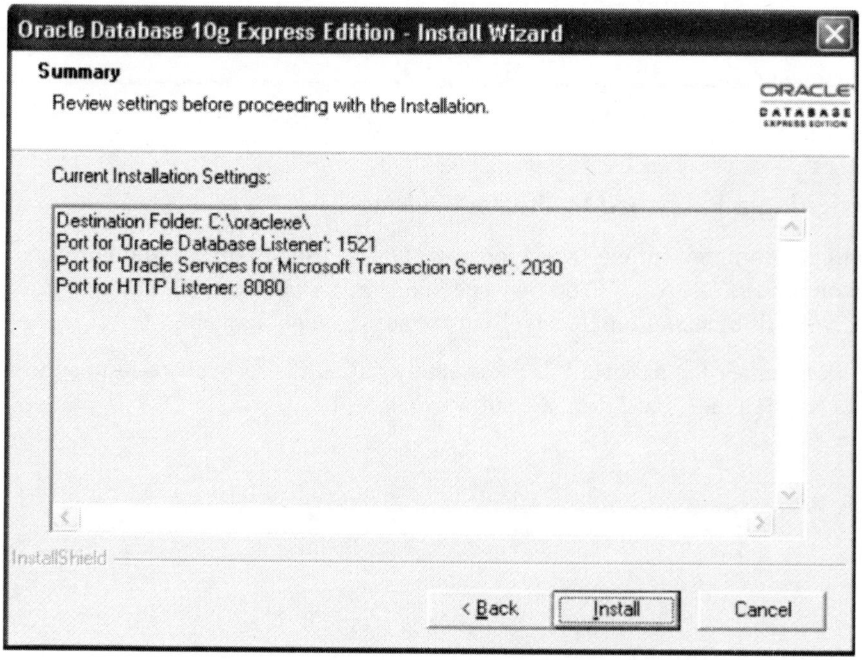

Figure 2.6   Summary of installation settings.

The Oracle Database Installation will start and will take almost 10 minutes on a Pentium 4 with 512 MB RAM machine/PC. You will be shown the status of installation as in Figure 2.7.

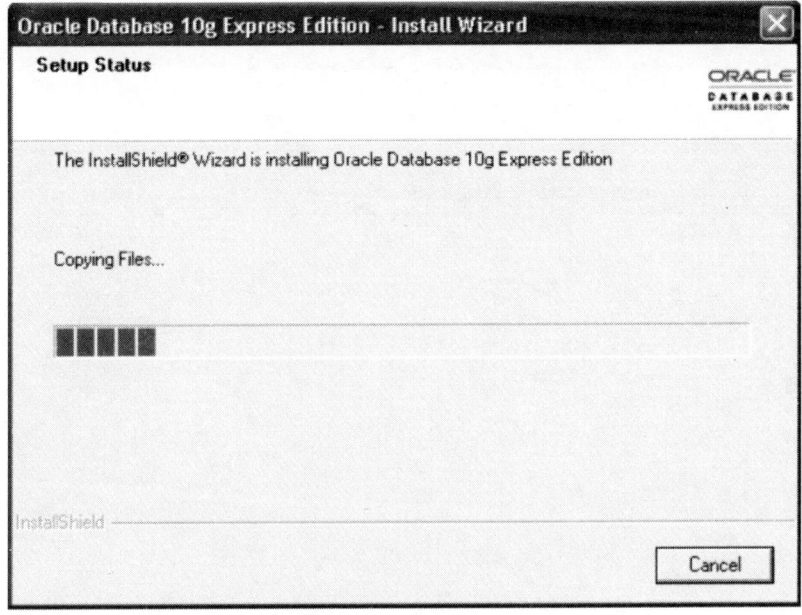

Figure 2.7   Installation of Oracle Express Edition.

On Completion you will see the Figure 2.8. Click "Finish".

Note: Verify that "Launch the Database homepage" is checked.

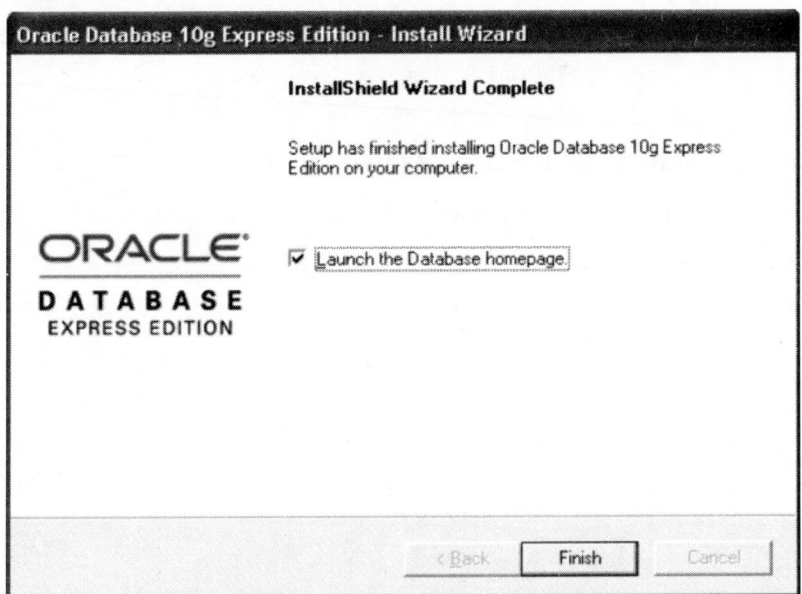

Figure 2.8   Installation Wizard Completion.

2.2.2   Logging in as "sys" User

On clicking "Finish", you will see Figure 2.9 on screen prompting for username and password. Type "sys" in Username field and "sys" in the Password field. Click "Login".

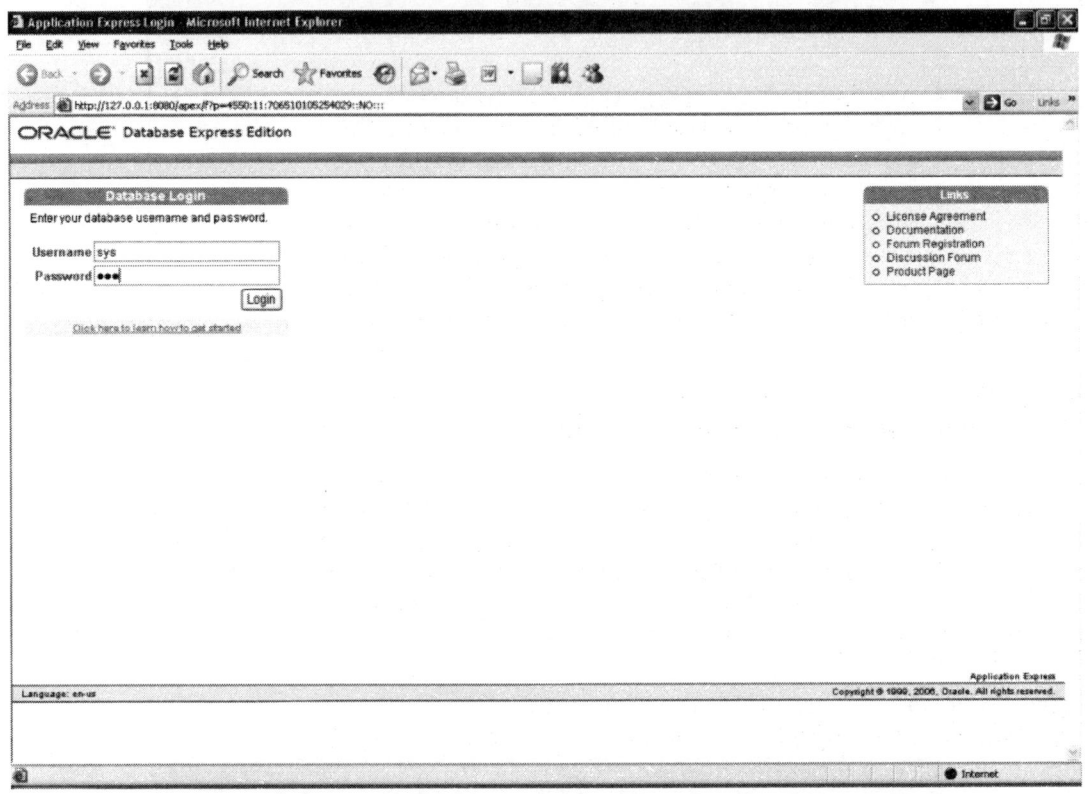

Figure 2.9   Login as "sys" user.

2.2.3   Creating a New Database User Named "scott"

Click on "Administration" → "Database Users" → "Create User" and you will see Figure 2.10 on screen.

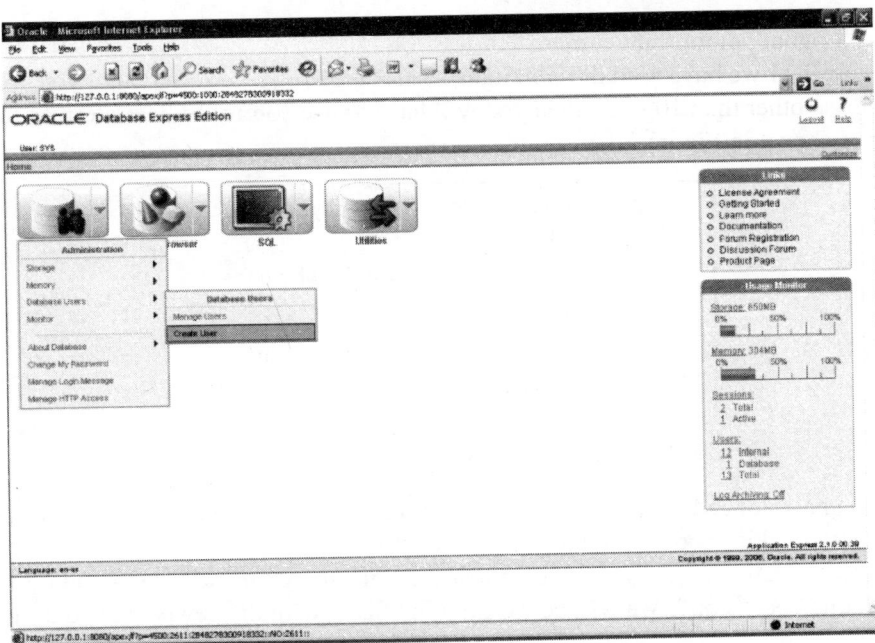

Figure 2.10   Creating a new user named "scott".

Enter "scott" in Username field, "tiger" in Password field, "tiger" in Confirm Password field and click "Create" button as shown in Figure 2.11.

Note: Check that "Unlocked" is mentioned in "Account Status" field.

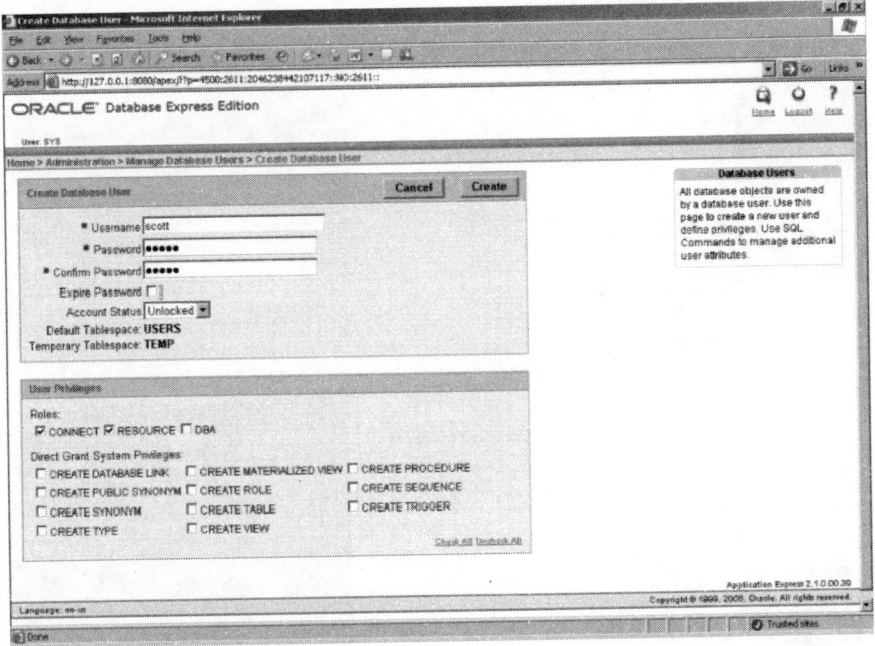

Figure 2.11   Specifying new users name and password.

Click "Logout" in topright corner.

In Figure 2.11 we have used the GUI interface for creating a new user but if you are using the Oracle database other than 10g XE, then you will have to use command line interface for creating a new user as shown in Figure 2.12.

```
SQL> connect sys/sys@xe as sysdba
Connected.
SQL> create user scott identified by tiger;
User created.
SQL> grant connect, resource to scott;
Grant succeeded.
```

Figure 2.12   Commands for creating new user.

First we have logged in as DBA(sys) then created a new user named "scott" with password "tiger". We will deal in more depth the GRANT command in Chapter 15.

Till now we have logged in as the database administrator named "sys" and created a new database user named "scott". We will be working in Oracle with the newly created user from now onwards.

2.2.4   Logging into the Oracle Database as "scott" User

Let us now log in to the Oracle database using the new username and password.

Go to "Start" → "Programs" → "Oracle Database 10g Express Edition" → "Run SQL command Line". Refer to Figure 2.13.

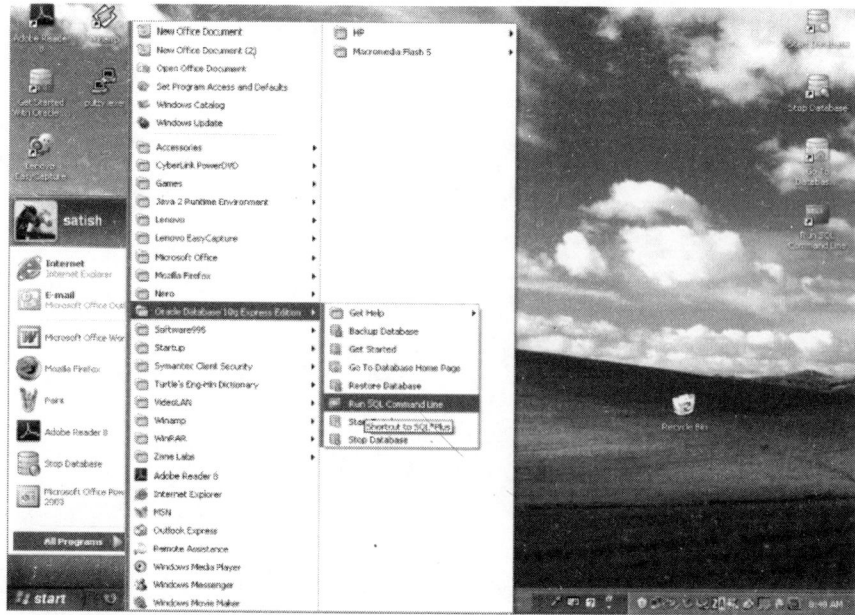

Figure 2.13   Logging to the Oracle database as "scott" user.

You will be greeted by Figure 2.14.

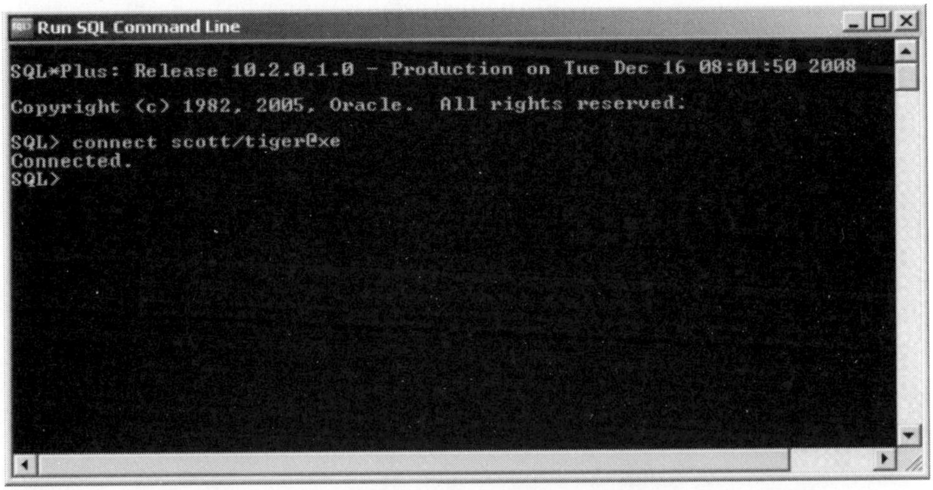

Figure 2.14   SQL Command Line.

Type the following command at SQL prompt

SQL> connect scott/tiger@xe

And you will receive the message "Connected".

We have installed Oracle Database Software and created a new user named "scott". In the next few chapters we will learn the Oracle database by logging in as the "scott" user.

2.3   TYPES OF DATABASE USERS

Oracle is a multi-user database management system and has predominantly two types of users:

1. DBA (Database Administrator)
2. Normal User

2.3.1   DBA

The "sys" user we have created is actually a DBA account. The DBA account has the privileges to perform various tasks as specified below:

- Manage database storage
- Administer users and security
- Manage schema objects
- Monitor and manage database performance
- Perform backup and recovery
- Schedule and automate jobs.

DBA has the authority to create new users, remove existing users or modify any of the environment variables or privileges assigned to other users.

2.3.2 Normal Database Users

The "scott" user we have created is actually a normal database user who has been allocated database space for creation, deletion and updation of various objects like tables, functions, procedures, etc. Moreover, by default the "scott" user has access to own objects only and cannot access objects owned by other users. The DBA has the authority to grant or remove various privileges to normal users.

2.4 CHANGING DISPLAY SETTINGS

If you do not like the screen with black background and white text then do the following:
Right click Mouse and Title bar of "Run SQL Command Line" and then "Properties". Refer to Figure 2.15.

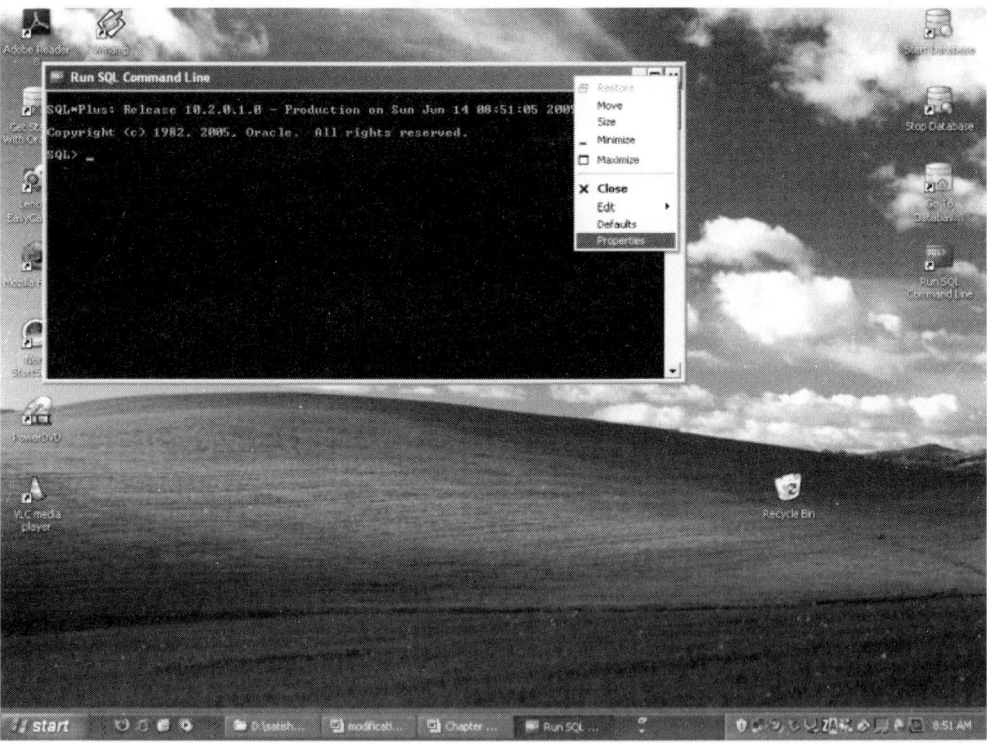

Figure 2.15 Changing display settings.

With "Screen Text" selected, click black color box (leftmost) as shown in Figure 2.16.

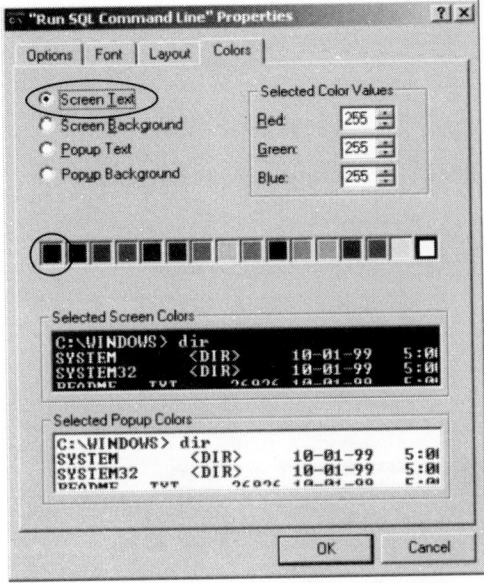

Figure 2.16   Changing text color.

Click "OK".

Repeat the same procedure for setting background color as white as shown in Figure 2.17.

With "Screen Background" selected, click white color box (rightmost) as shown in Figure 2.17.

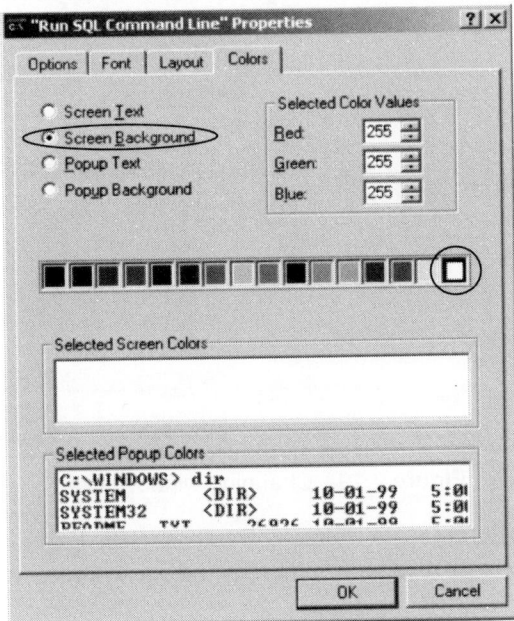

Figure 2.17   Changing background color.

Click "OK". Select the option "Modify shortcut that started this window" and press "OK". You will be prompted with Figure 2.18.

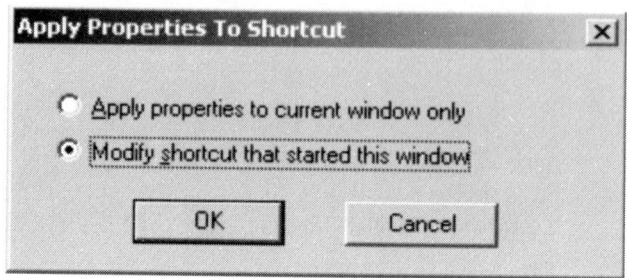

Figure 2.18   Apply properties.

Specify the width and height of Window as per your preferences in Figure 2.19 and click "OK".

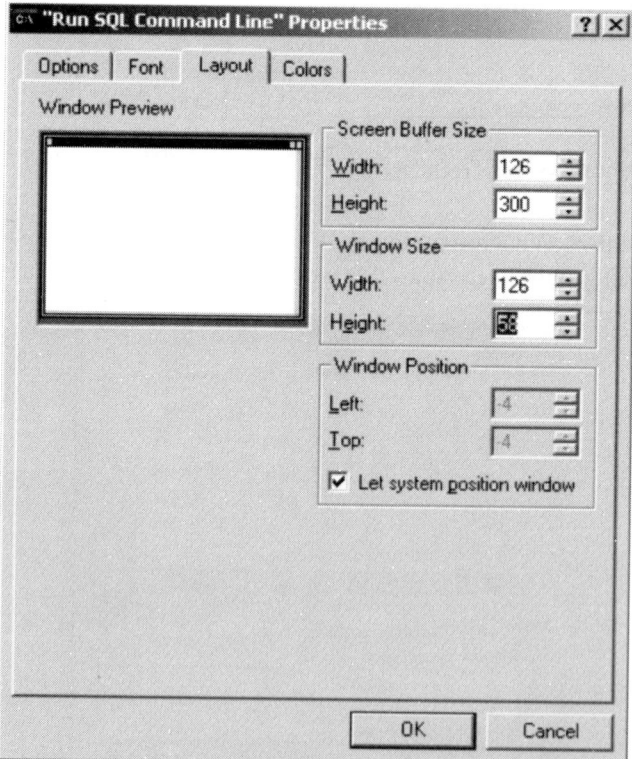

Figure 2.19   Changing window size.

Go to "Start" → "Programs" → "Oracle Database 10g Express Edition" → "Run SQL command Line". Now you will receive a white background screen with text in black color as shown in Figure 2.20.

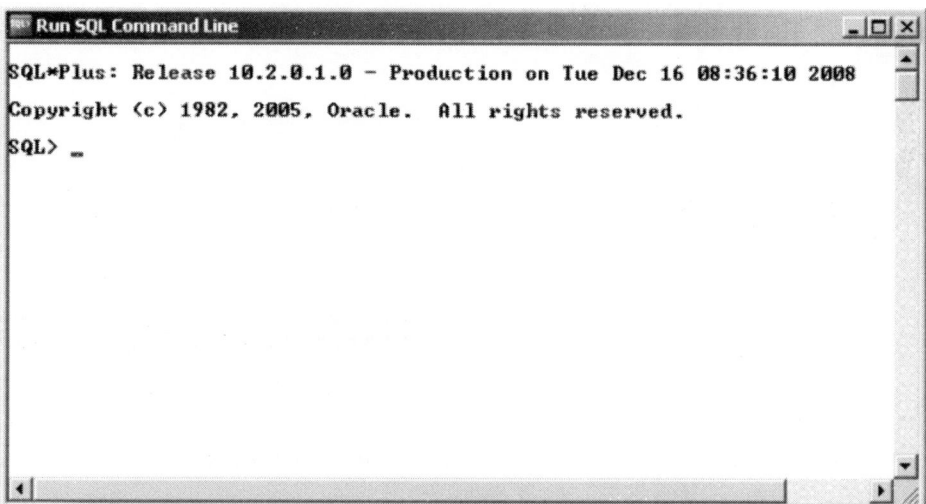

Figure 2.20 Modified login screen.

REVIEW QUESTIONS

1. Specify the minimum system requirements for installing the Oracle database 10g Express Edition.
2. Enlist the role of DBA. What are the differences between a DBA and a normal database user?
3. Is Oracle a multi-user database management system?

Introduction to Oracle

3.1 THREE MAJOR PRODUCTS OF ORACLE CORPORATION

Oracle Corporation has three major products:

1. **Oracle Database Server (DB)**—Storage, retrieval, manipulation of data.
2. **Oracle Developer Suite**—Used for developing GUI screens and reports.
3. **Oracle Application Server (AS)**—All screens and reports developed using Developer Suite are compiled and stored on AS.

Figure 3.1 is the architecture which is typically used by an organization.

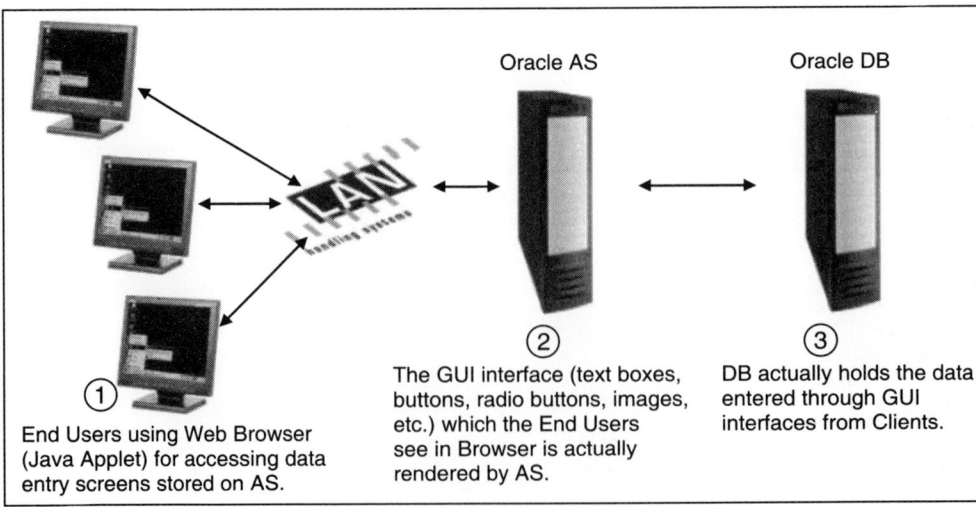

Figure 3.1 Typical database architecture.

3.1.1   Oracle DB (Database)

It is called the back-end software for storing, retrieving and manipulating data. It comprises the database engine which is responsible for managing the database.

To learn Oracle DB we have to learn 3 languages:

1. SQL
2. SQL *Plus
3. PL/SQL

SQL

SQL is an acronym for **Structured Query Language**. It is **a 4th Generation** language because it is quite similar to the normal English language and is used to perform various operations on database software like Oracle. SQL is a non-procedural language and does not support declaration of variables, conditional statements like IF ELSE, looping statements and therefore has several limitations.

SQL was originally known as **"SEQUEL" standing for Structured English Query Language**.

*SQL *Plus*

SQL*Plus is a proprietary language of Oracle Corporation and is an extension to the standard SQL language. It supports several new features in comparison to standard SQL and has reporting and formatting capabilities.

PL/SQL

SQL and SQL*Plus being 4th Generation languages are very easy to learn and use but at the same time have several limitations. SQL does not have provision for declaring variables, conditional statements like IF, looping controls like WHILE, DO WHILE, etc. PL/SQL stands for Procedural SQL which is an extension to the SQL language and has similar capabilities as other 3rd Generation languages. Moreover, SQL commands can be embedded in PL/SQL programs and hence called PL/SQL.

3.1.2   Oracle Developer Suite

It is the **IDE (Integrated Development Environment)** for developing the GUI screens (Graphical User Interface comprising of text boxes, radio buttons, images, videos, etc.). All screens developed using Developer Suite are compiled and kept on Oracle AS. The end users view the desired screens through their web browser, which is actually rendered on PC's by Application Sever.

IDE means various GUI components like text boxes, drop down lists, radio buttons. Images, sound and video can be incorporated into screens (data entry forms) by just dragging and dropping from menu.

3.1.3   Oracle AS (Application Server)

It **renders the GUI screens on end user PC** through a web browser. The source code of screens developed using Oracle Developer is compiled and stored on AS. Whenever an end user requests a specific screen through web browser, the screen is rendered by the AS.

Note: We will use the following abbreviations throughout the book.
DB: Database
AS: Application Server
IDE: Integrated Development Environment
Following **Synonyms** will be used interchangeably.
Client/PC/machine
Screen/Forms - Oracle calls data entry screens as Forms.
Web Browser: Any of the browsers like Internet Explorer, Firefox, Netscape, etc.

3.2 PRE-REQUISITES BEFORE LEARNING SQL

1. Oracle DB must be installed on your system. For installation, refer to Chapter 2.
2. To start Oracle Database Engine, Go to "Start" → "All Programs" → Oracle Database 10g Express Edition → Start Database. You will see Figure 3.2 on the screen saying "Oracle Service XE started successfully".

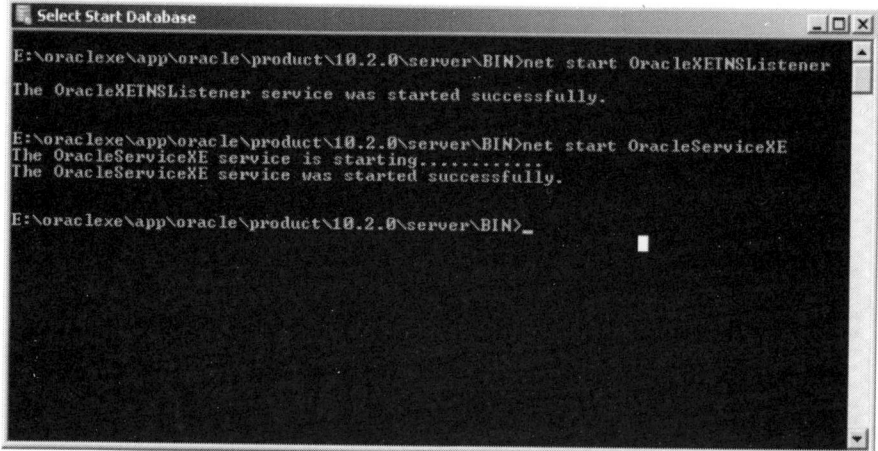

Figure 3.2   Starting Oracle Database.

3. Run SQL.

Go to "Start" → "All Programs" → Oracle Database 10g Express Edition → Run SQL Command and you will be presented Figure 3.3.

```
Run SQL Command Line

SQL*Plus: Release 10.2.0.1.0 - Production on Tue Oct 7 11:26:4
Copyright (c) 1982, 2005, Oracle.  All rights reserved.
SQL>
```

Figure 3.3   Running SQL Command Line.

Oracle is a multi-user RDBMS and therefore requires a username and password for each individual logging into the system. In Chapter 2, we have already created a user named "scott" with password "tiger".

So let us now connect as "scott" user onto the Oracle database by issuing the following commands. Refer to Figure 3.4.

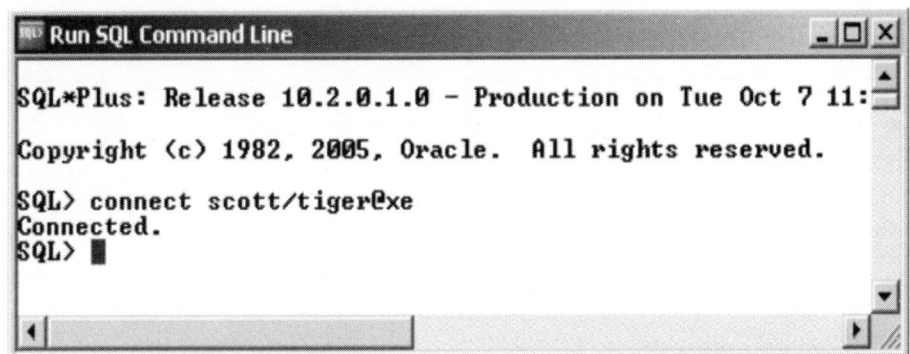

Figure 3.4   Connecting to Oracle Database as "scott" user.

Let us start with creation of a table as shown in Figure 3.5.

SQL>create table *student* (*rollno* number, *marks* number);

Table Created

Figure 3.5   Creating table.

"create", "table" are reserved words.

"student", "rollno", "marks" are names specified by you.

"number" is a reserved word specifying the data type. This means only digits from 0 to 9 can be entered in this field. We will explain more about data types in Chapter 4.

A table can be defined as a collection of rows and columns. A table is the basic entity for any Database Management System.

Note: We will use the following words interchangeably:

Row or Record

Column or Field

Let us now add rows/records into the student table (Figures 3.6 and 3.7).

SQL>insert into *student* values (*1,78*);

1 row created

Figure 3.6   Adding record.

Value 1 goes into the "rollno" field and value 78 goes into the "marks" field.

```
SQL> insert into student values (2,56);
1 row created
```

Figure 3.7   Adding record.

Now let us view the records that we have entered (Figure 3.8).

```
SQL> select * from student;
        ROLLNO        MARKS
            1           78
            2           56
2 rows selected
```

Figure 3.8   Viewing records added to STUDENT table.

"*" means display all fields.
"select", "from" are reserved words.
"student" is the name of table.
We can achieve the same result by issuing the command as shown in Figure 3.9.

```
SQL> select rollno, marks from student;
        ROLLNO        MARKS
            1           78
            2           56
2 rows selected
```

Figure 3.9   Specifying column names.

We have specified the fields explicitly instead of using "*" for all fields.

It is also possible that we change the sequence of fields while displaying records. Figure 3.10 contains the command for displaying records such that marks is shown before rollno.

```
SQL> select marks, rollno from student;
        MARKS        ROLLNO
           78            1
           56            2
2 rows selected
```

Figure 3.10   Displaying marks before rollno.

You must have noted that column headings appear completely in capital letters. If we want headings should appear as what we want then use double quotes as shown in Figure 3.11.

```
SQL>select rollno "RollNo", marks "Marks" from student;
        ROLLNO          MARKS
           1              78
           2              56
```

Figure 3.11   Changing column headings.

Now suppose that we wish to calculate percent of marks obtained out of 80. Refer to Figure 3.12 for the command.

```
SQL> select rollno, marks, marks / 80 *100 from student;
        ROLLNO          MARKS         MARKS/80*100
           1              78              97.5
           2              56              70
```

Figure 3.12   Percent of marks out of 80.

Again note that heading for per cent is appearing as the formula we have typed.
In order to specify a heading for per cent use the statement of Figure 3.13.

```
SQL> select rollno, marks, marks/80 *100 percent from student;
        ROLLNO          MARKS          PERCENT
           1              78              97.5
           2              56              70
```

Figure 3.13   Heading for percent column.

Here percent is called the **ALIAS NAME** for the calculated column. The ALIAS NAME affects the heading only.

3.3   ORACLE NAMING CONVENTIONS

There are certain rules which are to be followed while giving name to tables or column names.

- Names cannot be more than 30 characters in length.
- Names can contain letters(alphabets), digits and underscore(_).
- A name must start with a letter. It cannot start with any other character even underscore.
- Although Oracle allows $ and # in names but it is advisable not to use them.

3.4   CLASSIFICATION OF SQL COMMANDS

In order to learn SQL we will have to learn various commands or statements supported by SQL language. All the SQL commands can be broadly classified into five categories as shown in Figure 3.14.

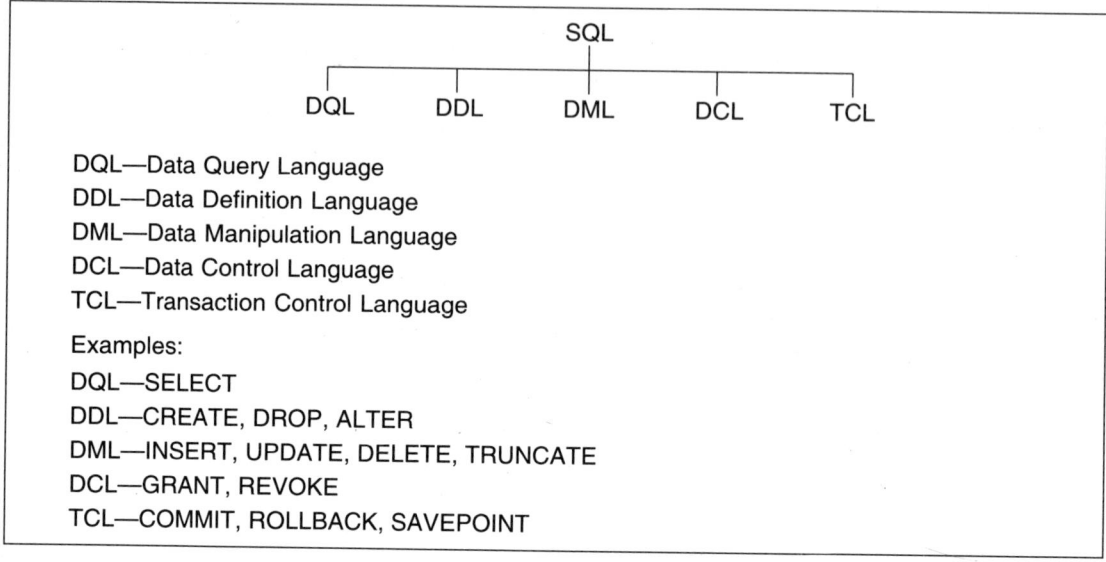

Figure 3.14 Classification of SQL commands.

3.4.1 Data Query Language (DQL)

These commands are used to view records from tables onto computer monitor. The actual data in the form of tables is stored onto the hard disk of Oracle Database Server and DQL commands enable us to view the information/records stored in database onto the monitor, for example, SELECT.

3.4.2 Data Definition Language (DDL)

DDL statements are used to create tables, remove tables and make changes to the table structure. Table structure refers to the number of columns and data types of columns and constraints which can be applied or revoked as desired, for example, CREATE, DROP, ALTER.

3.4.3 Data Manipulation Language (DML)

For adding new records, removing existing records or changing values of existing records we will use DML statements, for example, INSERT, UPDATE, DELETE.

3.4.4 Data Control Language (DCL)

Oracle is a multi user database management system. Each user has his own assigned area where his data is stored. By default one user cannot view, modify or delete the information stored in another user's area. Oracle has provision for allowing the owner to grant permissions on data owned by him to another user. These commands control how and to what extent one user can view, modify and delete information in another user's area, for example, GRANT, REVOKE.

3.4.5   Transaction Control Language (TCL)

Each operation which is done on database is called a Transaction. Transaction can be addition of new record, modification in values of existing records or deletion of existing records. Each transaction can be stored permanently or can be undone by using the transaction control statements, for example, COMMIT, ROLLBACK, SAVEPOINT.

We will learn each of the above mentioned commands in the next few chapters.

REVIEW QUESTIONS _____

1. Why is the Oracle database called the back-end software?
2. What does SQL stand for? Why is it called a 4th Generation language?
3. Is SQL a proprietary language of Oracle Corporation?
4. Which features does SQL not support as a language?
5. What is the difference between SQL, SQL*Plus and PL/SQL?
6. Which command is used to create a new table?
7. Specify the commands used to add records and view records from a table.
8. Explain the concept of Aliasing.
9. What is meant by the Oracle Naming Convention?
10. Explain the classification of SQL statements.

MULTIPLE CHOICE QUESTIONS _____

1. Which Oracle Product is responsible for storing the data?
   (a) Database Server
   (b) Application Server
   (c) Developer Suite
2. Which software does a client PC must have to access the deployed Forms and Reports on Application Server?
   (a) Windows Operating System
   (b) Browser
   (c) Oracle Database
3. SQL stands for
   (a) Simple Query Language
   (b) Structured Query Language
   (c) Structured English Query Language
4. PL/SQL stands for
   (a) Programmable Structured Query Language
   (b) Procedural Structured Query Language
   (c) Procedural Extension to SQL language

5. Which SQL command is used to make a new table?
    (a) ALTER
    (b) CREATE
    (c) INSERT

6. ALIASING refers to
    (a) Duplicate name to a table
    (b) Duplicate name to a column
    (c) Duplicate name to a calculated value
    (d) All of the above

7. What is the maximum length for a table or column name?
    (a) 50
    (b) 40
    (c) 30

8. The INSERT command falls into which category of the SQL commands?
    (a) DDL
    (b) DCL
    (c) DML

9. The database component which stores the data is
    (a) OBJECT
    (b) TABLE
    (c) VIEW

10. The SQL command used to create a new table is
    (a) NEW
    (b) CREATE
    (c) ADD
    (d) None

11. The SQL command for adding new records is
    (a) ADD
    (b) CREATE
    (c) INSERT
    (d) None

Oracle Data Types

4.1 INTRODUCTION

In Chapter 3, we created a table named "student" with two columns, namely "rollno" and "marks" of type NUMBER. NUMBER is known as the data type for the column and will only allow digits 0–9 to be input as value. Data type actually restricts the kind of digits, characters or special characters which can be supplied as value for that particular column.

4.2 DATA TYPE—A DEFINITION

Data type implies the set of numbers, characters, special characters which can be input as a value for a particular column of the table. A column whose type has been defined as NUMBER will not accept any character other than numerals (0–9), a decimal and +/– sign.

Oracle provides several other data types which are explained in the subsequent sections.

4.2.1 CHAR

Valid characters : 0–9, a–z, A–Z, special characters like $, %, &, etc.
Default size : 1
Minimum length : 1
Maximum length : 1
Example : Figure 4.1

```
SQL> create table student(rollno number, gender char);

Table created.

SQL> insert into student values (1,'M');

1 row created.

SQL> insert into student values (2,'F');

1 row created.

SQL> insert into student values (3,'MALE');
insert into student values (3,'MALE')

         *

ERROR at line 1:
ORA-12899: value too large for column "SCOTT"."STUDENT"."GENDER"
(actual: 4, maximum: 1)
```

Figure 4.1   Example of CHAR data type.

Note:

1. All CHARACTER values must be supplied within single quotes (e.g. gender).
    NUMBER values are supplied without quotes (e.g. rollno).
2. By default the size of CHAR data type is 1 character. Since we tried inserting 'MALE' which is 4 chars long, oracle gave error message.
3. We could have used CHAR(1) instead of CHAR with the same result.

4.2.2   CHAR(N)

Valid characters	:	0–9, a–z, A–Z, special characters like $,%,& etc.
Default size	:	N
Minimum length	:	1
Maximum length	:	2000
Characteristics	:	(a) **Fixed length:** If the value being entered has less number of characters than the specified N, then also the database will consume N bytes of memory space.
		(b) **Blank padded:** If the value being entered has less number of characters than the specified N, oracle appends blank space characters at the end of the value.
Example	:	Figure 4.2

```
SQL> create table student (rollno number, name char(10));

Table created.

SQL> insert into student values (1,'satish');

1 row created.

SQL> insert into student values (2,'neelesh');

1 row created.

SQL> select rollno, name, length(name) from student;

     ROLLNO          NAME          LENGTH(NAME)
        1             satish             10
        2             neelesh            10
```

Figure 4.2   Example of CHAR(N) data type.

Note:
1. LENGTH is an Oracle built-in function which gives the space occupied by a value. We will learn about Oracle built-in functions in Chapter 7.
2. 'satish' and 'neelesh' are of 6 and 7 characters respectively, still the space occupied is 10 characters.

4.2.3   VARCHAR2(N)

Valid characters	:	0–9, a–z, A–Z, special characters like $, %, &, etc.
Default size	:	N
Minimum length	:	1
Maximum length	:	4000
Characteristics	:	(a) **Variable length:** The space occupied by value is exactly equal to the number of characters in that value.
		(b) **Not blank padded:** Blank(spaces) are not appended at the end of data value of lesser size.
Example	:	Figure 4.3

```
SQL> create table student (rollno number(4), name varchar2(10));

Table created.

SQL> insert into student values (1,'satish');

1 row created.

SQL> insert into student values (2,'neelesh');
```

1 row created.

SQL> select rollno, name, length(name) from student;

ROLLNO	NAME	LENGTH(NAME)
1	satish	6
2	neelesh	7

Figure 4.3 Example of VARCHAR2(N) data type.

The space occupied by 'satish' is 6 and 'neelesh' is 7 and not 10 as was the case in CHAR data type.

Note:

1. Use CHAR data type for columns for which the data values will be of the same length in most or ALL of the records, for example, for Gender column use CHAR as it can have 'M' or 'F' only.

2. Use VARCHAR2 for columns in which values being entered will vary in size from record to record, for example, use VARCHAR2 for name field as name can vary from few characters to large strings. VARCHAR2 saves the valuable database (hard disk) space.

4.2.4 LONG

Similar to VARCHAR2 with maximum size of 2 GB.

Valid characters	:	0–9, a–z, A–Z, special characters like $,%,&, etc.
Default size	:	2 GB (Gigabytes)
Minimum length	:	1
Maximum length	:	2 GB (Gigabytes)
Characteristics	:	(a) **Variable length:** The space occupied by value is exactly equal to the number of characters in that value.
		(b) **Not blank padded:** Blank(spaces) are not appended at the end of data value of lesser size.

4.2.5 NUMBER(N)

Integer values with maximum N digits, e.g. NUMBER(7)

Valid characters	:	0–9, +, –
Default size	:	N (excluding + or – sign)
Minimum value	:	–9999999
Maximum value	:	+9999999
Example	:	Figure 4.4

```
SQL> create table test_number (a number(7));
Table created.

SQL> insert into test_number values (9999999);
1 row created.

SQL> insert into test_number values (–9999999);
1 row created.

SQL> insert into test_number values (99.99);
1 row created.

SQL> insert into test_number values (9999999.99);
insert into test_number values (9999999.99)
                                     *

ERROR at line 1:
ORA-01438: value larger than specified precision allowed for this column
SQL> select * from test_number;

          A

    9999999
   –9999999
        100
```

Figure 4.4   Example of NUMBER(N) data type.

Caution: When we insert 99.99, Oracle has automatically rounded it to 100. Since NUMBER(7) is INTEGER type so it discards decimal positions after rounding.

(If we supplied 99.23 then the value actually stored would be 99.)

Note: We cannot insert values greater than 9999999.

4.2.6   NUMBER(p, s)

This data type is used to store decimal numbers, for example, NUMBER(7, 2).

p: Precision : Total number of digits including digits after decimal point.

s: Scale : Total number of digits after decimal point.

Decimal values with maximum p-s digits to the left of decimal point and s number of digits to the right of decimal point.

Valid characters	:	0–9, +, –
Default size	:	p-s = 5 digits to the left of decimal point and s = 2 digits to the right of decimal point. (Excluding + or – sign and decimal)
Minimum value	:	–99999.99
Maximum length	:	+99999.99
Example	:	Figure 4.5

```
SQL> drop table test_number;
Table dropped.

SQL> create table test_number(a number(7,2));
Table created.

SQL> insert into test_number values (99999.99);
1 row created.

SQL> insert into test_number values (–99999.99);
1 row created.

SQL> insert into test_number values (123456.34);
 insert into test_number values (123456.34)
                  *
ERROR at line 1:
ORA-01438: value larger than specified precision allowed for this column

SQL> insert into test_number values (12345.3467);
1 row created.

SQL> insert into test_number values (12345.3423);
1 row created.

SQL> select * from test_number;

          A
     99999.99
    –99999.99
     12345.35
     12345.34
```

Figure 4.5   Example of NUMBER(p,s) Data Type.

Note:

1. The maximum number which can be entered is +99999.99 and the minimum number which can be entered is –99999.99.

2. Oracle gave error message when we tried to insert 123456.34 as the maximum number of digits to the left of decimal point is $5 (7 - 2)$ only.

3. On inserting 12345.3467 oracle did not give any error message but stored 12345.35 into table which can be seen from the select statement. It is because NUMBER(7,2) implies just two places to the right of decimal point and so Oracle rounded to two decimal places.

4. On inserting 12345.3423, Oracle stored 12345.34.

Caution:

Oracle gives error message whenever we try to insert numbers greater than the specified precision. But Oracle rounds the decimal portion to the number of places as specified while defining the data type.

4.2.7 NUMBER Data Type

Just by specifying NUMBER, we can store large numbers.

Positive numbers from 1×10^{-130} to $9.99 \dots 9 \times 10^{125}$ with up to 38 significant digits.

Negative numbers from -1×10^{-130} to $9.99 \dots 99 \times 10^{125}$ with up to 38 significant digits.

By 38 significant digits we mean the number can have 38 9's before the decimal point.

Note: Oracle stores numeric data in variable-length format.

4.2.8 DATE Data Type

DATE data type stores both date and time.

Before understanding DATE data type let us first see (Figure 4.6) how to view the current date and time.

```
SQL> select sysdate from dual;

SYSDATE
18-MAR-08

SQL> select to_char(sysdate,'dd/mm/yyyy hh24:mi:ss') from dual;

TO_CHAR(SYSDATE,'DD)
18/03/2008 14:14:17
```

Figure 4.6   Displaying current date and time.

Sysdate is system variable which stores the current date and time.

dd/mm/yyyy	implies show date as '18/03/2008' instead of '18-mar-08'.
hh24	implies show hour in 24-hour clock format
mi	implies show minutes
ss	implies show seconds

Dual is called a dummy table which is required to just complete the syntax of the SELECT statement. SQL being highly-structured language requires exact syntax for all statements. The "SELECT" statement must have the "FROM" clause.

In order to view date as well as time we need to use Oracle's built-in function "to_char". We will learn more about built-in functions in Chapter 7.

Let us create a column named "date_of_birth" for storing the students date of birth as shown in Figure 4.7.

```
SQL> create table student
  2 (
  3 rollno number(4),
  4 name varchar2(10),
  5 date_of_birth date
  6 );
```

Table created.

SQL> insert into student values (1,'satish',sysdate);

1 row created.

SQL> insert into student values (2,'rashmi','18-mar-08');

1 row created.

SQL> insert into student values (3,'neelesh','18-mar-2008');

1 row created.

SQL> insert into student values (4,'ruchi',to_date('24-mar-2008 10:00:00','dd-mon-yyyy hh24:mi:ss'));

1 row created.

SQL> select rollno, name, to_char(date_of_birth,'dd/mm/yyyy hh24:mi:ss') from student;

ROLLNO	NAME	TO_CHAR(DATE_OF_BIR
1	satish	18/03/2008 14:24:21
2	rashmi	18/03/2008 00:00:00
3	neelesh	18/03/2008 00:00:00
4	ruchi	24/03/2008 10:00:00

Figure 4.7   Storing DATE values.

For rollno 1 we had used sysdate, therefore, current date + time at that moment was inserted.

For rollno 2 we had used '17-mar-08', therefore, current date + time as 00:00:00 was inserted as we did not specify the time.

For rollno 3 we had used '17-mar-2008', therefore, current date + time as 00:00:00 was inserted as we did not specify the time.

Note: '17-mar-08' and '17-mar-2008' are known as the default date formats in Oracle. When we insert values using any of the two formats the default time that gets stored is 00:00:00.

For rollno 4 we specified both the date and time by using "to_date" built-in function.

4.2.9   TIMESTAMP

TIMESTAMP is similar to DATE data type with the additional information of fractions of seconds. This data type stores the date (dd-mon-yyyy) and time in hh.mi.ss.fractions_of_seconds AM/PM. By default 6 fractions are used for further dividing a second. Figure 4.8 demonstrates the use of TIMESTAMP data type.

```
SQL> create table temp(a timestamp);

Table created.

SQL> insert into temp values (systimestamp);

1 row created.

SQL> insert into temp values (systimestamp);

1 row created.

SQL> select * from temp;

                             A
                19-MAR-08 10.31.36.495053 AM
                19-MAR-08 10.31.42.195465 AM
```

Figure 4.8 TIMESTAMP data type example.

If you need to view the fractions of seconds up to 3 places only instead of default 6, use format (ff3) as shown in Figure 4.9.

```
SQL> select to_char(a,'ddmmyyyy hh:mi:ss AM ff3') from temp;

TO_CHAR(A,'DDMMYYYYHH:MI:SSAMF

19032008 10:31:36 AM 495
19032008 10:31:42 AM 195
```

Figure 4.9 TIMESTAMP fraction of seconds.

4.2.10 RAW(size) Data Type

This is used to store binary data like images, sound, videos, graphs, etc.
Its variable length data type with maximum size of 2000 bytes.

LONG RAW

It is also used to store binary data like images, sound, videos, graphs, etc.
Its variable length data type with maximum size of 2 GB.

4.2.11 Large Object Data Types

CLOB stands for Character Large Object. Variable length character data can have a maximum length of 4 GB.

BLOB stands for Binary Large Object. Variable length binary data can have a maximum length of 4 GB.

REVIEW QUESTIONS

1. What is the purpose of specifying data type for a column?
2. List the various data types supported by Oracle.
3. Differentiate between CHAR(N) and VARCHAR2(N) data types. In which conditions should VARCHAR2 be preferred to CHAR data type?
4. DATE data type stores date as well as time. How to view the time from a stored date value?
5. How to input time in date column?
6. If we want to store 2GB of character data then which data type should be used and why?
7. Which data types are available for storing binary data like images, videos, etc.?

MULTIPLE CHOICE QUESTIONS

1. Data type refers to
   (a) The minimum number of characters/digits that can be supplied as a value
   (b) The maximum number of characters/digits that can be supplied as a value
   (c) Set of allowed characters and digits
   (d) All of the above
2. How many characters can be stored in CHAR data type?
   (a) 1
   (b) 2
   (c) 3
   (d) Any number of characters
3. CHAR(N) is different from VARCHAR2(N)
   (a) CHAR is fixed length data type
   (b) CHAR is not blank padded but VARCHAR2 is blank padded
   (c) CHAR(N) and VARCHAR2(N) are the same
4. The maximum value that can be stored in NUMBER(5,3) is
   (a) 99999.999
   (b) 999.999
   (c) 99.999
   (d) 999.9
5. The maximum value which can be stored in NUMBER(5,5) is
   (a) 9.99999
   (b) 0.99999
   (c) 99999.9
6. DATE data type stores which of the following?
   (a) DATE
   (b) TIME
   (c) DATE + TIME

7. Which data type needs to be enclosed within single quotes?
   (a) CHAR
   (b) VARCHAR2
   (c) DATE
   (d) All of the Above

8. Which data type should be used to store names?
   (a) CHAR
   (b) VARCHAR2
   (c) CLOB

9. CHAR/VARCHAR2 can store
   (a) 0–9, a–z, A–Z
   (b) –,+,*,/
   (c) %,^,@,#
   (d) All of the above

10. To store movies of size > 650 MB, which data type should be used?
    (a) RAW
    (b) LONG RAW
    (c) BLOB
    (d) NONE

11. To store the bank account code like 'A10001', which data type should be used?
    (a) NUMBER(6)
    (b) CHAR(6)
    (c) VARCHAR2(6)

12. We want to add a column which would store the data+time+fraction of seconds when the record was added. Which data type would be used?
    (a) DATE
    (b) TIME
    (c) DATETIME
    (d) TIMESTAMP

LAB ASSIGNMENT

1. Create a table named DEPARTMENT with the following columns.

TABLE 4.1 Structure of DEPARTMENT table

Column name	Data type	Size
DEPARTMENT_NO	NUMBER	2
DEPARTMENT_NAME	VARCHAR2	20
LOCATION	VARCHAR2	10

2. Create a table named EMPLOYEE

TABLE 4.2   Structure of EMPLOYEE table

Column name	Data type	Size
EMPLOYEE_NO	NUMBER	4
EMPLOYEE_NAME	VARCHAR2	10
DATE_OF_JOINING	DATE	
DEPARTMENT_NO	NUMBER	2
GENDER	CHAR	1
SALARY	NUMBER	10,2
COMMISSION	NUMBER	10,2

3. Add the following records in the DEPARTMENT table

DEPARTMENT_NO	DEPARTMENT_NAME	LOCATION
10	FINANCE	BHOPAL
20	ACCOUNTS	INDORE
30	MANUFACTURING	BARODA
40	ENGINEERING	BANGALORE

4. Add the following records in the EMPLOYEE table

EMPNO	NAME	DATE OF JOINING	DEPT	GENDER	SAL	COMM
1111	SATISH	19-DEC-2008	10	M	10,000	1000
2222	RASHMI	01-JAN-1987	20	F	8,000	500
3333	RISHI	05-JUN-1976	10	M	7,000	400
4444	ANIL	16-APR-196710:10:10 AM	10	M	12,000	2000

5. List the details of all departments.
6. Find the names of all employees.
7. Display the Name, Department and Salary of all employees.
8. Display the Employee_no as "STAFFNO", EMPLOYEE_NAME as "Name" and DEPARTMENT_NO as "Dept" for all employees.
9. Show Employee Name along with TOTAL SALARY which is the SUM of SALARY and COMMISSION.
10. List Employee Name and Total Salary as SALARY+10% of SALARY + COMMISSION and show the heading of new computed column as "Total Salary".

Oracle Operators

5.1 INTRODUCTION

Oracle provides several operators for performing various mathematical, comparison and logical operations. Table 5.1 contains the list of various operators.

TABLE 5.1   List of Oracle Operators

Type of operator	Operators
Mathematical Operators	+, −, * , /
Comparison/Relational Operators	=, <. >, >=, <=, <> or !=
Logical/Boolean Operators	AND, OR, NOT
Special Operators	IN, IS, LIKE, BETWEEN

5.1.1 Mathematical Operators

The mathematical operators are used for performing mathematical operations like addition, subtraction, multiplication, division, etc.

Assume an "emp" table which contains information about employees (Figure 5.1).

EMPNO—Unique number assigned to each employee
ENAME—Employee Name
JOB—Category of job like MANAGER, CLERK, etc.
MGR—Contains the employee number of boss/senior to which the employee reports
HIREDATE—Date of joining in the company

SAL—Salary of employee
COMM—Commission earned by the employee
DEPTNO—Department Number to which the employee belongs

```
SQL>select * from emp;
```

EMPNO	ENAME	JOB	MGR	HIREDATE	SAL	COMM	DEPTNO
7369	SMITH	CLERK	7902	17-DEC-80	800	250	20
7499	ALLEN	SALESMAN	7698	20-FEB-81	1600	300	30
7521	WARD	SALESMAN	7698	22-FEB-81	1250	500	30
7566	JONES	MANAGER	7839	02-APR-81	2975	250	20
7654	MARTIN	SALESMAN	7698	28-SEP-81	2000	250	30
7698	BLAKE	MANAGER	7839	01-MAY-81	2850	250	30
9999	XEON	CLERK	7782	11-JAN-97	2000	300	50

Figure 5.1   Records in EMP table.

- **Display the sum of sal and commission as total salary for all employees (Figure 5.2).**

```
SQL>select empno, ename, sal+comm from emp;
```

EMPNO	ENAME	SAL+COMM
7369	SMITH	1050
7499	ALLEN	1900
7521	WARD	1750
7566	JONES	3225
7654	MARTIN	2250
7698	BLAKE	3100
9999	XEON	2300

Figure 5.2   Displaying TOTAL salary.

Note that 3rd column has been shown as "SAL+COMM" displaying the added value for "sal" and "comm" columns.

- **Display the column heading as "TOTAL" instead of "SAL+COMM".**

We will have to use alias name for this purpose as shown in Figure 5.3.

```
SQL>select empno,ename,sal+comm total from emp;
```

EMPNO	ENAME	TOTAL
7369	SMITH	1050
7499	ALLEN	1900
7521	WARD	1750
7566	JONES	3225
7654	MARTIN	2250
7698	BLAKE	3100
9999	XEON	2300

Figure 5.3   Specifying Alias names to computed columns.

Here total is called the **ALIAS NAME** for the **newly calculated column sal+comm.**
The above query (Figure 5.3) can be written as
SQL> select empno, ename, *sal+comm as total* from emp;
"AS" is a optional word which can be used to specify the ALIAS NAME. If we do not
supply "AS", then it is assumed as the alias name.
- **Find out what percent of salary is commission for all employees (Figure 5.4).**

SQL>select empno, ename, sal, comm, *comm/sal*100 as percent* from emp;

EMPNO	ENAME	SAL	COMM	PERCENT
7369	SMITH	800	250	31.25
7499	ALLEN	1600	300	18.75
7521	WARD	1250	500	40
7566	JONES	2975	250	8.40336134
7654	MARTIN	2000	250	12.5
7698	BLAKE	2850	250	8.77192982
9999	XEON	2000	300	15

Figure 5.4   Commission as percent of total salary.

- **Display the percent up to 2 places of decimal**

We can restrict the number of decimal places by using Oracle's built-in function named
round(), which is explained in detail in Chapter 7. Refer to Figure 5.5 for how to use ROUND()
built-in function.

SQL>select empno, ename, sal, comm, *round(comm/sal*100,2) as percent* from emp;

EMPNO	ENAME	SAL	COMM	PERCENT
7369	SMITH	800	250	31.25
7499	ALLEN	1600	300	18.75
7521	WARD	1250	500	40
7566	JONES	2975	250	8.4
7654	MARTIN	2000	250	12.5
7698	BLAKE	2850	250	8.77
9999	XEON	2000	300	15

Figure 5.5   Formatting percent to two decimal places.

- **Calculate bonus as 10 percent of (salary + commission) (Figure 5.6).**

SQL>select empno,ename,sal,comm,*10/100*(sal+comm) as bonus* from emp;

EMPNO	ENAME	SAL	COMM	BONUS
7369	SMITH	800	250	105
7499	ALLEN	1600	300	190
7521	WARD	1250	500	175
7566	JONES	2975	250	322.5
7654	MARTIN	2000	250	225
7698	BLAKE	2850	250	310
9999	XEON	2000	300	230

Figure 5.6   Calculating bonus.

5.1.2   Comparison or Relational Operators

The operators used to compare the values are called Comparison or Relational Operators which are listed in Table 5.2.

TABLE 5.2   List of comparison operators

Comparison Operator	Description
=	Equal to
<	Less than
>	Greater than
<=	Less than or equal to
>=	Greater than or equal to
<>	Not equal to
!=	Not equal to

- **List employees of department 20 only (Figure 5.7).**

SQL>select empno,ename,sal,comm,deptno from emp *where deptno=20;*

EMPNO	ENAME	SAL	COMM	DEPTNO
7369	SMITH	800	250	20
7566	JONES	2975	250	20

Figure 5.7   Displaying records satisfying specified condition.

WHERE is a clause of the SELECT statement which can be used to specify conditions for the records to be displayed.

- **List only those employees whose salary is more than 1000 (Figure 5.8).**

SQL>select empno,ename,sal,comm from emp *where sal>1000;*

EMPNO	ENAME	SAL	COMM
7499	ALLEN	1600	300
7521	WARD	1250	500
7566	JONES	2975	250
7654	MARTIN	2000	250
7698	BLAKE	2850	250
9999	XEON	2000	300

Figure 5.8   Using comparison operator.

- **List all those employees who are not in department 20 (means employees who are in any department other than department 20) (Figure 5.9).**

SQL>select empno, ename, sal, comm, deptno from emp *where deptno <>20*;

EMPNO	ENAME	SAL	COMM	DEPTNO
7499	ALLEN	1600	300	30
7521	WARD	1250	500	30
7654	MARTIN	2000	250	30
7698	BLAKE	2850	250	30
9999	XEON	2000	300	50

Figure 5.9 Using not equal to operator.

Note: <> and != can be used interchangeably.

5.1.3 Logical Operators/Boolean Operators

If we want to check for more than one condition in a single select query then we need to use the Boolean operators as specified in Table 5.3. Boolean operators can return only True or False for a given condition.

TABLE 5.3 List of Boolean operators

Boolean operator	Condition 1	Condition 2	Result
AND	TRUE	TRUE	TRUE
	TRUE	FALSE	FALSE
	FALSE	TRUE	FALSE
	FALSE	FALSE	FALSE
OR	TRUE	TRUE	TRUE
	TRUE	FALSE	TRUE
	FALSE	TRUE	TRUE
	FALSE	FALSE	FALSE

Boolean operator	Condition	Result
NOT	TRUE	FALSE
	FALSE	TRUE

AND—If any of the condition is FALSE, then it returns FALSE else TRUE.
OR—If any of the condition is TRUE, then it returns TRUE else FALSE.
NOT operator negates the given condition

- **List employees of department 30 who have salary more than 1500 (Figure 5.10).**

SQL>select empno, ename, sal, comm, deptno from emp *where deptno=30 and sal>1500;*

EMPNO	ENAME	SAL	COMM	DEPTNO
7499	ALLEN	1600	300	30
7654	MARTIN	2000	250	30
7698	BLAKE	2850	250	30

Figure 5.10 Using AND operator.

- **List employees whose salary ranges between 1000 and 2000(inclusive) (Figure 5.11).**

SQL>select empno, ename, sal, comm, deptno from emp *where sal >=1000 and sal<=2000;*

EMPNO	ENAME	SAL	COMM	DEPTNO
7499	ALLEN	1600	300	30
7521	WARD	1250	500	30
7654	MARTIN	2000	250	30
9999	XEON	2000	300	50

Figure 5.11   Boolean AND operator.

- **List employees whose salary is greater than 2000 or commission is greater than 300 (Figure 5.12).**

SQL>select empno, ename, sal, comm, deptno from emp *where sal>2000 OR comm>300;*

EMPNO	ENAME	SAL	COMM	DEPTNO
7521	WARD	1250	500	30
7566	JONES	2975	250	20
7698	BLAKE	2850	250	30

Figure 5.12   Boolean OR operator.

- **List employees who are in dept 20 and salary>1000 or any other department with salary>2000 (Figure 5.13).**

SQL>select empno, ename, sal, comm, deptno from emp *where deptno=20 and sal>2000 or deptno!=20 and sal>2000;*

EMPNO	ENAME	SAL	COMM	DEPTNO
7566	JONES	2975	250	20
7698	BLAKE	2850	250	30

Figure 5.13   Combining AND, OR operators.

Note:
- Combination of AND, OR and NOT Boolean operators can be used depending on the requirement.
- AND has higher precedence over OR operator, therefore, in situations requiring precedence of OR operator need to be enclosed within braces ().

NOT Operator

This negates the given condition.

- **List employees who are not in dept 10(other than 10) (Figure 5.14).**

SQL>select * from emp *where not deptno = 10;*							
EMPNO	**ENAME**	**JOB**	**MGR**	**HIREDATE**	**SAL**	**COMM**	**DEPTNO**
7369	SMITH	CLERK	7902	17-DEC-80	800	–	20
7499	ALLEN	SALESMAN	7698	20-FEB-81	1600	300	30
7566	JONES	MANAGER	7839	02-APR-81	2975	300	20
7902	FORD	ANALYST	7566	03-DEC-81	3000	–	20

Figure 5.14 NOT operator.

5.1.4 Special Operators

Oracle provides some special operators which enhance the capabilities of SQL statements. The special Operators are: IN, IS, LIKE and BETWEEN. Moreover, these operators can be used in conjunction with each other.

IN

- **List employees of dept 10 and 30 only (Figure 5.15).**

SQL> select * from emp *where deptno=10 or deptno=30;*							
EMPNO	**ENAME**	**JOB**	**MGR**	**HIREDATE**	**SAL**	**COMM**	**DEPTNO**
7499	ALLEN	SALESMAN	7698	20-FEB-81	1600	300	30
7839	KING	PRESIDENT	–	17-NOV-81	5000	–	10
7934	MILLER	CLERK	7782	23-JAN-82	1300	400	10

Figure 5.15 Display records of multiple departments.

Note: We have used Boolean operator OR and typed deptno twice because equal to operator can compare only one value at a time and therefore cannot be used for checking multiple value equality.

Caution: Following statements are wrong
   SQL>select * from emp where deptno=10,30;
   SQL>select * from emp where deptno=(10,30);

Oracle provides a **Special Operator called IN** which can be used to compare multiple values as in Figure 5.16.

SQL>select * from emp *where deptno IN (10, 30);*							
EMPNO	**ENAME**	**JOB**	**MGR**	**HIREDATE**	**SAL**	**COMM**	**DEPTNO**
7499	ALLEN	SALESMAN	7698	20-FEB-81	1600	300	30
7839	KING	PRESIDENT	–	17-NOV-81	5000	–	10
7934	MILLER	CLERK	7782	23-JAN-82	1300	400	10

Figure 5.16 IN Special operator.

NOT Boolean operator can be used with any other operator to negate the given condition. Suppose we want to list employees other than dept 10 and 30 (Figure 5.17).

SQL>select * from emp *where deptno not in (10,30);*							
EMPNO	**ENAME**	**JOB**	**MGR**	**HIREDATE**	**SAL**	**COMM**	**DEPTNO**
7369	SMITH	CLERK	7902	17-DEC-80	800	–	20
7566	JONES	MANAGER	7839	02-APR-81	2975	300	20
7902	FORD	ANALYST	7566	03-DEC-81	3000	–	20

Figure 5.17   Using NOT with IN operator.

BETWEEN

BETWEEN operator is used for checking the range of values.

- List of employees whose salary is between 2000 and 5000.

In Figure 5.11, we used Boolean operator as

SQL>select * from emp where sal>=2000 and sal<=5000;

Oracle provides a Special operator called BETWEEN for the same purpose.

SQL>select * from emp where sal **BETWEEN 2000 and 5000;**

Note: BETWEEN includes both the lower and upper limit values.

LIKE operator

LIKE is used for pattern matching searches.

- **List employees whose name starts with 'A' (Figure 5.18).**

SQL>select * from emp *where ename like 'A%';*							
EMPNO	**ENAME**	**JOB**	**MGR**	**HIREDATE**	**SAL**	**COMM**	**DEPTNO**
7876	ADAMS	CLERK	7788	12-JAN-83	1100	–	20
7499	ALLEN	SALESMAN	7698	20-FEB-81	1600	300	30

Figure 5.18   LIKE operator using '%'.

'A%' means that all employees whose name starts with 'A' and followed by any number of characters. **'%' is called the wild card character** which represents any number of characters including zero characters after 'A'.

- **List employees whose names have 'D' as 2nd character followed by any number of characters (Figure 5.19).**

SQL>select * from emp where *ename like '_D%';*							
EMPNO	**ENAME**	**JOB**	**MGR**	**HIREDATE**	**SAL**	**COMM**	**DEPTNO**
7876	ADAMS	CLERK	7788	12-JAN-83	1100	–	20

Figure 5.19   LIKE operator using '_'.

"_" underscore is also called a wild card character used for single character matching. '_D%' means 1st character can be any of the characters and 2nd character must be D followed by zero or more than zero number of characters.

- List employees whose name contains 'O' followed by any number of characters, followed by 'E' and then any number of characters.

SQL> select * from emp where ename like '%O%E%'.

The name contains both O and E and O must precede E.

IS operator

Before understanding the IS Operator we need to understand **a concept called NULL value**.

NULL values

Till now we have been adding records for employees with some salary and commission. Let us assume that a new employee has joined the company and his empno, ename and dept are known but his salary and commission have not been finalised. What we mean to say is that salary and commission for this new employee are not zero but rather UNKNOWN. **UNKNOWN values are called NULL value** in Oracle. **NULL is not blank spaces or zero**.

Now let us add the record for this new employee with unknown salary and commission (Figure 5.20).

SQL>insert into emp values (8000,'RAHUL','MANAGER',7839,'11-sep-1997',*null,null*,20);
SQL>select * from emp;

EMPNO	ENAME	JOB	MGR	HIREDATE	SAL	COMM	DEPTNO
7876	ADAMS	CLERK	7788	12-JAN-83	1100		20
8000	RAHUL	MANAGER	7839	11-SEP-97			20
7369	SMITH	CLERK	7902	17-DEC-80	800		20
7499	ALLEN	SALESMAN	7698	20-FEB-81	1600	300	30
7566	JONES	MANAGER	7839	02-APR-81	2975	300	20
7839	KING	PRESIDENT		17-NOV-81	5000		10
7902	FORD	ANALYST	7566	03-DEC-81	3000		20
7934	MILLER	CLERK	7782	23-JAN-82	1300	400	10

Figure 5.20 Inserting unknown values.

For inserting unknown values for a column we can just specify the word NULL.
There is one more way of providing NULL values for a particular column.

If we do not provide value for a particular column while using insert statement, then by default the value inserted is NULL. See the following statement.

SQL>insert into emp(empno, ename, job, mgr, hiredate, deptno) values (9000,'RASHMI','MANAGER',7839,'09-sep-1998',20);

We have supplied values for only empno, ename, job, mgr, hiredate, deptno and not for sal and comm column. Therefore, the default value which is stored in sal and comm column is NULL.

Now assume "emp" table with certain records where sal is NULL or commission is NULL or both are NULL (Figure 5.21).

```
SQL> select * from emp;
```

EMPNO	ENAME	JOB	MGR	HIREDATE	SAL	COMM	DEPTNO
7369	SMITH	CLERK	7902	17-DEC-80		300	10
7934	MILLER	CLERK	7782	23-JAN-82	1300		10
7839	KING	PRESIDENT		17-NOV-81	5000	400	10
7566	JONES	MANAGER	7839	02-APR-81			10

Figure 5.21   Employees with unknown salary and commission.

Let us now display the sal + comm as total salary for employees (Figure 5.22).

```
SQL>select empno,ename,sal,comm,sal + comm as total from emp;
```

EMPNO	ENAME	SAL	COMM	TOTAL
7369	SMITH		300	
7566	JONES			
7839	KING	5000	400	5400
7934	MILLER	1300		

Warning: TOTAL is right for KING only and blank for the rest of all. **Why so ?????** In fact, TOTAL for all employees Except KING has been displayed as NULL.

Figure 5.22   Total salary.

Now let us understand this behaviour of Oracle.

For SMITH, the sal is NULL and comm is 300. sal being NULL means not known. If sal is not known then sal + comm is also not known.

For JONES, the sal is not known and commission is also not known, therefore unknown + unknown is again an unknown.

For KING, the sal is 5000 and commission is 400, therefore, sal + com is 5400.

Caution: If any one of the two operands of a mathematical operator is NULL, then the result is also NULL. NULL implies NOT KNOWN and performing any mathematical operation on UNKNOWN value returns UNKNOWN.

Oracle provides a built-in function named **NVL()** which can be used to overcome this behaviour of Oracle for NULL values as shown in Figure 5.23. NVL stands for NULL VALUE.

```
SQL>select empno, ename, nvl(sal,0),nvl(comm,0),nvl(sal,0)+nvl(comm,0) as total from emp;
```

EMPNO	ENAME	NVL(SAL,0)	NVL(COMM,0)	TOTAL
7369	SMITH	0	300	300
7566	JONES	0	0	0
7839	KING	5000	400	5400
7934	MILLER	1300	0	1300

Figure 5.23   Using NVL() function.

Syntax of NVL() Function is given by:

NVL(column name, value to be assumed if NULL)

The first parameter of NVL() function is the column name. the second parameter tells the function to assume the specified value if NULL is found or else return the actual value.

When we say nvl(sal,0), it means that if the sal is NULL then assume it as zero or else take the actual value of sal column.

Similarly, nvl(sal,0)+nvl(comm,0) means assume the value of both sal and comm as zero if it is NULL and then add the two.

More about Oracle's built-in functions is discussed in Chapter 7.

Note: NULL value can be specified for any Data Type (NUMBER, CHAR, VARCHAR2, DATE etc.).

Let us list employees whose salary is not known or NULL (Figure 5.24).

```
SQL>select empno,ename,sal,comm from emp where sal=null;
no rows selected
```

Figure 5.24   Using EQUAL operator for displaying column with NULL value.

Although we had 2 employees, namely SMITH and JONES whose salary was not known or NULL but still they were not displayed. The reason is that a NULL value being unknown cannot be compared with anything(not even NULL). Two unknown values cannot be compared and hence records for SMITH and JONES are not displayed.

List employees whose salary is known or salary is NOT NULL (Figure 5.25).

```
SQL>select empno,ename,sal,comm from emp where sal<>null;
no rows selected
```

Figure 5.25   Using NOT EQUAL operator for salary other than NULL.

Although KING and MILLER had salary 5000 and 1300 respectively, still they were not displayed. When salary of KING 5000 is compared with NULL(Unknown) the net result is Unknown and hence the record is not displayed. Similar is the case for MILLER.

Now the question arises how to solve the above problem (Figures 5.24 and 5.25) of listing employees with unknown salary or known salary. Oracle provides a **Special Operator called IS** which comes handy while dealing with NULL values.

IS—a special operator to deal with NULL values

Let us find employees whose salary is unknown or NULL (Figure 5.26).

```
SQL>select empno,ename,sal,comm from emp where sal IS null;
```

EMPNO	ENAME	SAL	COMM
7369	SMITH	–	300
7566	JONES	–	–

Figure 5.26   IS operator.

Note: We have used special operator IS instead of '=' sign.

Find employees whose salary is known or NOT NULL (Figure 5.27).

```
select empno, ename, sal, comm from emp where sal IS NOT null;
```

EMPNO	ENAME	SAL	COMM
7839	KING	5000	400
7934	MILLER	1300	–

Figure 5.27   Using NOT in conjunction with IS.

Note: We have used the Boolean operator NOT in combination with IS operator.

Some authors say that the same purpose can be achieved by using NVL() function in the WHERE clause as shown in Figure 5.28.

Finding employees with NULL salary (Figure 5.28).

```
SQL>select empno, ename, sal, comm from emp where nvl(sal,0)=0;
```

EMPNO	ENAME	SAL	COMM
7369	SMITH		300
7566	JONES		

Figure 5.28   Finding employees with NULL salary using NVL().

Caution: There is a caveat in the above query (Figure 5.28). Suppose our table contained an employee XEON with zero salary. It means that he is not a permanent employee and is paid only commission and not salary.

Assume records in the EMP table as in Figure 5.29.

```
SQL>select empno, ename, sal, comm from emp ;
```

EMPNO	ENAME	SAL	COMM
7369	SMITH		300
7566	JONES		
7839	KING	5000	400
7934	MILLER	1300	
9999	XEON	0	400

Figure 5.29   Records in EMP table.

Let us again find the employees with unknown or NULL salary by using nvl(sal,0)=0 in the WHERE clause as shown in Figure 5.30.

SQL>select empno, ename, sal, comm from emp where nvl(sal,0)=0;

EMPNO	ENAME	SAL	COMM
7369	SMITH	–	300
7566	JONES	–	–
9999	XEON	0	400

Figure 5.30   Using NVL() for records with NULL values.

Actually we wanted employees with unknown or NULL salary and not the employees with zero salary. XEON has also been displayed which was not the intended objective. In such situations we have to use IS Operator for the intended purpose.

5.2   OPERATOR PRECEDENCE

The various operators that we have discussed so far follow a precedence rule. For example, 2+3*5 will evaluate to 2+15=17 because of higher precedence of multiplication over addition. **Table 5.4 contains the list of operators in order of the highest precedence to the lowest precedence.**

TABLE 5.4   Operator precedence

Precedence	Type of operator	Operator	Meaning
1	Binary	**	Exponentiation. Not supported by SQL Supported by PL/SQL
2	Unary	+, −	Single Operand
3	Binary	*, /	Multiplication, Division
4	Binary	+, −, ||	Addition, Subtraction and Concatenation
5	Comparison	=, <, >, <=, >=, <>, IS, IN, BETWEEN, LIKE	Comparing values
6	Boolean	NOT	Negation
7	Boolean	AND	Returns TRUE when both Conditions are TRUE
8	Boolean	OR	Returns TRUE if any of the Conditions is TRUE

Note: Operators at the same level of precedence have equal priority. This priority can be overridden by using () braces.

REVIEW QUESTIONS

1. Classify the various operators supported by Oracle.
2. Explain the concept of NULL values. How is NULL value different from empty string or zero?
3. Is it possible to use comparison operators with columns containing NULL values? If not, then specify the reason.
4. Is it possible to compare two NULL values?
5. What is the role of NVL() function?
6. Which operators are used for pattern matching queries?
7. What is the significance of "_" and "%" wild card characters?
8. Explain the concept of Operator Precedence. How can the precedence of operators be changed?

MULTIPLE CHOICE QUESTIONS

1. SQL commands are
   (a) Case sensitive
   (b) Not case sensitive but data stored is case sensitive
   (c) Case sensitive but data stored is not case sensitive
2. Adding NULL value to 100 gives
   (a) 100
   (b) NULL
   (c) BLANK
3. SELECT NULL||'TEST' FROM DUAL returns
   (a) TEST
   (b) NULLTEST
   (c) TEST
4. SELECT 'NULL'||'TEST' FROM DUAL returns
   (a) NULLTEST
   (b) NULL TEST
   (c) TEST
   (d) TEST
5. SELECT * FROM STUDENT WHERE MARKS>50 and MARKS<90 is equivalent to (assuming integer marks only)
   (a) WHERE MARKS BETWEEN 50 and 90
   (b) WHERE MARKS BETWEEN 51 and 89
   (c) WHERE MARKS BETWEEN 49 and 91
6. Which of the following statements is correct for displaying the employees of department 20 and 40 only?
   (a) SELECT * FROM EMP WHERE DEPTNO=20,40
   (b) SELECT * FROM EMP WHERE DEPTNO=(20,40)

    (c) SELECT * FROM EMP WHERE DEPTNO=20 OR DEPTNO=40

    (d) SELECT * FROM EMP WHERE DEPTNO NOT BETWEEN 20 AND 40

7. List employees whose name contains O followed by any character then followed by M

    (a) SELECT * FROM EMP WHERE ENAME LIKE 'O_M%';

    (b) SELECT * FROM EMP WHERE ENAME LIKE '%O_M%';

    (c) SELECT * FROM EMP WHERE ENAME LIKE '%O%M%';

8. What is the right syntax for inserting 19th FEB 1997 in a date column?

    (a) 19-FEB-98

    (b) 19-FEB-1998

    (c) 19-FEBRUARY-1998

    (d) 19/02/1998

9. Inserting '19-FEB-99' in a Date Column will actually store

    (a) 19-FEB-1999

    (b) 19-FEB-2099

    (c) 19-FEB-0099

10. Which of the following is correct for displaying employees with NULL salary?

    (a) WHERE sal = NULL

    (b) WHERE NVL(sal,)=0

    (c) WHERE sal is NULL

11. SELECT 2+3*4 FROM DUAL; will return

    (a) 20

    (b) 14

    (c) None of the above

LAB ASSIGNMENT

1. Refer to Table 4.2 and add the following records in the EMPLOYEE table.

EMPLOYEE NO.	EMPLOYEE NAME	DATE OF JOINING	DEPARTMENT NO.	GENDER	SALARY	COMMISSION
1111	SATISH	19-DEC-2008	10	M	10,000	1000
2222	RASHMI	01-JAN-1987	20	F	8000	500
3333	RISHI	05-JUN-1976	10	M	7000	400
4444	ANIL	16-APR-1967 10:10:10 AM	10	M	12,000	2000
5555	ANITA		30	F		1000
6666	NEELESH	20-MAY-1987	20	M	13,000	
7777	RUCHI	11-JUN-2000 13:20:10 PM		F		
8888	SARIKA			F		

2. Retrieve ALL the records from the EMPLOYEE table.
3. Retrieve the employee_no, name and salary from the EMPLOYEE table for all employees.
4. Retrieve the department_no, name, salary and commission for all employees.
5. Retrieve the department_no, employee_no and total salary as SALARY + 10% of SALARY + COMMISSION for all employees.
6. List employees who have joined the company after 1st APRIL 2000.
7. List the male employees of department 10 and 30.
8. List those employees who have SALARY more than 10,000.
9. List the employees of department 10 who earn more than 10,000.
10. Display employees who earned commission more than 1000 and belong to department 10 or have salary more than 10,000/- but do not belong to department 10.
11. List the employees with zero salary.
12. List the employees with unknown salary.
13. List the employees with either salary or commission unknown.
14. List the employees with both salary and commission unknown.
15. Display the employees whose name contains 'SA'.
16. Display the employees whose name starts with 'S' followed by any character then followed by 'T', followed by any number of characters.
17. Display the salary of employees as ZERO if unknown.

Integrity Constraints

6.1 INTRODUCTION

Oracle provides several ways of controlling what kind of data can be input into a table. The various controls/constraints are as follows:

1. PRIMARY KEY
2. NOT NULL
3. UNIQUE
4. DEFAULT
5. CHECK
6. FOREIGN KEY

Note: Key means a single column or a combination of columns.

6.2 CLASSIFICATION OF CONSTRAINTS

Constraints can be broadly classified as:

1. Column Level
2. Table Level

6.2.1 Column Level Constraints

When a constraint is applied to a single column then it is called a **Column Level Constraint**. This constraint will affect the values being entered for that particular column only irrespective of values of other columns.

6.2.2 Table Level Constraints

When a single constraint is applied to more than one column then it is called **Table Level Constraint**. These constraints impact the values being entered for a combination of column values, for example, salary can never be less than the commission is a table level constraint.

6.3 PRIMARY KEY

Primary key can be defined as the single column or combination of columns which uniquely identify a row in a table, for example, the rollno column in our "student_master" table is the primary key. No two students can have the same rollno and moreover rollno field cannot be left NULL in any case, for example, see Figure 6.1.

Primary Key = UNIQUE + NOT NULL + Automatic Indexed

```
SQL> create table student_master
  2 (
  3 rollno number(4) primary key,
  4 name varchar2(10)
  5 );

Table created.

SQL> insert into student_master values (1,'rahul');

1 row created.

SQL> insert into student_master values (2,'rashmi');

1 row created.

SQL> insert into student_master values (1,'test');
insert into student_master values (1,'test')
*
ERROR at line 1:
ORA-00001: unique constraint (SCOTT.SYS_C005312) violated
```

Figure 6.1   Creating primary key.

Note that when we try to insert rollno 1 with name "test", Oracle gives an error message saying unique constraint violated because rollno 1 already exists in the table.

Let us now try to insert a NULL value for a record as shown in Figure 6.2.

```
SQL> insert into student_master values (null,'abc');
insert into student_master values (null,'abc')
                     *
ERROR at line 1:
ORA-01400: cannot insert NULL into ("SCOTT"."STUDENT_MASTER"."ROLLNO")
```

Figure 6.2   Inserting NULL values in primary key column.

6.3.1 Composite Primary Key

Primary key can be defined for a combination of columns also. When a primary key consists of multiple columns, then it is called a **Composite Primary Key**.

Assume a table STUDENT having COLLEGE, ROLLNO and NAME columns. If we presume that students of different colleges can have the same rollno then we will have to declare COLLEGE + ROLLNO as the primary key, or in other words, the same rollno will repeat for all colleges.

ROLLNOs for COLLEGE "A": 1, 2, 3, 4, ...
ROLLNOs for COLLEGE "B": 1, 2, 3, 4, ...

To refer to a particular student we have to specify the college as well as the rollno within that college.

6.3.2 Defining a Composite Primary Key

We can define composite primary key as shown in Figure 6.3.

```
SQL> create table student_master
  2 (
  3 college varchar2(4),
  4 rollno number(4),
  5 name varchar2(10),
  6 primary key (college, rollno)
  7 );

Table created.

SQL> insert into student_master values ('OIST',1,'rashmi');
1 row created.

SQL> insert into student_master values ('OIST',2,'satish');
1 row created.

SQL> insert into student_master values ('OIST',3,'neelesh');
1 row created.

SQL> insert into student_master values ('RKDF',1,'ruchi');
1 row created.

SQL> insert into student_master values ('RKDF',2,'sarika');
1 row created.

SQL> insert into student_master values ('OIST',2,'test');
insert into student_master values ('OIST',2,'test')
*
ERROR at line 1:
ORA-00001: unique constraint (SCOTT.SYS_C005313) violated
```

Figure 6.3   Creating composite primary key.

By making college + rollno as the primary key, the same rollno cannot be supplied for OIST College. Rollno will be unique within the same college.

> **Note:**
> - A table can have one and only one primary key.
> - Primary key implies UNIQUE as well as NOT NULL values.
> - UNIQUE implies duplicate values cannot be entered.
> - NOT NULL implies value cannot be unknown(NULL) for any of the records.
> - Primary key columns are automatically indexed(Refer to Chapter 13 for more details).

6.4 NOT NULL

Specifying NOT NULL as constraint means that NULL values cannot be inserted for that particular field although duplicate values for that column can be entered. Figure 6.4 contains an example for specifying the NOT NULL constraint.

```
SQL> create table student
  2 (
  3 rollno number(4),
  4 name varchar2(10) not null,
  5 marks number(3) not null
  6 );

Table created.

SQL> insert into student values (1,'rashmi',20);
1 row created.

SQL> insert into student values (2,null,30);
insert into student values (2,null,30)
                            *
ERROR at line 1:
ORA-01400: cannot insert NULL into ("SCOTT"."STUDENT"."NAME")

SQL> insert into student values (3,'satish',null);
insert into student values (3,'satish',null)
                                       *
ERROR at line 1:
ORA-01400: cannot insert NULL into ("SCOTT"."STUDENT"."MARKS")

SQL> insert into student values (1,'rashmi',32);
1 row created.

SQL> insert into student values (1,'rashmi',32);
1 row created.
```

Figure 6.4   Defining NOT NULL constraint.

We are able to insert "rashmi" as name in multiple records but we cannot insert NULL values for name field.

6.5   UNIQUE

UNIQUE implies duplicate values for the same field cannot be entered but NULL values can be inserted for that column. Since two NULL values cannot be compared therefore UNIQUE constraint does not prevent from supplying NULL values, for example, see Figure 6.5.

```
SQL> create table student
  2 (
  3 rollno number(4) unique,
  4 name varchar2(10));

Table created.

SQL> insert into student values (1,'satish');

1 row created.

SQL> insert into student values (2,'rashmi');

1 row created.

SQL> insert into student values (1,'test');
insert into student values (1,'test')
*
ERROR at line 1:
ORA-00001: unique constraint (SCOTT.SYS_C005316) violated

SQL> insert into student values (null,'test');

1 row created.
```

Figure 6.5   Defining UNIQUE constraint.

6.6   DEFAULT

DEFAULT implies that if we do not specify a value for column in the INSERT statement, then the value specified in default clause gets inserted. Let us see an example shown in Figure 6.6. We want to insert a student with marks zero if marks not supplied in the INSERT statement.

```
SQL> create table student
  2 (
  3 rollno number(4),
  4 marks number(3) default 0
  5 );

Table created.

SQL> insert into student values (1, 10);
```

1 row created.

SQL> insert into student (rollno) values (2);

1 row created.

SQL> insert into student values (3, *null);*

1 row created.

SQL> insert into student values (4, 40);

1 row created.

SQL> select * from student;

ROLLNO	MARKS
1	10
2	0
3	
4	40

Figure 6.6 Defining DEFAULT constraint.

Notes:
1. While inserting record 2 we did not specify marks. So default value 0 was inserted.
2. In record 3 we forcibly inserted NULL for marks. DEFAULT has no impact if we provide NULL value for the column.
3. DEFAULT means that when we do not supply any value for that column then the value specified in default clause is inserted.

6.7 CHECK

The CHECK constraint allows verifying the values being supplied against specified condition, e.g. Figure 6.7 restricting marks between 0 and 100, specifying a list of colleges, etc.

```
SQL> create table student
  2 (
  3 rollno number(4),
  4 college varchar2(4) check (college in ('RKDF','OIST','PTL')),
  5 marks number(3) check (marks >=0 and marks <=100)
  6 );

Table created.

SQL> insert into student values (1,'RKDF',10);
```

1 row created.

SQL> insert into student values (2,'TEST',20);
 insert into student values (2,'TEST',20)
 *
ERROR at line 1:
ORA-02290: check constraint (SCOTT.SYS_C005317) violated

Figure 6.7   CHECK constraint.

Since 'TEST' was not specified as a valid college in the CHECK constraint, therefore, it was rejected. Note that data is case sensitive. If we try to insert "oist" in college column then it will also be rejected as shown in Figure 6.8.

We cannot insert a value less than 0 or more than 100 as per CHECK constraint put on marks column as shown in Figure 6.8.

SQL> insert into student values (3,'RKDF',-5);
 insert into student values (3,'RKDF',-5)
 *
ERROR at line 1:
ORA-02290: check constraint (SCOTT.SYS_C005318) violated

Figure 6.8   CHECK constraint on marks.

Note: CHECK constraint must be enclosed within brackets ( ).

Caution:
- SQL commands are not case sensitive, for example, SELECT, select, SeLect all are the same.
- Values supplied for records are case sensitive, for example, 'oist' is different from 'OIST', 'Oist', 'OIst'. Searching for college='OIST' will return exact match only.

The same CHECK constraint on marks column can be defined using the BETWEEN clause as shown in Figure 6.9.

```
SQL> create table student
   2 (
   3 rollno number(4),
   4 marks number(3) check (marks between 0 and 100)
   5 );

Table created.
```

Figure 6.9   Using BETWEEN operator in CHECK constraint.

6.7.1   CHECK Constraint on Multiple Columns

Let us create an "employee" table with "empno", "salary" and "commission" columns such that for any employee either salary or commission is non-zero. Figure 6.10 shows an example for the CHECK constraint.

```
SQL> create table employee
  2 (
  3 empno number(4),
  4 salary number(10,2),
  5 commission number(10,2),
  6 CHECK (salary > 0 or commission >0)
  7 );

Table created.

SQL> insert into employee values (1,100,20);
1 row created.

SQL> insert into employee values (2,200,0);
1 row created.

SQL> insert into employee values (3,0,30);
1 row created.

SQL> insert into employee values (4,0,0);
insert into employee values (4,0,0)
*
ERROR at line 1:
ORA-02290: check constraint (SCOTT.SYS_C005320) violated
```

Figure 6.10   CHECK constraint using OR operator.

6.8   FOREIGN KEY

Assume a situation wherein we have two tables, namely "studentmaster" and "studentdetails". The "studentmaster" table contains the rollno, name, age and address columns. The "studentdetails" table contains rollno, subject and marks columns.

We desire the following two functionalities:

1. The rollno and marks for a student can be entered in details table only when the specified rollno exists in the master table(**called PARENT table**).
2. The rollno from the master table cannot be deleted if corresponding rollno exists in details table(**called CHILD table**).

In such a scenario, we create primary key on rollno of master table and then reference the rollno field of details table to the primary key of master table as shown in Figure 6.11.

```
SQL>create table studentmaster
  2 (
  3 rollno number(4) primary key,
  4 name varchar2(10),
  5 age number(2),
  6 address varchar2(10)
  7 );
```

```
Table created.

SQL> create table studentdetails
 2 (
 3 rollno number(4) references studentmaster(rollno),
 4 subject varchar2(10),
 5 marks number(2)
 6 );

Table created.
```

Figure 6.11   Defining foreign key.

The foreign key can also be created using an alternative syntax (Figure 6.12).

```
SQL> create table studentdetails
   2 (
   3 rollno number(4),
   4 subject varchar2(10),
   5 marks number(2),
   6 foreign key (rollno) references studentmaster(rollno)
   7 );

Table created.
```

Figure 6.12   Alternative Syntax for defining foreign key.

Let us insert some records in both the tables (Figure 6.13).

```
SQL> insert into studentmaster values (1,'rashmi',25,'243,9-B');

1 row created.

SQL> insert into studentmaster values (2,'satish',30,'23,C');

1 row created.

SQL> select * from studentmaster;

     ROLLNO        NAME          AGE         ADDRESS
        1          rashmi         25         243,9-B
        2          satish         30         23,C

SQL> insert into studentdetails values (1,'maths',45);

1 row created.

SQL> insert into studentdetails values (1,'phy',56);

1 row created.
```

```
SQL> insert into studentdetails values (2,'maths',67);

1 row created.

SQL> insert into studentdetails values (3,'maths',66);
insert into studentdetails values (3,'maths',66)
*
ERROR at line 1:
ORA-02291: integrity constraint (SCOTT.SYS_C005322) violated - parent key not
found
```

Figure 6.13 Verifying working of foreign key.

Note:
1. We are able to insert marks for rollno 1 and 2 in details table because they exist in the master table.
2. When we tried inserting marks for rollno 3 in details table, Oracle gives ERROR message, as rollno 3 is not existing in the master table.

Now let us try to delete rollno 2 from the master table which is existing in details table (Figure 6.14).

```
SQL> delete from studentmaster where rollno=2;
delete from studentmaster where rollno=2
*
ERROR at line 1:
ORA-02292: integrity constraint (SCOTT.SYS_C005322) violated - child record found
```

Figure 6.14 Deleting record from master table.

We cannot delete rollno 2 from the master table as we have marks entered for that student in details tables. In order to achieve this we first need to delete rollno 2 from details table and then followed by deleting rollno 2 from the master table as shown in Figure 6.15.

```
SQL> delete from studentdetails where rollno=2;

1 row deleted.

SQL> delete from studentmaster where rollno=2;

1 row deleted.
```

Figure 6.15 Deleting record from detail table and then from master table.

Note:
- A foreign key can refer to a primary key only.
- A table can have multiple foreign keys referring to different tables for different columns.
- A table can have one and only one primary key.
- Defining foreign key establishes a PARENT/CHILD relationship between the two tables. Some authors name the PARENT/CHILD relation as MASTER/DETAIL relation.

- **Defining a foreign key implies two conditions:**
  1. We can insert only those records in the CHILD table for which corresponding records exist in the PARENT table.
  2. We can delete only those records from the PARENT table for which there are no corresponding records in the CHILD table.
- It is not necessary that the name of foreign key column should be the same as that of the primary key column of other table. The column names of primary key and foreign key may be different.

6.8.1 Defining Foreign Key on Multiple Columns

In Figure 6.11 we had just one column in details table which referenced the rollno column of the master table. Suppose we have a master table with composite primary key, then how to specify foreign key in such cases. Assume that master table has college + rollno as the primary key and detail table will reference this composite primary key. Figure 6.16 defines composite primary key and foreign key based on the composite primary key.

```
SQL> create table student_master(college char(10),rollno number(4),name
varchar2(10),address varchar2(10),
primary key (college,rollno));

Table created.

SQL> create table student_details(college char(10),rollno number(4),subject char(10),marks
number(3),
foreign key (college,rollno) references student_master(college,rollno));

Table created.
```

Figure 6.16 Foreign key on multiple columns.

6.8.2 Defining Multiple Foreign Keys

A table can have multiple foreign keys referring to different tables. Say, the "student_details" table has rollno as foreign key which refers to rollno of "student_master" table. Similarly, the "student_details" may have one more column named grade which would refer to the grade column of another table "student_grades". Refer to Figure 6.17.

```
SQL> create table student_master(rollno number(4),name char(10),address varchar2(10),
primary key (rollno));

Table created.

SQL> create table student_grades (grade char(2),description varchar2(20),primary key (grade));
Table created

SQL> create table student_details(rollno number(4),subject char(10),marks number(3),
  2 grade char(1),
```

```
3 primary key (rollno,subject),
4 foreign key (rollno) references student_master(rollno),
5 foreign key (grade) references student_grades(grade);

Table created.
```

Figure 6.17   Multiple foreign keys.

Student_details has the following keys:

1. Primary key (rollno, subject)
2. Foreign key rollno referring to rollno of student_master table
3. Foreign key grade referring to grade of student_grades table.

6.9   DATA DICTIONARY/META-DATA

Oracle maintains the information about the various objects like tables in the form of tables. In Database terminology this is called as **meta-data (data about data) or "Data Dictionary"**. Let us understand it through examples.

To know the number of tables in "scott" user area we can query a system table named "tab" as shown in Figure 6.18.

```
SQL> select * from tab;

            TNAME                    TABTYPE

     STUDENT_MASTER                   TABLE
     STUDENT_DETAILS                  TABLE
           STUDENT                    TABLE

3 rows selected.
```

Figure 6.18   Data dictionary.

Here "tab" is Oracle's internal table which stores the name and type of various objects created. From listing it is clear that we have three tables in our "scott" user, namely "student_master", " student_details" and "student".

6.9.1   Adding, Removing and Altering Constraints

The constraints we applied at the time of table creation can also be specified after the table has been created (without constraints).

Adding constraints and primary key after table creation

Suppose we forgot to specify primary key at the time of table creation. How do we add it later on? For example, see Figure 6.19 for adding constraint after the table has been created.

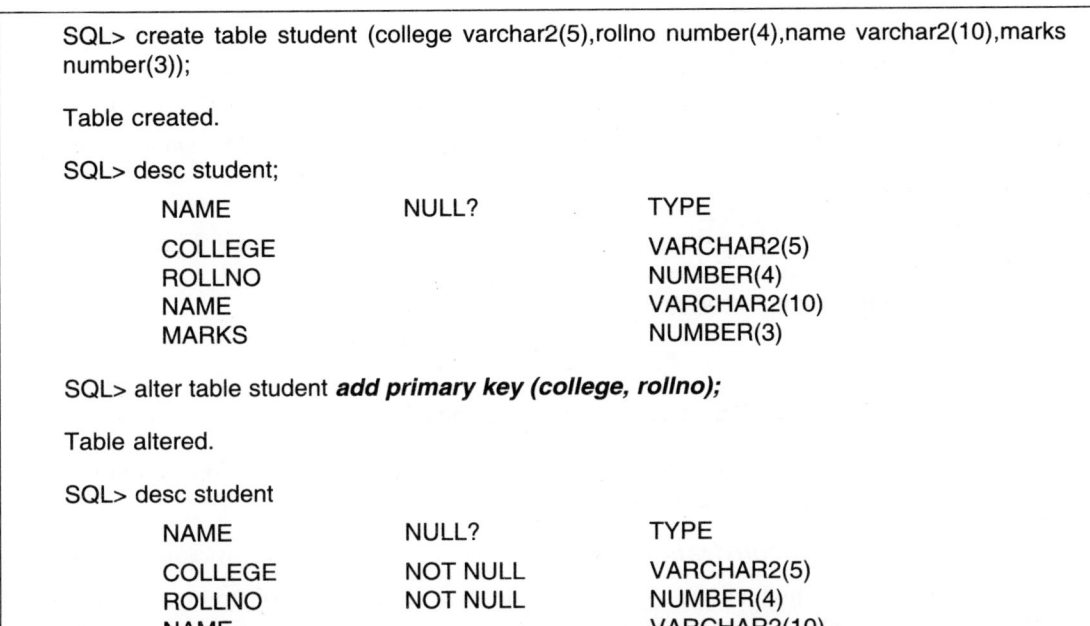

```
SQL> create table student (college varchar2(5),rollno number(4),name varchar2(10),marks
number(3));

Table created.

SQL> desc student;
        NAME                    NULL?                   TYPE
        COLLEGE                                         VARCHAR2(5)
        ROLLNO                                          NUMBER(4)
        NAME                                            VARCHAR2(10)
        MARKS                                           NUMBER(3)

SQL> alter table student add primary key (college, rollno);

Table altered.

SQL> desc student
        NAME                    NULL?                   TYPE
        COLLEGE                 NOT NULL                VARCHAR2(5)
        ROLLNO                  NOT NULL                NUMBER(4)
        NAME                                            VARCHAR2(10)
        MARKS                                           NUMBER(3)
```

Figure 6.19 Adding constraint after table creation.

Note: Display of "NOT NULL" against "college" and "rollno" is indicative of primary key. But still we cannot be sure as these fields could have been applied just "NOT NULL" constraint at the time of creation instead of primary key.

Let us query the Oracle's Data Dictionary tables (Figure 6.20) for finding out the primary key of the "student" table.

```
SQL> select constraint_name,constraint_type,table_name from user_constraints;

CONSTRAINT_NAME         C       TABLE_NAME
SYS_C004025             P       STUDENT
```

Figure 6.20 Data dictionary for constraints.

USER_CONSTRAINTS is an internal table of Oracle which stores the various constraints applied to a table.

Here, constraint_type='P' indicates that it is a primary key constraint.

Let us now find out the columns which are forming the primary key (Figure 6.21).

```
SQL> select constraint_name,table_name,column_name from user_cons_columns where
constraint_name='SYS_C004025';

CONSTRAINT_NAME             TABLE_NAME              COLUMN_NAME
    SYS_C004025                 STUDENT                 COLLEGE
    SYS_C004025                 STUDENT                 ROLLNO
```

Figure 6.21 Finding primary key columns.

As the "college" and "rollno" both are associated with the same constraint_name "SYS_C004025", therefore, both are forming the primary key.

Note: Whenever we declare a constraint at the time of table creation or add it afterwards, Oracle automatically assigns a unique constraint name starting with SYS_C followed by unique serial no.

Removing primary key

Primary key can be removed by using the ALTER table command as shown in Figure 6.22.

```
SQL> alter table student drop primary key;

Table altered.
```

Figure 6.22   Removing primary key.

Now if we try to select records from "user_constraints" and "user_cons_columns" data dictionary tables, no records will be shown for the "student" table.

Specifying user-defined constraint name

Oracle automatically assigns a unique constraint name to each and every constraint applied starting with 'SYS_C'. Oracle also provides a feature whereby we can assign our own-defined constraint names. Let us see an example (Figure 6.23).

User-defined constraint names can be declared at the time of creating table or afterwards using the "alter table" command.

```
SQL>create table student(college varchar2(5),rollno number(4),name varchar2(10),marks number(3),
constraint PK_STUDENT_COLLEGE_ROLLNO PRIMARY KEY (college,rollno));

Table created.

SQL> select constraint_name,constraint_type,table_name from user_constraints;

CONSTRAINT_NAME                    C       TABLE_NAME

PK_STUDENT_COLLEGE_ROLLNO  P       STUDENT
```

Figure 6.23   User-defined constraint names.

Note that we have used quite elaborate name for primary constraint starting with "PK", table name and followed by columns on which primary key has been defined.

Note: Experts suggest that we should prefer using elaborate user-defined constraint names so that we do not need to refer to data dictionary views for identifying constraints.

Moreover, user-defined constraints names are much easier to manage.

Adding user-defined constraint names afterwards

Let us first drop the existing primary key (Figure 6.24).

SQL> alter table student drop primary key;

Table altered.

Figure 6.24 Removing primary key.

The primary key can be dropped by using the user-defined constraint name as shown in Figure 6.25 which has the same result as given in the statement of Figure 6.24.

SQL> *alter table student drop constraint PK_STUDENT_COLLEGE_ROLLNO ;*

Table altered.

Figure 6.25 Removing primary key using user-defined constraint name.

Let us again add the Primary key with user-defined constraint name using the "alter" command (Figure 6.26).

SQL> alter table student *add constraint PK_STUDENT_COLLEGE_ROLLNO PRIMARY KEY (college,rollno);*

Table altered.

Figure 6.26 Adding primary key with user-defined constraint name.

6.10 ENABLING AND DISABLING CONSTRAINTS

Oracle provides a feature by which we can temporarily disable or enable constraints instead of dropping them permanently. Figure 6.27 specifies how to disable a constraint.

SQL> alter table student *disable constraint PK_STUDENT_COLLEGE_ROLLNO;*

Table altered.

SQL> insert into student values ('GEC',1,'satish',12);

1 row created.

SQL> insert into student values ('GEC',1,'test',14);

1 row created.

Figure 6.27 Disabling constraint.

We are now able to insert duplicate college and rollno combination since the primary key is disabled.

Data dictionary table "user_constraints" contains a column called "status" indicating the status (enabled/disabled) for constraints (Figure 6.28).

```
SQL> select constraint_name,constraint_type,table_name,status from user_constraints ;

CONSTRAINT_NAME                      C TABLE_NAME          STATUS
PK_STUDENT_COLLEGE_ROLLNO            P STUDENT            DISABLED
```

Figure 6.28 Status of a constraint.

Here we can see that the status of constraint "PK_STUDENT_COLLEGE_ROLLNO" is "DISABLED".

6.10.1 Enabling Constraints

Let us now enable back the primary key constraint as shown in Figure 6.29.

```
SQL> alter table student enable constraint PK_STUDENT_COLLEGE_ROLLNO;
alter table student enable constraint PK_STUDENT_COLLEGE_ROLLNO
*
ERROR at line 1:
ORA-02437: cannot validate (SCOTT.PK_STUDENT_COLLEGE_ROLLNO) - primary key
violated
```

Figure 6.29 Enabling constraint.

Oracle gave Error because we already have two records for college='GEC' and rollno=1. So when we are trying to enable primary key constraint, it failed. To get this working we will have to first delete any one of the two records (Figure 6.30).

```
SQL> select * from student;

COLLE    ROLLNO       NAME   MARKS
GEC      1            satish  12
GEC      1            test    14

SQL> delete from student where name='test';

1 row deleted.

SQL> commit;

Commit complete.

SQL> alter table student enable constraint PK_STUDENT_COLLEGE_ROLLNO;

Table altered.

SQL> insert into student values ('GEC',1,'test',14);
insert into student values ('GEC',1,'test',14)
*
ERROR at line 1:
ORA-00001: unique constraint (SCOTT.PK_STUDENT_COLLEGE_ROLLNO) violated
```

Figure 6.30 Removing duplicate records before enabling primary key.

Now since the PRIMARY KEY constraint is enabled, therefore, it is not allowing us to enter record with duplicate college, rollno.

REVIEW QUESTIONS

1. What do we mean by constraints? Which constraints are supported by Oracle?
2. Differentiate between Column and Table Level Constraints?
3. Define primary key. How can a single and multicolumn primary key be defined?
4. Explain the purpose of UNIQUE and NOT NULL constraints. How is primary key different from the above two constraints?
5. Can the DEFAULT constraint prevent input of NULL values?
6. Specify practical applications of the CHECK constraint.
7. What does foreign key signify?
8. What is Data Dictionary? Why is it called Meta-Data?
9. How to add constraints after the table has been created? Specify the command used for the same purpose.
10. How to remove a constraint?
11. What do we mean by enabling and disabling constraints?
12. Can we recover dropped constraints?

TRUE/FALSE

1. Constraints control the type of values that can be entered into a column.
2. A primary key implies UNIQUE as well as NOT NULL values.
3. A primary key can be defined on multiple columns with different data types.
4. A table must have at least one primary key.
5. A table can have multiple primary keys.
6. NULL values can be supplied for columns with UNIQUE constraint.
7. When no value is supplied for a column with DEFAULT constraint then the actual value stored in database is NULL.
8. Constraints cannot be applied on multiple columns.
9. A foreign key can refer to a primary key only.
10. A table can have multiple foreign keys.
11. A foreign key can refer to primary key of different table.
12. A foreign key can refer to primary key of the same table.
13. Dropped constraints can be recovered.
14. Name of foreign and primary keys must be the same.
15. Data type and size of foreign and primary keys must be the same.
16. Constraints can be given user-defined names.
17. Constraints can be enabled or disabled as desired.

LAB ASSIGNMENT

1. Create a DEPT table with the following columns and constraints.

TABLE 6.1   Structure of DEPT table

Column name	Data type	Size	Constraint
DEPTNO	NUMBER	2	PRIMARY KEY
DNAME	VARCHAR2	10	UNIQUE + NOT NULL
LOCATION	VARCHAR2	10	UNIQUE + NOT NULL

2. Create an EMP table with the following columns and constraints.

TABLE 6.2   Structure of EMP table

Column name	Data type	Size	Constraint
EMPNO	CHAR	4	PRIMARY KEY
ENAME	VARCHAR2	10	NOT NULL
JOB	VARCHAR2	10	
MGR	CHAR	4	
HIREDATE	DATE		NOT NULL
GENDER	CHAR	1	'M' OR 'F' ONLY
SAL	NUMBER	8,2	DEFAULT 0
COMM	NUMBER	8,2	DEFAULT 0
DEPTNO	NUMBER	2	FOREIGN KEY referring to DEPTNO of DEPT table

3. Add the following records into the DEPT table.

DEPTNO	DNAME	LOCATION
10	ACCOUNTING	NEW YORK
20	RESEARCH	DALLAS
30	SALES	CHICAGO
40	OPERATIONS	BOSTON

4. Add the following records into the EMP table.

EMPNO	ENAME	JOB	MGR	HIREDATE	GENDER	SAL	COMM	DEPTNO
7369	SMITH	CLERK	7902	17-DEC-1980	M	800	–	20
7499	ALLEN	SALESMAN	7698	20-FEB-1981 10:10:20 AM	F	1600	300	30
7521	WARD	SALESMAN	7698	22-FEB-1981	F	1250	500	30

(Contd.)

EMPNO	ENAME	JOB	MGR	HIREDATE	GENDER	SAL	COMM	DEPTNO
7566	JONES	MANAGER	7839	02-APR-1981	M	2975	–	20
7654	MARTIN	SALESMAN	7698	28-SEP-1981 13:20:33 PM	M	1250	1400	30
7698	BLAKE	MANAGER	7839	01-MAY-1981 14:15:40 PM	F	2850	-	30
7782	CLARK	MANAGER	7839	09-JUN-1981	M	2450	-	10
7788	SCOTT	ANALYST	7566	09-DEC-1982	M	3000	-	20
7839	KING	PRESIDENT	-	17-NOV-1981 23:10:30 PM	M	5000	-	10
7844	TURNER	SALESMAN	7698	08-SEP-1981 08:45:34 AM	M	1500	0	30

5. Add a table level constraint such that commission cannot be greater than the 30% of salary after the table has been created. Assign a user-defined constraint name CTBL_COMM_GT_30_SAL.

6. Add a new constraint with the name DEPT_CHK_LOCATION to the DEPARTMENT table such that LOCATION can be any one of the following cities NEW YORK, DALLAS, CHICAGO, BOSTON only.

7. Remove the UNIQUE constraint from LOCATION column of DEPT table.

8. It has been decided that the LOCATION of more than one department could be the same. So it is required to disable temporarily the UNIQUE constraint on LOCATION column.

9. Enable the disabled constraint on LOCATION column of the DEPT table.

CHAPTER

7

Oracle Built-in Functions

7.1 INTRODUCTION

The operations which are frequently performed on data are converted into standardized built-in functions so that a programmer does not need to invest time repeatedly for the same task. Providing built-in functions not only reduces the amount of coding but also reduces the mistakes occurring due to typographic and logical mistakes. For example, it is very common to round a fractional value to, say 2 digits of decimal point.

Oracle provides several built-in functions which can be broadly classified into 3 categories, namely SCALAR, AGGREGATE and LIST as shown in Figure 7.1.

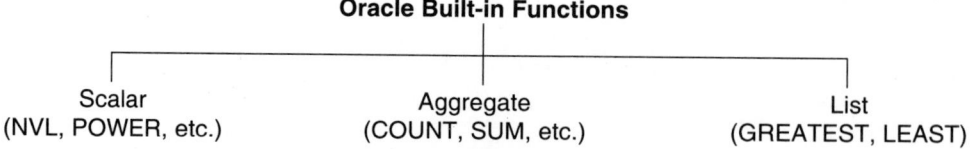

Oracle Built-in Functions

Scalar	Aggregate	List
(NVL, POWER, etc.)	(COUNT, SUM, etc.)	(GREATEST, LEAST)

Figure 7.1 Broad classification of built-in functions.

Caution: Oracle 10g has several new built-in functions which are not available in the earlier versions. So if you are working on any version below 10g some of the mentioned functions may not work, e.g. MEDIAN, RANK, DENSE_RANK.

7.1.1 Scalar Functions

These functions return value for each record or row in table.

Name: NVL

Acronym for: NULL Value
Syntax: NVL(fieldname , value to be substituted if NULL)
Applicable to: CHAR/VARCHAR2/NUMBER/DATE

Explanation: NVL () returns the specified value if the value in the corresponding column is NULL.

Assume "emp" table with records as shown in Figure 7.2.

```
SQL> select empno,deptno,sal,comm from emp;

    EMPNO        DEPTNO         SAL          COMM

     7369           20
     7499           30          1600          300
     7521           30          1250          500
     7566           20          2975
     7654           30          1250         1400
     7698           30          2850
     7782           10
```

Figure 7.2   Records in EMP table.

Note that salary of employees with NO salary (NULL) is not appearing in the SELECT statement. If we wish to show salary as zero for employees whose salary is NULL then we have to use the NVL function as shown in Figure 7.3.

- **Display salary and commission as zero if it is NULL.**

Figure 7.3 shows how to use the NVL() function.

```
SQL> select empno,deptno,nvl(sal,0),nvl(comm,0) from emp;

    EMPNO        DEPTNO       NVL(SAL,0)      NVL(COMM,0)

     7369           20             0               0
     7499           30           1600             300
     7521           30           1250             500
     7566           20           2975               0
     7654           30           1250            1400
     7698           30           2850               0
     7782           10             0               0
```

Figure 7.3   NVL() function.

We can use the NVL () function for CHAR and DATE data type also.

Suppose we want to display employee name as "XXX" if ename is not known and hiredate as "01-JAN-1000" where hiredate is not known.

Assume records in the "emp" table as shown in Figure 7.4.

```
SQL> select empno,ename,deptno,hiredate,sal from emp;
```

EMPNO	ENAME	DEPTNO	HIREDATE	SAL
7369		20		
7499		30		1600
7521	WARD	30	22-FEB-81	1250
7566	JONES	20	02-APR-81	2975
7654	MARTIN	30	28-SEP-81	1250
7698	BLAKE	30	01-MAY-81	2850
7782	CLARK	10	09-JUN-81	

Figure 7.4 Records in EMP table.

- **Display name as 'XXXX' if it is NULL.**

NVL() can be used for VARCHAR2 and Date data type also as shown in Figure 7.5.

```
SQL>select empno,nvl(ename,'XXXX'),deptno,nvl(hiredate,'01-jan-1000'),sal from emp;
```

EMPNO	NVL(ENAME,	DEPTNO	NVL(HIRED	SAL
7369	XXXX	20	01-JAN-00	
7499	XXXX	30	01-JAN-00	1600
7521	WARD	30	22-FEB-81	1250
7566	JONES	20	02-APR-81	2975
7654	MARTIN	30	28-SEP-81	1250
7698	BLAKE	30	01-MAY-81	2850
7782	CLARK	10	09-JUN-81	

Figure 7.5 NVL() for VARCHAR2 data type.

Note that by default Oracle displays only 2-digits of Year. This would mean that it will show "00" for "1000", "1900", "2000" years. But this is not acceptable. So we will have to use another oracle built-in function called to_char ().

- **Display hiredate as dd/mm/yyyy.**

The default display format for date data type can be modified by using the TO_CHAR() built in function (Figure 7.6).

```
SQL> select empno,nvl(ename,'XXXX'),deptno,to_char(nvl(hiredate,'01-jan-1000'),'dd/mm/
yyyy'),sal from emp;
```

EMPNO	NVL(ENAME,	DEPTNO	TO_CHAR(NV	SAL
7369	XXXX	20	01/01/1000	
7499	XXXX	30	01/01/1000	1600
7521	WARD	30	22/02/1981	1250
7566	JONES	20	02/04/1981	2975
7654	MARTIN	30	28/09/1981	1250
7698	BLAKE	30	01/05/1981	2850
7782	CLARK	10	09/06/1981	

Figure 7.6 TO_CHAR() for date data type.

Name: CONCAT or ||

Acronym for: Concatenation

Syntax: CONCAT (field1, field2)

Applicable To: CHAR/VARCHAR2/NUMBER/DATE

Explanation: This function combines or joins two fields into one.

Assume records in vehicle table containing registration of vehicles as shown in Figure 7.7.

```
SQL>describe vehicle;

        Name                    Null?           Type
        STATE                                   CHAR(2)
        ZONE                                    CHAR(2)
        CITY                                    CHAR(2)
        SR_NO                                   NUMBER(4)
        OWNER                                   VARCHAR2(10)
        ADDRESS                                 VARCHAR2(20)

SQL>select * from vehicle;
```

STATE	ZONE	CITY	SR_NO	OWNER	ADDRESS
MP	03	JB	1111	rashmi	45,shakti,bhopal
UP	01	LK	2222	anil	45,UIT,Lucknow
UP	02	PF	3333	rishi	2-mahrauli,Bareilli

Figure 7.7 Records in VEHICLE table.

Now we want to display vehicle registration as a single field like 'MP-03/JB-1111' for all vehicles. Since each value is in separate columns of table, therefore, we will have to use Concatenation built-in function as shown in Figure 7.8.

- **Display Vehicle Registration as Single Field.**

```
SQL>select state||'-'||zone||'/'||city||'-'||sr_no, owner, address from vehicle;
```

STATE||'-'||ZONE||'/'||CITY||'-'||SR_NO	OWNER	ADDRESS
MP-03/JB-1111	rashmi	45,shakti,bhopal
UP-01/LK-2222	anil	45,UIT,Lucknow
UP-02/PF-3333	rishi	2-mahrauli,Bareilli

Figure 7.8 Using Concatenation function.

Name: RPAD

Acronym for: Padding specified characters from right

Syntax: RPAD (string, no. of characters, character to be padded from right)

Explanation: This function inserts the specified character from right of string.

In the vehicle table we want each owner name to be displayed in 10 characters and if actual name contains less than 10 characters then fill the space with '*' from right. Figure 7.9 shows how to use RPAD() function.

```
SQL> select state,zone,city,sr_no, rpad(owner,10,'*'), address from vehicle;

   STATE      ZONE      CITY     SR_NO     RPAD(OWNER,10,'*')        ADDRESS
     MP        03        JB       1111      rashmi****           45,shakti,bhopal
     UP        01        LK       2222      anil******           45,UIT,Lucknow
     UP        02        PF       3333      rishi*****           2-mahrauli,Bareilli
```

Figure 7.9   RPAD().

Character to be padded is optional and by default it is taken as blank space.

Examples

RPAD('rahul',10)   'rahul' (5 blank spaces padded at right end)
RPAD('rahul',10,'*')   'rahul*****'
RPAD('This is test',20,'x')   'This is testxxxxxxxx'

Name: LPAD

Acronym for: Padding specified characters from left

Syntax: LPAD(string, no. of characters, character to be padded from left)

Explanation: Similar to RPAD() but inserts the specified character from left of string.

In the vehicle table we want each owner name to be displayed in 10 characters and if actual name contains less than 10 characters then fill the space with '*' from left. See Figure 7.10.

```
SQL> select state, zone, city, sr_no, lpad(owner,10,'*'), address from vehicle;

   STATE     ZONE      CITY     SR_NO     LPAD(OWNER,10,'*')        ADDRESS
     MP       03        JB       1111      ****rashmi           45,shakti,bhopal
     UP       01        LK       2222      ******anil           45,UIT,Lucknow
     UP       02        PF       3333      *****rishi           2-mahrauli,Bareilli
```

Figure 7.10   LPAD() function.

Character to be padded is optional and by default it is taken as blank space.

Examples

LPAD('rahul',10)   'rahul' (5 blank spaces padded at left end)
LPAD('rahul',10,'*')   '*****rahul'
LPAD('This is test',20,'x')   'xxxxxxxxThis is test'

Oracle DUAL table

The Oracle database contains a table named "DUAL" and is used for special purpose as indicated in Figure 7.11.

About DUAL

The DUAL table is a special one-row table present by default in all the Oracle database installations. It is suitable for use in selecting a pseudo-column such as SYSDATE or USER. Pseudo means that the column is not in the table but can still be used in the SQL statements like SELECT.

The table has a single VARCHAR2(1) column called DUMMY that has a value of "X"

SQL> desc dual;

Name	Null?	Type
DUMMY		VARCHAR2(1)

SQL> select * from dual;
D
-
X

SQL> select sysdate from dual;

SYSDATE

16-DEC-08

SQL> select user from dual;

USER

SCOTT

The same DUAL table can also be used to understand the functioning of various built-in functions. In the previous examples we applied the built-in functions to columns of tables. But now we will use the DUAL table for the same purpose.

Figure 7.11 About DUAL table.

Name: LTRIM
Acronym for : Left Trimming
Syntax: LTRIM(string, 'set of characters to be trimmed from left')

Explanation: This function trims/cuts the specified characters from string starting from left (Figure 7.12).

SQL>select *ltrim('123;rahul','2;31')* from *dual;*

LTRIM('123;RAHUL','1;32')

rahul

Figure 7.12 LTRIM().

Note: SQL is a highly structured language and the SELECT statement requires a "FROM" table clause. Instead of using an actual table we can use this DUAL table for testing functionality of built-in functions.

Explanation: LTRIM function starts reading the characters from left of string one by one. If the character exists in the 2nd parameter then that character is trimmed or removed. This **continues until the first character is encountered which is not in the 2nd parameter list**. In Figure 7.12, **LTRIM stops working as soon as the 'r' of 'rahul' is encountered**.

Caution: LTRIM works for set of characters and not for the sequence of characters.

Figure 7.13 shows an example wherein LTRIM is working for a set of characters and not for the sequence of characters.

```
SQL>select ltrim('123;ra;h1ul','2;31') from dual;
LTRIM('123;RA;H1UL','2;31')
ra;h1ul
```

Figure 7.13   LTRIM() example.

Note: ';' after 'A' and '1' after 'H' have not been trimmed.

Specifying the characters to be trimmed is optional and by default LTRIM trims the blank spaces from left of string (Figure 7.14).

```
SQL>select ltrim(' rahul') from dual;
LTRIM('RAHUL')
rahul
```

Figure 7.14   Default trimmed character is space.

Name: RTRIM
Acronym for: Right Trimming
Syntax: RTRIM(string, 'set of characters to be trimmed from right')

Explanation: This function trims the specified set of characters from string starting from right as shown in Figure 7.15.

```
SQL>select rtrim('123;rahul;21','2;31') from dual;
RTRIM('123;RAHUL;21','2;31')
123;rahul
```

Figure 7.15   RTRIM().

Note: ';', '2', '1' got trimmed from right only and not from left since we have used RTRIM().

We can use **function within a function** to achieve functionality of both. For example, we can use both LTRIM and RTRIM to trim desired characters both from left and right (Figure 7.16).

```
SQL>select ltrim(rtrim('123;rahul;21','2;31'),'2;31') from dual;
LTRIM(RTRIM('123;RAHUL;21','2;31'),'2;31')
rahul
```

Figure 7.16   Nesting built-in functions.

By default LTRIM trims blank spaces from left of string.

Name: TRIM

Acronym for: Left and Right Trimming for blank spaces only

Syntax: TRIM(string)

Explanation: This function trims the blank spaces from both left and right of string as shown in Figure 7.17.

SQL>select *trim('rahul')* from dual;

TRIM('RAHUL')

rahul

Figure 7.17   TRIM().

Note: We cannot specify set of characters to be trimmed in TRIM function.

Name: SUBSTR

Acronym for: Substring

Syntax: SUBSTR (string, start position, no. of characters)

Explanation: This function returns the specified no. of characters starting from the specified position.

Assume a table named vehicle1 (Figure 7.18) with single column for vehicle registration number (example MP-04/FE-2345).

SQL>select * from vehicle1;

VEHICLE_NO	OWNER	ADDRESS
MP-03/JB-1111	rashmi	45,shakti,bhopal
UP-01/LK-2222	anil	45,UIT,Lucknow
UP-02/PF-3333	rishi	2-mahrauli,Bareilli
UP-02/FF-4444	sanjay	123,samir apt

Figure 7.18   Records in VEHICLE1 table.

Now we want to list vehicles of state UP only (Figure 7.19).

SQL>select * from vehicle1 *where substr(vehicle_no,1,2)='UP';*

VEHICLE_NO	OWNER	ADDRESS
UP-01/LK-2222	anil	45,UIT,Lucknow
UP-02/PF-3333	rishi	2-mahrauli,Bareilli
UP-02/FF-4444	sanjay	123,samir apt

Figure 7.19   SUBSTR in WHERE Clause.

Now we want to list vehicles of state UP and zone 02 (Figure 7.20).

SQL>select * from vehicle1 *where substr(vehicle_no,1,2)='UP' and substr(vehicle_no,4,2)='02';*

VEHICLE_NO	OWNER	ADDRESS
UP-02/PF-3333	rishi	2-mahrauli,Bareilli
UP-02/FF-4444	sanjay	123,samir apt

Figure 7.20 SUBSTR in conjunction with AND.

We want only the sr_no for vehicles of UP state (Figure 7.21).

SQL>select substr(vehicle_no,10,4) from vehicle1 where *substr(vehicle_no,1,2)='UP';*
SUBSTR(VEHICLE_NO,10,4)

2222
3333
4444

Figure 7.21 Extracting serial no. using SUBSTR.

Name: LOWER
Acronym for: Lower Case
Syntax: LOWER(string)

Explanation: Converts uppercase characters to lowercase (Figure 7.22).

SQL>*select lower('Rahul Arora')* from dual;
LOWER('RAHULARORA')

rahul arora

Figure 7.22 LOWER().

Name: UPPER
Acronym for: Upper Case
Syntax: UPPER(string)

Explanation: Converts lowercase characters to uppercase (Figure 7.23).

SQL>select *upper('Rahul Arora')* from dual;
UPPER('RAHULARORA')
RAHUL ARORA

Figure 7.23 UPPER().

Name: INITCAP
Acronym for: Initial Capital
Syntax: INITCAP(string)

Explanation: Converts first character of every word to uppercase and rest to lowercase (Figure 7.24).

SQL>*select initcap('raHul aRora')* from dual;

INITCAP('RAHULARORA')

Rahul Arora

Figure 7.24   INITCAP().

Name: LENGTH
Acronym for: length of string
Syntax: LENGTH(string)

Explanation: Displays the number of characters in the specified string (Figure 7.25).

SQL>select empno, *length(empno), ename, length(ename)* from emp;

EMPNO	LENGTH(EMPNO)	ENAME	LENGTH(ENAME)
7369	4	SMITH	5
7566	4	JONES	5
7839	4	KING	4
7934	4	MILLER	6
9999	4	XEON	4

Figure 7.25   LENGTH().

Name: REPLACE
Acronym for: REPLACE
Syntax: REPLACE(string, 'existing sequence of chars', 'new sequence of chars')

Explanation: Replace specified sequence of characters with new sequence of characters (Figure 7.26).

SQL>select *replace('hello','he','xyz')* from dual;

REPLACE('HELLO','HE','XYZ')

xyzllo

Figure 7.26   REPLACE().

If we do not specify the new sequence of characters then the existing sequence is removed from the string (Figure 7.27).

select *replace('hello','he')* from dual;

REPLACE('HELLO','HE')

llo

Figure 7.27   New sequence is optional.

Name: DECODE
Syntax: decode(column , search1 , result1 [, searchN , resultN]... [, default])

Explanation: Displays result1 if value in column is search1
Displays result2 if value in column is search2
.
.
Displays resultN if value in column is searchN
If the column value does not match any of search1,search2 … searchn values then displays Default value

For example, assume records in employee table as shown in Figure 7.28.

```
SQL>select * from employee;

     EMPNO          ENAME          GRADE
      1111          rahul           E1
      2222          rishi           E2
      3333          rashmi          M1
      4444          samay           M2
      5555          ruchi           XX
      6666          neelesh
```

Figure 7.28   Records in EMPLOYEE table.

Now we want to display the grade as "ENGINEER" if grade='E1'
"SENIOR ENGINEER" if grade='E2'
"MANAGER" if grade='M1'
"SENIOR MANAGER" if grade='M2'
ELSE "NOT KNOWN"

To apply conditional display we can use DECODE() function as shown in Figure 7.29.

```
SQL>select empno, ename, grade, DECODE(grade,'E1','ENGINEER','E2','SENIOR
ENGINEER','M1','MANAGER','M2','SENIOR MANAGER','NOT KNOWN') from employee;

  EMPNO   ENAME    GRADE    DECODE(GRADE,'E1','ENGINEER','E2',
                            'SENIOR ENGINEER','M1','MANAGER','M2',
                            'SENIOR MANAGER', 'NOT KNOWN')

   1111   rahul     E1       ENGINEER
   2222   rishi     E2       SENIOR ENGINEER
   3333   rashmi    M1       MANAGER
   4444   samay     M2       SENIOR MANAGER
   5555   ruchi     XX       NOT KNOWN
   6666   neelesh            NOT KNOWN
```

Figure 7.29   DECODE().

Note: For both ruchi and neelesh the grade has been displayed as UNKNOWN. UNKNOWN forms the ELSE part of the DECODE function.

NAME: INSTR
ACRONYM FOR: In String
SYNTAX:
instr(string1, string2 [, start_position [, nth_appearance]])

string1 is the string to search.

string2 is the substring to search for in *string1*.

start_position is the position in *string1* where the search will start. This argument is optional. If omitted, it defaults to 1. The first position in the string is 1.

nth_appearance is the nth appearance of *string2*. This is optional. If omitted, it defaults to 1.

Note: If *string2* is not found in *string1*, then the **instr** Oracle function will return 0, for example, Figures 7.30, 7.31 and 7.32 show a few examples for INSTR function.

instr('Tech on the net', 'e')	would return 2; the first occurrence of 'e'
instr('Tech on the net', 'e', 1, 1)	would return 2; the first occurrence of 'e'
instr('Tech on the net', 'e', 1, 2)	would return 11; the second occurrence of 'e'
instr('Tech on the net', 'e', 1, 3)	would return 14; the third occurrence of 'e'
instr('Tech on the net', 'e', -3, 2)	would return 2.

Figure 7.30 Examples for INSTR function.

```
SQL>select instr('Tech on the net', 'e', 1, 3) from dual;
INSTR('TECHONTHENET','E',1,3)
14
```

Figure 7.31 INSTR().

INSTR can return occurrence of sequence of characters also (Figure 7.32).

```
SQL>select instr('this is test....this is test....this is test', 'this', 1, 1) from dual;
INSTR('THISISTEST....THISISTEST....THISISTEST','THIS',1,1)
1

SQL>select instr('this is test....this is test....this is test', 'this', 1, 2) from dual;
INSTR('THISISTEST....THISISTEST....THISISTEST','THIS',1,2)
17

SQL>select instr('this is test....this is test....this is test', 'this', 1, 3) from dual;
INSTR('THISISTEST....THISISTEST....THISISTEST','THIS',1,3)
33
```

Figure 7.32 Occurrence of sequence of characters.

TRANSLATE

The **translate** function replaces a sequence of characters in a string with another set of characters. However, it replaces a single character at a time. For example, it will replace the 1st character in the *string_to_replace* with the 1st character in the *replacement_string*. Then it will replace the 2nd character in the *string_to_replace* with the 2nd character in the *replacement_string*, and so on.

The syntax for the **translate** function is:

translate(string1, string_to_replace, replacement_string)
string1 is the string to replace a sequence of characters with another set of characters.
string_to_replace is the string that will be searched for in *string1*.

Replacement_string: All characters in the *string_to_replace* will be replaced with the corresponding character in the *replacement_string*, for example, see Figure 7.33.

translate('1tech23', '123', '456');	would return '4tech56'
translate('222tech', '2ec', '3it');	would return '333tith'

Figure 7.33   Translate.

7.1.2   Mathematical Functions

ABS

The syntax for the **abs** function is:
abs(number)

number is the number to convert to an absolute value. For example, see Figures 7.34 and 7.35.

abs(−23)	would return 23
abs(−23.6)	would return 23.6
abs(−23.65)	would return 23.65
abs(23.65)	would return 23.65
abs(23.65 * −1)	would return 23.65

Figure 7.34   ABS.

SQL>select *abs(12.345),abs(−34.567)* from dual;

ABS(12.345)	ABS(−34.567)
12.345	34.567

Figure 7.35   ABS.

SQRT

The **sqrt** function returns the square root of *n*.
The syntax for the **sqrt** function is:
sqrt(n)
where *n* is a positive number.
For example, see Figure 7.36.

sqrt(9)	would return 3
sqrt(37)	would return 6.08276253029822
sqrt(5.617)	would return 2.37002109695251

Figure 7.36   SQRT.

POWER

The **power** function returns *m* raised to the *n*th power.

The syntax for the **power** function is:

power(*m*, *n*)

where *m* is the base and *n* is the exponent.

For example, see Figure 7.37.

power(3, 2)	would return 9
power(5, 3)	would return 125
power(−5, 3)	would return −125
power(6.2, 3)	would return 238.328
power(6.2, 3.5)	would return 593.431934277892

Figure 7.37   Power.

CEIL

The **ceil** function returns the smallest integer value that is greater than or equal to a *number*.

The syntax for the **ceil** function is:

ceil(number)

where *number* is the value used to find the smallest integer value.

For example, see Figure 7.38.

ceil(32.65)	would return 33.
ceil(32)	would return 32.
ceil(−32.65)	would return −32.
ceil(−32)	would return −32.
Ceil(3.1)	Would return 4
Ceil(3.6)	Would return 4
Ceil(−3.1)	−3
Ceil(−3.6)	−3

Figure 7.38   CEIL.

FLOOR

The **floor** function returns the largest integer value that is equal to or less than a *number*.

The syntax for the **floor** function is:

floor(number)

where *number* is the value used to determine the largest integer value that is equal to or less than a number. For example, see Figure 7.39.

floor(5.9)	would return 5
floor(34.29)	would return 34
floor(−5.9)	would return −6

Figure 7.39   FLOOR.

EXP

The **exp** function returns *e* raised to the *n*th power, where *e* = 2.71828183.

The syntax for the **exp** function is:

exp(number)

where *number* is the power to raise *e* to the *n*th power.

For example, see Figure 7.40.

exp(3)	would return 20.0855369231877
exp(3.1)	would return 22.1979512814416
exp(−3)	would return 0.0497870683678639

Figure 7.40   EXP.

LOG

The **log** function returns the logarithm of *n* base *m*.

The syntax for the **log** function is:

log(*m*, *n*)

where *m* must be a positive number, except 0 or 1 and *n* also have to be a positive number.

For example, see Figure 7.41.

log(10, 20)	would return 1.30102999566398
log(2, 15)	would return 3.90689059560852
log(100, 1)	would return 0

Figure 7.41   LOG.

LN

The **ln** function returns the natural logarithm of a *number*.

The syntax for the **ln** function is:

ln(number)

where *number* must be greater than 0.

For example, see Figure 7.42.

ln(20)	would return 2.99573227355399
ln(25)	would return 3.2188758248682
ln(100)	would return 4.60517018598809
ln(100.5)	would return 4.61015772749913

Figure 7.42   LN.

SIGN

The **sign** function returns a value indicating the sign of a number.

The syntax for the **sign** function is:

sign(number)

where *number* is the number to test for its sign.

If *number* < 0, then sign returns −1.

If *number* = 0, then sign returns 0.

If *number* > 0, then sign returns 1.

For example, see Figure 7.43.

sign(−23)	would return −1
sign(−0.001)	would return −1
sign(0)	would return 0
sign(0.001)	would return 1
sign(23)	would return 1
sign(23.601)	would return 1

Figure 7.43 SIGN.

SIN

The **sin** function returns the sine of *n*.

The syntax for the **sin** function is:

sin(*n*)

where *n* is a number. It is an angle expressed in radians.

For example, see Figure 7.44.

sin(3)	would return 0.141120008059867
sin(5.2)	would return −0.883454655720153
sin(−5.2)	would return 0.883454655720153

Figure 7.44 SIN.

Similarly, Oracle has functions like cos(number), tan(number), asin(number), acos(number), atan(number), sinh(n), cosh(n), tanh(n).

MOD

The **mod** function returns the remainder of *m* divided by *n*.

The syntax for the **mod** function is:

mod(*m, n*)

The **mod** is calculated as:

$m - n * floor(m/n)$

Note: The **mod** function uses the floor function in its formula, whereas the **remainder function** uses the round function in its formula.

The mod function returns *m* if *n* is 0.

For example, Figure 7.45.

mod(15, 4)	would return 3
mod(15, 0)	would return 15
mod(11.6, 2)	would return 1.6
mod(11.6, 2.1)	would return 1.1
mod(−15, 4)	would return −3
mod(−15, 0)	would return −15

Figure 7.45 MOD.

REMAINDER

The **remainder** function returns the remainder of m divided by n.

The syntax for the **remainder** function is:

remainder(m, n)

The **remainder** is calculated as:

$$m - (n * X)$$

where X is the integer nearest m/n.

Note: The **remainder** function uses the round function in its formula, whereas the mod function uses the floor function in its formula.

For example, see Figure 7.46.

remainder(15, 6)	would return 3
remainder(15, 5)	would return 0
remainder(15, 4)	would return −1
remainder(11.6, 2)	would return −0.4
remainder(11.6, 2.1)	would return −1
remainder(−15, 4)	would return 1

Figure 7.46   REMAINDER.

ROUND

The **round** function returns a number rounded to a certain number of decimal places.

The syntax for the **round** function is:

round(number, [decimal_places])

where *number* is the number to round.

decimal_places is the number of decimal places to which the calculation is to be rounded off. This value must be an integer. If this parameter is omitted, the **round** function will round the number to 0 decimal places.

For example, see Figure 7.47.

round(125.315)	would return 125
round(125.315, 0)	would return 125
round(125.315, 1)	would return 125.3
round(125.315, 2)	would return 125.32
round(125.315, 3)	would return 125.315
round(−125.315, 2)	would return −125.32

Figure 7.47   ROUND.

TRUNC

The **trunc** function returns a number truncated/chopped to a certain number of decimal places.

The syntax for the **trunc** function is:

trunc(number, [decimal_places])

where *number* is the number to truncate.

decimal_places is the number of decimal places to which the calculation needs to be truncated. This value must be an integer. If this parameter is omitted, the **trunc** function will truncate the number to 0 decimal places.

For example, see Figure 7.48.

trunc(125.815)	would return 125
trunc(125.815, 0)	would return 125
trunc(125.815, 1)	would return 125.8
trunc(125.815, 2)	would return 125.81
trunc(125.815, 3)	would return 125.815
trunc(−125.815, 2)	would return −125.81
trunc(125.815, −1)	would return 120
trunc(125.815, −2)	would return 100
trunc(125.815, −3)	would return 0

Figure 7.48 TRUNC.

DISTINCT

Distinct returns the UNIQUE value for the specified column.

We want to list all the JOBs in the EMP table. Assume that JOB column has position of each employee stored as shown in Figure 7.49.

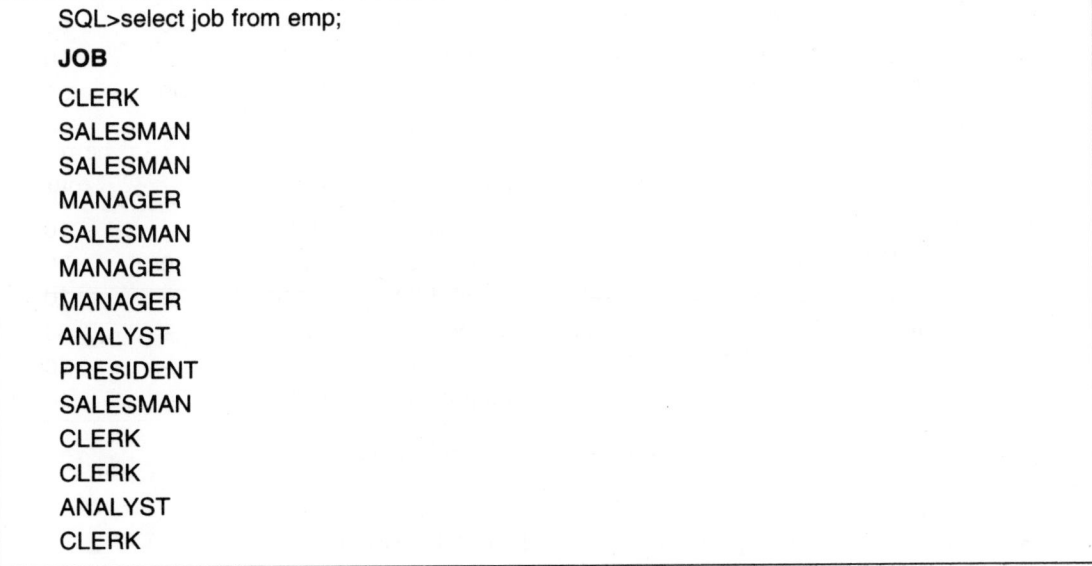

```
SQL>select job from emp;
JOB
CLERK
SALESMAN
SALESMAN
MANAGER
SALESMAN
MANAGER
MANAGER
ANALYST
PRESIDENT
SALESMAN
CLERK
CLERK
ANALYST
CLERK
```

Figure 7.49 JOB value in EMP table.

The statement of Figure 7.49 displayed JOB for each and every record in the EMP table.

We want to display the UNIQUE/DISTINCT JOBs we have in the EMP table. See Figure 7.50 on how to use DISTINCT function for columns.

```
SQL>select distinct job from emp;
JOB
CLERK
SALESMAN
PRESIDENT
MANAGER
ANALYST
```

Figure 7.50 DISTINCT.

7.1.3 Aggregate Functions

These functions work on group of records and not individual records. They calculate single value for a group of records. We can calculate single values for an entire table also.

Assume records in EMP table as shown in Figure 7.51.

EMPNO	ENAME	JOB	MGR	HIREDATE	SAL	COMM	DEPTNO
7369	SMITH	CLERK	7902	17-DEC-80	800	–	20
7499	ALLEN	SALESMAN	7698	20-FEB-81	1600	300	30
7521	WARD	SALESMAN	7698	22-FEB-81	1250	500	30
7566	JONES	MANAGER	7839	02-APR-81	2975	–	20
7654	MARTIN	SALESMAN	7698	28-SEP-81	1250	1400	30
7698	BLAKE	MANAGER	7839	01-MAY-81	2850	–	30
7782	CLARK	MANAGER	7839	09-JUN-81	2450	–	10
7788	SCOTT	ANALYST	7566	09-DEC-82	3000	–	20
7839	KING	PRESIDENT	–	17-NOV-81	5000	–	10
7844	TURNER	SALESMAN	7698	08-SEP-81	1500	0	30
7876	ADAMS	CLERK	7788	12-JAN-83	1100	–	20
7900	JAMES	CLERK	7698	03-DEC-81	950	–	30
7902	FORD	ANALYST	7566	03-DEC-81	3000	–	20
7934	MILLER	CLERK	7782	23-JAN-82	1300	–	10

Figure 7.51 Records in EMP table.

COUNT

- Finding number of employees/records in EMP table (Figure 7.52).

```
SQL>select count(*) from emp;
COUNT(*)
14
```

Figure 7.52 COUNT(*).

- Finding the number of Distinct/Unique JOBS we have (Figure 7.53).

```
SQL.select count(distinct job) from emp;
COUNT(DISTINCTJOB)
5
```

Figure 7.53   COUNT with DISTINCT.

We have JOB as CLERK, SALESMAN, MANAGER, ANALYST and PRESIDENT.

- How many JOBs we have in dept 10 (Figure 7.54).

```
SQL>select count(distinct job) from emp where deptno=10;
COUNT(DISTINCTJOB)
3
```

Figure 7.54   COUNTING distinct jobs in a department.

- Let us count the values for empno, sal and comm columns (Figure 7.55).

```
SQL>select count(ename),count(sal),count(comm) from emp;
```

COUNT(ENAME)	COUNT(SAL)	COUNT(COMM)
14	14	4

Figure 7.55   Counting for different columns.

Caution: Aggregate functions ignore NULL values in columns. As no record has NULL value for EMPNO and SAL therefore COUNT displayed 14. COMM column has NON-NULL values for 4 records only.

- Display the number of employees in each department (Figure 7.56).

```
SQL>select deptno, count(*) from emp group by deptno;
```

DEPTNO	COUNT(*)
30	6
20	5
10	3

Figure 7.56   Departmentwise count of employees.

We wanted the count of employees for all departments. As we want to calculate COUNT for group of records for each department, therefore, we used a NEW CLAUSE called **"GROUP BY"** clause. **This clause group records based on the same department and then calculates COUNT for each department (Figure 7.57).**

Grouping of Records

Group of Dept 10	7782	CLARK	MANAGER	7839	09-JUN-81	2450	–	10
	7839	KING	PRESIDENT	–	17-NOV-81	5000	–	10
	7934	MILLER	CLERK	7782	23-JAN-82	1300	–	10

	7566	JONES	MANAGER	7839	02-APR-81	2975	–	20
Group	7902	FORD	ANALYST	7566	03-DEC-81	3000	–	20
of	7876	ADAMS	CLERK	7788	12-JAN-83	1100	–	20
Dept 20	7369	SMITH	CLERK	7902	17-DEC-80	800	–	20
	7788	SCOTT	ANALYST	7566	09-DEC-82	3000	–	20
	7521	WARD	SALESMAN	7698	22-FEB-81	1250	500	30
Group	7844	TURNER	SALESMAN	7698	08-SEP-81	1500	0	30
of	7499	ALLEN	SALESMAN	7698	20-FEB-81	1600	300	30
Dept 30	7900	JAMES	CLERK	7698	03-DEC-81	950	–	30
	7698	BLAKE	MANAGER	7839	01-MAY-81	2850	–	30
	7654	MARTIN	SALESMAN	7698	28-SEP-81	1250	1400	30

Figure 7.57 Grouping records based on department.

The COUNT function is applied after GROUPING the records departmentwise.

Query of Figure 7.56 can be assigned to ALIAS name for the aggregate function COUNT as shown in Figure 7.58.

SQL>select deptno, count(*) **as "No.of Employees"** from emp group by deptno;	
DEPTNO	**No. of Employees**
30	6
20	5
10	3

Figure 7.58 Aliasing aggregate column.

- COUNT of employees in each department with salary > 2000 (Figure 7.59).

SQL>select deptno, count(*) as "No.of Employees" from emp **where sal>2000 group by deptno;**	
DEPTNO	**No. of Employees**
30	1
20	3
10	2

Figure 7.59 Aggregate functions with WHERE clause.

SUM

As the name suggests this aggregate function adds up the values of the specified columns.

- Display total salary(sal + comm) for all employees (Figure 7.60).

SQL>select **sum(sal),sum(comm),sum(nvl(sal,0)+nvl(comm,0))** from emp;		
SUM(SAL)	**SUM(COMM)**	**SUM(NVL(SAL,0)+NVL(COMM,0))**
29025	2200	31225

Figure 7.60 SUM().

Note:
- nvl() function has been used for SAL+COMM or else the result would be wrong. REFER NVL() function at the beginning of this chapter.
- NVL has not been used in sum(sal) and sum(comm) because aggregate functions ignore NULL values in columns but mathematical operators like +, –, *, / produce NULL if any of the values being operated are NULL.

- Show departmentwise TOTAL salary(sal + comm) (Figure 7.61).

SQL>select *deptno,sum(sal),sum(comm),sum(nvl(sal,0)+nvl(comm,0))* from emp *group by deptno;*			
DEPTNO	SUM(SAL)	SUM(COMM)	SUM(NVL(SAL,0)+NVL(COMM,0))
30	9400	2200	11600
20	10875	–	10875
10	8750	–	8750

Figure 7.61 Departmentwise total salary.

Note that departments are not appearing in the alphabetical order.

Let us arrange the query of Figure 7.61 in order of "deptno".

For arranging records in alphabetical order we will have to use the ORDER BY clause as in Figure 7.62.

SQL>select deptno,sum(sal),sum(comm),sum(nvl(sal,0)+nvl(comm,0)) from emp *group by deptno order by deptno;*			
DEPTNO	SUM(SAL)	SUM(COMM)	SUM(NVL(SAL,0)+NVL(COMM,0))
10	8750	–	8750
20	10875	–	10875
30	9400	2200	11600

Figure 7.62 GROUP with ORDER.

Note: The ORDER BY clause can appear only after the GROUP BY clause as SQL is a highly-structured language. We cannot use the ORDER BY clause before the GROUP BY clause.

GROUP BY HAVING clause

GROUP BY clause forms groups on the specified columns. Filter of these groups depends on some conditions which can be achieved by using GROUP BY HAVING clause.

- **Display departmentwise total salary such that only those departments are shown to which company is paying total salary of more than 9000 (Figure 7.63).**

SQL>select deptno,sum(sal) from emp group by deptno *having sum(sal)>9000* order by deptno;	
DEPTNO	SUM(SAL)
20	10875
30	9400

Figure 7.63 Groups satisfying certain conditions.

Department 10 has not been displayed as total salary being paid is 8750.

Note: The WHERE clause filters the individual records based on the specified criteria. The HAVING clause filters those groups which do not satisfy the specified criteria.
The HAVING clause can be used in conjunction with the GROUP BY clause only.

- **List the departments with more than three employees (Figure 7.64).**

```
SQL>select deptno,count(empno) empcount from emp
group by deptno having count(empno)>3 order by deptno;
```

DEPTNO	EMPCOUNT
20	5
30	6

Figure 7.64 HAVING clause with COUNT aggregate function.

GROUPING on multiple columns

The GROUP BY clause can be used with multiple columns also.

- **Display the amount of salary being paid jobwise for each department (Figure 7.65).**

```
SQL>select deptno,job,sum(sal) from emp
group by deptno,job
order by deptno,job;
```

DEPTNO	JOB	SUM(SAL)
10	CLERK	1300
10	MANAGER	2450
10	PRESIDENT	5000
20	ANALYST	6000
20	CLERK	1900
20	MANAGER	2975
30	CLERK	950
30	MANAGER	2850
30	SALESMAN	5600

Figure 7.65 Department, jobwise salary.

GROUP BY ROLLUP Clause

In the above query (Figure 7.65) jobwise total salary for each department was displayed using the GROUP BY Clause. But it is a common requirement that sub-total should also be shown on each department. The ROLLUP operator defines the sub-total as in Figure 7.66.

```
SQL>select deptno,job,sum(sal) from emp
group by rollup(deptno,job)
order by deptno,job;
```

DEPTNO	JOB	SUM(SAL)
10	CLERK	1300

10	MANAGER	2450
10	PRESIDENT	5000
10	–	8750
20	ANALYST	6000
20	CLERK	1900
20	MANAGER	2975
20	–	10875
30	CLERK	950
30	MANAGER	2850
30	SALESMAN	5600
30	–	9400
–	–	29025

Figure 7.66 ROLLUP.

Note: The ROLLUP operator not only calculates sub-total for each department but it also calculates grand total.

GROUP BY CUBE clause

The CUBE operator displays the group function value for the specified combination of columns. Suppose we want to display the total salary for each department, along with total salary for each type of job and total salary for each combination of DEPT and JOB then use the CUBE operator (Figure 7.67).

```
SQL>select deptno,job,sum(sal) from emp
group by cube(deptno,job);
```

DEPTNO	JOB	SUM(SAL)
–	–	29025
–	CLERK	4150
–	ANALYST	6000
–	MANAGER	8275
–	SALESMAN	5600
–	PRESIDENT	5000
10	–	8750
10	CLERK	1300
10	MANAGER	2450
10	PRESIDENT	5000
20	–	10875
20	CLERK	1900
20	ANALYST	6000
20	MANAGER	2975
30	–	9400
30	CLERK	950
30	MANAGER	2850
30	SALESMAN	5600

Figure 7.67 CUBE.

AVG

The **AVG** function returns the average value of an expression.

- **Display the average salary and commission of all employees (Figure 7.68).**

SQL>select *avg(sal),avg(comm)* from emp;	
AVG(SAL)	**AVG(COMM)**
2073.2142857	550

Figure 7.68   AVG.

No record has NULL salary, therefore, average salary has been calculated as 29025/14=2073.2142857.

For commission, the average has been calculated as 2200/4=550.

Explanation: ALLEN, WARD, MARTIN and TURNER had commission as 300, 500, 1400 and 0 respectively. Now the sum(comm) is 2200 but the number of non-NULL values in COMM column is 4 and not 14. As we have stated earlier, AGGREGATE functions ignore NULL values. So the AVERAGE comm has been calculated as 2200/4 and not 2200/14. This means that all the employees for which commission is not known or NULL are not taken into consideration for calculating the AGGREGATE function values. BLAKE and JAMES have not been counted for calculating AVERAGE value as they have NULL commission.

- **Find departmentwise average salary and commission (Figure 7.69).**

SQL>select *deptno,avg(sal) ,avg(comm)* from emp **group by deptno**;		
DEPTNO	**AVG(SAL)**	**AVG(COMM)**
30	1566.6666667	550
20	2175	–
10	2916.6666667	–

Figure 7.69   Departmentwise average salary and commission.

Caution: Refer to Figure 7.51, where we have 6 employees in department 30. The total salary is (1250 + 1500 + 1600 + 950 + 2850 + 1250 = 9400) and the average salary is 9400/6 = 1566.6666. Total commission is (500 + 0 + 300 + 1400 = 2200) and the average commission has been calculated as 2200/4 = 550 instead of 2200/6 = 366.6666 as records with NULL commission are not counted by the AVG function. We want to know average salary and commission including employees with NULL salary and commission. This means that we want to count the employees who have NULL salary and commission for calculating the AVERAGE values (Figure 7.70).

SQL>select deptno,avg(nvl(sal,0)) ,avg(nvl(comm,0)) from emp group by deptno;		
DEPTNO	**AVG(NVL(SAL,0))**	**AVG(NVL(COMM,0))**
30	1566.66666667	366.66666667
20	2175	0
10	2916.66666667	0

Figure 7.70   AVG with NVL.

Note: For department 30, the average commission has been calculated as 2200/6 = 366.66666667 because now the records with NULL commission has also been counted for calculating the AVERAGE value (NULL commission has been assumed as zero by using NVL() function).

MAX

The MAX function returns the maximum value of an expression.

- **Find the maximum salary and commission for the entire company (Figure 7.71).**

MAX(SAL)	MAX(COMM)
5000	1400

SQL>select max(sal),max(comm) from emp;

Figure 7.71 MAX.

- **Display departmentwise maximum salary and commission (Figure 7.72).**

SQL>select deptno,max(sal),max(comm) from emp group by deptno;

DEPTNO	MAX(SAL)	MAX(COMM)
30	2850	1400
20	3000	–
10	5000	–

Figure 7.72 Departmentwise MAX.

MIN

The MIN function returns the minimum value of an expression (Figure 7.73).

SQL>select deptno,min(sal),min(comm) from emp group by deptno;

DEPTNO	MIN(SAL)	MIN(COMM)
30	950	0
20	800	–
10	1300	–

Figure 7.73 MIN.

MEDIAN

The **median** function returns the median of an expression (Figure 7.74).

SQL>select *deptno,median(sal),median(comm)* from emp group by deptno;

DEPTNO	MEDIAN(SAL)	MEDIAN(COMM)
10	2450	–
20	2975	–
30	1375	400

Figure 7.74 MEDIAN.

STDDEV—Standard deviation

The **stddev** function returns the standard deviation of a set of numbers (Figure 7.75).

DEPTNO	STDDEV(SAL)	STDDEV(COMM)
30	668.331255	602.7713773
20	1123.33209	–
10	1893.62967	–

SQL>select *deptno,stddev(sal),stddev(comm)* from emp group by deptno;

Figure 7.75 STDDEV.

VARIANCE

The **variance** function returns the variance of a set of numbers.

CORR—Correlation function

The **corr** function returns the coefficient of correlation of a set of number pairs.

The syntax for the **corr** function is:

corr(*n, m*)

where *n* and *m* are the numbers use to calculate the cofficient of correlation.

The **corr** function requires at least two columns (Figure 7.76).

SQL>select deptno, corr(comm, sal) from emp group by deptno;

DEPTNO	CORR(COMM,SAL)
30	–.6992097
20	–
10	–

Figure 7.76 CORRELATION.

RANK

The **rank** returns the rank of a row within a group of rows.

We want to rank the employees in the order of increasing salary for each department. Say, in dept 10 MILLER should be ranked 1 (sal=1300) followed by CLARK (sal=2450) and then KING (sal=5000). See Figure 7.77.

SQL>select deptno, ename, sal,
rank() OVER (PARTITION BY deptno ORDER BY sal)
from emp;

DEPTNO	ENAME	SAL	RANK()OVER(PARTITIONBYDEPTNOORDERBYSAL)
10	MILLER	1300	1
10	CLARK	2450	2
10	KING	5000	3
20	SMITH	800	1
20	ADAMS	1100	2
20	JONES	2975	3
20	SCOTT	3000	4

20	FORD	3000	4
30	JAMES	950	1
30	MARTIN	1250	2
30	WARD	1250	2
30	TURNER	1500	4
30	ALLEN	1600	5
30	BLAKE	2850	6

Figure 7.77 RANK.

PARTITION BY is similar to GROUP BY which means assign ranks to records within each group of DEPT. ORDER BY sal implies rank employees in an increasing order of salary.

Note:
- Employees with the same salary have been assigned the same rank. For example, SCOTT and FORD of department 20 have been assigned the same rank 4.
- Whenever consecutive records with the same rank are found then the next rank number is skipped and incremented rank is allotted to the next record. For example, in department 30 MARTIN and WARD have the same salary, therefore, they got assigned the same rank 2. But note that the next employee TURNER has been assigned rank 4 instead of 3.

DENSE_RANK

This function is similar to RANK() Function. Therefore, mentioned problem in RANK() function (Figure 7.77) of skipping rank numbers on finding records with the same salary can be resolved using DENSE_RANK function (Figure 7.78).

```
SQL>select deptno,ename, sal,
dense_rank() OVER (PARTITION BY deptno ORDER BY sal)
from emp;
```

DEPTNO	ENAME	SAL	DENSE_RANK()OVER(PARTITIONBYDEPTNOORDERBYSAL)
10	MILLER	1300	1
10	CLARK	2450	2
10	KING	5000	3
20	SMITH	800	1
20	ADAMS	1100	2
20	JONES	2975	3
20	SCOTT	3000	4
20	FORD	3000	4
30	JAMES	950	1
30	MARTIN	1250	2
30	WARD	1250	2
30	TURNER	1500	3
30	ALLEN	1600	4
30	BLAKE	2850	5

Figure 7.78 DENSE RANK.

Note: Now in department 30, MARTIN and WARD have been assigned rank 2 and TURNER has been assigned rank 3 in continuity as against the RANK() function.

7.1.4 List Functions

These functions work on set of columns instead of rows.

GREATEST

The **greatest** function returns the greatest value in a list of expressions.

The syntax for the **greatest** function is:

greatest(*expr1, expr2, …, expr_n*)

where *expr1, expr2, …, expr_n* are the expressions that are evaluated by the greatest function.

If the datatypes of the expressions are different, all expressions will be converted to whatever datatype *expr1* is.

If the comparison is based on a character comparison, one character is considered greater than another if it has a higher character set value. For example, see Figure 7.79.

greatest(2, 5, 12, 3)	would return 12
greatest('2', '5', '12', '3')	would return '5'
greatest('apples', 'oranges', 'bananas')	would return 'oranges'
greatest('apples', 'applis', 'applas')	would return 'applis'

Figure 7.79 GREATEST.

Assume a table TEMPERATURE (Figure 7.80) with records containing the monthwise temperatures for two cities.

```
SQL>select * from temperature;
```

CITY	JAN	FEB	MAR	APR	MAY	JUN	JUL	AUG	SEP	OCT	NOV	DEC
BHOPAL	20	30	40	42	44	46	48	39	37	33	27	25
INDORE	21	32	41	43	44	50	48	39	37	33	27	25

Figure 7.80 Records in TEMPERATURE table.

We want the maximum temperature for the cities (Figure 7.81).

```
SQL>select city,greatest(jan,feb,mar,apr,may,jun,jul,aug,sep,oct,nov,dec) from temperature;
```

CITY	GREATEST(JAN,FEB,MAR,APR,MAY,JUN,JUL,AUG,SEP,OCT,NOV,DEC)
BHOPAL	48
INDORE	50

Figure 7.81 GREATEST.

LEAST

The **least** function returns the smallest value in a list of expressions.

The syntax for the **least** function is:

least(expr1, expr2, ... expr_n)

where *expr1, expr2, . expr_n* are the expressions that are evaluated by the least function.

If the datatypes of the expressions are different, all expressions will be converted to whatever datatype *expr1* is.

If the comparison is based on a character comparison, one character is considered smaller than another if it has a lower character set value.

Note: Having a NULL value in one of the expressions will return NULL as the **least** value.

Figures 7.82 and 7.83 contains examples for LEAST function.

least(2, 5, 12, 3)	would return 2
least('2', '5', '12', '3')	would return '12'
least('apples', 'oranges', 'bananas')	would return 'apples'
least('apples', 'applis', 'applas')	would return 'applas'
least('apples', 'applis', 'applas', null)	would return NULL

Figure 7.82 LEAST.

SQL>select city,*least(jan,feb,mar,apr,may,jun,jul,aug,sep,oct,nov,dec)* from temperature;

CITY	LEAST(JAN,FEB,MAR,APR,MAY,JUN,JUL,AUG,SEP,OCT,NOV,DEC)
BHOPAL	20
INDORE	21

Figure 7.83 LEAST.

7.1.5 Transformation Functions

These are basically SCALAR functions used to convert one data type to another.

TO_CHAR()

This function converts
- Number data type to character data type
- Date data type to character data type

Assume records in EMPLOYEE TABLE as shown in Figure 7.84.

Note: sal is of type NUMBER(10,4), i.e. we can supply salary up to 4 decimal places.

```
SQL> describe employee;
```

Name	Null?	Type
EMPNO		NUMBER(4)
ENAME		VARCHAR2(10)
GRADE		CHAR(2)
SAL		NUMBER(10,4)

```
SQL>select * from employee;
```

EMPNO	ENAME	GRADE	SAL
1111	rahul	E1	123.4567
2222	rishi	E2	123.236
3333	rashmi	M1	5145.2436
4444	samay	M2	2000
5555	ruchi	XX	3000.25
6666	neelesh	–	–

Figure 7.84 Records in EMPLOYEE table.

Now we want to display salary up to 2 places of decimal only (Figure 7.85).

SQL>select empno,ename,***to_char(sal,'99999.99')*** from employee;

EMPNO	ENAME	TO_CHAR(SAL,'99999.99')
1111	rahul	123.46
2222	rishi	123.24
3333	rashmi	5145.24
4444	samay	2000.00
5555	ruchi	3000.25
6666	neelesh	–

Figure 7.85   Converting Number to Character.

Figure 7.86 contains examples of **to_char()** function.

to_char(1210.73, '9999.9')	would return '1210.7'
to_char(1210.73, '9,999.99')	would return '1,210.73'
to_char(1210.73, '$9,999.00')	would return '$1,210.73'
to_char(21, '000099')	would return '000021'

Figure 7.86   TO_CHAR examples.

Converting date data type to character/string data type

The Default Date format of Oracle is dd-mon-yy. Recall that DATE data type stores both date and time.

Let us see the system date through system variable sysdate (Figure 7.87).

SQL>select sysdate from dual;
SYSDATE
03-OCT-08

Figure 7.87   SYSDATE.

Note: DUAL is a dummy table which is required to fulfil the syntax of the SQL SELECT command.

We want to know both the current date and time (Figure 7.88).

SQL>select ***to_char(sysdate, 'dd-mon-yyyy hh:mi:ss')*** from dual;
TO_CHAR(SYSDATE,'DD-MON-YYYYHH:MI:SS')
04-oct-2008 08:00:42

Figure 7.88   Date and Time.

The 2nd parameter of to_char() function is called **the format** in which we want oracle to display the date and time. ·

Figure 7.89 contains a list of valid parameters when the **to_char()** function is used to convert a date to a string. These parameters can be used in many combinations.

Parameter	Explanation
YEAR	Year, spelled out
YYYY	4-digit year
YYYYYY	Last 3, 2, or 1 digit(s) of year.
IYYIYI	Last 3, 2, or 1 digit(s) of ISO year.
Q	Quarter of year (1, 2, 3, 4; JAN–MAR = 1).
MM	Month (01–12; JAN = 01).
MON	Abbreviated name of month.
MONTH	Name of month, padded with blanks to length of 9 characters.
RM	Roman numeral month (I–XII; JAN = I).
WW	Week of year (1–53) where week 1 starts on the first day of the year and continues to the seventh day of the year.
W	Week of month (1–5) where week 1 starts on the first day of the month and ends on the seventh.
D	Day of week (1–7).
DAY	Name of day.
DD	Day of month (1–31).
DDD	Day of year (1–366).
DY	Abbreviated name of day.
J	Julian day; the number of days since January 1, 4712 BC.
HH	Hour of day (1–12).
HH12	Hour of day (1–12).
HH24	Hour of day (0–23).
MI	Minute (0–59).
SS	Second (0–59).
SSSSS	Seconds past midnight (0–86399).
FF	Fractional seconds.

Figure 7.89 List of format specifier for date data type.

Figure 7.90 contains examples for the **to_char** function applied to Date data type.

to_char(sysdate, 'yyyy/mm/dd');	would return '2003/07/09'
to_char(sysdate, 'Month DD, YYYY');	would return 'July 09, 2003'
to_char(sysdate, 'FMMonth DD, YYYY');	would return 'July 9, 2003'
to_char(sysdate, 'MON DDth, YYYY');	would return 'JUL 09TH, 2003'
to_char(sysdate, 'FMMON DDth, YYYY');	would return 'JUL 9TH, 2003'
to_char(sysdate, 'FMMon ddth, YYYY');	would return 'Jul 9th, 2003'

Figure 7.90 TO_CHAR examples for Date data type.

You will notice that in some examples, the *format_mask* parameter begins with "FM". This means that zeros and blanks are suppressed. This can be seen in the examples of Figure 7.91.

to_char(sysdate, 'FMMonth DD, YYYY');	would return 'July 9, 2003'
to_char(sysdate, 'FMMON DDth, YYYY');	would return 'JUL 9TH, 2003'
to_char(sysdate, 'FMMon ddth, YYYY');	would return 'Jul 9th, 2003'

Figure 7.91 Suppressing zeroes and blanks.

The zeros have been suppressed so that the day component shows as "9" as opposed to "09".

Let us apply the TO_CHAR() function to HIREDATE column of EMP table (Figure 7.92).

```
SQL>select empno,ename,to_char(hiredate,'dd/mm/yyyy hh24:mi:ss') from emp;
```

EMPNO	ENAME	TO_CHAR(HIREDATE,'DD/MM/YYYYHH24:MI:SS')
7369	SMITH	17/12/1980 08:24:00
7499	ALLEN	20/02/1981 11:31:12
7521	WARD	22/02/1981 06:00:00
7566	JONES	02/04/1981 08:24:00
7654	MARTIN	28/09/1981 11:31:12
7698	BLAKE	01/05/1981 06:00:00
7782	CLARK	09/06/1981 08:24:00
7788	SCOTT	09/12/1982 11:31:12
7839	KING	17/11/1981 06:00:00
7844	TURNER	08/09/1981 08:24:00
7876	ADAMS	12/01/1983 11:31:12
7900	JAMES	03/12/1981 06:00:00
7902	FORD	03/12/1981 06:00:00
7934	MILLER	23/01/1982 06:00:00

Figure 7.92   Displaying hiredate column in desired 24-hour format.

TO_DATE() Function

This function converts string to date data type.

Note that "23/10/2007" will come before "25/01/2006" if both values are considered as string. As strings follow alphabetical order therefore 23 comes before 25 and hence the ordering gets invalid. But if both are compared as dates then 25/01/2006 will appear before 23/10/2007.

The default DATE format of Oracle is "dd-MON-yy". If we want to insert new records in EMP table then we can use the default format for providing the HIREDATE as shown in Figure 7.93.

```
SQL>insert into emp values (1111,'RASHMI','MANAGER',7369,'24-AUG-97',3000,1000,10);

SQL>insert into emp values (2222,'RUCHI','MANAGER',7369,'12-OCT-07',3000,1000,10);

SQL>select * from emp where empno in (1111,2222);
```

EMPNO	ENAME	JOB	MGR	HIREDATE	SAL	COMM	DEPTNO
1111	RASHMI	MANAGER	7369	24-AUG-97	3000	1000	10
2222	RUCHI	MANAGER	7369	12-OCT-07	3000	1000	10

Figure 7.93   Inserting date values.

HIREDATE is displayed as dd-MON-yy but it is not clear from the 2-digit year that whether 97 indicates 1997 or 2007 for employee 1111. For employee 2222, year 07 means 1907 or 1997 or 2007 is also not clear. To identify the 4-digit year, let us use the TO_CHAR() function (Figure 7.94).

```
SQL>select empno, ename, to_char(hiredate,'dd/mm/yyyy') from emp where empno in
(1111,2222);
```

EMPNO	ENAME	TO_CHAR(HIREDATE,'DD/MM/YYYY')
1111	RASHMI	24/08/1997
2222	RUCHI	12/10/2007

Figure 7.94 Displaying date values in desired format.

Note: Oracle follows century concept for storing the dates. When we specify 97, it assumes as 1997 and when we specify 07 it takes as 2007(current century is 20th).

Oracle also allows us to insert DATE values in default date format by using 4 digits for the year as shown in Figure 7.95.

```
SQL>insert into emp values (3333,'RISHI','MANAGER',7369,'07-OCT-1977',3000,1000,10);
SQL>select empno, ename, to_char(hiredate,'dd/mm/yyyy') from emp;
```

EMPNO	ENAME	TO_CHAR(HIREDATE,'DD/MM/YYYY')
1111	RASHMI	24/08/1997
2222	RUCHI	12/10/2007
3333	RISHI	07/10/1977

Figure 7.95 Inserting date values in default format.

Till now we have been using the DEFAULT DATE format for inserting records.

What if we want to specify the DATE format in Indian style (dd/mm/yyyy) while inserting new records. We will have to use the built-in TO_DATE() function (Figure 7.96).

```
SQL>insert into emp values (4444,'NEELESH','SALESMAN',7369,to_date('01/07/1998','dd/mm/
yyyy'),4000, 200,30);
SQL>select empno,ename,to_char(hiredate,'dd/mm/yyyy'),sal,comm from emp;
```

EMPNO	ENAME	TO_CHAR(HIREDATE,'DD/MM/YYYY')	SAL	COMM
1111	RASHMI	24/08/1997	3000	1000
2222	RUCHI	12/10/2007	3000	1000
3333	RISHI	07/10/1977	3000	1000
4444	NEELESH	01/07/1998	4000	200

Figure 7.96 Inserting date values in desired format.

Oracle stores the default time as 12:00:00 as shown in Figure 7.97.

```
SQL>select empno,ename,to_char(hiredate,'dd/mm/yyyy hh:mi:ss'),sal,comm from emp;
```

EMPNO	ENAME	TO_CHAR(HIREDATE,'DD/MM/YYYYHH:MI:SS')	SAL	COMM
1111	RASHMI	24/08/1997 12:00:00	3000	1000
2222	RUCHI	12/10/2007 12:00:00	3000	1000
3333	RISHI	07/10/1977 12:00:00	3000	1000
4444	NEELESH	01/07/1998 12:00:00	4000	200

Figure 7.97 Default time stored is 12:00:00.

How do we specify both DATE and TIME while inserting new records? Figure 7.98 shows how to use TO_DATE() for inserting date as well as time while adding new records.

```
SQL>insert into emp values (5555,'ANIL','MANAGER',7566,to_date('15/03/1996 08:10:15','dd/
mm/yyyy hh:mi:ss'),2000,200,20);

SQL>select empno,ename,to_char(hiredate,'dd/mm/yyyy hh:mi:ss') from emp;

   EMPNO        ENAME        TO_CHAR(HIREDATE,'DD/MM/YYYYHH:MI:SS')
    1111        RASHMI              24/08/1997 12:00:00
    2222        RUCHI               12/10/2007 12:00:00
    3333        RISHI               07/10/1977 12:00:00
    4444        NEELESH             01/07/1998 12:00:00
    5555        ANIL                15/03/1996 08:10:15
```

Figure 7.98   Specifying date as well as time while inserting records.

Now we have specified the time as 08:10:15 along with the date.

We want to insert date and time as 4.00 PM. There are 2 ways, namely

1. Using 12-hour format
2. Using 24-hour format

Figure 7.99 contains the commands for both 12-hour and 24-hour format.

In 12-hour format, we will have to specify AM or PM and HH/HH12 format.

In 24-hour format, we need to use 16 for 4 PM and HH24 format.

```
SQL>insert into emp values (6666,'ANITA','SALESMAN',7566,to_date('09/01/1997 04:10:15
PM','dd/mm/yyyy hh:mi:ss PM'),2000,200,20);
OR
SQL>insert into emp values (6666,'ANITA','SALESMAN',7566,to_date('09/01/1997
16:10:15','dd/mm/yyyy hh24:mi:ss'),2000,200,20);
```

Figure 7.99   Specifying 12-hour and 24-hour format.

Note:

- The DEFAULT date format is dd-mon-yy both for inserting new values in DATE data type column and displaying date columns(if we insert year as 97 it will be stored as 1997 and 07 will be stored as 2007).
- While inserting date value, we can specify 4-digit year value also.
- To insert values for DATE column in our desired format, we will have to use TO_DATE() function.
- To display DATE column in our desired format, we will have to use TO_CHAR() function.

7.1.6   Oracle DATE Functions

Oracle provides various built-in functions to interact with DATE data type.

TO_CHAR()

This, as we have seen, is used to display both the DATE and TIME stored in a database column using format specifier.

TO_DATE()

As we have seen this is used to insert DATE and TIME values in DATE data type columns.
Let us now see some more functions which are applicable to DATE data type.

DATE arithmetic + and −

We can add or subtract a value from a DATE which gives the date on nth day from the given date. For example, if today is 08th Oct-2008 then sysdate+2 will return 10th Oct-2008 (Figure 7.100).

SQL> select sysdate, sysdate+2, sysdate-3 from dual;		
SYSDATE	**SYSDATE+2**	**SYSDATE-3**
08-OCT-08	10-OCT-08	05-OCT-08

Figure 7.100 Date arithmetic.

DATE difference

We can subtract one date from another which returns the number of days between the specified dates. Further, we can divide the number of days by 365 to get the number of years between 2 dates. For example, let us find out the number of years for various employees who served the company (Figure 7.101).

SQL>select empno,ename,sysdate - hiredate no_of_days,(sysdate - hiredate)/365 no_of_years from emp;			
EMPNO	**ENAME**	**NO_OF_DAYS**	**NO_OF_YEARS**
7369	SMITH	10157.3564814	27.8283739
7499	ALLEN	10092.3564814	27.6502917
7521	WARD	10090.3564814	27.6448122
7566	JONES	10051.3564814	27.5379629
7654	MARTIN	9872.3564814	27.047552
7698	BLAKE	10022.3564814	27.4585109
7782	CLARK	9983.3564814	27.3516615
7788	SCOTT	9435.3564814	25.8502917
7839	KING	9822.3564814	26.9105657
7844	TURNER	9892.3564814	27.1023465
7876	ADAMS	9401.3564814	25.757141
7900	JAMES	9806.3564814	26.86673
7902	FORD	9806.3564814	26.86673
7934	MILLER	9755.3564814	26.727004

Figure 7.101 Date difference.

Note that Oracle calculates the difference between 2 dates up to seconds and hence the net result is in decimals. We can further use ROUND() or TRUNC() functions to get the number of days or years as integer (Figure 7.102).

```
SQL>select empno,ename,round(sysdate - hiredate) no_of_days,round((sysdate - hiredate)/
365) no_of_years from emp;
    EMPNO       ENAME       NO_OF_DAYS      NO_OF_YEARS
     7369       SMITH          10157             28
     7499       ALLEN          10092             28
     7521       WARD           10090             28
      .
      .
      .
```

Figure 7.102   Date difference without decimal values.

Determining the age of employees from DOB (Date of Birth) using DATE difference. Assume STUDENT table with records as in Figure 7.103.

```
SQL>select rollno,name,to_char(date_of_birth,'dd/mm/yyyy'),marks from student;
   ROLLNO     NAME      TO_CHAR(DATE_OF_BIRTH,'DD/MM/YYYY')      MARKS
     1111    rashmi                 13/09/1981                    54
     3333    chetan                 01/03/1987                    45
     4444    rishi                  10/05/1995                    30
     5555    anil                   20/11/1994                    89
```

Figure 7.103   Records in STUDENT table.

We want to display the AGE of students from Date of Birth (Figure 7.104).

```
SQL>select rollno,name,date_of_birth,trunc((sysdate - date_of_birth)/365) AGE,marks from
student;
   ROLLNO     NAME      DATE_OF_BIRTH      AGE      MARKS
     1111    rashmi       13-SEP-81        27        54
     3333    chetan       01-MAR-87        21        45
     4444    rishi        10-MAY-95        13        30
     5555    anil         20-NOV-94        13        89
```

Figure 7.104   Calculating AGE of students.

ADD_MONTHS(date, N-number of months)

This returns the Date after N-number of months from the specified date. N can be positive or negative (Figure 7.105).

```
SQL>select sysdate, add_months(sysdate,2), add_months(sysdate,-2) from dual;
     SYSDATE      ADD_MONTHS(SYSDATE,2)      ADD_MONTHS(SYSDATE,-2)
    08-OCT-08          08-DEC-08                   08-AUG-08
```

Figure 7.105   ADD_MONTHS.

LAST_DAY(date)

This returns the last date of the specified month (Figure 7.106).

SQL>select sysdate, last_day(sysdate) from dual;	
SYSDATE	**LAST_DAY(SYSDATE)**
08-OCT-08	31-OCT-08

Figure 7.106 LAST_DAY.

Sysdate is of October, therefore, the last date of October is 31-Oct-2008.

MONTHS_BETWEEN(date 1, date 2)

This returns the number of months between specified dates (Figure 7.107).

SQL>select months_between('24-oct-2008','10-aug-2008') from dual;
MONTHS_BETWEEN('24-OCT-2008','10-AUG-2008')
2.451612

Figure 7.107 MONTHS_BETWEEN.

Note that Oracle takes seconds into consideration while doing any calculation on dates.

NEXT_DAY(date, day of the week)

Day of the week can be 'MON', 'TUE', 'WED', 'THU', 'FRI', 'SAT', 'SUN'.
This function returns the next date on which the specified DAY of the week will occur (Figure 7.108).

SQL>select sysdate, next_day(sysdate, 'FRI') from dual;	
SYSDATE	**NEXT_DAY(SYSDATE,'FRI')**
08-OCT-08	10-OCT-08

Figure 7.108 NEXT_DAY.

If today 08th Oct 2008 is Wednesday then the next date which is Friday is on 10th Oct 2008.

INTERVAL

Returns the new time offset by the specified INTERVAL(positive or negative) as shown in Figure 7.109.

SQL>select to_char(sysdate,'hh24:mi:ss'),to_char(sysdate + INTERVAL '10' MINUTE,'hh24:mi:ss') from dual;	
TO_CHAR(SYSDATE,'HH24:MI:SS')	**TO_CHAR(SYSDATE+INTERVAL'10'MINUTE,'HH24:MI:SS')**
09:03:27	09:13:27

Figure 7.109 INTERVAL.

INTERVAL can be in MINUTE/HOUR/SECOND.

TRUNC and ROUND

In 24-hour format, Oracle represents midnight as 00:00:00 and 12:00:00 as noon. Any time past 12:00:00 is PM.

Assume records in EMP table as in Figure 7.110.

```
SQL>select empno,ename,to_char(hiredate,'dd-mon-yyyy hh24:mi:ss') from emp;
```

EMPNO	ENAME	TO_CHAR(HIREDATE,'DD-MON-YYYYHH24:MI:SS')
7369	SMITH	17-dec-1980 16:05:14
7499	ALLEN	20-feb-1981 13:10:10
7521	WARD	22-feb-1981 19:20:16
7566	JONES	02-apr-1981 20:01:01
7654	MARTIN	28-sep-1981 11:03:02
7698	BLAKE	01-may-1981 00:00:00
7782	CLARK	09-jun-1981 08:10:10
7788	SCOTT	09-dec-1982 23:01:02
7839	KING	17-nov-1981 12:00:00
7844	TURNER	08-sep-1981 00:00:00
7876	ADAMS	12-jan-1983 23:59:59
7900	JAMES	03-dec-1981 00:00:00
7902	FORD	03-dec-1981 10:10:10
7934	MILLER	23-jan-1982 12:10:10

Figure 7.110   Records in EMP table.

Let us find the employees who have joined on 08-sep-1981 (Figure 7.111).

```
SQL>select empno,ename,to_char(hiredate,'dd-mon-yyyy hh24:mi:ss') from emp where
hiredate='08-sep1981';
```

EMPNO	ENAME	TO_CHAR(HIREDATE,'DD-MON-YYYYHH24:MI:SS')
7844	TURNER	08-sep-1981 00:00:00

Figure 7.111   WHERE clause for Date column.

Note: The DEFAULT time for any date value is 00:00:00. As TURNER joined on 08-sep1981 at 00:00:00 and we specified a WHERE condition without time, therefore the default time compared was 00:00:00.

Let us find employees who have joined on 28-sep-1981 as in Figure 7.112.

```
SQL>select empno,ename,to_char(hiredate,'dd/mm/yyyy hh24:mi:ss') from emp where
hiredate='28-sep-1981';

No Data Found
```

Figure 7.112   WHERE clause for Date column.

Note: Although MARTIN joined on 28-sep-1981 still it was not displayed. Because the hiredate for MARTIN is 28-sep-1981 with time as 11:03:02 and we have specified in WHERE clause "hiredate='28-sep-1981'" without time. A date without time specification is assumed as 00:00:00 time. Therefore, the actual query should be SQL>select empno, ename, to_char(hiredate,'dd/mm/yyyy hh24:mi:ss') from emp where hiredate='28-sep-1981 00:00:00';

Now how to specify the WHERE clause so that it displays MARTIN.

There are 2 ways to do this.

1. We should know the exact time (Figure 7.113).

SQL>select empno,ename,to_char(hiredate,'dd-mon-yyyy hh24:mi:ss') from emp where hiredate=to_date('28-sep-1981 11:03:02','dd-mon-yyyy hh24:mi:ss');

EMPNO	ENAME	TO_CHAR(HIREDATE,'DD-MON-YYYYHH24:MI:SS')
7654	MARTIN	28-sep-1981 11:03:02

Figure 7.113 Using time also for date column.

Here we have used to_date() function to specify the time also in 24-hour format.

2. We can use Oracle's built-in function named TRUNC.
TRUNC removes the time part from DATE value (Figure 7.114).

SQL>select empno,ename,to_char(hiredate,'dd-mon-yyyy hh24:mi:ss') from emp where TRUNC(hiredate)='28-sep-1981';

EMPNO	ENAME	TO_CHAR(HIREDATE,'DD-MON-YYYYHH24:MI:SS')
7654	MARTIN	28-sep-1981 11:03:02

Figure 7.114 Removing Time component.

Here we are asking Oracle to remove the TIME component from hiredate field and compare it with '28-sep-1981'. So now comparison is made based on purely DATE component and not time.

Figure 7.115 has some examples for applying TRUNC on date values.

DATE value 24 HR Format	AM/PM/NOON	TRUNC(date)
08-sep-1981 10:01:01	AM	08-sep-1981 00:00:00
08-sep-1981 12:00:00	NOON	08-sep-1981 00:00:00
08-sep-1981 16:01:01	PM	08-sep-1981 00:00:00
08-sep-1981 23:59:59	PM	08-sep-1981 00:00:00
08-sep-1981 00:00:00	AM	08-sep-1981 00:00:00

Figure 7.115 Examples of TRUNC(date).

Whatever be the TIME component TRUNC chops the TIME component.

ROUND()

This function when applied to DATE data type rounds the date to the nearest date which is greater than the specified date. For example, see Figure 7.116.

DATE value 24 HR Format	AM/PM/NOON	ROUND(date)
08-sep-1981 10:01:01	AM	08-sep-1981 00:00:00
08-sep-1981 12:00:00	NOON	09-sep-1981 00:00:00
08-sep-1981 16:01:01	PM	09-sep-1981 00:00:00
08-sep-1981 23:59:59	PM	09-sep-1981 00:00:00
08-sep-1981 00:00:00	AM	08-sep-1981 00:00:00

Figure 7.116 Examples of ROUND(date).

Caution: DATE + any time beyond 12:00:00(NOON) is rounded to NEXT DATE.

Let us apply both ROUND and TRUNC functions to EMP table (Figure 7.117).

```
SQL>select empno, ename, to_char(hiredate,'dd/mm/yy hh24:mi:ss'), to_char(round(hiredate),
'dd/mm/yy hh24:mi:ss'), to_char(trunc(hiredate),'dd/mm/yy hh24:mi:ss') from emp;
```

EMPNO	ENAME	TO_CHAR (HIREDATE, 'DD/MM/YYHH24:MI:SS')	TO_CHAR (ROUND(HIREDATE), 'DD/MM/YYHH24:MI:SS')	TO_CHAR (TRUNC(HIREDATE), 'DD/MM/YYHH24:MI:SS')
7369	SMITH	17/12/80 16:05:14	18/12/80 00:00:00	17/12/80 00:00:00
7499	ALLEN	20/02/81 13:10:10	21/02/81 00:00:00	20/02/81 00:00:00
7521	WARD	22/02/81 19:20:16	23/02/81 00:00:00	22/02/81 00:00:00
7566	JONES	02/04/81 20:01:01	03/04/81 00:00:00	02/04/81 00:00:00
7654	MARTIN	28/09/81 11:03:02	28/09/81 00:00:00	28/09/81 00:00:00
7698	BLAKE	01/05/81 00:00:00	01/05/81 00:00:00	01/05/81 00:00:00
7782	CLARK	09/06/81 08:10:10	09/06/81 00:00:00	09/06/81 00:00:00
7788	SCOTT	09/12/82 23:01:02	10/12/82 00:00:00	09/12/82 00:00:00
7839	KING	17/11/81 12:00:00	18/11/81 00:00:00	17/11/81 00:00:00
7844	TURNER	08/09/81 00:00:00	08/09/81 00:00:00	08/09/81 00:00:00
7876	ADAMS	12/01/83 23:59:59	13/01/83 00:00:00	12/01/83 00:00:00
7900	JAMES	03/12/81 00:00:00	03/12/81 00:00:00	03/12/81 00:00:00
7902	FORD	03/12/81 10:10:10	03/12/81 00:00:00	03/12/81 00:00:00
7934	MILLER	23/01/82 12:10:10	24/01/82 00:00:00	23/01/82 00:00:00

Figure 7.117 ROUND and TRUNC on Hiredate.

REVIEW QUESTIONS

1. What are built-in functions? What is the advantage of having rich library of built-in functions?
2. Differentiate between scalar, aggregate and list functions.
3. Explain the significance of NVL() function.
4. What are Aggregate functions?
5. List the various Transformation functions.
6. How to insert both date and time in DATE data type column? How to view the date and time components stored in date field?
7. How to calculate the AGE from Date of Birth?

MULTIPLE CHOICE QUESTIONS

1. SCALAR functions operate on
   - (a) Columns of records
   - (b) Each row of table
   - (c) Set of rows of a table

2. LIST functions operate on
   - (a) Set of columns
   - (b) Set of rows
   - (c) Every row

3. Which is TRUE about CONCAT and "||"?
   - (a) CONCAT can combine 2 strings only.
   - (b) CONCAT can combine multiple strings but "||" cannot.
   - (c) "||"can combine multiple strings but CONCAT cannot.

4. Which is the correct syntax for specifying a unknown value for CHAR/VARCHAR2 data type?
   - (a) 'NULL'
   - (b) "NULL"
   - (c) NULL
   - (d) None of the above.

5. Which built-in function can be used to extract specified number of characters from a string?
   - (a) INSTR
   - (b) DECODE
   - (c) SUBSTR
   - (d) TO_CHAR

6. SELECT ROUND(TO_DATE('12/02/2009 10:10:10','dd/mm/yyyy hh24:mi:ss')) FROM DUAL; will return
   - (a) 12-FEB-09
   - (b) 12-FEB-2009
   - (c) 13-FEB-09
   - (d) 13-FEB-2009

7. SELECT ROUND(TO_DATE('12/02/2009 14:10:10','dd/mm/yyyy hh24:mi:ss')) FROM DUAL; will return
   - (a) 12-FEB-09
   - (b) 12-FEB-2009
   - (c) 13-FEB-09
   - (d) 13-FEB-2009

8. SELECT TRUNC(TO_DATE('12/02/2009 10:10:10','dd/mm/yyyy hh24:mi:ss')) FROM DUAL; will return
   - (a) 12-FEB-09
   - (b) 12-FEB-2009
   - (c) 13-FEB-09
   - (d) 13-FEB-2009

9. SELECT TRUNC(TO_DATE('12/02/2009 14:10:10','dd/mm/yyyy hh24:mi:ss')) FROM DUAL; will return
    (a) 12-FEB-09
    (b) 12-FEB-2009
    (c) 13-FEB-09
    (d) 13-FEB-2009
10. What is the default DATE format?
    (a) DD-MON-YY
    (b) DD-MON-YYYY
    (c) Both (a) and (b) are correct
11. The function which can be used to implement IF ELSE type of construct is
    (a) SUBSTR
    (b) IF_ELSE
    (c) DECODE
    (d) None of the above
12. Which of the following is not a transformational function?
    (a) TO_CHAR
    (b) TO_DATE
    (c) DECODE

LAB ASSIGNMENT

Assume a CUSTOMER ORDER system with the following three tables:

1. **CUSTOMER:** Contains the details of various customers such that each customer has been assigned a UNIQUE Identification named CUSTOMER_ID.
2. **PRODUCT:** Contains the details of various products manufactured in the company. Each product has a unique identification number called PRODUCT_CODE.
     The first two characters of product code indicate the type of product. For example, 'CD' indicates CD PLAYER, 'TV' indicates Television, etc.
3. **ORDER:** This table contains the information about various orders received from customers.

TABLE 7.1   CUSTOMER

Column name	Data type	Size	Constraint
CUSTOMER_ID	CHAR	6	PRIMARY KEY. Must start with 'C'
CUSTOMER_NAME	VARCHAR2	20	NOT NULL
ADDRESS	VARCHAR2	20	UNIQUE
CITY	VARCHAR2	20	
PINCODE	NUMBER	6	
STATE	VARCHAR2	20	
BALANCE_DUE	NUMBER	8,2	

TABLE 7.2 PRODUCT

Column name	Data type	Size	Constraint
PRODUCT_CODE	CHAR	6	PRIMARY KEY
PRODUCT_NAME	VARCHAR2	20	UNIQUE
QTY_AVAILABLE	NUMBER	5	
COST_PRICE	NUMBER	8,2	
SELLING_PRICE	NUMBER	8,2	

TABLE 7.3 ORDER

Column name	Data type	Size	Constraint
ORDER_NO	CHAR	6	
ORDER_DATE	DATE		
CUSTOMER_ID	CHAR	6	
PRODUCT_CODE	CHAR	6	
QUANTITY	NUMBER	5	

Primary Key: ORDER_NO+ORDER_DATE+CUSTOMER_ID+PRODUCT_CD.

The same customer can place order for more than one product in single order.

4. Add the following records in the CUSTOMER table

CUST.ID	NAME	ADDRESS	CITY	PIN	STATE	BAL
C10001	ASNANI BROTHERS	243,9-B	BHOPAL	462024	MP	5000
C10002	SINGH ASSOCIATES	E1, 23	BHOPAL	462020	MP	3000
C10003	GUPTA SALES	100, G-APART	GURGAON	110234	HA	1000
C10004	SINHA DISTRIBUTERS	21, GANDHINAGAR	CHITTAUR	230011	RJ	7000
C10005	ARORA CO.	28, 2-C	BHOPAL	462021	MP	3300

5. Add the following records in the PRODUCT table

PRODUCT.CD	NAME	QTY.AV	COST PRICE	SELLINGPRICE
CD0001	Philips CD A230	10	2000	3000
CD0002	Samsung D100	20	2500	3200
TV0001	Samsung T101	30	10000	12000
TV0002	Samsung T222	12	12000	14000
TV0003	Philips 1022	14	9000	12000
TV0004	Philips 2002	11	15000	18000
RF0001	Godrej Q1023	25	10000	13000
RF0002	Godrej D1024	23	16000	18000
RF0003	Whirlpool W123	12	20000	20000

6. Add the following records in the ORDER table

ORDER NO	ORDER DATE	CUST.ID	PROD.CD	QTY
O10001	11-FEB-2008 11:10:10 AM	C10001	CD0001	10
O10002	12-FEB-2008 16:12:23 PM	C10001	TV0001	20
O10003	11-FEB-2008 18:20:15 PM	C10002	RF0001	12
O10003	11-FEB-2008 20:30:34 PM	C10002	TV0004	15
O10004	25-MAR-200913:23:34 PM	C10003	TV0003	11
O10004	25-MAR-200913:23:34 PM	C10003	RF0002	5

7. Apply UNIQUE constraint on CUSTOMER_ID + PRODUCT_CODE on the ORDER table.

8. Define a foreign key on CUSTOMER_ID of the ORDER table referring to CUSTOMER_ID of CUSTOMER TABLE.

9. Define a foreign key on PRODUCT_CODE of ORDER table referring to PRODUCT_CODE of the PRODUCT table.

10. List the customer names whose balance due is more than 4000/-.

11. For all the products display the product name along with Net Profit as Selling Price – Cost Price.

12. Count the total number of orders from the ORDER table.

13. Count the customerwise number of orders.

14. Calculate profit earned on each order.

15. Calculate the average selling price of all the products.

16. Calculate the maximum and minimum quantity of products which have been ordered till date and display them as "MAX.QTY" and "MIN.QTY" respectively.

17. Display the products whose selling price is more than equal to 5000.

18. Display the orders placed during 2008.
   (**Hint:** TO_CHAR(ORDER_DATE,'YYYY')='2008')

19. List the yearwise number of orders placed.

20. Display monthwise, customerwise number of orders with minimum and maximum quantity ordered.

21. Display the customer with maximum due balance.

22. Display the customer with minimum due balance.

23. Display the top 3 customers with maximum due balances.
   (**Hint:** Refer to Chapter 12)

24. List the customer names for which we have orders in hand.
   (**Hint:** Join ORDER and CUSTOMER TABLE and then SELECT DISTINCT CUSOMER_NAME from CUSTOMER table such that QUANTITY in ORDER table is not zero.)

25. How many orders do we have for CD-PLAYERS?

26. How many orders do we have for each type of product?

27. Display orderwise, categorywise, total quantity sold. Display category as 'CD-PLAYERS', 'TELEVISION', 'REFRIGERATOR'.

    (**Hint:** use DECODE and SUBSTR)

28. Display customer namewise number of orders placed in MORNING and AFTERNOON.

29. Find the customerwise last order placed.

30. Display the customerwise average number of orders placed.

31. Identify the customers whose name contains 'BAJAJ'.

32. What would be the date 10 days from today?

33. 29/02/2009 would be falling on which day (Mon, Tue, …)?

34. Find 4 to the power of 6.

35. Find the square root of 365.

Adding, Deleting and Modifying Records

8.1 ADDING RECORDS

DBMS is basically a collection of data in the form of tables with rows and columns. The first step to create a database is to add new records.

8.1.1   Inserting Values of Different Data Types

Although we have discussed adding new records with different data type columns in previous chapters but we will summarize it here for clarity.

CHARACTER data type

The Character/String values can be regarded as input which use single quotes.

NUMBER data type

The NUMBER data type value can be regarded as input directly without any quotes.

DATE data type

The Date data type value can be regarded as input using single quotes if the value being supplied is in default oracle format (dd-mon-yy or dd-mon-yyyy). To insert in desired format we have to use the TO_DATE() built-in function with format specifier as indicated in Chapter 7.

8.1.2   Adding NULL Values

Any data type can be supplied unknown value by specifying NULL.

Caution: Do not use NULL with quotes as it will store the text 'NULL' instead of Unknown value.

Let us create a table named "student" with columns of different data types and add Records (Figure 8.1).

```
SQL> create table student (rollno char(4),name varchar2(10),date_of_birth date,
    2 marks number(3));
Table created.

SQL> insert into student values ('1111','satish','14-oct-83',59);
1 row created.

SQL> insert into student values ('2222','rashmi','13-sep-1981',45);
1 row created.

SQL> insert into student values ('3333','anil',NULL,56);
1 row created.

SQL> insert into student values ('4444','rishi','07-oct-1972',null);
1 row created.

SQL> insert into student values ('5555',null,'07-jan-1993',87);
1 row created.

SQL> select * from student;
```

ROLL	NAME	DATE_OF_B	MARKS
2222	rashmi	13-SEP-81	45
3333	anil		56
4444	rishi	07-OCT-72	
5555		07-JAN-93	87
1111	satish	14-OCT-83	59

```
SQL> insert into student values ('6666','anita', 2 to_date('11/01/1970 10:10:10','dd/mm/yyyy
hh24:mi:ss'),34);

1 row created.

SQL> select rollno,name,to_char(date_of_birth,'dd/mm/yyyy hh24:mi:ss') dob, 2 marks from
student;
```

ROLL	NAME	DOB	MARKS
2222	rashmi	13/09/1981 00:00:00	45
3333	anil		56
4444	rishi	07/10/1972 00:00:00	
5555		07/01/1993 00:00:00	87
1111	satish	14/10/1983 00:00:00	59
6666	anita	11/01/1970 10:10:10	34

```
6 rows selected.
```

Figure 8.1 Adding values of different data types.

Note: Character data type values are enclosed in single quotes.

Number data type does not require quotes.

Date data type:

> Values are enclosed in single quotes. Format specifier is optional.
>
> If we supply date component only then the time stored is 00:00:00.
>
> The time component can be specified using built-in function TO_DATE() with format specifier.
>
> To display both Date and Time use TO_CHAR() built-in function.

8.1.3 String Substitution for Adding Multiple Records

It is quite cumbersome and requires a lot of typing if we want to insert many records. Oracle has a provision called "String Substitution" which comes very handy in such scenarios. String substitution uses the symbol '&' and '&&' as shown in Figure 8.2.

```
SQL> create table std (college char(4),rollno number,name varchar2(10), marks number(3));

Table created.

SQL> insert into std values ('&p_college',&p_rollno,'&p_name',&p_marks);
Enter value for p_college: OIST
Enter value for p_rollno: 1111
Enter value for p_name: satish
Enter value for p_marks: 34
old 1: insert into std values ('&p_college',&p_rollno,'&p_name',&p_marks)
new 1: insert into std values ('OIST',1111,'satish',34)

1 row created.

SQL> /
Enter value for p_college: OIST
Enter value for p_rollno: 2222
Enter value for p_name: rashmi
Enter value for p_marks: 56
old 1: insert into std values ('&p_college',&p_rollno,'&p_name',&p_marks)
new 1: insert into std values ('OIST',2222,'rashmi',56)

1 row created.
```

Figure 8.2 Using string substitution (Single '&').

Explanation: '&p_college' tells Oracle to ask for the value of "p_college" string when the Insert statement is executed. Single quote is required as the COLLEGE column is of Character data type. Single quote is not required for marks as it is of Number data type.

Note that Oracle prompts to enter value for all substitution strings.

Once all substitution strings have been supplied values from keyboard, Oracle converts the entire statement with the specified values. This is indicated by the *"new 1: insert into std values ('OIST',1111,'satish',34)"*.

To add a new record just type "/" at SQL prompt and press the "ENTER" key. Oracle will repeat the earlier steps. "/" repeats the previously executed SQL statement.

Suppose we have to enter multiple records for the students of the same college, say "OIST". Oracle provides '&&' as Substitution string which stores the value once supplied for the current SQL session (Figure 8.3).

```
SQL> insert into std values ('&&p_college',&p_rollno,'&p_name',&p_marks);
Enter value for p_college: OIST
Enter value for p_rollno: 3333
Enter value for p_name: anil
Enter value for p_marks: 23
old 1: insert into std values ('&&p_college',&p_rollno,'&p_name',&p_marks)
new 1: insert into std values ('OIST',3333,'anil',23)

1 row created.

SQL> /
Enter value for p_rollno: 4444
Enter value for p_name: rishi
Enter value for p_marks: 69
old 1: insert into std values ('&&p_college',&p_rollno,'&p_name',&p_marks)
new 1: insert into std values ('OIST',4444,'rishi',69)

1 row created.
```

Figure 8.3 Using string substitution (double '&&').

Note that value for p_college was prompted for the first INSERT statement and not for the next INSERT statement which is executed by / at SQL prompt.

Oracle has temporarily stored the value 'OIST' in the session string 'p_college' and will store it till the session is exited or another single ampersand substitution string is used with the same name in the subsequent statements.

8.2   DELETING RECORDS

Deleting implies removing the records from a table which are no longer required.

Assume "student_details" table with records as shown in Figure 8.4.

```
SQL> select * from student_details;
```

ROLLNO	SUBJECT	MARKS
1	MATHS	12
1	PHY	23
2	MATHS	34
3	MATHS	35
4	MATHS	38
4	PHY	45

6 rows selected.

Figure 8.4   Records in STUDENT_DETAILS table.

- **Deleting all records from a table.**

We want to delete/remove all records from the STUDENT_DETAILS table (Figure 8.5).

```
SQL> delete from student_details;

6 rows deleted.

SQL> select * from student_details;

no rows selected
```

Figure 8.5   Removing all records.

All records have been removed on issuing the "delete" command.

- **Deleting specific records.**

Now assume the table with the original data, that is, 6 records (Figure 8.4).

Delete records of rollno 4. Records of rollno 4 can be deleted by using the WHERE clause as shown in Figure 8.6.

```
SQL> delete from student_details where rollno=4;

2 rows deleted.
```

Figure 8.6   Remove specific records.

- **Deleting specific records using Boolean operators (AND, OR).**

Again, assume the table with the original data, that is, 6 records (Figure 8.4).

Figure 8.7 contains the statement for deleting the record containing marks of MATHS subject for rollno 4.

```
SQL> delete from student_details where rollno=4 and subject='MATHS';

1 row deleted.
```

Figure 8.7   Using Boolean operators in DELETE command.

Similarly, we can use the "OR" logical operator in the "WHERE" clause of delete statement depending on the requirement.

- **Deleting records from one table depending on records in another table.**

We need to delete those rollno's from "student_master" table for which marks have not been entered in "student_details" table (in a single SQL statement). Assume data in master and detail tables as shown in Figure 8.8.

```
SQL> select * from student_master;
    ROLLNO NAME
         1 satish
         2 rashmi
         4 nilesh
```

SQL> select * from student_details;

ROLLNO	SUBJECT	MARKS
1	MATHS	12
1	PHY	23
2	MATHS	34
3	MATHS	35

Figure 8.8   Records in master and detail tables.

Rollno 4 is in master table but does not have marks entered in details table.

Figure 8.9 shows the command for removing those records from master table for which there are no records in detail table.

SQL> delete from student_master where rollno **NOT IN** (select rollno from student_details);

1 row deleted.

SQL> select * from student_master;

ROLLNO NAME
   1 satish
   2 rashmi

Figure 8.9   Using NOT IN for deletion operation.

Here we have used the "NOT IN" operator for achieving the desired result. The sub-query "select rollno from student_details" returns 1,1,2,3 and then the delete statement finds rollno 4 in outer query which is not in 1,1,2,3 and will delete the same.

8.3   UPDATING/MODIFYING DATA VALUES

Updating refers to changing or modifying values in columns of existing records. Assume data in "student_master" table as shown in Figure 8.10.

SQL> select * from student_master;

ROLLNO	NAME	MARKS
1	satish	10
2	rashmi	8
3	nilesh	13
4	ruchi	16
5	sarika	7

Figure 8.10   Records in master table.

- **Updating all records.**

Let us add 5 marks to marks obtained by every student (Figure 8.11).

```
SQL> update student_master set marks=marks+5;
5 rows updated.

SQL> select * from student_master;

        ROLLNO          NAME            MARKS
          1             satish           15
          2             rashmi           13
          3             nilesh           18
          4             ruchi            21
          5             sarika           12
```

Figure 8.11   Modifying values of all records.

- **Updating specific column value for a specific record.**

Figure 8.12 shows how to change the name of rollno 3 to 'vivek'.

```
SQL> update student_master set name='vivek' where rollno=3;
1 row updated.

SQL> select * from student_master;

        ROLLNO          NAME            MARKS
          1             satish           10
          2             rashmi            8
          3             vivek            13
          4             ruchi            16
          5             sarika            7
```

Figure 8.12   Modifying specific column value.

- **Updating multiple columns in single update statement.**

Figure 8.13 contains statement for changing the name to 'rishi' and marks to 11 for rollno 5.

```
SQL> update student_master set name='rishi', marks=11 where rollno=5;

1 row updated.

SQL> select * from student_master;

        ROLLNO          NAME            MARKS
          1             satish           10
          2             rashmi            8
          3             vivek            13
          4             ruchi            16
          5             rishi            11
```

Figure 8.13   Modifying multiple column values.

Note: The "WHERE" clause of update statement can contain logical operators like "AND", "OR".

- **Updating table using IN operator.**

Assume master and details table with records as shown in Figure 8.14.

```
SQL> select * from student_master;
```

ROLLNO	NAME	CITY
1	satish	BHOPAL
2	rashmi	AJMER
3	rishi	BHOPAL
4	shama	AJMER
5	nilesh	DELHI

```
SQL> select * from student_details;
```

ROLLNO	SUBJECT	MARKS
1	MATHS	12
1	PHY	23
2	MATHS	14
2	PHY	21
3	MATHS	34
4	MATHS	43
5	MATHS	20

Figure 8.14   Records in master and detail table.

We want to add 5 marks to the MATHS subject for all students who live in the city of BHOPAL (Figure 8.15).

```
SQL> update student_details set marks=marks + 5
2 where subject='MATHS'
3 and rollno in (select rollno from student_master where city='BHOPAL');

2 rows updated.

SQL> select * from student_details;
```

ROLLNO	SUBJECT	MARKS
1	MATHS	17
1	PHY	23
2	MATHS	14
2	PHY	21
3	MATHS	39
4	MATHS	43
5	MATHS	20

Figure 8.15   Using Boolean and IN operators.

The sub-query "select rollno from student_master where city='BHOPAL'" executes first and returns rollno 1,2. Now update the statement—adds 5 marks for records having rollno in 1,2 and subject='MATHS'.

8.4 SAVING AND UNDOING CHANGES IN DATA

Oracle provides certain features for saving records and undoing changes. Let us first understand the saving part of it.

Let us create a master table and insert a few records (Figure 8.16).

```
SQL> create table student_master(rollno number(4),name varchar2(10));

Table created.

SQL> insert into student_master values (1,'satish');

1 row created.

SQL> insert into student_master values (2,'rashmi');

1 row created.

SQL> insert into student_master values (3,'nilesh');

1 row created.
```

Figure 8.16 Saving records.

Now if instead of typing "exit" at the SQL prompt, you just click the "cross" button at the righttop of SQL Screen and login again and then select records from master table as shown in Figure 8.17, since we closed the SQL window by clicking the cross button on the righttop of SQL window.

```
SQL> select * from student_master;

no rows selected
```

Figure 8.17 Records not saved.

Oracle has not saved your data because you have killed that particular SQL session forcibly. Now what exactly "exit" command do. When you issue the "exit" command at SQL prompt, oracle automatically saves the data inserted/updated/deleted and then exits the SQL prompt screen.

8.4.1 COMMIT

What we normally call "save" is called "commit" in Oracle. All the records inserted, updated or deleted are saved to the database only when we explicitly issue the "commit" statement or use the "exit" command.

Now issue the same insert statements as in Figure 8.16 and then type "commit" at SQL Prompt and then press the cross symbol at the righttop of SQL screen. Now login again and select records from master table. What did you observe? This time the records were intact because we issued the "commit" command before closing the SQL prompt screen.

Conclusion

1. To save the changes(insert/update/delete), we need to issue the "commit" command.
2. The "exit" command can also be used to save the changes and it will store the data till last statement. "exit" first issues "commit" and then closes the SQL Prompt screen.
3. DDL statements like "create" do not require commit. Only DML statements like "insert, update, delete" require commit for saving changes.
4. If we just click the cross button at the righttop of SQL Prompt screen, all the changes till last "commit" only are saved.

8.4.2 ROLLBACK

What we normally call "Undo" is called "rollback" in Oracle.

Let us see an example (Figure 8.18).

```
SQL> create table student_master(rollno number(4),name varchar2(10));

Table created.

SQL> insert into student_master values (1,'satish');

1 row created.

SQL> insert into student_master values (2,'rashmi');

1 row created.

SQL> commit;

Commit complete.

SQL> insert into student_master values (3,'nilesh');

1 row created.

SQL> insert into student_master values (4,'ruchi');

1 row created.

SQL> select * from student_master;

    ROLLNO NAME
        1 satish
        2 rashmi
        3 nilesh
        4 ruchi

SQL> rollback;

Rollback complete.

SQL> select * from student_master;

    ROLLNO NAME
        1 satish
        2 rashmi
```

Figure 8.18 ROLLBACK.

We issued the "commit" statement after inserting rollno 1 and 2. Then we inserted rollno 3, and 4 followed by rollback. What "rollback" did is undo all the changes made till last "commit". Therefore, on selecting records from master table after "rollback", only rollno 1 and 2 existed in the database.

Caution: We can rollback to last COMMIT only.

8.4.3   Savepoint

Oracle provides a feature wherein we can define savepoints in between various DML (insert, update, delete) operations so that at a later stage we can rollback changes to a specific savepoint. In Figure 8.19, we have created two savepoints and rolled back to 2nd savepoint.

```
SQL> insert into student_master values (1,'satish');
1 row created.

SQL> insert into student_master values (2,'rashmi');
1 row created.

SQL> savepoint sp1;
Savepoint created.

SQL> insert into student_master values (3,'nilesh');
1 row created.

SQL> insert into student_master values (4,'ruchi');
1 row created.

SQL> savepoint sp2;
Savepoint created.

SQL> insert into student_master values (5,'sarika');

1 row created.

SQL> select * from student_master;
        ROLLNO          NAME
          1             satish
          2             rashmi
          3             nilesh
          4             ruchi
          5             sarika

SQL> rollback to savepoint sp2;

SQL> select * from student_master;
        ROLLNO          NAME
          1             satish
          2             rashmi
          3             nilesh
          4             ruchi
```

Figure 8.19   Savepoint.

Note that rollno 5 is not available as we have rolled back to savepoint sp2.
In Figure 8.20, we have rolled back to savepoint sp1.

```
SQL> rollback to savepoint sp1;

Rollback complete.

SQL> select * from student_master;

        ROLLNO          NAME
           1            satish
           2            rashmi
```

Figure 8.20 Savepoint.

Note that rollno 3 and 4 are not displayed as we have rolled back to savepoint sp1.

Caution: If we issue "commit" statement then all savepoints are lost.

Now we will create two savepoints sp1 and sp2 and then issue a commit statement. Figure 8.21 shows that we cannot rollback to specific savepoints whenever a commit is executed.

```
SQL>truncate table student_master;

Table Truncated

SQL> insert into student_master values (1,'satish');

1 row created.

SQL> insert into student_master values (2,'rashmi');

1 row created.

SQL> savepoint sp1;

Savepoint created.

SQL> insert into student_master values (3,'nilesh');

1 row created.

SQL> insert into student_master values (4,'ruchi');

1 row created.

SQL> savepoint sp2;

Savepoint created.

SQL> insert into student_master values (5,'sarika');

1 row created.

SQL> commit;

Commit complete.
```

```
SQL> select * from student_master;
       ROLLNO              NAME
           1               satish
           2               rashmi
           3               nilesh
           4               ruchi
           5               sarika

SQL> rollback to sp1;
rollback to sp1
*
ERROR at line 1:
ORA-01086: savepoint 'SP1' never established
```

Figure 8.21   COMMIT disables all save points.

8.5   TRUNCATE

If we want to delete all records permanently, we first issue the "delete" statement followed by the "commit". Instead we can just use a single statement "truncate" to achieve the same (Figure 8.22).

```
SQL> select * from student_master;

       ROLLNO          NAME          CITY
           1           satish        BHOPAL
           2           rashmi        AJMER
           3           rishi         BHOPAL
           4           shama         AJMER
           5           nilesh        DELHI

SQL> truncate table student_master;

Table truncated.

SQL> select * from student_master;

no rows selected

SQL> rollback;

Rollback complete.

SQL> select * from student_master;

no rows selected
```

Figure 8.22   TRUNCATE.

Caution: Rollback statement cannot recover the truncated records.

8.5.1 Differences between DELETE and TRUNCATE

- Deleted records can be restored using rollback. Truncated records cannot be restored because they are removed permanently.
- In the DELETE statement we can specify the WHERE clause thereby specifying which records to be deleted. TRUNCATE removes all records.
- On executing the DELETE statement all database triggers are fired, whereas in using the TRUNCATE statement database triggers are not fired. As such, TRUNCATE is faster and doesn't use as much undo space as DELETE.

We will be learning about database triggers in the Chapter titled "Database Triggers".

8.6 DROP

A table has two aspects, namely

1. The structure – Number of Columns, Data Type of Columns and constraints like PRIMARY KEY, NOT NULL, UNIQUE, etc.
2. The Data – The records or rows.

The DROP command is used to destroy the entire table along with contents. The *"drop" will remove all the records and destroy the table structure also*. Moreover, dropped tables cannot be recovered using the ROLLBACK command.

The TRUNCATE command permanently removes the records only and not the structure. Records truncated cannot be rolled back.

The DELETE command removes the desired records (all or depending on WHERE clause) but records removed using the DELETE command can be recovered using ROLLBACK command. The DELETE command does not affect the table structure.

To remove the structure as well as data of "student_master" table issue the commands as shown in Figure 8.23.

```
SQL>drop table student_master;
Table dropped

SQL> desc student_master;
ERROR:
ORA-04043: object student_master does not exist

SQL> select * from student_master;
select * from student_master
     *
ERROR at line 1:
ORA-00942: table or view does not exist

SQL> rollback;
Rollback complete.
```

```
SQL> select * from student_master;
select * from student_master
       *
ERROR at line 1:
ORA-00942: table or view does not exist
```

Figure 8.23   DROP command.

REVIEW QUESTIONS

1. Why are the NUMBER values not enclosed in quotes whereas CHARACTER strings need to be enclosed in single quotes?
2. How to add NULL values for different data types?
3. What is the purpose of String Substitution? What is the difference between single and double ampersand?
4. Which Oracle operator needs to be used for deleting records from one table based on records from another table?
5. Explain COMMIT, ROLLBACK and SAVEPOINT.
6. Differentiate between DELETE, TRUNCATE and DROP.

TRUE/FALSE

1. CHAR and VARCHAR2 data type values need to be enclosed in single quotes.
2. NUMBER data type values may or may not be enclosed in single quotes.
3. The DEFAULT Date format is 'DD/MM/YYYY'.
4. To insert NULL value in CHAR/VARCHAR2 column NULL should be enclosed within single quotes.
5. To supply time component along with DATE for a column the function used is TO_DATE().
6. To display TIME component of a DATE column the function used is TO_CHAR().
7. DATE data type stored DATE + TIME.
8. String Substitution && stores the values for current session only.
9. The DELETE command removes the records permanently.
10. The TRUNCATE command can be used with WHERE clause.
11. The trunacted records cannot be rolled back.
12. It is possible to modify values of multiple columns in the same UPDATE statement.
13. The committed records cannot be rolled back.
14. All SAVEPOINTS are lost after a COMMIT statement.

LAB ASSIGNMENT

Refer to Table 7.1 for the CUSTOMER ORDER tables

1. Change the city of 'ASNANI BROTHERS' from BHOPAL to INDORE.
2. Change the address of 'SINGH ASSOCIATES' to 'E2, 24-C' and BALANCE to 10,000.
3. Increase the cost price of CD-PLAYERS by 10% and selling price by 12%.
4. Increase the cost price of CD-PLAYERS by 10% and refrigerators by 15%.
   (*Hint:* Both requirements cannot be fulfilled by single UPDATE statement)
5. Change the Selling Price of Televisions to Cost Price + 20% profit.
6. A new order has been placed by 'SINGH ASSOCIATES' for product 'RF0003' for a quantity of 25 items dated 12-JAN-2009 at 10:10:10 AM.
7. List the customers who have not placed any order in the past 15 days.
8. Change the quantity for the order placed by 'ASNANI BROTHERS' to 33 for product 'TV0001'.
9. Remove 'SINHA DISTRIBUTORS' from the CUSTOMER table.
10. It has been decided that all products with selling price less than 5000 will not be sold. Remove the products with selling price less than 5000.
11. Remove the customers from the CUSTOMER table who have not placed any order in the last 1 year.
12. Delete those products from the PRODUCT table for which there are no corresponding records in the ORDER table.

Sorting

9.1 INTRODUCTION

Sorting refers to arranging records in a specified sequence maybe alphabetically or by value. For a university we would like to arrange student records by rollno or college or maybe first by college and then followed by rollno. This sorting can be achieved by the "ORDER BY" clause of select statement.

9.2 SORTING ON SINGLE COLUMN

Consider a student_master table with structure and records as shown in Figure 9.1.

```
SQL> desc student_master

        Name              Null?           Type
        COLLEGE                           VARCHAR2(4)
        ROLLNO                            NUMBER(4)
        NAME                              VARCHAR2(15)
        MARKS                             NUMBER(3)

SQL> select * from student_master;

        COLL       ROLLNO       NAME         MARKS
        RKDF        1           sanjay        12
        RKDF        2           salaj         34
        OIST        3           rahul         23
```

PTL	4	sunil	45
OIST	5	neelesh	43
RKDF	6	ruchi	21
RKDF	7	sarika	49
RKDF	8	satish	32

8 rows selected.

Figure 9.1 Master table structure and records.

9.2.1 Arranging Records by College in Ascending Order

The ORDER BY clause can be used to arrange records in the specific order (Figure 9.2).

SQL> select * from student_master **order by college;**

COLL	ROLLNO	NAME	MARKS
OIST	3	rahul	23
OIST	5	neelesh	43
PTL	4	sunil	45
RKDF	1	sanjay	12
RKDF	2	salaj	34
RKDF	6	ruchi	21
RKDF	7	sarika	49
RKDF	8	satish	32

8 rows selected.

Figure 9.2 Arranging records in ascending order.

Note: Ascending order is implied by default whenever we use "ORDER BY" clause.

The ascending order can be specified after "ORDER BY" clause (Figure 9.3) which produces the same output as ORDER BY statement of Figure 9.2.

SQL> select * from student_master **order by college asc;**

COLL	ROLLNO	NAME	MARKS
OIST	3	rahul	23
OIST	5	neelesh	43
PTL	4	sunil	45
RKDF	1	sanjay	12
RKDF	2	salaj	34
RKDF	6	ruchi	21
RKDF	7	sarika	49
RKDF	8	satish	32

8 rows selected.

Figure 9.3 Arranging records in ascending order.

9.3 SORTING ON MULTIPLE COLUMNS

Now we want to arrange records first by college in ascending order and then followed by marks in descending order. This means that students will be shown in order of their descending marks within a college such that the highest scorer is displayed first followed by the next highest scorer. If two or more students have the same marks then they will be shown adjacent to each other. See Figure 9.4 for achieving the desired result.

```
SQL> select * from student_master order by college asc,marks desc;

     COLL        ROLLNO        NAME        MARKS

     OIST           5          neelesh        43
     OIST           3          rahul          23
     PTL            4          sunil          45
     RKDF          7          sarika         49
     RKDF          2          salaj          34
     RKDF          8          satish         33
     RKDF          6          ruchi          21
     RKDF          1          sanjay         12

8 rows selected.
```

Figure 9.4 Sorting on multiple columns.

Note: "asc" implies ascending order.
"desc" implies descending order.
"asc" cannot be replaced by "ascending"
"desc" cannot be replaced by "descending".

The statement in Figure 9.5 will arrange the records displaying the lowest scorer first followed by the next lowest (marks ascending) and so on irrespective of college.

```
SQL> select * from student_master order by marks;

     COLL        ROLLNO        NAME        MARKS

     RKDF          1          sanjay         12
     RKDF          6          ruchi          21
     OIST           3          rahul          23
     RKDF          8          satish         33
     RKDF          2          salaj          34
     OIST           5          neelesh        43
     PTL            4          sunil          45
     RKDF          7          sarika         49

8 rows selected.
```

Figure 9.5 Arranging in the order of marks.

The statement in Figure 9.6 will arrange the records displaying the highest scorer first followed by the next highest (marks descending) and so on irrespective of college.

```
SQL> select * from student_master order by marks desc;

        COLL        ROLLNO        NAME        MARKS

        RKDF          7          sarika         49
        PTL           4          sunil          45
        OIST          5          neelesh        43
        RKDF          2          salaj          34
        RKDF          8          satish         33
        OIST          3          rahul          23
        RKDF          6          ruchi          21
        RKDF          1          sanjay         12

    8 rows selected.
```

Figure 9.6   Arranging in the order of marks descending.

9.4   SORTING ON A COLUMN WITH NULL VALUES

NULL indicates an unknown value and therefore records with NULL values are listed at the end while sorting in ascending order.

Let us insert a few records where name is null or marks is null. Then we will select records in order of marks (Figure 9.7).

```
SQL> insert into student_master values ('OIST',9,null,31);

1 row created.

SQL> insert into student_master values ('OIST',10,'abc',null);

1 row created.

SQL> insert into student_master values ('OIST',11,'xyz',null);

1 row created.

SQL> select * from student_master order by marks;

        COLL        ROLLNO        NAME        MARKS

        RKDF          1          sanjay         12
        RKDF          6          ruchi          21
        OIST          3          rahul          23
        OIST          9                         31
        RKDF          8          satish         33
        RKDF          2          salaj          34
        OIST          5          neelesh        43
        PTL           4          sunil          45
        RKDF          7          sarika         49
        OIST          10         abc
        OIST          11         xyz

    11 rows selected.
```

Figure 9.7   Sorting on NULL values.

Note: Students with null marks are displayed at the end.

9.4.1   Displaying the Records with NULL Value on Top

We can display the students with NULL marks on top using the "ORDER BY NULLS FIRST" clause (Figure 9.8).

```
SQL> select * from student_master order by marks nulls first;

      COLL        ROLLNO        NAME        MARKS
      OIST          10          abc
      OIST          11          xyz
      RKDF           1          sanjay        12
      RKDF           6          ruchi         21
      OIST           3          rahul         23
      OIST           9                        31
      RKDF           8          satish        33
      RKDF           2          salaj         34
      OIST           5          neelesh       43
      PTL            4          sunil         45
      RKDF           7          sarika        49

11 rows selected.
```

Figure 9.8   Displaying NULL column values on TOP.

Note:
1. By default nulls are shown at last. We can also specify the "nulls last" in ORDER BY.
2. The "nulls first" feature is available from Oracle9i onwards only. If you have earlier versions of oracle then using "nulls first" will produce error.

9.5   COMBINING WHERE AND ORDER BY CLAUSES

SQL is highly-structured language and requires the WHERE clause to appear before the ORDER BY clause.

Students of OIST College only can be displayed in order of descending marks as shown in Figure 9.9.

```
SQL> select * from student_master where college='OIST' order by marks desc;

      COLL        ROLLNO        NAME        MARKS
      OIST          10          abc
      OIST          11          xyz
      OIST           5          neelesh       43
      OIST           9                        31
      OIST           3          rahul         23
```

Figure 9.9   Using WHERE and ORDER BY.

Note: "marks desc" has displayed the students with NULL marks on top.

Caution: Always keep in mind that data is case sensitive "abc" is different from "ABC", "aBc", "Abc", etc.

Suppose we have inserted records as shown in Figure 9.10 (with college='oist' in small case)

```
SQL> insert into student_master values ('oist',12,'test',30);
1 row created.

SQL> select * from student_master where college='OIST';

    COLL        ROLLNO        NAME        MARKS

    OIST          3           rahul         23
    OIST          5           neelesh       43
    OIST          9                         31
    OIST         10           abc
    OIST         11           xyz
```

Figure 9.10 Uppercase and lowercase are different.

Note: The record we just inserted does not appear in the select statement because of case sensitive data.

For resolving the problem of Figure 9.10 we can use OR Boolean operator (Figure 9.11).

```
SQL> select * from student_master where college='OIST' or college='oist';

    COLL        ROLLNO        NAME        MARKS

    OIST          3           rahul         23
    OIST          5           neelesh       43
    OIST          9                         31
    OIST         10           abc
    OIST         11           xyz
    oist         12           test          30

6 rows selected.
```

Figure 9.11 Dealing with uppercase and lowercase data.

Alternatively, we can use oracle built-in function UPPER (). Refer to Chapter 7.

SQL> select * from student_master where upper(college)='OIST';

Note: The upper (fieldname) function converts each and every character to upper case.

9.6 SORTING ON DATE COLUMN

Assume an "EMP" table (Figure 9.12) where we have a column named hiredate which indicates the date of joining in the company. Now we want to display the employees in descending order of joining date.

```
SQL> select * from emp order by hiredate desc;
```

EMPNO	ENAME	JOB	MGR	HIREDATE	SAL	COMM	DEPTNO
7876	ADAMS	CLERK	7788	12-JAN-83	1100	–	20
7788	SCOTT	ANALYST	7566	09-DEC-82	3000	–	20
7934	MILLER	CLERK	7782	23-JAN-82	1300	–	10
7902	FORD	ANALYST	7566	03-DEC-81	3000	–	20
7900	JAMES	CLERK	7698	03-DEC-81	950	–	30
7839	KING	PRESIDENT	–	17-NOV-81	5000	–	10
7654	MARTIN	SALESMAN	7698	28-SEP-81	1250	1400	30
7844	TURNER	SALESMAN	7698	08-SEP-81	1500	0	30
7782	CLARK	MANAGER	7839	09-JUN-81	2450	–	10
7698	BLAKE	MANAGER	7839	01-MAY-81	2850	–	30
7566	JONES	MANAGER	7839	02-APR-81	2975	–	20
7521	WARD	SALESMAN	7698	22-FEB-81	1250	500	30
7499	ALLEN	SALESMAN	7698	20-FEB-81	1600	300	30
7369	SMITH	CLERK	7902	17-DEC-80	800	–	20

Figure 9.12   Records in EMP table.

Caution: Do not use TO_CHAR() built-in function for DATE columns in ORDER BY Clause because it converts DATE data type to text and the entire sorting will be wrong.

Example: As per text comparison "31/12/2007" will appear after "01/01/2008" as "3" is higher in alphabetical sequence then "0". As per DATE comparison 31/12/2007 comes before 01/01/2008.

Refer to Figure 9.13 where we have sorted on date column after applying TO_CHAR() function.

```
SQL>select * from emp order by to_char(hiredate,'dd/mm/yyyy');
```

EMPNO	ENAME	JOB	MGR	HIREDATE	SAL	COMM	DEPTNO
7698	BLAKE	MANAGER	7839	01-MAY-81	2850	-	30
7566	JONES	MANAGER	7839	02-APR-81	2975	-	20
7902	FORD	ANALYST	7566	03-DEC-81	3000	-	20
7900	JAMES	CLERK	7698	03-DEC-81	950	-	30
7844	TURNER	SALESMAN	7698	08-SEP-81	1500	0	30
7782	CLARK	MANAGER	7839	09-JUN-81	2450	-	10
7788	SCOTT	ANALYST	7566	09-DEC-82	3000	-	20

FIGURE 9.13   TO_CHAR() should not be used for sorting on date data type.

Note: In Figure 9.13 as we have used TO_CHAR() function in ORDER BY clause therefore the records have been arranged in alphabetical sequence rather than as per Date semantics.

TRUE/FALSE

1. The "ORDER BY column-name" and the "ORDER BY column-name ASC" are the same.
2. If we SORT on a column having NULL values, then the records with NULL values are displayed first.
3. TO_CHAR() function can be used to arrange records based on a DATE column.
4. "ASC" and "ASCENDING" can be used interchangeably for arranging records.

LAB ASSIGNMENT

Refer to Table 7.1 for the CUSTOMER ORDER system:

1. Display the customers from the CUSTOMER table such that the customer with maximum due balance is displayed at the top.
2. Arrange the customers first by STATE and then by NAME.
3. Display the CD-PLAYERS in the decreasing order of selling price followed by increasing order of cost price.
4. Assuming some of the customers for whom PINCODE is not available, display the list of such customers such that they are displayed at the top.
5. List the orders such that the most recent orders are displayed first. Show the number of days when the last order was placed.

10

Table Operations—Altering Structure

10.1 INTRODUCTION

In the previous chapters we have learnt insertion, updation and deletion of records. Let us turn our focus on modifying the existing structure of a table. By structure we mean column names, data types and constraints. This chapter focuses on modifying the table name, column names and data types. We have learnt about changing the constraints like PRIMARY KEY, NOT NULL, UNIQUE in Chapter 6.

Caution: If you have installed any version of Oracle Database below 10g then some of the specified commands may not work.

10.2 RENAMING A TABLE

Figure 10.1 shows the command to change the name of "student_master" table to "student".

```
SQL> rename student_master to student;

Table renamed.

SQL> desc student;
        Name            Null?              Type
        ROLLNO                             NUMBER(4)
        NAME                               VARCHAR2(10)
        CITY                               VARCHAR2(15)
```

```
SQL> desc student_master;
ERROR:
ORA-04043: object student_master does not exist
```

Figure 10.1   Rename table.

Table "student_master" no longer exists and is now known as "student".

10.3   ADDING COLUMNS TO A TABLE

Let us add an extra column of "age" in student table (Figure 10.2).

```
SQL> alter table student add (age number(2));

Table altered.

SQL> desc student
```

Name	Null?	Type
ROLLNO		NUMBER(4)
NAME		VARCHAR2(10)
CITY		VARCHAR2(15)
AGE		NUMBER(2)

Figure 10.2   Adding column.

Note: The new column will always be added at the end of last column. We cannot add new columns in between existing columns or at the first position.

10.4   REMOVING COLUMNS FROM A TABLE

Let us remove column city from the table (Figure 10.3).

```
SQL> alter table student drop column city;

Table altered.

SQL> desc student;
```

Name	Null?	Type
ROLLNO		NUMBER(4)
NAME		VARCHAR2(10)
AGE		NUMBER(2)

Figure 10.3   Remove existing column.

10.5   INCREASING WIDTH OF A COLUMN

Figure 10.4 shows how to increase the width of name column to 15 characters.

```
SQL> alter table student modify (name varchar2(15));

Table altered.

SQL> desc student;

      Name            Null?              Type
      ROLLNO                             NUMBER(4)
      NAME                               VARCHAR2(15)
      AGE                                NUMBER(2)
```

Figure 10.4   Increasing column size.

10.6   DECREASING WIDTH OF A COLUMN

Figure 10.5 shows the command for decreasing the width of "name" column to 10 again.

```
SQL> alter table student modify (name varchar2(10));

Table altered.

SQL> desc student

      Name            Null?              Type
      ROLLNO                             NUMBER(4)
      NAME                               VARCHAR2(10)
      AGE                                NUMBER(2)
```

Figure 10.5   Decreasing column size.

Now let us further decrease the width of "name" column to 5 characters as shown in Figure 10.6.

```
SQL> alter table student modify (name varchar2(5));
alter table student modify (name varchar2(5))
                            *
ERROR at line 1:
ORA-01441: cannot decrease column length because some value is too big
```

Figure 10.6   Decreasing column width.

As the "name" field already contains values which are more than 5 characters in length therefore oracle refuses to reduce the size.

Note: Column size can be reduced only in two cases.
1. All the records contain NULL value for that column.
2. The size of data which is already present is less than or equal to the new size specified.

10.7   CHANGING DATA TYPE OF A COLUMN

We can change data type from CHAR to VARCHAR2 and vice-versa, i.e. again we change the data type of "name" column from varchar2 to char. The Alter table command can be used to change the data type as in Figure 10.7.

SQL> alter table student *modify (name char(10));*

Table altered.

SQL> desc student;

Name	Null?	Type
ROLLNO		NUMBER(4)
NAME		CHAR(10)
CITY		VARCHAR2(15)

Figure 10.7   Changing VARCHAR2 to CHAR.

Note: We can change the data type from char to varchar2 and vice-versa provided the new size is more than or equal to the size of the existing data values.

10.7.1   Changing Number Data Type to CHAR

Figure 10.8 shows how to change the data type of "rollno" column from number(4) to char(4).

SQL> alter table student *modify (rollno char(4));*
alter table student modify (rollno char(4))
          *

ERROR at line 1:
ORA-01439: column to be modified must be empty to change data type

Figure 10.8   Changing NUMBER to CHAR.

Note: We cannot change the data type from NUMBER to CHAR/VARCHAR2 and vice versa. First we need to empty the data values for the column and then modify it to the new data type (Figure 10.9).

SQL> update student set rollno=null;

5 rows updated.

SQL> alter table student modify (rollno char(4));

Table altered.

SQL> desc student

Name	Null?	Type
ROLLNO		CHAR(4)
NAME		CHAR(10)
CITY		VARCHAR2(15)

Figure 10.9   Changing NUMBER to CHAR.

10.8   COPYING A TABLE

A table has two components: Structure and Records. Structure refers to column names, data types and constraints. Records refer to the data which is available in the table.

To copy structure as well as records we can use the "CREATE TABLE" command with "SELECT AS Clause" as shown in Figure 10.10.

```
SQL>create table employee (empno number(4) primary key,
name varchar2(10) not null,
address varchar2(10) unique);

Table created

SQL> insert into employee values (1111,'satish','243,saket');
1 row created.

SQL> insert into employee values (2222,'rashmi','27,ajmer');
1 row created.

SQL> commit;

SQL> create table employee_new as select * from employee;

Table created

SQL> desc employee_new;
```

Name	Null?	Type
EMPNO		NUMBER(4)
NAME	NOT NULL	VARCHAR2(10)
ADDRESS		VARCHAR2(10)

```
SQL> select * from employee_new;
```

EMPNO	NAME	ADDRESS
1111	satish	243,saket
2222	rashmi	27,ajmer

Figure 10.10   Copying table with structure and records.

Column names, data types have been copied from "employee" table to the new "employee_new" table along with the records.

10.8.1   Copying a Table Specifying Different Column Names

We can use the aliasing concept to specify different column names for the new table as in Figure 10.11.

```
SQL> create table employee_diff as select empno as staffno,name as ename,address as
addr from employee;

Table created.

SQL> desc employee_diff;
```

Name	Null?	Type
STAFFNO		NUMBER(4)
ENAME	NOT NULL	VARCHAR2(10)
ADDR		VARCHAR2(10)

Figure 10.11 Different column names for the new table.

10.8.2 Copying Table Structure Only and Not Records

We can just copy the structure excluding records by using a WHERE clause with a condition which always evaluates to FALSE for every record in base table (Figure 10.12).

```
SQL> create table employee_structure as select * from employee where 1=2;

Table created.

SQL> desc employee_structure;
```

Name	Null?	Type
EMPNO		NUMBER(4)
NAME	NOT NULL	VARCHAR2(10)
ADDRESS		VARCHAR2(10)

```
SQL> select * from employee_structure;

no rows selected
```

Figure 10.12 Copying structure only.

Caution: Copying a table into new table does not copy the constraints except NOT NULL. Be careful as all constraints are not applied to the newly created table except the NOT NULL constraint.

REVIEW QUESTIONS

1. While renaming a table, is the original table name lost?
2. Can we add columns in between the existing columns or as the first/last column?
3. What are the conditions under which Oracle does not allow to decrease the size of a column?
4. What is the procedure to decrease the size of a column?
5. Can we change a columns data type from NUMBER to CHAR and vice versa?
6. How to copy an entire table (including structure and records)?

7. How to copy a table structure only?
8. While copying a table are the constraints copied too for the newly created table?

TRUE/FALSE

1. The TRUNCATE TABLE command permanently removes the table structure as well as records.
2. The DROPPED table cannot be recovered.
3. Renaming a table removes the original table.
4. It is not possible to ADD Columns in between the existing columns.
5. Columns can be added only after the last column.
6. Data length of a column can be increased without affecting the data values.
7. Data length of a column can be reduced without affecting the data values.
8. CHAR and NUMBER data type can be interchanged without affecting the data values.
9. A column can be renamed.
10. Copying a table into a new table maintains the integrity constraints and indexes for the new table.

LAB ASSIGNMENT

Refer to the CUSTOMER ORDER tables in Chapter 7 (Table 7.1).

1. Change the name of the CUSTOMER table to the CUSTOMER_MASTER.
2. Add new columns named "TELEPHONE" of data type NUMBER(11) and "FAX" of data type NUMBER(11) in the CUSTOMER table. Can we specify the columns in between where the new columns has been placed?
3. Remove the column "FAX" and add a column "EMAIL" of VARCHR2(10) in the CUSTOMER TABLE.
4. Increase the size of EMAIL column by 10.
5. Modify the size of the COST_PRICE column to 7,2.
6. Change the data type of TELEPHONE column of the CUSTOMER table to VARCHAR2(15) so that we can store hyphen to segregate ISD and STD codes, for example, 91-0755-4289528.
7. We are updating the COST_PRICE and SELLING_PRICE to new values. But before doing so we want to take a backup of PRODUCT table with "PRODUCT_BKUP". Create the backup table with complete structure and records from the PRODUCT table.

Joins

11.1 INTRODUCTION

Till now we have been selecting records from a single table at a time like DEPT and EMP. What if we need to select the columns from more than one table in a single query? Let us assume that we want to display department description followed by the list of various employees in that department. As department description is given in the DEPT table and the details of employees are given in the EMP table, therefore, we have to use a concept called "Join" in order to achieve the desired result.

Assume DEPARTMENT and EMPLOYEE tables with records as shown in Figure 11.1.

```
SQL> select * from department;

      DEPT_NO                    DEPT_NAME
          10                     MANUFACTURING
          20                     ENGINEERING
          30                     SALES
          40                     FINANCE

SQL>select emp_no,emp_name,designation,salary,commission,dept_no from employee;
```

EMP_NO	EMP_NAME	DESIGNATION	SALARY	COMMISSION	DEPT_NO
1000	KING	CEO	20000	–	10
2001	SCOTT	General Manager	15000	–	10
2002	JOHN	General Manager	14000	–	20
2003	SUSE	General Manager	14500	–	30
3004	MARUTI	Manager	13100	857	20
9999	XEON	Manager	12300	789	50

Figure 11.1 DEPARTMENT and EMPLOYEE tables.

Note:
- No employee belongs to department 40
- Employee 9999 named "XEON" is in the department 50 which is not available in the DEPARTMENT table.

11.2   CLASSIFICATION OF JOINS

Joins can be classified as shown in Figure 11.2.

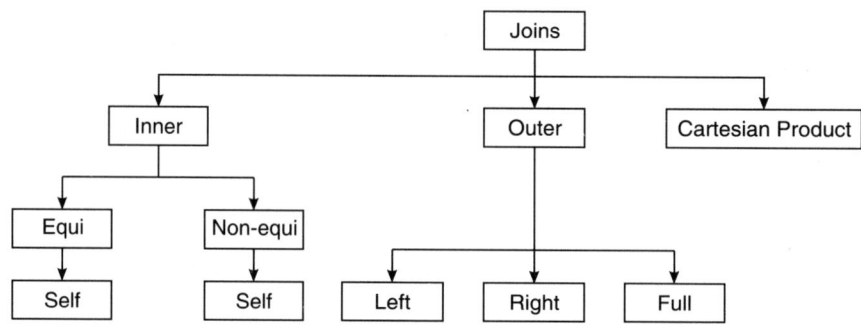

Figure 11.2   Classification of Joins.

11.2.1   Inner Joins

Joins which are based on the selection of matching records between tables is called an **Inner Join**. Inner joins can be further categorized as Equi and Non-Equi.

Inner equi join

When the two tables are joined using EQUAL TO operator then that join is called **Inner Equi Join**.

Inner non-equi join

When the two tables are joined using any comparison operator (<,>,<=,>=,!=) other than EQUAL TO operator then that join is called **Inner Non-Equi Join**.

Example of inner equi join

We want to display the department name, emp_no, emp_name, salary and commission from the tables of Figure 11.1. Figure 11.3 shows the inner equi join statement.

```
SQL> select department.dept_name, employee.emp_no, employee.emp_name,
employee.salary, employee.commission
from employee, department
where employee.dept_no=department.dept_no;
```

DEPT_NAME	EMP_NO	EMP_NAME	SALARY	COMMISSION
MANUFACTURING	1000	KING	20000	–
MANUFACTURING	2001	SCOTT	15000	–
ENGINEERING	2002	JOHN	14000	–
SALES	2003	SUSE	14500	–
ENGINEERING	3004	MARUTI	13100	857

Figure 11.3   Inner equi join.

In the query of Figure 11.3, each record from the EMPLOYEE table is fetched and its corresponding record in the DEPARTMENT table is searched for matching record for dept_no. The dept_name is displayed from the DEPARTMENT table and the rest of the columns are displayed from the EMPLOYEE table.

Each column name has been preceded by table name with dot(.) operator. This is essential when columns with the same name exist in both the tables. We could have skipped the table names before emp_no, emp_name, salary and commission as there are no fields with the same name in the DEPARTMENT table.

Note: As no employee belonged to the department 40, therefore, the department "FINANCE" was not displayed in the query. Secondly, as employee 9999 belonged to dept_no 50 for which there is no record in the DEPARTMENT table, therefore, it is not displayed by the query too. This is what we mean by the inner query. Only matching records of both the tables are shown discarding all others.

Notice the "WHERE" clause specifying the join of two tables based on matching dept_no column.

The WHERE clause of the join statement is known as the **JOIN CONDITION**.

The Join Condition may involve more than one column.

Aliasing

In the query of Figure 11.3, each of the columns have been preceded by the table name, say, department.dept_name, employee.emp_no, etc. Oracle provides a facility called aliasing whereby we can assign a short name to the tables being joined and use those alias names for preceding the column names.

The query of Figure 11.3 can be written in the following way also:

SQL> **select b.dept_name, a.emp_no, a.emp_name, a.salary, a.commission**
from employee a, department b
where a.dept_no=b.dept_no;

We have given alias name "a" to the DEPARTMENT table and alias name "b" to the EMPLOYEE table in the FROM Clause. Then we have used these names for prefixing the various columns selected.

Note: These alias names are temporary and will not be available in the next SQL command/session/login.

Example of inner non-equi join

The inner joins which are based on any comparison operator other than EQUAL TO are called **Non-Equi joins**. These are not commonly used and therefore have been explained at the end of this chapter. Refer to Section 11.2.5.

11.2.2   Outer Joins

In Figure 11.3 query, although the employee 9999 existed in the EMPLOYEE table but was not displayed as the department 50 to which he belonged did not exist in the DEPARTMENT table.

Similarly, the department number 40 which existed in the DEPARTMENT table for which there is no employee in the EMPLOYEE table was also not displayed.

So we need to have a facility of displaying non-matching records also in the two tables. We will make use of a concept called "Outer" joins to achieve the desired output.

Classification of outer joins

Outer joins can be classified as

Left outer join

Right outer join

Full outer join

Left outer join

Now we want that employee 9999 should also be displayed. For this we will have to use an outer join so that not only matching records are displayed but also the records which are in the EMPLOYEE table but their corresponding dept_no is not available in the DEPARTMENT table are also listed (Figure 11.4).

```
SQL> select
b.dept_name,a.dept_no,a.emp_no,a.emp_name,a.salary,a.commission
from employee a,department b
where a.dept_no=b.dept_no(+);
```

DEPT_NAME	DEPT_NO	EMP_NO	EMP_NAME	SALARY	COMMISSION
MANUFACTURING	10	2001	SCOTT	15000	–
MANUFACTURING	10	1000	KING	20000	–
ENGINEERING	20	3004	MARUTI	13100	857
ENGINEERING	20	2002	JOHN	14000	–
SALES	30	2003	SUSE	14500	–
–	50	9999	XEON	12300	789

Figure 11.4   Left outer join.

Note: "(+)" on the DEPARTMENT table side in the WHERE clause indicates that even if the dept_no of an employee in the EMPLOYEE table is not existing in the DEPARTMENT table then also show the employee details. Moreover, note that department name for employee 9999 is not appearing.

Right outer join

In the query of Figure 11.4, employee 9999 was displayed with unknown department but note that the department 40 for which there are no employees in the EMPLOYEE table is still not displayed.

We can use right outer joins similar to the left outer joins so that all departments for which there are no employees in the EMPLOYEE table are also listed by the query (Figure 11.5).

```
SQL> select b.dept_name,a.dept_no,a.emp_no,a.emp_name,a.salary,a.commission
from employee a,department b
where a.dept_no(+)=b.dept_no;
```

DEPT_NAME	DEPT_NO	EMP_NO	EMP_NAME	SALARY	COMMISSION
MANUFACTURING	10	1000	KING	20000	–
MANUFACTURING	10	2001	SCOTT	15000	–
ENGINEERING	20	2002	JOHN	14000	–
SALES	30	2003	SUSE	14500	–
ENGINEERING	20	3004	MARUTI	13100	857
FINANCE	–	–	–	–	–

Figure 11.5 Right outer join.

Note: We have placed "(+)" on the EMPLOYEE table. Now the department 40 with name "FINANCE" got displayed although there were no employees in that department.

Full outer joins

Full outer joins are not supported by Standard SQL.

It might occur to our mind that just as we have right and left outer joins, there must be an outer join which displays non-matching records from both the tables. Full outer join implies that the employee 9999 whose dept_no 50 is not in the DEPARTMENT table should be displayed as well as department 40 (FINANCE) of the DEPARTMENT table for which there is no employee should also be displayed. But full outer joins are not supported by Standard SQL. In Figure 11.6 we have placed (+) on both tables for a full outer join but Oracle gives an error message.

```
SQL>select b.dept_name,a.dept_no,a.emp_no,a.emp_name,a.salary,a.commission
from employee a,department b
where a.dept_no(+)=b.dept_no(+);
```
❌ ORA-01468: a predicate may reference only one outer-joined table

Figure 11.6 Full outer join.

Note: SQL language has two standards:
1. **Standard SQL**
2. **ANSI SQL**

Standard SQL does not support full outer join.
ANSI SQL supports full outer join.

The Oracle database supports both Standard and ANSI SQL.

ANSI SQL join syntax

The Standard and ANSI SQL have different syntax for the commands. Let us see the ANSI SQL commands (Figures 11.7,11.8, 11.9 and 11.10) for all kinds of joins—inner-equis, outer (left, right and full join/joins).

```
SQL>select b.dept_name,a.dept_no,a.emp_no,a.emp_name,a.salary,a.commission
from employee a inner join department b
on a.dept_no=b.dept_no;
```

DEPT_NAME	DEPT_NO	EMP_NO	EMP_NAME	SALARY	COMMISSION
MANUFACTURING	10	1000	KING	20000	–
MANUFACTURING	10	2001	SCOTT	15000	–
ENGINEERING	20	2002	JOHN	14000	–
SALES	30	2003	SUSE	14500	–
ENGINEERING	20	3004	MARUTI	13100	857

Figure 11.7   ANSI SQL—inner equi join.

Note: ANSI SQL uses a much cleaner syntax than standard SQL. Note the use of "INNER JOIN" and the "ON" clause. Secondly "(+)" symbol has not been used.

```
SQL>select b.dept_name,a.dept_no,a.emp_no,a.emp_name,a.salary,a.commission
from employee a left outer join department b
on a.dept_no=b.dept_no;
```

DEPT_NAME	DEPT_NO	EMP_NO	EMP_NAME	SALARY	COMMISSION
MANUFACTURING	10	2001	SCOTT	15000	–
MANUFACTURING	10	1000	KING	20000	–
ENGINEERING	20	3004	MARUTI	13100	857
ENGINEERING	20	2002	JOHN	14000	–
SALES	30	2003	SUSE	14500	–
–	50	9999	XEON	12300	789

Figure 11.8   ANSI SQL—left outer join.

Note: Note the usage of "left outer join" and the "on" clause. Secondly, "(+)" symbol has not been used.

```
SQL>select b.dept_name,a.dept_no,a.emp_no,a.emp_name,a.salary,a.commission
from employee a right outer join department b
on a.dept_no=b.dept_no;
```

DEPT_NAME	DEPT_NO	EMP_NO	EMP_NAME	SALARY	COMMISSION
MANUFACTURING	10	1000	KING	20000	–
MANUFACTURING	10	2001	SCOTT	15000	–
ENGINEERING	20	2002	JOHN	14000	–
SALES	30	2003	SUSE	14500	–
ENGINEERING	20	3004	MARUTI	13100	857
FINANCE	–	–	–	–	–

Figure 11.9   ANSI SQL—right outer join.

Note: Note the usage of "right outer join" and the "on" clause. Secondly, "(+)" symbol has not been used.

```
SQL>select b.dept_name,a.dept_no,a.emp_no,a.emp_name,a.salary,a.commission
from employee a full outer join department b
on a.dept_no=b.dept_no;
```

DEPT_NAME	DEPT_NO	EMP_NO	EMP_NAME	SALARY	COMMISSION
MANUFACTURING	10	2001	SCOTT	15000	–
MANUFACTURING	10	1000	KING	20000	–
ENGINEERING	20	3004	MARUTI	13100	857
ENGINEERING	20	2002	JOHN	14000	–
SALES	30	2003	SUSE	14500	–
–	50	9999	XEON	12300	789
FINANCE	–	–	–	–	–

Figure 11.10 ANSI SQL—full outer join.

Note: Note the usage of "full outer join" and the "on" clause. Secondly, "(+)" symbol has not been used. Both employee XEON and department FINANCE have been displayed.

11.2.3 Cartesian Product

A join in which each record of table 1 gets associated with each and every record of table 2 is called a **Cartesian Product** (Figure 11.11).

```
SQL> select b.dept_name,a.dept_no,a.emp_no,a.emp_name,a.salary,a.commission
from employee a, department b
order by a.emp_no;
```

DEPT_NAME	DEPT_NO	EMP_NO	EMP_NAME	SALARY	COMMISSION
FINANCE	10	1000	KING	20000	–
SALES	10	1000	KING	20000	–
ENGINEERING	10	1000	KING	20000	–
MANUFACTURING	10	1000	KING	20000	–
FINANCE	10	2001	SCOTT	15000	–
SALES	10	2001	SCOTT	15000	–
MANUFACTURING	10	2001	SCOTT	15000	–
ENGINEERING	10	2001	SCOTT	15000	–

.
.
.
.

Figure 11.11 Cartesian product.

Note:
- No WHERE clause has been used. This means that whenever we do not use the WHERE clause while joining two tables then the result is Cartesian product. Each and every record of table 1 gets associated to each and every record of table 2. Hence, the total number of records returned is m*n where m is the number of rows in table 1 and n is the number of rows in table 2.
- Each employee has appeared 4 times in the listing because each employee record in the EMPLOYEE table got associated with each dept_no in the DEPARTMENT table.
- Cartesian product is practically useless.

11.2.4 Self-joins

When a table is joined with its own then it is called a "Self-join".

Assume that the EMPLOYEE table has one more column named "SENIOR_EMP_NO" which indicates the senior/boss of each employee. In other words, SENIOR_EMP_NO field will contain the emp_no of his boss.

See Figure 11.12 for understanding the hierarchy of employees. KING is the CEO and three people SCOTT, JOHN and SUSE report to him. HENRY, JORD and WILLIAMS report to SCOTT and so on. Here we have shown one branch only and Emp.No is within braces.

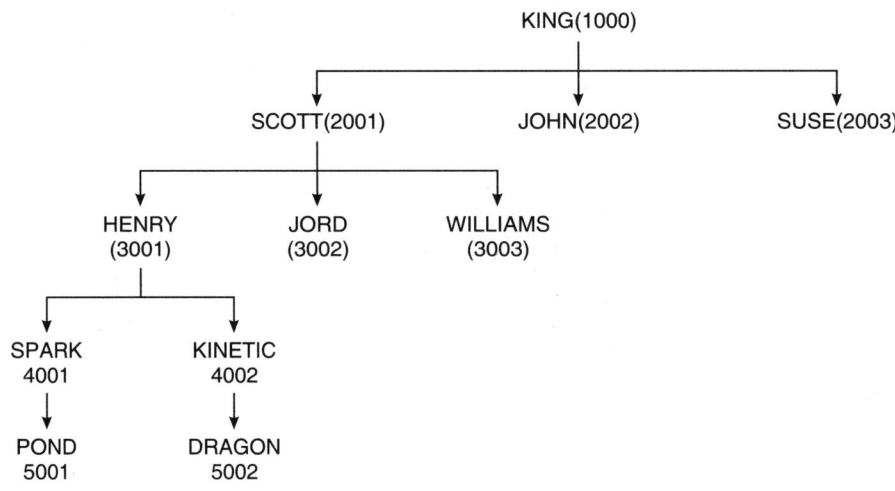

Figure 11.12 Hierarchy of employees.

Now we want to display the emp_no, emp_name, senior_emp_no and name of senior along with employees salary and commission.

The name of senior/boss is not available in the EMPLOYEE table. How do we achieve this?

We will make two copies of EMPLOYEE table (X and Y) and then join X.senior_emp_no=Y.emp_no so that X will contain name of employee and Y will contain name of senior/boss. SENIOR_EMP_NO field of X is joined with EMP_NO of Y (Figure 11.13).

```
SQL> select x.emp_no,x.emp_name "Emp.Name",x.salary,x.commission,
x.senior_emp_no,y.emp_name "Sr.Name"
from employee x, employee y
where x.senior_emp_no=y.emp_no
order by x.emp_no;
```

EMP_NO	Emp.Name	SALARY	COMMISSION	SENIOR_EMP_NO	Senior.Name
2001	SCOTT	15000	–	1000	KING
2002	JOHN	14000	–	1000	KING
2003	SUSE	14500	–	1000	KING
3001	HENRY	13600	1000	2001	SCOTT
3002	JORD	12000	950	2001	SCOTT

3003	WILLIAMS	12100	850	2001	SCOTT
3004	MARUTI	13100	857	2002	JOHN
3005	SANTRO	12200	800	2002	JOHN
3006	PIAGGIO	10000	700	2003	SUSE
3006	TANGO	11000	760	2003	SUSE
4001	SPARK	10000	600	3001	HENRY
4002	KINETIC	11000	700	3001	HENRY
4003	JONATHAN	8500	850	3002	JORD

Figure 11.13 Self-join.

Note that the KING who is CEO of the company doesn't have a Senior/Boss and therefore is not listed in the query of Figure 11.13 as we have used inner equi-join. What if we want to display the CEO also?

We will use the right outer join as shown in Figure 11.14.

```
SQL> select x.emp_no,x.emp_name "Emp.Name",x.salary,x.commission,
x.senior_emp_no,y.emp_name "Senior.Name"
from employee x, employee y
where x.senior_emp_no=y.emp_no(+)
order by x.emp_no;
```

EMP_NO	Emp.Name	SALARY	COMMISSION	SENIOR_EMP_NO	Senior.Name
1000	KING	20000	–	–	–
2001	SCOTT	15000	–	1000	KING
2002	JOHN	14000	–	1000	KING
2003	SUSE	14500	–	1000	KING
3001	HENRY	13600	1000	2001	SCOTT
3002	JORD	12000	950	2001	SCOTT
3003	WILLIAMS	12100	850	2001	SCOTT
3004	MARUTI	13100	857	2002	JOHN
3005	SANTRO	12200	800	2002	JOHN
3006	PIAGGIO	10000	700	2003	SUSE

Figure 11.14 Right outer join in self-joins.

11.2.5 Non-equi Joins

The inner joins which use any comparison operator except EQUAL TO are called non-equi joins. Although they are not required often but prove very handy in certain situations.

Assume two tables, namely EMPLOYEE and PRODUCT as shown in Figure 11.15. The PRODUCT table contains the list of products with validity dates (offer_start_date and offer_end_date). Whenever a new employee joins he is eligible for certain products as gift depending on his date of joining. If his date of joining is between the offer_start_date and offer_end_date then he is eligible for that product as gift.

```
SQL>select * from employee;

       EMPNO          ENAME          DATE_OF_JOINING
       1111           satish             14-OCT-09
       2222           vivek              11-SEP-09
       3333           anup               01-APR-09
       1111           vijay              20-DEC-09

SQL>select * from product;

   PRODUCT_ID      PRODUCT      OFFER_START_DATE      OFFER_END_DATE
        1             TV            01-OCT-09             30-OCT-09
        2             DVD           01-SEP-09             20-OCT-09
```

Figure 11.15   EMPLOYEE and PRODUCT.

We want to know the employees and the products for which they are eligible as gifts. Note that in such a situation there is no joining condition on equality possible. We will have to use other comparison operators for joining the two tables (Figure 11.16).

```
SQL>select * from employee a, product b
where a.date_of_joining >= b.offer_start_date
and a.date_of_joining <= b.offer_end_date;
```

EMPNO	ENAME	DATE_OF_ JOINING	PRODUCT _ID	PRODUCT	OFFER_ START_DATE	OFFER_ END_DATE
1111	satish	14-OCT-09	1	TV	01-OCT-09	30-OCT-09
1111	satish	14-OCT-09	2	DVD	01-SEP-09	20-OCT-09
2222	vivek	11-SEP-09	2	DVD	01-SEP-09	20-OCT-09

Figure 11.16   Non-Equi Join Example (Standard SQL).

Here we have used ">=" and "<=" comparison operators rather than "="
"satish" is eligible for both TV and DVD.
"vivek" is eligible for DVD only.
Figure 11.17 shows the ANSI SQL command for non-equi join.

```
SQL>select * from employee inner join product on
employee.date_of_joining >= product.offer_start_date
and employee.date_of_joining <= product.offer_end_date;
```

Figure 11.17   Non-Equi Join Example (ANSI SQL).

Deleting duplicate records using non-equi join

Assume that by mistake the products have got duplicated in the PRODUCT table (Figure 11.18).

```
SQL>select * from product;

  PRODUCT_ID      PRODUCT      OFFER_START_DATE      OFFER_END_DATE
       1            TV            01-OCT-09             30-OCT-09
       2            DVD           01-SEP-09             20-OCT-09
       1            TV            01-OCT-09             30-OCT-09
       2            DVD           01-SEP-09             20-OCT-09
```

Figure 11.18 Duplicate records in the PRODUCT table.

Now we want to remove the duplicate records. Before we achieve this we need to understand a pseudo-column named "ROWID" which stands for ROW IDENTIFICATION. Each record in the Oracle database has a unique physical location on Hard Disk referred to as ROWID. No two rows can have the same ROWID. See Figure 11.19.

```
SQL>select rowid,product_id,product,offer_start_date,offer_end_date from product;

  ROWID              PRODUCT_ID    PRODUCT     OFFER_         OFFER_
                                               START_DATE     END_DATE
AAADxLAABAAAKiaAAC       1           TV        01-OCT-09      30-OCT-09
AAADxLAABAAAKiaAAD       2           DVD       01-SEP-09      20-OCT-09
AAADxLAABAAAKiaAAG       1           TV        01-OCT-09      30-OCT-09
AAADxLAABAAAKiaAAH       2           DVD       01-SEP-09      20-OCT-09
```

Figure 11.19 ROWID.

Now we can use the ROWID concept to delete the duplicate rows whose ROWID is less than the row with MAXIMUM ROWID for the same product. For example, product_id 1 has two records with ROWID's as "**AAADxLAABAAAKiaAAC**" and "**AAADxLAABAAAKiaAAG**". See Figure 11.20.

```
SQL> delete from product x
where rowid < (select max(rowid) from product y
where  y.product_id=x.product_id);

2 row(s) deleted.

SQL>select rowid,product_id,product,offer_start_date,offer_end_date from product;

  ROWID              PRODUCT_ID    PRODUCT     OFFER_         OFFER_
                                               START_DATE     END_DATE
AAADxLAABAAAKiaAAG       1           TV        01-OCT-09      30-OCT-09
AAADxLAABAAAKiaAAH       2           DVD       01-SEP-09      20-OCT-09
```

Figure 11.20 Removing duplicate records using non-equi join.

Note: We have made two copies of the same table as X and Y and then joined them on PRODUCT_ID which is the primary key column. This join condition must include all the columns which are a part of the primary key. For each product the record with MAXIMUM ROWID appears in the inner SELECT and the outer DELETE command removes all the records with ROWID's below the MAXIMUM ROWID.

REVIEW QUESTIONS

1. What do we mean by Joins? In what situations do we need to join tables?
2. Differentiate between the inner and outer joins? Under what situations are outer joins more appropriate than the Inner Joins?
3. If the EMP table had a defined Foreign Key on DEPTNO column referring to DEPTNO column of the DEPT table at the time of table creation then will inner and outer joins(left and right both) produce the same result?
4. What is the significance of right and left outer joins?
5. Is the Cartesian product of two tables of any use?
6. Explain the concept of using ALIAS names for tables being joined. Is it necessary to use ALIAS names whenever tables are joined?

LAB ASSIGNMENT

Refer to Table 7.1 for the CUSTOMER ORDER system
1. Display the product names which have been supplied to ASNANI BROTHERS.
2. Find out the product names and their quantity which have been delivered in the month of FEBRUARY.
3. Find out the product names and their quantity which have been delivered in the current month.
4. Display the product code and description of high demand products. The products with demand of more than 10 are high demand products.
5. List the customer names who have bought more than 20 Televisions.
6. Find the product name, customer name and total quantity purchased by various customers.
7. Find the product name, customer name and total quantity for only those orders in which more than 20 items have been ordered.
8. Display ORDER_NO, ORDER_DATE, CUSTOMER_NAME, PRODUCT_NAME and QUANTITY from the CUSTOMER ORDER system tables.
9. In the above query display those customers also who have not placed any order.
10. Find the CUSTOMER_NAMEs who have placed ORDER within two days.
11. Display the CUSTOMER_NAME along with the Total Quantity and Selling Price at which items are being bought.
12. Generate a report displaying CUSTOMER_NAME along with the TOTAL DUE BALANCE.
13. Display the total Sale Amount and Quantity for each customer. The report should display CUSTOMER_NAME instead of CUSTOMER_ID.

Advanced Queries Using Special Operators

12.1 INTRODUCTION

Oracle provides some special operators for performing specific queries. We have learned about various mathematical, relational and logical operators in Chapter 5. In Chapter 5, we have also mentioned the usage of special operators, namely IN, IS, BETWEEN, LIKE in conjunction with NOT operator. This chapter focuses on using the special operators for advanced or more complicated scenarios.

Assume two tables "STUDENT_MASTER" and "STUDENT_DETAILS" as shown in Figure 12.1.

```
SQL> select * from student_master;

       COLLEGE        ROLLNO        NAME
        GEC             1           satish
        GEC             2           rashmi
        RKDF            3           rishi
        RKDF            4           anil

SQL> select * from student_details;

       ROLLNO         SUBJECT       MARKS
         1             MATHS          12
         1             PHY            23
         2             MATHS          34
         3             MATHS          35
```

Figure 12.1 STUDENT_MASTER and STUDENT_DETAILS.

12.2 IN OPERATOR

The IN operator checks for the equality of a set of values.

- **Display college, rollno and name of the students for which marks have been entered in details table (Figure 12.2).**

SQL> select * from student_master where *rollno IN (select rollno from student_details);*

COLLEGE	ROLLNO	NAME
GEC	1	satish
GEC	2	rashmi
RKDF	3	rishi

Figure 12.2 IN operator.

Here the **inner select statement**("select rollno from student_details") is called the **sub-query** and the **outer select** statement("select * from student_master where rollno in") is called the **main query**. The sub-query is executed first returning rollno 1,2 and 3 from details table for which marks have been entered. Now the main query executes for master table for those rollnos which are returned through sub-query.

When the sub-query executes the entire query reduces to:

SQL>select * from student_master where rollno IN (1,2,3)

Note: The IN operator is equivalent to "=ANY" operator. Some of the authors prefer to using "=ANY" operator as it is more clear in understanding.

Caution: The relational operators cannot be used in such scenarios because they compare only two values. Following statement is incorrect.

SQL> select * from student_master where *rollno = (select rollno from student_details);*

⊗ **ORA-01427: single-row subquery returns more than one row**

Right-hand side of the EQUAL operator should not return multiple values.
If the sub-query is going to return a single value then the query will not produce error.
To compare a column value with a set of values we have to use the IN operator.

12.3 NOT IN OPERATOR

NOT is a negation operator which can be used in conjunction with the IN operator for reversing the desired condition.

- **Display college, rollno and name of the students for which marks have not been entered into details table (Figure 12.3).**

SQL> select * from student_master where rollno **NOT IN** (select rollno from student_details);

COLLEGE	ROLLNO	NAME
RKDF	4	anil

Figure 12.3 NOT IN operator.

The sub-query is executed first returning rollno 1,2,3, then the main query is executed and returns 4.

12.4   EXISTS

An EXISTS condition tests for the existence of rows in a sub-query.

- **Display college, rollno and name of those students for which marks have been entered in details tables (Figure 12.4).**

```
SQL> select * from student_master a
  2 where EXISTS
  3 (select * from student_details b
  4 where a.rollno=b.rollno);

       COLLEGE          ROLLNO          NAME
         GEC               1            satish
         GEC               2            rashmi
         RKDF              3            rishi
```

Figure 12.4   EXISTS operator.

For each rollno in the master table, Oracle searches for the corresponding record in details table based on rollno. If the corresponding rollno is found in details table, then it displays that rollno and if the corresponding rollno is not found in details table, then it is not displayed. This has been achieved by using the EXISTS operator and joining the two tables on rollno(equi-join).

Differences Between IN and EXISTS Operators

The working of EXISTS and IN operators is slightly different with the same result.

The EXISTS operator only checks for the existence of matching records in details table whereas the IN operator checks whether the returned rollnos in sub-query are in the master table.

Secondly, while using the EXISTS operator, we need to equi-join tables which is not required in the IN operator.

Thirdly, in the EXISTS operator for each record found in the main query, Oracle searches for the matching records in details table(sub-query). The main query executes first and for each record found, the corresponding records are searched in details table.

As the EXISTS operator only checks for the existence of records in the sub-query for each record found in the master table, therefore, the sub-query can use any value in the SELECT clause. Following query gives the same result as the query shown in Figure 12.4.

SQL>select * from student_master a where EXISTS
(select 1 from student_details b where a.rollno=b.rollno);

Note that we have used "select 1" instead of "select *" in sub-query with the same result.

12.5   NOT EXISTS

- **Display college, rollno and name of those students for which marks have not been entered in details tables (Figure 12.5).**

```
SQL> select * from student_master a
  2 where NOT EXISTS
  3 (select * from student_details b
  4 where a.rollno=b.rollno)

     ROLLNO          NAME
        4             nilesh
```

Figure 12.5   NOT EXISTS.

The working of Figure 12.5 query is similar to Figure 12.4 only with the difference that now Oracle displays only those records for which corresponding rollno is not in details table.

NOT negation operator has been used in conjunction with EXISTS operator for the desired results.

12.6   SET OPERATORS

There may be situations where we need to combine results from more than one query. To accomplish this, Oracle supports SET operators, namely UNION, UNION ALL, INTERSECT, MINUS. Generally SET operations are applied on multiple SELECT statements. The records returned by each SELECT statement are treated as a SET of values and the final result is obtained depending on the SET operator used.

12.6.1   INTERSECT Operator

This operator finds the common values in sets.

- **Display the rollnos which are in both master and details table (Figure 12.6).**

```
SQL> select rollno from student_master
  2 intersect
  3 select rollno from student_details;

     ROLLNO
        1
        2
        3
```

Figure 12.6   INTERSECT.

INTERSECT gives those rollnos which are common in both master and details table.

"select rollno from student_master"   returns 1,2,3,4
"select rollno from student_details"   returns 1,1,2,3
INTERSECT operator   returns 1,2,3

The SET operators are similar to the mathematical SET theory and can be represented by Venn Diagram (Figure 12.7).

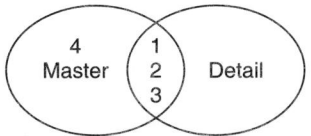

Figure 12.7   Venn diagram: INTERSECT.

Note: The select statements with set operators are called compound queries and the individual select statements are called component queries.

Caution: Two SELECT statements can be combined in a SET operation only if they satisfy the following conditions:

1. Both the queries must return the same number of columns.
2. The data type of columns in the second query must match with the data type of corresponding columns in the first query.
3. The data types do not need to be the same if those in the second result set can be automatically converted by Oracle (using implicit casting) to types compatible with those in the first result set.

- **Display the college, rollno and name of students for which marks have been entered in details table.**

In Figure 12.6 query, we displayed only the rollnos common in both master and details table. Here we want to display college, rollno and name of students which are common in both the tables (Figure 12.8).

```
SQL>select * from student_master
  2 where rollno IN
  3 (
  4 select rollno from student_master
  5 intersect
  6 select rollno from student_details
  7 );

    COLLEGE          ROLLNO          NAME
      GEC               1            satish
      GEC               2            rashmi
      RKDF              3            rishi
```

Figure 12.8   INTERSECT as sub-query.

The INTERSECT sub-query is executed first returning 1,2,3 and then the main query is executed returning college,rollno,name for rollno 1,2 and 3.

12.6.2   UNION Operator

The UNION operator returns the values which exist in either of the two queries.

Display all the rollnos which exist either in the master or in the details table (Figure 12.9).

```
SQL> select rollno from student_master
2 union
3 select rollno from student_details;
    ROLLNO
      1
      2
      3
      4
```

Figure 12.9   UNION.

UNION means display the rollnos returned from both the queries.

Caution: UNION suppresses the display of the same repeated values.
STUDENT_MASTER has rollno 1,3,4
STUDENT_DEAILS has rollno 1,1,2,3

UNION returns 1,2,3,4 instead of 1,3,4,1,1,2,3

UNION ALL

In certain situations we may need to display all the values returned from both *the queries*. The UNION operator has an additional clause called ALL which displays the duplicate values also (Figure 12.10).

```
SQL> select rollno from student_master
  2 UNION ALL
  3 select rollno from student_details;

    ROLLNO
      1
      2
      3
      4
      1
      1
      2
      3
```

Figure 12.10   UNION ALL.

Rollno 1,2,3,4 are displayed from the master table and 1,1,2,3 are displayed from the details table.

ORDER BY clause in SET operations

In order to arrange the final result of any SET operator, we can use the ORDER BY clause at the end of the last SELECT statement. To sort the results of the above query on rollno, use the command as shown in Figure 12.11.

```
SQL>select rollno from student_master
union all
select rollno from student_details
order by rollno;

        ROLLNO
          1
          1
          1
          2
          2
          3
          3
          4
```

Figure 12.11   ORDER BY in SET operators.

Note: The ORDER BY clause has been specified in the second SELECT statement but it operates on the final result of the SET operator. We cannot use the ORDER BY clause in the individual SELECT statements.

Referencing columns in ORDER BY clause using position

We can reference the columns in the ORDER BY clause by their position in the result set. Assume that we have separate tables storing the student information for various years. Suppose we have two tables, namely STUDENT_MASTER_20062007 and STUDENT_MASTER_20072008 containing information of students for the years 2006–2007 and 2007–2008 respectively (Figure 12.12).

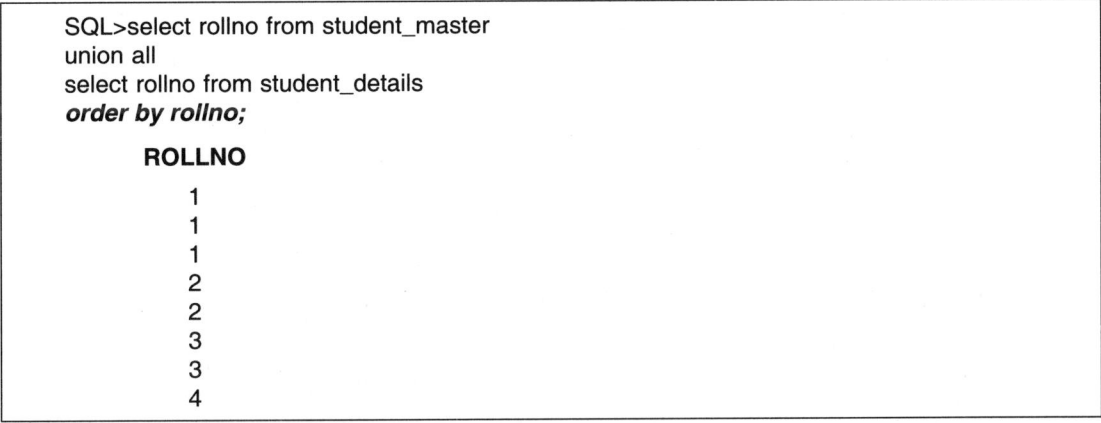

```
SQL>select * from student_master_20062007;

        COLLEGE          ROLLNO          NAME
          GEC               1            satish
          GEC               2            rashmi
          RKDF              3            rishi
          RKDF              4            anil
SQL>select * from student_master_20072008;

        COLLEGE          ROLLNO          NAME
          GEC               1            anita
          GEC               2            deepa
          GEC               3            jaya
```

Figure 12.12   Two separate master tables for different years.

- **Display the student information from the tables of Figure 12.12 in the order of year, college, rollno and name (Figure 12.13).**

```
SQL>select '2006-2007' year,college,rollno,name from student_master_20062007
union
select '2007-2008' year,college,rollno,name from student_master_20072008
order by college,year,rollno,name;
```

YEAR	COLLEGE	ROLLNO	NAME
2006-2007	GEC	1	satish
2006-2007	GEC	2	rashmi
2007-2008	GEC	1	anita
2007-2008	GEC	2	deepa
2007-2008	GEC	3	jaya
2006-2007	RKDF	3	rishi
2006-2007	RKDF	4	anil

Figure 12.13   ORDER By column names in SET operators.

The ORDER BY clause in Figure 12.13 query can be specified using the position of columns also as shown in Figure 12.14.

```
SQL>select '2006-2007' year,college,rollno,name from student_master_20062007
union
select '2007-2008' year,college,rollno,name from student_master_20072008
order by 2,1,3,4;
```

Figure 12.14   Using position of columns in ORDER BY clause.

1 => year, 2 => college, 3 => rollno, 4 => name

Referring columns by position in the ORDER BY clause is very useful when the individual SELECT statements have different column names. Suppose we have two tables, namely table A with ROLLNO as column and table B with ENROLL as column. Now to join the result set from table A and table B, we can use UNION and specify the column position for sorting. Specifying column name in sorting the final result set is not possible as the column names are different in the individual SELECT statements. See Figure 12.15.

```
SQL> desc table_a;
      Name              Null?           Type
      COLLEGE                           CHAR(4)
      ROLLNO                            NUMBER(4)
      NAME                              VARCHAR2(10)

SQL> desc table_b;
      Name              Null?           Type
      COLLEGE                           CHAR(4)
      ENROLL                            NUMBER(4)
      NAME                              VARCHAR2(10)

SQL>select college,rollno from table_a
UNION
select college,enroll from table_b
order by college,enroll;
   ⊗ ORA-00904: "ENROLL": invalid identifier
```

Figure 12.15   Using position of columns in ORDER BY clause.

To solve the problem of Figure 12.15, we have two options:

1. We can use the same alias name for both ROLLNO and ENROLL and then use that alias name in the ORDER BY clause.
2. We can use position of column in the ORDER BY clause.

Refer to Figure 12.16 for how to use alias name or position in the ORDER BY clause.

```
SQL>select college,rollno roll from table_a
UNION
select college,enroll roll from table_b
order by college,roll;

OR

SQL>select college,rollno from table_a
UNION
select college,enroll from table_b
order by college,2;
```

Figure 12.16 ORDER BY alias name or position.

12.6.3 MINUS Operator

The MINUS operator takes the result set of one SELECT statement, and removes those rows that are also returned by a second SELECT statement.

- **Display the students whose marks have not been entered in the details table (Figure 12.17).**

```
SQL>select rollno from student_master
MINUS
select rollno from student_details;

        ROLLNO

           4
```

Figure 12.17 MINUS operator.

12.6.4 Summary of SET Operators

Table 12.1 summarizes the various SET operators.

TABLE 12.1 List of SET operators

Operator	Result
UNION ALL	Combines the results of two SELECT statements into one result set.
UNION	Combines the results of two SELECT statements into one result set, and then eliminates any duplicate rows from that result set.
MINUS	Takes the result set of one SELECT statement, and removes those rows that are also returned by the another SELECT statement.
INTERSECT	Returns only those rows that are returned by each of the two SELECT statements.

12.7   TOP-N QUERIES

The task of retrieving the top or bottom N-rows from a table (by salary, sales amount, marks, etc.) is often referred to as a "top-N query". This task is fairly common in the application development. Assume the master and the details tables with records as shown in Figure 12.18.

```
SQL> select * from student_master;

    ROLLNO          NAME            CITY
       1            satish          BHOPAL
       2            rashmi          AJMER
       3            rishi           BHOPAL
       4            shama           AJMER
       5            nilesh          DELHI

SQL> select * from student_details;

    ROLLNO        SUBJECT          MARKS
       1           MATHS            12
       1           PHY              23
       2           MATHS            14
       2           PHY              21
       3           MATHS            34
       4           MATHS            43
       5           MATHS            20
```

Figure 12.18   Master and details tables.

- **Give the rollno and marks of student who has scored highest in MATHS subject, in other words, give the rollno and marks of student who has topped in MATHS subject (Figure 12.19).**

```
SQL> select * from student_details
where marks = (select max(marks) from student_details where subject='MATHS');

    ROLLNO        SUBJECT          MARKS
       4           MATHS            43
```

Figure 12.19   Highest scorer of MATHS subject.

The sub-query "select max(marks) from student_details where subject='MATHS'" returned 43 and then the main query was executed "where marks=43".

- **Display rollno, name and city of student who has topped in MATHS subject.**

The difference between this query and the query of Figure 12.19 is that here we need to access columns of the master table depending on the values fetched from details table. Figure 12.20 specifies the query for this requirement.

```
SQL> select * from student_master where rollno in
   (
   select rollno from student_details
   where marks = (select max(marks) from student_details where
   subject='MATHS')
   );


ROLLNO          NAME   CITY
4          shama   AJMER
```

Figure 12.20   Master table columns for the specified condition based on values in details table.

The sub-query "select max(marks) from student_details where subject='MATHS'" returned 43, then the query "select rollno from student_details where marks =43" returned rollno 4, followed by the main query returning rollno, name, city from the master table where rollno=4.

- **Display the rollno, marks of the top three students of MATHS subject (Figure 12.21).**

```
SQL> select * from student_details
   2 where subject='MATHS'
   3 order by marks desc;


ROLLNO          SUBJECT          MARKS

4               MATHS            43
3               MATHS            34
5               MATHS            20
2               MATHS            14
1               MATHS            12
```

Figure 12.21   Students in the order of descending marks.

In Figure 12.21 query, we are able to get all the students in decreasing order of marks for MATHS subject.

But our intention is to get the top three students only and we have displayed all students in the order of descending marks. Figure 12.22 contains the query for retrieving the top three students for MATHS subject.

```
SQL>select * from
   (
   select * from student_details
   where subject='MATHS'
   order by marks desc
   )
   where rownum<=3;

ROLLNO          SUBJECT          MARKS

4               MATHS            43
3               MATHS            34
5               MATHS            20
```

Figure 12.22   Top-N query.

The output of the sub-query is the same as shown in Figure 12.19.

We are able to restrict to the top three students by using "where rownum<=3".

- **Display rollno, name, city, marks of the top three students of MATHS subject (Figure 12.23).**

```
SQL>select * from
(
select a.rollno,a.name,a.city,b.marks
from student_master a,student_details b
where b.subject='MATHS'
and a.rollno=b.rollno
order by b.marks desc
)
where rownum<=3;
```

ROLLNO	NAME	CITY	MARKS
4	shama	AJMER	43
3	rishi	BHOPAL	34
5	nilesh	DELHI	20

Figure 12.23   Name of the top three students.

As we wanted to display name, city which are in the master table and marks which is in details table we had to join the two tables. In the sub-query, we arranged records by descending order of marks in MATHS subject. Then in the main query we selected just the top three records by using "rownum<=3".

12.8   SERIAL NUMBER GENERATION

Generating serial number for the records is a common requirement. ROWNUM can be used for displaying the serial number.

Assume the student table with data as shown in Figure 12.24.

```
SQL> select rownum "S.No.", rollno,name,marks from student;
```

S.No.	ROLLNO	NAME	MARKS
1	1	satish	25
2	2	nilesh	23
3	3	rashmi	21
4	4	piyush	13
5	5	ruchi	30

Figure 12.24   STUDENT table.

Here, rownum has given us the required serial no.

12.8.1   Generating Serial Number for Queries with ORDER BY Clause

Displaying the serial number for students in ORDER of MARKS and NAME. In Figure 12.25, we have selected rownum with the ORDER BY clause for generating serial number.

```
SQL> select rownum "S.No.", rollno,name,marks from student order by marks;
```

S.No.	ROLLNO	NAME	MARKS
4	4	piyush	13
3	3	rashmi	21
2	2	nilesh	23
1	1	satish	25
5	5	ruchi	30

```
SQL> select rownum "S.No.", rollno,name,marks from student order by name;
```

S.No.	ROLLNO	NAME	MARKS
2	2	nilesh	23
4	4	piyush	13
3	3	rashmi	21
5	5	ruchi	30
1	1	satish	25

Figure 12.25   Serial number with ORDER BY clause.

It is clear from the result that rownum is not giving the required serial number generation when used with the "ORDER BY" clause.

Reason: The rownum is assigned as soon as the records are fetched from database before sorting. When record 1 is fetched it is assigned rownum 1, when record 2 is fetched it is assigned rownum 2 and so on. The "ORDER BY" clause is executed only after the records have been fetched from database and assigned rownum in sequence. Therefore, using rownum for assigning serial no. will always fail with the "ORDER BY" clause.

Figure 12.26 contains the query which generates serial number with the ORDER BY clause.

```
SQL>select rownum "S.No.",rollno,name,marks from
  2 (
  3 select * from student order by name
  4 )
  5* order by rownum;
```

S.No.	ROLLNO	NAME	MARKS
1	2	nilesh	23
2	4	piyush	13
3	3	rashmi	21
4	5	ruchi	30
5	1	satish	25

Figure 12.26   Serial number generation for queries with ORDER BY clause.

In Figure 12.26, we have used the "ORDER BY" clause in the sub-query and then selected rownum in the main query. The sub-query is returning the records in the desired "ORDER BY" clause and after that the main query is assigning ROWNUM as serial number to records returned by the sub-query.

12.9   MATRIX QUERY/REPORT

A query which displays a single value for combination of 2 columns is called a MATRIX report.

Assume an EMP table with records as shown in Figure 12.27 containing the employee information like name, department, salary and commission.

```
SQL>select * from emp;
```

EMPNO	ENAME	JOB	MGR	HIREDATE	SAL	COMM	DEPTNO
7369	SMITH	CLERK	7902	17-DEC-80	800	–	20
7499	ALLEN	SALESMAN	7698	20-FEB-81	1600	300	30
7521	WARD	SALESMAN	7698	22-FEB-81	1250	500	30
7566	JONES	MANAGER	7839	02-APR-81	2975	–	20
7654	MARTIN	SALESMAN	7698	28-SEP-81	1250	1400	30
7698	BLAKE	MANAGER	7839	01-MAY-81	2850	–	30
7782	CLARK	MANAGER	7839	09-JUN-81	2450	–	10
7788	SCOTT	ANALYST	7566	09-DEC-82	3000	–	20
7839	KING	PRESIDENT	–	17-NOV-81	5000	–	10
7844	TURNER	SALESMAN	7698	08-SEP-81	1500	0	30
7876	ADAMS	CLERK	7788	12-JAN-83	1100	–	20
7900	JAMES	CLERK	7698	03-DEC-81	950	–	30
7902	FORD	ANALYST	7566	03-DEC-81	3000	–	20
7934	MILLER	CLERK	7782	23-JAN-82	1300	–	10

Figure 12.27   EMP table.

Now we want to display a matrix report containing jobwise departmentwise total salary as shown in Figure 12.28.

JOB	DEPT10	DEPT20	DEPT30	DEPT40
CLERK	1300	1900	950	–
SALESMAN	–	–	5600	–
PRESIDENT	5000	–	–	–
MANAGER	2450	2975	2850	–
ANALYST	–	6000	–	–

Figure 12.28   Matrix report.

In other words, we want total salary being given to each department for various categories of employee (JOB) like CLERK, SALESMAN, MANAGER, etc.

Figure 12.29 contains the query for producing the output as shown in Figure 12.28.

```
SQL>SELECT job,
          sum(decode(deptno,10,sal)) DEPT10,
          sum(decode(deptno,20,sal)) DEPT20,
          sum(decode(deptno,30,sal)) DEPT30,
          sum(decode(deptno,40,sal)) DEPT40
       FROM emp
    GROUP BY job;
```

Figure 12.29   Matrix report query.

The sum(decode(deptno,10,sal)) will return the sal column only for department 10 employees as we have used the DECODE function (Refer to Chapter 7 for explanation of the DECODE function). We have given ALIAS name "DEPT10" to this column.

sum(decode(deptno,20,sal)) will return the sal column only for department 20 employees as we have used the DECODE function. We have given ALIAS name "DEPT20" to this column.

12.10 HIERARCHICAL QUERIES

Oracle is a RDBMS (Relational Database Management System) but it can also be used for storing hierarchical information.

EMP table has one more column named "mgr" – manager which indicates the manager/boss of each employee. In other words, mgr field will contain the empno of his boss.

See Figure 12.30 for understanding the hierarchy of employees. KING is the President and the 3 people JONES, BLAKE and CLARK report to him. SCOTT and FORD report to JONES and so on.

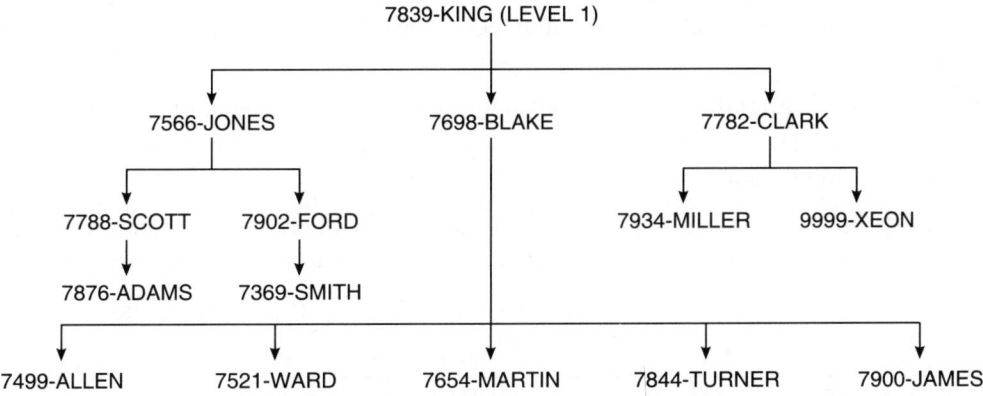

Figure 12.30 Hierarchy of employees.

For hierarchical records there is associated LEVEL number with each record.
For example,
KING is at LEVEL 1,
JONES, BLAKE and CLARK are at level 2.
SCOTT, FORD, ALLEN, WARD, MARTIN, TURNER, JAMES, MILLER, XEON at LEVEL 3.
ADAMS, SMITH at LEVEL 4. LEVEL pseudo-column can be used to display the levels as shown in Figure 12.31.

```
SQL>select LEVEL, empno, ename, mgr from emp
START WITH ename='KING'
CONNECT BY PRIOR empno=mgr;
```

LEVEL	EMPNO	ENAME	MGR
1	7839	KING	–
2	7566	JONES	7839
3	7788	SCOTT	7566

4	7876	ADAMS	7788
3	7902	FORD	7566
4	7369	SMITH	7902
2	7698	BLAKE	7839
3	7499	ALLEN	7698
3	7521	WARD	7698
3	7654	MARTIN	7698
3	7844	TURNER	7698
3	7900	JAMES	7698
2	7782	CLARK	7839
3	7934	MILLER	7782

Figure 12.31   LEVEL pseudo-column.

LEVEL is a pseudo-column which indicates the LEVEL in hierarchy of employees.

Pseudo means it is a column which actually does not exist in the EMP table but can be selected in a query.

START WITH defines the starting point or rather the topmost employee from where we have to trace down the tree(which is KING). For hierarchical queries we need to specify the START WITH clause.

CONNECT BY PRIOR specifies the relationship between 2 columns empno and mgr. PRIOR empno=mgr implies that we are following a top-down hierarchy. We will see later that we can also use bottom-up hierarchy queries.

Although the query of Figure 12.31 has displayed the top-to-bottom LEVEL for each employee but the display is not intuitive. It means that it is not very clear as to who is reporting whom.

Let us rewrite the query of Figure 12.31 which will align the employees as per hierarchy (Figure 12.32).

```
SQL>select LEVEL, empno, lpad(ename, level*10,'*'),mgr from emp
START WITH ename='KING'
CONNECT BY PRIOR empno=mgr;
```

LEVEL	EMPNO	LPAD(ENAME,LEVEL*10,'*')	MGR
1	7839	******KING	–
2	7566	***************JONES	7839
3	7788	*************************SCOTT	7566
4	7876	***********************************ADAMS	7788
3	7902	*************************FORD	7566
4	7369	***********************************SMITH	7902
2	7698	***************BLAKE	7839
3	7499	*************************ALLEN	7698
3	7521	*************************WARD	7698
3	7654	*************************MARTIN	7698
3	7844	*************************TURNER	7698
3	7900	*************************JAMES	7698
2	7782	***************CLARK	7839
3	7934	*************************MILLER	7782

Figure 12.32   Aligning records as per LEVEL.

Now it is very clear that JONES, BLAKE and CLARK are reporting to KING. We have used LPAD() function to introduce the number of '*' depending on LEVEL of employee.

The query of Figure 12.32 can also be written as given in Figure 12.33.

```
SQL>select LEVEL,empno,lpad(ename,level*10,'*'),mgr from emp
START WITH mgr IS NULL
CONNECT BY PRIOR empno=mgr;
```

Figure 12.33   Using START WITH clause.

KING is the President of the company and so the company does not have a Boss (mgr column is NULL). Therefore, to specify the Top starting employee we can use either START WITH ename='KING' OR START WITH mgr is NULL.

Display the employees reporting to BLAKE only. This can be achieved with START WITH clause as shown in Figure 12.34.

```
SQL>select LEVEL,empno,lpad(ename,level*10,'*'),mgr from emp
START WITH ename='BLAKE'
CONNECT BY PRIOR empno=mgr;
```

LEVEL	EMPNO	LPAD(ENAME,LEVEL*10,'*')	MGR
1	7698	*****BLAKE	7839
2	7499	***************ALLEN	7698
2	7521	****************WARD	7698
2	7654	**************MARTIN	7698
2	7844	**************TURNER	7698
2	7900	**************JAMES	7698

Figure 12.34   START WITH parameter.

Display bottom-up hierarchy starting from JAMES. Figure 12.35 contains the query for bottom-up hierarchy.

```
SQL>select LEVEL,empno,lpad(ename,level*10,'*'),mgr from emp
START WITH ename='JAMES'
CONNECT BY empno=PRIOR mgr;
```

LEVEL	EMPNO	LPAD(ENAME,LEVEL*10,'*')	MGR
1	7900	*****JAMES	7698
2	7698	**************BLAKE	7839
3	7839	************************KING	–

Figure 12.35   Bottom-up hierarchy.

For bottom-up hierarchy we have used **"CONNECT BY empno=PRIOR mgr;"**. Note that we have placed the PRIOR word on mgr side instead of on empno side for bottom-up hierarchy.

LEVEL pseudo-column can be used in WHERE clause also.

We want to list hierarchy starting from KING up to 2 LEVELS only (Figure 12.36).

```
SQL>select LEVEL, empno, lpad(ename, level*10,'*'),mgr from emp
WHERE LEVEL<=2
START WITH ename='KING'
CONNECT BY PRIOR empno=mgr;
```

LEVEL	EMPNO	LPAD(ENAME,LEVEL*10,'*')	MGR
1	7839	******KING	–
2	7566	**************JONES	7839
2	7698	**************BLAKE	7839
2	7782	**************CLARK	7839

Figure 12.36   LEVEL in WHERE clause.

Oracle provides a function called **sys_connect_by_path**() which displays entire hierarchy for each employee as shown in Figure 12.37.

```
SQL>select LEVEL, empno, lpad(ename, level*10,'*'), mgr,
sys_connect_by_path(ename,'->') path from emp
START WITH ename='KING'
CONNECT BY PRIOR empno=mgr;
```

LEVEL	EMPNO	LPAD(ENAME,LEVEL*10,'*')	MGR	PATH
1	7839	******KING	–	->KING
2	7566	**************JONES	7839	->KING->JONES
3	7788	***********************SCOTT	7566	->KING->JONES->SCOTT
4	7876	********************************ADAMS	7788	->KING->JONES->SCOTT->ADAMS
3	7902	***********************FORD	7566	->KING->JONES->FORD
4	7369	********************************SMITH	7902	->KING->JONES->FORD->SMITH
2	7698	**************BLAKE	7839	->KING->BLAKE
3	7499	***********************ALLEN	7698	->KING->BLAKE->ALLEN
3	7521	***********************WARD	7698	->KING->BLAKE->WARD
3	7654	***********************MARTIN	7698	->KING->BLAKE->MARTIN
3	7844	***********************TURNER	7698	->KING->BLAKE->TURNER
3	7900	***********************JAMES	7698	->KING->BLAKE->JAMES
2	7782	**************CLARK	7839	->KING->CLARK
3	7934	***********************MILLER	7782	->KING->CLARK->MILLER

Figure 12.37   Displaying hierarchy path.

12.11   CASE

Oracle provides a CASE statement which is similar to IF-THEN-ELSE of other languages. The syntax for the **case** statement is:

```
CASE [ expression ]
   WHEN condition_1 THEN result_1
   WHEN condition_2 THEN result_2
   ...
   WHEN condition_n THEN result_n
   ELSE result
END
```

The *expression* is optional. It is the value that you are comparing to the list of conditions. (i.e. condition_1, condition_2, ..., condition_n)

condition_1 to condition_n must be the same datatype. Conditions are evaluated in the order listed. Once a *condition* is found to be true, the **case** statement will return the result and not evaluate the conditions further.

result_1 to result_n must be the same datatype. This is the value returned once a *condition* is found to be true.

Note: If no *condition* is found to be true, then the **case** statement will return the value in the ELSE clause.

If the ELSE clause is omitted and no *condition* is found to be true, then the **case** statement will return NULL.

Assume STUDENT table as in Figure 12.38.

```
SQL>select * from student;

    ROLLNO          NAME          MARKS
    1111            rashmi         54
    2222            ajay           68
    3333            chetan         45
    4444            rishi          30
    5555            anil           89
```

Figure 12.38   STUDENT table.

We want to assign grades to students depending on the following conditions.
Marks >= 80 then GRADE A
60<MARKS<80 then GRADE B
40<MARKS<=60 then GRADE C
ELSE GRADE D

The query for conditional display can be achieved using CASE statement as in Figure 12.39.

```
SQL>select rollno, name, marks,
case
when marks >=80 then 'GRADE A'
when marks>=60 and marks<80 then 'GRADE B'
when marks>=40 and marks<60 then 'GRADE C'
else 'GRADE D'
end GRADE
from student;

    ROLLNO          NAME          MARKS          GRADE
    1111            rashmi         54             GRADE C
    2222            ajay           68             GRADE B
    3333            chetan         45             GRADE C
    4444            rishi          30             GRADE D
    5555            anil           89             GRADE A
```

Figure 12.39   CASE statement.

Every CASE must have an END followed by ALIAS NAME to that CASE logic.

Here we have given the ALIAS NAME "GRADE" to the CASE logic.

When CASE values are to be checked for EQUALITY only and not any other comparison operator like <, <, >=, <=, <> then we can use the alternative form of case statement as shown in Figure 12.41.

Assume EMPLOYEE table as in Figure 12.40.

EMPNO	ENAME	GRADE	SAL
1111	rahul	E1	123.4567
2222	rishi	E2	123.236
3333	rashmi	M1	5145.2436
4444	samay	M2	2000
5555	ruchi	XX	3000.25
6666	neelesh	–	–

Figure 12.40   EMPLOYEE table.

```
SQL>select empno,ename,grade,
case grade
when 'E1' then 'ENGINEER'
when 'E2' then 'SENIOR ENGINEER'
when 'M1' then 'MANAGER'
when 'M2' then 'SENIOR MANAGER'
else 'UNKNOWN'
end grade_description
from employee;
```

EMPNO	ENAME	GRADE	GRADE_DESCRIPTION
1111	rahul	E1	ENGINEER
2222	rishi	E2	SENIOR ENGINEER
3333	rashmi	M1	MANAGER
4444	samay	M2	SENIOR MANAGER
5555	ruchi	XX	UNKNOWN
6666	neelesh	–	UNKNOWN

Figure 12.41   CASE with equality comparison only.

Here we have not used "when grade='E1' then", as equality operator is assumed while using this syntax.

REVIEW QUESTIONS

1. What is the difference between relational EQUAL (=) operator and the IN operator?
2. Differentiate between the EXISTS and the IN operator.
3. Explain the various SET Operators.
4. Is it possible to use the ORDER BY clause in the individual SELECT statements with queries using SET operators?

5. What advantage does the referencing of ORDER BY columns by position has over referencing by name?

6. How are TOP-N queries performed in SQL? What is the purpose of ROWNUM in solving TOP-N queries?

7. How can serial number be generated for the desired sequence of records?

8. Generate a matrix report displaying collegewise count of students.

9. How can hierarchical data be stored using the relational tables? Explain the various clauses which can be used with hierarchical queries.

10. Explain the significance of the CASE statement. Can the CASE statement be used with various relational operators like <,>,<=,>= and !=?

MULTIPLE CHOICE QUESTIONS

Refer to Table 7.1 for the CUSTOMER ORDER System

1. For comparing the value of a column against a set of values, the operator used is
   (a) EQUAL TO
   (b) =ANY
   (c) IN
   (d) (b) and (c) are correct

2. For listing the customer names who have placed order to us, the correct statement is
   (a) Select customer_name from CUSTOMER where customer_id = (select customer_id from ORDER);
   (b) Select customer_name from CUSTOMER where customer_id = select customer_id from ORDER;
   (c) Select customer_name from CUSTOMER where customer_id IN (select customer_id from ORDER);

3. Which of the following statements is correct?
   (a) IN operator checks for the equality against a set of values
   (b) EXISTS operator checks for the equality against a set of values
   (c) IN and EXISTS operator are the same

4. Which of the following is not a SET operator?
   (a) IN
   (b) UNION
   (c) INTERSECT
   (d) MINUS

5. Which is TRUE about the EXISTS operator?
   (a) The sub-query is executed first followed by the main query
   (b) Main query executes first followed by the sub-query
   (c) For each record fetched in the main query corresponding records are checked for existence in records returned by sub-query.

6. Which of the following is not correct about the SET operators?
   (a) They combine result of more than one query
   (b) The individual component of queries cannot contain ORDER BY clause
   (c) The ORDER BY clause specified in the last SELECT decides the final ORDER in which records are displayed.

7. The operator which displays duplicate values from multiple SELECT statements is
   (a) UNION
   (b) UNION ALL
   (c) DISINCT

8. Which is not TRUE about SET operators?
   (a) The number of columns in each SELECT statement must be the same
   (b) The name of columns must be the same
   (c) The data type of columns must match

9. The ORDER BY clause with SET operators can reference columns by
   (a) Name
   (b) Position
   (c) Both Name and Position

10. The PSEUDO column which can be used to view TOP-N records is
    (a) LEVEL
    (b) ROWID
    (c) ROWNUM

11. The PSEUDO column which can be used to generate serial number is
    (a) LEVEL
    (b) ROWID
    (c) ROWNUM

12. The clause of SELECT statement which can provide the IF-ELSE logic is
    (a) DECODE
    (b) TRANSLATE
    (c) CASE

LAB ASSIGNMENT

Refer to Tables 7.1 and 7.2 of the CUSTOMER ORDER System
1. Display the customer names who are in MP or HA.
2. Display the customers who have placed some order. Use IN and EXISTS operators.
3. List the product names for which we have orders.
4. Show the product names for which we have no orders.
5. Find the customer names that have not placed any order for the last 1 month.
6. List the customer codes that have placed orders using SET operator.
7. Display customer codes that have not placed any order using SET operator.
8. Display the customer names who have placed some order using SET operator.

9. Find the customer who has placed maximum number of orders for televisions.
10. Find the top 2 customers who have placed maximum number of orders for cd-players.
11. List the customer names in the order of decreasing quantity ordered.
12. Generate serial number for the above query.
13. Develop a matrix report indicating the quantity of each type of product ordered against each customer. Type of product implies television, cd-player etc.
14. We want to classify the customers based on the quantity of various products ordered in certain categories as follows:

Quantity ordered	Category of customer
1<qty<10	C
10<qty<20	B
Qty>=20	A

Indexing

13.1 INTRODUCTION

Index is an object which can be defined as the ordered list of values of a column or combination of columns used for faster searching and sorting of data.

Oracle assigns a unique identification number to every record in the database called **"ROWID"—Row Identification**. It contains the physical address/location of a record in the database (hard disk).

ROWID is a **pseudo-column** associated with each and every record of a table and is represented by **radix values** as shown in Figure 13.1.

SQL> select *rowid,* college, rollno, name, gender from student;				
ROWID	**COLLE**	**ROLLNO**	**NAME**	**G**
AAADZ2AAEAAAAGkAAA	OIST	1	satish	M
AAADZ2AAEAAAAGkAAB	PTL	2	rashmi	F
AAADZ2AAEAAAAGkAAC	RKDF	3	rishi	M
AAADZ2AAEAAAAGkAAD	PTL	4	nilesh	M
AAADZ2AAEAAAAGkAAE	PTL	5	ruchi	F

Figure 13.1 ROWID.

Additional Information: The ROWID format is in 10 bytes:

- bits 1 to 32 (bytes 1 to 4): data object id (0-4294967295)
- bits 33 to 44 (byte 5 and half byte 6): file number inside the tablespace (0-4095)
- bits 45 to 64 (half byte 6 and bytes 7 and 8): block number inside the database file (0-1048575)
- bits 65 to 80 (bytes 9 and 10): row number inside the block (0-65535)

When printed, each field is displayed in radix 64 (A-Za-z0-9+/)

By default whenever we search for records with the "WHERE" clause, Oracle looks for the desired records sequentially. This takes considerable time for the retrieval of records. Therefore, Oracle provides an object called "Index" which can be used to speed up the searching of records.

When we select records for college='PTL', Oracle fetches the first record, compares the college with 'PTL', as 'OIST' not matching, therefore, the first record is not displayed. It fetches the next record, finds college name matching, and displays the record and so on. This is known as sequential searching and takes considerable time in retrieving records from tables containing huge number of records.

To speed up the retrieval of records for college column we will create an index on it (Figure 13.2).

```
SQL> create index ind_student_college on student(college);
Index created.
```

Figure 13.2 Creating index.

where ind_student_college is user-defined name for index object.

On creating index on college column, Oracle stores a structure as shown in Figure 13.3 in the database.

COLLEGE	ROWID
OIST	AAADZ2AAEAAAAGkAAA
PTL	AAADZ2AAEAAAAGkAAB
PTL	AAADZ2AAEAAAAGkAAD
PTL	AAADZ2AAEAAAAGkAAE
RKDF	AAADZ2AAEAAAAGkAAC

Figure 13.3 Index organization.

Now when we search for records of 'PTL' college, Oracle sequentially scans the first record in index object, finds mismatch, ignores. Next record is fetched, finds matching college, picks the rowid and fetches the record by rowid from the database. This process continues till the non-match record of "RKDF" college is found. If we had lakhs of records for PTL college then the searching would obviously be faster while using indexes rather than sequential search.

Oracle also arranges the records in index object based on indexed column (college). Note that the colleges are alphabetically arranged in order. Actually this sorting on indexed column along with rowid enhances the retrieval speed of records.

13.2 REMOVING INDEX

To remove the index, the DDL statement DROP INDEX can be used (Figure 13.4).

```
SQL> drop index ind_student_college;
Index dropped.
```

Figure 13.4 Removing index.

13.3   CREATING INDEX ON MULTIPLE COLUMNS

Index object can be created on multiple columns (Figure 13.5).

```
SQL> create index ind_student_college_rollno on student(college,rollno);

Index created.
```

Figure 13.5   Index on multiple columns.

Here index has been created for both college and rollno in combination.

13.4   TYPES OF INDEXES

Indexes are classified on two parameters, namely

  1. Depending on data values: UNIQUE/NON-UNIQUE
  2. Depending on data structure being employed for indexing: B-Tree/Bitmap

13.4.1   Non-unique

The index we created in Figure 13.2 on college is NON-UNIQUE index, that is, the values in college column may repeat in various records. We have three records for PTL college.

13.4.2   Unique

Suppose we frequently select records based on rollno, then we will create UNIQUE index on rollno column. By UNIQUE we mean that duplicate rollnos cannot exist in different records of the same table. Figure 13.6 contains command for creating unique index.

```
SQL> create unique index ind_unique_student_rollno on student(rollno);

Index created.
```

Figure 13.6   Creating unique index.

Note: Oracle automatically creates UNIQUE index for the PRIMARY KEY columns and UNIQUE constraint columns. That is why we cannot insert duplicate values.

13.4.3   B-Tree

Oracle uses the B-Tree structure by default for indexes. For the student table of Figure 13.2, Oracle maintains the index structure in the database as shown in Figure 13.7. This is an abstract representation of the B-Tree.

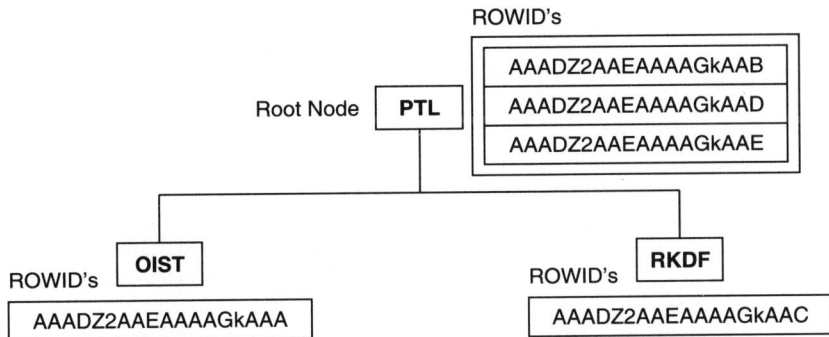

Figure 13.7 Abstract representation of B-Tree.

As "PTL" lies alphabetically after "OIST" and before "RKDF", therefore, it becomes the root node. Now when we search for records of RKDF college, Oracle starts at root node, compares it with "RKDF", finds that "RKDF" is alphabetically after "PTL", so it starts searching on the right-hand tree of "PTL" node. This process of cascading down the tree continues till the matching records are found.

Note: The B-Tree index should be used when a column has a large number of distinct values. There will be several colleges, therefore, we will create the B-Tree index for college column.

13.4.4 Bitmap Indexes

The Bitmap index is used for columns having a few distinct values. For example, in the student table, "gender" have just two values "M" or "F". If our query frequently based on "gender" then we should create the Bit-Map index on "gender" column as shown in Figure 13.8.

```
SQL> create bitmap index ind_bitmap_student_gender on student(gender);

Index created.
```

Figure 13.8 Creating Bitmap index.

Figure 13.9 shows an abstract representation of the Bitmap Index.

GENDER	ROWID's(we have shown just last 3 chars of ROWID)				
	AAA	AAB	AAC	AAD	AAE
M	1	0	1	1	0
F	0	1	0	0	1

Figure 13.9 Abstract representation of Bitmap index.

Whenever we search for all "M" or "F" students, then the Bitmap index is used for faster retrieval. A single bit is associated to each ROWID indicating gender.

13.5   INDEXING ON ORACLE BUILT-IN FUNCTIONS

Assume a VEHICLE table with information about vehicles registered (Figure 13.10).

```
SQL>desc vehicle;
         Name                    Null?              Type
      REGISTRATION_NO                            CHAR(13)
      OWNER                                      VARCHAR2(10)
      ADDRESS                                    VARCHAR2(30)

SQL>select * from vehicle;

   REGISTRATION_NO          OWNER              ADDRESS
      MP-04,NK-4602          satish             243,9-B,saket
      MP-04,AB-3234          rashmi             N-21,shakti
      UP-01,EU-5678          rishi              C-32,alkapuri
```

Figure 13.10   VEHICLE table.

Here the first two characters of the "registration_no" column indicate the state in which the vehicle has been registered.

To query vehicles based on a STATE (MP, UP, etc.) which is a part of the "registration_no" column, we will have to use oracle built-in function.

Let us display vehicles of state MP (Figure 13.11).

```
SQL> select * from vehicle where substr(REGISTRATION_NO,1,2)='MP';

   REGISTRATION_          OWNER           ADDRESS
      MP-04,NK-4602        satish          243,9-B,saket
      MP-04,AB-3234        rashmi          N-21,shakti
```

Figure 13.11   Vehicles of state MP.

Here we have used the "SUBSTR" built-in function of Oracle.

Caution: Oracle does not use the indexes when functions (both built-in and user-defined) are used in the WHERE clause even if the column "registration_no" is indexed.

If we frequently need to query on "state" derived from "registration_no" column, then we will have to create index on "registration_no" column with SUBSTR function (Figure 13.12).

```
SQL> create index ind_vehicle_substr_reg_no on vehicle (substr(registration_no,1,2));
Index created.
```

Figure 13.12   Creating index on built-in functions.

Now all queries using SUBSTR(registration_no,1,2) in "WHERE" and "ORDER BY" clause will use the defined index.

13.6 SITUATIONS WHEN ORACLE USES INDEXES

1. The "WHERE" clause of the "SELECT" statement uses the indexed Column.
2. The "ORDER BY" clause of the "SELECT" statement uses the indexed Column.
3. When two tables are joined on the indexed column.

13.7 SITUATIONS WHEN ORACLE DOES NOT USE INDEXES

1. The "SELECT" statement does not contain the "WHERE" or "ORDER BY" clause.
2. The "WHERE" clause contains a column which is not indexed.
3. The "ORDER BY" clause contains a column which is not indexed.

13.8 ADVANTAGES OF INDEXES

1. Faster retrieval of records using indexed columns in the "WHERE" clause.
2. Faster retrieval and sorting of records using the indexed columns in the "ORDER BY" clause.
3. Faster retrieval of records when joining tables on the indexed columns.

13.9 DISADVANTAGES OF INDEXES

The DML operations like INSERT, UPDATE, DELETE consume more time for indexed tables as index processing must be done for each record. Index is a separate organization/structure which is maintained for each and every index created. Whenever a DML operation is performed then the changes are reflected in the base table as well as the index structure is modified to incorporate the new changes.

13.10 DATA DICTIONARY TABLES FOR INDEXES

Drop all the indexes created till now and create indexes as shown in Figure 13.13.

```
SQL> create index ind_student_college on student(college);

Index created.

SQL> create unique index ind_uniq_student_rollno on student(rollno);

Index created.

SQL> create bitmap index ind_bitmap_student_gender on student(gender);

Index created.
```

Figure 13.13 New indexes.

"ind_student_college" is a normal (default B-Tree) index on "college" column.
"ind_uniq_student_rollno" is a normal unique index on "rollno" column.
"ind_bitmap_student_gender" is a Bit-Map index on "gender" column.

The **user_indexes** and **user_ind_columns** are the data dictionary tables containing information about the indexes (Figures 13.14 and 13.15).

```
SQL> select index_name,index_type,table_name from user_indexes
  2 where table_name='STUDENT';
```

INDEX_NAME	INDEX_TYPE	TABLE_NAME
IND_STUDENT_COLLEGE	NORMAL	STUDENT
IND_UNIQ_STUDENT_ROLLNO	NORMAL	STUDENT
IND_BITMAP_STUDENT_GENDER	BITMAP	STUDENT

Figure 13.14   Data dictionary for indexes.

Now we want to know the columns on which indexes have been created (Figure 13.15).

```
SQL> select index_name,table_name,column_name
  2 from user_ind_columns where table_name='STUDENT';
```

INDEX_NAME	TABLE_NAME	COLUMN_NAME
IND_STUDENT_COLLEGE	STUDENT	COLLEGE
IND_UNIQ_STUDENT_ROLLNO	STUDENT	ROLLNO
IND_BITMAP_STUDENT_GENDER	STUDENT	GENDER

Figure 13.15   Data dictionary for indexes.

Caution: When a table is dropped, all the indexes created on that table are also dropped.

REVIEW QUESTIONS

1. What is the purpose of indexing?
2. How does indexing help in faster searching and sorting of records?
3. What is ROWID and what information does it contain?
4. Explain the various types of indexes. When will we use B-Tree and Bitmap indexes and why?
5. Is it possible to apply indexes while applying built-in functions to columns?
6. List the conditions when Oracle uses and does not use the index object.
7. Enlist the advantages and disadvantages of indexes.

MULTIPLE CHOICE QUESTIONS

1. Which is not correct about indexes?
   (a) Indexes are created for faster search and retrieval.
   (b) Indexes slowdown the DML operations.
   (c) Indexes improve the performance of DML operations.

2. The default type of index generated by Oracle is
   (a) Bit-Map
   (b) B-Tree
   (c) Non-unique
   (d) b and c are correct

3. The pseudo-column which represents the physical location of records is
   (a) ROWNUM
   (b) ROWID
   (c) RID

4. Bit-Map index should be used where
   (a) Number of distinct values for a column is high.
   (b) Number of distinct values for a column is low.

TRUE/FALSE

1. Oracle uses indexes for all the SELECT statements.

2. Indexes are used in the WHERE and ORDER by clauses.

3. Indexes are not used when the WHERE clause does not use an indexed column.

4. Indexes reduce the performance of the DML statements.

5. Indexing all columns is a good practice as in some or the other situation the WHERE clause would use any of the column values.

6. Indexes are independent objects from tables.

7. All indexes are dropped as soon as a table is dropped.

LAB ASSIGNMENT

Refer to Table 7.1 for CUSTOMER ORDER System

1. Create Unique index on customer_id of the CUSTOMER table.

2. Create Unique index on ORDER_NO, CUSTOMER_ID and PRODUCT_CD of ORDER table.

3. Add an additional column named CATEGORY in the CUSTOMER table which will contain 'A', 'B' or 'C' indicating the class of customer. Create a Bitmap index on the CATEGORY column.

4. Create a Non-unique index on first two characters of PRODUCT_CD in the PRODUCT table.

Oracle Security—Privileges

14.1 INTRODUCTION

Oracle is a multi-user RDBMS and provides a secure environment such that the objects owned by a user are by default not accessible to the other users. It provides the facility that the owner of an object can grant various permissions to other database users as per requirement. Object implies tables, views, synonyms, functions procedures, etc.

The various permissions on objects are called **privileges**. For example, the user "scott" may give permission to user "john" for selecting records from the "student' table. "john" can only "select" records from the "student" table. He won't be able to insert, update or delete records from scott's "student" table.

Let us first create a user named "john" to understand the concept of permissions.

Go To -> Start -> Programs -> Oracle Database 10g Express Edition ->
Go To Database Home Page -> Supply username as sys and password as sys. -> Administration -> Database Users. You will be shown Figure 14.1 on screen.

Click "Create" button. This will display Figure 14.2 on screen.
Enter Username as "john"
Password "john"
Confirm Password as "john"
Verify that all options in "User Privilege" section are checked EXCEPT "DBA"

Click "Create" button.

Alternatively, we can use the command line interface for creating a new user (Refer to Figure 2.12 of Chapter 2).

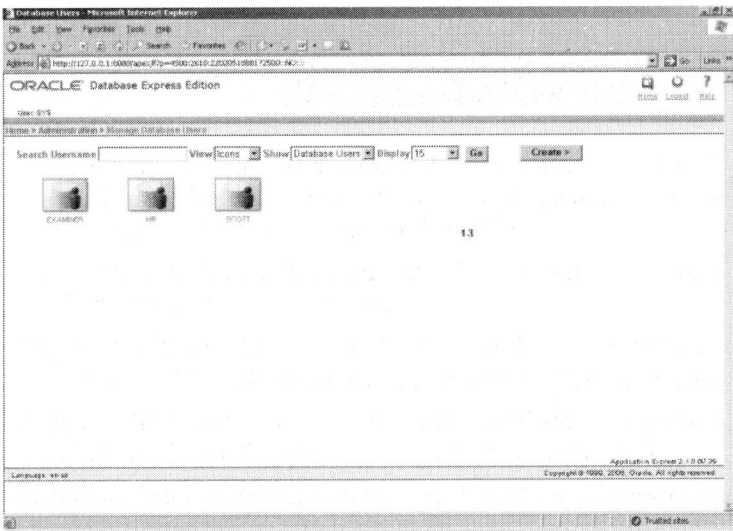

Figure 14.1   Web-based interface for creating new database users.

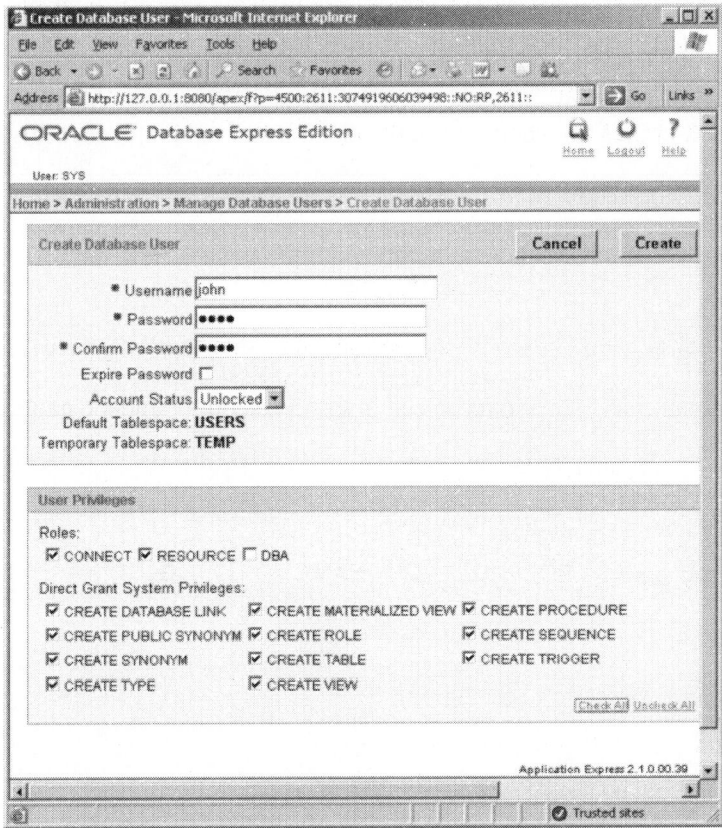

Figure 14.2   Creating new user named "john".

Now open SQL Prompt (Start -> All Programs -> Oracle Database 10g Express Edition-> Run SQL Command line). See Figure 14.3.

```
SQL> connect john/john@xe
Connected.
SQL> select * from scott.student;
select * from scott.student
       *
ERROR at line 1:
ORA-00942: table or view does not exist
```

Figure 14.3 Logging as JOHN user.

Here, "john" user is trying to view records in the "student" table of "scott" user (referred as scott.student). Note that "john" is not able to view the records of "student" table. It is because by default the objects (table) created by "scott" can be viewed, inserted, updated or deleted by the owner "scott" only. If required, the "scott" user can give specific permissions on his own objects to other users.

14.2 GRANTING PERMISSIONS

Let us allow "john" user to view and insert records in scott's student table. First, we will have to log in as scott user and then give permission of select, insert to "john" user (Figure 14.4).

```
SQL> connect scott/scott@xe
Connected.
SQL> grant select, insert on student to john;

Grant succeeded.
```

Figure 14.4 SCOTT giving permission on his objects to JOHN.

Now again connect as john and try select, insert into scott's "student" table as in Figure 14.5.

```
SQL> connect john/john@xe
Connected.
SQL> select * from scott.student;
```

COLLE	ROLLNO	NAME	G
OIST	1	satish	M
PTL	2	rashmi	F
RKDF	3	rishi	M
PTL	4	nilesh	M
PTL	5	ruchi	F

```
SQL> insert into scott.student values ('OIST',6,'anil','M');

1 row created.

SQL> select * from scott.student;
```

COLLE	ROLLNO	NAME	G
OIST	1	satish	M
PTL	2	rashmi	F
RKDF	3	rishi	M
PTL	4	nilesh	M
PTL	5	ruchi	F
OIST	6	anil	M

6 rows selected.

Figure 14.5 JOHN accessing SCOTT's tables.

Note that "john" user is now able to select and insert records into the "student" table of "scott" user.

Let us see if "john" can "update" and "delete" records from the "student" table (Figure 14.6).

```
SQL> update scott.student set name='test' where rollno=1;
update scott.student set name='test' where rollno=1
             *

ERROR at line 1:
ORA-01031: insufficient privileges

SQL> delete from scott.student where rollno=1;
delete from scott.student where rollno=1
           *

ERROR at line 1:
ORA-01031: insufficient privileges
```

Figure 14.6 JOHN cannot execute UPDATE and DELETE.

Oracle gives error message saying "insufficient privileges".

14.3 WHAT A USER CAN GRANT?

A user can grant privileges on any object he/she owns. Different objects have different permissions to be assigned to other users as specified in Table 14.1.

TABLE 14.1 Permissions on objects

Object	Privileges
Table	select, insert, update, delete, alter, index
Views, Materialized Views	select, insert, update, delete
Sequence	select, alter
Functions, Procedures, Packages	execute
Index	execute

We will learn about the various objects referenced here in later chapters.

14.4 GRANTING PERMISSION FOR ALL OPERATIONS

Suppose "scott" wants to grant ALL privileges (select, insert, update, delete, alter, index) on the "student" table to "john". SCOTT can grant all kinds of permissions on an object to JOHN by using ALL clause of the GRANT statement (Figure 14.7).

```
SQL> grant all on student to john;

Grant succeeded.
```

Figure 14.7 Granting ALL privileges.

Here "all" indicates every possible permission on that particular object.

14.5 GRANTING PERMISSIONS TO ALL USERS

If we want to grant certain permissions to all other users of the database then we can use the "PUBLIC" keyword as shown in Figure 14.8.

```
SQL> grant select, insert on student to public;

Grant succeeded.
```

Figure 14.8 Granting permissions to all database users.

Now every user can select and insert records into scott's student table.

Caution: Be careful while granting permissions to public. You will not come to know which user has done what on your table.

14.6 ALLOWING GRANTEE TO FURTHER GRANT THE PERMISSIONS TO OTHER USERS

"scott" gave select, insert permission on the "student" table to "john". Now "john" cannot carry forward the same permission to other users on "scott.student" table. But if we want that the grantee (john) should be able to assign the permissions to other users, then "scott" will have to use a clause called "WITH GRANT OPTION" in grant statement (Figure 14.9).

```
SQL> connect scott/scott@xe

Connected.

SQL> grant select,insert on student to john with grant option;

Grant succeeded.
```

Figure 14.9 Allowing grantee to further grant permissions.

Let us create one more user named "suse".

Till now we have been creating users using the GUI interface(Start -> Programs -> Oracle Database 10g Express Edition -> Go to database Home Page -> Login as sys/sys" -> Database Users -> Create.

This time let us use the SQL Command Prompt for creating new user "suse". We have to login as "sys" as in Figure 14.10.

```
SQL> connect sys/sys@xe as sysdba;
Connected.
SQL> create user suse identified by "suse";

User created.

SQL> grant connect, resource to suse;

Grant succeeded.
```

Figure 14.10 Creating new user with SQL Command Prompt.

Here identified by <password> is the password assigned to "suse" user.

Log in as "john" as shown in Figure 14.11 and grant permission to "suse".

```
SQL> connect john/john@xe
Connected.

SQL> grant select on scott.student to suse;
Grant succeeded.
```

Figure 14.11 JOHN granting privileges on Scott's table to "suse".

Now "john" is able to grant select permission on Scott's student table to "suse" (Figure 14.11) because "scott" user specified "WITH GRANT OPTION" in the grant statement (Figure 14.9).

Log in as "suse" and SELECT records from Scott's student table as shown in Figure 14.12.

```
SQL> connect suse/suse@xe
Connected.
SQL> select * from scott.student;

        COLLE        ROLLNO        NAME        G

        OIST          1            satish      M
        PTL           2            rashmi      F
        RKDF          3            rishi       M
        PTL           4            nilesh      M
        PTL           5            ruchi       F
        OIST          6            anil        M

6 rows selected.
```

Figure 14.12 "Suse" viewing records from Scott's table.

14.7 DATA DICTIONARY VIEWS

Assume the following scenario.

1. Scott has given select and insert permissions on student table to John WITH ADMIN OPTION.
2. John has given select permission on employee table to Scott WITHOUT ADMIN OPTION.
3. John has given select permission on Scott's student table to suse WITHOUT ADMIN OPTION.

There are mainly three data dictionary tables which contain information about the privileges as shown in Figure 14.13.

SQL>select * from dictionary where table_name like 'USER_TAB_PRIVS%';

TABLE_NAME	COMMENTS
USER_TAB_PRIVS	Grants on objects for which the user is the owner, grantor or grantee
USER_TAB_PRIVS_MADE	All grants on objects owned by the user
USER_TAB_PRIVS_RECD	Grants on objects for which the user is the grantee

---

Figure 14.13 Data dictionary for privileges.

USER_TAB_PRIVS_MADE contains the list of privileges given to other users

USER_TAB_PRIVS_RECD contains the privileges received from other users

USER_TAB_PRIVS contains the privileges granted to other users as well as received from other users.

In Figure 14.14 we have logged in as "SCOTT" and viewed records from the three data dictionary tables related to privileges.

```
SQL>connect scott/tiger
Connected
SQL>select * from user_tab_privs;
```

GRANTEE	OWNER	TABLE_NAME	GRANTOR	PRIVILEGE	GRANTABLE
SCOTT	JOHN	EMPLOYEE	JOHN	SELECT	NO
SUSE	SCOTT	STUDENT	JOHN	SELECT	NO
JOHN	SCOTT	STUDENT	SCOTT	SELECT	YES
JOHN	SCOTT	STUDENT	SCOTT	INSERT	YES

```
SQL>select * from user_tab_privs_made;
```

GRANTEE	TABLE_NAME	GRANTOR	PRIVILEGE	GRANTABLE
JOHN	STUDENT	SCOTT	INSERT	YES
JOHN	STUDENT	SCOTT	SELECT	YES
SUSE	STUDENT	JOHN	SELECT	NO

```
SQL>select * from user_tab_privs_recd;
```

OWNER	TABLE_NAME	GRANTOR	PRIVILEGE	GRANTABLE
JOHN	EMPLOYEE	JOHN	SELECT	NO

Figure 14.14 Viewing privileges from data dictionary.

OWNER => The creator of object is the owner.

GRANTEE => The user who has been given the privilege.

GRANTOR => User who has given the privilege. The object owner may permit a user to further grant privileges on the objects owned by him to other users. For example, Scott has given select and insert permissions on the student table to John along with GRANT OPTION. Now John has further given privileges to suse user on Scott's student table.

GRANTABLE => Whether the user who has been granted permission can further grant the privileges to other users. YES implies can further grant the privileges and NO indicates cannot further grant the privileges.

14.8 REVOKING OR WITHDRAWING GRANTED PRIVILEGES

The privileges granted can be revoked or withdrawn by using the REVOKE command.

Suppose Scott user wants to withdraw the insert permission on the student table from John user (Figure 14.15).

```
SQL> revoke insert on student from john;

Revoke succeeded.

SQL>select * from user_tab_privs_made;
```

GRANTEE	TABLE_NAME	GRANTOR	PRIVILEGE	GRANTABLE
JOHN	STUDENT	SCOTT	SELECT	YES
SUSE	STUDENT	JOHN	SELECT	NO

Figure 14.15 Withdrawing permissions.

14.9 GRANTING PRIVILEGES ON SPECIFIC COLUMNS

The privileges can be granted on specific columns of a table also. Suppose Scott wants to permit John user to be able to perform update on name column of the student table (Figure 14.16).

```
SQL> grant update(name) on student to john;
Grant succeeded.

SQL>select * from user_col_privs_made;
```

GRANTEE	TABLE_NAME	COLUMN_NAME	GRANTOR	PRIVILEGE	GRANTABLE
JOHN	STUDENT	NAME	SCOTT	UPDATE	NO

Figure 14.16 Granting column level permissions.

REVIEW QUESTIONS

1. What does privilege mean?
2. Can a user grant permissions on objects owned by other users?
3. What is the difference between granting permission to ALL users and ALL operations?
4. How can a user grant permission to another user in such a way that the grantee can further cascade the permissions onto other users?
5. List the various Data Dictionary views which contain information about the privileges given and received.
6. Which command is used to withdraw permissions on objects?
7. Is it possible to grant privileges on columns of a table instead of on the entire table?

LAB ASSIGNMENT

1. Create two new users named "PATRICK" with password "PATRICK" and "JONATHAN" with password "JONATHAN" using SQL*Plus. Grant them sufficient privileges so that they can create, drop, alter tables and perform DML operations in their respective areas/schema.
2. Log in as "PATRICK" and create the CUSTOMER ORDER table as specified in Lab Assignment of Chapter 7.
3. Permit the "JONATHAN" user to be able to INSERT and DELETE records from the CUSTOMER table.
4. Log in as "JONATHAN" and perform some INSERT and DELETE commands on the CUSTOMER table in PATRICK schema.
5. Log in as "JONATHAN" and allow all the database users to have SELECT permission on the CUSTOMER table.
6. Grant the INSERT permission to "JONATHAN" such that "JONATHAN" can further grant the INSERT permission to other database users.
7. "PATRICK" wants to know all the privileges he has extended to other users.
8. "PATRICK" wants to withdraw the DELETE permission from all users.
9. "PATRICK" wants to give the UPDATE permission on ADDRESS and STATE column of the CUSTOMER table to "JONATHAN".

CHAPTER

15

Oracle Security—Roles

15.1 INTRODUCTION

In Chapter 14 we learned about how we can grant and revoke permissions. Let us turn our attention to an object called "Role" which is basically a group of permissions assigned to a single name. All the permissions granted to a role can be allocated to any user just by assigning the single role name to that user.

A user must have permission for creating roles. Log in as "sys" user to grant permission to "scott" user for creating role as shown in Figure 15.1.

```
SQL> connect sys/sys@xe as sysdba
Connected.
SQL> grant create role to scott;
Grant succeeded.
```

Figure 15.1 Allowing SCOTT user to create roles.

15.2 CREATING ROLE AND ASSIGNING PRIVILEGES TO ROLE

Log in as "scott" to create a role and assign certain privileges to that role (Figure 15.2).

```
SQL> create role role_operator;
Role created.
SQL> grant select, insert, update on student to role_operator;
Grant succeeded.
```

Figure 15.2 Creating role.

Here we have created a role for operators named "role_operator" and assigned select, insert, update permissions to it.

15.3   ASSIGNING ROLE TO USERS

If "scott" user needs to assign the same set of privileges to a number of users then instead of using multiple privileges, one for each user, the users can be assigned roles. Figure 15.3 shows how to grant roles to users.

```
SQL> grant role_operator to john;

Grant succeeded.

SQL> grant role_operator to suse;

Grant succeeded.
```

Figure 15.3   Granting roles to users.

The "john" and "suse" users have been granted select, insert, update permissions on scott's student table.

15.4   REVOKING PRIVILEGES FROM ROLE

Let us revoke update permission from "role_operator" role (Figure 15.4).

```
SQL> revoke update on student from role_operator;

Revoke succeeded.
```

Figure 15.4   Revoking privileges from role.

15.5   DROPPING ROLES

Roles can be removed from database with the Drop Role command as shown in Figure 15.5.

```
SQL> drop role role_operator;

Role dropped.
```

Figure 15.5   Removing roles.

15.6   PASSING ON ROLES TO OTHER USERS

Grantor can grant role to a user such that the grantee can further grant those roles to other users provided grantor assigns the specified role with admin option (Figure 15.6).

```
SQL> create role role_operator;

Role created.

SQL> grant select, insert on student to role_operator;

Grant succeeded.

SQL> grant role_operator to john with admin option;

Grant succeeded.
```

Figure 15.6   Grantor granting role with admin option.

As "scott" has assigned role with admin option, therefore, john can pass on the "role_operator" to other users as shown in Figure 15.7.

```
SQL> connect john/john@xe
Connected.

SQL> grant role_operator to suse;

Grant succeeded.

SQL> connect suse/suse@xe
Connected.

SQL> select * from scott.student;
```

ROLLNO	NAME	CITY
1	satish	BHOPAL
2	rashmi	AJMER
3	rishi	BHOPAL
4	shama	AJMER
5	nilesh	DELHI

Figure 15.7   Grantee further granting the role to other users.

15.7   GRANTING PRIVILEGES ON SPECIFIC COLUMNS TO ROLES

If we want to assign update permission on name column of student table to john, then we will assign the required permission to role "role_operator". Since role_operator is already assigned to "john", therefore, "john" will get the update permission in turn. Figure 15.8 shows how to grant privilege on specific columns to roles.

```
SQL> grant update (name) on student to role_operator;
Grant succeeded.
```

Figure 15.8   Privilege on specific columns.

Caution: Before granting a column-specific INSERT privilege, determine if the table contains any columns on which NOT NULL constraints are defined. Granting selective insert capability without including the NOT NULL columns prevents the user from inserting any rows into the table. To avoid this situation, make sure that each NOT NULL column is either insertable or has a non-NULL default value. Otherwise, the grantee will not be able to insert rows into the table and will receive an error.

15.8   DATA DICTIONARY FOR ROLES

Data Dictionary table "user_role_privs" can be queried to know all the roles which are owned by the user "scott" as shown in Figure 15.9.

```
SQL> select * from user_role_privs;
```

USERNAME	GRANTED_ROLE	ADM	DEF	OS_
SCOTT	CONNECT	NO	YES	NO
SCOTT	RESOURCE	NO	YES	NO
SCOTT	ROLE_OPERATOR	YES	YES	NO

Figure 15.9   Data Dictionary for roles.

Here "scott" has been granted CONNECT and RESOURCE roles which are Oracle's built-in roles. We will learn more about these predefined roles at the end of this chapter. "scott" also owns a role named "role_operator" which contains select, insert, update on the student table. This information can be found in "user_tab_privs" Data Dictionary table (Figure 15.10).

```
SQL> select * from user_tab_privs order by grantee;
```

GRANTEE	OWNER	TABLE_NAME	GRANTOR	PRIVILEGE	GRA	HIE
ROLE_OPERATOR	SCOTT	STUDENT	SCOTT	INSERT	NO	NO
ROLE_OPERATOR	SCOTT	STUDENT	SCOTT	SELECT	NO	NO
ROLE_OPERATOR	SCOTT	STUDENT	SCOTT	UPDATE	NO	NO

Figure 15.10   Data Dictionary for privileges.

To view all the privileges assigned to "scott" user, query "user_sys_privs" is shown in Figure 15.11.

```
SQL> select * from user_sys_privs;
```

USERNAME	PRIVILEGE	ADM
SCOTT	CREATE DATABASE LINK	NO
SCOTT	CREATE SYNONYM	NO
SCOTT	CREATE ROLE	NO
SCOTT	CREATE VIEW	NO
SCOTT	CREATE TYPE	NO
SCOTT	CREATE MATERIALIZED VIEW	NO
SCOTT	CREATE PROCEDURE	NO

SCOTT	UNLIMITED TABLESPACE	NO
SCOTT	CREATE PUBLIC SYNONYM	NO
SCOTT	CREATE TABLE	NO
SCOTT	CREATE TRIGGER	NO
SCOTT	CREATE SEQUENCE	NO

Figure 15.11 Data Dictionary for all privileges.

15.9 PRE-DEFINED ROLES

Oracle provides three pre-defined roles, namely CONNECT, RESOURCE and DBA.

15.9.1 CONNECT Role

The user will only be able to CONNECT to the Oracle database. The only privilege given is CREATE SESSION. The user cannot create objects like Tables, Views, etc. This role becomes meaningful only with the addition of access to specific tables belonging to other users and the privileges to select, insert, update and delete rows in these tables.

Let us create a user named "xeno" who is not assigned any role (Figure 15.12).

```
SQL> connect sys/sys@xe as sysdba;
Connected.
SQL> create user xeno identified by xeno;

User created.

SQL> connect xeno/xeno@xe
ERROR:
ORA-01045: user XENO lacks CREATE SESSION privilege; logon denied


Warning: You are no longer connected to ORACLE.
```

Figure 15.12 Creating new user "xeno".

Note that "xeno" user does not have the permission to even CONNECT to the Oracle database.

Let us now grant CONNECT role to "xeno" (Figure 15.13) so that he is able to log in to the Oracle database.

```
SQL> connect sys/sys@xe as sysdba;
Connected.
SQL> grant connect to xeno;

Grant succeeded.

SQL> connect xeno/xeno@xe
Connected.
```

Figure 15.13 Allowing XENO to CONNECT to Oracle database.

"xeno" is now able to connect to the Oracle database.

But he cannot create any object (Figure 15.14) as he still does not have the RESOURCE ROLE assigned.

```
SQL> create table a (a number);
create table a(a number)
      *
ERROR at line 1:
ORA-01031: insufficient privileges
```

Figure 15.14   XENO cannot create objects.

15.9.2   RESOURCE Role

Assigning the RESOURCE role to a user provides the following privileges.

CREATE DATABASE LINK
CREATE SYNONYM
CREATE ROLE
CREATE VIEW
CREATE TYPE
CREATE MATERIALIZED VIEW
CREATE PROCEDURE
CREATE PUBLIC SYNONYM
CREATE TABLE
CREATE TRIGGER
CREATE SEQUENCE

The RESOURCE Role is used for normal users who are allowed to create various objects.

Let us assign RESOURCE role to "xeno" user so that he can create tables (Figure 15.15).

```
SQL> connect sys/sys@xe as sysdba;
Connected.
SQL> grant RESOURCE to xeno;

Grant succeeded.

SQL> connect xeno/xeno@xe
Connected.
SQL> create table a(a number);

Table created.
```

Figure 15.15   Allowing XENO to create objects.

Note: "role_sys_privs" data dictionary can be used to see all the ROLES and the corresponding privileges assigned to a user.

15.9.3   DBA Role

The DBA role implies all system privileges WITH ADMIN OPTION. A user with the DBA role assigned can grant all privileges to any user. He can create, alter and drop users. He can insert, update, delete, drop other users objects. "sys" user that we have been using till now for creating users has the DBA role assigned to it. Any normal user can be extended the DBA role (Figure 15.16).

```
SQL> connect sys/sys@xe as sysdba;
Connected.
SQL>
SQL> grant DBA to scott;

Grant succeeded.

SQL> connect scott/scott@xe as sysdba;
Connected.
SQL> create user jane identified by jane;

User created.
```

Figure 15.16   Granting DBA role to normal users.

Here "scott" has been assigned the "DBA" role by "sys" user. Now "scott" can also perform all the operations just as the "sys" user.

Caution: Avoid granting the DBA role to normal users. DBA can drop an entire database user with all the objects owned by him in a single command.

REVIEW QUESTIONS

1. What do we mean by a ROLE?
2. How is a ROLE different from a PRIVILEGE?
3. What privileges must a user have in order to be able to CREATE ROLES? Who can assign this privilege?
4. Under what circumstances ROLES should be created instead of assigning privileges to individual database users?
5. Specify the steps of defining new roles and then assigning them to users.
6. Is it possible for other users to use the roles created by other users?
7. Explain the purpose of various Pre-defined Roles.

LAB ASSIGNMENT

Refer to Table 7.1 of the CUSTOMER ORDER database and Lab Assignment of Chapter 14.

1. Log in as Oracle DBA and assign privilege for creating roles to "PATRICK" user.
2. Log in as "PATRICK" and create a new role named "ROLE_MODIFY".

3. Assign INSERT and UPDATE privilege on the CUSTOMER table to the new role. Also add the provision of UPDATE on NAME column of PRODUCT table. Allocate the new role to "JONATHAN".

4. Modify the role such that "JONATHAN" can further grant the role to other users.

5. Remove the UPDATE privilege on the CUSTOMER table from the role.

6. Remove the role "ROLE_MODIFY".

CHAPTER 16

Sequences and Synonyms

16.1 SEQUENCES

16.1.1 Introduction

Oracle supports an object called SEQUENCE which can be used to generate numbers in a sequence. This can be used to generate values for primary keys.

16.1.2 Creating Sequence

Sequences can be created using the CREATE SEQUENCE command which has the following syntax:

```
CREATE SEQUENCE <sequence-name>
START WITH <integer-value>
INCREMENT BY <integer-value>
MAXVALUE <integer-value> OR NOMAXVALUE
MINVALUE <integer-value> OR NOMINVALUE
CYCLE OR NOCYCLE
CACHE OR NOCACHE
ORDER OR NOORDER
```

START WITH <integer-value>:   Specify the 1st sequence number to be generated.

INCREMENT BY <integer-value>:   The integer number by which sequence number should be incremented for generating the next number. If it is positive then values are ascending and if it is negative then values are descending. The default value is 1.

MAXVALUE <integer-value>:   If the increment value is positive then MAXVALUE determines the maximum value up to which the sequence numbers will be generated.

NOMAXVALUE: Specifies a maximum value of 10^27 for an ascending sequence or –1 for a descending sequence.

MINVALUE <integer-value>:   If the increment value is negative then MINVALUE determines the minimum value up to which the sequence numbers will be generated.

NOMINVALUE: Specifies a minimum value of 1 for an ascending sequence and –10^26 for a descending sequence.

CYCLE: Causes the sequences to automatically recycle to minvalue when maxvalue is reached for ascending sequences; for descending sequences, it causes a recycle from minvalue back to maxvalue.

NOCYCLE: Sequence numbers will not be generated after reaching the maximum value for ascending sequences or minimum value for descending sequences.

CACHE: Specifies how many values are pre-allocated in buffers for faster access. Default value is 20.

NOCACHE: Sequence numbers are not pre-allocated.

ORDER: Generates the numbers in a serial order.

NORDER: Generates the numbers in a random order.

We will create a sequence named "SEQ_EMPNO" with certain parameters as shown in Figure 16.1.

```
SQL>create sequence seq_empno
    start with 1000
    increment by 1
    maxvalue 9999
    nocycle
    cache 2
    order
    /
Sequence created.
```

Figure 16.1   Creating sequence object.

16.1.3   Initializing Sequence

A sequence needs to be initialized before being used. Every sequence is initialized by a pseudo-column NEXTVAL. Initialization means the START WITH <value> is assigned to the sequence (Figure 16.2).

```
SQL> select seq_empno.nextval from dual;
        NEXTVAL
          1000
```

Figure 16.2 Initializing sequence.

16.1.4 Determining the Last Running Sequence Number

We can query the sequence for the currently held value by using the pseudo-column CURRVAL meaning current value as shown in Figure 16.3.

```
SQL> select seq_empno.currval from dual;
        CURRVAL
          1000
```

Figure 16.3 Current value in sequence.

16.1.5 Accessing the Successive Sequence Values

The consecutive sequence values can be accessed by using the NEXTVAL pseudo-column. NEXTVAL increments the previous value in sequence object by the value specified in INCREMENT BY clause (Figure 16.4).

```
SQL> select seq_empno.nextval from dual;
        NEXTVAL
          1001
```

Figure 16.4 Consecutive sequence values.

Example: Assume that we want to generate EMPNO whenever a new employee joins the company without having to remember the EMPNO allotted to last employee hired. We will use the sequence created in Figure 16.1 for assigning the EMPNO to new employees. Figure 16.5 shows how to use sequence for EMPNO values.

```
SQL> insert into emp(empno,ename,sal,comm,deptno) values
(seq_empno.nextval,'SATISH',8000,500,10);

1 row created.

SQL> select * from emp;
```

EMPNO	ENAME	JOB	MGR	HIREDATE	SAL	COMM	DEPTNO
1002	SATISH	–	–	–	8000	500	10

Figure 16.5 Using sequence in INSERT command.

Here we have used the sequence.nextval for accessing the next serial number.

16.1.6   Modifying Sequence

It may be required later on to change certain parameters of an already created sequence. Suppose we want to change the INCREMENT value to 2 instead of 1 which we defined at the time of sequence creation (Figure 16.1). Figure 16.6 uses the ALTER SEQUENCE command for modifying sequence parameters.

```
SQL> alter sequence seq_empno INCREMENT BY 2;
Sequence altered.

SQL> select seq_empno.currval from dual;

    CURRVAL
       1002

SQL> select seq_empno.nextval from dual;

    NEXTVAL
       1004
```

Figure 16.6   Altering sequence parameters.

16.1.7   Data Dictionary for Sequences

All the sequences along with the values of various parameters are stored in data dictionary table "USER_SEQUENCES" as shown in Figure 16.7.

```
SQL>select * from user_sequences;
```

SEQUENCE NAME	MIN VALUE	MAX VALUE	INCREMENT BY	CYCLE FLAG	ORDER FLAG	CACHE SIZE	LAST NUMBER
SEQ_EMPNO	1	9999	2	N	Y	2	1008

Figure 16.7   Data dictionary for sequences.

16.1.8   Dropping Sequence

The DROP sequence-name can be used to remove the sequence object from the database (Figure 16.8).

```
SQL> drop sequence seq_empno;
Sequence dropped.
```

Figure 16.8   Removing sequence from database.

16.2   SYNONYMS

16.2.1   Introduction

Synonyms are alternative names for an existing object which are permanently stored in database. We have used alias names for accessing tables with shorter names in various queries of Chapter 11.

The difference is that these alias names are of temporary nature and are lost from one query to another, whereas synonyms are permanent alias names for objects.

The various objects for which synonyms can be created are as follows.

- Tables
- Views
- Materialized views
- Stored function
- Stored procedures
- Packages
- Sequences
- Synonyms

16.2.2 Who Can Create Synonyms?

A user who has CREATE SYNONYM privilege can create the synonyms.

Let us login as SYS DBA and grant CREATE SYNONYM privilege to SCOTT user (Figure 16.9).

```
SQL> connect sys/sys@xe as sysdba
Connected.

SQL> grant create synonym to scott;
Grant succeeded.
```

Figure 16.9 Allowing SCOTT to create synonym.

Now SCOTT user can create and use synonyms.

Let us create a synonym named "EMPLOYEE" for "EMP" table as shown in Figure 16.10.

```
SQL> create synonym EMPLOYEE for EMP;
Synonym created.
SQL>select * from emp;
```

EMPNO	ENAME	JOB	MGR	HIREDATE	SAL	COMM	DEPTNO
7369	SMITH	CLERK	7902	17-DEC-80	800	–	20
7499	ALLEN	SALESMAN	7698	20-FEB-81	1600	300	30

....

```
SQL>select * from employee;
```

EMPNO	ENAME	JOB	MGR	HIREDATE	SAL	COMM	DEPTNO
7369	SMITH	CLERK	7902	17-DEC-80	800	–	20
7499	ALLEN	SALESMAN	7698	20-FEB-81	1600	300	30

Figure 16.10 Creating synonym.

Now EMP and EMPLOYEE are referring to the same table EMP. All DDL, DML operations can be performed on EMPLOYEE synonym just as if they are being performed on EMP table.

16.2.3 Granting Privileges

Granting privileges on the SYNONYM grants the privileges on the actual object.

Suppose SCOTT user gives SELECT permission on EMPLOYEE synonym to JOHN user then JOHN user will actually be given the specified permission on both the synonym and the actual table (Figure 16.11).

```
SQL>connect scott/tiger@xe
SQL> grant select on employee to john;
Grant succeeded.

SQL> connect john/john@xe
Connected.
SQL> select * from scott.employee;
```

EMPNO	ENAME	JOB	MGR	HIREDATE	SAL	COMM	DEPTNO
7369	SMITH	CLERK	7902	17-DEC-80	800	–	20
7499	ALLEN	SALESMAN	7698	20-FEB-81	1600	300	30

```
SQL> select * from scott.emp;
```

EMPNO	ENAME	JOB	MGR	HIREDATE	SAL	COMM	DEPTNO
7369	SMITH	CLERK	7902	17-DEC-80	800	–	20
7499	ALLEN	SALESMAN	7698	20-FEB-81	1600	300	30

Figure 16.11   Granting privilege on synonym.

JOHN can refer to the SCOTT's EMP table using SCOTT.EMP or SCOTT.EMPLOYEE because both are actually referring to the same table EMP.

Permission on SYNONYM EMPLOYEE has actually been granted on EMP table.

If SCOTT grants SELECT privilege on EMP table to JOHN then it is advisable that JOHN user creates the SYNONYM for SCOTT's EMP table in his area so that he does not need to qualify EMPLOYEE table with SCOTT username as "SCOTT.EMPLOYEE" for referring to SCOTT's EMP table (Figure 16.12).

```
SQL> connect scott/tiger@xe
Connected.
SQL> grant select on emp to john;
Grant succeeded.

SQL> connect john/john@xe
Connected.

  QL> create synonym EMPLOYEE for scott.emp;
  ynonym created.

SQL> select * from employee;
```

EMPNO	ENAME	JOB	MGR	HIREDATE	SAL	COMM	DEPTNO
7369	SMITH	CLERK	7902	17-DEC-80	800	–	20

Figure 16.12   Grantee(John) creating synonym for grantors(Scott) table.

Note that now JOHN has specified just the Synonym Name for accessing SCOTT's EMP table.

16.2.4   Data Dictionary for Synonyms

"USER_SYNONYMS" is the data dictionary for synonyms (Figure 16.13).

SQL>select * from *user_synonyms*;			
SYNONYM_NAME	**TABLE_OWNER**	**TABLE_NAME**	**DB_LINK**
EMPLOYEE	SCOTT	EMP	–

Figure 16.13   Data dictionary for synonyms.

16.2.5   Dropping Synonyms

The DROP SYNONYM command can be used to remove synonym (Figure 16.14).

```
SQL>drop synonym employee;
Synonym Dropped
```

Figure 16.14   Removing synonym.

Caution: Dropping SYNONYM will not drop the actual table.
    Dropping an actual object will not drop the synonyms but all operations using synonyms will fail indicating that the synonym is not valid.

CHAPTER 17

Views and Materialized Views

17.1 INTRODUCTION

Till now we have learned about creating, inserting, updating, deleting, dropping and altering of tables. A table is just one of the several objects supported by oracle. Let us study an object called "VIEW".

Before learning about views, the "scott" user should have the permission of creating views. Granting permission to normal users like "scott" for creating various objects is the task of "sys" oracle user which is known as the DBA (Database Administrator). So let us login as "sys" and permit "scott" user for creating views.

Go To -> Start -> Programs -> Oracle Database 10g Express Edition ->.

Go To Database Home Page -> Supply username as sys and password as sys. -> Administration -> Database Users -> Click "SCOTT" -> You will be presented with Figure 17.1.

Check that all the checkboxes in the "User Privileges" section are ticked.

Click "Alter User" button on topright corner of the Manage Database User' section.

Now user "scott" has got the permission of creating various objects like SYNONYMS, TYPE, VIEWS, MATERIALIZED VIEWS, ROLE, PROCEDURE, SEQUENCE, TRIGGER, etc.

Alternatively, we can use the command line interface for creating a new user (Refer to Figure 2.12 of Chapter 2). By default normal users do not have the privilege of creating views. So DBA has to permit "scott" user to be able to create views.

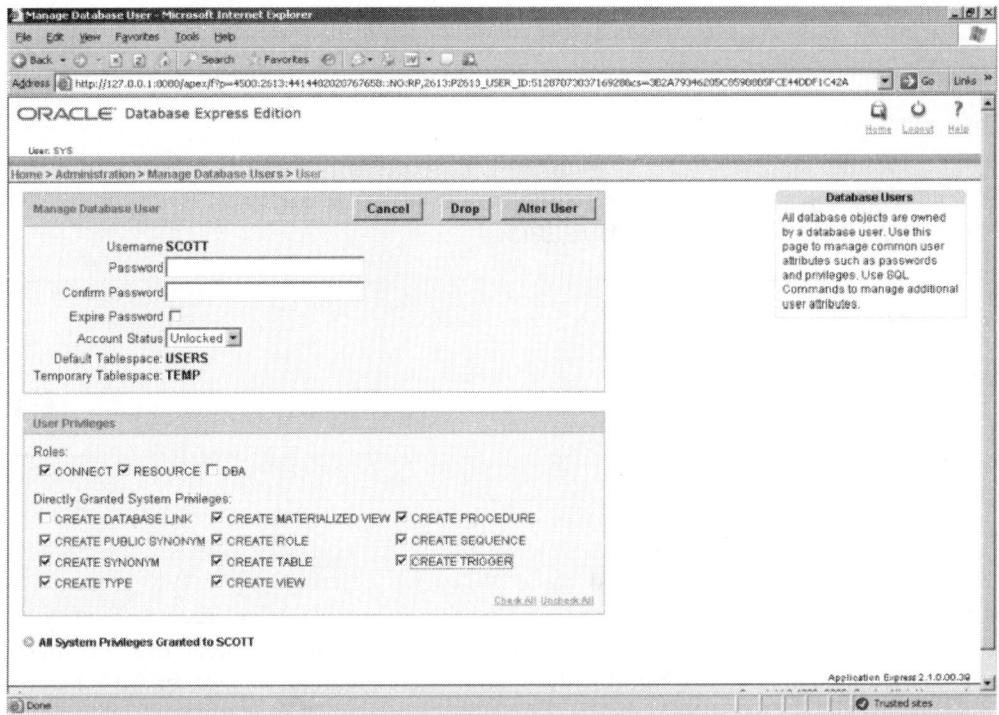

Figure 17.1 New User Creation Screen.

17.2 VIEW—CREATING AND ACCESSING

A view is a pre-defined query on one or more tables. Let us understand it with an example.

Return to "SQL Prompt" of "scott" user.

Assume "student" table with columns and records as shown in Figure 17.2.

SQL> select * from student;			
COLLE	**ROLLNO**	**NAME**	**MARKS**
GEC	1	satish	25
GEC	2	nilesh	23
OIST	3	rashmi	21
OIST	4	piyush	13
GEC	5	ruchi	30

Figure 17.2 STUDENT table.

We want that the examiner who is checking the copies has access to just rollno and marks. He should not have access to college and name column. Instead of creating a separate table for examiners we will create a VIEW comprising of just rollno and marks field from "student" table (Figure 17.3).

```
SQL> create view vw_student as select rollno,marks from student;

View created.

SQL> desc vw_student;

        Name                    Null?                   Type
        ROLLNO                  NOT NULL                NUMBER(4)
        MARKS                   NUMBER(3)

SQL> select * from vw_student;

        ROLLNO          MARKS
        1               25
        2               23
        3               21
        4               13
        5               30
```

Figure 17.3   Creating view.

Here "vw_student" is user-defined name. When we described view "vw_student", oracle shows that it has only two columns rollno and marks. When we select records from view, the records were actually fetched from the actual table "student". What we mean to say is that oracle just stores the SQL statement specified at the time of view creation. Whenever we select records from view, oracle internally fetches records from underlying table "student". Such tables are called **"base"** tables because they form a base from which views are created. The actual data resides in the base tables only. **In other words, view can be thought of as a pre-defined query**.

17.3   CHANGING THE NAMES OF COLUMNS IN A VIEW

We can assign different names to columns of base tables in a view as shown in Figure 17.4.

```
SQL> create view vw_student_new as select rollno enroll_no,marks marks_obtained from
student;

Table created.

SQL> desc vw_student_new;

        Name                    Null?                   Type
        ENROLL_NO                                       NUMBER(4)
        MARKS_OBTAINED                                  NUMBER(3)

SQL> select * from vw_student_new;

        ENROLL_NO                       MARKS_OBTAINED
        1                               25
        2                               23
        3                               21
        4                               13
        5       .                       30
```

Figure 17.4   Assigning different names in views to columns of base table.

Here we have assigned "enroll_no" name to "rollno" column of "student" table and "marks_obtained" to "marks".

Now the "scott" user can give permissions to "examiner" user for inserting, updating and deleting just the rollno and marks column. The "examiner" user will not know the actual table name and the actual field names of the base table. The "examiner" cannot know the college and name of any student.

Let us now create a new Oracle user called "examiner".

Go To -> Start -> Programs -> Oracle Database 10g Express Edition ->.

Go To Database Home Page -> Supply username as sys and password as sys. -> Administration -> Database Users -> Click "Create" Button. You will be presented with Figure 17.5.

Type Username as "examiner"
Password as "examiner"
Confirm Password as "examiner"

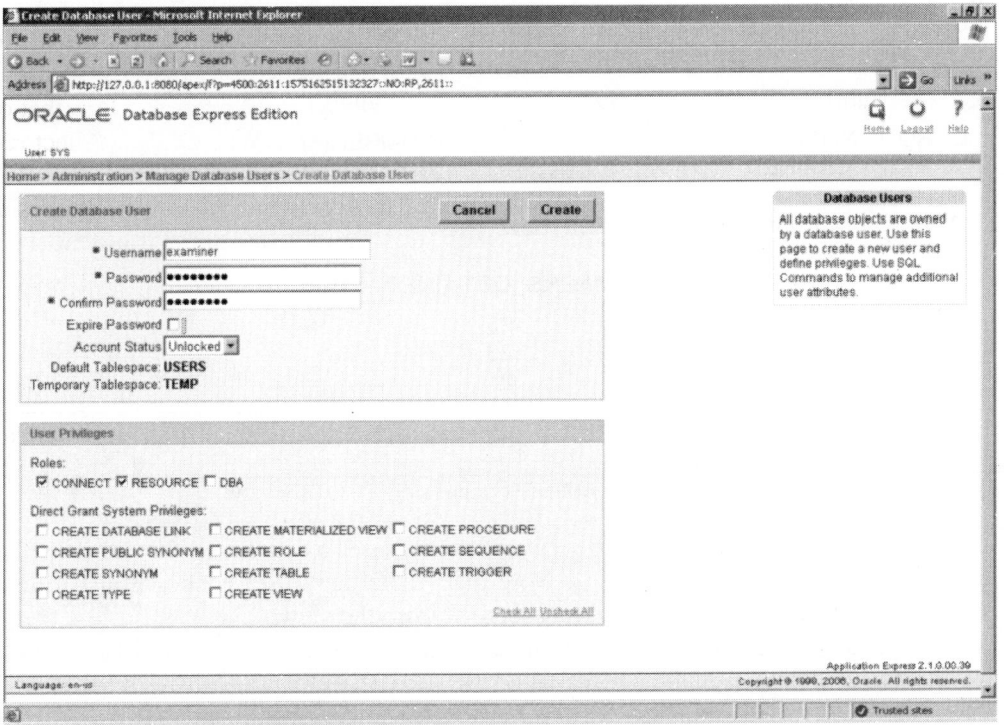

Figure 17.5 New user creation screen.

Click the "Create" button.

Now we will log in as "scott" and grant permission to "examiner" for viewing records from view "vw_student_new" (See Figure 17.6).

```
SQL>connect scott/tiger@xe

Connected

SQL> grant select,insert,update,delete on vw_student_new to examiner;

Grant succeeded.
```

Figure 17.6   Granting permission on view to examiner.

Lets first create the user "examiner"
Again login as "sys" user.
Now connect as "examiner" user and issue the commands as shown in Figure 17.7.

```
SQL> connect examiner/examiner@xe
Connected.
SQL>
SQL>
SQL>
SQL> desc scott.vw_student_new;
```

Name	Null?	Type
ENROLL_NO		NUMBER(4)
MARKS_OBTAINED		NUMBER(3)

```
SQL> select * from scott.vw_student_new;
```

ENROLL_NO	MARKS_OBTAINED
1	25
2	23
3	21
4	13
5	30

Figure 17.7   EXAMINER accessing SCOTT's view.

Here, "examiner" user can refer to views of "scott" user by prefixing the username before the view name ("scott.vw_student_new"). Note that "examiner" user is shown just rollno and marks column while describing and selecting records from the view.

Let us see how "examiner" can insert, update and delete records (Figure 17.8).

```
SQL> insert into scott.vw_student_new values (6,33);
1 row created.

SQL>commit;
Commit complete.

SQL> select * from scott.vw_student_new;
```

ENROLL_NO	MARKS_OBTAINED
1	25
2	23
3	21
4	13
5	30
6	33

6 rows selected.

Figure 17.8 DML operations on SCOTT's view.

Again connect to the "scott" user and select data from "vw_student_new" view and student table as shown in Figure 17.9.

```
SQL> connect scott/scott@xe
Connected.
SQL> select * from vw_student_new;
```

ENROLL_NO	MARKS_OBTAINED
1	25
2	23
3	21
4	13
5	30
6	33

6 rows selected.

```
SQL> select * from student;
```

COLLE	ROLLNO	NAME	MARKS
GEC	1	satish	25
GEC	2	nilesh	23
OIST	3	rashmi	21
OIST	4	piyush	13
GEC	5	ruchi	30
	6		33

6 rows selected.

Figure 17.9 SCOTT accessing base table and view.

Note:
1. The "examiner" user added rollno 6 with marks 33 in scott's view which actually got inserted in "student" table. Since "examiner" user did not have permission to insert college and name, therefore, NULL values were inserted into college and name columns.
2. Only "scott" user can provide college and name to a rollno.
3. The same logic is applied to update and delete operations.

Conclusion
1. A view is a pre-defined query on one or more tables.
2. Retrieving information from a view is done in the same manner as retrieving from a table.
3. With some views you can also perform DML operations (delete, insert, and update) on the base tables (discussed in section 17.4.1).
4. Views do not store data, they only access rows in the base tables—avoid data redundancy.
5. View can hide the underlying base tables and columns—data security.
6. By writing complex queries as a view, we can hide complexity from an end user.
7. View only allows a user to access certain rows in the base tables. We can create a view with the "WHERE" clause also.

17.4 CLASSIFICATION OF VIEWS

Views can be classified as updateable views and non-updateable views.

17.4.1 Updateable Views

By updateable we mean to say that one can insert, update, and delete records from view. Actually all the DML operations are performed on the base table.
View with the following characteristics is called an updateable view.

1. It is created from a single table.
2. It includes all the PRIMARY KEYS and NOT NULL columns of base table.
3. Aggregate functions like SUM,AVG,MAX have not been used.
4. It should not have DISTINCT, GROUP BY, HAVING clauses.
5. It must not use constants, strings or value expressions like salary * 2.
6. It must not contain function calls (e.g. RPAD, SUBSTR, etc.).
7. If a view is defined from another view then that view must also be updateable.

17.4.2 Non-updateable Views

Non-updateable means we cannot insert, update, delete records from that view.
View with the following characteristics is called a non-updateable view.

1. It is created from more than one table.
2. It has DISTINCT, GROUP BY, HAVING clause. Even if view is derived from single table but contains any of these clauses then it is not updateable.
3. It does not include all the PRIMARY KEYS and NOT NULL columns of base tables.

17.5 VIEW FROM MULTIPLE TABLES

Views can be created from more than one table but such views are not updateable. Non-updateable means that we cannot INSERT, UPDATE or DELETE records for such views. Even if we include all the PRIMARY KEYS, NOT NULL columns of all the base tables then also such views are not updateable.

Let us create a view from student_master and student_details having the following columns:

Rollno   Name   Total_marks

where rollno and name will be from student_master table.

Total_marks will be sum of marks obtained in all subjects by a particular student from student_details table (Figure 17.10).

```
SQL> create or replace view vw_student_new as
  2  select a.rollno,a.name,sum(b.marks) total_marks
  3  from student_master a,student_details b
  4  where a.rollno=b.rollno
  5  group by a.rollno,a.name;

View created.

SQL> desc vw_student_new;
```

Name	Null?	Type
ROLLNO	NUMBER(4)	
NAME	VARCHAR2(10)	
TOTAL_MARKS	NUMBER	

```
SQL> select * from vw_student_new;
```

ROLLNO	NAME	TOTAL_MARKS
1	satish	35
5	nilesh	20
2	rashmi	35
3	rishi	34
4	shama	43

Figure 17.10 View from multiple tables.

Firstly, we have used the "create or replace view vw_student_new" command which means that create the view even if it is already existing by the same name. In other words, if the view with the name "vw_student_new" is already existing then it will be over-written with the new select statement.

Secondly, we have supplied an alias name "total_marks" to the sum(b.marks) field. Views containing AGGREGATE functions like SUM must provide alias names to columns being aggregated.

17.5.1 Inserting into Non-updateable Views

Let us try to insert new record into the view "vw_student_new" as shown in Figure 17.11.

```
SQL> insert into vw_student_new values (6,'test',40);
insert into vw_student_new values (6,'test',40)
     *
ERROR at line 1:
ORA-01779: cannot modify a column which maps to a non key-preserved table
```

Figure 17.11 Inserting records into non-updateable views.

Oracle gives error message if we try to insert records into non-updateable views.

17.5.2   Updating Non-updateable Views

Let us perform UPDATE operation on non-updateable view (Figure 17.12).

```
SQL> update vw_student_new set total_marks=100 where rollno=1;
update vw_student_new set total_marks=100 where rollno=1
      *
ERROR at line 1:
ORA-01732: data manipulation operation not legal on this view
```

Figure 17.12   Updating column values of non-updateable views.

17.5.3   Deleting from Non-updateable Views

Let us perform DELETE operation on Non-updateable view (Figure 17.13).

```
SQL> delete from vw_student_new where rollno=1;
delete from vw_student_new where rollno=1
      *
ERROR at line 1:
ORA-01732: data manipulation operation not legal on this view
```

Figure 17.13   Deleting records from non-updateable views.

Since the view is based on more than one table and uses aggregate functions, therefore, DML operations like INSERT, UPDATE and DELETE cannot be performed.

17.6   AUTOMATIC/ONLINE REFLECTION OF DATA IN VIEWS

The most important aspect of views is that there is an immediate reflection of changes in base table data onto the view.

Suppose we update the marks of MATHS subject of rollno 1 to 50 and select records from the view (Figure 17.14).

```
SQL> select * from vw_student_new;

    ROLLNO        NAME        TOTAL_MARKS
         1        satish               35
         5        nilesh               20
         2        rashmi               35
         3        rishi                34
         4        shama                43

SQL> update student_details set marks=50 where rollno=1 and subject='MATHS';
1 row updated.

SQL> select * from vw_student_new;
```

ROLLNO	NAME	TOTAL_MARKS
1	satish	73
5	nilesh	20
2	rashmi	35
3	rishi	34
4	shama	43

Figure 17.14 Updating base table values.

Note: The total marks for rollno 1 changed from 35 to 73 in view also.

17.7   DATA DICTIONARY TABLES FOR VIEWS

17.7.1   Identifying the Views Created by User

To know all the views that have been created by "scott" user we can select data from data dictionary table "user_objects" (See Figure 17.15).

```
SQL> select object_name,object_type,created from user_objects
  2* where object_type='VIEW';
```

OBJECT_NAME	OBJECT_TYPE	CREATED
VW_STUDENT_NEW	VIEW	26-MAR-08

Figure 17.15 Data dictionary for views.

17.7.2   Finding the Source Code of Views

The data dictionary table "user_views" contains the text used for creating the view as shown in Figure 17.16.

```
SQL> select view_name,text from user_views where view_name='VW_STUDENT_NEW';

VIEW_NAME

TEXT

VW_STUDENT_NEW
select a.rollno,a.name,sum(b.marks) total_marks
from student_master a,student_de
```

Figure 17.16 Source code of views.

Note that only 80 characters text of the view has been displayed. It is because the default display length of "long" data type is 80 in Oracle. The "text" column of "user_views" is of data type "long". We will have to increase it to display the entire text of view (See Figure 17.17).

```
SQL> set long 200
SQL> select view_name,text from user_views where view_name='VW_STUDENT_NEW';

VIEW_NAME

TEXT

VW_STUDENT_NEW
select a.rollno,a.name,sum(b.marks) total_marks
from student_master a,student_details b
where a.rollno=b.rollno
group by a.rollno,a.name
```

Figure 17.17 Increasing display width of LONG data type column.

Here we increased the display length of long data type to 200 instead of 80 which is default.

17.8 REMOVING VIEWS

Views can be removed by using the command "DROP VIEW" as in Figure 17.18.

```
SQL> drop view vw_student_new;

View dropped.

SQL> desc vw_student_new;
ERROR:
ORA-04043: object vw_student_new does not exist


SQL> select * from vw_student_new;
select * from vw_student_new
              *
ERROR at line 1:
ORA-00942: table or view does not exist
```

Figure 17.18 Removing a view.

17.9 MATERIALIZED VIEW

We have studied an object named "Views" which may be defined as a pre-defined query based on one or more tables. Whenever records are selected from a view the corresponding records are fetched from the base tables only. Now if the base tables have lakhs of records and the view produces summary information for the entire set of records then every time the view query is executed the records are fetched from the base tables, summarized columns calculated and the result displayed. This can become a bottleneck for the performance of database server.

Oracle10g/11g provides an object called Materialized View which stores the records fetched from base tables into its own area. When a materialized view is queried the records are fetched from the local copy of the records in the view which have already been fetched from base tables.

17.9.1 Differences between Normal Views and Materialized Views

Materialized views store a local copy of the base table records whereas normal views always fetch records from the base tables.

Any changes in the base tables are immediately reflected in the normal views. But changes made to the base tables are not reflected immediately in the materialized views. Although we can specify time intervals at which changes in base tables are reflected in the materialized view.

17.9.2 When to Use Materialized Views?

- When base tables have lakhs of records and summaries are executed against all or large number of records of base table quite frequently.
- The data does not change frequently. The volume of INSERT, UPDATE and DELETE operations is considerably low.
- Any changes in base tables need not be reflected immediately in view. There can be some minimum allowed time delay between the changes in base tables to be reflected in materialized view data.

17.9.3 Who Can Create Materialized Views?

A user must have "create materialized view" privilege. The Oracle DBA has to grant the required privilege to SCOTT user (Figure 17.19).

```
SQL> connect sys/sys@orcl11g as sysdba
Connected.
SQL> grant create materialized view to scott;
Grant succeeded.
```

Figure 17.19   Granting materialized view creation permission to SCOTT.

17.9.4 Creating Materialized Views

In its simplest form we can create materialized view without specifying any parameters as shown in Figure 17.20.

```
SQL>connect scott/tiger@orcl11g
Connected.

SQL> create materialized view mvw_emp_dept AS
select b.dept_name,sum(a.salary) salary,sum(a.commission) commission
from employee a,department b
where a.dept_no=b.dept_no
group by b.dept_name;

Materialized view created.

SQL> select * from mvw_emp_dept;
```

DEPT_NAME	SALARY	COMMISSION
MANUFACTURING	52700	2800
ENGINEERING	39300	1657
SALES	35500	1460

Figure 17.20   Creating materialized view.

Now let us add a new record in EMPLOYEE table and see whether the changes are reflected in materialized view (Figure 17.21).

```
SQL> insert into employee values (9999,'XEON','12-FEB-2008',15000,1200,10,1000);

1 row created.

SQL> commit;

Commit complete.

SQL> select * from mvw_emp_dept;
```

DEPT_NAME	SALARY	COMMISSION
MANUFACTURING	52700	2800
ENGINEERING	39300	1657
SALES	35500	1460

Figure 17.21   Changes in base table not automatically reflected in materialized view.

Caution: There has been no impact on the records in materialized view as it has **stored a local copy of the records from the two tables** at the time of view creation.

17.9.5   Refreshing the Materialized Views

What if we want to reflect the latest chances incorporated in the base tables in materialized view.

We will have to manually execute a command named REFRESH using the DBMS_MVIEW package so that materialized view reflects the latest status of records in base tables (Figure 17.22).

```
SQL> execute DBMS_MVIEW.REFRESH('MVW_EMP_DEPT','c');
PL/SQL procedure successfully completed.

SQL> select * from mvw_emp_dept;
```

DEPT_NAME	SALARY	COMMISSION
MANUFACTURING	67700	4000
ENGINEERING	39300	1657
SALES	35500	1460

Figure 17.22   Refreshing materialized view.

DBMS_MVIEW.REFRESH has two parameters: **Materialized View** and **REFRESH option**. REFRESH has 3 options, namely

1. fast ('f') – This option fetches only the changed records from base tables into materialized view.
2. complete('c') – Re-create the materialized view from scratch.
3. force('?c') – First attempt fast if fails then use complete.

Refreshing all materialized views

All Materialized Views can be refreshed in a single command as in Figure 17.23.

```
SQL>execute DBMS_MVIEW.REFRESH_ALL;
```

Figure 17.23 Refreshing all materialized views.

Options for materialized views

REFRESH: We have already seen the REFRESH option which can have 3 values: fast, complete and force. These options can be specified at the time of view creation also.

ON COMMIT: The changes in base tables are reflected in the materialized view when they are committed.

ON DEMAND: The changes in base tables are reflected in the materialized view only by manually using the REFRESH command.

FOR UPDATE: By default the materialized views are read-only. We can create updateable materialized view by using this option.

START WITH: The first time when the materialized view will be created. We can specify some date.

NEXT: The next time when the materialized view will be automatically refreshed.

Note: Materialized views can be automatically refreshed by using the START WITH <date> NEXT <date>.

Let us re-create the materialized view of Figure 17.20 with some of the options mentioned above as shown in Figure 17.24.

```
SQL>drop materialized view mvw_emp_dept ;
Materialized view dropped.

SQL>create materialized view mvw_emp_dept
REFRESH COMPLETE
START WITH SYSDATE NEXT SYSDATE+1
as
select b.dept_name,sum(a.salary) salary,sum(a.commission) commission
from employee a,department b
where a.dept_no=b.dept_no
group by b.dept_name;
```

Figure 17.24 Materialized view with some parameters.

START WITH SYSDATE NEXT SYSDATE+1: View will be created and refreshed right now (sysdate) and thereafter once every day at the same time (SYSDATE+1).

REFRESH COMPLETE: Every time the view is re-created.

Examples for refresh intervals

SYSDATE + 1/12 will refresh every 2 hr
SYSDATE + 1/24 will refresh every 1 hr
SYSDATE + 1/48 will refresh every 1/2 hr
SYSDATE + 1/96 will refresh every 15 minutes
SYSDATE + 1/192 will refresh every 7.5 minutes
SYSDATE + 1/384 will refresh every 3.25 minutes

NEXT NEXT_DAY(TRUNC(SYSDATE)),'MONDAY')+12/24 will refresh every Monday at noon. This finds the next Monday from current date, removes the time component (TRUNC) and adds 12-hours.

REVIEW QUESTIONS

1. Define view and explain its purpose.
2. What privilege a user must have in order to create views?
3. Is it possible to draw a view from multiple tables? Can a view be drawn from another view or a combination of base table and views?
4. How is it possible that the data in view reflects the dynamic addition, deletion or updated records of base tables?
5. What do we mean by updateable and non-updateable views? Explain with practical examples.
6. Why a view containing AGGREGATE functions is non-updateable?
7. Specify the data dictionary tables containing information about various views created by the user.
8. Does deleting a record from updateable view removes the record from base table?
9. Differentiate between normal views and materialized views. Under what circumstances should materialized views be preferred to normal views?
10. Which command is used to refresh the contents of materialized view manually?

LAB ASSIGNMENT

Refer to Table 7.1 of the CUSTOMER ORDER database
1. Create a view named "VW_CUST_BAL" which will display customer names with balances more than 4000.
2. Add a new customer named "AHUJA CO." with a balance of 6000 through the view "VW_CUST_BAL".
3. Create a view named "VW_CITY_BAL" which will contain citywise total balances.
4. Create a view "VW_CUST_QTY" to display Customer Namewise Product Categorywise total quantity ordered.(Product Category implies TV, CD, RF, etc.)
5. Create a view "VW_PRODUCT_QTY" to display Product Namewise average quantity of products ordered.

CHAPTER 18

SQL *Plus Reporting

18.1 INTRODUCTION

SQL*Plus is an extension to SQL language. SQL*Plus is a proprietary language of Oracle Corporation and supports all the features of Standard SQL. It has Reporting and Formatting capabilities for generating reports in a desired format.

Assume EMP table with records as in Figure 18.1.

EMPNO	ENAME	JOB	MGR	HIREDATE	SAL	COMM	DEPTNO
7369	SMITH	CLERK	7902	17-DEC-80	800	–	20
7499	ALLEN	SALESMAN	7698	20-FEB-81	1600	300	30
7521	WARD	SALESMAN	7698	22-FEB-81	1250	500	30
7566	JONES	MANAGER	7839	02-APR-81	2975	–	20
7654	MARTIN	SALESMAN	7698	28-SEP-81	1250	1400	30
7698	BLAKE	MANAGER	7839	01-MAY-81	2850	–	30
7782	CLARK	MANAGER	7839	09-JUN-81	2450	–	10
7788	SCOTT	ANALYST	7566	09-DEC-82	3000	–	20
7839	KING	PRESIDENT	–	17-NOV-81	5000	–	10
7844	TURNER	SALESMAN	7698	08-SEP-81	1500	0	30
7876	ADAMS	CLERK	7788	12-JAN-83	1100	–	20
7900	JAMES	CLERK	7698	03-DEC-81	950	–	30
7902	FORD	ANALYST	7566	03-DEC-81	3000	–	20
7934	MILLER	CLERK	7782	23-JAN-82	1300	–	10

Figure 18.1 Records in EMP table.

237

18.2   GENERATING SQL*PLUS REPORT

To generate means we want a physical hard copy (on paper) for the list of all employees. To print such a report on paper we first need to copy the output of select statement into a file, say "report.lst".

The command which is used to move the output of SELECT statement to a file is "SPOOL filename". Figure 18.2 shows how to use the SPOOL command for moving the output of SELECT statement into a file on hard disk.

```
SQL> spool report.lst
SQL> select empno,ename,hiredate,sal from emp;
```

EMPNO	ENAME	HIREDATE	SAL
7369	SMITH	17-DEC-80	800
7499	ALLEN	20-FEB-81	1600
7521	WARD	22-FEB-81	1250
7566	JONES	02-APR-81	2975
7654	MARTIN	28-SEP-81	1250
7698	BLAKE	01-MAY-81	2850
7782	CLARK	09-JUN-81	2450
7788	SCOTT	09-DEC-82	3000
7839	KING	17-NOV-81	5000
7844	TURNER	08-SEP-81	1500
7876	ADAMS	12-JAN-83	1100
7900	JAMES	03-DEC-81	950
7902	FORD	03-DEC-81	3000
7934	MILLER	23-JAN-82	1300

```
SQL> spool off
```

Figure 18.2   Moving output of SELECT into a file on hard disk.

The spool report.lst creates a file named "report.lst". Now onwards output of any SQL command like SELECT, INSERT, UPDATE, DELETE will be appended to the file "report.lst". This appending of output of the SQL commands will continue till we specify SQL*Plus not to append any further output by specifying the "spool off" command.

Note: We can specify just "spool report" instead of "report.lst". Extension LST stands for Listing and default extension for any spool file is ".lst".

The "Spool off" command ends the appending of any further output of SQL commands.

Caution: SPOOL report.lst causes the output of the SELECT command to be written to file named "report.lst" which is in the temporary memory area called buffer. The SPOOL OFF causes the contents of the buffer file to be written to file on Hard Disk with the same name. If you forget to issue the SPOOL OFF command then the output won't be written to the file on Hard Disk.

Let us now see the contents of report.lst file (Figure 18.3).

```
SQL>edit report.lst
```

Figure 18.3   Viewing contents in report.lst file.

You will see the Notepad document as shown in Figure 18.4.

```
 report.LST - Notepad                                          _ | □ | X |
File   Edit   Format   View   Help
SQL> select empno,ename,hiredate,sal from emp;

     EMPNO ENAME        HIREDATE             SAL
---------- ---------- ---------- ----------
      7369 SMITH        17-DEC-80            800
      7499 ALLEN        20-FEB-81           1600
      7521 WARD         22-FEB-81           1250
      7566 JONES        02-APR-81           2975
      7654 MARTIN       28-SEP-81           1250
      7698 BLAKE        01-MAY-81           2850
      7782 CLARK        09-JUN-81           2450
      7788 SCOTT        09-DEC-82           3000
      7839 KING         17-NOV-81           5000
      7844 TURNER       08-SEP-81           1500
      7876 ADAMS        12-JAN-83           1100

     EMPNO ENAME        HIREDATE             SAL
---------- ---------- ---------- ----------
      7900 JAMES        03-DEC-81            950
      7902 FORD         03-DEC-81           3000
      7934 MILLER       23-JAN-82           1300

14 rows selected.

                                          Ln 1, Col 1
```

Figure 18.4   Output of SQL command spooled to a file.

The EDIT command invokes the default editor which is Notepad for Windows Operating System.

"report.lst" is a file containing the output of the SELECT command. This file can be printed on the attached printers through File-> Print Command.

Note: "spool filename" and "spool off" are SQL*Plus commands which may or may not be terminated by ";"

18.3   SQL*PLUS ENVIRONMENT VARIABLES

SQL*Plus has some system variables/environment variables which decide the reporting parameters. Let us understand the various parameters.

18.3.1   PAGESIZE

This variable determines the number of lines which comprise a page. Default value is 14. As soon as 14 lines are printed on a page, SQL*Plus creates a page break and remaining records get printed on the next page.

Note that column headings repeat on each page break.

We can display the default pagesize by using the "show"command (Figure 18.5).

```
SQL> show pagesize
pagesize 14
```

Figure 18.5   SHOW parameter value.

To change the default pagesize we can use the "set" command (Figure 18.6).

```
SQL> set pagesize 23
SQL> show pagesize
pagesize 23
```

Figure 18.6   Changing PAGESIZE value.

Let us create a sql file named "sqlplus1.sql" (Figure 18.7) with commands as shown in Program 18.1.

```
SQL>edit sqlplus1.sql
```

Figure 18.7   Creating sqlplus1.sql.

Program 18.1   sqlplus1.sql—Generating report in a file named report.lst

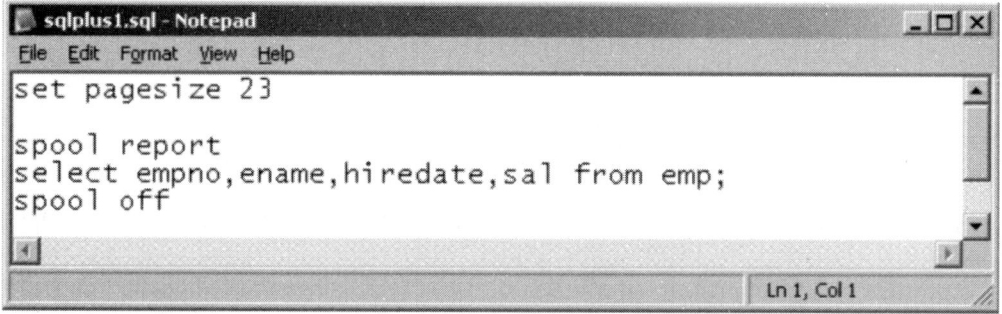

Save the file and exit.

Let us execute the program and view the report.lst file (Figure 18.8).

```
SQL> @sqlplus1
```

EMPNO	ENAME	HIREDATE	SAL
7369	SMITH	17-DEC-80	800
7499	ALLEN	20-FEB-81	1600
7521	WARD	22-FEB-81	1250
7566	JONES	02-APR-81	2975
7654	MARTIN	28-SEP-81	1250
7698	BLAKE	01-MAY-81	2850
7782	CLARK	09-JUN-81	2450

7788	SCOTT	09-DEC-82	3000
7839	KING	17-NOV-81	5000
7844	TURNER	08-SEP-81	1500
7876	ADAMS	12-JAN-83	1100
7900	JAMES	03-DEC-81	950
7902	FORD	03-DEC-81	3000
7934	MILLER	23-JAN-82	1300

14 rows selected.

Figure 18.8   Running sqlplus1.sql program.

All the commands which have been written in sqlplus1.sql file can be executed by using @sqlplus1 at the SQL prompt.

Let us view the report.lst file (Figure 18.9).
SQL>edit report.lst

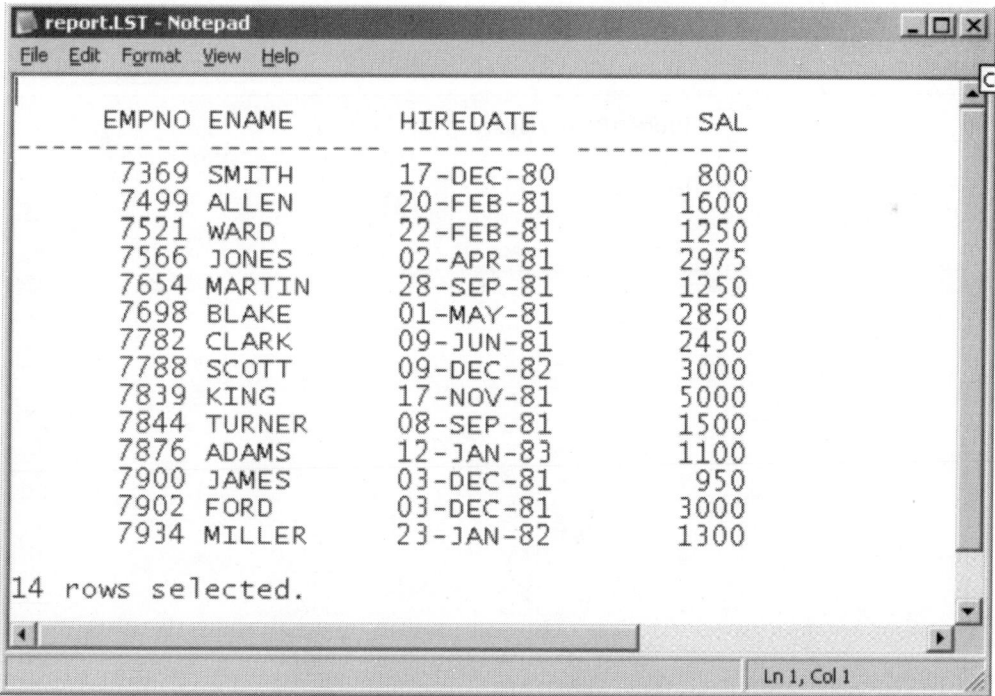

Figure 18.9   Output of Program 18.1.

Note that all 14 records have got displayed on single page as now the pagesize is 23 instead of 14 which is default.

18.3.2   TERM

Program 18.1 (sqlplus1.sql) displayed records on screen as well as generated a spool file named "report.lst". Suppose the report comprised of thousands of records then the screen would have kept scrolling for long before you are able to view the report.lst file. To stop SQL*Plus from displaying records on screen we can use a command "set term off" where term stands for "screen terminal".

Create sqlplus2.sql (Program 18.2) and add statement "set term off".

SQL>edit sqlplus2.sql

Program 18.2   sqlplus2.sql (Using TERM).

```
set term off
set pagesize 23

spool report
select empno,ename,hiredate,sal from emp;
spool off
```

Now when we run Program 18.2 (Figure 18.10), the records are not displayed on screen but the output of select statement goes to the report.lst file.

```
SQL> @sqlplus2
SQL>
```

Figure 18.10   Running sqlplus2.sql.

Let us view the report.lst file (Figure 18.11).

SQL>edit report.lst

Figure 18.11   Output of Program 18.2.

18.3.3 TTITLE and BTITLE—Adding Top and Bottom Titles in Reports

Now we want to add a title to the report specifying the company name, say "PEPSI Company Limited" at the top center. Then in the 2nd line we want to display "List of Employees" then followed by the report.

At the bottom of page, we want to display "For Private Use Only".

Create new file sqlplus3.sql (Program 18.3).

SQL>edit Sqlplus3.sql

Program 18.3 sqlplus3.sql—using ttitle and btitle.

```
set term off
set pagesize 23

ttitle center 'PEPSI Company Limited' skip 1 -
center 'List of Employees' skip 2

btitle center '——————————————————' skip 1 -
center 'For Private Use Only' skip 1 -
center '——————————————————'

spool report
select empno,ename,hiredate,sal from emp;
spool off
```

Run the program 18.3 (sqlplus3.sql) and view report.lst (Figure 18.12).

SQL>@sqlplus3

SQL>edit report.lst

```
                    PEPSI Company Limited
                     List of Employees

     EMPNO          ENAME          HIREDATE          SAL
     7369           SMITH          17-DEC-80         800
     7499           ALLEN          20-FEB-81         1600
     7521           WARD           22-FEB-81         1250
     7566           JONES          02-APR-81         2975
     7654           MARTIN         28-SEP-81         1250
     7698           BLAKE          01-MAY-81         2850
     7782           CLARK          09-JUN-81         2450
     7788           SCOTT          09-DEC-82         3000
     7839           KING           17-NOV-81         5000
     7844           TURNER         08-SEP-81         1500
     7876           ADAMS          12-JAN-83         1100
     7900           JAMES          03-DEC-81         950
     7902           FORD           03-DEC-81         3000
     7934           MILLER         23-JAN-82         1300
                    For Private Use Only
14 rows selected.
```

Figure 18.12 Output of Program 18.3.

Here ttitle stands for Top Title which gets printed on the top of every page.

The ttitle can be followed by "center", "left" or "right" which indicate the title's justification. If we do not specify justification type then default is "left".

Justification is followed by actual text which has to be displayed at the top of the page.

"skip 1" moves the control to next line.

"-" is called line continuation character. If ttitle command exceeds more than 1 line then we can continue the command on the next line by using "-" as the rightmost character.

"skip 2" moves the control to next two lines. Observe one blank line between the "List of Employees" and the heading "EMPNO" of the first column.

Here btitle stands for bottom title. It is similar to ttitle but prints specified text at the bottom of every page.

18.3.4 Changing Display Width for NUMBER Data Types

Note that in Figure 18.12 empno, sal and comm being number data types are being displayed in 10 characters. This is the default setting of SQL*Plus reports. We want to increase this width to, say, 15 characters. We can use the NUMWIDTH parameter as in Figure 18.13 to adjust the field display size.

```
SQL> show numwidth
numwidth 10
SQL> set numwidth 15
```

Figure 18.13   Changing NUMWIDTH.

Now numwidth environment variable will affect all the columns of number data type. See program 18.4 where we have set numwidth to 15 and provided "EMP.ID" heading to the EMPNO column.

Program 18.4   sqlplus4.sql (Using numwidth).

```
set term off
set pagesize 23
set numwidth 15

column empno heading "EMP.ID"

ttitle center 'PEPSI Company Limited' skip 1 -
center 'List of Employees' skip 2

btitle center '——————————————————————' skip 1 -
center 'For Private Use Only' skip 1 -
center '——————————————————'

spool report
select empno,ename,hiredate,sal from emp;
spool off
```

Figure 18.14 displays the output of Program 18.4.

```
                        PEPSI Company Limited
                          List of Employees

   EMP.ID          ENAME          HIREDATE          SAL
    7369           SMITH          17-DEC-80          800
    7499           ALLEN          20-FEB-81         1600
    7521           WARD           22-FEB-81         1250
    7566           JONES          02-APR-81         2975
    7654           MARTIN         28-SEP-81         1250
    7698           BLAKE          01-MAY-81         2850
    7782           CLARK          09-JUN-81         2450
    7788           SCOTT          09-DEC-82         3000
    7839           KING           17-NOV-81         5000
    7844           TURNER         08-SEP-81         1500
    7876           ADAMS          12-JAN-83         1100
    7900           JAMES          03-DEC-81          950
    7902           FORD           03-DEC-81         3000
    7934           MILLER         23-JAN-82         1300

                        For Private Use Only
 14 rows selected.
```

Figure 18.14   Output of Program 18.4.

Note: empno, sal and comm all being number data type have been displayed in 15 characters.

Now we want to restrict empno to just 6 digits as the heading "EMP.ID" has 6 characters and each empno is of 4 digits (Figure 18.15).

```
SQL> column empno heading "EMP.ID" format 999999
SQL> select empno,ename,hiredate,sal,comm from emp;

PEPSI Company Limited
List of Employees

   EMP.ID          ENAME          HIREDATE          SAL          COMM
    7369           SMITH          17-DEC-80          800
    7499           ALLEN          20-FEB-81         1600           300
    7521           WARD           22-FEB-81         1250           500
    7566           JONES          02-APR-81         2975
    7654           MARTIN         28-SEP-81         1250          1400
    7698           BLAKE          01-MAY-81         2850
    7782           CLARK          09-JUN-81         2450
    7788           SCOTT          09-DEC-82         3000
```

Figure 18.15   Format display length of EMPNO.

18.3.5   Formatting Number Data Types

Suppose we want that "sal" should be shown in Dollars and separated by comma for value in thousands with 2 places of decimal (Figure 18.16).

```
SQL> column sal heading "Salary" format $99,999.99
SQL> select empno,ename,hiredate,sal,comm from emp;

PEPSI Company Limited
List of Employees
```

EMP.ID	ENAME	HIREDATE	Salary	COMM
7369	SMITH	17-DEC-80	$800.00	
7499	ALLEN	20-FEB-81	$1,600.00	300
7521	WARD	22-FEB-81	$1,250.00	500
7566	JONES	02-APR-81	$2,975.00	

Figure 18.16   Format SAL column.

18.3.6   Formatting Date Data Type

We want to display hiredate as "dd/mm/yyy" instead of default "dd-mon-yy" format.

For this we will have to select the hiredate in desired format using to_char() built-in function (Figure 18.17).

```
SQL> select empno,ename,to_char(hiredate,'dd/mm/yyyy')
date_of_joining,sal,comm from emp;

                    PEPSI Company Limited
                      List of Employees
```

EMP.ID	ENAME	DATE_OF_JO	Salary	COMM
7369	SMITH	17/12/1980	$800.00	
7499	ALLEN	20/02/1981	$1,600.00	300
7521	WARD	22/02/1981	$1,250.00	500
7566	JONES	02/04/1981	$2,975.00	
7654	MARTIN	28/09/1981	$1,250.00	1400

Figure 18.17   Format HIREDATE column.

Here we have assigned an alias name "date_of_joining" to the to_char(hiredate,'dd/mm/yyyy') field selected from emp table.

Note that heading of hiredate after applying to_char() has become "DATE_OF_JO", because default size for display of aliased date field is 10. We want that this heading should appear in full, i.e. "DATE_OF_JOINING". For this we will have to increase the format size of hiredate column to 15 (Figure 18.18).

```
SQL> col  date_of_joining heading 'Date.of.joining' format a15
SQL> select empno,ename,to_char(hiredate,'dd/mm/yyyy')
date_of_joining,sal,comm from emp;
```

```
                        PEPSI Company Limited
                          List of Employees

      EMP.ID      ENAME      Date.of.joining     Salary      COMM

       7369       SMITH        17/12/1980        $800.00
       7499       ALLEN        20/02/1981       $1,600.00      300
       7521       WARD         22/02/1981       $1,250.00      500
       7566       JONES        02/04/1981       $2,975.00
       7654       MARTIN       28/09/1981       $1,250.00     1400
       7698       BLAKE        01/05/1981       $2,850.00
       7782       CLARK        09/06/1981       $2,450.00
```

Figure 18.18   Format HIREDATE column.

Here "format a15" implies 15 character (indicated by "a") spaces will be used to display the specified column.

> **Note:** SQL*Plus allows usage of just first 4 characters of various parameters.
> For example, "format a15" is equivalent to "for a15".
> "heading 'Date.Of.Joining'" is equivalent to "head 'Date.Of.Joining'"

18.3.7   FEEDBACK

Every time we select records it displays a message "14 rows selected". This is actually known as "feedback" from oracle for every SQL command. We can stop Oracle from giving such feedback (Figure 18.19).

```
SQL>set feedback off
```

Figure 18.19   Stopping feedback.

Now selecting records will produce the same output as before except the feedback.

18.3.8   Displaying Date of Report Generation and PAGE No.

We want the date of report generation to be printed on left top and page no. on right top of each page.

Create a new file sqlplus5.sql as shown in Program 18.5.

SQL>edit sqlplus5.sql

Program 18.5   sqlplus5.sql (report Date and Page Numbering).

```
set term off
set pagesize 23
set numwidth 15

column empno heading "EMP.ID" format 999999
column sal for $99,999.99 heading 'Salary'
column today noprint new_value todays_date
```

```
ttitle left todays_date center 'PEPSI Company Limited' right 'PAGE : ' sql.pno skip 1 -
center 'List of Employees' skip 2

btitle center '────────────────────' skip 1 -
center 'For Private Use Only' skip 1 -
center '────────────────────'

spool report
select to_char(sysdate,'dd/mm/yyyy') today ,deptno,empno,ename,hiredate,sal from emp
order by deptno,empno;
spool off
```

Displaying today's date on left top

Step 1. In SELECT statement include a column *"to_char(sysdate,'dd/mm/yyyy') today"* with alias name *"today"*

Step 2. Specify *"column today noprint new_value todays_date".*

"noprint" tells SQL*Plus not to print the "today" column of select statement along with other columns for each record of EMP table. If this is not specified then each record displayed is accompanied by today column as the first column with value "16/08/2008". *"new_value todays_date"* tells SQL*Plus to assign a new name to the "today" column of SELECT statement.

Step 3. Now we want the today's date value "16/08/2008" to be displayed on top left of every page. For this we specified "ttitle *left todays_date* center..."

Displaying page numbers

Displaying page numbers is quite easy. We just specified "ttitle *left todays_date* center 'PEPSI Company Limited' *right 'PAGE : ' sql.pno"* where 'PAGE :' is static text and actual page numbers are shown by SQL*Plus internal variable named sql.pno.

Let us run the Program 18.5 and view the report.lst (Figure 18.20).

```
SQL> @sqlplus5
SQL> edit report.lst
```

Figure 18.20   Running and viewing output.

Figure 18.21 displays the output of Program 18.5.

16/08/2008		PEPSI Company Limited List of Employees		PAGE :	1
DEPTNO	**EMP.ID**	**ENAME**	**HIREDATE**	**Salary**	
10	7782	CLARK	09-JUN-81	$2,450.00	
10	7839	KING	17-NOV-81	$5,000.00	
10	7934	MILLER	23-JAN-82	$1,300.00	
20	7369	SMITH	17-DEC-80	$800.00	

20	7566	JONES	02-APR-81	$2,975.00
20	7788	SCOTT	09-DEC-82	$3,000.00
20	7876	ADAMS	12-JAN-83	$1,100.00
20	7902	FORD	03-DEC-81	$3,000.00
30	7499	ALLEN	20-FEB-81	$1,600.00
30	7521	WARD	22-FEB-81	$1,250.00
30	7654	MARTIN	28-SEP-81	$1,250.00
30	7698	BLAKE	01-MAY-81	$2,850.00
30	7844	TURNER	08-SEP-81	$1,500.00
30	7900	JAMES	03-DEC-81	$950.00

For Private Use Only

14 rows selected.

Figure 18.21   Output of Program 18.5 - Report.lst.

Requirement: We want that report should show total salary and commission for each department.

18.3.9 Calculating Summaries

We want to display the departmentwise total of salary and commission for each department as well as Grand Total at the end of report.

To achieve this, SQL*Plus provides 2 commands namely BREAK and COMPUTE.
Create a new file sqlplus6.sql with commands as in Program 18.6.
SQL>Edit sqlplus6.sql

Program 18.6   sqlplus6.sql (computing summaries/sub-totals).

```
set term off
set pagesize 25
set numwidth 15

column empno heading "EMP.ID" format 999999
column sal for $99,999.99 heading 'Salary'
column today noprint new_value todays_date

break on report on deptno skip 3
compute sum label 'DEPT TOTAL:' of sal comm on  deptno
compute sum of sal comm on  report

ttitle left todays_date center 'PEPSI Company Limited' right 'PAGE : ' sql.pno skip 1 -
center 'List of Employees' skip 2

btitle center '————————————————' skip 1 -
center 'For Private Use Only' skip 1 -
center '————————————————'

spool report
select to_char(sysdate,'dd/mm/yyyy') today ,deptno,empno,ename,hiredate,sal from emp
order by deptno,empno;
spool off
```

The new commands used are as follows:

break on report on deptno skip 3
compute sum label 'DEPT TOTAL:' of sal comm on deptno
compute sum label 'GRAND TOTAL:' of sal comm on report

Here break instructs the SQL*Plus to stop displaying records on the change of value for the specified column. Here we have mentioned that display of records must stop at change in deptno and report. We can also specify the number of lines which must be skipped before starting off with next deptno (SKIP 3).

Compute statement specified to display SUM on change in deptno and report.

Compute statement can also specify a LABEL to the TOTAL's being displayed. The default label is 'SUM' if not specified.

Let us run the Program 18.6 (sqlplus6.sql) and view the contents of output file (Figure 18.22).

SQL>@sqlplus6.sql
SQL>edit report.lst

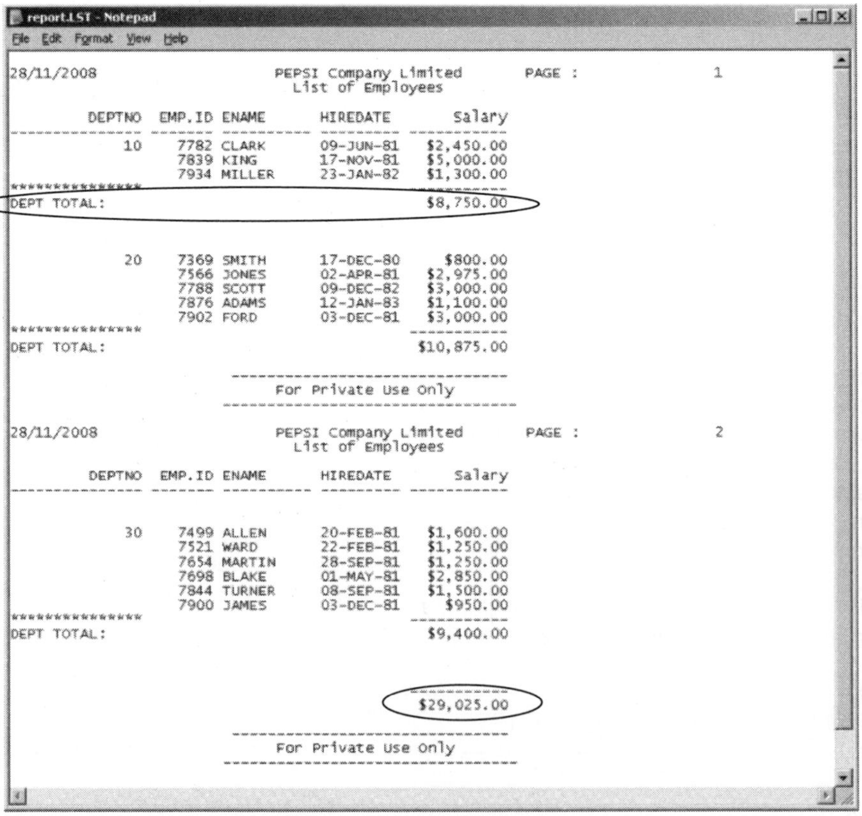

Figure 18.22 Output of Program 18.6.

Note: Just as we have used SUM as the aggregate function for displaying total we can use other aggregate functions like AVG, MAX, MIN, and COUNT also.

As we have skipped three lines on change in deptno, we can also skip a full page by specifying the SKIP PAGE clause. Suppose we want that each departments report should be on separate page then we will have to use the following break statement:

break on deptno skip page

Caution: Be careful while using break statements as the ORDER BY clause must be used along with it for proper results.

Note: All the reports generated by SQL*Plus are Character Based Text Reports. Character Based Report means we cannot use Bold, Italic, Underline formats and moreover the report cannot contain GUI objects like images, graphs, etc. For GUI reports Oracle has a separate Tool called "Oracle Developer Reports Builder".

18.4   PASSING PARAMETERS TO REPORT

We want that on running the report it should ask for department for which the report is to be generated and should print report for that particular department only.

Here we can use the variable substitution feature of SQL*Plus for taking the department as input parameter for the report and the WHERE clause for matching the department.

Note that to read values using substitution variables we must set the terminal ON or else the SQL Prompt will not ask for any value to be entered. Program 18.7 uses the substitution variable for DEPTNO.

Program 18.7   Sqlplus7.sql - Passing parameters for report.

```
set term on
set pagesize 25
set numwidth 15

column empno heading "EMP.ID" format 999999
column sal for $99,999.99 heading 'Salary'
column today noprint new_value todays_date

break on report on deptno skip 3
compute sum label 'DEPT TOTAL:' of sal comm on  deptno
compute sum of sal comm on  report

ttitle left todays_date center 'PEPSI Company Limited' right 'PAGE : ' sql.pno skip 1 -
center 'List of Employees' skip 2

btitle center '————————————————————' skip 1 -
center 'For Private Use Only' skip 1 -
center '————————————————————'

spool report
select to_char(sysdate,'dd/mm/yyyy') today ,deptno,empno,ename,hiredate,sal from emp
where deptno=&dep_no
order by deptno,empno;
spool off
```

Figure 18.23 displays the execution and output file of Program 18.7.

```
SQL> @sqlplus7
Enter value for dep_no: 30
old   2: where deptno=&dep_no
new   2: where deptno=30


05/03/2009                    PEPSI Company Limited              PAGE :    1
                                List of Employees

       DEPTNO        EMP.ID         ENAME         HIREDATE          Salary
           30        7499           ALLEN         20-FEB-81      $1,600.00
                     7521           WARD          22-FEB-81      $1,250.00
                     7654           MARTIN        28-SEP-81      $1,250.00
                     7698           BLAKE         01-MAY-81      $2,850.00
                     7844           TURNER        08-SEP-81      $1,500.00
                     7900           JAMES         03-DEC-81        $950.00
       DEPT TOTAL:                                               $9,400.00



                              $9,400.00

                          For Private Use Only

    6 rows selected.
```

Figure 18.23   Output of Program 18.7.

18.4.1   User-defined Prompt Message for Input Parameters

We want that the report before running should ask "**Please enter department:**" instead of the default message "*Enter value for dep_no:*"

SQL*Plus has command named ACCEPT with PROMPT for this purpose as shown in Program 18.8.

Program 18.8   Sqlplus8.sql (user defined prompt messages).

```
set term on
set pagesize 25
set numwidth 15


accept v_dep_no number prompt 'Please enter department:'

column empno heading "EMP.ID" format 999999
column sal for $99,999.99 heading 'Salary'
column today noprint new_value todays_date

break on report on deptno skip 3
compute sum label 'DEPT TOTAL:' of sal comm on  deptno
compute sum of sal comm on  report
```

```
ttitle left todays_date center 'PEPSI Company Limited' right 'PAGE : ' sql.pno skip 1 -
center 'List of Employees' skip 2

btitle center '——————————————————' skip 1 -
center 'For Private Use Only' skip 1 -
center '——————————————————'

spool report
select to_char(sysdate,'dd/mm/yyyy') today ,deptno,empno,ename,hiredate,sal from emp
where deptno=&v_dep_no
order by deptno,empno;
spool off
```

Figure 18.24 shows the execution of Program 18.8.

```
SQL> @sqlplus8
Please enter department:30
old   2: where deptno=&v_dep_no
new   2: where deptno=30
```

Figure 18.24   Running Program 18.8 (sqlplus8.sql).

accept v_dep_no number prompt 'Please enter department:'

The ACCEPT clause implies that read variable named v_dep_no of NUMBER data type. The PROMPT clause implies the message to be prompted on screen.

Note: v_dep_no is used in both the ACCEPT and WHERE clause.

REVIEW QUESTIONS

1. What do we mean by reporting and formatting?
2. Which command is used to move the result of SELECT statement into a file? What is the default extension of such files?
3. Is it possible to perform formatting like Bold, Italic, Underline through SQL*Plus report?
4. Which command is used to invoke the default editor of the Operating System?
5. How can we view the settings for all environment variables? (Hint: Use the SHOW ALL command).
6. Explain the purpose of PAGESIZE and LINESIZE settings.
7. How can we specify formatting for NUMBER and CHARACTER Data Type?
8. Which environment variable prints the PAGE No.?
9. What are the commands to print SUB-TOTALS and GRAND-TOTALS?
10. Which commands are used to specify user-defined messages for input parameters?

LAB ASSIGNMENT _____

Refer to Tables 7.1, 7.2 and 7.3 for CUSTOMER ORDER database:

1. Generate a report named "myreport.lst" displaying customer namewise outstanding balance such that the balance is shown with dollar symbol and up to 2 places of decimals.

2. Generate the above report in a file named "myreport.txt". (Hint: SPOOL myreport.txt)

3. Generate a single report such that list of all customers is followed by the list of all products. (Hint: Specify the two different SELECT statements one below the other)

4. Develop a report showing Customer Namewise, Product Namewise TOTAL Quantity ordered. Also calculate the sub-totals for each Customer and Grand Total on report.

5. For the above report create page break for each customer.

6. For the above report add a Title at the top of each page with the following text "Synonym Inc.". Add the 2nd line "Bhopal, M.P". The report should display "For Internal Use Only" at the bottom of each page.

7. For the above report display the date of report generation at right bottom of each page along with PAGE No.'s at the right top of each page.

19

PL/SQL

19.1   INTRODUCTION

PL/SQL stands for Procedural SQL. It is an extension to the 4th Generation language SQL. PL/SQL is a 3rd generation language like C, C++, Java having branching, looping and conditional statements.

19.2   DRAWBACKS OF SQL—NEED FOR A PROCEDURAL EXTENSION TO SQL

The need for a procedural extension to SQL was because of some drawbacks associated with SQL.

1. SQL does not have procedural capabilities, that is, it does not have conditional statement like IF..ELSE, looping statements like FOR, WHILE and branching statements like GOTO.
2. SQL statements are passed on to the Oracle Database Engine one at a time for compilation and execution.
3. When an error occurs in any of the SQL statements, Oracle displays its own built-in error messages which are quite unfriendly in most of the cases. In PL/SQL we can assign our own Error messages.

Note: PL/SQL is a 3rd generation language like C, C++, Java having procedural capabilities. It is an extension to the 4th generation language SQL.

19.3   ADVANTAGES OF PL/SQL

1. PL/SQL has procedural capabilities like conditional statement, branching, looping.
2. PL/SQL has embedded SQL, that is, we can write SQL statements within a PL/SQL program.

3. We can declare variables within PL/SQL blocks and use them for intermediate calculations.
4. It is a block structured language which means that an entire block of statements are passed on to the oracle engine for compilation and execution.
5. PL/SQL facilitates dealing of Oracle's built-in error messages and allows users to define their own error messages.

19.4   STRUCTURE OF PL/SQL BLOCK

All programming languages have a definite structure. Figure 19.1 shows the structure of a PL/SQL program.

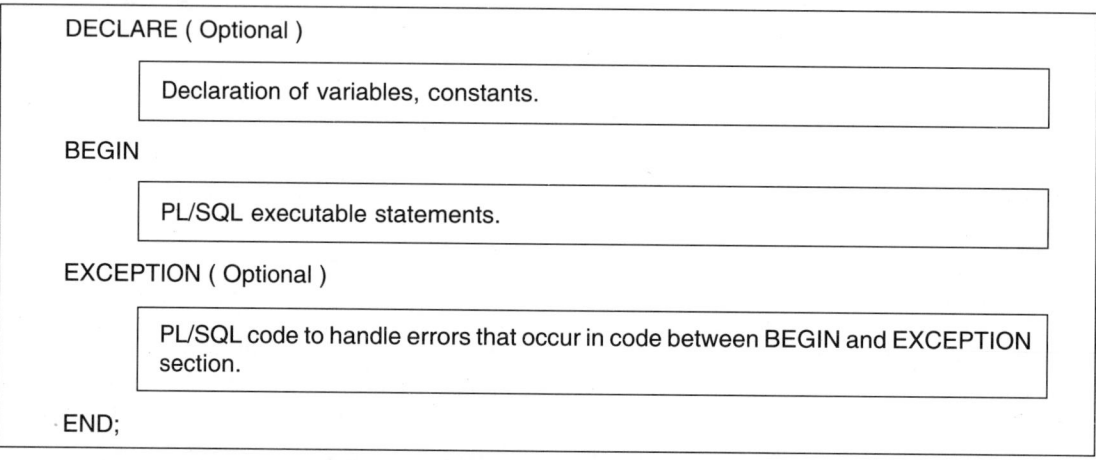

Figure 19.1   Structure of PL/SQL block.

DECLARE: Variables and constants are declared within this section and we may initialize them with values.

BEGIN: It contains the PL/SQL statements which implement the actual programming logic. This section contains conditional statements like IF..ELSE, looping statements like FOR WHILE and branching statements like GOTO and calculations.

EXCEPTION: The errors generated on execution of PL/SQL statements above this section are handled here. Error can arise due to syntax, logical or failure of validation rules.

Note:
1. BEGIN and END; are compulsory sections of any PL/SQL program.
2. DECLARE and EXCEPTION are optional sections.

19.5   PROGRAM TO DISPLAY "HELLO! WORLD" ON SCREEN

We will develop this program in a file named "a.sql".Go To SQL Prompt. Type "edit a" and press enter key.

SQL> edit a

Notepad editor will be invoked. Type the code as shown in Program 19.1.

Program 19.1   a.sql (Displaying "Hello World").

```
set serveroutput on
begin
dbms_output.put_line('Hello! World');
end;
/
```

File -> Save.

File -> Exit. You will be returned to SQL Prompt.

Run the program in a.sql file as shown in Figure 19.2.

```
SQL> @a
Hello! World

PL/SQL procedure successfully completed.
```

Figure 19.2   Running Hello World program.

What we have done is that we created a file named "a.sql" by using the Windows default editor called "Notepad". Now to run the code written in a.sql file we have used "@" symbol followed by filename (here a). For running program in a.sql file, we can either write "@a" or "@a.sql".

Note:

1. The default extension of all PL/SQL files is .sql.
2. All statements within BEGIN and END are terminated by semi-colon(;).
3. BEGIN is not ended by semi-colon.
4. END is terminated by semi-colon.
5. The program must be ended by a forward slash "/" which should be the first character on the last line.
6. "set serveroutput on" enables the PL/SQL program to display output on screen.
7. dbms_output is oracle built-in package(we will learn about this later).
8. put_line is built-in procedure for displaying output on screen of "dbms_output" package.

19.6   PROGRAM TO CALCULATE AREA OF A CIRCLE

Let us write a program to calculate area of a circle which will ask us to enter radius and then calculate and display the result on screen. Here we will be using some variables and constants which are analogously available in other 3rd generation languages like C, C++, Java, etc. See Program 19.2 for the code.

SQL>edit a

Program 19.2   a.sql (Area of a Circle).

```
a - Notepad                                                    _□×
File  Edit  Format  View  Help
set serveroutput on
declare
        pi constant number:=3.14;
        radius number:=&radius;
        area number;
begin
        area:=pi *  radius * radius;
        dbms_output.put_line('Area is : '||area);
end;
/
```

Let us execute the Program 19.2 as in Figure 19.3.

```
SQL> @a
Enter value for radius: 10
old 3: radius number:=&radius;
new 3: radius number:=10;
Area is : 314

PL/SQL procedure successfully completed.
```

Figure 19.3   Running Program 19.2.

In this program we have declared variables.

"pi" has been declared as constant of data type number with fixed value of 3.14. What we mean by constant is that this value of pi cannot be changed throughout this program.

"radius" has been declared as of type number and has been assigned a value by using substitution variable "&radius".

"area" is declared of type number.

Area has been calculated using the formula pi * square of radius.

Note that we have used ":=" symbol for assigning values to variables. C language uses '=' for assignment and '==' for comparison. Oracle uses ':=' for assignment and '=' for comparison of values.

19.7   PROGRAM FOR AREA OF A CIRCLE USING ORACLE BUILT-IN FUNCTIONS

Instead of calculating area as "pi * radius * radius", we could have used oracle's built-in function named "power" as in Program 19.3.

Program 19.3 a.sql (Area of a Circle using CONSTANT variable).

```
set serveroutput on
declare
    pi constant number:=3.14;
    radius number:=&radius;
    area number;
begin
    area:=pi * power(radius,2);
    dbms_output.put_line('Area is : '||area);
end;
/
```

19.8 CONDITIONAL STATEMENT—IF

IF statement is used to transfer the control of program depending on a specified condition. Suppose we want to know the greater of given 2 numbers then we can use the IF statement for comparing the 2 values.

19.8.1 Simplest IF Statement

The simplest IF statement takes the following format

```
IF <condition> THEN
    <statements>;
END IF;
```

19.8.2 IF Statement with ELSE Part

The IF statement can have a ELSE part also

```
IF <condition> THEN
    <statements>;
ELSE
    <statements>;
END IF;
```

19.8.3 Nested IF Statement

One IF can be made a part of the ELSE of other IF.

```
IF <condition-1> THEN
    <statements>;
ELSE
    IF <Condition-2> THEN
            <Statements>;
```

```
      ELSE
            <Statements>;
            . . . . . . . . . . . . .
      END IF:
   END IF;
```

19.8.4   Alternative Syntax for Nested IF

```
IF <condition-1> THEN
   <statements>;
ELSIF <condition-2> THEN
   <statements>;
ELSIF <condition-3> THEN
   <statements>;
. . . . . . . . . . . . . . . . . . . .
. . . . . . . . . . . . . . . . . . . .
. . . . . . . . . . . . . . . . . . . .
ELSE
   <statements>;
END IF;
```

19.8.5   IF ... END IF Example

We have an employee table with structure and records as shown in Figure 19.4.

```
SQL> desc employee;
      Name                    Null?              Type
      EMPLOYEE_ID                                NUMBER(4)
      SALARY                                     NUMBER(5)

SQL> select * from employee;

         EMPLOYEE_ID              SALARY
              1                    1000
              2                   15000
              3                    5000
              4                   17000
```

Figure 19.4   Records in EMPLOYEE table.

19.9   PROGRAM USING IF ... END IF CONSTRUCT

We will input employee_id and calculate commission based on salary (Table 19.1) and display the employee _id and commission if it is more than 5000/-, else we will display the message that "Employee Does not have commission more than 5000".

TABLE 19.1 Criteria for calculating commission

Salary	Commission(% of salary)
If salary < 1000	10%
If salary between 1001 and 5000	20%
If salary >5000	30%

Edit plsql2.sql and write the code as in Program 19.4.

SQL>edit plsql2

Program 19.4 plsql2.sql – program using IF statement.

```
set serveroutput on
declare
   v_employee_id number(4);
   v_salary number(5);
   v_commission    number(5):=0;
begin
   select employee_id,salary into v_employee_id,v_salary from employee
   where employee_id=&empid;

   if v_salary < 1000 then
            v_commission:=10/100*v_salary;
   end if;

   if v_salary between 1000 and 5000 then
            v_commission:=20/100*v_salary;
   end if;

   if v_salary > 5000 then
            v_commission:=30/100*v_salary;
   end if;


   if v_commission > 5000 then
            dbms_output.put_line('Employee Id : '||v_employee_id
            ||' '||'Commission : '||v_commission);
   else
            dbms_output.put_line('Employee Id : '||v_employee_id
            ||' '||' Does Not have commission more than 5000');
   end if;
end;
/
```

Let us first execute Program 19.4 as shown in Figure 19.5 and then we will discuss various components of it.

```
SQL> @plsql2 .
Enter value for empid: 1
old 7: where employee_id=&empid;
new 7: where employee_id=1;
Employee Id : 1 Does Not have commission more than 5000

PL/SQL procedure successfully completed.
```

Figure 19.5   Running program 19.4 with employee_id=1.

As salary of employee_id 1 is 1000, therefore, commission is 10/100*1000=100.

As commission is not more than 5000, therefore, it displayed the message "Employee Id : 1 Does Not have commission more than 5000".

Now let us again run the Program 19.4 for employee_id 4 as in Figure 19.6.

```
SQL> @plsql2
Enter value for empid: 4
old 7: where employee_id=&empid;
new 7: where employee_id=4;
Employee Id : 4 Commission : 5100

PL/SQL procedure successfully completed.
```

Figure 19.6   Running program 19.4 with employee_id=4.

Salary of employee_id 4 is 17000, therefore, commission=30/100*17000=5100 which is greater than 5000 so it displayed "Employee Id : 4 Commission : 5100".

Let us now understand the various parts of the Program 19.4.

We have declared 3 variables of data type NUMBER, namely

v_employee_id number(4);

v_salary number(5);

v_commission number(5):=0;

Then we have selected the values of employee_id and salary column into the variables v_employee_id and v_salary. Note that SELECT is a SQL statement and has been used in PL/SQL code with the only difference that we have to select the values of columns "INTO" variables.

IF <condition> THEN <statements> END IF has been used to implement the logic for calculation of commission. Note that IF has a corresponding END IF.

Then we have displayed the employee_id with commission using dbms_output.put_line with IF ELSE statement.

IF <condition1> THEN

    <statements>;

ELSE

    <statements>;

END IF:

Note that we have the concatenation characters "||" to display the employee id along with commission.

TIP: Oracle displayed statements like "old" and "new" indicating that we supplied employee_id 4 as input using substitution variable &empid. The display of substitution variables can be hidden by using the command "set verify off" as shown in Program 19.5.

Program 19.5 plsql2a.sql - Setting Verification off.

```
set verify off
set serveroutput on
declare
    v_employee_id number(4);
    v_salary number(5);
    v_commission    number(5):=0;
begin
    select employee_id,salary into v_employee_id,v_salary from employee
    where employee_id=&empid;
    if v_salary < 1000 then
            v_commission:=10/100*v_salary;
    end if;

    if v_salary between 1000 and 5000 then
            v_commission:=20/100*v_salary;
    end if;

    if v_salary > 5000 then
            v_commission:=30/100*v_salary;
    end if;

    if v_commission > 5000 then
            dbms_output.put_line('Employee Id : '||v_employee_id
            ||' '||'Commission : '||v_commission);
    else
            dbms_output.put_line('Employee Id : '||v_employee_id
            ||' '||' Does Not have commission more than 5000');
    end if;
end;
/
```

Let us execute the Program 19.5 as shown in Figure 19.7.

```
SQL> @plsql2a
Enter value for empid: 1
Employee Id : 1 Does Not have commission more than 5000

PL/SQL procedure successfully completed.
```

Figure 19.7 Running Program 19.5.

Note that now "old" and "new" for substitution variables was not displayed on screen.

19.10 USING IF ... ELSIF ... ELSIF ... ELSE ... END IF

The Program 19.5 can also be developed using "IF ... ELSIF ... ELSIF ... ELSE ... END IF" construct as shown in Program 19.6.

Program 19.6   plsql3.sql–Using IF..ELSIF construct.

```
set serveroutput on
declare
    v_employee_id number(4);
    v_salary number(5);
    v_commission     number(5):=0;
begin
    select employee_id,salary into v_employee_id,v_salary from employee
    where employee_id=&empid;

    if v_salary < 1000 then
            v_commission:=10/100*v_salary;
    elsif v_salary between 1000 and 5000 then
            v_commission:=20/100*v_salary;
    elsif v_salary > 5000 then
            v_commission:=30/100*v_salary;
    end if;

    if v_commission > 5000 then
            dbms_output.put_line('Employee Id : '||v_employee_id
            ||' '||'Commission : '||v_commission);
    else
            dbms_output.put_line('Employee Id : '||v_employee_id
            ||' '||' Does Not have commission more than 5000');
    end if;
end;
/
```

The advantage of using Nested IF is that the moment one of the IF clauses is satisfied, the rest of ELSIF statements are not executed. Whereas in case of IF ... END IF, IF...END IF, even if the first IF condition is satisfied then also all the other IF statements are also executed for checking the condition.

Note: The performance of Nested IF construct is much better than the IF ... END IF ... IF ... END IF construct.

Let us see one more example to understand the PL/SQL programming.

We have a table named "tbl_bank_account" which contains account_id, name of account holder and balance. We want to write a program which will be supplied account_id and amount to be withdrawn. The program will check the existence of specified account_id in the bank and if the account_id does not exist then it will display the error message. If the account exists then it will check that if on withdrawing the required amount the balance left is not less than 1000(minimum account balance). The program will also update the new balance after specified amount withdrawal. Figure 19.8 shows the structure and records in "tbl_bank_account".

```
SQL> desc tbl_bank_account

        Name                    Null?                    Type
        ACCOUNT_ID                                       CHAR(13)
        NAME                                             VARCHAR2(10)
        BALANCE                                          NUMBER(12,2)

SQL> select * from tbl_bank_account;

    ACCOUNT_ID    NAME    BALANCE
    A123456789012 satish  2000

plsql4.sql
```

Figure 19.8   TBL_BANK_ACCOUNT.

Program 19.7 contains the code for achieving the desired requirement for bank account transaction.

> **Program 19.7**   plsql4.sql–Program for withdrawing amount from bank account.

```
set verify off
set serveroutput on
declare
    v_min_bal constant number(5):=1000; --Minimum Bank Balance is 1000
    v_count number(1);
    v_account_id char(13);
    v_balance number(12,2);
    v_new_balance number(12,2);
begin
    --check whether the given account exists in bank or not.
    select count(*) into v_count from tbl_bank_account
    where account_id='&&account_id';

    if v_count = 0 then --implies account does not exist in bank
            dbms_output.put_line('Account Does Not Exist');
    else                --account exists in bank
            select account_id,balance into v_account_id,v_balance
            from tbl_bank_account where account_id='&&account_id';

            --check the new balance
            if v_balance - &&v_withdrawal_amount < v_min_bal then
                    dbms_output.put_line('Specified Amount Cannot be WithDrawn');
                    dbms_output.put_line('New balance left is less than 1000');
            else
    update tbl_bank_account set balance=balance - &&v_withdrawal_amount
                    where account_id='&&account_id';
                    commit;
```

```
                        v_new_balance:=v_balance - &&v_withdrawal_amount;
                        dbms_output.put_line('Amount WithDrawn :
'||&&v_withdrawal_amount);
                        dbms_output.put_line('New Balance : '||v_new_balance);
                end if;

        end if; --end if of v_count > 0
    end;
    /
```

Comments in PL/SQL Code

Comments are not executed by PL/SQL Compiler. Single line comments are specified using two dashes in continuity (- -) and multiple line comments are specified using "/*....................*/". Comments are added to improve the readability and are also used to provide information about the various logics applied for better understanding of the program code. Some programmers even specify the name and the date on which a program was developed along with the purpose for proper documentation.

Understanding the program 19.7

We have declared a constant variable "v_min_bal" specifying the minimum balance that must be available after withdrawal of desired amount.

We have checked the existence of given account by selecting count(*) into "v_count". Remember that count returns 0 if record is not found in table.

If account exists then we have checked whether the balance after withdrawal will be less than 1000(v_min_bal) or not. If new balance is less than 1000 then display message "'Specified Amount Cannot be WithDrawn". If new balance is greater than or equal to 1000 then update the new balance in "tbl_bank_account" and display on screen the new balance amount.

Two hyphens " - -" means Remarks or Comments added for program readability. These statements are not executed by Oracle PL/SQL compiler.

Let us run the Program 19.7 for account id 1111 which does not exist in our BANK and withdraw an amount of 1000 (Figure 19.9).

```
SQL> @plsql4
Enter value for account_id: 1111
Enter value for v_withdrawal_amount: 1000
Account Does Not Exist

PL/SQL procedure successfully completed.
```

Figure 19.9   Running Program 19.7.

Let us run the Program 19.7 for account id 'A123456789012' and withdraw amount 500 (see Figure 19.10).

```
SQL> select * from tbl_bank_account;

        ACCOUNT_ID              NAME            BALANCE
        A123456789012           satish          2000

SQL> @plsql4
Enter value for account_id: A123456789012
Enter value for v_withdrawal_amount: 500
Amount WithDrawn : 500
New Balance : 1500

PL/SQL procedure successfully completed.

SQL> select * from tbl_bank_account;

        ACCOUNT_ID              NAME            BALANCE
        A123456789012           satish          1500
```

Figure 19.10 Running Program 19.7.

After withdrawal of Rs. 500/- the new balance left is 1500/-.
Let us withdraw Rs. 800/- from the same account (see Figure 19.11).

```
SQL> select * from tbl_bank_account;

        ACCOUNT_ID              NAME            BALANCE
        A123456789012           satish          1500

SQL> @plsql4
Enter value for account_id: A123456789012
Enter value for v_withdrawal_amount: 800
Specified Amount Cannot be WithDrawn
New balance left is less than 1000

PL/SQL procedure successfully completed.

SQL> select * from tbl_bank_account;

        ACCOUNT_ID              NAME            BALANCE
        A123456789012           satish          1500
```

Figure 19.11 Running Program 19.7.

We could not withdraw 800/- as the balance left would be $1500 - 800 = 700$ and the minimum balance left after withdrawal must be 1000.

19.11 ITERATIVE CONTROLS/LOOPING CONTROLS

When we need to execute a block of statements repeatedly for a certain number of times then we have to use loops.

Oracle provides three looping controls, namely: Simple LOOP; WHILE LOOP; FOR LOOP.

19.11.1 Simple LOOP

Program 19.8 shows the SIMPLE loop construct for displaying numbers from 1 to 10.

Program 19.8   plsql5.sql. this program print numbers from 1 to 10.

```
Set serveroutput on
declare
   i number;
begin
   i:=0;
   loop
            i:=i+1;
            exit when i>10;
            dbms_output.put_line(i);
   end loop;
end;
/
```

All statements to be repeated are placed within LOOP and END LOOP. Statements between LOOP and END LOOP are executed till the EXIT condition is satisfied. Value of variable i is initialized to 0 before entering the loop and when the value of I reaches 11 then the loop is ended and the program control is transferred to the statement next to "END LOOP;".

It is important to initialize the value of LOOP controlling variable(i) and to increment its value within loop so that at some point of time the condition is not satisfied and the EXIT statement is executed which breaks the execution of statements within LOOP..END LOOP and transfers the control of program to the statement following "END LOOP;".

Caution:
1. Note that no semi-colon is placed after LOOP.
2. Every LOOP ... END LOOP must have an exit condition specified by "EXIT WHEN <condition>" or else it becomes an infinite loop.

Let us run the Program 19.8 as in Figure 19.12.

```
SQL> @plsql5
   1
   2
   3
   4
   5
   6
   7
   8
   9
  10
PL/SQL procedure successfully completed.
```

Figure 19.12   Running plsql5.sql.

19.11.2   WHILE LOOP

The WHILE LOOP first checks the condition and then executes the statements if condition is satisfied. Program 19.9 uses the WHILE LOOP for displaying the numbers from 1 to 10.

Program 19.9   plsql6.sql Display 1 to10 using WHILE LOOP.

```
set serveroutput on
declare
    i number;
begin
    i:=1;
    while i<=10 loop
            dbms_output.put_line(i);
            i:=i+1;
    end loop;
end;
/
```

Output of this program is the same as Program 19.8.

19.11.3   FOR LOOP

The FOR LOOP is used when we know the number of iterations in advance. If we know that this set of statements will be executed n times (here 10) then use FOR LOOP. Program 19.10 shows the usage of FOR LOOP for displaying the numbers from 1 to 10.

Program 19.10   plsql7.sql display 1 to 10 Using FOR LOOP.

```
set serveroutput on
begin
    for i in 1..10 loop
            dbms_output.put_line(i);
    end loop;
end;
/
```

Note:
1. FOR variables (i) does not need initialization UNLIKE other loops (Simple, WHILE).
2. No EXIT condition is specified. The LOOP automatically breaks on "i" reaching 10.
3. "i" is automatically incremented by 1(default).

FOR REVERSE LOOP

Oracle FOR LOOP supports reverse option for counting down the numbers (Program 19.11).

Program 19.11   plsql8.sql display 10 to 1 in reverse order.

```
set serveroutput on
begin
    for i in reverse 1..10 loop
            dbms_output.put_line(i);
    end loop;
end;
/
```

Figure 19.13 shows the output of Program 19.11.

```
SQL> @plsql8
10
 9
 8
 7
 6
 5
 4
 3
 2
 1
PL/SQL procedure successfully completed.
```

Figure 19.13   Running Program 19.11.

Changing the Increment value by N

Now let us see how to change the increment value by N instead of 1 which is default in FOR LOOP. Suppose we want to increment numbers by 2. See Program 19.12.

Program 19.12   plsql9.sql—changing increment value.

```
set serveroutput on
begin
    for i in 1..10 loop
            dbms_output.put_line(i);
            i:=i+2;
    end loop;
end;
/
```

Let us execute the Program 19.12 as in Figure 19.14.

```
SQL> @plsql9
i:=i+2;
  *
ERROR at line 4:
ORA-06550: line 4, column 3:
```

PLS-00363: expression 'I' cannot be used as an assignment target
ORA-06550: line 4, column 3:
PL/SQL: Statement ignored

Figure 19.14 Running Program 19.12.

We cannot increment the variable "i" using the assignment operator i:=i+2 in FOR LOOP.

What we can do is to achieve the desired increment (say 2 or 3). The solution is to use MOD oracle built-in function which returns the remainder portion of a division as shown in Program 19.13. This program will print all even numbers from 1 … 10.

Program 19.13 plsql10.sql—printing even numbers.

```
set serveroutput on
begin
   for i in 1..10 loop
            if mod(i,2)=0 then
                     dbms_output.put_line(i);
            end if;
   end loop;
end;
/
```

19.12 USING DML STATEMENTS WITHIN PL/SQL

PL/SQL being procedural extension to SQL can use the various SQL DML commands within its code.

Let us see an example using FOR LOOP involving the INSERT command.

We want to calculate area of a circle starting with radius 5 and ending with radius 15. We also need to store both radius and corresponding calculated area in TBL_AREA table having two columns radius and area. In Figure 19.15 we have created the table "TBL_AREA" and Program 19.14 contains the code.

```
SQL> create table tbl_area(radius number(2),area number(5));

Table created.
```

Figure 19.15 Creating table TBL_AREA.

Program 19.14 plsql11.sql—DML statements within PL/SQL.

```
declare
   pi constant number(5,2):=3.14;
   area number;
begin
   for radius in 5..15 loop
            area:=pi * radius * radius;
            insert into tbl_area values (radius,area);
   end loop;
   commit;
end;
/
```

Figure 19.16 shows the execution of Program 19.14.

```
SQL> @plsql11

PL/SQL procedure successfully completed.

SQL> select * from tbl_area;

       RADIUS              AREA
          5                 79
          6                113
          7                154
          8                201
          9                254
         10                314
         11                380
         12                452
         13                531
         14                615
         15                707

11 rows selected.
```

Figure 19.16   Running Program 19.14.

19.13   GOTO

GOTO statement transfers the control of program unconditionally. In contrast to the IF statement GOTO can transfer the control of program to any position in the PL/SQL block. Let us recode the BANK ACCOUNT program (Program 19.7: plsql4.sql) using GOTO construct (Program 19.15).

Program 19.15   plsql12.sql (using GOTO).

```
set verify off
set serveroutput on
declare
    v_min_bal constant number(5):=1000; --Minimum Bank Balance is 1000
    v_count number(1);
    v_account_id char(13);
    v_balance number(12,2);
    v_new_balance number(12,2);
begin
    --check whether the given account exists in bank or not.
    select count(*) into v_count from tbl_bank_account
    where account_id='&&account_id';

    if v_count = 0 then --implies account does not exist in bank
            GOTO ACCOUNT_NOT_FOUND;
```

```
    else            --account exists in bank
            select account_id,balance into v_account_id,v_balance
            from tbl_bank_account where account_id='&&account_id';

            --check the new balance
            if v_balance - &&v_withdrawal_amount < v_min_bal then
                    dbms_output.put_line('Specified Amount Cannot be WithDrawn');
                    dbms_output.put_line('New balance left is less than 1000');
            else
                    update tbl_bank_account set balance=balance -
            &&v_withdrawal_amount
                    where account_id='&&account_id';
                    commit;
                    v_new_balance:=v_balance - &&v_withdrawal_amount;
                    dbms_output.put_line('Amount WithDrawn :
'||&&v_withdrawal_amount);
                    dbms_output.put_line('New Balance : '||v_new_balance);
            end if;

    end if; --end if of v_count > 0


<<ACCOUNT_NOT_FOUND>>
    dbms_output.put_line('Account Does Not Exist');
end;
/
```

Any PL/SQL block can be assigned a name by using << and >>. The GOTO statement can transfer the program control to these named blocks specifying the assigned name like "GOTO *ACCOUNT_NOT_FOUND" without << and >>.*

Caution: It is generally considered not a good programming practice to use the GOTO statement extensively. As it is an unconditional transfer of program control to any specified point in program, therefore, logical clarity is lost and may at times lead to infinite loops.

REVIEW QUESTIONS

1. What does PL/SQL stands for? Specify the drawbacks of SQL language.
2. What are the compulsory and optional parts of a PL/SQL block?
3. Which command must be executed so that output of programs can be displayed on screen?
4. What is the assignment operator in PL/SQL?
5. How can constant values be declared?
6. Can we use Oracle built-in functions within PL/SQL blocks?
7. Which conditional statement should be preferred—Simple or Nested and why?
8. Can we embed INSERT, UPDATE and DELETE SQL commands within PL/SQL? What is the difference between syntax of SQL SELECT and PL/SQL SELECT?

9. Which looping controls are supported by Oracle? Specify the situations where various loops can be used.

10. Why the GOTO statements should be avoided?

LAB ASSIGNMENT

1. Write a PL/SQL block to calculate square of a number.
2. Write a program to calculate the area of a triangle.
3. Develop a program to convert temperature in Celsius to Fahrenheit and vice versa.
4. Write a program to find the greatest of the three numbers.
5. Write a program to find factorial of a given number.
6. Write a program which will accept marks of three subjects, namely maths, physics and chemistry. Calculate the average marks and display the total grade as per the following conditions:

   IF average marks < 40 then Grade C
   IF average marks between 40 and 70 then Grade B
   ELSE Grade A

7. Write a program which will accept EMPNO and calculate BONUS as per the following criteria

Salary+Comm	BONUS(% of salary+comm.)
Less than 1500	5%
1500-4000	10%
4001-8000	15%
>8000	20%

8. Write a program to display first 10 even numbers.
9. Write a program to display first 10 those numbers which are divisible by 5 and 7 both.
10. Write a program which will accept EMPNO and will calculate various components of salary as follows:

    BASIC=SAL
    DA=10% of BASIC
    HRA=20% of BASIC
    GRAND SALARY=BASIC+DA+HRA+COMM
    INCOME TAX=15% of (BASIC+DA+HRA)
    NET SALARY=GRAND SALARY – INCOME TAX

11. Develop a program to sum the digits of a specified 5 digit number.
12. Develop a program to reverse the digits of a 5 digit number.
13. Develop a program to calculate the net electricity bill payment as per the number of units used

Units consumed	Rate
0–100	Rs. 0.5 per unit
100–200	Rs. 1.0 per unit excess of 100
200–300	Rs. 1.5 per unit excess of 200
>300	Rs. 3.0 per unit excess of 300

Stored Functions

20.1 INTRODUCTION

Stored functions are logically grouped PL/SQL statements which perform a specific task. They can also be defined as PL/SQL blocks that take parameters, perform some action and return a single value to the calling program.

20.2 STRUCTURE OF FUNCTION

Stored function comprises of three sections, namely Declarative, Executable and Exception Handling as shown in Figure 20.1.

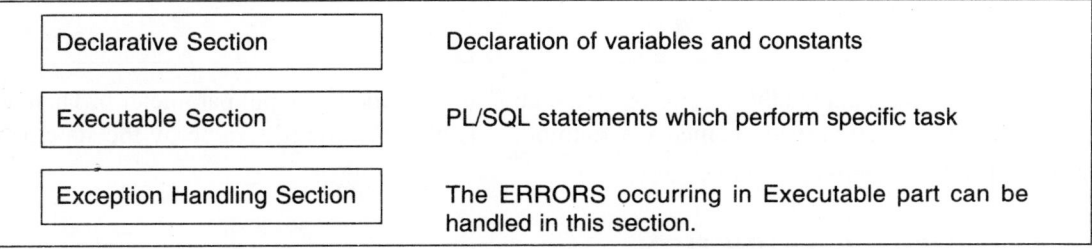

Declarative Section	Declaration of variables and constants
Executable Section	PL/SQL statements which perform specific task
Exception Handling Section	The ERRORS occurring in Executable part can be handled in this section.

Figure 20.1 Components of Stored Function.

Figure 20.2 shows the syntax of Function Declaration.

```
create or replace function function_name(parameters)
return data_type is                            ⎫
    /* local variables declaration */          ⎬  Declarative Section
begin                                          ⎭
    PL/SQL statements;                         ⎫
    ………………..                                    ⎬  Executable Section
    ………………..                                    ⎬
    ………………..                                    ⎭
exception                                      ⎫
    PL/SQL statements for handling ERRORS      ⎬  Error Handling
End;                                           ⎭
/
```

Figure 20.2   Syntax of Function Declaration.

Here, *function_name* and *data_type* are provided by us.

Note: The local variable declaration is not preceded by DECLARE keyword.

20.3   FUNCTION TO CALCULATE POWER OF 3 FOR GIVEN NUMBER

Let us now see a practical example. We want to create our own function called "CUBE" which will return three times of the number supplied as input. If our input is 5 it will return $5^3=125$. Program 20.1 contains the code for creating CUBE function.

Program 20.1   Function1.sql—function to calculate cube of a number.

```
create or replace function fn_cube(p number)
return number is
    y number;
begin
    y:=p * p * p;
    return y;
end;
/
```

Here, we have named the function as "fn_cube" and supplied an input parameter p. Then we have declared a local variable named y as number. y is assigned the p^3 value by the statement y:=p*p*p and the value is returned by using the RETURN statement.

20.4   COMPILING A FUNCTION

To compile a function we need to run the function1.sql program (Figure 20.3).

```
SQL> @function1

Function created.
```

Figure 20.3   Compiling a function.

20.5 CALLING A FUNCTION

A function can be called in two ways.

1. It can be called in the SELECT statement as shown in Figure 20.4.

```
SQL> select fn_cube(5) from dual;

    FN_CUBE(5)

        125
```

Figure 20.4 SELECT statement using stored function.

Dual is called a dummy table which is required to just complete the syntax of the SELECT statement. SQL being highly-structured language requires exact syntax for all statements. The "SELECT" statement must have the "FROM" clause.

2. Function can be called within a PL/SQL program also as shown in Program 20.2.

Program 20.2 Function2.sql—volume of a cube.

```
/*
PL/SQL program to find volume of a cube
The program is supplied length of the side of cube
It calls a function fn_cube() to calculate the side^3
*/
set serveroutput on
declare
    side      number:=&side;
    volume number;
begin
    volume:=fn_cube(side);
    dbms_output.put_line('Volume is : '||volume);
end;
/
```

Here function2.sql uses the function fn_cube() created in Program 20.1. Note that while declaring the function we specified "return number" in the 2nd line which means that the calling program must receive the number value returned from fn_cube() to a variable of type number only (e.g. volume).

20.6 WHY CALLED "STORED FUNCTION"?

Oracle stores not only the source code of functions but also the compiled code in its database. That is why all functions in Oracle are called "STORED FUNCTIONS".

Whenever a function is created, Oracle automatically performs the following steps:

1. Compiles the function.
2. Stores the compiled code into database.
3. Stores the function source code in database. The "user_source" data dictionary can be queried to see the text of all functions defined.

20.7 TROUBLE SHOOTING ERRORS

If there are syntax errors in function code then on compiling, Oracle does not show the errors on screen. To see the errors encountered we need to use a command "show errors". Let us revisit our fn_cube() and introduce an error as shown in Program 20.3.

Let us introduce an error by replacing the assignment operator with equal to operator in the statement calculating y

$$y = p * p * p$$

Program 20.3 Function3.sql—debugging errors in functions.

```
create or replace function fn_cube(p number)
return number is
    y number;
begin
    y=p * p * p;
    return y;
end;
/
```

Now when we compile the function by typing @function3 (Figure 20.5), we receive the message that function has been created with compilation errors. But the errors are not shown.

```
SQL> @function3

Warning: Function created with compilation errors.
```

Figure 20.5 Compilation does not show error.

To display the actual errors we have to type a command "show errors" (Figure 20.6).

```
SQL> show errors
Errors for FUNCTION FN_CUBE:

LINE/COL ERROR

5/3 PLS-00103: Encountered the symbol "=" when expecting one of the following:
    := . ( @ % ;

6/2 PLS-00103: Encountered the symbol "RETURN"
```

Figure 20.6 Displaying error messages.

Oracle shows the line/column on which error has been encountered along with the error message.

Actually the "show errors" command queries a data dictionary view named "user_errors" for displaying the errors encountered. We can query the error messages from data dictionary as shown in Figure 20.7.

```
SQL> select line,position,substr(text,1,100) from user_errors;
LINE POSITION
SUBSTR(TEXT,1,100)
    5    3
PLS-00103: Encountered the symbol "=" when expecting one of the following:
    := . ( @ % ;
    6    2
PLS-00103: Encountered the symbol "RETURN"
```

Figure 20.7 Data dictionary for errors.

Here "text" column of "user_errors" is of type varchar2(4000). Therefore, for ease of display we have selected only first 100 characters of the text column using substr function.

20.8 STATUS OF A FUNCTION

If a function is not properly compiled or has some errors then Oracle maintains the status as VALID/INVALID for each function created in a data dictionary view named "user_object" as shown in Figure 20.8.

```
SQL> select object_name,object_type,status from user_objects where object_name=
'FN_CUBE';
```

OBJECT_NAME	OBJECT_TYPE	STATUS
FN_CUBE	FUNCTION	INVALID

Figure 20.8 Status of function.

Since we had encountered error message while compiling the function, therefore, its status is INVALID. The moment function gets compiled without error the status is updated as "VALID".

20.9 PROGRAM TO CHECK EXISTENCE OF BANK ACCOUNT USING FUNCTIONS

Let us now create a function named "check_account_id" which will receive account_id as parameter and will check the existence of that account in "tbl_bank_account". It will return 1 if account exists and 0 if account does not exist.

Assume BANK ACCOUNT table with structure and records as in Figure 20.9.

```
SQL> desc tbl_bank_account;
```

Name	Null?	Type
ACCOUNT_ID		CHAR(13)
BALANCE		NUMBER(12,2)

```
SQL> select * from tbl_bank_account;
```

ACCOUNT_ID	BALANCE
A012345678901	2000

Figure 20.9 Table structure and records in TBL_BANK_ACCOUNT.

The function for checking the existence of bank account is shown in Program 20.4.

Program 20.4   Function4.sql – checking existence of specified bank account.

```
create or replace function check_account_id(p_account_id char)
return char is
v_count number(1);
begin
   select count(*) into v_count from tbl_bank_account
   where account_id=p_account_id;

   if v_count > 0 then --account_id exists
           return 1;
   else
           return 0;
   end if;
end;
/
```

This function receives an input parameter named p_account_id and returns a character data type (0 or 1). We have declared a local variable named v_count which will contain 1 if corresponding account_id exists and 0 when account_id does not exist in tbl_bank_account.

Let us compile the function check_account_id as in Figure 20.10.

```
SQL> @function6

Function created.
```

Figure 20.10   Compiling Program 20.4.

Figure 20.11 shows the working of function of Program 20.4.

```
SQL> select check_account_id('1111') from dual;

CHECK_ACCOUNT_ID('1111')

0

SQL> select check_account_id('A012345678901') from dual;

CHECK_ACCOUNT_ID('A012345678901')

1
```

Figure 20.11   Using CHECK_ACCOUNT_ID function.

Caution: The data type for the parameter and the data type for return statement cannot specify the size. If we specify the data type size for parameter or return data type then Oracle gives error message.

Suppose we specify the data type for parameter "p_account_id" of check_account_id function (see Program 20.5).

Program 20.5 Function5.sql – specifying parameter size.

```
create or replace function check_account_id(p_account_id char(13))
return char is
v_count number(1);
begin
    select count(*) into v_count from tbl_bank_account
    where account_id=p_account_id;

    if v_count > 0 then --account_id exists
            return 1;
    else
            return 0;
    end if;
end;
/
```

Here, we have specified a size of 13 for p_account_id. Let us compile and see the result as shown in Figure 20.12.

```
SQL> @function5

Warning: Function created with compilation errors.

SQL> show errors
Errors for FUNCTION CHECK_ACCOUNT_ID:

LINE/COL ERROR

1/44 PLS-00103: Encountered the symbol "(" when expecting one of the following:
    := ) , default varying character large
    The symbol ":=" was substituted for "(" to continue.
```

Figure 20.12 Compiling Program 20.5.

Oracle gave an error message as we had specified char(13) for the parameter "p_account_id".

20.10 BOOLEAN PL/SQL DATA TYPE

PL/SQL supports a data type named BOOLEAN which can contain values TRUE or FALSE.

Now we will re-create the function5 (Program 20.4) using return type as BOOLEAN. See Program 20.6 for the code.

Program 20.6   Function6.sql—using BOOLEAN data type.

```
create or replace function check_account_id(p_account_id char)
return boolean is
v_count number(1);
begin
   select count(*) into v_count from tbl_bank_account
   where account_id=p_account_id;

   if v_count > 0 then --account_id exists
           return true;
   else
           return false;
   end if;
end;
/
```

Let us compile the Program 20.6 as shown in Figure 20.13.

```
SQL> @function6

Function created.
```

Figure 20.13   Compiling Program 20.6.

Let us try to use the function of Program 20.6 in the select statement (Figure 20.14).

```
SQL> select check_account_id('1111') from dual;
select check_account_id('1111') from dual
       *
ERROR at line 1:
ORA-06552: PL/SQL: Statement ignored
ORA-06553: PLS-382: expression is of wrong type
```

Figure 20.14   Using CHECK_ACCOUNT_ID function in SELECT.

Note: Oracle gives error message in the SELECT statements using functions returning BOOLEAN data type. Functions returning BOOLEAN data type can be used in other functions, procedures or PL/SQL blocks where value returned from these functions can be assigned to variables of Data Type BOOLEAN.

20.10.1   Using BOOLEAN Data Type for Checking Existence of Bank Account

Let us create a PL/SQL block making use of the function (Program 20.6) returning BOOLEAN data type. See Program 20.7 for the code.

Program 20.7 Function7.sql – PL/SQL block calling function6.sql with BOOLEAN return type.

```
set serveroutput on
declare
   v_check_account_id boolean;
begin
   v_check_account_id:=check_account_id('&account_id');
   if v_check_account_id = TRUE then --account exists
          dbms_output.put_line('Account Exists');
   end if;

   if v_check_account_id = FALSE then --account does not exist
          dbms_output.put_line('Account Does Not Exist');
   end if;
end;
/
```

Here, we have declared a variable "v_check_account_id" of type BOOLEAN. Then we have assigned the value TRUE or FALSE into this variable depending on the existence of particular account_id in tbl_bank_account.

Note:
1. BOOLEAN data type variables can be assigned just two values: TRUE/FALSE.
2. TRUE/FALSE are case insensitive. We can use either small case or upper case letters.

20.11   DROPPING A FUNCTION

A function can be removed from the database by using the DROP FUNCTION command (Figure 20.15).

```
SQL>drop function check_account_id;

Function dropped.
```

Figure 20.15   Removing a function.

20.12   GRANTING EXECUTE PERMISSION ON FUNCTION TO OTHER USERS

Suppose we need to allow user "john" to use our function "check_account_id", then we need to grant execute permission on the function to "john" user as shown in Figure 20.16.

```
SQL> grant execute on check_account_id to john;

Grant succeeded.

SQL> connect john/john@xe
Connected.
SQL> select scott.check_account_id('1111') from dual;

SCOTT.CHECK_ACCOUNT_ID('1111')

0
```

Figure 20.16   Granting EXECUTE permission on functions.

First as "scott" we granted execute permission on "check_account_id" to "john".
Then we logged in as "john" and used the function as "scott.check_account_id".

Caution: When a user grants execute permission on a function/procedure, the other user automatically gains the permission on all the DML operations on all objects being accessed within that function/ procedure even if he does not have access to individual DML operations on those objects.

20.13   REVOKING EXECUTE PERMISSION ON FUNCTION FROM OTHER USER

Execute permission on a function to other user can be withdrawn using the REVOKE command (Figure 20.17).

```
SQL> connect scott/scott@xe
Connected.
SQL> revoke execute on check_account_id from john;

Revoke succeeded.

SQL> connect john/john@xe
Connected.
SQL> select scott.check_account_id('1111') from dual;
select scott.check_account_id('1111') from dual
       *
ERROR at line 1:
ORA-00904: : invalid identifier
```

Figure 20.17   Removing EXECUTE permission on function.

20.14   FUNCTIONS CANNOT USE DDL STATEMENTS WITHIN THEM

Oracle does not allow functions to use DDL statements like "CREATE", "DROP" or "ALTER" in executable section as shown in Program 20.8.

Program 20.8   Function8.sql—DDL statements cannot be used within PL/SQL.

```
create or replace function check_ddl
return char is
begin
    insert into tbl_bank_account values ('1111111111111',1300);
    commit;
    drop table tbl_bank_account;
end;
/
```

On compiling the Oracle gives error message as shown in Figure 20.18.

```
SQL> @function8
Warning: Function created with compilation errors.

SQL> show errors
Errors for FUNCTION CHECK_DDL:
LINE/COL ERROR

6/2 PLS-00103: Encountered the symbol "DROP" when expecting one of the following:
    begin case declare end exception exit for goto if loop mod
    null pragma raise return select update while with
    <an identifier> <a double-quoted delimited-identifier>
    <a bind variable> << close current delete fetch lock insert
    open rollback savepoint set sql execute commit forall merge
    pipe
```

Figure 20.18   DDL statements cannot be used within functions.

Note:
1. DML operations are allowed within PL/SQL programs (functions, procedures, etc.).
2. DDL operations are not allowed.
3. When a function fails compilation then all the DML operations are also rolled back. The record with account_id '1111111111111' has not been inserted into the table due to failure in compilation of DDL statement.

20.15   VIEWING THE SOURCE CODE FOR STORED FUNCTION

Oracle stores the source code of all functions in data dictionary view named "user_source" (Figure 20.19).

```
SQL> select text from user_source where name='CHECK_ACCOUNT_ID';
TEXT

function check_account_id(p_account_id char)
return char is
v_count number(1);
begin
    select count(*) into v_count from tbl_bank_account
    where account_id=p_account_id;
    if v_count > 0 then —account_id exists
            return 1;
    else
            return 0;
    end if;
end;
```

Figure 20.19   Source code of functions.

20.16   FORMAL AND ACTUAL PARAMETERS

Refer to the CHECK_ACCOUNT_ID function (Program 20.7: function7.sql). The parameter p_account_id which is defined while creating the function is called "Formal Parameter" as at the time of Function compilation its value is not known. When this function is passed a value from SELECT or other PL/SQL programs then it is called an Actual Parameter.

```
create or replace function check_account_id(p_account_id char)
Here p_account_id is called the Formal Parameter.

v_check_account_id:=check_account_id('1111');
    Here '1111' is the actual parameter value.

select check_account_id('1111') from dual;
    Here '1111' is the actual parameter value.
```

20.17   A FUNCTION RETURNS A SINGLE VALUE

A function may contain several RETURN statements but only one of them returns the value. The RETURN statement returns the value to the calling program and stops further execution of function code. So in any case the function value is returned by the first executed RETURN statement discarding the rest of the RETURN statements. In our CHECK_ACCOUNT_ID function we have two RETURN statements but for a given account_id, only one of them will be executed.

REVIEW QUESTIONS _____

1. Define a Function. What is the purpose of using Functions?
2. Why the user-defined functions are called "Stored Functions" in Oracle?
3. Which command is used to view the errors on compilation? Compilation errors are stored in which data dictionary table?
4. What do we mean by status of a function? How can we find the current status of a function?
5. How can a function be called from other PL/SQL blocks?
6. What is the risk involved if a user has granted execute permission to other users on his functions?
7. Is it possible to use DDL statements within functions?
8. What does formal and actual parameters signify?
9. Can a function return more than one value? Can a function have multiple return statements?

LAB ASSIGNMENT _____

1. Create a function named "SimpleInterest" for calculating the simple interest. The function will receive Principal, Rate and Interest and it will calculate S.I. using P*R*T/100 and will return the same to calling program.

2. Create a function named "CALC_GRAND_SAL" which will receive EMPNO as parameter and calculate the GRAND SALARY as sum of SAL, COMM and 10% of SAL+COMM.

3. Write a function named Fibonacci for generating the Fibonacci series. Use recursion for the function.(0 1 1 2 3 5 8…9).

Refer to CUSTOMER ORDER table of Chapter 7 Lab Assignment.

4. Create a function named "PRODUCT_DESCRIPTION" which will receive PRODUCT_CD as parameter and will return corresponding description as Television for TVxxxxx, CD-PLAYER for CDxxxxx and so on.

(Hint: use SUBSTR() within function).

5. Create a function named "CALC_DISCOUNTED_PRICE" which will receive CUSTOMER_CODE and ORDER_NO. If the ORDER_DATE is before 01-apr-2008 then the selling price should be shown with 5% discount and if the ORDER_DATE is after 01-apr-2008, then the selling price should be discounted to 10%.

Stored Procedures

21.1 INTRODUCTION

A procedure is a logically grouped set of SQL and PL/SQL statements that perform a specific task. It is named PL/SQL block that is compiled and stored into the database.

21.2 ADVANTAGES OF PROCEDURES

1. *Modular Programming:* We can break a large program into smaller, more manageable well-defined units.
2. *Reusable:* Procedures can be used repeatedly executing the same logic without recompiling. Different users can use the same procedure.
3. *Improve Database Security:* We can restrict database access by allowing other users to access data through stored procedures.
4. *Performance:* Oracle keeps compiled code for procedures which improves performance.

Once Oracle has fetched compiled code into the memory, the cached version is then used by all consecutive calls from the same/other users without reading the compiled code from hard disk.

21.3 WHY CALLED "STORED PROCEDURES"?

Oracle stores both the source code and compiled code of procedures in database, therefore, procedures in Oracle are called "Stored Procedures".

21.4   SIMILARITIES BETWEEN PROCEDURES AND FUNCTIONS

The similarities between procedures and functions are:

1. Both are named PL/SQL blocks performing specific tasks.
2. Both provide the same advantages as listed in section 21.2.
3. Both can receive and return parameter values.
4. Both can be created without any input parameters.

21.5   DIFFERENCES BETWEEN PROCEDURES AND FUNCTIONS

The differences between procedures and functions are:

1. A function explicitly returns a single value to calling program through the "RETURN" statement. A procedure can return multiple values to the calling program using the OUT type parameters. But procedure cannot return values using the RETURN statement. The RETURN statement in procedure cannot pass values back to calling program.
2. While creating procedure we do not specify the RETURN type unlike Functions.

21.6   COMPONENTS OF PROCEDURES

Procedures comprise of three sections as shown in Figure 21.1.

Declarative Section	Declaration of variables and constants
Executable Section	PL/SQL statements which perform specific task
Exception Handling Section	The ERRORS occurring in Executable part can be handled in this section.

Figure 21.1   Structure of Stored Procedure.

Figure 21.2 shows the syntax of a Procedure Declaration.

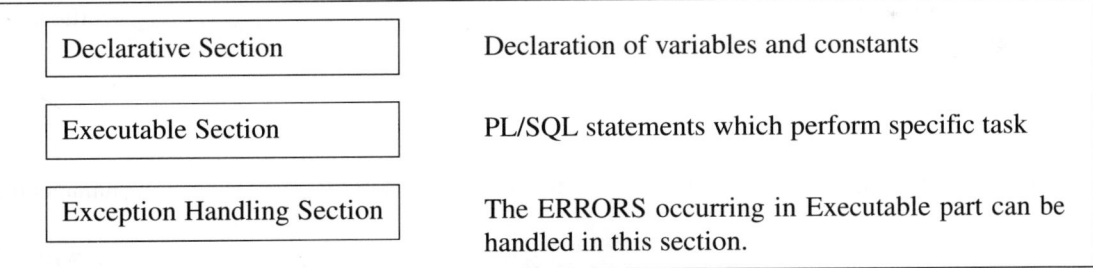

```
create or replace procedure procedure_name(parameters) is
    /* local variables declaration */              } Declarative Section
begin
    PL/SQL statements;
    ...................
    ...................                             } Executable Section
    ...................
exception
    PL/SQL statements for handling ERRORS           } Error Handling
End;
/
```

Figure 21.2   Syntax for procedural declaration.

Here, *procedure_name* is any user-defined name.

Note: The local variable declaration is not preceded by DECLARE keyword.

Let us now see a practical example. We want to develop a procedure named "proc_withdrawal" which will receive account_id and amount to be withdrawn. It will first check whether the specified account exists or not. If account does not exist it will display the message for non-existence and if the account exists it will check whether the new balance after desired withdrawal is at least 1000 (MINIMUM BALANCE).

Program 21.1 contains the code for "proc_withdrawal".

Program 21.1   procedure1.sql—procedure for withdrawing amount from bank.

```
set serveroutput on
create or replace procedure proc_withdrawal(p_account_id char, p_withdrawal_amount number)
is
MIN_BALANCE        constant number:=1000;
v_balance          number;
v_new_balance      number;
v_count            number(2);
begin
    select count(*) into v_count from tbl_bank_account
    where account_id=p_account_id;

    if v_count = 0 then
            dbms_output.put_line('Account Does Not Exist');
    else
            select balance into v_balance from tbl_bank_account
            where account_id=p_account_id;

            v_new_balance := v_balance - p_withdrawal_amount;

            if v_new_balance < MIN_BALANCE then
                    dbms_output.put_line('Cannot WithDraw');
            else
                    update tbl_bank_account set balance = v_new_balance
                    where account_id=p_account_id;
                    commit;
                    dbms_output.put_line('New balance : '||v_new_balance);
            end if;
    end if;
end;
/
```

Here, we have created a procedure named "proc_withdrawal". Two parameters have been created, namely p_account_id and p_withdrawal_amount. The working is quite intuitive. First we have checked the existence of account id by selecting count(*) into v_count. Remember that COUNT(*) returns 0 if matching record is not found. If v_count = 0 then we have displayed the appropriate message for non-existent account.

If account id existed then we have calculated the new balance. If new balance after withdrawal is less than 1000(MIN_BALANCE) then the person cannot withdraw money. If new balance >= 1000 then the account is updated for the new balance.

Note:
1. No size has been specified for the data type of both parameters.
2. Procedure declaration does not have the RETURN type statement before "IS".

21.7   COMPILING A PROCEDURE

We need to run the procedure1.sql script to compile the procedure (Figure 21.3).

```
SQL> @procedure1

Procedure created.
```

Figure 21.3   Compile procedure.

21.8   EXECUTING A PROCEDURE

"exec" is the command which executes the procedure.

Let us execute the procedure for account 1111 which does not exist in our table (Figure 21.4).

```
SQL> exec proc_withdrawal('1111',100);
Account Does Not Exist

PL/SQL procedure successfully completed.
```

Figure 21.4   Executing procedure.

Let us execute the procedure for account 'A012345678901' which exists in our table with a balance of 2000/- as shown in Figure 21.5.

```
SQL> exec proc_withdrawal('A012345678901',400);
New balance : 1600

PL/SQL procedure successfully completed.

SQL> select * from tbl_bank_account;

ACCOUNT_ID        BALANCE

A012345678901     1600
```

Figure 21.5   Executing procedure.

Let us again withdraw 800/- from the same account as in Figure 21.6.

```
SQL> exec proc_withdrawal('A012345678901',800);
Cannot WithDraw

PL/SQL procedure successfully completed.

SQL> select * from tbl_bank_account;

ACCOUNT_ID        BALANCE

A012345678901     1600
```

Figure 21.6   Execute procedure.

The procedure has displayed the message "Cannot Withdraw" as the new balance would be less than 1000/- after withdrawal of 800/- from 1600/-.

21.9   SOURCE CODE OF A PROCEDURE

Oracle stores the source code in data dictionary view named "user_source" as shown in Figure 21.7.

```
SQL> select text from user_source where name='PROC_WITHDRAWAL';

TEXT

procedure proc_withdrawal(p_account_id char,p_withdrawal_amount number) is
MIN_BALANCE constant number:=1000;
v_balance number;
v_new_balance number;
v_count number(2);
begin
    select count(*) into v_count from tbl_bank_account
    where account_id=p_account_id;

    if v_count = 0 then
            dbms_output.put_line('Account Does Not Exist');
    else
            select balance into v_balance from tbl_bank_account
            where account_id=p_account_id;

            v_new_balance := v_balance - p_withdrawal_amount;

            if v_new_balance < MIN_BALANCE then
                    dbms_output.put_line('Cannot WithDraw');
            else
                    update tbl_bank_account set balance = v_new_balance
                    where account_id=p_account_id;
                    commit;
                    dbms_output.put_line('New balance : '||v_new_balance);
            end if;
    end if;
end;

28 rows selected.
```

Figure 21.7   Source code of procedures.

21.10   DROPPING A PROCEDURE

Figure 21.8 shows the command to drop a procedure.

```
SQL>drop procedure proc_withdrawal;

Procedure dropped.
```

Figure 21.8   Dropping procedure.

21.11   CALLING A PROCEDURE FROM ANOTHER PROGRAM

Let us make one more procedure proc_deposit for depositing money into the account. Program 21.2 contains the code for creating "proc_deposit".

Program 21.2   procedure2.sql—procedure for depositing money in bank account.

```
set serveroutput on
create or replace procedure proc_deposit(p_account_id char,p_deposit_amount number)
is
v_count             number;
v_new_balance       number;
begin
    select count(*) into v_count from tbl_bank_account
    where account_id=p_account_id;

    if v_count = 0 then
            dbms_output.put_line('Account Does Not Exist');
    else
update tbl_bank_account set balance = balance + p_deposit_amount
            where account_id=p_account_id;
            commit;
            select balance into v_new_balance from tbl_bank_account
            where account_id=p_account_id;
            dbms_output.put_line('New balance : '||v_new_balance);
    end if;
end;
/
```

Let us compile and run the procedure as in Figure 21.9.

```
SQL> @procedure2

Procedure created.

SQL> select * from tbl_bank_account;

ACCOUNT_ID        BALANCE

A012345678901     1600
```

```
SQL> exec proc_deposit('A012345678901',300);
New balance : 1900

PL/SQL procedure successfully completed.

SQL> select * from tbl_bank_account;

ACCOUNT_ID        BALANCE

A012345678901     1900
```

Figure 21.9   Compiling and executing "proc_deposit".

Now we will make an unnamed PL/SQL block which will ask for whether to withdraw or deposit money. On specifying the option, it will call upon the proc_withdrawal or proc_deposit procedures. See Program 21.3 for the code.

Program 21.3   procedure3.sql—unnamed PL/SQL block calling stored procedures.

```
set serveroutput on

accept v_option number prompt 'Select 1 or 2 : '
accept v_account_id char prompt 'Enter Account id : '
accept v_amount char prompt 'Enter Amount : '

begin
    /**************************************/
    /********* 1. WithDrawal ************/
    /********* 2. Deposit ************/
    /**************************************/

    if &v_option=1 then
            proc_withdrawal('&v_account_id',&v_amount);
    elsif &v_option=2 then
            proc_deposit('&v_account_id',&v_amount);
    end if;
end;
/
```

First we have asked to input the option 1 or 2. If the option supplied is 1 then the procedure "proc_withdrawal" is called and if the option chosen is 2 then "proc_deposit" is called.

Note:
1. A procedure can be called in another program by just specifying its name along with parameters.
2. A procedure can be executed on SQL prompt by using the "exec" command.

Let us execute the procedure as shown in Figure 21.10.

```
SQL> select * from tbl_bank_account;

ACCOUNT_ID      BALANCE

A012345678901    1900

SQL> @procedure3
Select 1 or 2 : 1
Enter Account id : A012345678901
Enter Amount : 200
old        7:       if &v_option=1 then
new        7:       if     1=1 then
old        8:              proc_withdrawal('&v_account_id',&v_amount);
new        8:              proc_withdrawal('A012345678901',200);
old        9:       elsif &v_option=2 then
new        9:       elsif 1=2 then
old       10:              proc_deposit('&v_account_id',&v_amount);
new       10:              proc_deposit('A012345678901',200);
New balance : 1700

PL/SQL procedure successfully completed.

SQL> select * from tbl_bank_account;

ACCOUNT_ID      BALANCE

A012345678901    1700
```

Figure 21.10   Executing procedure3.sql.

In Figure 21.10, we have executed the procedure3.sql and chosen 1 for withdrawing an amount of Rs. 200/- from account A012345678901. After withdrawing 200/- from existing balance of 1900/-, the new balance is 1700/-.

21.12   PARAMETER PASSING

There are three modes in which a parameter can be passed from calling program to a called program (function or procedure), namely IN, OUT and IN OUT.

21.12.1   IN Mode

This is the default mode of parameter passing. We have to pass a value from calling program to IN parameter of called program. The value can be a constant, literal, initialized variable or expression. The IN parameter cannot be assigned a value within the called program.

21.12.2   OUT Mode

This mode of parameter is used to return value from called program to calling program. The OUT parameter must be assigned some value in the called program. The value of OUT parameter cannot be assigned to other variable in called program. The calling program must pass a variable name for OUT parameter. The calling program cannot specify literal, constant or expression for a OUT parameter.

21.12.3 IN OUT Mode

If we need to pass on values from calling program to called program and at the same time require that called program should return value then we use IN OUT parameter mode.

Note: If you are conversant with C language then IN parameter is similar to "passing by value" and OUT parameter is similar to "passing by reference".

See Programs 21.4 and 21.5 for understanding the concept of IN and OUT parameters. Program 21.4 accepts three parameters in different modes: "a" has been specified as "IN", "b" as OUT and "c" as IN OUT. In Program 21.5, we have created an unnamed PL/SQL block for passing parameters to procedure created in Program 21.4. Elaborate comments have been added to assist you in understanding the concept.

Program 21.4 procedure4.sql—program to understand various parameter modes.

```
clear screen
set serveroutput on

/*********** Called procedure *****************************/
create or replace procedure proc_parameters(a in number,b out number,c in out number)
is
begin
    dbms_output.put_line('*** Called Procedure : Begin ***');
    dbms_output.put_line('a= '||a);
    dbms_output.put_line('"a" has been assigned the value 10 from calling program');
    dbms_output.put_line('*************************************************************');

    dbms_output.put_line('b= '||b);
    dbms_output.put_line('"b" being defined as OUT parameter has not been assigned any value');
    dbms_output.put_line('although we have passed the value 11 through "y" from calling program');
    dbms_output.put_line('*************************************************************');

    dbms_output.put_line('c= '||c);
    dbms_output.put_line('"c" being defined as IN OUT has been assigned the value 22');
    dbms_output.put_line('from calling program through variable z');
    dbms_output.put_line('*************************************************************');

    --a:=111; ERROR: IN parameter cannot be assigned value in called procedure
    b:=100; --b,c being declared as OUT parameter therefore they can be assigned
            --values within the called procedure.
    c:=c+100;

    dbms_output.put_line('*** Called Procedure : After modifying values ***');
    dbms_output.put_line('Value of IN parameter "a" cannot be modified within called program');
    dbms_output.put_line('Value of OUT parameters "b","c" can be modified within called program');
    dbms_output.put_line('a= '||a);
    dbms_output.put_line('b= '||b);
    dbms_output.put_line('c= '||c);
end;
/
```

Program 21.5 procedure5.sql—unnamed PL/SQL block calling procedures.

```
*****************************************************************/
/*********** Unnamed PL/SQL block ( Calling Program ) **************/
/** this PL/SQL blocks calls the procedure proc_parameters declared in Program 21.4 ***/
/****************************************************************/

declare
    y number:=11;
    z number:=22;
begin
    dbms_output.put_line(' *** Main Program : Begin ***');
    dbms_output.put_line('x= '||y);
    dbms_output.put_line('y= '||z);
    dbms_output.put_line('*************************************');

    proc_parameters(10,y,z);

    dbms_output.put_line('*** Main Program : After calling procedure ***');
    dbms_output.put_line('y= '||y);
    dbms_output.put_line('z= '||z);
    dbms_output.put_line('*************************************');
    dbms_output.put_line('NOTE that values of "y" and "z" has got modified by called program');
    dbms_output.put_line('as "b" and "c" parameters have been defined to be of type OUT');

    --IN parameter "a" can be assigned value(here 10) from calling program
    --b and c being OUT parameters must be supplied variables / variable =———expressions

    --proc_parameters(10,20,z);
    --ERROR : 2nd parameter(b OUT) cannot be assigned value from —calling program

    --2nd parameter must be a variable / variable expression. It cannot be a
    --value as 20 over here.
end;
/
```

Let us run the procedure4.sql as in Figure 21.11.

```
SQL>@procedure4

Procedure created.

*** Main Program : Begin ***
x= 11
y= 22
************************************************************
*** Called Procedure : Begin ***
a= 10
"a" has been assigned the value 10 from calling program
************************************************************
```

```
b=
"b" being defined as OUT parameter has not been assigned any value
although we have passed the value 11 through "y" from calling program
*************************************************************
c= 22
"c" being defined as IN OUT has been assigned the value 22
from calling program through variable z
*************************************************************
*** Called Procedure : After modifying values ***
Value of IN parameter "a" cannot be modified within called program
Value of OUT parameters "b","c" can be modified within called program
a= 10
b= 100
c= 122
*** Main Program : After calling procedure ***
y= 100
z= 122
*************************************************************
NOTE that values of "y" and "z" has got modified by called program
as "b" and "c" parameters have been defined to be of type OUT

PL/SQL procedure successfully completed.
```

Figure 21.11   Running procedure4.sql.

Here, we have first declared a procedure named "proc_parameter". Three parameters have been defined: "a" as IN, "b" as OUT and "c" as "IN OUT".

Then we have declared an unnamed PL/SQL block which calls upon this procedure.

First we have assigned values 11 and 22 to variable "y" and "z" respectively. We have displayed their values. Then we have called upon procedure proc_parameters as follows:

proc_parameters(10,y,z);

we have passed value 10 to IN parameter "a" of procedure, variable "y" to OUT parameter "b" and variable "z" to IN OUT parameter "c".

"a" has been defined as IN parameter, therefore, we have to pass a value to "a". We cannot pass a variable or variable expression for IN type.

"b" has been defined as OUT parameter, therefore, we must pass variable to it. We cannot pass a value to OUT parameter.

"c" has been defined as both IN OUT parameter. As it is OUT parameter we must pass a variable name to it.

Let us see the working of Called Procedure.

First we have displayed the values of parameters "a", "b" and "c".
Note that "a" got assigned 10.
"b" was not assigned any value as it is of type OUT.
"c" got assigned 22 as it is of type IN/OUT.

Since "a" is a IN parameter, therefore, we cannot assign any value within the called program, e.g. a:=111; will give error message.

"b" and "c" being OUT parameters and can be assigned any value within the called program.

Then we have displayed the value for "a", "b" and "c" which are 10, 100, 122.

Now the execution returns to the calling program after the statement "proc_parameters (10,y,z);".
Now we have displayed the value for "y" and "z" which are 100 and 122 respectively. Since "y" and "z" were passed to OUT parameters "b" and "c", therefore, any changes to the values of "a" and "b" in the called procedure is also reflected in the calling program.

REVIEW QUESTIONS

1. Define a procedure and provide reasons for which they should be used.
2. Why procedures in Oracle are called "Stored Procedures"?
3. Which distinct feature differentiates a function from a procedure?
4. How are stored procedures called from other programs? Can stored procedures be executed on SQL prompt?
5. Specify the data dictionary table which stores the source code of functions and procedures.
6. What are the various modes of parameter passing? Explain each mode with examples.

LAB ASSIGNMENT

Refer to Tables 7.1 and 7.2 of the CUSTOMER ORDER database.
1. Create a procedure named "PROC_SELLING_PRICE" which will receive CUSTOMER_CODE as parameter. For each order by that customer, the procedure will determine the new selling price based on the following criteria. If the order quantity is between 1 and 5 then new selling price should be displayed as 5 percent discounted. If the order quantity is between 5 and 10 then new selling price should be displayed as 10 percent discounted or else 20 percent discounted.

22

Oracle Packages

22.1 INTRODUCTION

A package is a collection of stored functions, procedures and exceptions. A package is compiled and stored in database as an object. Suppose we are developing several applications like payroll, HR, accounting, etc. then we can group together the functions and procedures of individual applications into separate units called "PACKAGE". Each package will have its own set of functions and procedures related to the specific application. The facility of grouping together all related functions, procedures into one unit is called package.

For a banking application we may group together the following into single unit called "Package".

1. A function for checking the existence of an account_id in tbl_bank_account.
2. A procedure for withdrawal of money.
3. A procedure for depositing money.

22.2 ADVANTAGES OF PACKAGES

1. All related functions and procedures can be grouped together in a single unit called "package".
2. Packages ease the process of granting privileges. A privilege given on package passes on the granted privileges on all the functions and procedures defined within the package.
3. All the functions and procedures within a package can share variables among them. The variables can be of simple data types like NUMBER or complex types like cursors.
4. Packages enable to perform "overloading" of functions and procedures.
5. Packages improve performance by loading the multiple objects into memory at once, therefore, subsequent calls to related programs do not require physical I/O(from hard disk).

22.3 COMPONENTS OF PACKAGES

A package comprises 2 parts

1. A specification: It contains the list of various functions / procedure names which will be a part of the package.
2. *A body:* This contains the actual PL/SQL code implementing the logics of functions and procedures declared in "specification".

22.4 CREATING A PACKAGE

Let us create a package named "package_bank" which consists of the following:

1. A function named "fn_check_account_id" which will check for the existence of the specified account_id in bank.
2. A procedure named "proc_withdrawal" which will first check for the existence of an account_id using function "fn_check_account_id". If the account exists, it will deduct the withdrawal amount from the specified account.
3. A procedure name "proc_deposit" which will first check for the existence of an account_id using function "fn_check_account_id". Then it will add the amount to be deposited to the existing balance.

Step 1 Defining package specification

Program 22.1 shows how to create package specification.

Program 22.1 package1.sql—package specification.

```
create or replace package package_bank as
function fn_check_account_id(p_account_id char)
    return char;
procedure proc_withdrawal(p_account_id char,p_withdrawal_amount number);
procedure proc_deposit(p_account_id char,p_deposit_amount number);
end;
/
```

Step 2 Creating package body

Program 22.2 shows how to create package body.

Program 22.2 package2.sql—package body.

```
set serveroutput on

create or replace package body package_bank is
function fn_check_account_id(p_account_id char)
return char
is
v_count     number(1);
begin
    select count(*) into v_count from tbl_bank_account
    where account_id=p_account_id;
```

```
      if v_count=0 then --account does not exist in tbl_bank_account
            return 0;
      else                          --account exists in tbl_bank_account
            return 1;
      end if;
end;
procedure proc_withdrawal(p_account_id char,p_withdrawal_amount number)
is
v_account_exists    char;
v_balance           number;
v_new_balance            number;
begin
   v_account_exists:=fn_check_account_id(p_account_id);

   if v_account_exists='0' then
            dbms_output.put_line('Account Does Not Exist');
   else
            select balance into v_balance
            from tbl_bank_account where account_id=p_account_id;

            v_new_balance:=v_balance - p_withdrawal_amount;

            update tbl_bank_account set balance=v_new_balance
            where account_id=p_account_id;
            commit;
            dbms_output.put_line('New Balance : '||v_new_balance);
   end if;
end; --end of procedure proc_withdrawal
procedure proc_deposit(p_account_id char,p_deposit_amount number)
is
v_account_exists    char;
v_balance           number;
v_new_balance            number;
begin
   v_account_exists:=fn_check_account_id(p_account_id);

   if v_account_exists='0' then
            dbms_output.put_line('Account Does Not Exist');
   else
            update tbl_bank_account set balance=balance + p_deposit_amount
            where account_id=p_account_id;
            commit;
            dbms_output.put_line('Amount Deposited');
   end if;
end;         --end of procedure proc_deposit
/* ALL global variables are declared here */
begin — this begin corresponds to package initialization
   dbms_output.put_line('PACKAGE EXAMPLE');
end;
/
```

22.5   CALLING PACKAGE FUNCTIONS AND PROCEDURES

Assume records in tbl_bank_account as in Figure 22.1.

```
SQL> select * from tbl_bank_account;

ACCOUNT_ID        NAME   BALANCE

A123456789012     satish    1500
```

Figure 22.1   Records in TBL_BANK_ACCOUNT.

22.6   EXECUTING PACKAGE FUNCTION

Figure 22.2 shows the syntax for executing function within a package.

```
SQL> select package_bank.fn_check_account_id('1111') from dual;

PACKAGE_BANK.FN_CHECK_ACCOUNT_ID('1111')

0

SQL> select package_bank.fn_check_account_id('A123456789012') from dual;

PACKAGE_BANK.FN_CHECK_ACCOUNT_ID('A123456789012')

1
```

Figure 22.2   Executing package function.

Package functions are called by specifying package_name.(dot) function_name.

Package function "fn_check_account_id" has returned 0 for non-existent accounts and 1 for existing account.

22.7   EXECUTING PACKAGE PROCEDURE

Package procedure can be executed by the "exec" command as in Figure 22.3.

```
SQL> exec package_bank.proc_deposit('1111',100);
Account Does Not Exist

PL/SQL procedure successfully completed.
```

Figure 22.3   Executing package procedure.

Note that proc_deposit has called upon fn_check_account_id and has displayed an appropriate message.

Let us deposit Rs. 1000/- in account A123456789012 as shown in Figure 22.4.

```
SQL> select * from tbl_bank_account;

ACCOUNT_ID          NAME   BALANCE

A123456789012       satish   1500

SQL> exec package_bank.proc_deposit('A123456789012',1000);
Amount Deposited

PL/SQL procedure successfully completed.

SQL> select * from tbl_bank_account;

ACCOUNT_ID          NAME   BALANCE

A123456789012       satish   2500
```

Figure 22.4   Deposit amount.

Let us now withdraw 400/- from the same account as shown in Figure 22.5.

```
SQL> select * from tbl_bank_account;

ACCOUNT_ID          NAME   BALANCE

A123456789012       satish   2500

SQL> exec package_bank.proc_withdrawal('A123456789012',400);
New Balance : 2100

PL/SQL procedure successfully completed.

SQL> select * from tbl_bank_account;

ACCOUNT_ID          NAME   BALANCE

A123456789012       satish   2100
```

Figure 22.5   Withdraw amount.

22.8   GRANTING PRIVILEGES ON PACKAGES TO OTHER USERS

Figure 22.6 shows the command for giving access on packages to "john" user.

```
SQL> grant execute on package_bank to john;

Grant succeeded.
```

Figure 22.6   Granting privileges on packages.

Let us connect as john and execute the package procedure in "scott" user (Figure 22.7).

```
SQL> connect john/john@xe
Connected.
SQL> select * from scott.tbl_bank_account;
select * from scott.tbl_bank_account
       *
ERROR at line 1:
ORA-00942: table or view does not exist

SQL> exec scott.package_bank.proc_withdrawal('A123456789012',200);

PL/SQL procedure successfully completed.
```

Figure 22.7   Other user accessing package procedure.

"john" can call packages of "scott" user by specifying user_name.package_name.procedure_name with parameters.

Caution: Although "john" user does not have the permission to even view the records of scott.tbl_bank_account but he has been granted execute permission on package_bank, therefore, he is able to perform update operation on tbl_bank_account of scott user.

22.9   REVOKING PRIVILEGES ON PACKAGES FROM OTHER USERS

Figure 22.8 shows how to remove execute privilege on package from john user.

```
SQL> connect scott/scott@xe
Connected.
SQL> revoke execute on package_bank from john;

Revoke succeeded.
```

Figure 22.8   Removing privileges on package.

22.10   DROPPING PACKAGE

Figure 22.9 shows how to remove a package from database.

```
SQL> drop package package_bank;

Package dropped.
```

Figure 22.9   Removing package.

22.11   DATA DICTIONARY FOR PACKAGE SPECIFICATION

Figure 22.10 displays the package specification from data dictionary "USER_SOURCE".

```
SQL> select text from user_source where name='PACKAGE_BANK' and type='PACKAGE';

package package_bank as
function fn_check_account_id(p_account_id char)
 return char;
procedure proc_withdrawal(p_account_id char,p_withdrawal_amount number);
procedure proc_deposit(p_account_id char,p_deposit_amount number);
end;
```

Figure 22.10   Data dictionary for package specification.

22.12   DATA DICTIONARY FOR PACKAGE BODY

Figure 22.11 displays the package body from data dictionary "USER_SOURCE".

```
SQL> select text from user_source where name='PACKAGE_BANK' and type='PACKAGE BODY';

package body package_bank is
function fn_check_account_id(p_account_id char)
return char
is
v_count number(1);
begin
    select count(*) into v_count from tbl_bank_account
    where account_id=p_account_id;

    if v_count=0 then          --account does not exist in tbl_bank_accoun
            return 0;
    else                       --account exists in tbl_bank_account
            return 1;
    end if;
end;

procedure proc_withdrawal(p_account_id char,p_withdrawal_amount number)
is
v_account_exists char;
...............................
...............................
...............................
```

Figure 22.11   Data dictionary for package body.

22.13   STATUS OF PACKAGES

Oracle maintains the status of objects as "VALID/INVALID" in data dictionary called "user_objects". It maintains separate status for package specification and package body as shown in Figure 22.12.

```
SQL> column object_name format a30
SQL> select object_name,object_type,created,status from user_objects where
object_name='PACKAGE_BANK';
```

OBJECT_NAME	OBJECT_TYPE	CREATED	STATUS
PACKAGE_BANK	PACKAGE	06-APR-08	VALID
PACKAGE_BANK	PACKAGE BODY	06-APR-08	VALID

Figure 22.12   Status of package.

REVIEW QUESTIONS

1. Define a package and explain the purposes for which packages should be used.
2. What are the steps for creating a functional package?
3. How can package functions and procedures be called from other programs?
4. When a privilege is granted to other user on a package does he gain privileges on the inner functions and procedures also?
5. What are the data dictionary tables for finding the package specification and body?

LAB ASSIGNMENT

Refer to Tables 7.1 and 7.2 of the CUSTOMER ORDER database

1. Create a function named "PRODUCT_DESCRIPTION" which will receive PRODUCT_CD as parameter and will return corresponding description as television for TVxxxxx, cd-player for CDxxxxx and so on.

   (Hint: use SUBSTR() within function).

2. Create a function named "CALC_DISCOUNTED_PRICE" which will receive CUSTOMER_CODE and ORDER_NO. If the ORDER_DATE is before 01-apr-2008 then the selling price should be shown with 5% discount and if the ORDER_DATE is after 01-apr-2008 then the selling price should be discounted to 10%.

3. Create a procedure named "PROC_SELLING_PRICE" which will receive CUSTOMER_CODE as parameter. For each order by that customer, the procedure will determine the new selling price based on the following criteria. If the order quantity is between 1 and 5 then new selling price should be displayed as 5 percent discounted. If the order quantity is between 5 and 10 then new selling price should be displayed as 10 percent discounted or else 20 percent discounted.

4. Create a package named "PACKAGE_CUSTOMER" which will contain the functions created in Q1, Q2 and as well as the procedure of the Question 3.

Exception Handling in PL/SQL

23.1 INTRODUCTION

We have discussed the various sections of PL/SQL program, namely DECLARE, BEGIN and END. Let us now learn about the section named EXCEPTION which deals with the handling of errors that are encountered while executing the statements within BEGIN and END section. Whenever an error is encountered in the statements within the BEGIN and END section, Oracle displays the error number along with a message indicating the type of error.

Exception means that something has gone wrong and we need to halt the program execution immediately. The program can halt on encountering pre-defined Oracle exceptions or user-defined exceptions.

23.2 CLASSIFICATION OF ERRORS

The classification of errors is shown in Figure 23.1.

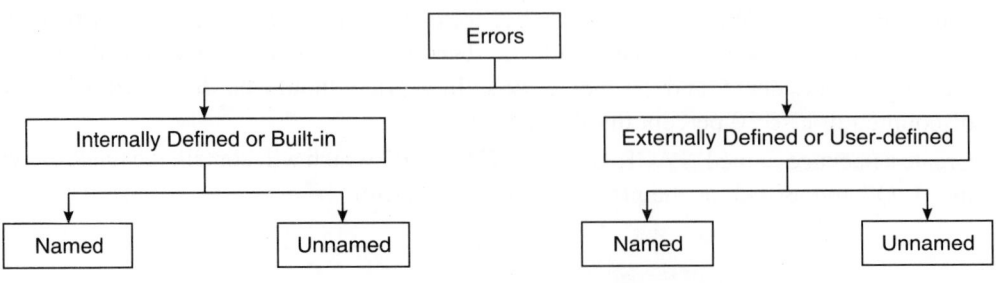

Figure 23.1 Classification of errors.

23.2.1   Internally Defined or Built-in Errors

These errors are pre-defined and are automatically raised by Oracle whenever an error is encountered. Each error is assigned a unique number and a message.

These can be further classified as Named and Unnamed.

Named errors

These pre-defined errors have been assigned names by Oracle. They can be referred to by the name instead of number and some of them have been listed in Table 23.1.

TABLE 23.1   Examples of named errors

Error No.	Error Name	Raised When
ORA-01422	TOO_MANY_ROWS	When a SELECT statement returns more than one row.
ORA-01403	NO_DATA_FOUND	When a SELECT statement does not return any row.
ORA-06502	VALUE_ERROR	Raised when the data type or data size is invalid.
ORA-00001	DUP_VAL_ON_INDEX	Raised whenever a SQL statement tries to enter duplicate values for a column which has unique index.
ORA-01476	ZERO_DIVIDE	When division by zero occurs.
ORA-01722	INVALID_NUMBER	When a character is supplied for a number data type.

Unnamed errors

These are also pre-defined errors with unique error number but do not have an assigned name. They are generated automatically whenever an error occurs, displaying a unique error number.

These are referred to by the general name "OTHERS". **OTHERS stands for all other exceptions not explicitly named**.

Table 23.2 contains a list of Unnamed exceptions from oracle website (http://download.oracle.com/docs/cd/B14117_01/server.101/b10744/toc.htm).

TABLE 23.2   Unnamed errors webpage

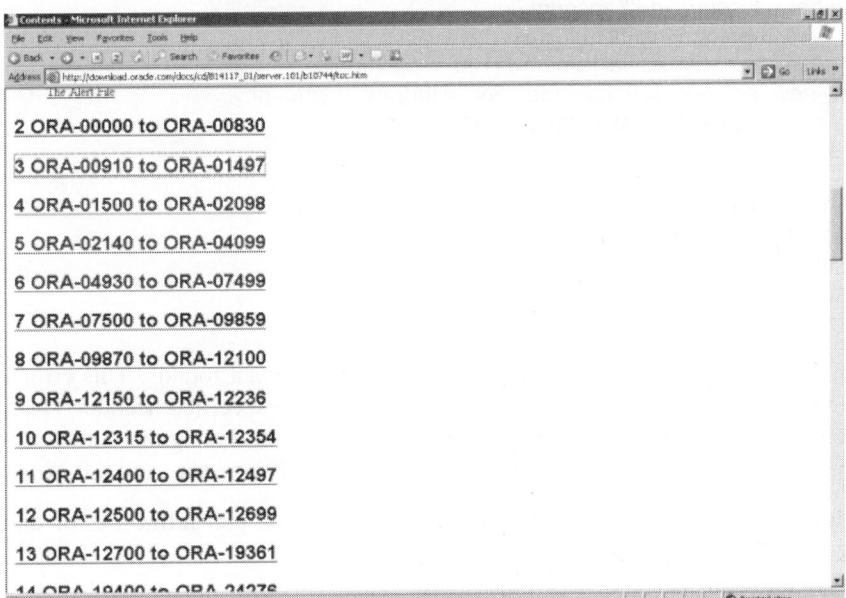

Handling pre-defined named exceptions

Refer to Program 23.1 which contains an unnamed PL/SQL block for withdrawal of money from a bank account without any EXCEPTION section.

Program 23.1 exception1.sql—without exception section.

```
/*** this is a simple program for withdrawal of money
    without any validations and no exception section *******/
declare
            v_account_id      char(13);
            v_balance         number;
            v_new_balance     number;
begin
            select account_id,balance into v_account_id,v_balance from tbl_bank_account where
            account_id='&account_id';

            v_new_balance := v_balance - &v_withdrawal_amount;

            update tbl_bank_account set balance=v_new_balance
            where account_id=v_account_id;

            commit;
end;
/
```

Let us run the Program 23.1 for account id 1111 which is not in tbl_bank_account as shown in Figure 23.2.

```
SQL> @exception1
Enter value for account_id: 1111
old 7: where account_id='&account_id';
new 7: where account_id='1111';
Enter value for v_withdrawal_amount: 100
old 9: v_new_balance := v_balance - &v_withdrawal_amount;
new 9: v_new_balance := v_balance - 100;
declare
*
ERROR at line 1:
ORA-01403: no data found
ORA-06512: at line 6
```

Figure 23.2 Running Program 23.1.

Note: Oracle has returned an error message "ORA-01403: no data found". This error has occurred because the SELECT statement did not find any record for the specified account 1111. So an error message having unique id "ORA-01403" was executed by Oracle saying that "no data found". This message is not very intuitive in the sense that it does not specify the exact cause of error.

Now let us use the EXCEPTION section to handle this pre-defined error and assign it a proper error message. See Program 23.2 for the sample code.

Program 23.2 exception2.sql—exception section for handling pre-defined exceptions.

```
/*** this is a simple program for withdrawal of money
     without any validations but with EXCEPTION Section
     to handle pre-defined exceptions *********/
set serveroutput on

declare
          v_account_id      char(13);
          v_balance         number;
          v_new_balance     number;
begin
          select account_id,balance into v_account_id,v_balance from tbl_bank_account
          where account_id='&&account_id';

          v_new_balance := v_balance - &v_withdrawal_amount;

          update tbl_bank_account set balance=v_new_balance
          where account_id=v_account_id;

          commit;

exception
          when NO_DATA_FOUND then
                    dbms_output.put_line('Account id : '||'&&account_id'||
                    ' DOES NOT EXIST');
end;
/
```

Here "NO_DATA_FOUND" is a pre-defined named exception.
Let us run the Program 23.2 with account id 1111 as in Figure 23.3.

```
SQL> @exception2
Enter value for account_id: 1111
old 7:          where account_id='&&account_id';
new 7:          where account_id='1111';
Enter value for v_withdrawal_amount: 100
old 9:          v_new_balance := v_balance - &v_withdrawal_amount;
new 9:          v_new_balance := v_balance - 100;
old 18:         dbms_output.put_line('Account id : '||'&&account_id'||
new 18:         dbms_output.put_line('Account id : '||'1111'||

Account id : 1111 DOES NOT EXIST

PL/SQL procedure successfully completed.
```

Figure 23.3 Running Program 23.2.

What exactly has happened that on encountering pre-defined error "ORA-01403 : no data found", Oracle instead of executing its default code has executed the code specified by us in the exception section.

Caution:
1. Whenever any exception is encountered the control of program moves to the EXCEPTION section without executing the statements followed next to the point where exception occurred. EXCEPTION is a method of exiting normal program execution with proper messages.
2. All the statements that were executed prior to the point of exception are rolled back if EXCEPTION is encountered.

Handling exceptions other than those defined in the EXCEPTION section

It is quite possible that we may miss out writing code for some exception. Therefore, Oracle provides a facility of displaying OTHER exceptions also as shown in Program 23.3.

Program 23.3   exception3.sql—handling OTHER exceptions.

```
set serveroutput on
declare
    v_account_id      char(13);
    v_balance         number;
    v_new_balance     number;
    v_calc            number;
begin
    select 1/0 into v_calc from dual;

    select account_id,balance into v_account_id,v_balance from tbl_bank_account
    where account_id='&&account_id';

    v_new_balance := v_balance - &v_withdrawal_amount;

    update tbl_bank_account set balance=v_new_balance
    where account_id=v_account_id;

    commit;

exception
    when NO_DATA_FOUND then
            dbms_output.put_line('Account id : '||'&&account_id'||
            ' DOES NOT EXIST');
    when OTHERS then
            dbms_output.put_line(SQLCODE||' '||SQLERRM);
end;
/
```

Here we have generated a "Divide by zero" error prior to the SELECT statement. In EXCEPTION section, we have defined "NO_DATA_FOUND" error as before but we have also defined that in other cases errors show the Oracle's built-in error number (SQLCODE) and error message (SQLERRM).

23.2.2   User-defined Exceptions

These are explicitly declared and raised by user. **User-defined exceptions can again be divided into two categories:** 1. Named and 2. Unnamed.

User-defined Named Exceptions

These exceptions are defined by name and are raised explicitly by user. Let us consider a table "employee" with records as shown in Figure 23.4.

```
SQL> select * from employee;
        EMPID           SALARY          COMMISSION
          1              4000             1000
          2              5000             6000
```

Figure 23.4   Records in EMPLOYEE table.

We will make a PL/SQL block for incrementing the commission of specified employee by 500. But if in any case commission is greater than the salary then we must exit the program with appropriate message. See Program 23.4 which meets the specified requirement.

Program 23.4   exception4.sql—user-defined named exceptions.

```
set serveroutput on

declare
    v_empid number(4);
    v_salary number;
    v_commission    number;
    EXP_COMM_GT_SAL EXCEPTION;
begin
    select empid,salary,commission into v_empid,v_salary,v_commission
    from employee where empid='&&empid';

    if v_commission > v_salary then --exit the program with proper message
            RAISE exp_comm_gt_sal;
    else
            update employee set commission=commission + 500
            where empid=v_empid;
            commit;
    end if;

EXCEPTION
    When EXP_COMM_GT_SAL then
            dbms_output.put_line('Commission greater than salary for employee : '||v_empid);
            dbms_output.put_line('Program Terminated with Error Condition');
    when OTHERS then
            dbms_output.put_line(SQLERRM);
end;
/
```

We have defined EXP_COMM_GT_SAL as of type EXCEPTION in DECLARE section. Then we have raised(called) the exception by "RAISE EXP_COMM_GT_SAL" statement. In the EXCEPTION section we have specified the code which has to be executed when this exception is raised.

Note: User-defined exceptions need to be declared and raised by user only.

Let us run the Program 23.4 for empid 2 as in Figure 23.5.

```
SQL> @exception4
Enter value for empid: 2
old 8:         from employee where empid='&&empid';
new 8:         from employee where empid='2';
Commission greater than salary for employee : 2
Program Terminated with Error Condition

PL/SQL procedure successfully completed.
```

Figure 23.5 Running Program 23.4.

User-defined unnamed exceptions

Oracle provides a feature wherein we can RAISE exceptions by our own assigned error number and message without specifying a name to it. Program 23.5 contains the code for user-defined unnamed exception.

Program 23.5 exception5.sql—user-defined unnamed exceptions.

```
set serveroutput on

declare
    v_empid number(4);
    v_salary number;
    v_commission     number;
begin
    select empid,salary,commission into v_empid,v_salary,v_commission
    from employee where empid='&&empid';

    if v_commission > v_salary then --exit the program with proper message

    RAISE_APPLICATION_ERROR(-20000,'Commission more than Salary');

    else
            update employee set commission=commission + 500
            where empid=v_empid;
            commit;
    end if;

EXCEPTION
    when OTHERS then
            dbms_output.put_line(SQLERRM);
end;
/
```

Here we have not declared any exception, rather we have raised the exception using " RAISE_APPLICATION_ERROR" with a error number and a message. We can use the number error numbers from –20000 to –20999 for our own defined errors. Oracle reserves the rest error numbers for its internal exception handling.

Let us run the exception5.sql for empid 2 as shown in Figure 23.6.

```
SQL> @exception5
old 7: from employee where empid='&&empid';
new 7: from employee where empid='2';
ORA-20000: Commission more than Salary

PL/SQL procedure successfully completed.
```

Figure 23.6 Running Program 23.5.

Assigning name and Error number to user-defined exception

A user-defined exception can be assigned a name and an error number by using PRAGMA pre-compiler directive. This directive binds the specified error number to a user-defined exception name. In Program 23.6, we have declared an exception named "EXP_COMM_GT_SAL" and then we have used the PRAGMA EXCEPTION_INIT to bind number -20000 to EXP_COMM_GT_SAL.

Program 23.6 exception6.sql—naming a User-defined exception.

```
set serveroutput on

declare
    v_empid number(4);
    v_salary number;
    v_commission    number;
    EXP_COMM_GT_SAL    EXCEPTION;
    PRAGMA EXCEPTION_INIT(EXP_COMM_GT_SAL,-20000);
begin
    select empid,salary,commission into v_empid,v_salary,v_commission
    from employee where empid='&&empid';

    if v_commission > v_salary then --exit the program with proper message
            RAISE EXP_COMM_GT_SAL;
    else
            update employee set commission=commission + 500
            where empid=v_empid;
            commit;
    end if;

EXCEPTION
    when EXP_COMM_GT_SAL then
dbms_output.put_line(SQLERRM||' '||'Commission Greater Than Salary');
    when OTHERS then
            dbms_output.put_line(SQLERRM);
end;
/
```

On encountering the error we have raised "EXP_COMM_GT_SAL" for which corresponding code has been written in EXCEPTION section.

Let us run Program 23.6 for empid 2 as in Figure 23.7.

```
SQL> @exception6
Enter value for empid: 2
old 9: from employee where empid='&&empid';
new 9: from employee where empid='2';
ORA-20000: Commission Greater Than Salary

PL/SQL procedure successfully completed.
```

Figure 23.7   Running Program 23.6.

Note that Oracle has now shown ORA-20000 as error number and the corresponding message "Commission Greater Than Salary".

23.3   CONTINUING AFTER AN EXCEPTION IS RAISED

Whenever an exception is raised the normal program execution is aborted with the control moving to EXCEPTION section. The statements below the point where exception occurred are not executed. But what if we want to continue with the statements which are below the point where exception occurred.

Let us see an example. We have table "test" with 2 columns "a" and "b". We want to calculate the ratio a/b for record where b=0 and store it in table "result". See Program 23.7.

Program 23.7   exception7.sql—continuing after an exception.

```
drop table test;
create table test (a number, b number);
insert into test values (10,3);
insert into test values (21,0);
insert into test values (34,3);
commit;

drop table result;
create table result (result number);

set serveroutput on
declare
    v_ratio number;
begin
    select a/b into v_ratio from test where b=0;

    insert into result values (v_ratio);
exception
    WHEN ZERO_DIVIDE THEN
            dbms_output.put_line('Division By Zero Occurred');
    WHEN OTHERS THEN
            dbms_output.put_line(SQLERRM);
end;
/
select * from result;
```

Let us execute the Program 23.7 as shown in Figure 23.8.

```
SQL> @exception7

Table dropped.

Table created.

1 row created.

1 row created.

1 row created.

Commit complete.

Table dropped.

Table created.

Division By Zero Occurred

PL/SQL procedure successfully completed.

no rows selected
```

Figure 23.8 Running Program 23.7.

Note that no records have been inserted in the "result" table as the ZERO_DIVIDE error is encountered in the SELECT statement, Oracle exits the program and moves control to the exception section. The INSERT statement just after the SELECT statement is not executed.

Now let us make a program which will insert the ratio 0 for record where b=0 even after the ZERO_DIVIDE error is encountered. See Program 23.8 for the code.

Program 23.8 exception8.sql—continuing after an exception is raised.

```
set serveroutput on
declare
   v_ratio number;
begin
   begin
           select a/b into v_ratio from test where b=0;
   exception
           WHEN ZERO_DIVIDE THEN
                   v_ratio:=0;
   end;
   insert into result values (v_ratio);
exception
   WHEN OTHERS THEN
           dbms_output.put_line(SQLERRM);
end;
/
select * from result;
```

Here we have defined 2 blocks of BEGIN … END. The outer block has BEGIN, EXCEPTION and END section. The outer block encloses the inner block which contains BEGIN, EXCEPTION and END. "ZERO_DIVIDE" is in the inner block and "OTHERS" is in the outer block.

When the SELECT statement is executed "ZERO_DIVIDE" exception is encountered, the control of program moves to EXCEPTION section of the inner block and assigns value 0 to v_ratio. Then this value of v_ratio is inserted into the result table by the INSERT statement which is outside the inner blocks exception section and will always be executed.

Let us run the Program 23.8 as shown in Figure 23.9.

```
SQL> @exception8

PL/SQL procedure successfully completed.

     RESULT

        0
```

Figure 23.9 Running Program 23.8.

23.4 DISPLAYING USER-DEFINED MESSAGES FOR PRE-DEFINED (NAMED OR UNNAMED) EXCEPTIONS

User-defined messages can be associated with named as well as unnamed pre-defined exceptions. Program 23.9 shows how to specify user-defined messages for pre-defined exceptions.

Program 23.9 exception9.sql—displaying user-defined messages.

```
set serveroutput on

declare
    v_empid        number(4);
    v_salary       number;
    v_commission   number;
    v_ratio        number;
begin
    select 1/0 into v_ratio from dual;

    select empid,salary,commission into v_empid,v_salary,v_commission
    from employee where empid='&&empid';

EXCEPTION
    WHEN OTHERS THEN
    dbms_output.put_line('************************************');
    dbms_output.put_line('** Default Error Message by Oracle **');
    dbms_output.put_line('————————————————————————');
    dbms_output.put_line(SQLERRM);

    dbms_output.put_line('************************************');
```

```
        dbms_output.put_line('User Defined Error Message');
        dbms_output.put_line('————————————————————');

        if SQLERRM LIKE 'ORA-01403%' then
                dbms_output.put_line('Record for specified employee DOES NOT EXIST');
        end if;

        if SQLERRM LIKE 'ORA-01476%' then
                dbms_output.put_line('Division By Zero Not Allowed');
        end if;

    end;
    /
```

Here, we have displayed default Oracle error messages using SQLERRM and in EXCEPTION section we have used IF clauses for 2 exceptions numbered 01403 and 01476 and displayed our own messages.

REVIEW QUESTIONS

1. What do we mean by exception? What does handling exceptions signify?
2. Can exceptions be handled in SQL commands?
3. What is the difference between internal and external exceptions?
4. Differentiate between Named and Unnamed Errors.
5. Is it possible to resume the program execution where exception has occurred through EXCEPTION Section?
6. What do SQLCODE and SQLERRM contain?
7. Why the user-defined exceptions need to be explicitly raised?
8. How can we assign an ERROR No. to a user-defined exception?
9. Can we associate user-defined messages to pre-defined exceptions? If yes, then how?

24

Cursors

24.1 HOW ARE SQL STATEMENTS PROCESSED BY ORACLE?

Oracle performs a set of tasks for executing any SQL statement.

1. Reserves an area in memory called private SQL area.
2. Populates this area with appropriate data.
3. Processes the data in memory.
4. Frees the memory area when execution completes.

Example: SELECT college, rollno, nvl(marks,0) from student
WHERE college='OIST'
ORDER BY college, rollno;

To execute the above statement Oracle reserves an area in memory and populates with all records in student table, rejects records which do not satisfy WHERE clause, applies NVL function to marks column, arranges the records in ascending order of college, rollno and then displays the records to user.

24.2 WHAT IS CURSOR?

Cursor is the work area which Oracle reserves for internal processing of SQL statements. The data which is stored in the cursor is called **Active Data Set**.

24.3 PURPOSE OF CURSOR/WHEN TO USE CURSOR?

Within PL/SQL a SELECT statement cannot return more than one row at a time. So in order to process some group of rows (more than one row) for implementing certain logic to all the records of that group, we need to use cursors. Although in cursors also only one row is selected at any given time.

When we have to process a set of records and not a single record then we have to use cursors.

24.4 CLASSIFICATION OF CURSORS

Cursors can be broadly classified as:

Implicit or Internal—Managed by Oracle itself.

Explicit or User-defined—Managed explicitly by users/programmers.

24.4.1 Implicit Cursors

For any SQL statement Oracle uses implicit cursors for its internal processing. Even if we execute a SELECT statement Oracle reserves a private SQL area in memory(called cursor), populates that area with data and rejects record which do not satisfy WHERE clause and then applies ORDER BY clause and displays the records to the client/user. Figure 24.1 represents the private SQL area along with active data set for a query from client.

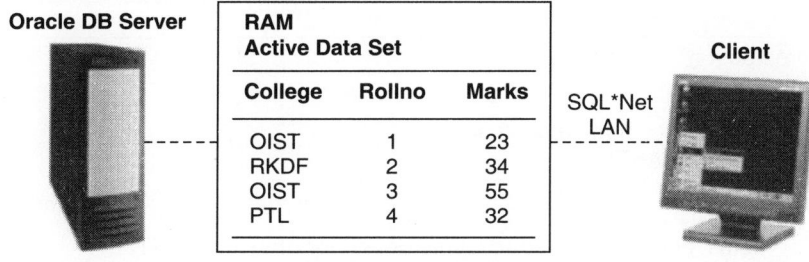

Figure 24.1 Cursor.

Implicit cursor variables

Each implicit cursor has associated with its certain variables which are listed in Table 24.1.

TABLE 24.1 List of implicit cursor variables

Cursor attribute	Cursor variable	Description
%ISOPEN	SQL%ISOPEN	The Oracle database automatically opens and closes the implicit cursor associated with any select, insert, update or delete statement. As such the SQL%ISOPEN always returns FALSE for implicit cursors.
%FOUND	SQL%FOUND	Returns TRUE if SELECT returns one/more than one row, INSERT creates a row, UPDATE, DELETE affect one or more than one rows.
%NOTFOUND	SQL%NOTFOUND	Is logical opposite of %FOUND.
%ROWCOUNT	SQL%ROWCOUNT	Returns the number of rows affected by an insert, update, delete or select statement.

Although we need not use this attribute for implicit cursors which are internally used by Oracle but let us try to see the values in these variables whenever a SQL statement is fired.

Assume a table "tbl_bank_account" with columns and records as in Figure 24.2.

```
SQL> select * from tbl_bank_account;

    ACCOUNT_ID          BRANCH          BALANCE          STATUS
    A123456789012       SHAKTI          2000             ACTIVE
    B123456789012       KOLAR           1000             ACTIVE
    C123456789012       SHAKTI          4000             ACTIVE
```

Figure 24.2 Records in TBL_BAN_ACCOUNT.

Here BRANCH is the area where bank is located.

STATUS can be ACTIVE or INACTIVE. Whenever no transactions are done in an account for more than 1 year then the account is inactivated.

We will update the status of all accounts in "SHAKTI" area to INACTIVE as branch has been closed and we will display the values of various CURSOR attributes. See Program 24.1 for the code.

Program 24.1 cursor1.sql—implicit cursor variables.

```
set serveroutput on

begin
    update tbl_bank_account set status='INACTIVE'
    where branch='SHAKTI';

    IF SQL%FOUND THEN
            dbms_output.put_line('Accounts Found for branch SHAKTI');
    END IF;

    IF SQL%NOTFOUND THEN
            dbms_output.put_line('NO Accounts for branch SHAKTI');
    END IF;

    IF SQL%ROWCOUNT > 0 then
            dbms_output.put_line(SQL%ROWCOUNT||' account(s) Inactivated');
    ELSE
            dbms_output.put_line('NO Active account(s) Found');
    END IF;
end;
/
```

Let us run the Program 24.1 as shown in Figure 24.3.

```
SQL> @cursor1
Accounts Found for branch SHAKTI
2 account(s) Inactivated

PL/SQL procedure successfully completed.
```

Figure 24.3 Running Program 24.1.

As 2 records were updated belonging to branch "SHAKTI", therefore, SQL%FOUND returned TRUE and the desired message was displayed.

SQL%NOTFOUND returned FALSE and the corresponding message was not displayed.

SQL%ROWCOUNT returned 2, therefore, the message "2 account(s) Inactivated" was displayed.

Note: SQL%ISOPEN will always return FALSE for implicit cursors as the cursor is closed as soon as the SQL statement is processed.

24.4.2   Explicit Cursors

The cursors which are declared by user are called Explicit Cursors. The user has to declare the cursor, open cursor to reserve memory area and populate data, fetch records from the Active Data Set one at a time, apply the processing logic and then close the cursor.

Explicit cursor variables/attributes

Each explicit cursor has associated with its certain variables, which have been listed in Table 24.2.

TABLE 24.2   List of explicit cursor variables

Cursor attribute	Cursor variable	Description
%ISOPEN	SQL%ISOPEN	The Oracle database automatically opens and closes the implicit cursor associated with any select, insert, update or delete statement. As such the SQL%ISOPEN always returns FALSE for implicit cursors.
%FOUND	SQL%FOUND	Returns TRUE if SELECT returns one/more than one row, INSERT creates a row, UPDATE, DELETE affect one or more than one rows.
%NOTFOUND	SQL%NOTFOUND	Is logical opposite of %FOUND.
%ROWCOUNT	SQL%ROWCOUNT	Returns the number of rows affected by an insert, update, delete or select statement.

Steps involved in using explicit cursors

1. Declare a cursor that specifies the SQL statement to be processed.
2. OPEN the cursor—this will reserve a memory area and will populate the memory with required records.
3. LOOP for all the records in cursor (Active Data Set).
4. FETCH one record at a time from Active Data Set.
5. Apply the processing logic to one record at a time.
6. Exit the LOOP when no records are found or else repeat the loop.
7. CLOSE the cursor—free the memory area occupied by Active Data Set.

For example, Assume 3 tables with structure and records as shown in Figure 24.4.

```
SQL> desc tbl_bank_account;

    Name                        Null?              Type

    ACCOUNT_ID                                     CHAR(13)
    BRANCH                                         VARCHAR2(10)
    BALANCE                                        NUMBER(7,2)
    STATUS                                         VARCHAR2(10)
    ACCOUNT_TYPE                                   VARCHAR2(10)

SQL> desc tbl_bank_transactions;

    Name                        Null?              Type

    ACCOUNT_ID                                     CHAR(13)
    TRANSACTION_DATE                               DATE
    WITHDRAWAL_AMT                                 NUMBER(7,2)
    DEPOSIT_AMT                                    NUMBER(7,2)

SQL> desc tbl_bank_audit;

    Name                        Null?              Type

    ACCOUNT_ID                                     CHAR(13)
    DATE_OF_INACTIVATION                           DATE
    ACCOUNT_TYPE                                   VARCHAR2(10)
```

Figure 24.4   Records in bank account and transactions.

"tbl_bank_account" contains the account_id, branch, balance amount, status (ACTIVE/INACTIVE) —depending on whether any transactions have been done in the past 1 year or not and account type as SAVINGS or CURRENT.

"tbl_bank_transactions" records each and every withdrawal and deposit action along with the date of transaction.

"tbl_bank_audit" : whenever any account is inactivated then the account_id, account_type along with date of inactivation will be recorded in this table.

Develop a program which will inactivate all those accounts in which no transactions have occurred in the past 1 year. Moreover, our program will insert a record in "tbl_bank_audit" specifying the account_id which is inactivated and the date of inactivation. See Program 24.2 for the code.

Program 24.2   cursor2.sql—using CURSOR.

```
/*
As we have to process group of records for which no transactions
have occurred in the last 1 year therefore we will have to use cursor
*/
set serveroutput on
```

```
declare
    v_account_id              char(13);
    v_account_type            varchar2(10);

    cursor c1 is select account_id,account_type from tbl_bank_account
    where account_id in (select account_id from tbl_bank_transactions
    group by account_id having sysdate - MAX(transaction_date) > 365);
begin
    open c1;
    loop
            fetch c1 into v_account_id,v_account_type;
            exit when c1%notfound;

            update tbl_bank_account set status='INACTIVE'
            where account_id=v_account_id;
            commit;

insert into tbl_bank_audit (account_id,date_of_inactivation,account_type)
            values (v_account_id,sysdate,v_account_type);
            commit;
    end loop;
close c1;
end;
/
```

In Program 24.2, we have declared a cursor c1 which will return account id's for which no transactions have occurred for the last 1 year. Note that we have used an inner query with the GROUP BY clause which returns account "A123456789012" and "C123456789012". MAX(transaction_date) returns the date of last transaction and sysdate—MAX(transaction_date) returns the difference in days which has been compared with 1 year (365 days).

OPEN c1: Reserves a memory area in RAM and populates the cursor with 2 records for account id's - "A123456789012" and "C123456789012".

Then we have used a LOOP for implementing the desired logic for each record returned by the cursor.

FETCH c1 into v_account_id, v_account_type actually moves the pointer to first record in Active Data set, that is, account id "A123456789012", assigns the value of account_id column to variable v_account_id and value of account_type column to v_account_type.

The UPDATE statement updates the status to "INACTIVE" for account id "A123456789012".

The INSERT statement inserts the account id, account_type and sysdate as date of inactivation.

On reaching the END LOOP, the program control transfers to the LOOP statement.

Next record is fetched by the FETCH statement and the same process is repeated for the account id "C123456789012".

Assume the records in 3 tables for a BANK as in Figure 24.5.

```
SQL> select * from tbl_bank_account;

    ACCOUNT_ID          BRANCH       BALANCE      STATUS        ACCOUNT_TY

    A123456789012       SHAKTI       2000         ACTIVE        SAVINGS
    B123456789012       KOLAR        1000         ACTIVE        SAVINGS
    C123456789012       SHAKTI       4000         ACTIVE        CURRENT

SQL> select * from tbl_bank_transactions;

    ACCOUNT_ID          TRANSACTION       WITHDRAWAL        DEPOSIT
                        _DATE             _AMT              _AMT

    A123456789012       03-APR-07         100               0
    A123456789012       06-APR-07         200               0
    A123456789012       05-APR-07         0                 500
    B123456789012       10-APR-08         1000              0
    C123456789012       01-APR-07         0                 3000

SQL> select * from tbl_bank_audit;

no rows selected
```

Figure 24.5 Sample records in BANK tables.

Let us execute the Program 24.2 assuming sysdate as "10-apr-08" (Figure 24.6).

```
SQL> @cursor2
DOC>As we have to process group of records for which no transactions
DOC>have occurred in last 1 year therefore we will have to use cursor
DOC>*/

PL/SQL procedure successfully completed.

SQL> select * from tbl_bank_account;

    ACCOUNT_ID          BRANCH       BALANCE      STATUS        ACCOUNT_TY

    A123456789012       SHAKTI       2000         INACTIVE      SAVINGS
    B123456789012       KOLAR        1000         ACTIVE        SAVINGS
    C123456789012       SHAKTI       4000         INACTIVE      CURRENT

SQL> select * from tbl_bank_audit;

        ACCOUNT_ID              DATE_OF_I           ACCOUNT_TY

        A123456789012           10-APR-08           SAVINGS
        C123456789012           10-APR-08           CURRENT
```

Figure 24.6 Running Program 24.2.

Status of Accounts A123456789012 and C123456789012 has become "INACTIVE" as no transactions has occurred within 365 days in "TBL_BANK_TRANSACTIONS".

24.5   DECLARING TYPE OF THE VARIABLES (TYPE)

In Program 24.2 we have declared v_account_id as char(13). We need to describe the table tbl_bank_account for knowing the data type and size of columns and then use the same type and size in declaring variables.

Oracle provides a facility whereby we can specify the same data type and size for variables as in the table by specifying table_name.column_name%TYPE as follows:

```
Declare
        v_account_id     tbl_bank_account.account_id%TYPE;
        v_account_type   tbl_bank_account.account_type%TYPE;
........................
...........................
```

This means that our local variable "v_account_id" will be assigned the same data type and size as that of the "account_id" column of "tbl_bank_account".

Note: Use of %TYPE reduces the risk of program from failing when the data type or size of columns in table are changed.

24.6   CURSOR DATA TYPE

We can define a variable of type cursor. In Program 24.2, if cursor contained many columns then for each column we need to declare separate local variables for holding the values fetched from cursor records. In Program 24.2, we have declared two variables v_account_id and v_account_type for the two columns account_id and account_type selected in cursor.

Oracle provides a facility whereby we can declare a single variable of type cursor. Program 24.3 is the example code for Program 24.2 using cursor variable.

Program 24.3   cursor3.sql (CURSOR variable).

```
/*
As we have to process group of records for which no transactions
have occurred in last 1 year therefore we will have to use cursor
*/
set serveroutput on

declare
    cursor c1 is select account_id,account_type from tbl_bank_account
    where account_id in (select account_id from tbl_bank_transactions
    group by account_id having sysdate - MAX(transaction_date) > 365);

    c1_rec  c1%rowtype;
begin
    open c1;
    loop
```

```
                fetch c1 into c1_rec;
                exit when c1%notfound;

                update tbl_bank_account set status='INACTIVE'
                where account_id=c1_rec.account_id;
                commit;

                insert into tbl_bank_audit
                (account_id,date_of_inactivation,account_type)
                values (c1_rec.account_id,sysdate,c1_rec.account_type);
                commit;
        end loop;
    close c1;
    end;
    /
```

In Program 24.3, we have not declared the two variables v_account_id and v_account_type.
We have declared a variable c1_rec as of c1%rowtype. What this means is that c1_rec variable will have two variables, namely c1_rec.account_id and c1_rec.account_type each referring to the columns selected in CURSOR c1.

"fetch c1 into c1_rec;" means that cursor c1's account_id value has been fetched into c1_rec.account_id and c1's account_type value is fetched into c1_rec.account_type.

In the UPDATE statement we have compared account_id to c1_rec.account_id.

Similarly, INSERT values have been derived from c1_rec.account_id and c1_rec.account_type.

24.7 CURSOR FOR LOOP

Till now we have specified statements to OPEN, LOOP, FETCH and CLOSE cursors. Oracle provides a CURSOR FOR LOOP which automatically does all the operations like OPEN, LOOP, FETCH and CLOSE. Program 24.4 is the same Program as 24.3 using CURSOR FOR LOOP.

Program 24.4   cursor4.sql (CURSOR FOR LOOP).

```
set serveroutput on

declare
    cursor c1 is select account_id,account_type from tbl_bank_account
    where account_id in (select account_id from tbl_bank_transactions
    group by account_id having sysdate - MAX(transaction_date) > 365);

    c1_rec   c1%rowtype;
begin
    for c1_rec in c1 loop

                update tbl_bank_account set status='INACTIVE'
                where account_id=c1_rec.account_id;
                commit;
```

```
                    insert into tbl_bank_audit
                    (account_id,date_of_inactivation,account_type)
                    values (c1_rec.account_id,sysdate,c1_rec.account_type);
                    commit;
           end loop;
     end;
     /
```

Note: OPEN, LOOP, FETCH and CLOSE statements have not been used. Oracle automatically performs these operations when we use CURSOR FOR LOOP.

24.8 PARAMETERIZED CURSORS

The *parameter makes the cursor more reusable.* Instead of hardcoding a value into the WHERE clause of a query to select particular information, you can use a parameter and then pass different values to the WHERE clause each time a cursor is opened.

Assume 2 tables, namely "tbl_bank_account" and "tbl_bank_new_accounts".

Tbl_bank_account contains the accounts existing in the bank.

Tbl_bank_new_accounts contains the list of new accounts to be added in tbl_bank_account.

It is quite possible that an account which is already existing in tbl_bank_account is again entered in tbl_bank_new_accounts. Figure 24.7 shows the existing as well as new records and account A123456789012 is appearing in both the records.

```
SQL> select * from tbl_bank_account;

    ACCOUNT_ID BRANCH          BALANCE STATUS          ACCOUNT_TY

    A123456789012 SHAKTI          2000 ACTIVE            SAVINGS
    B123456789012 KOLAR           3000 ACTIVE            CURRENT
    C123456789012 SHAKTI          5000 ACTIVE            SAVINGS

SQL> select * from tbl_bank_new_accounts;

    ACCOUNT_ID BRANCH          BALANCE STATUS          ACCOUNT_TY

    A123456789012 SHAKTI          2000 ACTIVE            SAVINGS
    P123456789012 ARERA           5000 ACTIVE            SAVINGS
    X123456789012 KOLAR          10000 ACTIVE            SAVINGS
    Q123456789012 KOLAR           800 ACTIVE             SAVINGS
```

Figure 24.7 Records in BANK.

We will write a Program 24.5 which will insert records from tbl_bank_new_accounts into tbl_bank_account. Before inserting NEW accounts we have to check whether that account already exists in tbl_bank_account or not. If exists then display message that "Account already Exists" or else insert the new account into tbl_bank_account.

We will define 2 cursors one for tbl_bank_new_accounts and another for tbl_bank_account with account_id of 1st cursor passed as a parameter. See Program 24.5 for the code.

Program 24.5 cursor5.sql (Parameterized Cursor).

```
set serveroutput on

declare
    cursor c_bank_new_accounts is select * from tbl_bank_new_accounts;
    c_bna    c_bank_new_accounts%rowtype;

    cursor c_bank_account(p_account_id char) is select * from tbl_bank_account
    where account_id=p_account_id;
    c_ba c_bank_account%rowtype;
begin
    open c_bank_new_accounts;
    loop
            fetch c_bank_new_accounts into c_bna;
            exit when c_bank_new_accounts%notfound;

            open c_bank_account(c_bna.account_id);

            fetch c_bank_account into c_ba;
                    if c_bank_account%found then
                    dbms_output.put_line('Account Id : '||c_bna.account_id||
                    ' Already Exists');
            else
                    insert into tbl_bank_account values (c_bna.account_id,c_bna.branch,
                    c_bna.balance,c_bna.status,c_bna.account_type);
                    commit;
            end if;

            close c_bank_account;
    end loop;
    close c_bank_new_accounts;
end;
```

Cursor c_bank_new_acccounts fetches all records from tbl_bank_new_accounts.

For each record fetched by cursor c_bank_new_acccounts, cursor c_bank_account is opened by passing the account_id of c_bank_new_acccounts(c_bna) as parameter. If corresponding record found in tbl_bank_account then message is displayed that "Account Already Exists" and if not found then new account is inserted into tbl_bank_account.

Note: The cursor c_bank_account is opened and then closed at the end of every account_id fetched in c_bank_new_accounts.

Let us run the Program 24.5 and view the contents of tbl_bank_account (Figure 24.8).

```
SQL> @cursor5
Account Id : A123456789012 Already Exists

PL/SQL procedure successfully completed.
```

```
SQL> select * from tbl_bank_account;
```

ACCOUNT_ID BRANCH	BALANCE STATUS	ACCOUNT_TY
A123456789012 SHAKTI	2000 ACTIVE	SAVINGS
B123456789012 KOLAR	3000 ACTIVE	CURRENT
C123456789012 SHAKTI	5000 ACTIVE	SAVINGS
Q123456789012 KOLAR	800 ACTIVE	SAVINGS
P123456789012 ARERA	5000 ACTIVE	SAVINGS
X123456789012 KOLAR	10000 ACTIVE	SAVINGS

6 rows selected.

Figure 24.8 Running Program 24.5.

24.9 PARAMETERIZED CURSOR FOR LOOP

The same Program 24.5 (cursor5.sql) can be written using CURSOR FOR LOOP as shown in Program 24.6. Here we learn how to pass parameters using CURSOR FOR LOOP.

Program 24.6 cursor6.sql (Parameterized CURSOR FOR LOOP).

```
set serveroutput on

declare
    cursor c_bank_new_accounts is select * from tbl_bank_new_accounts;
    c_bna    c_bank_new_accounts%rowtype;

    cursor c_bank_account(p_account_id char) is select * from tbl_bank_account
    where account_id=p_account_id;
    c_ba c_bank_account%rowtype;
begin
    for c_bna in c_bank_new_accounts loop
            for c_ba in c_bank_account(c_bna.account_id) loop
                    if c_bank_account%found then
                        dbms_output.put_line('Account Id :
                            '||c_bna.account_id||' Already EXists');
                    else
                            insert into tbl_bank_account values
                            (c_bna.account_id,c_bna.branch,
                            c_bna.balance,c_bna.status,c_bna.account_type);
                            commit;
                    end if;
            end loop;
    end loop;
end;
/
```

REVIEW QUESTIONS

1. What operations are performed by Oracle for displaying the result of a SELECT statement?
2. Define cursor and Active Data Set.
3. Specify the situations which will need CURSORS.
4. What are the various types of Cursors? Differentiate between Implicit and Explicit cursors.
5. Explain the purpose of various cursor variables.
6. What are the steps involved in defining and using explicit cursors? What does OPENING and CLOSING a cursor signify?
7. FETCH moves the cursor pointer to the next record. Can it be used to jump to desired record in Active Data Set?
8. Is it necessary to use some LOOPING construct to deal with Active Data Set?
9. What is the advantage of using TYPE for various PL/SQL variables?
10. What is CURSOR Data Type and how does it help in coding?
11. Explain the CURSOR FOR LOOP and the advantages it offers over the traditional LOOPS.
12. Explain the concept of Parameterized Cursors with an example.

LAB ASSIGNMENT

1. Create a PL/SQL program using cursors which will display the EMPNO, ENAME, SAL and COMM on screen from EMP table for department 20 and 30 in the order of department number. (Hint: Use CURSOR and DBMS_OUTPUT.PUT_LINE)
2. For the program developed in Question1, display the column headings also.
3. Write a PL/SQL block to delete all the employees of department 20 with salary more than 3000 and check if at least one row has been processed. Use the SQL%FOUND attribute and move the deleted records in EMP_HISTORY table.
4. Write a PL/SQL block to increment the salary of employees of department 30 by 20%. If the number of employees affected by salary hike is more than 5 then ROLLBACK or else COMMIT the change.
5. Develop a PL/SQL program which will receive department number as parameter. Declare a CURSOR which will select all employees of that department, raise the salary by 15%, updates the new salary in EMP table and at the same time adds records in EMP_TRANSACTIONS table containing EMPNO, DATE_OF_RAISE and NEW_SALARY.
6. Write a PL/SQL block using CURSOR FOR LOOP which will display the top 5 salaried employees from EMP table and add those employees in a new table named "EMP_TOP_EARNERS".
7. Refer to the CUSTOMER ORDER tables of Chapter 7 Lab Assignment.

   Create a table named "CUSTOMER_STATUS" with 3 columns CUSTOMER_NAME, LAST_ORDER_DATE and STATUS. Add all the customers who have not placed any order for the past 6 months into this table specifying the last date on which an order was placed. Secondly, mark the status of such customers as 'D GRADE'.

Database Triggers

25.1 DATABASE TRIGGER

A trigger is a PL/SQL block that is associated with a table, stored in database and executed implicitly/automatically in response to a specific data manipulation event.

The data manipulation events for which a trigger gets automatically executed are: Insert, Update and Delete.

A trigger is a database object like a table or view which is stored in the database and is always executed when the event for which it is defined occurs. It does not matter if the event is triggered by some SQL statement, PL/SQL, utilities like SQL*Loader or front end data entry screens developed using Developer 10g, Visual Basic or web applications using ASP, JSP, etc.

25.2 COMPONENTS OF TRIGGER

1. **Triggering SQL statement:**   The SQL statements on execution of which the defined trigger code fires is called Triggering SQL statement. For example, INSERT, UPDATE and DELETE.
2. **Trigger action:**   The PL/SQL block which gets executed when the Triggering SQL statement is executed.
3. **Trigger restriction:**   We can specify under what condition the trigger should fire.

25.3 TYPES OF TRIGGERS

Oracle has 13 triggers. See Figure 25.1 for the list of triggers.

25.3.1 Classification of Triggers

The classification of triggers based on whether they fire/execute before or after the triggering statement.

BEFORE TRIGGERS

AFTER TRIGGERS

25.3.2 Classification Based on Whether the Trigger Fires for Each Record or Table

STATEMENT LEVEL (TABLE LEVEL)

ROW LEVEL

25.3.3 Classification Based on the DML Operation (Triggering Event)

INSERT

UPDATE

DELETE

Therefore, there can be 12 types of triggers in Oracle (Figure 25.1) based on the above classification (Section 25.3).

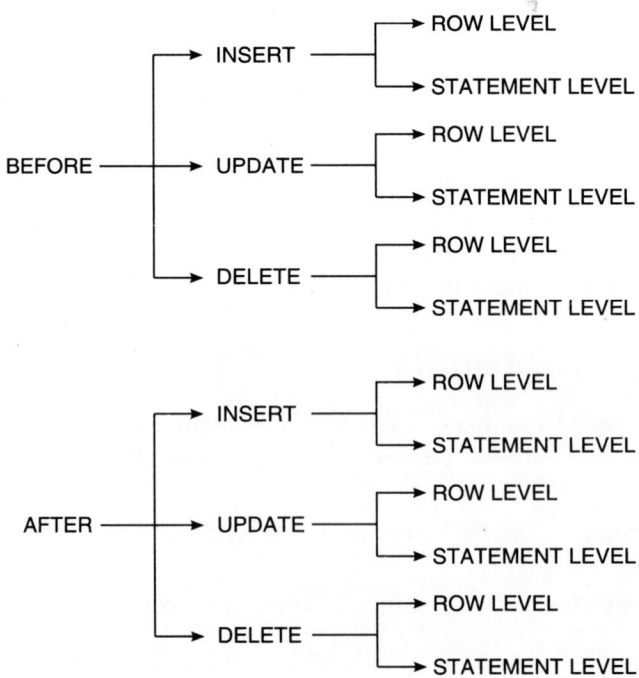

Figure 25.1 Classification of triggers.

Note: The 13th trigger is called **INSTEAD OF** which is discussed at the end of this chapter (Section 25.6).

Before triggers

These triggers are fired before the triggering SQL statement (INSERT, UPDATE, DELETE) is executed. The execution of triggering SQL statement can be stopped depending on the various conditions to be fulfilled in BEFORE trigger.

After triggers

These triggers are fired after the triggering SQL statement (INSERT, UPDATE, DELETE) is executed. The triggering SQL statement is anyhow executed first followed by the code of trigger.

> **Note:**
> *Oracle has 13 triggers:* 1–12 are based on the various combinations of BEFORE or AFTER, DML operation and ROW or STATEMENT level.
>   13th Trigger is INSTEAD OF and is used for Non-Updateable views.

Statement level or table level

These triggers are fired for each DML operation being performed on a table. We cannot access the column values for records being inserted, updated or deleted as it is meant for the table and not for the individual records.

Example: Suppose we want to keep a record of the date and time when a DML operation was performed on the "employee" table. We are not concerned with the rows for which DML operation is performed. We just want to record the DML operation(INSERT, UPDATE or DELETE) and the date on which it was performed on table "employee" in table "tbl_audit". Figure 25.2 contains the structure of TBL_AUDIT table.

```
SQL> desc tbl_audit;
    Name                        Null?              Type
    TABLE_NAME                                     VARCHAR2(10)
    DML_OPERATION                                  VARCHAR2(6)
    DATE_OF_DML                                    DATE
```

Figure 25.2   Structure of TBL_AUDIT.

We will write a STATEMENT/TABLE LEVEL trigger (Program 25.1) as we are not bothered to identify the rows on which DML operations are performed. We just need to identify the date on which a DML operation was performed on the table "employee".

Program 25.1   trigger1.sql (Statement level trigger).

```
create or replace trigger trig_employee_audit
after insert or update or delete on employee
begin
    if INSERTING then
            insert into tbl_audit values ('EMPLOYEE','INSERT',sysdate);
    end if;
    if UPDATING then
            insert into tbl_audit values ('EMPLOYEE','UPDATE',sysdate);
    end if;
```

```
        if DELETING then
                insert into tbl_audit values ('EMPLOYEE','DELETE',sysdate);
        end if;

end;
/
```

Let us create the trigger using Program 25.1 as shown in Figure 25.3.

```
SQL> @trigger1

Trigger created.
```

Figure 25.3   Creating trigger of Program 25.1.

Now let us insert, update and delete few records from the EMPLOYEE table and see the status of tbl_audit as in Figure 25.4.

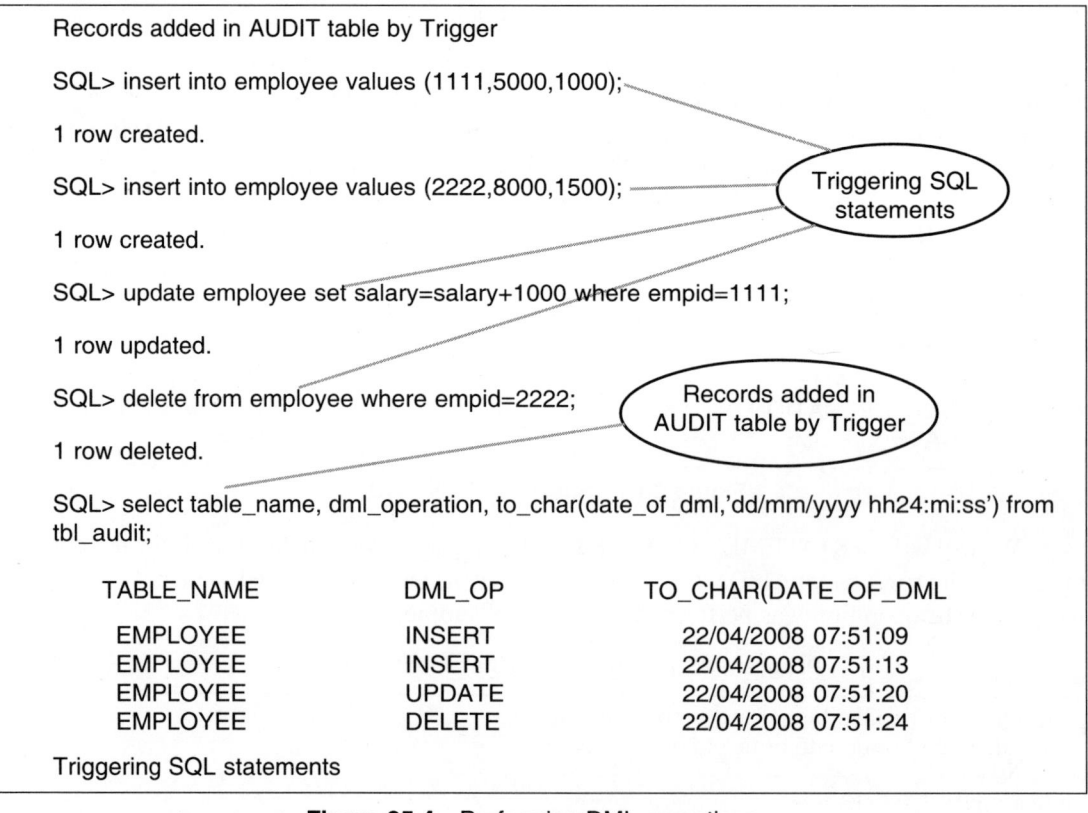

Figure 25.4   Performing DML operations.

Note: We generally use statement level triggers for the purpose of DML auditing only.

In Program 25.1, insert operation has been identified by reserved word "INSERTING". Similarly update and delete have been identified using "UPDATING" and "DELETING" reserved words. We could have written BEFORE trigger instead of AFTER also. For STATEMENT level triggers BEFORE and AFTER do not differ in logic. The only point is that if we write BEFORE trigger then the trigger code is executed first followed by the triggering DML statement.

ROW LEVEL TRIGGERS

These triggers are fired for each and every record which is inserted or updated or deleted from a table.

In the STATEMENT level triggers, we cannot access the values of individual rows being inserted, updated or deleted. Suppose we want to implement a logic that when a new employee is being added then in no case the commission be greater than the salary. The same logic is to be applied while updating values for either salary or commission. In such situations we have to access the values of rows being inserted, updated or deleted then we have to use ROW LEVEL triggers.

First we need to check the values whether commission is less than salary or not, therefore, we will create a BEFORE ROW LEVEL trigger, because the trigger code has to be executed for each and every row being inserted or updated. Program 25.2 contains the code for creating a ROW LEVEL BEFORE trigger.

Program 25.2   trigger2.sql (ROW LEVEL BEFORE trigger).

```
create or replace trigger trig_employee_sal_gt_comm
before insert or update on employee
for each row
begin
   if inserting then
         if :new.salary < :new.commission then
                 raise_application_error('-20000','INSERT Error:
                 Commission CANNOT be GREATER THAN Salary');
         end if;
   end if;

   if updating then
         if :new.salary < :new.commission then
                 raise_application_error('-20001','UPDATE Error:
                 Commission CANNOT be GREATER THAN Salary');
         end if;
   end if;

end;
/
```

Note that in Program 25.2, we have declared trigger as "BEFORE' and "FOR EACH ROW" (indicating row level trigger). Secondly, we have used a variable named "new.column_name" for accessing the values being inserted. The values specified in the INSERT command on SQL Prompt can be referred to **:NEW.COLUMN**.

Let us create the trigger from code of Program 25.2 and insert a new record as in Figure 25.5 such that sal > comm.

```
SQL> @trigger2

Trigger created.

SQL> insert into employee values (3333,9000,2000);

1 row created.
```

Figure 25.5   Creating trigger and adding records with sal > comm.

As salary > commission, therefore, record got inserted into employee table.
Let us try to insert a record where salary < commission as shown in Figure 25.6.

```
Trigger Code execution
SQL> insert into employee values (4444,5000,7000);          Triggering SQL
   insert into employee values (4444,5000,7000)               statements
             *
ERROR at line 1:
ORA-20000: INSERT Error: Commission CANNOT be GREATER THAN Salary
ORA-06512: at "SCOTT.TRIG_EMPLOYEE_SAL_GT_COMM", line 4
ORA-04088: error during execution of trigger                 Trigger Code
'SCOTT.TRIG_EMPLOYEE_SAL_GT_COMM'                              execution
```

Figure 25.6   Adding record with sal < comm.

When we tried to insert empid 4444 with salary=5000 and commission=7000 such that commission > salary then Oracle returned an error message from our trigger code along with an appropriate message.

Let us try to update a record such that after updation salary will become less than commission as in Figure 25.7.

```
SQL> update employee set salary=900 where empid=3333;
update employee set salary=900 where empid=3333
       *
ERROR at line 1:
ORA-20001: UPDATE Error: Commission CANNOT be GREATER THAN Salary
ORA-06512: at "SCOTT.TRIG_EMPLOYEE_SAL_GT_COMM", line 10
ORA-04088: error during execution of trigger 'SCOTT.TRIG_EMPLOYEE_SAL_GT_COMM'
```

Figure 25.7   Modify a record such that sal becomes less than commission.

Note:
1. ROW LEVEL BEFORE TRIGGERS can be used for data validation.
2. Since we have written a BEFORE trigger, therefore, we can check for specific conditions before triggering the SQL statement to be executed. We can even fail the execution of triggering SQL statement by using "raise_application_error".

Example: Let us see a practical example for ROW LEVEL trigger.

We have a table named "tbl_audit_employee" with structure as shown in Figure 25.8.

```
SQL> desc tbl_audit_employee;

   Name                          Null?              Type

   EMPID                                            NUMBER(4)
   OPERATION                                        VARCHAR2(6)
   OLD_SAL                                          NUMBER(5)
   NEW_SAL                                          NUMBER(5)
   OLD_COMM                                         NUMBER(5)
   NEW_COMM                                         NUMBER(5)
   DATE_OF_DML                                      DATE
```

Figure 25.8   Structure of TBL_AUDIT_EMPLOYEE.

We want that when a new record is inserted into employee table then corresponding empid, salary, commission should also get inserted into tbl_audit_employee along with the operation name "INSERT" and the date on which it was inserted. In this example, we will insert the salary and commission being specified in the DML INSERT statement into old_sal and old_comm column of tbl_audit_employee.

Secondly, whenever a UPDATE DML is executed then we want to insert the old and as well as the new salary and commission into the tbl_audit_employee table.

Thirdly, whenever a DELETE is executed we want to insert the record into tbl_audit_employee such that salary and commission go to the old_sal and old_comm column of tbl_audit_employee.

Refer to Table 25.1 for summary of all the requirements.

Program 25.3 contains the code for meeting the requirements specified in Table 25.1.

TABLE 25.1   tbl_audit_employee

OPERATION	Empid	Operation	Old_sal	New_sal	Old_comm	New_comm	Date of DML
INSERT	xxxx	INSERT	:new.salary	NULL	:new.commission	NULL	sysdate
UPDATE	xxxx	UPDATE	:old.salary	:new.salary	:old.commission	:new.commission	sysdate
DELETE	xxxx	DELETE	:old.salary	NULL	:old.commission	NULL	sysdate

Note:
1. :old.column_name and :new.column_name are reserved words of Oracle indicating the OLD and NEW values of columns
2. While INSERTING we can access only :new values
3. While UPDATING we can access both :old and :new values
4. While DELETING we can access only :old values.

Program 25.3   trigger3.sql (ROW LEVEL AFTER trigger).

```
create or replace trigger trig_audit_employee
after insert or update or delete on employee
```

```
          for each row
          begin
             if INSERTING then
                      insert into tbl_audit_employee values
                      (:new.empid,'INSERT',:new.salary,NULL,:new.commission,
                      NULL,sysdate);
             end if;

             if UPDATING then
                      insert into tbl_audit_employee values
                      (:new.empid,'UPDATE',:old.salary,:new.salary,
                      :old.commission,:new.commission,sysdate);

             end if;

             if DELETING then
                      insert into tbl_audit_employee values
                      (:old.empid,'DELETE',:old.salary,NULL,
                      :old.commission,NULL,sysdate);

             end if;

          end;
          /
```

In the STATEMENT level trigger of previous section (Program 25.1), we had kept an audit for DML operations at the table level. We could not access the old and new values for records being inserted or manipulated.

In Program 25.3 we have kept the audit at record level by using the ROW LEVEL trigger. Secondly, as we are not doing any data validation before the execution of triggering the SQL statement, therefore, we created an AFTER trigger.

Understanding :OLD and :NEW in ROW LEVEL triggers

We will create a trigger named "trig_employee_display" (Program 25.4) for which EACH DML operation on "employee" table will display the contents in :old and :new variables.

Program 25.4   trigger4.sql—example of :OLD and :NEW.

```
create or replace trigger trig_employee_display
before insert or update or delete on employee
for each row
begin
   if INSERTING then
            dbms_output.put_line('NEW SAL: '||:new.salary);
            dbms_output.put_line('NEW COMM: '||:new.commission);
            dbms_output.put_line('OLD SAL: '||:old.salary);
            dbms_output.put_line('OLD COMM: '||:old.commission);
   end if;
```

```
    if UPDATING then
            dbms_output.put_line('NEW SAL: '||:new.salary);
            dbms_output.put_line('NEW COMM: '||:new.commission);
            dbms_output.put_line('OLD SAL: '||:old.salary);
            dbms_output.put_line('OLD COMM: '||:old.commission);

    end if;

    if DELETING then
            dbms_output.put_line('NEW SAL: '||:new.salary);
            dbms_output.put_line('NEW COMM: '||:new.commission);
            dbms_output.put_line('OLD SAL: '||:old.salary);
            dbms_output.put_line('OLD COMM: '||:old.commission);
    end if;

end;
/
```

Let us create the trigger by running trigger4.sql as in Figure 25.9.

```
SQL>@trigger4

Trigger Created
```

Figure 25.9 Creating trigger from Program 25.4.

In Figure 25.10, we have performed some DML operations to see the impact of trigger on :OLD and :NEW values for all the three operations (INSERT, UPDATE and DELETE).

```
SQL> insert into employee values (1,5000,1000);                    Actual Triggering
NEW SAL: 5000                                                       SQL statement
NEW COMM: 1000
OLD SAL:                  Trigger Execution
OLD COMM:


1 row created.                                      Feedback of triggering SQL statement

SQL> update employee set salary=8000 where empid=1;
NEW SAL: 8000
NEW COMM: 1000
OLD SAL: 5000
OLD COMM: 1000

1 row updated.

SQL> update employee set salary=10000,commission=3000 where empid=1;
NEW SAL: 10000
NEW COMM: 3000
OLD SAL: 8000
OLD COMM: 1000
```

```
1 row updated.

SQL> delete from employee where empid=1;
NEW SAL:
NEW COMM:
OLD SAL: 10000
OLD COMM: 3000

1 row deleted.
Actual Triggering SQL statement
Feedback of triggering SQL statement
Trigger Execution
```

Figure 25.10   Performing DML operations to see the impact of trigger.

For the INSERT command new salary and commission have been displayed but old salary and commission are NULL because for a new record there are no existing values in the table.

While UPDATING records, the existing values in table are referred to as :OLD and the values being supplied (in triggering SQL statement) are accessed as :NEW.

For DELETE operation there is no value for :NEW and therefore they are shown as NULL. DELETE which implies that the record is already existing and displays existing values in table as :OLD.

Note:

1. Feedback like "1 row inserted", "1 row updated", "1 row deleted" are appearing after the execution of our defined trigger. This means that as we have defined BEFORE trigger, therefore, our trigger code is executed first followed by the execution of actual triggering SQL statement (INSERT, UPDATE, DELETE).
2. If we do not supply any values to a column in the UPDATE statement then both :old.columnname and :new.columnname have the old value.

Accessing column values in ROW LEVEL triggers

If we are declaring trigger for INSERT operation then the new values being inserted can be accessed using :new.columnname.

If trigger is written for UPDATE then the new values being updated can be accessed using :new.columnname and old values can be accessed using :old.columnname.

If trigger is written for DELETE then the existing values of various columns can be accessed using :old.columnname. Refer to Table 25.2.

TABLE 25.2   Accessibility of old and new values for triggers

Trigger type	:OLD	:NEW
INSERT	No	Yes
UPDATE	Yes	Yes
DELETE	Yes	No

Note: We cannot access column values for the STATEMENT LEVEL triggers as they are meant for the entire table and not for the individual record.

25.4 TRIGGERS FOR APPLYING CONSTRAINTS

Triggers can be used to apply integrity constraints.

Example 1: Any record which is inserted or updated in the table "EMP", we must first check whether the commission is less than/equal to salary or not. If commission > salary, then do not execute the INSERT or UPDATE statement. Program 25.5 contains the code.

Program 25.5 trigger5.sql—integrity constraint through trigger.

```
set serveroutput on

create or replace trigger trig_emp_check_sal_gt_comm
BEFORE INSERT OR UPDATE ON EMP
FOR EACH ROW
begin
   if INSERTING then
           if :new.sal<:new.comm then
                   RAISE_APPLICATION_ERROR('-20101','RECORD NOT
                   INSERTED:::SALARY CANNOT BE LESS THAN COMMISSION');
           end if;
   end if;

   if UPDATING then
           if :new.sal<:new.comm then
                   RAISE_APPLICATION_ERROR('-20102','RECORD NOT
                   UPDATED:::SALARY CANNOT BE LESS THAN COMMISSION');
           end if;
   end if;
end;
/
```

Let us create the trigger from Program 25.5 and execute an INSERT statement such that salary is less than commission (Figure 25.11).

```
SQL> @trigger5

Trigger created.

SQL> insert into emp(empno,ename,deptno,sal,comm) values (9999,'XEON',10,7000,9000);
insert into emp(empno,ename,deptno,sal,comm) values (9999,'XEON',10,7000,9000)
     *
ERROR at line 1:
ORA-20101: RECORD NOT INSERTED:::SALARY CANNOT BE LESS THAN COMMISSION
ORA-06512: at "SCOTT.TRIG_EMP_CHECK_SAL_GT_COMM", line 4
ORA-04088: error during execution of trigger 'SCOTT.TRIG_EMP_CHECK_SAL_GT_COMM'
```

Figure 25.11 Creating trigger from Program 25.5.

Example 2: For any new employee always add the name in capital letters even if the INSERT statement uses lower or mixed case. See Program 25.6 for code.

Program 25.6 trigger6.sql—constraint through trigger.

```
set serveroutput on

create or replace trigger trig_emp_check_ename
BEFORE INSERT OR UPDATE ON EMP
FOR EACH ROW
begin
    if INSERTING then
            :new.ename:=UPPER(:new.ename);
    end if;

    if UPDATING then
            :new.ename:=UPPER(:new.ename);
    end if;
end;
/
```

Let us create the trigger from Program 25.6 and issue an INSERT command (Figure 25.12).

```
SQL> @trigger6
Trigger created.
SQL> insert into emp(empno,ename,deptno,sal,comm) values (9999,'xEon',10,9000,1000);
1 row created.
SQL> select * from emp where empno=9999;
```

EMPNO	ENAME	JOB	MGR	HIREDATE	SAL	COMM	DEPTNO
9999	XEON	–	–	–	9000	1000	10

Figure 25.12 Creating trigger from Program 25.6.

Although we supplied mixed case xEon as ENAME in the triggering SQL statement but the trigger before inserting the records has converted the ENAME to uppercase.

25.5 DIFFERENCES BETWEEN DATABASE TRIGGERS AND STORED PROCEDURES

Both are named PL/SQL blocks performing some specific task but are different in the following two respects.

- Procedures are explicitly executed by user or called within other PL/SQL blocks. Triggers are implicitly or automatically executed when triggering SQL statement is issued.
- Procedures can receive parameters but triggers do not have this option.

25.6 INSTEAD OF TRIGGER

We have studied non-updateable views (Section 17.4.2) in Chapter 17. The views which are derived from more than one table, even if it contains PRIMARY KEYS and NOT NULL columns of all the tables, then also the view remains non-updateable. We cannot perform any of the DML operations on such views. Oracle provides a trigger named INSTEAD OF which can be used to make the non-updateable views updateable.

Assume that we have defined a view based on EMP and DEPT table containing EMPNO, ENAME, DEPTNO and DNAME columns. Now we cannot perform INSERT operation on this view. To achieve this we will create a INSTEAD OF trigger on this view.

Triggering the INSERT command will specify EMPNO, ENAME, DEPT and DNAME. The INSERT command will add record in the non-updateable view. We will create a INSTEAD OF trigger on the view so that record isn't actually added to the view but rather to the underlying base tables. The trigger will look for the existence of specified EMPNO in EMP table and if the record does not exist then the employee will be added into the base table "EMP".

Similarly for the newly inserted EMPNO if the specified DEPTNO does not exist in DEPT table then the trigger will issue the INSERT command on DEPT table.

See Program 25.7 for the trigger code.

Program 25.7   Trigger7.sql—INSTEAD OF trigger.

```
set serveroutput on

create or replace view vw_emp_dept as select a.empno,a.ename,a.deptno,b.dname
from emp a, dept b
where a.deptno=b.deptno;

create or replace trigger trig_emp_dept
INSTEAD OF INSERT ON VW_EMP_DEPT
FOR EACH ROW
declare
    v_cnt number:=0;
begin
    if :new.empno is null then
            raise_application_error(-20101,'EMPNO CANNOT BE NULL');
    end if;

    if :new.deptno is null then
            raise_application_error(-20102,'DEPTNO CANNOT BE NULL');
    end if;

    select count(*) into v_cnt from emp where empno=:new.empno;
    if v_cnt=0 then
            insert into emp(empno,ename,deptno) values (:new.empno,:new.ename,:new.deptno);
    else
            dbms_output.put_line('EMPNO ALREADY EXISTS');
    end if;

    select count(*) into v_cnt from dept where deptno=:new.deptno;
    IF v_cnt=0 then
            insert into dept(deptno,dname) values (:new.deptno,:new.dname);
    ELSE
            dbms_output.put_line('DEPTNO ALREADY EXISTS');
    END IF;
end;
/
```

First we have a created view named "VW_EMP_DEPT" followed by the INSTEAD OF trigger on that view. If the triggering INSERT command does not specify EMPNO or DEPTNO then the trigger raises exception through "RAISE_APPLICATION_ERROR". If both EMPNO and DEPTNO are specified then the trigger looks for the existence of specified EMPNO in table EMP. If the EMPNO already exists, it displays appropriate message "'EMPNO ALREADY EXISTS" or else inserts the new employee in the EMP table.

Similar logic has been applied to DEPTNO and DNAME.

Let us create the INSTEAD OF trigger as in Figure 25.13 and ADD a new record.

```
SQL> @trigger7
View created.

Trigger created.

SQL> insert into vw_emp_dept values (9999,'XEON',99,'FINANCE');
1 row created.
SQL>commit;
```

Figure 25.13   Creating INSTEAD OF trigger.

Figure 25.14 shows the records from VIEW and the Base table.

```
SQL> select * from vw_emp_dept;
```

EMPNO	ENAME	DEPTNO	DNAME
9999	**XEON**	**99**	**FINANCE**
7369	SMITH	20	RESEARCH
7499	ALLEN	30	SALES
7521	WARD	30	SALES
7566	JONES	20	RESEARCH
7654	MARTIN	30	SALES
7698	BLAKE	30	SALES
7782	CLARK	10	ACCOUNTING
7788	SCOTT	20	RESEARCH
7839	KING	10	ACCOUNTING
7844	TURNER	30	SALES
7876	ADAMS	20	RESEARCH
7900	JAMES	30	SALES
7902	FORD	20	RESEARCH
7934	MILLER	10	ACCOUNTING

```
SQL> select * from emp;
```

EMPNO	ENAME	JOB	MGR	HIREDATE	SAL	COMM	DEPTNO
9999	**XEON**	–	–	–	–	–	**99**
7369	SMITH	CLERK	7902	17-DEC-80	800	–	20
7499	ALLEN	SALESMAN	7698	20-FEB-81	1600	300	30
7521	WARD	SALESMAN	7698	22-FEB-81	1250	500	30

7566	JONES	MANAGER	7839	02-APR-81	2975	–	20
7654	MARTIN	SALESMAN	7698	28-SEP-81	1250	1400	30
7698	BLAKE	MANAGER	7839	01-MAY-81	2850	–	30
7782	CLARK	MANAGER	7839	09-JUN-81	2450	–	10
7788	SCOTT	ANALYST	7566	09-DEC-82	3000	–	20
7839	KING	PRESIDENT	–	17-NOV-81	5000	–	10
7844	TURNER	SALESMAN	7698	08-SEP-81	1500	0	30
7876	ADAMS	CLERK	7788	12-JAN-83	1100	–	20
7900	JAMES	CLERK	7698	03-DEC-81	950	–	30
7902	FORD	ANALYST	7566	03-DEC-81	3000	–	20
7934	MILLER	CLERK	7782	23-JAN-82	1300	–	10

SQL>select * from dept;

DEPTNO	DNAME	LOC
99	**FINANCE**	**–**
10	ACCOUNTING	NEW YORK
20	RESEARCH	DALLAS
30	SALES	CHICAGO
40	OPERATIONS	BOSTON

Figure 25.14 Records in VIEW and BASE tables.

The new record inserted in view has been actually added in the EMP and DEPT table because of the INSTEAD OF trigger.

25.7 DATA DICTIONARY FOR TRIGGERS

USER_TRIGGERS contains the information about triggers as shown in Figure 25.15.

Table	Column	Comment
USER_TRIGGERS	TRIGGER_NAME	Name of the trigger
	TRIGGER_TYPE	Type of the trigger (when it fires)—BEFORE/AFTER and STATEMENT/ROW
	TRIGGERING_EVENT	Statement that will fire the trigger—INSERT, UPDATE and/or DELETE
	TABLE_OWNER	Owner of the table that this trigger is associated with
	BASE_OBJECT_TYPE	–
	TABLE_NAME	Name of the table that this trigger is associated with
	COLUMN_NAME	The name of the column on which the trigger is defined over
	REFERENCING_NAMES	Names used for referencing to OLD, NEW and PARENT values within the trigger

WHEN_CLAUSE	WHEN clause must evaluate to true in order for triggering body to execute
STATUS	If DISABLED then trigger will not fire
DESCRIPTION	Trigger description, useful for re-creating trigger creation statement
ACTION_TYPE	–
TRIGGER_BODY	Action taken by this trigger when it fires

Figure 25.15 Data dictionary for triggers.

Let us view the trigger text for all the triggers.

Figure 25.16 shows the trigger code from Data Dictionary. If required we can use the WHERE clause for finding the trigger text for specific triggers.

```
SQL> set long 2000
SQL> select trigger_body from user_triggers;
   begin
        if INSERTING then
            if :new.sal<:new.comm then
                    RAISE_APPLICATION_ERROR('-20101','RECORD NOT
                    INSERTED:::SALARY CANNOT BE LESS THAN COMMISSION');
            end if;
        end if;

        if UPDATING then
            if :new.sal<:new.comm then
                    RAISE_APPLICATION_ERROR('-
                    20102','RECORD NOT UPDATED:::SALARY
                    CANNOT BE LESS THAN COMMISSION');
            end if;
        end if;
   end;
```

Figure 25.16 Trigger code from data dictionary.

25.8 REMOVING TRIGGER

A trigger can be removed permanently from database using the DROP command—DROP TRIGGER triggername;

25.9 ENABLING AND DISABLING TRIGGERS

Triggers can be temporarily disabled or enabled using the ALTER TRIGGER command. We want to disable the trigger TRIG_EMP_CHECK_ENAME (Figure 25.17).

```
SQL> alter trigger TRIG_EMP_CHECK_ENAME disable;

Trigger altered.
```

Figure 25.17   Disable trigger.

Now this trigger will not be active till we issue the ENABLE command as shown in Figure 25.18.

```
SQL> alter trigger TRIG_EMP_CHECK_ENAME enable;

Trigger altered.
```

Figure 25.18   Enabling trigger.

REVIEW QUESTIONS

1. What is a trigger? What are the various components of a trigger?
2. Explain the classification of triggers. How many triggers are supported by Oracle?
3. What is the difference between TABLE LEVEL and ROW LEVEL triggers? Which of the two allow access to :OLD and :NEW values?
4. Which keywords can be used to identify the INSERT, UPDATE and DELETE operation?
5. Can a BEFORE trigger cancel the triggering SQL statement?
6. Which trigger type can be used for data validation?
7. Explain the concept of :OLD and :NEW pseudo-columns for ROW LEVEL triggers.
8. Can triggers be used to apply integrity constraints?
9. Differentiate Stored Procedures from Triggers.
10. Explain the purpose of INSTEAD OF trigger.
11. Which Data Dictionary table contains the information about triggers?
12. Is it possible to disable or enable a trigger as and when required?

LAB ASSIGNMENT

1. For the EMP table, create a trigger such that the department to which he belongs must exist in the DEPT table. (Do not use referential integrity constraint for this example.)
2. Create a trigger on EMP table such that no employees salary can be less than 5000. If it is less than 5000, then display appropriate message.
3. Create a trigger on EMP table so that Deletion operation cannot be performed on Sundays.
4. Create a trigger such that if the commission is not specified while adding a new employee then the default commission should be taken as 10% of salary.

5. Create a table named TBL_EMP_TOTAL with DEPTNO, SALARY, COMM columns. This table will contain the departmentwise total salary and commission. Create a trigger on EMP table such that whenever a new employee joins or existing employee data is updated or deleted then the corresponding changes in TBL_EMP_TOTAL are automatically applied.

6. Create a trigger on EMP table such that it restricts the entry of duplicate EMPNO.

7. Create a trigger on EMP table such that whenever a record is deleted it is moved to a history table named "EMP_HISTORY" with the same structure as EMP table. The EMP_HISTORY will contain additional column "DATE_OF_DELETION" to store the date on which a record was removed.

Oracle Flashback Technology

26.1 INTRODUCTION

All business organizations have a well-defined backup procedure for the entire database and use various media like Hard Disk, Magnetic Tapes, etc. for the same purpose. The basic purpose is to recover the data in case anything goes wrong with the running server hardware, Operating System or Data Corruption due to power failures, etc. Recovering data from Magnetic Tapes is a very cumbersome procedure and may take several hours for recovering a single table. Oracle from version 9i provides several features to address the simple data recovery needs.

26.2 SITUATIONS WHERE FLASHBACK TECHNOLOGY CAN BE USED

- Erroneous insert, update or delete transactions
- Erroneous DROP TABLE statements
- Erroneous batch job or widespread application errors have modified entire database.

26.3 SITUATIONS WHERE FLASHBACK TECHNOLOGY CANNOT BE USED

- Deleted data files and loss of data due to media failure cannot be handled by Flashback Technology.

26.4 WHO CAN USE FLASHBACK?

A user can use FLASHBACK feature only if he has been granted the privilege for the same by SYS user (DBA).

Let us connect SYS user and grant the required privilege to SCOTT user (Figure 26.1).

```
SQL> connect sys/sys@orcl11g as sysdba;
Connected.

SQL> grant flashback any table to scott;
Grant succeeded.
```

Figure 26.1   Granting flashback facility on all tables to SCOTT.

Now SCOTT can use FLASHBACK feature on all the tables owned by him.

SYS could have provided FLASHBACK facility on a specific table also to SCOTT. In that case "ANY TABLE" will be replaced by "ON username.table_name" as in Figure 26.2.

```
SQL> grant flashback on scott.student to scott;

Grant succeeded.
```

Figure 26.2   Granting flashback facility on specific table to SCOTT.

SCOTT will be able to use FLASHBACK feature for STUDENT table only.

26.5   FEATURES OF ORACLE FLASHBACK TECHNOLOGY

Oracle Flashback Technology has the following features:

Flashback Query
Flashback Table
Flashback Drop
Flashback Database

Caution: Oracle10g Express Edition supports only Flashback Query and Flashback DROP. To test the functionality of Flashback Table and Database you need to install Enterprise Edition.

We have tested the Flashback Table and Database commands on **Oracle11g Enterprise Edition**.

26.5.1   Flashback Query

This feature provides the facility of running queries against the database, viewing results as they would have appeared at a specified time. Suppose we have erroneously inserted, updated or deleted records from a table and want to view the original data at a specified date and time, then Flashback Query can help us to retrieve the same.

The status of a table can be viewed using the two mechanisms, namely

1. Using Date and Time
2. Using SCN (System Change Number)

FLASHBACK Query Using Date and Time

This enables us to view the data at a specified date and time. Refer to Figure 26.3 wherein we have added a few records and noted the date and time. After that we have added/deleted/updated a few more records and issued commit.

```
SQL> create table student(college varchar2(4),rollno number(4),name varchar2(10)
,marks number(3));

Table created.

SQL> insert into student values ('GEC',1,'satish',54);
1 row created.

SQL> insert into student values ('GEC',2,'rashmi',67);
1 row created.

SQL> commit;
Commit complete.

SQL> select to_char(sysdate,'dd/mm/yyyy hh24:mi:ss') from dual;
TO_CHAR(SYSDATE,'DD
_____
09/02/2009 10:12:29

SQL> insert into student values ('RKDF',1,'anil',78);
1 row created.

SQL> insert into student values ('OIST',1,'rishi',48);
1 row created.

SQL> commit;
Commit complete.

SQL> delete from student where name='rashmi';
1 row deleted.

SQL> update student set marks=99 where name='satish';
1 row updated.

SQL> commit;
Commit complete.

SQL> select * from student;
```

COLL	ROLLNO	NAME	MARKS
GEC	1	satish	99
RKDF	1	anil	78
OIST	1	rishi	48

Figure 26.3 Adding, deleting and updating records.

Now SCOTT user wants to know the status of STUDENT table at 10:12:29 AM. We can use the flashback query as shown in Figure 26.4.

```
SQL> select * from student as of timestamp to_timestamp('09/02/2009 10:12:29','dd/mm/
yyyy hh24:mi:ss')

    COLL            ROLLNO          NAME            MARKS

    GEC               1             satish            54
    GEC               2             rashmi            67
```

Figure 26.4 Using Flashback query with date and time.

Note that all the changes after the specified point of time have not been displayed. Impact of INSERT, DELETE and UPDATE statements after the specified time have not been shown even after the COMMIT was executed.

SCOTT can perform the point-in-time recovery using the "AS OF TIMESTAMP" clause with specified format.

FLASHBACK Query Using SCN

Oracle Database maintains a System Change Number to track every change occurring in the database. We can trace back to a specified SCN.

To know the SCN at a given point-in-time the user must have EXECUTE privilege on DBMS_FLASHBACK built-in package which is granted by the SYS DBA (Figure 26.5).

```
SQL> connect sys/sys@xe as sysdba;
Connected.

SQL> grant execute on dbms_flashback to scott;
Grant succeeded.
```

Figure 26.5 Granting execute privilege on DBMS_FLASHBACK package.

We can find the SCN at any point by using the get_system_change_number function of the DBMS_FLASHBACK package as shown in Figure 26.6.

```
SQL> connect scott/tiger@xe
Connected.

SQL> select * from student;

    COLL            ROLLNO          NAME            MARKS

    GEC               1             satish            99
    RKDF              1             anil              78
    OIST              1             rishi             48

SQL> select dbms_flashback.get_system_change_number from dual;
GET_SYSTEM_CHANGE_NUMBER

1170629
```

Figure 26.6 Determining the SCN.

In Figure 26.7 we have performed some DELETE and UPDATE operations.

SQL> delete from student where name='satish';
1 row deleted.

SQL> update student set marks=88 where name='anil';
1 row updated.

SQL> commit;
Commit complete.

SQL> select * from student;

COLL	ROLLNO	NAME	MARKS
RKDF	1	anil	88
OIST	1	rishi	48

Figure 26.7   Performing delete and update operations.

We can view the status of a table (Figure 26.8) to a point-in-time referring to the previous SCN NO. of Figure 26.6.

SQL> select * from student *as of scn 1170629;*

COLL	ROLLNO	NAME	MARKS
GEC	1	satish	99
RKDF	1	anil	78
OIST	1	rishi	48

Figure 26.8   Flashback using SCN.

Recovering a table with original records

The FLASHBACK Queries can be used to re-create a table with the original data after having performed several DML operations on the table. We will create a new table specifying AS OF SCN or AS OF TIMESTAMP Clause, then DROP the table followed by RENAMING the new table as shown in Figure 26.9.

SQL> create table student_new as select * from student as of SCN 1170629;
Table created.

SQL> drop table student;
Table dropped.

SQL> rename student_new to student;
Table renamed.

SQL> select * from student;

COLL	ROLLNO	NAME	MARKS
GEC	1	satish	99
RKDF	1	anil	78
OIST	1	rishi	48

Figure 26.9   Recovering original table.

26.5.2 Flashback Table

As we can perform point-in time recovery of records using "AS OF [TIMESTAMP | SCN]", similarly Oracle provides a feature for recovering a table to a certain point-in-time.

Oracle Flashback Table provides the ability to recover a table to a specified point in time in the past very quickly, easily, and without taking any part of the database offline. In many cases, Flashback Table eliminates the need to perform more complicated point-in-time recovery operations. Flashback Table restores tables while automatically maintaining associated attributes such as current indexes, triggers and constraints, and not requiring the DBA to find and restore the application-specific properties. Using Flashback Table causes the contents of one or more individual tables to revert to their state at some past SCN or time.

Flashback Table uses information in the undo tablespace to restore the table. This provides significant benefits over media recovery in terms of ease of use, availability and faster restoration of data.

Prerequisites for using Flashback Table

The prerequisites for performing a FLASHBACK TABLE operation are as follows:

- User must have been granted the FLASHBACK ANY TABLE system privilege or user must have the FLASHBACK object privilege on the table.
- User must have SELECT, INSERT, DELETE, and ALTER privileges on the table.
- Undo information retained in the undo tablespace must go far enough back in time to satisfy the specified target point in time or SCN for the FLASHBACK TABLE operation.
- Row movement must be enabled on the table for which you are issuing the FLASHBACK TABLE statement. User can enable row movement with the following SQL statement: ALTER TABLE *table_name* ENABLE ROW MOVEMENT;

Flashback table using Timestamp

Figure 26.10 shows how to perform flashback table using Timestamp.

```
SQL> connect scott/tiger@xe
Connected.
SQL> select * from student;

        COLL        ROLLNO        NAME        MARKS

        GEC           1           satish        99
        RKDF          1           anil          78
        OIST          1           rishi         48
        LNCT          1           anita         34

SQL> alter table student enable row movement;
Table altered.

SQL> select to_char(sysdate,'dd/mm/yyyy hh24:mi:ss') from dual;
TO_CHAR(SYSDATE,'DD

09/02/2009 11:31:42
```

```
SQL> insert into student values ('XXX',1,'test',55);
1 row created.

SQL> commit;
Commit complete.

SQL> flashback table student to timestamp to_timestamp('09/02/2009 11:31:42','dd/mm/yyyy
hh24:mi:ss');
Flashback complete.

SQL> select * from student;
```

COLL	ROLLNO	NAME	MARKS
GEC	1	satish	99
RKDF	1	anil	78
OIST	1	rishi	48
LNCT	1	anita	34

Figure 26.10 Flashback table using Timestamp.

Flashback Table using SCN

Flashback table command can be used for a SCN as follows:

```
SQL>flashback table student to SCN 1170629;
```

Note: Flashback Table restores tables while automatically maintaining associated attributes such as current indexes, triggers and constraints, and not requiring the DBA to find and restore the application-specific properties.

26.5.3   Oracle Flashback DROP

Until now we have learned that a DROPPED table cannot be recovered unless and until we have taken backup on secondary media like Hard Disk or Tape. In other words, the DROPPED table cannot be recovered from the live database. But Oracle provides a feature known as FLASHBACK DROP which can undo the DROP TABLE command without accessing the backup media like Tape which is generally very time consuming.

What is RECYCLEBIN?

Oracle maintains a space called RECYCLEBIN and whenever a table is dropped, the table along with associated objects like INDEXES, CONSTRAINTS, TRIGGERS are moved to the RECYCLEBIN with system-generated names starting with BIN$.

How tables and objects are stored in RECYCLEBIN?

Whenever a table is dropped, the table along with its associated attributes like INDEXES, CONSTRAINTS, TRIGGERS are moved to the RECYCLEBIN with new names starting with BIN$. Every dropped object is stored in RECYCLEBIN with a unique global name along with the original name which can be seen by the "show recyclebin" command as in Figure 26.11.

```
SQL> drop table student;
Table dropped.

SQL> show recyclebin;
        ORIGINAL          RECYCLEBIN          OBJECT          DROP
          NAME              NAME               TYPE           TIME

STUDENT BIN$JkoaU4NCToKtH82fpNYfUA==$0 TABLE       2009-02-11:08:08:31
```

Figure 26.11 Contents of recyclebin.

The "SHOW RECYCLEBIN" command displays the contents of the RECYCLEBIN. Note that it stores the original name along with the newly assigned name starting with BIN$ and also stores the date and time at which the object was dropped.

SCOTT user can recover the dropped table using "FLASHBACK TABLE STUDENT TO BEFORE DROP". Now let us assume that SCOTT user creates a new table with the name "STUDENT" after dropping the previous STUDENT table (Figure 26.12).

```
SQL> create table student (institution char(4),enrollno number(4),stdname varcha
r2(10), marks number(4));
Table created.

SQL> drop table student;
Table dropped.
```

Figure 26.12 Creating and dropping a table.

Figure 26.13 shows the status of recycle bin after the STUDENT table was dropped for the firsttime, then again created and again dropped (Figure 26.12). In such situations, Oracle will store a copy of both the tables with different names along with date and time when the table was dropped.

```
SQL> show recyclebin;

ORIGINAL NAME   RECYCLEBIN NAME   OBJECT TYPE DROP TIME

STUDENT    BIN$JIX7BwuVShq3LRyhjJVfZg==$0 TABLE   2009-02-11:08:18:02

STUDENT    BIN$JkoaU4NCToKtH82fpNYfUA==$0 TABLE   2009-02-11:08:08:31
```

Figure 26.13 Status of recyclebin.

Note: RECYCLEBIN has two objects with the same ORIGINAL NAME.

Now SCOTT wants to recover the 1st STUDENT table.

FLASHBACK TABLE STUDENT TO BEFORE DROP will recover the most recently dropped table. To recover the 1st table we will have to refer to RECYCLEBIN name "BIN$JIX7BwuVShq3LRyhjJVfZg==$0" as shown in Figure 26.14.

```
SQL> flashback table "BIN$JIX7BwuVShq3LRyhjJVfZg==$0" to before drop;
Flashback complete.
```

Figure 26.14   Recover table from recyclebin.

Caution: As recyclebin object names have special, small and upper case characters, therefore, we need to enclose names in double quotes.

Rename While Recovering Table from FLASHBACK DROP

Figure 26.15 shows how tables can be renamed while recovering with the FLASHBACK DROP command.

```
SQL> flashback table "BIN$JkoaU4NCToKtH82fpNYfUA==$0" to before drop rename to
student_new;

Flashback complete.

SQL> select * from student_new;
```

COLL	ROLLNO	NAME	MARKS ADDRESS
GEC	1	satish	99
RKDF	1	anil	78
OIST	1	rishi	48
XXX	1	test	55
LNCT	1	anita	34

Figure 26.15   Renaming flashback drop table.

Note: "SHOW RECYCLEBIN" command actually queries a Data Dictionary table named "USER_RECYCLEBIN". RECYCLEBIN is synonym for "USER_RECYCLEBIN".

SQL>show recyclebin

IS EQUIVALENT TO

SQL>select ORIGINAL_NAME, OBJECT_NAME, TYPE, DROPTIME, DROPSCN from user_recyclebin;

ORIGINAL_N	OBJECT_NAME	TYPE	DROPTIME	DROPSCN
STUDENT	BIN$I0P6VRoYQ/y4d4bn3Dk05A==$0	TABLE	2009-02-12:21:57:16	1234655

How much space is allocated for recyclebin?

The amount of space allocated for recycle bin can be specified by Oracle DBA. If you are using "Oracle 11g Enterprise Manager" then the location as well as the amount of space for recyclebin can be specified (Figure 26.16).

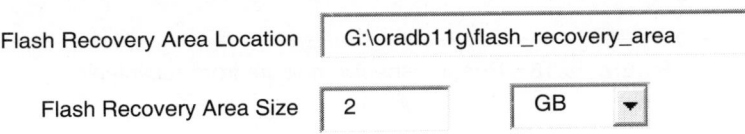

Flash Recovery Area Location   G:\oradb11g\flash_recovery_area

Flash Recovery Area Size   2   GB

Figure 26.16   Space for recyclebin.

What if the recyclebin space gets filled up?

Assuming that we have dropped so many objects that 2 GB of recyclebin is full. Now if we drop any more objects then the 1st object which was moved to recyclebin gets over written. The policy followed is First-In First-Out. Therefore, we can never be sure up to what time a particular dropped object will be available in the recyclebin.

Emptying recyclebin

The PURGE command is used to empty the recycle bin. Figure 26.17 shows how the PURGE command can be used to empty the recyclebin.

```
SQL> show recyclebin;

ORIGINAL NAME   RECYCLEBIN NAME   OBJECT TYPE DROP TIME

STUDENT   BIN$I0P6VRoYQ/y4d4bn3Dk05A==$0 TABLE   2009-02-12:21:57:16

SQL> purge recyclebin;

Recyclebin purged.

SQL> show recyclebin;
```

Figure 26.17   Emptying recyclebin.

Purging specific objects from recyclebin

The PURGE command can be used to remove the specific objects from recyclebin as shown in Figure 26.18.

```
SQL> drop table student_new;
Table dropped.

SQL> show recyclebin;

ORIGINAL NAME     RECYCLEBIN NAME     OBJECT TYPE DROP TIME

STUDENT_NEW   BIN$xXGPuXKBThSTjFUc5RPTww==$0 TABLE   2009-02-12:22:31:56

SQL> purge table student_new;
Table purged.
OR
SQL>purge table "BIN$xXGPuXKBThSTjFUc5RPTww==$0";
Table purged.

SQL> show recyclebin;
SQL>
```

Figure 26.18   Purging specific objects from recyclebin.

Specifying Oracle not to use recyclebin

Oracle provides an option in the DROP command so that object being removed does not move to recyclebin (Figure 26.19).

```
SQL> drop table STUDENT purge;
Table dropped.

SQL> show recyclebin;
SQL>
```

Figure 26.19 Dropping without using recyclebin.

26.5.4 Flashback Database

Oracle is a multi-user database and database refers to the data of all users. By Flashback Database we are referring to point-in time recovery of data of all users. This feature is used generally by the DBA to restore entire database for application/user wide erroneous DML operations. Assuming that some DML commands have modified the database value in several of SCOTT users tables, then the task of identifying individual tables and restoring the original tables with Flashback Table or Flashback Drop may not be feasible. So in such cases it is appropriate to use flashback database feature.

For the flashback database to work, the database must be running in archive log mode and the flashback feature must be enabled. Let us login as DBA and start the database in archive log mode and enable the flashback database feature (Figure 26.20).

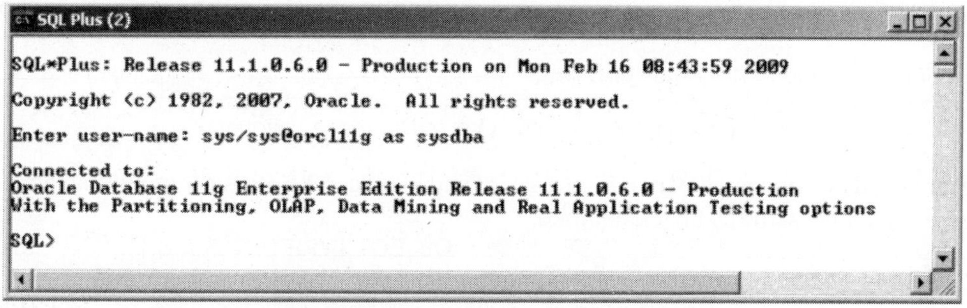

Figure 26.20 Logging as "sys" user.

Note that we have logged in as SYS DBA and the CONNECT description "orcl11g" refers to the SID name of Oracle Database11 g.

The Oracle Database start up involves 3 phases, namely

1. Start an Instance
2. Mount the Database
3. Open the Database.

The ARCHIVE LOG mode and FLASBACK DATABASE feature can be enabled only when the database is mounted but not open. Refer to Oracle's Database Administration Guide for more details on the various modes and the STARTUP and SHUTDOWN procedure.

We will first SHUTDOWN the database (Figure 26.21).

```
SQL> shutdown
Database closed.
Database dismounted.
ORACLE instance shutdown.
SQL>
```

Figure 26.21   Shutting down database.

Assuming that database is installed in G:\oradb11g folder which performs the following steps:

Go to "Start" -> "Run" -> Type "cmd" in box and click OK

C:\>Documents and Settings\satish>*G:*
G:\>*cd oradb11g\product\11.1.0\db_1\BIN*

Start the Oracle Listener as shown in Figure 26.22.

```
G:\oradb11g\product\11.1.0\db_1\BIN>LSNRCTL.EXE start

LSNRCTL for 32-bit Windows: Version 11.1.0.6.0 - Production on 16-FEB-2009 09:01:49
Copyright (c) 1991, 2007, Oracle. All rights reserved.

Listener using listener name LISTENER has been started
The command completed successfully

G:\oradb11g\product\11.1.0\db_1\BIN>
```

Figure 26.22   Starting Oracle Database Listener.

Start a SQL session as shown in Figure 26.23 and login as SYSDBA for mounting the database in archive log mode with flashback enabled.

```
G:\oradb11g\product\11.1.0\db_1\BIN>sqlplus

SQL*Plus: Release 11.1.0.6.0 - Production on Mon Feb 16 09:06:36 2009
Copyright (c) 1982, 2007, Oracle. All rights reserved.

Enter user-name: / as sysdba
Connected to an idle instance.

SQL> startup mount
ORACLE instance started.

Total System Global Area 426852352 bytes
Fixed Size 1333648 bytes
Variable Size 306185840 bytes
```

```
Database Buffers 113246208 bytes
Redo Buffers 6086656 bytes
Database mounted.

SQL> alter database archivelog;
Database altered.

SQL> alter database flashback on;
Database altered.
```

Figure 26.23   Starting SQL session.

The "startup mount" command starts the Database instance and mounts it without opening for connection by other database users.

Now we can shutdown and restart the database in normal mode so that users can CONNECT.

We will now shutdown and restart the database (Figure 26.24) after having switched the database to archive log and flashback mode as in Figure 26.23.

```
SQL> shutdown
ORA-01109: database not open
Database dismounted.
ORACLE instance shutdown.

SQL> startup
ORACLE instance started.

Total System Global Area 426852352 bytes
Fixed Size 1333648 bytes
Variable Size 306185840 bytes
Database Buffers 113246208 bytes
Redo Buffers 6086656 bytes
Database mounted.
Database opened.
SQL>
```

Figure 26.24   Shutting down and starting the Oracle Database.

Let us connect as SCOTT and find the DATE and TIME for point-in-time recovery later as in Figure 26.25.

```
SQL>connect scott/tiger@orcl11g
Connected

SQL> select to_char(sysdate,'dd/mm/yyyy hh24:mi:ss') from dual;
TO_CHAR(SYSDATE,'DD

16/02/2009 09:17:38
```

```
SQL> select * from tab;

          TNAME                    TABTYPE

          DEPT                     TABLE
          EMP                      TABLE
          STUDENT                  TABLE
```

Figure 26.25   Determining date and time.

At 16/02/2009 09:17:38, SCOTT user has 3 tables. Let us now perform some DDL and DML commands (Figure 26.26).

```
SQL> update emp set sal=sal+1000;
14 rows updated.

SQL> commit;
Commit complete.

SQL> create table student_master(rollno number(4),name varchar2(10),marks number(3));
Table created.

SQL> insert into student_master values (1111,'satish',35);
1 row created.

SQL> insert into student_master values (2222,'rashmi',56);
1 row created.

SQL> commit;

Commit complete.
```

Figure 26.26   Performing DDL and DML operations.

Assuming that all the DDL and DML commands executed after 16/02/2009 09:17:38 have to be reverted back, we can use the FLASHBACK DATABASE command.

But these operations can be performed by SYS DBA only. In Figure 26.27, we have logged in as SYSDBA and started the Oracle database in MOUNT mode.

```
SQL>connect sys/sys@orcl11g as sysdba;
Connected.

SQL> shutdown immediate
Database closed.
Database dismounted.
ORACLE instance shutdown.

SQL> startup mount
ORACLE instance started.
```

```
Total System Global Area 426852352 bytes
Fixed Size 1333648 bytes
Variable Size 306185840 bytes
Database Buffers 113246208 bytes
Redo Buffers 6086656 bytes
Database mounted.
SQL>
```

Figure 26.27 SYSDBA mounting the Oracle database.

Database must be mounted and not open for FLASHBACK database to work. In Figure 26.28, SYSDBA has issued flashback database command for a specific timestamp.

```
SQL> flashback database to timestamp to_timestamp('16/02/2009 09:17:38','dd/mm/yyyy
hh24:mi:ss');

Flashback complete.
```

Figure 26.28 FLASHBACK DATABASE.

Now we will restart the database in the OPEN mode (Figure 26.29) so that normal users such as SCOTT can login and find whether all the DDL and DML operations of Figure 26.26 have got reverted.

```
SQL>shutdown
SQL>exit

G:\oradb11g\product\11.1.0\db_1\BIN>LSNRCTL.EXE start
G:\oradb11g\product\11.1.0\db_1\BIN>sqlplus

SQL*Plus: Release 11.1.0.6.0 - Production on Mon Feb 16 09:40:17 2009
Copyright (c) 1982, 2007, Oracle. All rights reserved.
Enter user-name: / as sysdba
Connected to an idle instance.

SQL> startup mount
ORACLE instance started.
Total System Global Area 426852352 bytes
Fixed Size 1333648 bytes
Variable Size 306185840 bytes
Database Buffers 113246208 bytes
Redo Buffers 6086656 bytes
Database mounted.

SQL> alter database open resetlogs;

Database altered.
```

Figure 26.29 Mounting and opening the Oracle database.

Here "alter database open resetlogs;" actually restarts the database in the open mode so that other users can login.

Let us login as SCOTT and see the impact of FLASHBACK database as in Figure 26.30.

```
SQL> connect scott/tiger@orcl11g
Connected.

SQL>select * from tab;

        TNAME                    TABTYPE

        DEPT                     TABLE
        EMP                      TABLE
     STUDENT                     TABLE
```

Figure 26.30   Verifying impact of FLASHBACK database.

Note that the changes (DDL and DML) performed in Figure 26.26 have been reverted. In Figure 26.26, we had updated salary and created a new table STUDENT_MASTER with addition of some records, which are not available after we have flashed back the database to 16/02/2009 09:17:38 point in time. We can also verify that the SALARY has been restored to the original status dated 16/02/2009 09:17:38.

Normalization

27.1 INTRODUCTION

Normalization is the process of reducing redundancy and inconsistency of data. Redundancy refers to duplication/repetition of the same values at different places and inconsistency refers to incorrect information. Redundancy leads to inconsistency. The term Data Integrity is generally used to refer to both redundancy and inconsistency.

Normalization also simplifies the queries and DML operations.

27.2 NORMALIZATION TERMINOLOGY

It is important to understand the terminology related to normalization. Assume an EMPLOYEE table as shown in Table 27.1.

TABLE 27.1 EMPLOYEE table

EMP_NO	EMP_NAME	SKILL_ID	SKILL	VOTER_ID
1	Satish	1	Oracle	V1
1	Satish	2	Sybase	V1
1	Satish	3	Ingress	V1
2	Rashmi	4	DB2	V2
2	Rashmi	1	Oracle	V2
3	Rishi	5	Informix	V3
4	Anil			V4
5	Anita	6	MS-SQL	V5
5	Anita	4	DB2	V5

Attribute

Column or field is called an attribute (e.g. EMP_NO, EMP_NAME, SKILL).

Key

Key is single column or combination of columns (e.g. EMPNO, EMP_NAME, SKILL, EMP_NO+EMP_NAME, EMP_NO+SKILL, etc).

Superkey

A superkey is a column or set of columns that uniquely identifies rows within a table. In other words, two distinct rows are always guaranteed to have distinct superkeys.

Following are the superkeys in the EMPLOYEE table (Table 27.1):

EMP_NO+SKILL
EMP_NO+EMP_NAME+SKILL
EMP_NO+SKILL+VOTER_ID
EMP_NAME+SKILL
EMP_NAME+SKILL+VOTER_ID
VOTER_ID+SKILL
EMP_NO+EMP_NAME+SKILL+VOTER_ID

Note: SKILL or SKILL_ID both can be used interchangeably for superkey.

Following are not the superkeys:
EMP_NO+EMP_NAME—2 rows with the same EMP_NO and NAME for EMP 1,2,5.
EMP_NO+VOTER_ID—2 rows with the same EMP_NO and VOTER_ID for EMP 1,2,5.
EMP_NAME+VOTER_ID—The same reason as above.

Candidate key

A candidate key is a minimal superkey, that is, a superkey for which we can say that no proper subset of it is also a superkey. Table 27.2 specifies the various keys and whether those keys are candidate key or not.

TABLE 27.2 Candidate keys

Key	Candidate key or not
EMP_NO+SKILL	Candidate key
EMP_NO+EMP_NAME+SKILL	No Candidate key as subset, EMP_NO+SKILL is the superkey.
EMP_NO+SKILL+VOTER_ID	No Candidate key as subset, EMP_NO+SKILL is the superkey.
EMP_NAME+SKILL	Candidate key
EMP_NAME+SKILL+VOTER_ID	No Candidate key as subset, EMP_NAME+SKILL is the superkey. Moreover, subset VOTER_ID+SKILL is also a superkey.
VOTER_ID+SKILL	Candidate key
EMP_NO+EMP_NAME+SKILL+VOTER_ID	No Candidate key as subset, EMP_NO+SKILL, EMP_NAME+SKILL, and VOTER_ID+SKILL all are the super keys.

Non-prime attribute

A non-prime attribute is an attribute that does not occur in any candidate key. Employee Address would be a non-prime attribute in the EMPLOYEE table.

Primary key

Most DBMS requires a table to be defined as having a single unique key, rather than a number of possible unique keys. A primary key is a key which the database designer has designated for this purpose. For example, in the employee table we can designate any of the candidate keys as primary key:

> EMP_NO+SKILL
> EMP_NAME+SKILL
> VOTER_ID+SKILL

> Let us specify EMP_NO+SKILL as the primary key.

Alternate key

All candidate keys other than the primary keys are called alternate keys. In our example EMP_NAME+SKILL and VOTER_ID+SKILL are the alternate keys.

Functional dependence

A column Y is said to be functionally dependent on column X if each value of X determines the value of Y. For example, DATE_OF_BIRTH is functionally dependent on EMP_NO or EMP_NAME.

Transitive dependence

If Y is functionally dependent on X and Z is functionally dependent on Y and Z can be determined by X then it is called transitive dependence.

> X -> Y and Y-> Z implying X -> Z

> Z is said to be transitively dependent on X.
> We will see a practical example in Section 27.3.3 (3rd Normal Form).

Note:
Superkey: All column combinations which uniquely identify a row in a table.
Candidate Keys: Minimal superkey which uniquely identify a row in a table.
Primary Key: A Candidate key which has been designated for uniquely identifying rows in a table.
Alternate Keys: Candidate keys other than the primary key.

27.3 NORMALIZATION PROCESS

It involves a series of steps for modifying the structure used for storing information in various forms known as First Normal Form, Second Normal Form, Third Normal Form, etc.

27.3.1   First Normal Form—Eliminate Repeating Groups

A table is said to be in the First Normal Form if it satisfies the following criteria:

    1.   There are no repeating groups.
    2.   Each column contains atomic values only.

Assume an EMPLOYEE table (Table 27.3) which contains information about the employee along with the various projects completed.

TABLE 27.3   EMPLOYEE table

EMP_ID	NAME	JOB_CD	JOB_TITLE	PROJECT	COMPLETION DATE	DURATION DAYS
1111	Satish	A	Analyst	Railway Reservation	01/02/2008	90
1111	Satish	A	Analyst	Library Management	31/03/2008	60
2222	Rashmi	P	Programmer	Railway Reservation	01/02/2008	45
2222	Rashmi	P	Programmer	Library Management	31/03/2008	42
2222	Rashmi	P	Programmer	Hospital Management	10/08/2008	20

EMP_ID: Unique Identification given to each employee
NAME: Name of the Employee.
JOB_CD: Job Code 'A' => Analyst, 'P' => Programmer.
JOB_TITLE: 'A' => Analyst, 'P' => Programmer.
PROJECT: Project on which employee has worked.
COMPLETION_DATE: Date on which particular project was completed.
DURATION_DAYS: Number of days in which project was completed.

Each employee will have a single JOB_CD.

Each employee may have completed multiple projects. "Satish" has done 2 projects, namely Railway and Library as Analyst.

Many employees could have worked in the same project. "Satish" and "Rashmi" both have worked on Railway and Library Project.

This structure (Table 27.3) has several problems:

Problem 1:   The same employee's information has been repeated several times once for each project. We have been told twice that Satish is Analyst and thrice that Rashmi is a Programmer. This is called redundancy because of the repeating group.

Problem 2:   If an employee completes a new project then we will have to take care that employee's information like EMP_ID, NAME, JOB_CD and JOB_TITLE are entered correctly.

Problem 3:   For a new employee who doesn't have any project, we will have to supply NULL values for PROJECT, COMPLETION_DATE and DURATION.

Problem 4:   For a new project which has not been assigned to an Employee, we will have to store NULL values for EMP_ID, NAME, JOB_CD and JOB_TITLE.

Problem 5: If we want to change the JOB_CD of "Satish" then we need to do that in 2 records. If we forgot to change the same, say in one of the records then it will lead to incorrect information. This is called inconsistency. Redundancy leads to inconsistency.

To bring Table 27.3 in 1st Normal Form, we need to split the table into two parts as shown in Figure 27.1.

TABLE 27.4   EMP

EMP_ID	Name	Job_CD	JOB_TITLE
1111	Satish	A	Analyst
2222	Rashmi	P	Programmer

TABLE 27.5   EMP_PROJECT

EMP_ID	Project	Completion date	Duration
1111	Railway Reservation	01/02/2008	90
1111	Library Management	31/03/2008	60
2222	Railway Reservation	01/02/2008	45
2222	Library Management	31/03/2008	42
2222	Hospital Management	10/08/2008	20

Figure 27.1   Splitting Table 27.3 into two tables for complying with First Normal Form.

Table 27.4 and Table 27.5 resolve some of the problems associated with problem 1 of Table 27.3. This problem has been solved. Repeating group has been removed. Information about each employee is at a single place without repetition.

Problem 2 has also been solved. When an employee completes a new project, his Name and Job Code will be entered in a single record. The project he has completed will be entered in EMP_PROJECT table as a single record. Note that EMP_ID has to be repeated in EMP_PROJECT table because in the Relational Systems this is the linkage key between the EMPLOYEE and PROJECTS. We cannot call the EMP_ID of EMP_PROJECT table as the repeating group.

Problem 3 has been solved. Adding a new employee who has not been assigned any project is straightforward.

Problem 4 has not been solved. Adding a new project which has not been assigned to any employee, will need NULL value for EMP_ID.

Problem 5 can also be solved by changing JOB_CD of an employee which requires changes in just one record of EMP table.

27.3.2   Second Normal Form—Eliminate Redundant Data

A table is said to be in the second Normal Form if and only if

1. It is in the First Normal Form.
2. Every non-prime attribute is fully functionally dependent on candidate key.

Procedure for conversion to second Normal Form.

The procedure for converting to second Normal Form is:

1. Identify the candidate keys.
2. Identify the non-prime attributes which are fully functionally dependent on candidate key.
3. Create a separate table for the combination of candidate key and fully functionally dependent on non-prime attributes.

Table 27.4 (EMP) is in first and second Normal Form. There are no repeating groups. EMP_ID is the candidate key and every non-prime attribute like NAME, JOB_CD and JOB_TITLE are fully functionally dependent on candidate key. Y is fully functionally dependent on X if value of Y can be determined by the value of X. NAME, JOB_CD, JOB_TITLE can be determined from the EMP_ID. If we know the EMP_ID, all other known non-prime attributes can be based on the candidate key (EMP_ID).

Table 27.5 (EMP_PROJECT) is neither in first nor in second Normal Form. PROJECT and COMPLETION_DATE have been repeated for employees having worked on the same project. COMPLETION_DATE is fully functionally dependent on PROJECT only and must be moved to a separate table. Secondly, DURATION_DAYS is fully functionally dependent on EMP_ID+PROJECT, which is the candidate key. DURATION_DAYS is not fully functionally dependent on PROJECT. So, we should have a separate table containing EMP_ID, PROJECT and DURATION_DAYS.

Table 27.5 (EMP_PROJECT) should be further splitted into two tables to satisfy first and second Normal Form as shown in Figure 27.2.

TABLE 27.6 EMP

EMP ID	NAME	JOB_CD	JOB_TITLE
1111	Satish	A	Analyst
2222	Rashmi	P	Programmer

TABLE 27.7 PROJECT

Project	Completion Date
Railway Reservation	01/02/2008
Library Management	31/03/2008
Hospital Management	10/08/2008

TABLE 27.8 EMP_PROJECT

EMP_ID	Project	Duration
1111	Railway Reservation	90
1111	Library Management	60
2222	Railway Reservation	45
2222	Library Management	42
2222	Hospital Management	20

Figure 27.2 Splitting table 27.5 into two tables.

PROJECT (Table 27.7)
No repeating groups, therefore table is in first Normal Form.
Candidate Key: PROJECT
Non-Prime Attribute: COMPLETION_DATE

As COMPLETION_DATE is fully functionally dependent on candidate key, therefore, it is in second Normal Form.

EMP_PROJECT (Table 27.8)
No repeating groups, therefore, table is in first Normal Form.
Candidate Key: EMP_ID+PROJECT
Non-Prime Attribute: DURATION_DAYS

As DURATION_DAYS is fully functionally dependent on candidate key, therefore, it is in second Normal Form.

Note that in EMP_PROJECT table although we have specified the same project in multiple records but it cannot be called as repeating group because EMP_ID+PROJECT is the candidate key and establishes the link between EMP_ID and PROJECT for determining the DURATION_DAYS.

The second Normal Form has helped us in reducing the redundancy to a great extent. JOB_CD and JOB_TITLE appear once for each employee. COMPLETION_DATE is also specified once for each PROJECT.

EMP_PROJECT is in second Normal Form but still has some drawbacks. If we have an employee who has not been assigned any project then we will have to supply NULL value for PROJECT and DURATION_DAYS. Secondly, if a new project has started which has not been assigned to any employee then EMP_ID will have to be supplied NULL value.

27.3.3   Third Normal Form—Eliminate Transitive Dependence

A table is said to be in third Normal Form if every non-prime attribute is non-transitively dependent on the candidate key. Let us first understand what we mean by transitive dependence.

A relation must satisfy two conditions to be called transitive dependence. C is said to be transitively dependent on A if it satisfies the following conditions (Figure 27.3):

Condition 1. Attribute C depends on attribute B and attribute B depends on attribute A.

Condition 2. Attribute A is not dependent on B OR B is not dependent on C.

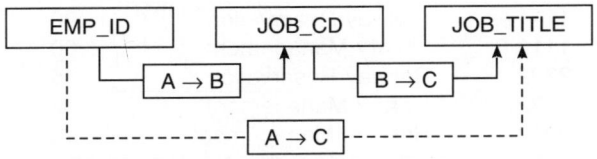

Figure 27.3 Transitive dependence.

Refer to Table 27.6 (EMP) in second Normal Form.

EMP ID	NAME	JOB_CD	JOB_TITLE
1111	Satish	A	Analyst
2222	Rashmi	P	Programmer

In this table, JOB_CD is functionally dependent on EMP_ID and JOB_TITLE is functionally dependent on JOB_CD.

JOB_CD is functionally dependent on JOB_TITLE but EMP_ID is not functionally dependent on JOB_CD. Therefore, we can say that JOB_TITLE is transitively dependent on EMP_ID.

The problem with Table 27.6 is that we may erroneously assign the same JOB_CD say 'A' to the some other TITLE other than 'ANALYST'.

To bring the Table 27.6 in third Normal Form, we need to break this transitive dependence. We should move the transitive dependence to separate table JOB as shown in Figure 27.4.

TABLE 27.9 EMP

EMP ID	Name	JOB_CD
1111	Satish	A
2222	Rashmi	P

TABLE 27.10 JOB

JOB_CD	JOB_TITLE
A	Analyst
P	Programmer

TABLE 27.11 PROJECT

PROJECT	COMPLETION DATE
Railway Reservation	01/02/2008
Library Management	31/03/2008
Hospital Management	10/08/2008

TABLE 27.12 EMP_PROJECT

EMP ID	Project	Duration
1111	Railway Reservation	90
1111	Library Management	60
2222	Railway Reservation	45
2222	Library Management	42
2222	Hospital Management	20

Figure 27.4 Breaking transitive dependence.

EMP (Table 27.9)
Candidate Key: EMP_ID

Non-Prime Attributes: NAME, JOB_CD

Every non-prime attribute is fully functionally dependent on the candidate key.

No non-prime attribute is transitively dependent on the candidate key.

JOB (Table 27.10)

Candidate Key: JOB_CD

Non-Prime Attributes: JOB_TITLE

Every non-prime attribute is non-transitively dependent on the candidate key.

27.3.4 Fourth Normal Form—Isolate Independent Multiple Relationships

The Fourth Normal Form talks of multi-valued dependency.

Assume an EMPLOYEE Table 27.13 which stores information about Projects and Skills possessed by an employee. An employee may be assigned multiple projects and he may have multiple skills for each project. We are assuming that there is no relationship between the projects and the skills.

TABLE 27.13 EMPLOYEE

EMP_ID	PROJECT_ID	SKILL
1111	Railway Reservation	Oracle
1111	Railway Reservation	JSP
1111	Railway Reservation	ASP.NET
1111	Library Management	SQL Server
1111	Library Management	PHP

Candidate Key: EMP_ID+PROJECT_ID+SKILL

As there are no non-prime attributes, therefore, the table is in the third Normal Form. This table has two independent multi-valued dependencies.

Each employee has multiple projects:

EMP_ID ->-> PROJECT

Each employee has multiple skills:

EMP_ID ->-> SKILL

SKILL does not depend on PROJECT and vice-versa. Multi-valued dependencies lead to lot of redundancy which in turn may lead to inconsistencies.

Suppose EMP_ID 1111 has got a new project then we will have to supply NULL values for SKILL. If employee has acquired a new skill then we will have to supply NULL value for the project. As there is no relationship between PROJECT and SKILL, therefore, we have two independent multi-valued dependencies. The fourth Normal Form suggests removal of independent multi-valued dependencies into separate tables as shown in Figure 27.5.

TABLE 27.14 EMP_PROJECT

EMP_ID	PROJECT
1111	Railway Reservation
1111	Library Management

TABLE 27.15 EMP_SKILL

EMP_ID	SKILL
1111	Oracle
1111	JSP
1111	ASP.NET
1111	SQL Server
1111	PHP

Figure 27.5 Breaking independent multi-valued dependency.

Adding a new project for an employee is easy. New SKILL can be added independent of project.

Caution: If we assume that there is a relationship between PROJECT and SKILL also then the table is already in the fourth Normal Form. It means that Railway Reservation project requires skills on Oracle, JSP and ASP.NET. In this situation the candidate key is EMP_ID+PROJECT_ID+SKILL and there are no non-prime attributes. Now we do not have independent multi-valued dependency and Table 27.16 is in the normal form.

TABLE 27.16 EMPLOYEE (Relationship exists between Project and Skills)
—Fourth Normal Form

EMP_ID	PROJECT_ID	SKILL
1111	Railway Reservation	Oracle
1111	Railway Reservation	JSP
1111	Railway Reservation	ASP.NET
1111	Library Management	SQL Server
1111	Library Management	PHP

27.3.5 Fifth Normal Form—Project Join Normal Form (PJ/NF)

Assume an EMP table (Table 27.17) in which there is a relationship between the PROJECT and SKILL. An employee may have skills appropriate for a project and he may have skills which are not required in a project.

TABLE 27.17 EMP

EMP_ID	PROJECT_ID	SKILL
1111	Railway Reservation	Oracle
1111	Railway Reservation	JSP
1111	Library Management	PHP
2222	Railway Reservation	Oracle

The process of splitting a table into two tables is called **Projection**. Suppose we split Table 27.17 into two tables as shown in Figure 27.6.

TABLE 27.18 EMP_PROJECT

EMP_ID	Project
1111	Railway Reservation
1111	Library Management
2222	Railway Reservation

TABLE 27.19 EMP_SKILL

EMP_ID	Skill
1111	Oracle
1111	JSP
1111	PHP
2222	Oracle

Figure 27.6 Projection.

It appears that the two new tables (Tables 27.18 and 27.19) are exact representation of the original table (Table 27.17). So it should be possible to reach the original table from these two tables. We will join the two tables so that we reach the original table based on the common key which is EMP_ID. Table 27.20 shows the result of joining EMP_PROJECT and EMP_SKILL on EMP_ID column.

TABLE 27.20 EMP obtained by joining EMP_PROJECT and EMP_SKILL

RECORD_NO	EMP_ID	PROJECT	SKILL
1	1111	Railway Reservation	Oracle
2	1111	Railway Reservation	JSP
3	1111	Railway Reservation	PHP
4	1111	Library Management	Oracle
5	1111	Library Management	JSP
6	1111	Library Management	PHP
7	2222	Railway Reservation	Oracle

For each record of EMP_ID 1111 in EMP table, we have correspondingly three records in the SKILL table. Therefore, we have got 6 records for EMP_ID 1111 in the resultant join of the two tables. Record numbers 3, 4, 5 are spurious records which did not exist in the original table. This problem occurred because we lost the relationship between the PROJECT and SKILL by splitting the table into two projections.

Table 27.17 is in the Fourth Normal Form but it cannot be splitted into two projections and then recombined to produce the original table. This structure (27.17) can be normalized to fifth form by splitting it into three tables as shown in Figure 27.7.

TABLE 27.21   EMP_PROJECT

EMP_ID	Project
1111	Railway Reservation
1111	Library Management
2222	Railway Reservation

TABLE 27.22   EMP_SKILL

EMP_ID	Skill
1111	Oracle
1111	JSP
1111	PHP
2222	Oracle

TABLE 27.23   PROJECT_SKILL

Project	Skill
Railway Reservation	Oracle
Railway Reservation	JSP
Library Management	PHP

Figure 27.7   Fifth Normal Form.

To get back to the original table (Table 27.17) we need to join the above three tables (Tables 27.21, 27.22 and 27.23).

First, we will join EMP_PROJECT (Table 27.21) and EMP_SKILL (Table 27.22) based on the common key EMP_ID. See Table 27.24 for the result of joining Tables 27.21 and 27.22.

TABLE 27.24   EMP_PROJECT_SKILL

EMP_ID	Project	Skill
1111	Railway Reservation	Oracle
1111	Railway Reservation	JSP
1111	Railway Reservation	PHP
1111	Library Management	Oracle
1111	Library Management	JSP
1111	Library Management	PHP
2222	Railway Reservation	Oracle

Note that we have got 3 spurious records which have been highlighted because the project and skill have not yet been taken into account.

Now we will join this intermediate Table 27.24 with Table 27.23 PROJECT_SKILL based on the common keys PROJECT and SKILL (see Table 27.25).

TABLE 27.25 Joining EMP_PROJECT_SKILL and PROJECT_SKILL

EMP_ID	Project	Skill
1111	Railway Reservation	Oracle
1111	Railway Reservation	JSP
1111	Library Management	PHP
2222	Railway Reservation	Oracle

27.3.6 BCNF—Boyce Code Normal Form

A table is said to be in BCNF if it satisfies following conditions:

1. It is in third Normal Form
2. All non-trivial functional dependencies(X->Y) depend on the superkey(X).

BCNF is between the 3rd and 4th normal forms.

Assume a TENNIS COURT table (Table 27.26) which contains information about various courts, their available timing and Rate.

TABLE 27.26 TENNIS_COURT

COURT_NO	START_TIME	END_TIME	RATE_CATEGORY
1	08:00	09:00	ECONOMY
1	10:00	11:00	ECONOMY
1	17:00	19:00	STANDARD
2	08:00	09:00	PREMIUM
2	10:00	11:00	PREMIUM
2	18:00	20:00	PREMIUM-PLUS

COURT_NO

COURT 1 => Hard Court which has two pricing categories, namely ECONOMY and STANDARD.

COURT 2 => Grass Court which has two pricing categories, namely PREMIUM and PREMIUM-PLUS

RATE_CATEGORY

ECONOMY—This rate is applicable to COURT 1 and can be used by members only.

STANDARD—This rate is applicable to COURT 1 and can be used by non-members only.

PREMIUM—This rate is applicable to COURT 2 and can be used by members only.

PREMIUM-PLUS—This rate is applicable to COURT 2 and can be used by non-members only.

Note: ECONOMY and STANDARD rates do not apply to COURT 2.

PREMIUM and PREMIUM-PLUS rates do not apply to COURT 1.

The problem with this table structure (Table 27.26) is that it does not restrict the condition that ECONOMY and STANDARD rates apply to COURT 1 only. Similarly, it does not restrict the condition that PREMIUM and PREMIUM-PLUS rates apply to COURT 2 only. COURT has non-trivial functional dependency on RATE_OF_CATEGORY. BCNF implies that determining attribute RATE_CATEGORY should be the candidate key in such case.

To make Table 27.26 in BCNF, we need to split it into two tables as shown in Figure 27.8.

TABLE 27.27   RATE

Rate_Category	Court	Member_tag
ECONOMY	1	Yes
STANDARD	1	No
PREMIUM	2	Yes
PREMIUM-PLUS	2	No

TABLE 27.28   COURT

Court	Start time	End time	Member tag
1	08:00	09:00	Yes
1	10:00	11:00	Yes
1	17:00	19:00	No
2	08:00	09:00	Yes
2	10:00	11:00	Yes
2	18:00	20:00	No

Figure 27.8   BCNF.

Now both Tables 27.27 and 27.28 are the following BCNF:

RATE Table—Candidate key is RATE_CATEGORY and COURT + MEMBER_TAG.

COURT Table—Candidate key is COURT+START_TIME and COURT+END_TIME.

In this structure different courts cannot have the same RATE_CATEGORY.

Entity Relationship Diagram (ERD)

28.1 INTRODUCTION

ERD is a database design tool which is used to identify the various entities and relationship which exists between them for proper understanding of the entire database to be designed. It is a detailed logical representation of the entities, associations and data elements for a database.

28.2 COMPONENTS OF ERD

ERD comprises of 3 components, namely Entities, Attributes and Relationships.

ENTITIES—Person, place, object, event or concept about which data is to be stored. It represents a set of objects in the real world that share the same properties. For example:

Person: Employee, student, patient

Place: School, college, warehouse

Object: Product, machine, car

Event: Registration, renewal, sale

Concept: Course, syllabus

ATTRIBUTES—Each entity has certain characteristics. For example, a student has the following attributes–ROLLNO, NAME, ADDRESS, PHONE, etc.

RELATIONSHIPS—Association between the instances of one or more entity types.

There can be 3 types of relationships between any two entities:

1. One-to-one (1:1): One instance of entity A is related to exactly one instance of entity B.
2. One-to-many (1:M): One instance of entity A is related to multiple instances of entity B.
3. Many-to-many (M:N): One instance of entity A is related to multiple instances of entity B and one instance of entity B is related to multiple instances of entity A.

28.3 ERD NOTATION

There are two notations which can be used to pictorially depicted entities, relations and attributes. These are Chen Model and Crow Foot Model.

28.3.1 Chen Model

Figure 28.1 shows the Notation used by Chen Model for ER-Diagrams.

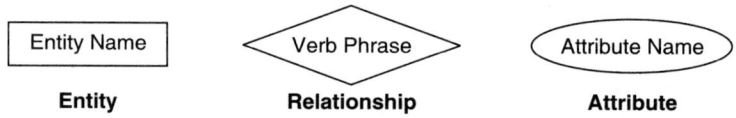

| Entity | Relationship | Attribute |

Figure 28.1 Chen notation symbols for ERD.

Entities are represented by rectangular box.

Attributes are specified through ellipse.

Relationships are indicated by diamond box and lines are drawn between the related entities along with the type of relation (1:1, 1:many, many: many).

Example of one-to-one

For a Professor heading a specific department, the ERD-using Chen Notation would be as shown in Figure 28.2.

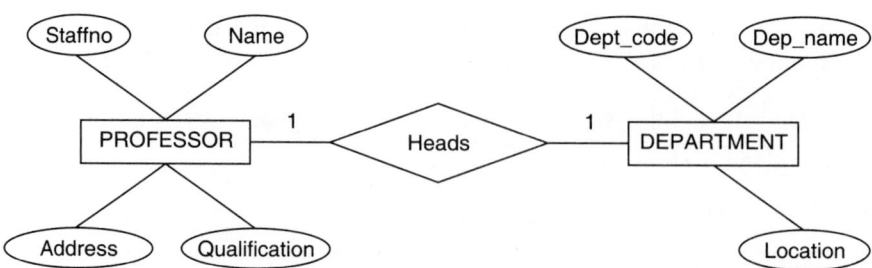

Figure 28.2 Chen Model.

Each Professor heads a specific department and each department is headed by one Professor. Therefore, the relationship is 1:1 which is indicated by placing 1 on the line joining entities to relation. Attributes have been displayed in ellipse.

28.3.2 Crow Foot Model

Crow Foot Model uses the same symbols for entities and attributes as Chen Model. The relationship is indicated by connecting lines with special symbols to reflect the relationship as shown in Figure 28.3.

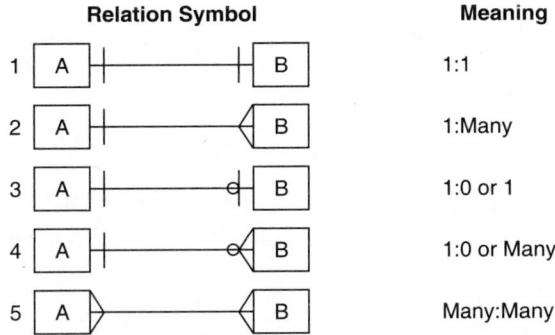

Figure 28.3 Crow Foot Notation for ERD.

Relation Symbol 1: Each instance of A is linked to single instance of B and vice versa. It is a mandatory relation. Mandatory implies that for each A, there must be one B. It is not possible that there is no B for a given A.

Relation Symbol 2: Each instance of A is linked to multiple instances of B. Each instance of B has correspondingly only one instance of A. It is a mandatory relation. Each A will have at least one B.

Relation Symbol 3: Each instance of A is linked to zero or 1 instance of B which means that for a given A there may not be any instance of B or just one instance of B. It is an optional relation. "A" may not have a corresponding B.

Relation Symbol 4: Each instance of A is linked to zero or many instances of B. It is an optional relation.

Relation Symbol 5: Each instance of A is linked to many instances of B and vice versa. It is also a mandatory relation. Each A will have at least one B.

The relation of Figure 28.2 using Crow Foot Model is shown in Figure 28.4.

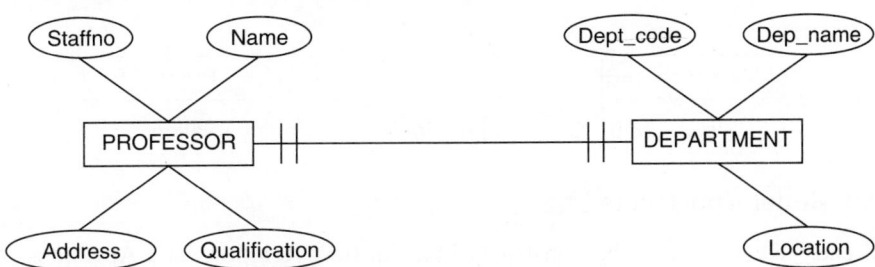

Figure 28.4 Crow Foot Model.

The ratio of Professor to Department is 1:1, therefore, two vertical lines at Department end. The ratio of Department to Professor is also 1:1, therefore, two vertical lines at Professor end.

Example of 1:many

An EMPLOYEE may have multiple DEPENDENTS but a DEPENDENT can belong to a single EMPLOYEE only. The Chen Model would be as shown in Figure 28.5.

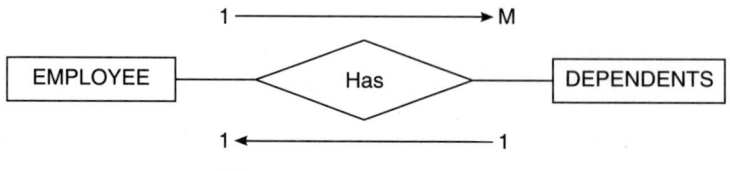

Figure 28.5   1:M relation.

1-M implies that an EMPLOYEE will have many DEPENDENTS and 1-1 implies that a DEPENDENT can belong to one EMPLOYEE only. The Craw Foot Model for Figure 28.5 has been shown in Figure 28.6.

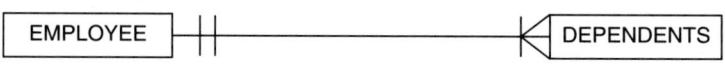

Figure 28.6   1:M relation.

Vertical line with 3 bars on DEPENDENTS side implies 1: Many relation from EMPLOYEE to DEPENDENTS. An EMPLOYEE can have multiple DEPENDENTS. Two vertical lines on EMPLOYEE side imply 1:1 relation from DEPENDENTS to EMPLOYEE. A DEPENDENT can belong to one EMPLOYEE only.

Many:Many Example

An EMPLOYEE may be executing multiple projects and a single project may be employing multiple employees. This is called many:many or M:N relation and has been depicted using both models in Figures 28.7 and 28.8.

Figure 28.7   Chen model for many:many relation.

Figure 28.8   Crow foot model for many:many relation.

28.3.3   ER Model Constructs

We have already seen some of the constructs like Entities, Relations and Attributes. Let us see some other important constructs as shown in Figure 28.9.

Symbols

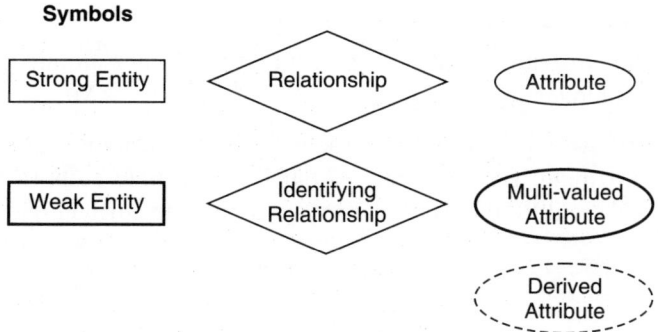

Figure 28.9 ER model constructs.

28.3.4 Entity Classification

Entities can be classified as Strong or Weak.

Strong entity

An entity which exists on its own and does not depend on other entities for its existence. A strong entity is uniquely identifiable by combination of some characteristics. For example, EMPLOYEE, STUDENT, COLLEGE are strong entities. A STUDENT can be identified by his name, address, etc.

Weak entity

An entity whose existence depends on another entity is called a weak entity. A weak entity has no meaning without the existence of other entities. The entity on which the weak entity depends is called the identifying owner or simply owner. A weak entity does not have its identity without owner entity. For example, each employee may have dependents and in such case dependents cannot exist without the employee in our ER-Diagram (Figure 28.10).

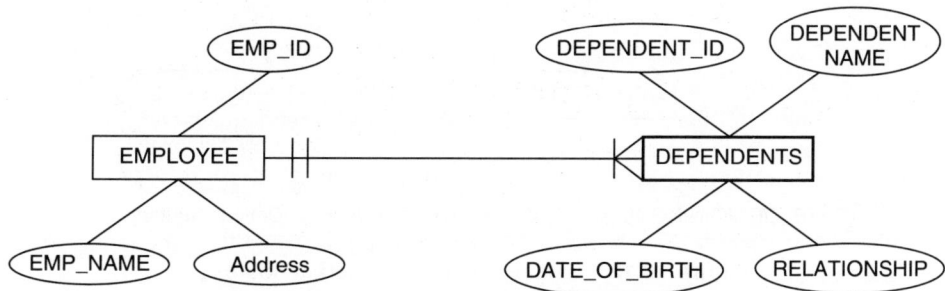

Figure 28.10 Strong and weak entities.

An employee may or may not have any dependents and he may have many dependents (0:Many). A dependent must belong to an employee (1:1). Each entity has its own attributes.

28.3.5 Attribute Classification

Attributes can be classified on various parameters.

Classification based on number of components

Simple attribute: An attribute is said to be a simple if it contains atomic or single values only and does not contain any hidden or implied values. EMP_ID, EMP_NAME are the simple attributes.

Composite attribute: An attribute which is actually a representation of more components is called a Composite Attribute. For example, ADDRESS attribute comprises of HOUSE_NO, COLONY, CITY, STATE and PIN_CODE and so is a composite attribute. See Figure 28.11.

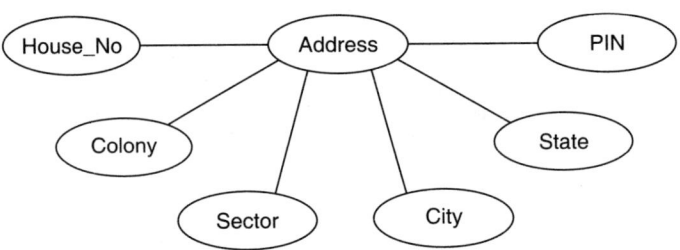

Figure 28.11   Composite attribute.

Classification based on number of values

Single-valued: The attributes which have a single value for a given entity is called a single-valued attribute. For example, EMP_ID, EMP_NAME, ADDRESS.

Multi-valued: An attribute which has many values for a given instance of entity is called a multi-valued attribute. For example, each employee may have skills on several software. See Figure 28.12.

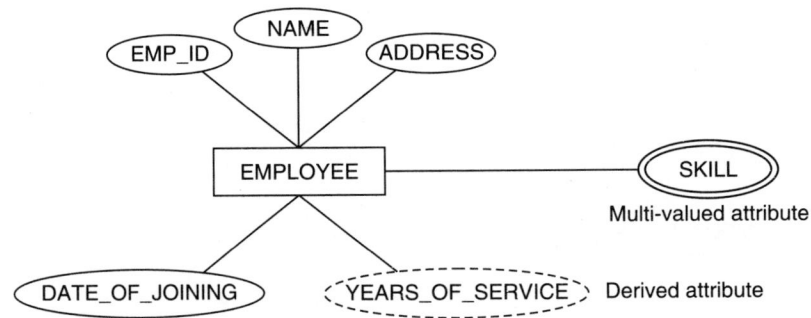

Figure 28.12   Single- and multi-valued attributes.

Classification based on derivation—Stored and Derived

Stored attributes: Attributes which are an integral part of the entity like EMP_ID, NAME and DATE_OF_JOINING.

Derived attributes: Attributes which are derived from stored attributes and provide some additional information about the entity are called Derived Attributes. For example, Years of Service for an employee can be calculated by subtracting DATE_OF_JOINING from the current date. See Figure 28.12.

28.3.6   Relationship Degree

Degree of relationship refers to the number of entities participating in a relation.

Unary: An entity is linked to other entities of the same type. See Figure 28.13.

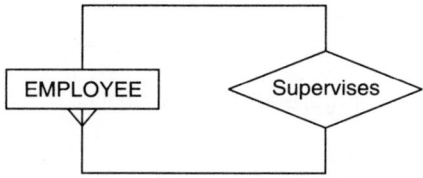

Figure 28.13   Unary.

An employee may supervise or monitor many employees.

Binary: An entity is linked to the other entity of different type. The relationship may be 1:1, 1:many or many:many and two entities are involved. See Figure 28.14.

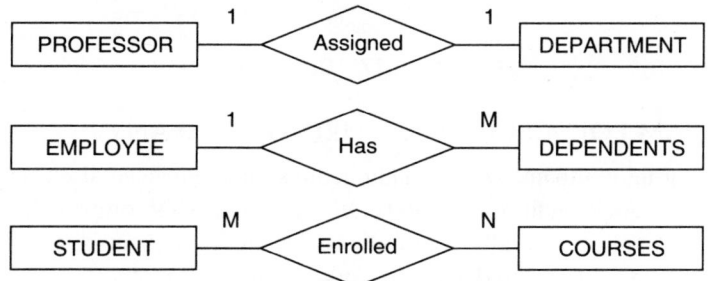

Figure 28.14   Binary.

Ternary: Three different entities are simultaneously related to each other. For example, a supplier may supply different parts to different projects. See Figure 28.15.

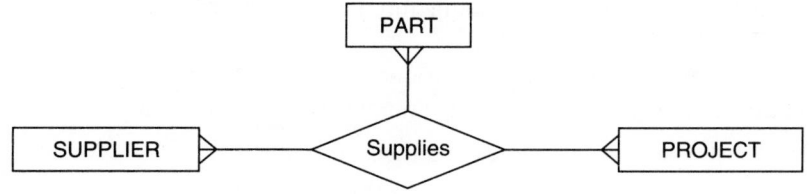

Figure 28.15   Ternary.

28.3.7   Cardinality of a Relation

Cardinality of a relation refers to a number of instances of one entity which are linked to another entity. For example, an EMPLOYEE can have many dependents. The minimum number of dependents an employee can have is zero and the maximum number of dependents can be, say, M. The cardinality of relation from EMPLOYEE to DEPENDENT is (0,M).

Similarly, a DEPENDENT can belong to one employee only. The minimum number of employees for a dependent is 1 and the maximum number of employees for a dependent is also 1. Therefore, the cardinality from DEPENDENT to EMPLOYEE is (1,1) as shown in Figure 28.16.

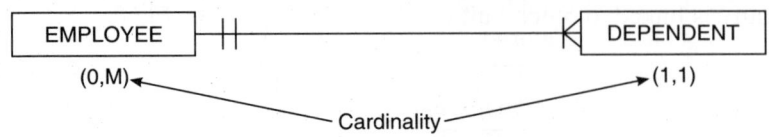

Figure 28.16   Cardinality.

We can provide another example.

An employee may be assigned zero or more projects. But a project must be assigned to same employee. A project is assigned at least one employee or may be assigned to many employees (Figure 28.17).

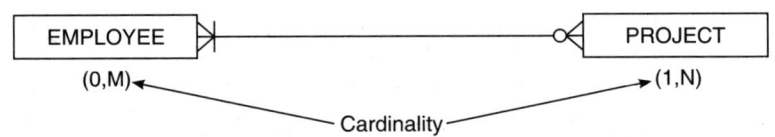

Figure 28.17   Cardinality.

28.4   ER DIAGRAM FOR A MANUFACTURING COMPANY

Assume a manufacturing company which manufactures and sells several electronic products like Television, Refrigerator, Air-Conditioner, CD/DVD Players, etc. This company has a list of suppliers who supply various components for different products. Several components assembled together form a product. A product will be manufactured in many work centres. Customers can order multiple products.

The various entities would be

PRODUCT – Company produces several products
COMPONENT – Each product uses components
VENDOR – Components are supplied by Vendors
WORK CENTRE – Products are manufactured in work centres
CUSTOMER – Purchase products
ORDER – Customers place orders for products
EMPLOYEE – Employees assemble the components on work centres.

Figure 28.18 lists the various entities and their attributes.

Entity	Attributes
PRODUCT	Product_Id, Description and Price
COMPONENT	Component_id, Name, Cost
SUPPLIER	Supplier_Id, Supplier_Name, Supplier_Address, Supplier_rating
WORK CENTRE	Work_Center_Id, Location
ORDER	Order_No, Order_Date
CUSTOMER	Customer_Id, Name, Address, Pin
EMPLOYEE	Employee_Id, Name, Address, Skill

Figure 28.18   Attributes of various entities.

Relationship between entities

Each product contains several components. A product has at least one component and may comprise of several components. A component must belong to a product and the same component can be used in multiple products. The attribute of the relationship between product and component is the quantity of the component which a product requires.

Company has a list of suppliers who supply various components. A SUPPLIER may not be supplying any component and may supply several components. A component must be supplied by at least one SUPPLIER or several SUPPLIERS may provide the same component. The attribute of the relationship between PRODUCT and SUPPLIER is the quantity being supplied and Unit Price.

Each product will be manufactured in single or multiple work centres. A work centre may not produce a product and may produce several products.

Each work centre will have one or more employees and an employee would be working in single work centre only.

A customer may not place any order and may place multiple orders. But a ORDER will belong to a specific customer only. There is a 0:Many relationship between CUSTOMER and ORDER, 1:1 relationship between ORDER and CUSTOMER.

Each order may contain single product or multiple products and the same product may be demanded in many ORDERS.

Relationship attributes

Certain attributes exist due to the relationship between the entities. For example, a supplier supplies components in a specific quantity and unit price. These two attributes have no meaning for either SUPPLIER or COMPONENT entities. They exist due to the relationship between the two types of entities. All attributes, depend on the relationship, have been indicated by black-coloured ellipses.

Figure 28.19 shows the complete ER-Diagram for the manufacturing company.

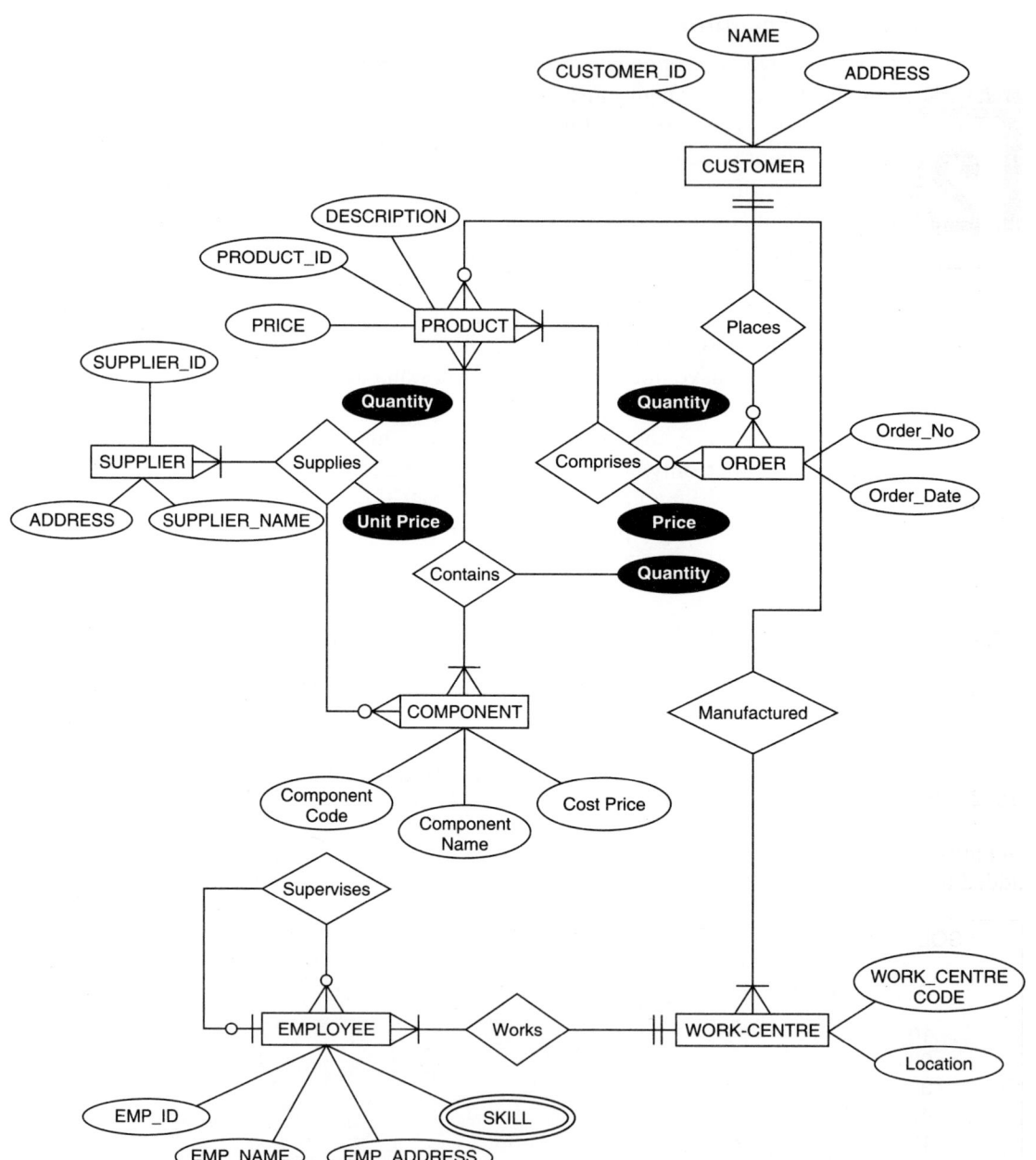

Figure 28.19   ERD for a manufacturing company.

Oracle FAQ

29.1 INTRODUCTION

This chapter provides answers to the most commonly asked questions regarding how to perform certain operations in Oracle. This chapter utilizes the various concepts learned in the previous sections.

29.2 ELIMINATING DUPLICATE ROWS IN A TABLE

Suppose we have a DEPARTMENT table with 4 records. By mistake the same 4 records have been added to the same table as shown in Figure 29.1. Now we want to remove the duplicate records.

```
SQL> select * from department;

DEPT_NO DEPT_NAME

    10 MANUFACTURING
    20 ENGINEERING
    30 SALES
    40 FINANCE
    10 MANUFACTURING
    20 ENGINEERING
    30 SALES
    40 FINANCE

8 rows selected.
```

Figure 29.1 Table with duplicate records.

There are two methods which can be used to solve the problem of duplicate records.

Method 1

ROWID pseudo-column is the unique identification or unique physical location of each record in database. No two records can have the same ROWID.

We can use the ROWID for deleting duplicate rows as shown in Figure 29.2.

```
SQL> DELETE FROM DEPARTMENT A WHERE ROWID > (
  2 SELECT min(rowid) FROM DEPARTMENT B
  3 WHERE A.dept_no = B.dept_no);
  4 rows deleted.
```

Figure 29.2   Removing duplicate records using ROWID (Method 1).

The two tables have been joined on the PRIMARY KEY dept_no and the duplicate record is deleted using the MIN(rowid) group function. The record with higher ROWID is deleted as ">" has been used.

Method 2

This is a very crude method of removing duplicate records. It involves the following three steps. See Figure 29.3.

1. Create a new table using DISTINCT * from the existing table.
2. Remove the existing table.
3. Rename the new table to the original name.

```
SQL> create table DEPARTMENT_NEW as select distinct * from DEPARTMENT;
Table created.

SQL> drop table DEPARTMENT;
Table dropped.

SQL> rename DEPARTMENT_NEW to DEPARTMENT;
Table renamed.
```

Figure 29.3   Removing duplicate records (Method 2).

Caution: Whenever a table is created from the existing table then all the constraints of the original table are not applied to the new table. You will have to recreate the constraints on the new table.

29.3 GENERATING PRIMARY KEY VALUES

It is a common requirement to generate the primary key values for a table. Assume EMPLOYEE table where we have not allotted EMPNO initially to any of the employees. We want to allocate UNIQUE values for EMPNO column for each employee.

There are three methods which can be used for generating Primary Key values.

Method 1: Using ROWNUM Pseudo-Column

ROWNUM can be used for generating Primary Key values as shown in Figure 29.4.

```
SQL> update employee set emp_no=rownum;
12 rows updated.

SQL> select emp_no,emp_name,salary,dept_no from employee order by emp_no;
```

EMP_NO	EMP_NAME	SALARY	DEPT_NO
1	KING	20000	1
2	SCOTT	15000	10
3	JOHN	14000	20
4	SUSE	14500	30
5	HENRY	13600	10
.			
.			
.			

Figure 29.4 Primary key generation using ROWNUM.

Note: EMP_NO's will be assigned from 1 to N. We cannot specify a starting number and increment value for the subsequent numbers.

Method 2: Using SEQUENCE

Sequences can be used to specify Starting Number and increment values as in Figure 29.5.

```
SQL> update employee set emp_no=null;
12 rows updated.

SQL> create sequence seq_emp_no start with 5555 increment by 1;
Sequence created.

SQL> select seq_emp_no.nextval from dual;

  NEXTVAL

  5555

SQL> update employee set emp_no= seq_emp_no.nextval ;
12 rows updated.

SQL> select emp_no,emp_name,salary from employee;
```

EMP_NO	EMP_NAME	SALARY
5556	KING	20000
5557	SCOTT	15000
5558	JOHN	14000

Figure 29.5 Primary key generation using SEQUENCE.

Method 3: Using CURSOR

Assigning Unique EMPNO in the ORDER of department and then by employee name is not possible by using either of the above two methods. We will use CURSOR to fetch records in the order of department and then by name and will maintain a variable which will be incremented for each employee and assigned. See Figure 29.6 for the code.

```
SQL>edit forupdate.sql
declare
    cursor c1 is select * from employee order by dept_no,emp_name;
    c1_rec   c1%rowtype;
    v_emp_no number(4);
begin
    v_emp_no:=8888;
    for c1_rec in c1 loop
            update employee set emp_no=v_emp_no where
            emp_no=c1_rec.emp_no;
            v_emp_no:=v_emp_no+1;
    end loop;
end;
/
commit;
```

Figure 29.6   Assigning primary key value for ORDERED records.

Let us execute the program of Figure 29.6 for generating the serial number as shown in Figure 29.7.

```
SQL> @forupdate
PL/SQL procedure successfully completed.

Commit complete.

SQL> select emp_no,emp_name,salary,dept_no from employee order by dept_no,emp_name;
```

EMP_NO	EMP_NAME	SALARY	DEPT_NO
8888	KING	20000	1
8889	HENRY	13600	10
8890	JORD	12000	10
8891	SCOTT	15000	10
.			
.			
.			

Figure 29.7   Running program of Figure 29.6.

29.4   GENERATING SERIAL NUMBER FOR RECORDS DISPLAYED IN A SPECIFIED ORDER

We can use the ROWNUM pseudo-column for generating the serial number but this concept fails when records are fetched in a specified order using ORDER BY clause (Figure 29.8).

```
SQL> select rownum "Sr.No", dept_no, emp_no, emp_name, salary from employee order by
dept_no,emp_name;
```

Sr.No	DEPT_NO	EMP_NO	EMP_NAME	SALARY
1	1	1	KING	20000
5	10	5	HENRY	13600
6	10	6	JORD	12000
2	10	2	SCOTT	15000
7	10	7	WILLIAMS	12100
12	10	12	XEON	15000

Figure 29.8 ROWNUM fails when records are ordered.

Note that Serial Numbers have not been generated properly as ORDER BY clause has been used. Figure 29.9 shows the SQL statement for generating serial number for an ORDERED list.

```
SQL> select rownum "Sr.No",dept_no,emp_no,emp_name,salary from
(select * from employee order by dept_no,emp_name)
order by rownum
```

Sr.No	DEPT_NO	EMP_NO	EMP_NAME	SALARY
1	1	1	KING	20000
2	10	5	HENRY	13600
3	10	6	JORD	12000
4	10	2	SCOTT	15000
5	10	7	WILLIAMS	12100
6	10	12	XEON	15000
7	20	3	JOHN	14000
8	20	8	MARUTI	13100
9	20	9	SANTRO	12200

Figure 29.9 Generating serial no. for ORDERED List.

The inner SELECT fetches the records in the desired ORDER and the Outer SELECT uses the ROWNUM for this sorted list of records.

29.5 COPYING A TABLE

A table comprises mainly three components, namely
  Structure—Table name, column names and data types
  Data—Records
  Constraints—Primary, Unique, Not Null, etc.

Caution: We can copy the Structure and records but we cannot copy the constraints from one table to another.

29.5.1 Copying both Structure and Data

Figure 29.10 shows the SQL command for copying both structure and records into a new table from an existing table.

```
SQL> create table employee_new as select dept_no,emp_no,emp_name,salary from employee;
Table created.

SQL> select * from employee_new;
            DEPT_NO        EMP_NO       EMP_NAME       SALARY
               1              1           KING          20000
               10             2           SCOTT         15000
               20             3           JOHN          14000
               30             4           SUSE          14500
               10             5           HENRY         13600
               10             6           JORD          12000
```

Figure 29.10   Copying both structure and records.

If we want all columns of base table then use "SELECT *". Secondly, we can specify WHERE clause also for restricting the records to be copied into the new table.

29.5.2   Copying Structure Only and Not Data

Figure 29.11 shows the command for copying the structure only and not the records into a new table from an existing table.

```
SQL> create table new_employee as select dept_no,emp_no,emp_name,salary from employee
where 1=2;
Table created.

SQL> select * from new_employee;
no rows selected

SQL> desc new_employee;
      Name                  Null?            Type
      DEPT_NO                                NUMBER(2)
      EMP_NO                                 NUMBER(4)
      EMP_NAME                               VARCHAR2(10)
      SALARY                                 NUMBER(8,2)
```

Figure 29.11   Copying structure only.

Where 1=2 evaluates to FALSE for every record fetched from the EMPLOYEE table; as such, only the structure is copied and not the record.

29.6   GENERATING MATRIX OR CROSS TAB OR PIVOT REPORT

There are 3 Methods for generating Matrix or Cross Tab or Pivot Report.

29.6.1   Using DECODE

Refer to Section12.9 of Chapter 12.

29.6.2   Using CASE Statement

Refer to Section 12.11 of Chapter 12.

Display Designationwise total salary for each department. Figure 29.12 shows the CASE statement for generating the matrix report.

```
SQL> select designation,
  2 sum(case when dept_no=10 then salary end) dept10,
  3 sum(case when dept_no=20 then salary end) dept20,
  4 sum(case when dept_no=30 then salary end) dept30,
  5 sum(case when dept_no=40 then salary end) dept40,
  6 sum(salary) total
  7 from employee group by designation;
```

DESIGNATION	DEPT10	DEPT20	DEPT30	DEPT40	TOTAL
Manager	37700	25300	21000		84000
Clerk	12000	8500			20500
Executive	21000				21000
General Manager	15000	14000	14500		43500
Salesman	16500	17000	17000		50500
CEO	20000				20000

6 rows selected.

Figure 29.12   Matrix report using CASE.

Figure 29.13 contains the command for displaying the total salary as Zero wherever it is NULL.

```
SQL> select designation,
  2 sum(case when dept_no=10 then salary else 0 end) dept10,
  3 sum(case when dept_no=20 then salary else 0 end) dept20,
  4 sum(case when dept_no=30 then salary else 0 end) dept30,
  5 sum(case when dept_no=40 then salary else 0 end) dept40,
  6 sum(salary) total
  7 from employee group by designation;
```

DESIGNATION	DEPT10	DEPT20	DEPT30	DEPT40	TOTAL
Manager	37700	25300	21000	0	84000
Clerk	12000	8500	0	0	20500
Executive	21000	0	0	0	21000
General Manager	15000	14000	14500	0	43500
Salesman	16500	17000	17000	0	50500
CEO	20000	0	0	0	20000

6 rows selected.

Figure 29.13   CASE with ELSE option.

29.6.3   Using PIVOT Operator

Oracle 11g supports a new operator named PIVOT which can be used to generate matrix reports as shown in Figure 29.14.

Note: **PIVOT** operator will not work if you are using any Oracle version below 11g.

```
SQL> select * from
2 (
3 select designation,dept_no,salary
4 from employee a
5 )
6 pivot
7 (
8 sum(salary)
9 for dept_no in (10,20,30,40)
10 )
11* order by designation;
```

DESIGNATION	10	20	30	40
CEO	20000			
Clerk	12000	8500		
Executive	21000			
General Manager	15000	14000	14500	
Manager	37700	25300	21000	
Salesman	16500	17000	17000	

6 rows selected.

Figure 29.14   Using PIVOT operator for matrix reports.

SALARY is to be Pivoted for intersection of designation and dept_no.

29.6.4   UNPIVOT Operator

UNPIVOT Operator does the opposite of PIVOT operator. It converts a Pivoted/Matrix report into normal relational table.

Suppose we have a Pivoted table EMPLOYEE_MATRIX generated by PIVOT Operator as shown in Figure 29.15.

```
SQL>create table employee_matrix as
select * from
(
select designation,dept_no,salary
from employee a
)
pivot
(
sum(salary)
for dept_no in (10,20,30,40)
)
order by designation;
```

Figure 29.15   Creating PIVOT table EMPLOYEE_MATRIX.

Again we want to flatten the matrix into designationwise salary and departmentwise salary. We can use the UNPIVOT operator to perform the opposite of PIVOT operation as shown in Figure 29.16.

```
SQL> select * from employee_matrix
  3 unpivot
  4 (
  5 salary
  6 for dept_no in ("10","20","30","40")
  7 )
  8* order by designation,dept_no;
```

DESIGNATION	DEPT_NO	SALARY
CEO	10	20000
Clerk	10	12000
Clerk	20	8500
Executive	10	21000
General Manager	10	15000
General Manager	20	14000
General Manager	30	14500
Manager	10	37700
Manager	20	25300
Manager	30	21000
Salesman	10	16500
Salesman	20	17000
Salesman	30	17000

13 rows selected.

Figure 29.16   Unpivoting pivoted table.

29.7   HOW TO ADD A DAY/HOUR/MINUTE/SECOND TO A DATE VALUE?

It is possible to add or subtract fractions from a date value (Figure 29.17).

```
SQL>select
  2 to_char(sysdate,'dd/mm/yyyy hh24:mi:ss')               today,
  3 to_char(sysdate+1,'dd/mm/yyyy hh24:mi:ss')             one_day,
  4 to_char(sysdate+1/24,'dd/mm/yyyy hh24:mi:ss')          one_hour,
  5 to_char(sysdate +1/(24*60),'dd/mm/yyyy hh24:mi:ss')    one_minute,
  6* to_char(sysdate + 1/(24*60*60),'dd/mm/yyyy hh24:mi:ss')  one_second from dual;
```

TODAY	ONE_DAY	ONE_HOUR	ONE_MINUTE	ONE_SECOND
13/03/2009 10:04:46	14/03/2009 10:04:46	13/03/2009 11:04:46	13/03/2009 10:05:46	13/03/2009 10:04:47

Figure 29.17   Adding Day/Hour/Minute/Second to current date.

29.8 DISPLAYING AMOUNTS IN WORDS

In words implies that 245.37 should be displayed as Two hundred Forty five and Thirty seven paise.

Oracle has a Julian Date format which converts a number into Julian year and then Julian year can be used to spell the desired value as shown in Figure 29.18.

```
SQL> select to_date('3456','J') from dual;

TO_DATE('

18-jun-03

SQL> select to_char(to_date('3456','J'),'JSP') from dual;

TO_CHAR(TO_DATE('3456','J'),'JSP')

THREE THOUSAND FOUR HUNDRED FIFTY-SIX
```

Figure 29.18 Julian spelling.

"J" implies convert the specified integer into Julian date. "JSP" stands for Julian spelling with all words in upper case. We can use "jsp" for all small case and "Jsp" for initial capital case.

Limitations of using Julian spelling

- Minimum value is 1 and maximum value is 5373484. If we have numbers greater than the upper limit, Julian spelling cannot be used.
- Julian spelling works for integer values only. To handle the decimal places also we will have to divide the value in two parts before and after decimal and apply Julian spelling separately.

Figure 29.19 shows how to use Julian spelling for decimal numbers.

```
SQL>select 'Rs.' ||decode(trunc(3456.89),0,'Zero',
to_char(to_date(trunc(3456.89),'J'),'Jsp'))|| ' and ' ||
decode(trunc(mod(3456.89,1)*100),0,'Zero',
to_char(to_date(trunc(mod(3456.89,1)*100),'J'),'Jsp'))|| 'Paise'
from dual;

'RS.'||DECODE(TRUNC(3456.89),0,'ZERO',TO_CHAR(TO_DATE(TRUNC(345

Rs. Three Thousand Four Hundred Fifty-Six and Eighty-Nine Paise
```

Figure 29.19 Julian spelling for decimal numbers.

trunc(3456.89) returns the integer part
to_date(trunc(3456.89),'J') converts integer to Julian Date
to_char(to_date(trunc(3456.89),'J'),'Jsp')) spells the Julian Date
mod(3456.89,1)*100 returns 89

For numbers more than 5373484 we cannot use the JSP format. So we will create a user-defined function named fn_words() which will receive a value as input and will return the corresponding value in words.

For this function we will create a table named "words" containing spelling of integers from 0 to 99 as shown in Figure 29.20.

```
SQL>select * from words order by num;

        NUM                 TEXT
         0              Zero
         1              One
         2              Two
         3              Three
         4              Four
         .
         .
         .
        97              Ninety Seven
        98              Ninety Eight
        99              Ninety Nine
```

Figure 29.20 Table WORDS.

Figure 29.21 contains the code for function "fn_words" which uses the spellings from the WORDS table.

```
SQL>create or replace function fn_words(rupees in number)
return char is
wordret char(130); —this will return the spelling in words
ones number:=0;
hundred number:=0;
thou number:=0;
lakh number:=0;
crore number:=0;
dec number:=0;
begin
select trunc((rupees) - trunc(rupees,-2),0),
(trunc((rupees) - trunc(rupees,-3),0)-trunc((rupees) - trunc(rupees,-2),0))/100 ,
(trunc((rupees) - trunc(rupees,-5),0)-trunc((rupees) - trunc(rupees,-3),0))/1000,
(trunc((rupees) - trunc(rupees,-7),0)-trunc((rupees) - trunc(rupees,-5),0))/100000 ,
trunc(rupees,-7)/10000000 ,
(rupees - trunc(rupees,0))*100
into ones, hundred, thou, lakh, crore, dec
from dual;
select decode (crore,0,' ', rtrim(f.text)|| 'crore')||
 decode (lakh,0,' ', rtrim(d.text)|| 'lakh')||
 decode (thou,0,' ',rtrim(c.text)|| 'thousand')||
 decode (hundred,0,' ',rtrim(b.text)|| 'hundred')||
 decode (ones,0,' ',rtrim(a.text))||

decode (dec,0,' ', 'and' || rtrim(e.text) || 'paise')
into wordret
from words a, words b, words c, words d, words e, words f
where a.num = ones and
        b.num = hundred and
        c.num = thou and
```

```
      d.num = lakh and
      e.num = dec and
      f.num = crore;
   return(wordret);
end;
/
```

Function Created

```
SQL> select fn_words(3456.89) from dual;
FN_WORDS(3456.89)
```

three thousand four hundred fifty six and eighty nine paise

Figure 29.21   Creating function for number spelling.

29.9   GENERATING OUTPUT WITH LINEFEEDS

The SELECT statement displays the tabular output as shown in Figure 29.22.

```
SQL> select emp_no,emp_name,designation from employee;
         EMP_NO        EMP_NAME        DESIGNATION
           1000         KING           CEO
           2001         SCOTT          General Manager
```

Figure 29.22   SELECT displays tabular output.

We desire an output such that each column value is displayed on a separate line as shown in Figure 29.23.

```
EMPNO: 1000
NAME: KING
DESIGNATION: CEO

EMPNO: 2001
NAME: SCOTT
DESIGNATION: General Manager
```

Figure 29.23   Displaying each column value on separate line.

We can introduce linefeed between various columns of records by using the built-in function "CHR(10)". CHR(10) implies line feed character (Figure 29.24).

```
SQL>select 'EMPNO: '||emp_no||chr(10)||'NAME: '
||emp_name||chr(10)
||'DESIGNATION:' ||designation||chr(10)
||'—————————'||chr(10) from employee;
```

Figure 29.24   Using CHR(10) for linefeed.

The statement of Figure 29.24 produces the output as shown in Figure 29.23.

29.10 GENERATING CSV OUTPUT

To move a table records from one database system to another database the easiest way is to generate a comma separated values (CSV) file from source database and then load the CSV output into the target database. We will use the SQL*Plus reporting capabilities to generate a text file by(a.sql) SQL>edit a.sql as shown in Figure 29.25.

```
set term off
set pagesize 0
set verify off
set feedback off
set colsep ','

spool sample.txt
select emp_no,emp_name,date_of_joining,designation from employee;
spool off
```

Figure 29.25   Generating CSV output.

Let us run a.sql (Figure 29.26) program for generating the CSV output and view the contents of sample.txt file (Figure 29.27).

```
SQL>@a
SQL>edit sample.txt
```

Figure 29.26   Running Program of Figure 29.25.

```
sample.txt - Notepad
File  Edit  Format  View  Help
      1000,KING      ,01-JAN-08,CEO
      2001,SCOTT     ,11-FEB-08,General  Manager
      2002,JOHN      ,23-FEB-08,General  Manager
      2003,SUSE      ,19-MAR-08,General  Manager
      3001,HENRY     ,25-MAR-08,Manager
      3002,JORD      ,30-APR-08,Manager
      3003,WILLIAMS  ,30-APR-08,Manager
      3004,MARUTI    ,02-MAY-08,Manager
      3005,SANTRO    ,10-MAY-08,Manager
      3006,TANGO     ,14-JUN-08,Manager
      3006,PIAGGIO   ,24-JUN-08,Manager
      4001,SPARK     ,11-JUL-08,Executive
      5001,POND      ,11-JUL-08,Salesman
      5002,DRAGON    ,11-JUL-08,Clerk
      4002,KINETIC   ,20-JUL-08,Executive
      5003,MILLIAN   ,11-JUL-08,Salesman
      5004,WOZER     ,11-JUL-08,Clerk
      4003,JONATHAN  ,11-JUL-08,Salesman
      4004,MAGGI     ,11-JUL-08,Salesman
      4005,RAMEN     ,11-JUL-08,Salesman
      4006,SAUCER    ,11-JUL-08,Salesman
```

Figure 29.27   sample.txt file generated by a.sql.

29.10.1 Loading CSV Data into Oracle Database

Suppose that we have a text file containing records in CSV format as shown in Figure 29.27. We want to load this data into Oracle table, say named "load_employee". Oracle has a utility called SQL*Loader which can be used for this purpose. In Figure 29.28, we have created the table "LOAD_EMPLOYEE" from "EMPLOYEE". Assume that this LOAD_EMPLOYEE table is in another Oracle database and we want to copy the records from EMPLOYEE table. What we can do is that we generate a CSV file from source database and load that CSV file into the other database table.

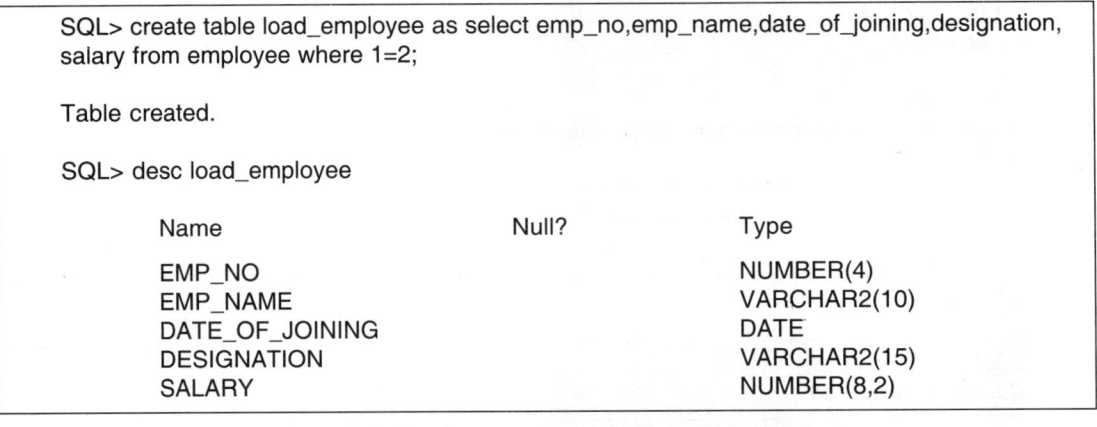

```
SQL> create table load_employee as select emp_no,emp_name,date_of_joining,designation,
salary from employee where 1=2;

Table created.

SQL> desc load_employee

        Name                        Null?              Type

        EMP_NO                                         NUMBER(4)
        EMP_NAME                                       VARCHAR2(10)
        DATE_OF_JOINING                                DATE
        DESIGNATION                                    VARCHAR2(15)
        SALARY                                         NUMBER(8,2)
```

Figure 29.28   Create table "LOAD_EMPLOYEE".

Assume **sample.txt** has CSV records as shown in Figure 29.29. Place this file in the Oracle Home Directory G:\oradb11g\product\11.1.0\db_1\BIN\sample.txt.

```
1000,KING,              CEO,                    01-JAN-08,2345.89
2001,SCOTT,             General Manager,        11-FEB-08,1234.45
```

Figure 29.29   Sample.txt CSV File.

SQL*Loader uses a control file with the extension. CTL for loading the data from CSV file into a table of the Oracle Database. We will create a "load.ctl" file as shown in Figure 29.30.
SQL>edit load.ctl

```
LOAD DATA
INFILE sample.txt
APPEND INTO TABLE LOAD_EMPLOYEE
FIELDS TERMINATED BY ','
(
emp_no,
emp_name,
designation,
date_of_joining,
salary
)
```

Figure 29.30   LOAD.CTL File for SQL*Loader.

29.10.2 Invoking SQL*Loader

SQL*Loader is a command line utility and we will have to switch to command mode.

Click Start->Run->CMD and Press OK

Change to the Oracle Home directory using the CD command as shown in Figure 29.31.

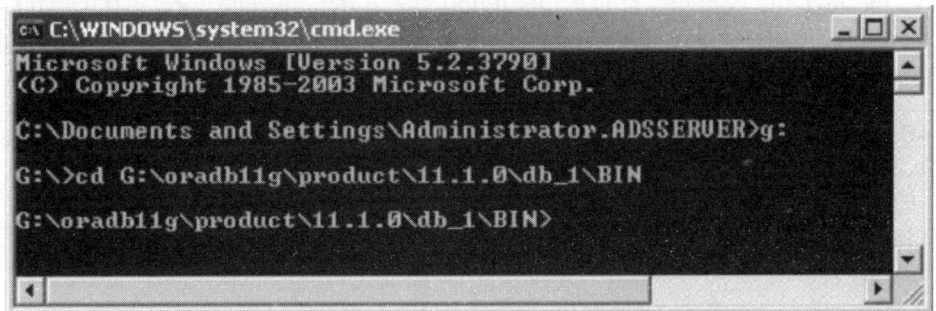

Figure 29.31 Changing to the Oracle Home directory.

Issue the sqlldr command which invokes the SQL*Loader as shown in Figure 29.32.

Figure 29.32 Invoking SQL*Loader.

Now let us view the records in LOAD_EMPLOYEE table (Figure 29.33).

SQL> select * from load_employee;

EMP_NO	EMP_NAME	DATE_OF_J	DESIGNATION	SALARY
1000	KING	01-JAN-08	CEO	2345.89
2001	SCOTT	11-FEB-08	General Manager	1234.45

Figure 29.33 Records loaded in LOAD_EMPLOYEE.

Let us now understand the load.ctl file

- The LOAD DATA statement is required at the beginning of the control file.
- The name of the file containing data follows the keyword INFILE.
- The INTO TABLE statement is required to identify the table to be loaded into. The INTO TABLE can be preceded by the INSERT or APPEND. For the INSERT, the table must be

empty. The APPEND command, adds the records of the text file into table in addition to the existing records.
- FIELDS TERMINATED BY ',' indicates the terminating symbol which has been used to delimit the individual column values.
- Last is the sequence of columns enclosed within braces.
- As the text file contains DATE OF JOINING in default date format (DD-MON-YY), therefore, loader successfully loads the records. Suppose the text file had date values in the dd/mm/yyyy format then the CTL will be modified as shown in Figure 29.34.

```
LOAD DATA
INFILE sample.txt
APPEND INTO TABLE LOAD_EMPLOYEE
FIELDS TERMINATED BY ','
 (
emp_no,
emp_name,
designation,
date_of_joining DATE 'dd/mm/yyyy',
salary
)
```

Figure 29.34   Loading date value which is not in default format.

The records in CSV format can also be specified within the .CTL file as shown in Figure 29.35.

```
LOAD DATA
INFILE *
APPEND INTO TABLE LOAD_EMPLOYEE
FIELDS TERMINATED BY ',' OPTIONALLY ENCLOSED BY " "
 (
emp_no,
emp_name,
designation,
date_of_joining DATE 'dd/mm/yyyy',
salary
)
BEGINDATA
1000,KING, "CEO", 01/01/2008,2345.89
2001,"SCOTT", General Manager, 11/02/2008,1234.45
```

Figure 29.35   Specifying records to be loaded in CTL File itself.

INFILE * implies that records are specified in the same CTL file.
OPTIONALLY ENCLOSED BY " " implies that Oracle should ignore double quotes for column values. The values may or may not be enclosed within double quotes.
BEGINDATA marks the beginning of records.

29.10.3   Loading CSV Data with Position (Fixed Format)

The position of values for fields is specified along with the data type as shown in Figure 29.36.

```
LOAD DATA
INFILE *
APPEND INTO TABLE LOAD_EMPLOYEE
(
emp_no              position(1:4)      integer external,
emp_name            position(6:14)     char,
designation         position(16:30)    char,
date_of_joining     position(32:41)    DATE 'dd/mm/yyyy',
salary              position(43:49)    decimal external
)
BEGINDATA
1000 KING           CEO                01/01/2008 2345.89
2001 SCOTT          General Manager 11/02/2008 1234.45
```

Figure 29.36   Specifying position and data type in CTL File.

As we have specified the position for each column value, therefore, commas are not required in data. Secondly, FIELDS TERMINATED BY has not been used.

29.10.4   Loading Delimited Free Format File

Assume that our text file has different delimiters for different fields. In Figure 29.37, semi-colon is the delimiter for date_of_joining field whereas rest of the fields have comma as delimiter.

Secondly, we want to generate key values for EMP_NO field.

```
LOAD DATA
INFILE *
APPEND INTO TABLE load_employee
FIELDS TERMINATED BY "," OPTIONALLY ENCLOSED BY " "
(
emp_no SEQUENCE(MAX,1),
emp_name,
designation,
date_of_joining date 'dd/mm/yyyy' terminated by ":",
salary
)
BEGINDATA
KING ,"CEO" ,01/01/2008:2345.89
"SCOTT" ,General Manager,11/02/2008:1234.45
```

Figure 29.37   Load2.ctl—Different delimiter for different fields.

Records in BEGINDATA section do not have value for EMP_NO. Value for EMP_NO column has been generated using the SEQUENCE(MAX,1) which adds 1 to the Maximum value in that column and assigns it to the specific record. Secondly, DATE_OF_JOINING value does not have comma as delimiter rather has colon as delimiter. Before loading the data in load2.ctl file, let us first delete all the previous records in LOAD_EMPLOYEE as shown in Figure 29.38.

```
SQL> truncate table load_employee;
Table truncated.
```

Figure 29.38   Remove existing records.

Go to command prompt and execute sqlldr comand as shown in Figure 29.39.

```
G:\oradb11g\product\111~1.0\db_1\BIN>sqlldr userid=scott/tiger control=load2.ctl
```

SQL*Loader: Release 11.1.0.6.0 - Production on Fri Apr 3 10:21:47 2009

Copyright (c) 1982, 2007, Oracle. All rights reserved.

Commit point reached - logical record count 2

Figure 29.39   SQLLDR for load2.ctl.

Let us see the records inserted into LOAD_EMOPLOYEE table through SQLLDR (Figure 29.40).

```
SQL> select * from load_employee;
```

EMP_NO	EMP_NAME	DESIGNATION	DATE_OF_J	SALARY
1	KING	CEO	01-JAN-08	2345.89
2	SCOTT	General Manager	11-FEB-08	1234.45

Figure 29.40   Records in LOAD_EMPLOYEE.

Oracle 11*g* New Features

30.1 INTRODUCTION

This chapter focuses on the various new features that have been introduced in the Oracle 11g database. If you are using any version below 11g, then the statements specified in this chapter will not work.

30.2 NEW FEATURES IN ORACLE 11*g*

30.2.1 PIVOT and UNPIVOT Operators

Oracle 11g provides two new operators, namely PIVOT and UNPIVOT. PIVOT is used for generating Matrix/Cross-Tab reports and UNPIVOT does the opposite of PIVOT.

PIVOT operator

We have seen the use of DECODE and CASE statement for generating Matrix Reports in Section 29.6. But both these methods are not very intuitive and therefore Oracle 11g provides an operator named "PIVOT" for the same purpose. The interesting part is that it also provides an UNPIVOT operator for flattening the PIVOT report.

Assume an EMPLOYEE table which has EMP_NO, NAME, DESIGNATION, DEPT_NO and SALARY. We want to produce a matrix report displaying designationwise and departmentwise total salary. Figure 30.1 shows how to use PIVOT operator for generating the desired cross-tab report.

```
SQL> select * from
2 (
3 select designation,dept_no,salary
4 from employee a
5 )
6 pivot
7 (
8 sum(salary)
9 for dept_no in (10,20,30,40)
10 )
11* order by designation;
```

DESIGNATION	10	20	30	40
CEO	20000			
Clerk	12000	8500		
Executive	21000			
General Manager	15000	14000	14500	
Manager	37700	25300	21000	
Salesman	16500	17000	17000	

6 rows selected.

Figure 30.1   Using PIVOT operator for matrix report.

SALARY is to be Pivoted for intersection of designation and dept_no.

UNPIVOT operator

UNPIVOT operator does the opposite of PIVOT operation and generates the table from which pivoted output was produced. Suppose we have a Pivoted table EMPLOYEE_MATRIX as created in Figure 30.2. Now we want to flatten the matrix into relational table like the employee containing designationwise and departmentwise salary (Figure 30.3).

```
SQL>create table employee_matrix as
select * from
(
select designation,dept_no,salary
from employee a
)
pivot
(
sum(salary)
for dept_no in (10,20,30,40)
)
order by designation;
```

Figure 30.2   Creating PIVOT table.

```
SQL> select * from employee_matrix
3 unpivot
4 (
5 salary
6 for dept_no in ("10","20","30","40")
7 )
8* order by designation,dept_no
```

DESIGNATION	DEPT_NO	SALARY
CEO	10	20000
Clerk	10	12000
Clerk	20	8500
Executive	10	21000
General Manager	10	15000
General Manager	20	14000
General Manager	30	14500
Manager	10	37700
Manager	20	25300
Manager	30	21000
Salesman	10	16500
Salesman	20	17000
Salesman	30	17000

13 rows selected.

Figure 30.3   UNPIVOT operator.

30.2.2   Virtual Columns

Oracle 11g provides a feature of virtual columns. Virtual column is a column which is not a field in the table but rather a non-existent column whose value depends on some other columns of the table. For example, in EMP table, it is very commonly required to calculate total salary which is the sum of salary and commission. Now in every SELECT statement, we need to use salary + commission as total salary. This can be avoided by creating a virtual column named total_salary as shown in Figure 30.4.

```
SQL>create table employee (emp_no number(4),emp_name varchar2(10),salary
number,commission number,
total_salary as (salary+commission));
Table Created

SQL> insert into employee(emp_no,emp_name,salary,commission) values
(1111,'satish',10000,1000);
1 row created.

SQL> insert into employee(emp_no,emp_name,salary,commission) values
(2222,'rashmi',9000,null);
1 row created.
```

```
SQL> insert into employee(emp_no,emp_name,salary,commission) values (3333,'anil',null,800);
1 row created.
```

```
SQL> select * from employee;
```

EMP_NO	EMP_NAME	SALARY	COMMISSION	TOTAL_SALARY
1111	satish	10000	1000	11000
2222	rashmi	9000		
3333	anil		800	

Figure 30.4   Virtual columns.

Caution: We cannot specify a value for virtual column in any of the DML operations like INSERT, UPDATE, DELETE. As virtual column value is derived from actual columns, therefore, we cannot specify value for virtual columns.

We should have used NVL() function for the virtual column as any of the two values may be NULL and hence the total salary will be shown as NULL.

SQL>create table employee (emp_no number(4),emp_name varchar2(10),salary number,commission number, total_salary as *(nvl(salary,0)+nvl(commission,0))*);

Note: A virtual column cannot be based on another virtual column.

In Figure 30.5, we have attempted to base a virtual column "c" on virtual column "b".

```
SQL> create table temp(a number,b as (a+1),c as (b+1));
create table temp(a number,b as (a+1),c as (b+1))
 *
ERROR at line 1:
ORA-54012: virtual column is referenced in a column expression
```

Figure 30.5   A virtual column cannot be based on another virtual column.

Here "b" is a virtual column and we have tried to create a virtual column "c" based on the virtual column "b" which is not allowed.

30.2.3   Case-sensitive Username and Passwords

All versions below 11g do not store username and password taking uppercase or lowercase in consideration. The user SCOTT with password TIGER can log on to database using any combination of uppercase or lowercase characters. For example

SQL>connect scott/tiger
is equivalent to
SQL>connect Scott/TIGer
is equivalent to
SQL>connect SCOTT/TIGER

Oracle 11g stores the username and password with case-sensitivity. SCOTT is different from Scott, sCott, scott, etc.

Let us change the password of SCOTT user to TigeR as shown in Figure 30.6.

```
SQL> connect sys/sys@orcl11g as sysdba;
Connected.

SQL> alter user scott identified by TigeR;
User altered.

SQL> connect scott/tiger
ERROR:
ORA-01017: invalid username/password; logon denied
Warning: You are no longer connected to ORACLE.

SQL> connect scott/TigeR
Connected.
```

Figure 30.6 Changing password of SCOTT user with case consideration.

Now SCOTT user has to specify the password in the exact case.

Oracle 11g provides commands for enabling and disabling case-sensitive username and password facility. A parameter named "SEC_CASE_SENSITIVE_LOGON" indicates whether case-sensitivity has been enabled or disabled. The status can be determined by the "SHOW PARAMETER" command (Figure 30.7).

```
SQL> connect sys/sys@orcl11g as sysdba;
Connected.
SQL> SHOW PARAMETER SEC_CASE_SENSITIVE_LOGON
```

NAME	TYPE	VALUE
sec_case_sensitive_logon	boolean	TRUE

Figure 30.7 Determining case sensitivity.

TRUE => Case-sensitive
FALSE => Case-insensitive
Case-sensitivity can be disabled using the ALTER SYSTEM command (Figure 30.8).

```
SQL> ALTER SYSTEM SET SEC_CASE_SENSITIVE_LOGON = FALSE;
System altered.

SQL> connect scott/tiger@orcl11g
Connected.
```

Figure 30.8 Disabling case sensitivity.

Now SCOTT is able to connect without caring about the uppercase or lowercase characters.

30.2.4 DDL with WAIT Option

Suppose a table has uncommitted transaction in a SQL session. Now if some other SQL session tries to modify the table structure using the DDL command then Oracle returns an error message "resource busy and acquire with NOWAIT specified or timeout expired" (See Figure 30.9, Time 4, Session 2).

Time	Session 1	Session 2
1	SQL>connect scott/tiger	
2	SQL>create table tbl_lock (a number); Table Created.	
3	SQL>insert into tbl_lock values(100); 1 row created.	SQL>connect scott/tiger
4		SQL>alter table tbl_lock modify (a number(10,2)); ERROR at line 1: ORA-00054: resource busy and acquire with NOWAIT specified or timeout expired.
5		SQL> ALTER SESSION SET ddl_lock_timeout=30; Session altered. SQL> alter table tbl_lock modify (a number(7,2)); alter table tbl_lock modify (a number(7,2)) * ERROR at line 1: ORA-00054: resource busy and acquire with NOWAIT specified or timeout expired **(Now the DDL command will wait for 30 seconds before throwing the error)**

Figure 30.9 DDL with WAIT option.

Oracle 11g provides a timeout to be specified for DDL statements. The DDL command waits for the specified time before throwing the "resource busy" error (See Figure 30.9_Time 5 Session2).

30.2.5 Query Result Cache

Oracle 11g provides a feature wherein we can cache the results of a query in SGA (System Global Area) for better performance on executing the same query again. If the table being queried has fewer records then the impact of Result Cache is not apparent. So to demonstrate the concept of Query Result Cache, we will create a table with 8,00,000 records using FOR LOOP (Figure 30.10).

```
SQL>create table TBL_QUERY_RESULT_CACHE(a number);
Table Created.

SQL> begin
 2 for i in 1..800000 loop
 3 insert into TBL_QUERY_RESULT_CACHE values (i);
 4 end loop;
 5 commit;
```

```
  6 end;
  7 /
PL/SQL procedure successfully completed.

SQL> set timing on

SQL> select sum(a) from TBL_QUERY_RESULT_CACHE;
 SUM(A)
 _____
3.2000E+11
Elapsed: 00:00:00.25
```

Figure 30.10   Creating table for testing query result cache.

In Figure 30.11, we have specified Oracle to use the result cache.

```
SQL> select /*+ result_cache */ sum(a) from TBL_QUERY_RESULT_CACHE;

SUM(A)

3.2000E+11
Elapsed: 00:00:00.37

SQL> select /*+ result_cache */ sum(a) from TBL_QUERY_RESULT_CACHE;

SUM(A)

3.2000E+11
Elapsed: 00:00:00.01
```

Figure 30.11   Verifying query result cache.

In Figure 30.10, SET TIMING ON displays the time taken to execute a SQL statement. The first SELECT took .25 seconds. In the second SELECT (Figure 30.11), Oracle has been specified to use RESULT_CACHE for storing the results in cache memory and it took .37 seconds (nearly equal to the earlier time of .25 seconds). Now the results have got stored in cache and any further SELECT will use the data in cache instead of fetching records from data blocks. The third SELECT used the data in cache and therefore took just .01 seconds.

30.2.6 PL/SQL Function Result Cache

Just as Oracle 11g provides Query Result Cache, similarly it has provision to store functions and procedures in cache memory for faster consecutive retrieval and execution. We will create a function named fn_add() for addition of two numbers with specification for caching function result as shown in Figure 30.12, SQL>edit a.sql.

```
set serveroutput on
create or replace function fn_add(a in number,b in number)
return number
```

```
result_cache
is
 c number;
begin
 c:=a+b;
 return (c);
end;
/
```

Figure 30.12   Function result cache.

Let us create the function by executing the a.sql file of Figure 30.12 and see the impact of function result cache in Figure 30.13.

```
SQL> @a
Function Created

SQL>set timing on
SQL> select fn_add(sum(a),sum(a)) from tbl_query_result_cache;
FN_ADD(SUM(A),SUM(A))

6.4000E+11

Elapsed: 00:00:00.73
SQL> select fn_add(sum(a),sum(a)) from tbl_query_result_cache;
FN_ADD(SUM(A),SUM(A))

6.4000E+11

Elapsed: 00:00:00.18
```

Figure 30.13   Generating function with result cache specification.

The 1st time fn_add() took 0.73 seconds for all records of tbl_query_result_cache table. As we had specified RESULT_CACHE clause at the time of creating the function therefore it got stored in cache when called for the 1st time. On 2nd time the cache already had the fn_add() available and took just 0.18 seconds for all records.

Note that on the next time the same function was executed and the time taken has drastically reduced from .73 to .18.

30.2.7   READ ONLY and READ-WRITE Tables

Oracle 11g provides a facility wherein we can make a table Read-Only or Read-Write by the ALTER TABLE command. If the status is set to Read-Only, no DDL and DML operation is permitted. DDL and DML can be executed only if the status has been changed to READ-WRITE. Earlier to Oracle 11g the tables were read-write for the owner but now it is possible to make the tables read-only for the owner also as shown in Figure 30.14.

```
SQL> alter table department read only;
Table altered.

SQL> insert into department values (99,'TEST');
insert into department values (99,'TEST')
     *
ERROR at line 1:
ORA-12081: update operation not allowed on table "SCOTT"."DEPARTMENT"

SQL> update department set dept_name='TEST' where dept_no=20;
update department set dept_name='TEST' where dept_no=20
     *
ERROR at line 1:
ORA-12081: update operation not allowed on table "SCOTT"."DEPARTMENT"

SQL> alter table department read write;
Table altered.

SQL> insert into department values (99,'TEST');
1 row created.
```

Figure 30.14   READ ONLY and READ-WRITE tables.

30.2.8   Automatic Sub-program In-lining

Whenever a call is made to functions, it increases the overhead of maintaining a STACK. If the sub-program is being called within a loop, then the overhead multiplies for each call. Oracle 11g provides a feature called "Sub-program In-lining" which reduces the overhead associated with procedure calls while maintaining the modularity of the existing code. In-lining basically means that the source code of called sub-program is placed at the point of call and executed. As such there is no overhead for saving the current status of calling program on STACK and then executing the sub-program code.

The process of sub-program in-lining is controlled by the PLSQL_OPTIMIZE_LEVEL parameter and the INLINE pragma. The default value for PLSQL_OPTIMIZE_LEVEL is 2 and the value of INLINE pragma determines whether the in-lining will be used or not. PLSQL_OPTIMIZE_LEVEL with value 3 implies that in-lining will be used automatically.

We will make a function named fn_add() for addition of 2 numbers and call it within a PL/SQL block within a FOR LOOP 1 crore times. See Figure 30.15.

PLSQL_OPTIMIZE_LEVEL is set to 2 and in-lining has not been used.

SQL>edit c.sql

```
ALTER SESSION SET PLSQL_OPTIMIZE_LEVEL=2;

SET SERVEROUTPUT ON
DECLARE
 v_start_time NUMBER;
 v_result NUMBER;
```

```
FUNCTION fn_add(p1 IN NUMBER,p2 IN NUMBER)
RETURN NUMBER AS
BEGIN
RETURN p1 + p2;
END;

BEGIN
v_start_time := DBMS_UTILITY.get_time;

FOR i IN 1 .. 10000000 LOOP
PRAGMA INLINE (fn_add, 'NO''); //in-lining will not be used
v_result := fn_add(1, i);
END LOOP;

DBMS_OUTPUT.put_line('Elapsed Time:' || (DBMS_UTILITY.get_time - v_start_time)/100 ||
'secs');
END;
/
```

Figure 30.15 Creating a function and calling it without using In-lining.

In Figure 30.16 we have executed the program of Figure 30.15.

```
SQL> @c
Session altered.

Elapsed Time: 4 secs

PL/SQL procedure successfully completed.
```

Figure 30.16 Executing program of Figure 30.15.

Note that in program of Figure 30.15, in-lining has not been used and the time taken is 4 seconds.

Now we will use in-lining through PRAGMA directive and observe the time taken as shown in Figure 30.17.

SQL>edit c.sql

```
ALTER SESSION SET PLSQL_OPTIMIZE_LEVEL=2;

SET SERVEROUTPUT ON
DECLARE
v_start_time NUMBER;
v_result NUMBER;

FUNCTION fn_add(p1 IN NUMBER,p2 IN NUMBER)
RETURN NUMBER AS
BEGIN
RETURN p1 + p2;
END;
```

```
BEGIN
v_start_time := DBMS_UTILITY.get_time;

FOR i IN 1 .. 10000000 LOOP
PRAGMA INLINE (fn_add, 'YES'); //in-lining will be used
v_result := fn_add(1, i);
END LOOP;

DBMS_OUTPUT.put_line('Elapsed Time: ' || (DBMS_UTILITY.get_time - v_start_time)/100 || '
secs');
END;
/
```

Figure 30.17 Program using In-lining.

In Figure 30.18, we have executed the program with in-lining and observe the drastic decrease in execution time for function calls.

```
SQL> @c
Session altered.

Elapsed Time: 1.96 secs

PL/SQL procedure successfully completed.
```

Figure 30.18 Running program in Figure 30.17 with In-lining.

30.2.9 Parameter Passing

Oracle 11g provides three notations for passing parameters to functions and the second procedures.

- Positional—The first value passed is assigned to the first parameter, the second value to the second parameter and so on. The position determines the value which will be assigned to a parameter.
- Named—The parameter values can be passed in any sequence specifying the name along with the value to be passed.
- Mixed—Combination of the above two methods.

For example, we will create a procedure named proc_add which will receive two numbers and display its SUM (Figure 30.19).

SQL>edit a.sql

```
set serveroutput on
create or replace procedure proc_add(a in number,b in number) is
 c number;
begin
 c:=a+b;
 dbms_output.put_line('Sum of '||a||' and '||b||' is :'||c);
end;
/
```

Figure 30.19 Creating procedure proc_add().

Let us create the procedure of Figure 30.19 as shown in Figure 30.20.

```
SQL> @a
Procedure created.
```

Figure 30.20   Creating procedure of Figure 30.19.

Let us use the three types of notations for passing parameters as shown in Figure 30.21.

```
Positional Parameters
SQL> exec proc_add(10,20);
Sum of 10 and 20 is :30

PL/SQL procedure successfully completed.

Named Parameters
SQL> exec proc_add(b=>10,a=>20);
Sum of 20 and 10 is :30

PL/SQL procedure successfully completed.

Mixed Parameters
SQL> exec proc_add(10,b=>20);
Sum of 10 and 20 is :30

PL/SQL procedure successfully completed.

SQL> exec proc_add(b=>20,10);
BEGIN proc_add(b=>20,10); END;
            *
ERROR at line 1:
ORA-06550: line 1, column 22:
PLS-00312: a positional parameter association may not follow a named
association
ORA-06550: line 1, column 7:
PL/SQL: Statement ignored
```

Figure 30.21   Using the three notations for parameter passing.

30.2.10   CONTINUE Statement in PL/SQL

Oracle 11g introduced the CONTINUE statement which can be used to return the program control from a point within a LOOP to the starting of LOOP. Earlier versions of Oracle required the use of IF and GOTO statement.

Figure 30.22 finds the odd numbers in the range of 1 to 10. Firstly, the IF statement has been used and then the same program, using CONTINUE, has been written.

    SQL>edit d.sql

```
set serveroutput on
declare
i number:=0;
begin
loop
    exit when i>10;
    i:=i+1;

    if MOD(i,2)<>0 then /*Odd Number*/
            dbms_output.put_line(i);
    else
            NULL; /*Do Nothing*/
    end if;
end loop;
end;
/
declare
i number:=0;
begin
loop
    exit when i>10;
    i:=i+1;
    CONTINUE WHEN MOD(i,2)=0; /*if EVEN return to starting of LOOP*/
    dbms_output.put_line(i);
end loop;
end;
/
```

Figure 30.22   PL/SQL continue statement.

Let us execute the program of Figure 30.22 as shown in Figure 30.23.

```
SQL> @d
1
3
5
7
9
PL/SQL procedure successfully completed.
1
3
5
7
9
PL/SQL procedure successfully completed.
```

Figure 30.23   Executing program in Figure 30.22.

Note: CONTINUE can be used with or without WHEN condition. EXIT of PL/SQL is similar to BREAK of C language and CONTINUE is similar to CONTINUE of C language.

EXIT transfers the control of program out of the LOOP whereas CONTINUE transfers the control of program to the starting of LOOP.

30.2.11 Referring SEQUENCE Values in PL/SQL

Earlier to Oracle 11g referring to Sequence values within PL/SQL required using SELECT INTO variable Clause which is not very intuitive (Figure 30.24).

SQL>edit a.sql

```
create sequence seq_temp start with 1000 increment by 1;
set serveroutput on

declare
a number;
begin
--a:=SEQ_TEMP.nextval; --Sequence value cannot be directly assigned
/*
Error PLS-00357: Table,View Or Sequence reference 'SEQ_TEMP.NEXTVAL' 9. not allowed
in this context
*/

select SEQ_TEMP.nextval into a from dual;

dbms_output.put_line(a);
end;
/
SQL> @a
Sequence created.
1000
PL/SQL procedure successfully completed.
```

Figure 30.24   Accessing sequence values in PL/SQL (earlier to Oracle 11g).

Note that before Oracle 11g we cannot assign a Sequence value to a variable in PL/SQL (a:=SEQ_TEMP.nextval). The only way to use sequence values within PL/SQL was to use SELECT sequence.nextval into variable.

Oracle 11g allows us to refer to sequence values in a very intuitive way as shown in Figure 30.25.

SQL>Edit b.sql

```
create sequence seq_temp start with 1000 increment by 1;
set serveroutput on

declare
a number;
begin
  a:=SEQ_TEMP.nextval;
  dbms_output.put_line(a);
end;
/
```

Figure 30.25   Sequence value can be directly assigned to variables (Oracle 11g).

30.2.12   Trigger Enhancements

Execution order of triggers

If we have created two triggers for INSERT operation FOR EACH ROW on a table then which one will fire first is not sure. Sometimes trigger1 will execute first followed by trigger2 and sometimes trigger2 may fire before trigger1. Oracle 11g provides a feature wherein we can specify the execution sequence while creating the triggers.

We will create two triggers, namely "trigger1" and "trigger2" on INSERT for DEPARTMENT table (Figure 30.26).

SQL>edit a.sql

```
create or replace trigger dept_trigger1
before insert on department
for each row
begin
 dbms_output.put_line('Trigger1 executed');
end;
/

create or replace trigger dept_trigger2
before insert on department
for each row
begin
 dbms_output.put_line('Trigger2 executed');
end;
/

set serveroutput on
insert into department values (99,'TEST');
```

Figure 30.26   Two triggers on the same table and for same operation.

Let us create the two triggers in Figure 30.26 as shown in Figure 30.27.

```
SQL> @a
Trigger created.
Trigger created.

Trigger2 executed
Trigger1 executed

1 row created.
```

Figure 30.27   Creating triggers as in Figure 30.26.

Note that trigger2 got executed first followed by trigger1. Earlier to Oracle 11g which trigger will execute first is not known. Sometimes trigger1 may execute first followed by trigger2 and sometimes trigger2 may execute before trigger1. What if we wanted trigger1 to execute first always followed by trigger2. This cannot be achieved in Oracle10g or earlier. In Oracle 11g we can specify the sequence of execution at the time of trigger creation as shown in Figure 30.28.

SQL>Edit b.sql

```
create or replace trigger dept_trigger1
before insert on department
for each row
begin
 dbms_output.put_line('Trigger1 executed');
end;
/

create or replace trigger dept_trigger2
before insert on department
for each row
follows dept_trigger1
begin
 dbms_output.put_line('Trigger2 executed');
end;
/

set serveroutput on
insert into department values (99,'TEST');
```

Figure 30.28   Execution order of triggers.

In Figure 30.29, we have created the triggers in Figure 30.28.

```
SQL> @b
Trigger created.
Trigger created.

Trigger1 executed
Trigger2 executed

1 row created.
```

Figure 30.29   Creating triggers as in Figure 30.28.

Now trigger1 executed before trigger2.

Installation of Oracle Database 12*c*

31.1 INTRODUCTION

In Chapter 2 we have seen the installation of Oracle Express Edition 10g. In this Chapter we will demonstrate installation of Oracle 12c. As Oracle 12c introduces the concept of Pluggable Databases, it automatically installs and configures a Container Database named ORCL and a pluggable database PDBORCL. We will understand the concept and working of both Container and Pluggable database later in this Chapter.

31.2 INSTALLATION OF ORACLE 12C DATABASE

Follow the steps as mentioned below to install Oracle 12c database.

31.2.1 Download the Oracle Database 12c Software from Oracle Site

Assuming that we have two files downloaded, namely winx64_12c_database_1of2.zip and winx64_12c_database_2of2.zip in the folder D:\Oracle12c_CD\.

Now create two folders named Disk1 and Disk2 within D:\Oracle12c_CD\.

Extract the winx64_12c_database_1of2.zip file in D:\Oracle12c_CD\Disk1 and winx64_12c_database_2of2.zip in D:\Oracle12c_CD\Disk2.

Copy all the files from D:\Oracle12c_CD\Disk2\database\stage\Components
To
D:\Oracle12c_CD\Disk1\database\stage\Components.

Figure 31.1 Displays the contents of D:\Oracle12c_CD\Disk2\database\stage\Components.

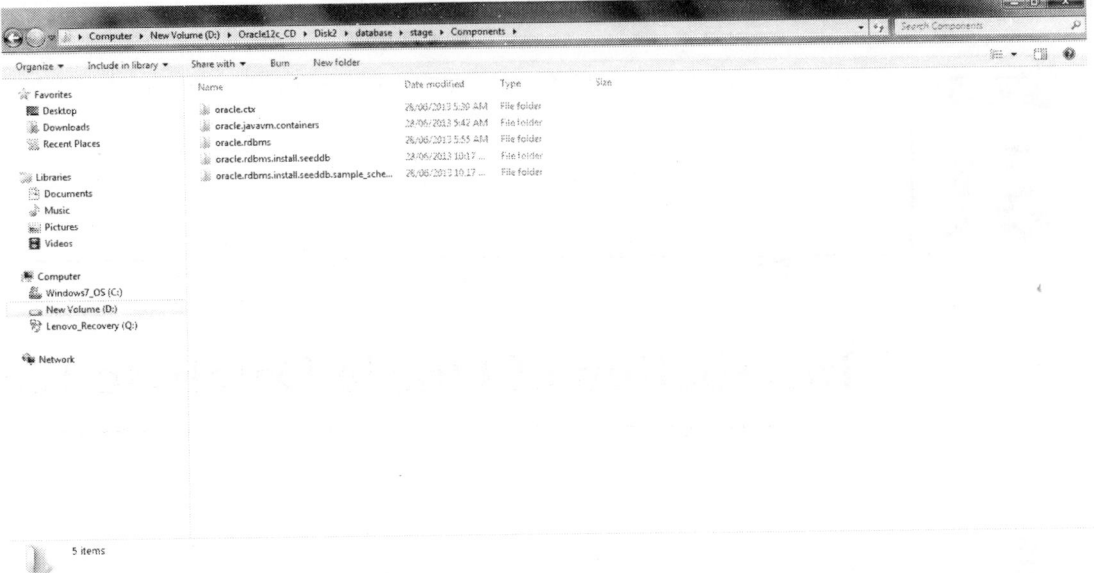

Figure 31.1   Contents of D:\Oracle12c_CD\Disk2\database\stage\Components.

31.2.2   Run the setup.exe from D:\Oracle12c_CD\Disk1\database as shown in Figure 31.2

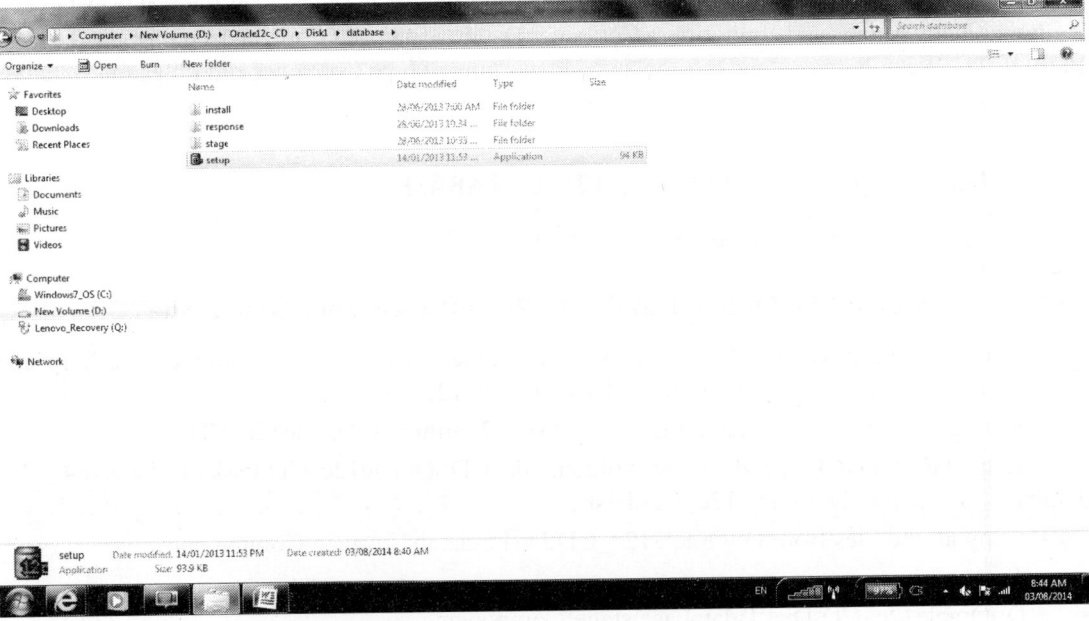

Figure 31.2   Location of setup.exe.

The installer will check for minimum RAM and display requirements as shown in Figure 31.3.

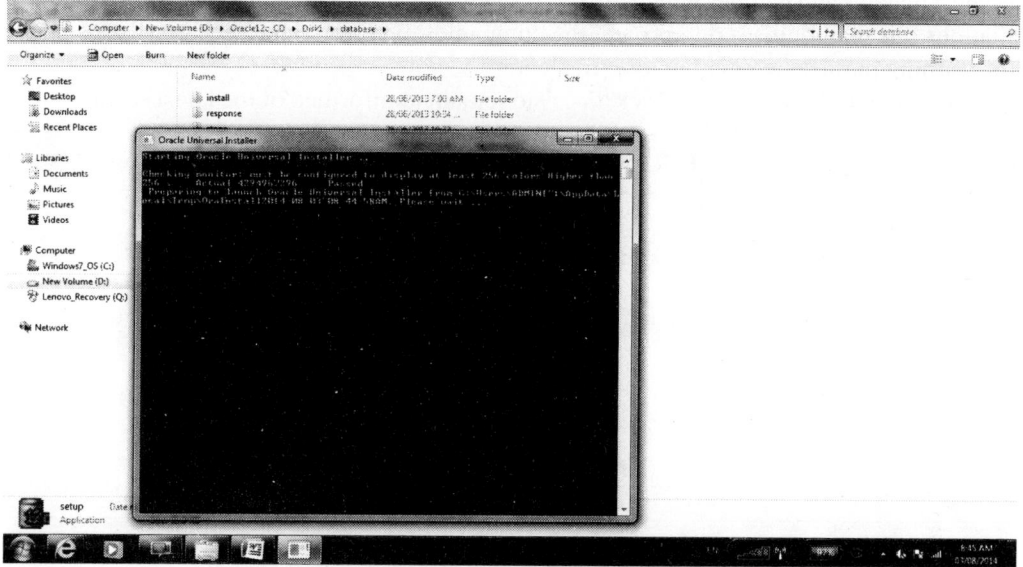

Figure 31.3   Check for hardware requirements.

A dialogue box for Security Updates configuration appears, as shown in Figure 31.4.

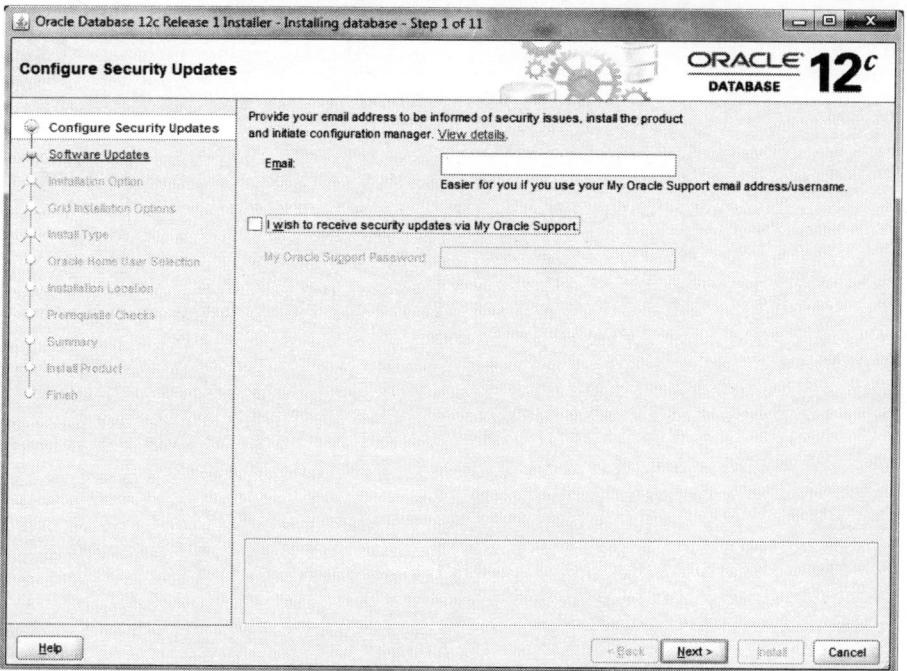

Figure 31.4   Security Updates Dialogue box.

Uncheck the option "I wish to receive security updates…". This will disable the deployment of the latest updates and patches which are regularly provided by Oracle Corporation. In Enterprise installations this feature is used to protect the companies data from latest security loops and holes but for learning purpose we may ignore this feature.

In next screen (Figure 31.5), Click "Yes" to remain uninformed of the latest security updates.

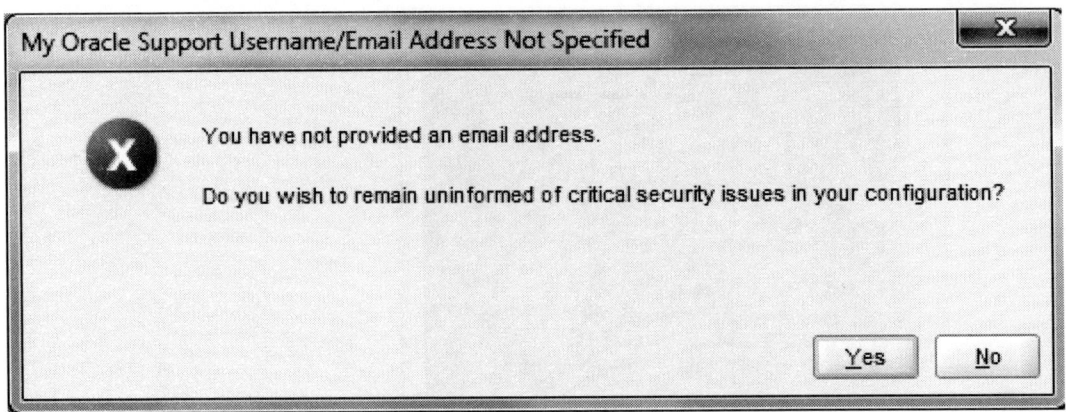

Figure 31.5   Security issues.

Next choose "Skip software updates" and click Next as shown in Figure 31.6.

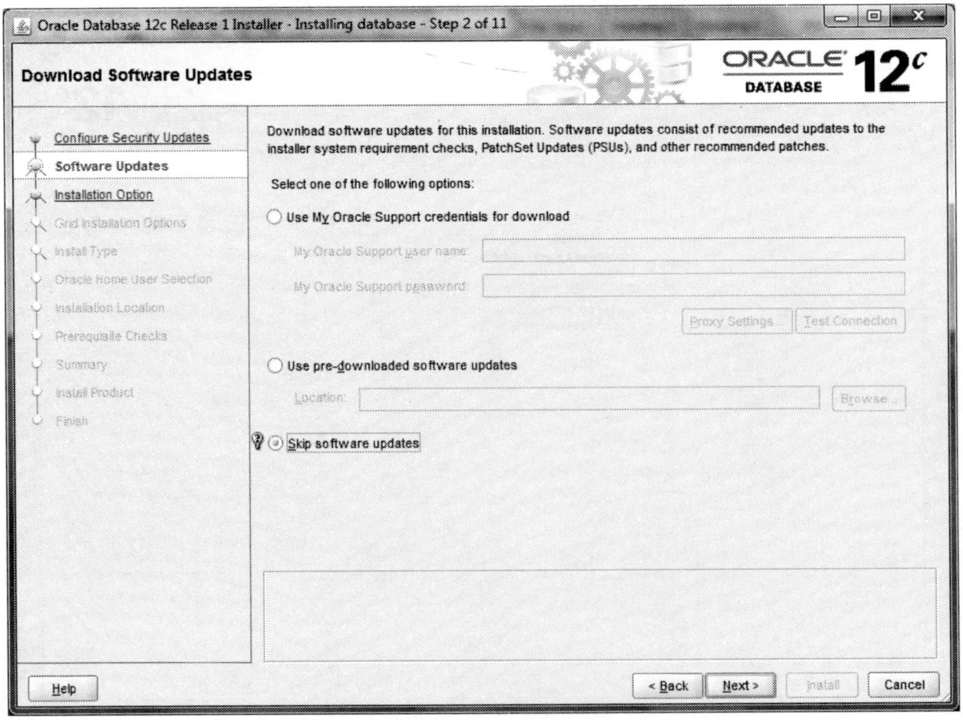

Figure 31.6   Skip software updates.

As shown in Figure 31.7, select "Create and Configure a database".

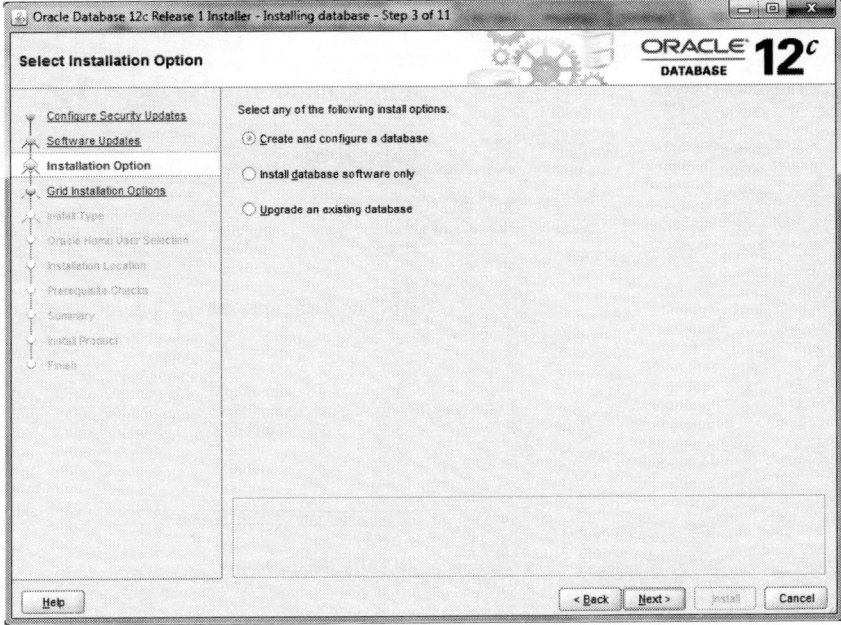

Figure 31.7   Create and configure a database.

In next screen (Figure 31.8), choose "Server Class".

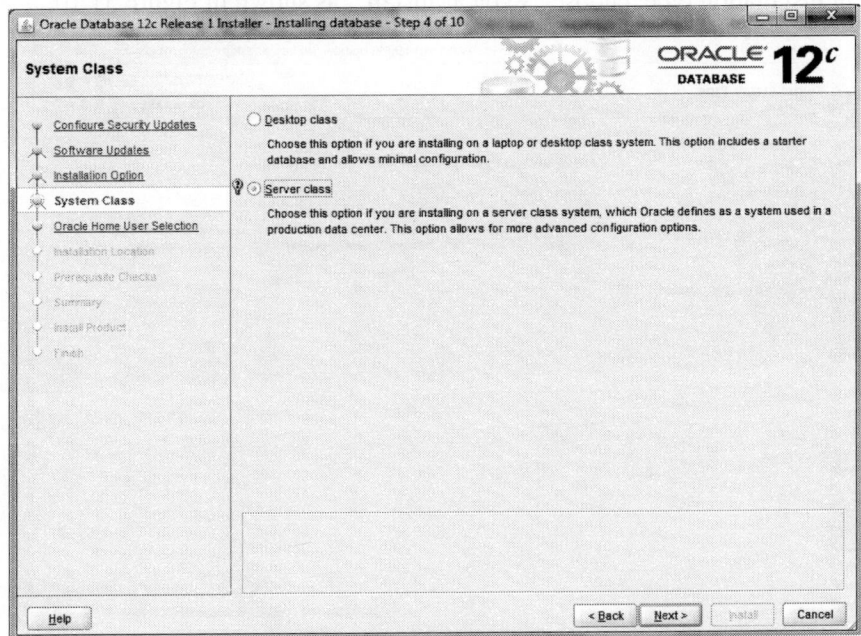

Figure 31.8   Server class.

Next in Grid Installation Option, choose "Single Instance Database Installation", as shown in Figure 31.9.

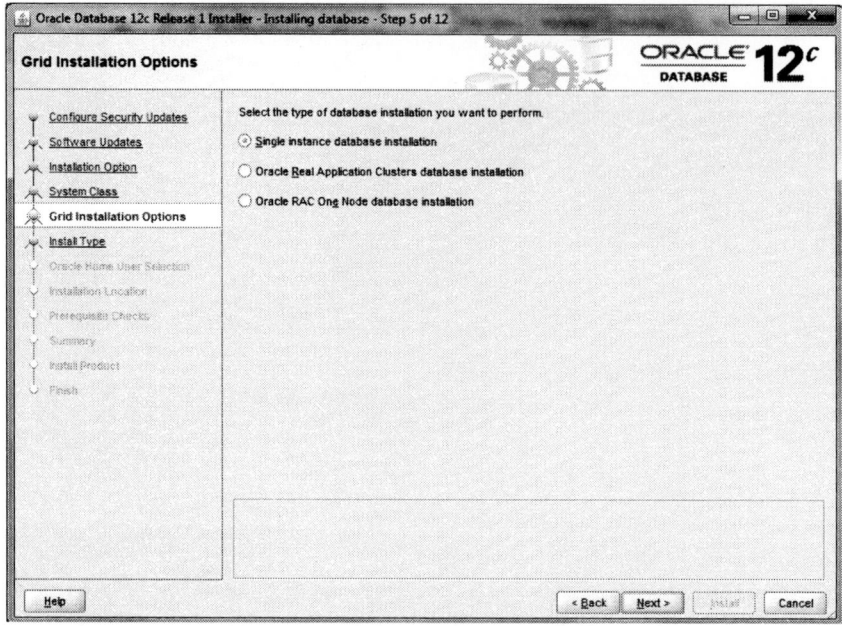

Figure 31.9 Grid installation option.

Then in installation type, choose "Typical Install", as shown in Figure 31.10.

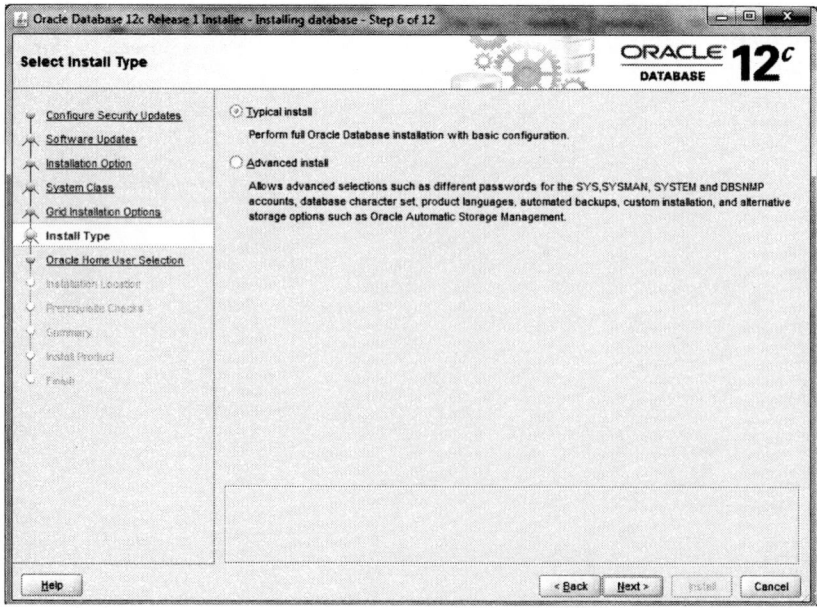

Figure 31.10 Installation type.

Next choose 'Create New Windows User' and specify username as 'oracle' and password as 'oracle123', as shown in Figure 31.11.

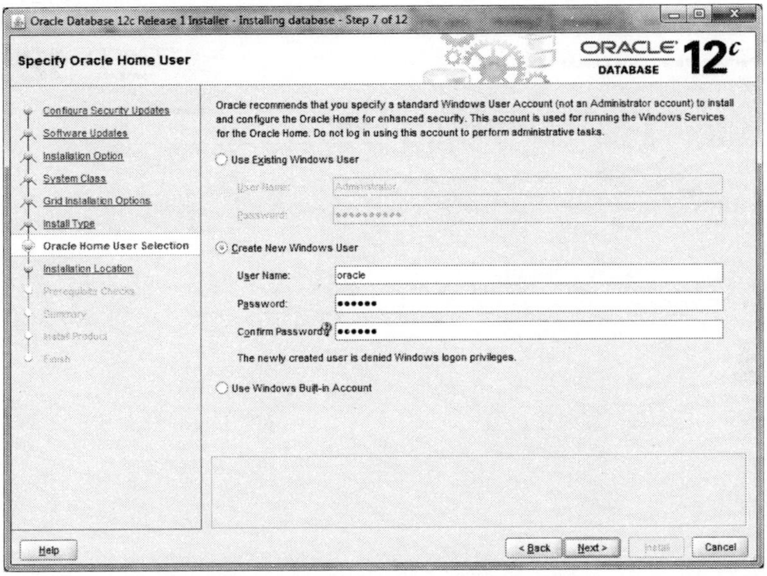

Figure 31.11   Oracle home user.

Next you will have to specify the path where Oracle database will be installed. By default, the Oracle base will specify "C:\app\oracle". Here we have changed it to "D:\app\oracle". In the administrative password, specify "system". This is the DBA's credential to perform various operations. Tick the option "Create as container database", and specify the Pluggable database name as "pdborcl12c".

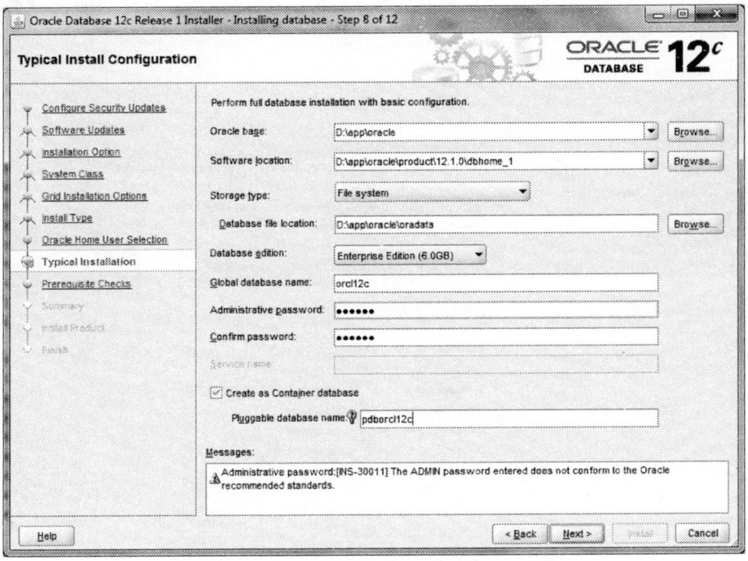

Figure 31.12   Oracle installation folder.

Click next and installation will continue with a progress bar for pre-requisite checks as shown in Figure 31.13.

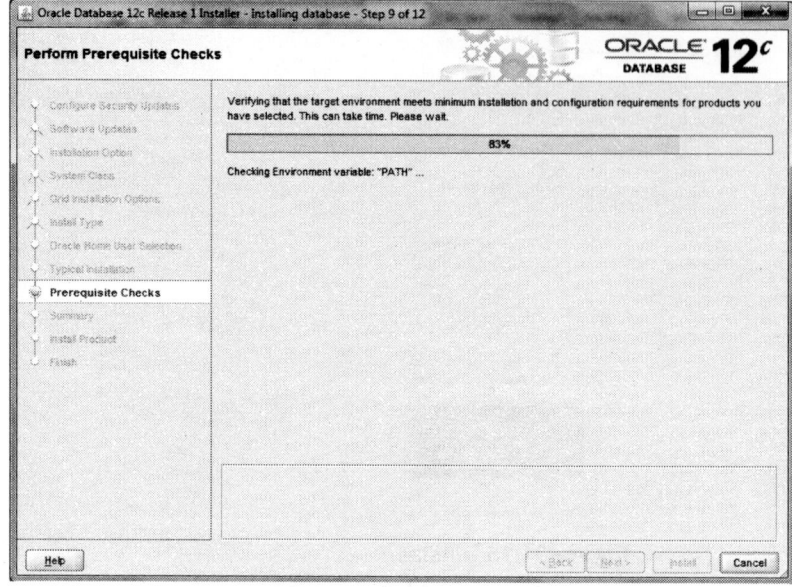

Figure 31.13 Progress bar.

After few seconds, you will be shown a summary of all the options you have chosen during the previous steps (Figure 31.14).

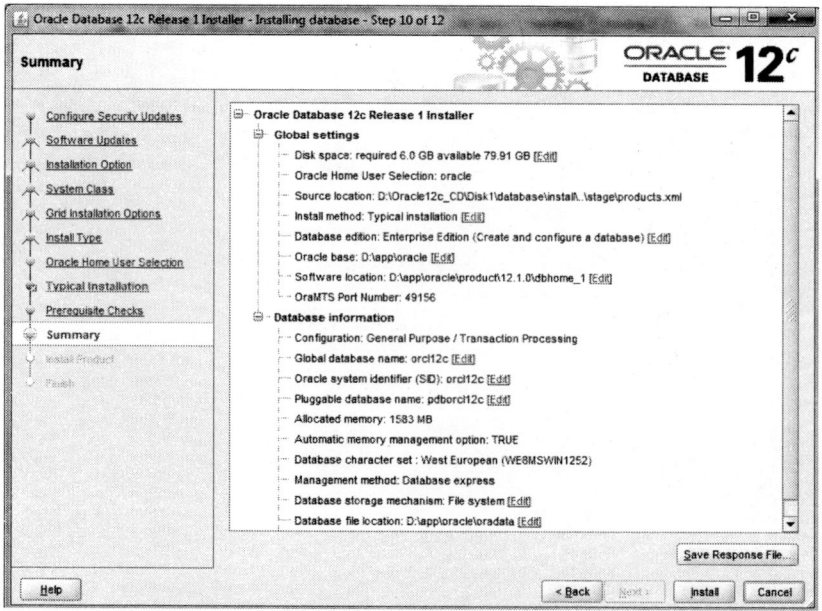

Figure 31.14 Summary of various options chosen.

Click 'Install' and the installation will proceed with a progress bar as shown in Figure 31.15.

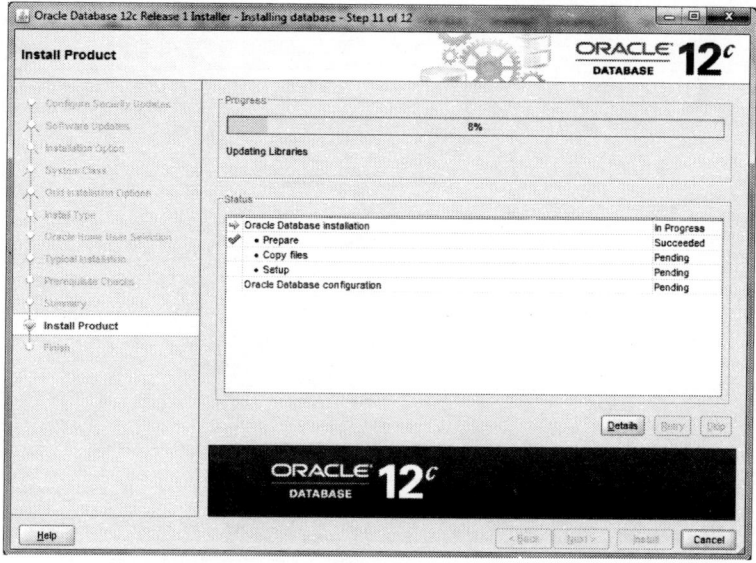

Figure 31.15   Installation progress bar.

If you are installing the Oracle 12c software on a machine with Intel Core i5 processor and 4 GB RAM, it will take around 15–20 minutes. After few minutes you will see Database Configuration Assistant as shown in Figure 31.16. Oracle 12c has a concept of Container and Pluggable databases which will be explained in detail later in this chapter. Referring Figure 13.14, a Container database is created with Instance name as "orcl12c" and a pluggable database will be created with the instance name "pdborcl12c".

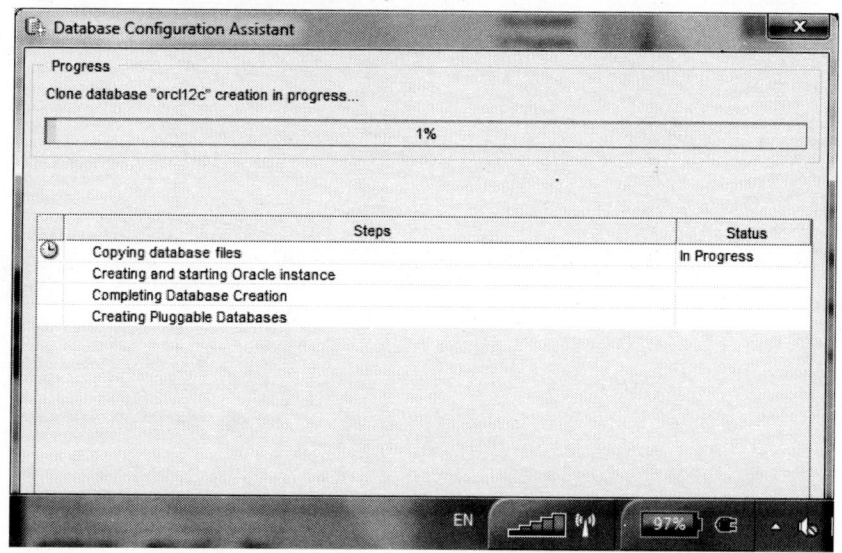

Figure 31.16   Database configuration assistant.

If you want to see the various stages of installation, click on "Activity Log" as shown in Figure 31.17.

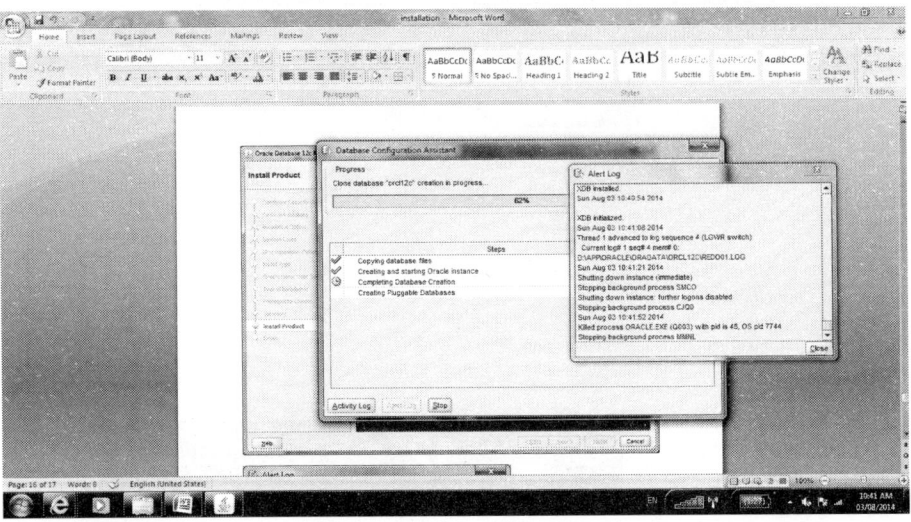

Figure 31.17 Activity log.

Once the installation is complete, you will see the screen as shown in Figure 31.18. Oracle database has broadly two categories of database users: DBA and normal user. SYSTEM user has the DBA privilege. Click on the Password Management button to change the password for SYS and SYSTEM user.

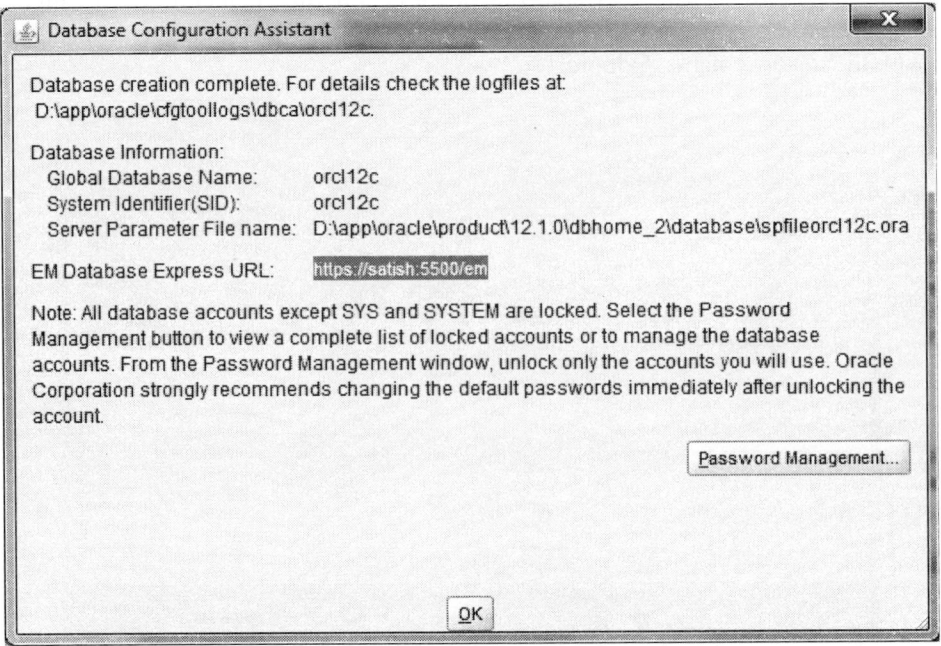

Figure 31.18 Database installation completion.

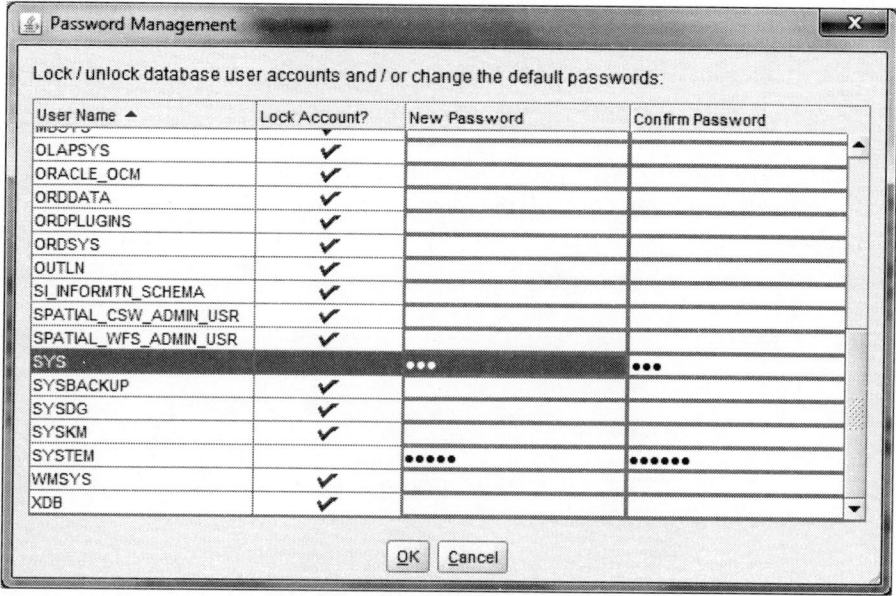

Figure 31.19   Password management.

Change the password of both SYS and SYSTEM user as "SYS" and "SYSTEM" respectively. You can keep the password as per your preference. Click OK and after few minutes you will see the Installation Complete message as shown in Figure 31.20.

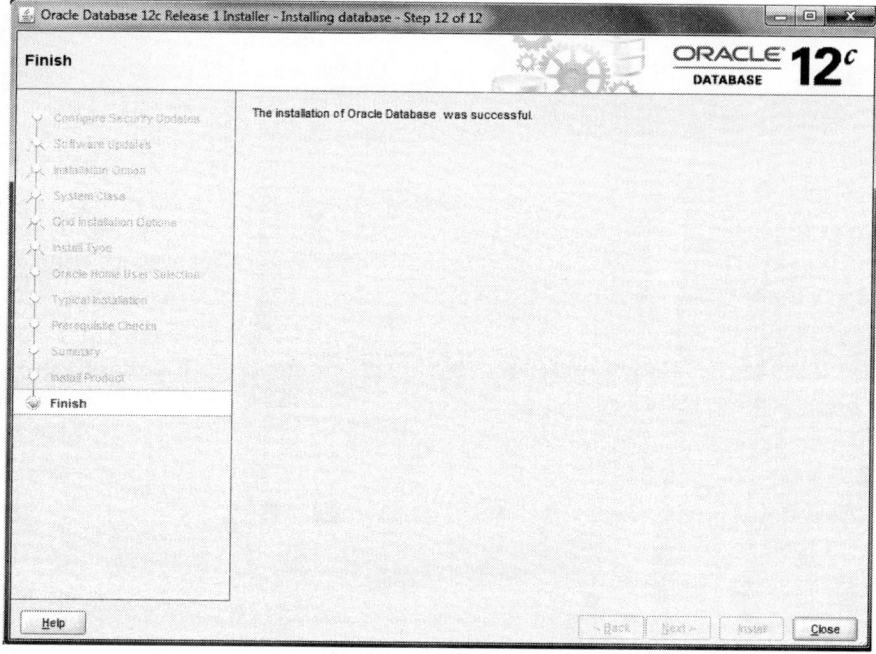

Figure 31.20   Installation completion.

31.3 DISABLE ORACLE DATABASE STARTUP AT BOOT

After Oracle database is installed it is configured to automatically start at every boot. As database software is resource hungry from processing and RAM point of view it may slow down the startup time of your PC. We will now disable the startup of Oracle Database software when the PC boots. Go to "Control Panel" -> "Administrative Tools" -> "Services". Search for "OracleServiceORCL12C" and access the Properties by right clicking the mouse as shown in Figure 31.21. Select the Startup Type as Manual.

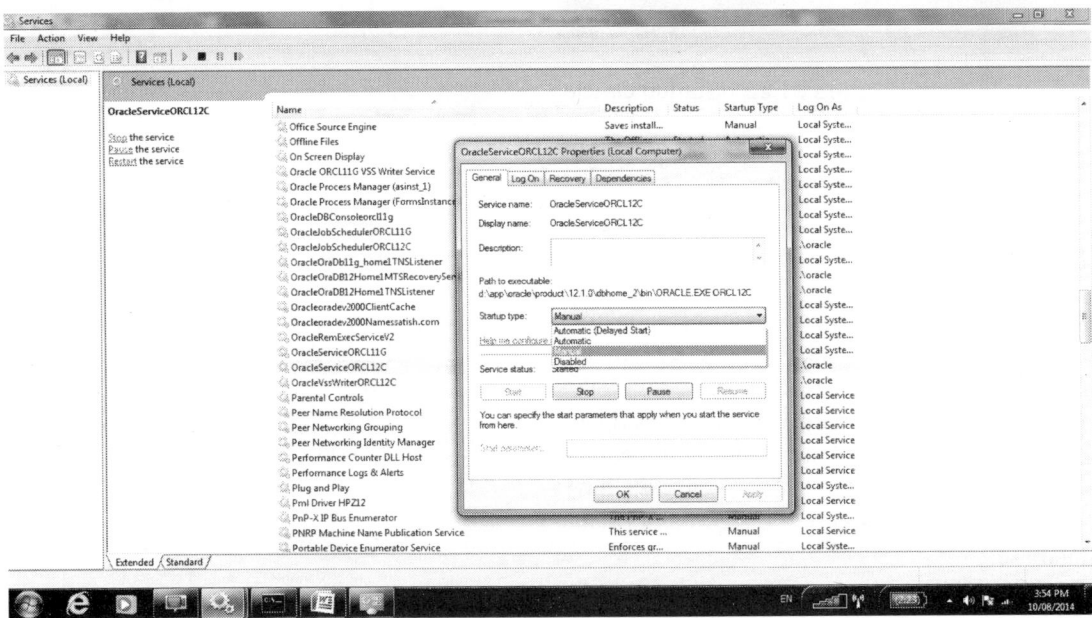

Figure 31.21   Disable Oracle startup at boot.

Click Apply.

Now onwards when the PC starts the Oracle Service will not be automatically loaded in the RAM. We will need to start the Oracle Service manually when we want to work with the database. To do so, go to **Contol Panel** -> **Administrative Tools** -> **Services**, locate OracleServiceORCL12C -> Right Click -> Select Start.

The services can be started and stopped through command line interface also. Click on "Windows Start" button. In the search programs and files textbox, type "cmd" and press "Enter".

On the command line, type following command to start the Oracle Database as shown in Figure 31.22.

C:\Users\Administrator> net start OracleServiceORCL12C

Figure 31.22   Startup Oracle database through command line.

To stop the Oracle Database service, type the following command:
C:\Users\Administrator> net stop OracleServiceORCL12C

31.4   CREATE A USER IN CONTAINER AND PLUGGABLE DATABASE

Before we start working on Oracle 12c database, we need to understand some basic architectural design of this new database version by Oracle Corporation. When we install Oracle 12c it creates a Container Database. Refer Figure 31.12 where Global Database Name has been specified as orlc12c which is in fact the Container Database and a Pluggable Database Name has been specified as pdborcl12c. In this new version of Oracle Database, a container database may comprise one or more Pluggable databases. In our case we have just one pluggable database as pdborcl12c.

Now, we will login to the container database as DBA and then create user in the Pluggable database.

Start the Oracle Database and login to the SQL prompt as shown in Figure 31.23.

Figure 31.23   Starting SQL plus session.

Enter username as system/system as sysdba as shown in Figure 31.24.

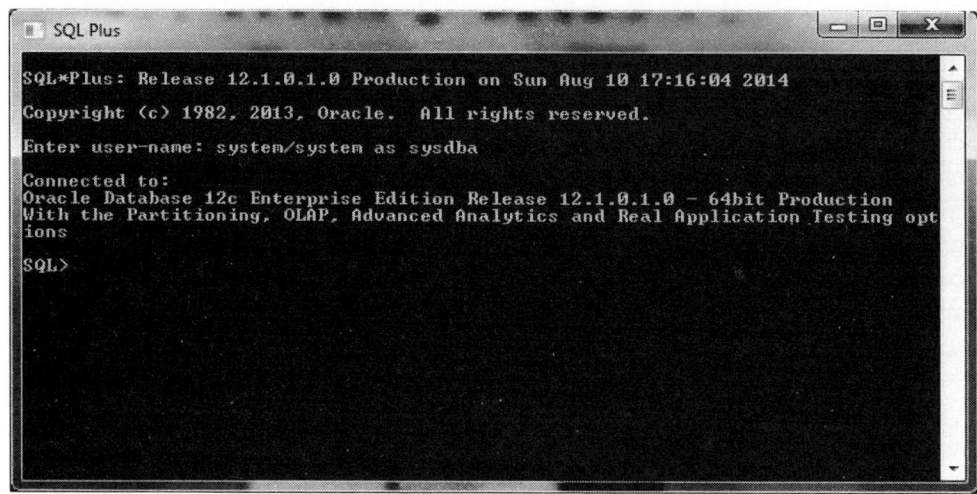

Figure 31.24 Connecting as SYSTEM user with DBA privilege.

Type 'show con_name' on the SQL prompt (Refer Figure 31.25).

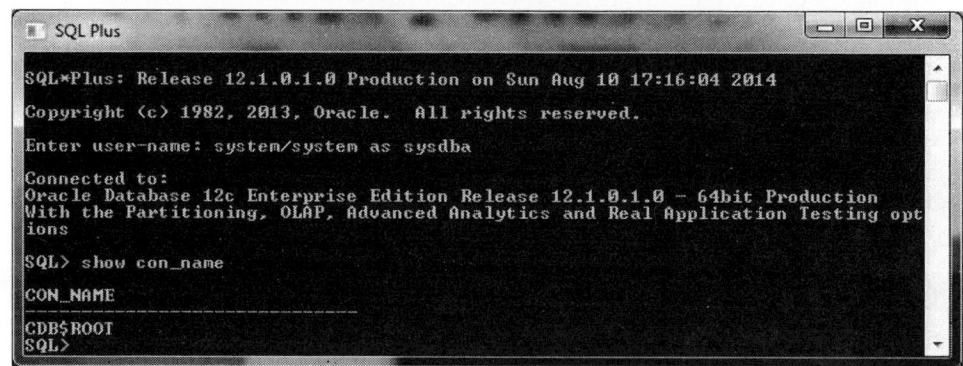

Figure 31.25 Displaying the current database connection.

Show con_name command displays the Container Database name as "CDB$ROOT" where CDB stands for Container Database.

Now, let us try to create a database user named "satish" with password "asnani" as shown in Figure 31.26.

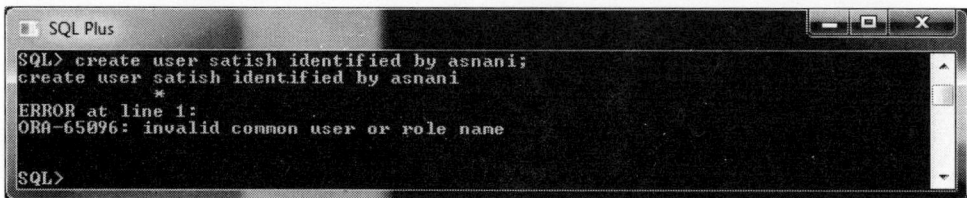

Figure 31.26 Creating a user named "satish".

We have received an error message saying "invalid common user or role name". Actually Oracle 12c supports two types of users: common and local. The default type is local, and we cannot create a local user in Container database by default. We can only create a common user in container database by specifying c## before the username as shown below

```
SQL>connect system/system as sysdba
SQL>create user c##satish identified by asnani;
c## implies container database user.
SQL>grant connect,resource to c##satish;
SQL>connect c##satish/asnani@orcl12c
OR simply
SQL>connect c##satish/asnani
```

By specifying c## it will login to the container database.

Instead of using the CONNECT command on SQL prompt, we can invoke the same by running the SQLPlus from the Programs menu as shown in Figure 31.27a. Figure 31.27b shows the command to start SQL Plus session through command line interface.

(a) Through GUI.

(b) Through command line.

Figure 31.27   Running SQL plus session.

Common user belongs to Container Database as well as current and future Plugged in databases. They can perform operations in both Container and Plugged databases based on privileges assigned.

Local user belongs to a specific Plugged database only.

Let us now create a local user named "mishkin" in plugged database PDBORCL12C.

SQL>connect system/system as sysdba
SQL>alter session set container=pdborcl12c;
Now, we are connected as sysdba on the plugged database instance PDBORCL12c.
SQL> show con_name

CON_NAME

PDBORCL12C

This database needs to be started before any operation can be performed like creating a user.
SQL> startup;
Pluggable Database opened.
SQL> create user mishkin identified by cat;

User created.

SQL> grant connect, resource to mishkin;

Grant succeeded.

Let us now see how "mishkin" user can connect to the Plugged Database named PDBORCL12C from SQL Plus prompt.

For this we need to make an entry for the PDBORCL12C plugged database in the tnsnames.ora file located at following location:

D:\app\oracle\product\12.1.0\dbhome_2\NETWORK\ADMIN

Assuming that Oracle Database 12c has been installed in the D:\app folder.

Referring to Figure 31.28, please note that we have created an entry PDBORCL12C in the tnsnames.ora file.

```
ORCL12C =
  (DESCRIPTION =
    (ADDRESS = (PROTOCOL = TCP)(HOST = localhost)(PORT = 1521))
    (CONNECT_DATA =
      (SERVER = DEDICATED)
      (SERVICE_NAME = orcl12c)
    )
  )

PDBORCL12C =
  (DESCRIPTION =
    (ADDRESS = (PROTOCOL = TCP)(HOST = localhost)(PORT = 1521))
    (CONNECT_DATA =
      (SERVER = DEDICATED)
      (SERVICE_NAME = pdborcl12c)
    )
  )
```

Figure 31.28 Entries in tnsnames.ora.

Let us connect as "mishkin" and create a table named "test" followed by adding a record
SQL> connect mishkin/cat@pdborcl12c;
Connected.
SQL> create table test (a number);

Table created.

SQL> insert into test values (1);
insert into test values (1)
  *
ERROR at line 1:
ORA-01950: no privileges on tablespace 'SYSTEM'
At this stage the user "mishkin" can create tables, but will not be able to INSERT records into any of the tables.

Although discussion of Oracle Database internal structure like tablespaces and datafiles is beyond the scope of this book, but we at least need to understand the above ERROR message and solve it. When we create a user, we need to specify a logical structure called tablespace which ultimately refers to a physical datafile on hard disk. But if we do not specify a tablespace name while creating a user, then the default tablespace assigned is SYSTEM. Moreover every user needs to be allotted a quota on the tablespace before he can perform DML operations. When we allot a quota, then the DML privileges are automatically assigned to the user for that tablespace. The above error message is indicating that the user "mishkin" has not been assigned any quota on the SYSTEM tablespace. Now, we will assign 100 MB of quota to "mishkin" user.
SQL> conn system/system@pdborcl12c;
Connected.
SQL> alter user mishkin quota 100M on system;

User altered.
Here we have allotted only 100 MB of storage space to user "mishkin" in SYSTEM tablespace. We could have allotted unlimited space by using following command as SYSDBA.
SQL> alter user mishkin quota unlimited on system;
We should avoid allotting UNLIMITED quota to any user.
Now, user "mishkin" can perform DML operations
SQL> connect mishkin/cat@pdborcl12c;
Connected.
SQL> insert into t values (1);
1 row created.
SQL> select * from t;

     A

     1
It is not recommended to store user data in SYSTEM tablespace. The SYSTEM tablespace should be solely used by SYSTEM user. We should create separate tablespace for each user.

Let us now create a tablespace and a datafile specific to "mishkin" user. We can create a tablespace and associate it with a datafile in single command.

SQL> create tablespace tbsp_mishkin datafile

'D:\app\oracle\oradata\orcl12c\pdb_hr\mishkin1.dbf' siz-e 1G;

We have created a tablespace named "tbsp_mishkin" and assigned a datafile named "mishkin1.dbf" of size 1 GB in the specified folder.

Tablespace created.

Now, we will re-create user "mishkin" and assign the tablespace "tbsp_mishkin"

SQL> drop user mishkin;

SQL> create user mishkin identified by cat default tablespace tbsp_mishkin;

SQL> grant connect, resource to mishkin;

SQL> alter user mishkin quota 100M on tbsp_mishkin;

Now, the "mishkin" user can connect and create tables within the separately allotted tablespace "tbsp_mishkin".

31.5   ARCHITECTURE OF ORACLE DATABASE 12c

After having created a common user "satish" in Container database and a local user "mishkin" in Plugged Database, let us try to understand the architecture of Oracle 12c Database.

31.5.1   Container and Pluggable Database

Oracle 12c database comprises one Container Database – CDB and one or more Pluggable databases PDBs within that CDB. The default container database is called "root" container.

31.5.2   Components of Container Database

Every Container Database comprises following:

1. Exactly one root: The root container is named CDB$ROOT. A common user is a database user known in every container.

2. Exactly one seed PDB: Whenever a container database is created a template PDB named "seed" is also created automatically. This seed PDB is named "PDB$SEED". We can create new PDBs based on that template seed PDB. We cannot add or remove objects from seed.

3. One or more PDBs: We can create multiple PDBs within the CDB$ROOT. For example, we may create separate PDBs for HR and SALES application.

The container database will have a DBA who can manage the container as well as all other pluggable databases. In Figure 31.29, we can have separate DBAs for HR and SALES PDB. The container DBA is responsible for starting and stopping the pluggable databases.

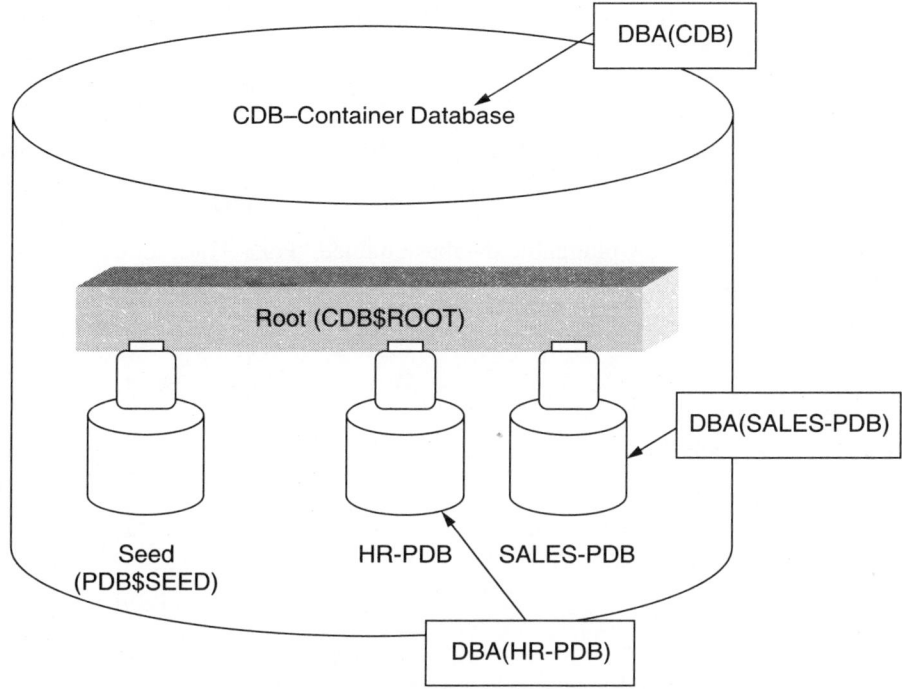

Figure 31.29   Oracle12c architecture.

31.5.3   Creating a New Pluggable Database

Let us now create a new pluggable database named "PDB_HR". There are four techniques of creating a PDB:

1. Create a PDB by using the seed
2. Create a PDB by cloning an existing PDB or non-CDB
3. Create a PDB by plugging an unplugged PDB into a CDB
4. Create a PDB by using a non-CDB

As of now we will create a PDB using SEED (Method I) which is the template provided within Container database.

SQL> create pluggable database pdb_hr admin user system_hr identified by system_hr roles=(dba)

file_name_convert

= ('D:\app\oracle\oradata\orcl12c\pdbseed\', 'D:\app\oracle\oradata\orcl12c\pdb_hr\');

Pluggable database created.

When we create a new PDB it must be assigned a DBA account. Here we have specified DBA as system_hr with password system_hr. Container database contains a SEED template based on which we can create a new PDB. The data files of SEED are located in "D:\app\oracle\oradata\ orcl12c\pdbseed\" folder and by file_name_convert clause we are asking Oracle database to create database files for the new PDB based on the datafiles of the SEED template database.

The SEED folder D:\app\oracle\oradata\orcl12c\pdbseed will have three files, namely
PDBSEED_TEMP01.DBF
SYSAUX01.DBF
SYSTEM01.DBF
And the PDB_HR database folder - D:\app\oracle\oradata\orcl12c\PDB_HR will also contain
the same filenames. This happens because we have created a new PDB_HR with SEED as the
template database.

After having created a new pluggable database named "PDB_HR", let us now create a user
named "nilesh" with password "parker".

SQL> alter session set container=pdb_hr;

Session altered.

SQL> show con_name

CON_NAME
_____

PDB_HR

SQL> startup;
Pluggable Database opened.
SQL> create user nilesh identified by parker;

User created.

SQL> grant connect, resource to nilesh;

Grant succeeded.
SQL>alter user nilesh quota 100M on system;

User altered.
User "nilesh" can now connect to PDB_HR database and perform various operations.

31.6 SQL DEVELOPER

SQL Developer is a free GUI tool which is automatically installed with Oracle Database 12c. This
tool provides a very easy to use graphical interface to perform various tasks which are done through
command line S`QL prompt. We need not to remember various commands for various operations.

Go To Windows Start -> All Programs -> Oracle- OraDB12Home1 -> Application
Development -> SQL Developer as shown in Figure 31.30.

As soon as you launch the SQL Developer for first time, it will ask you the location of JRE as shown in Figure 31.31.

Figure 31.30   Starting SQL developer.

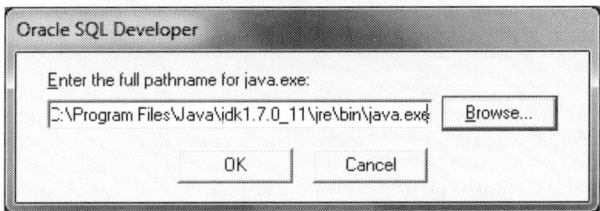

Figure 31.31   Specifying location of java.exe.

Specify the location of JRE on your system. In my case, it is C:\Program Files\Java\jre7\ jdk1.7.0_11\jre\bin\java.exe.

SQL Developer will get launched displaying screenshot as shown in Figure 31.32.

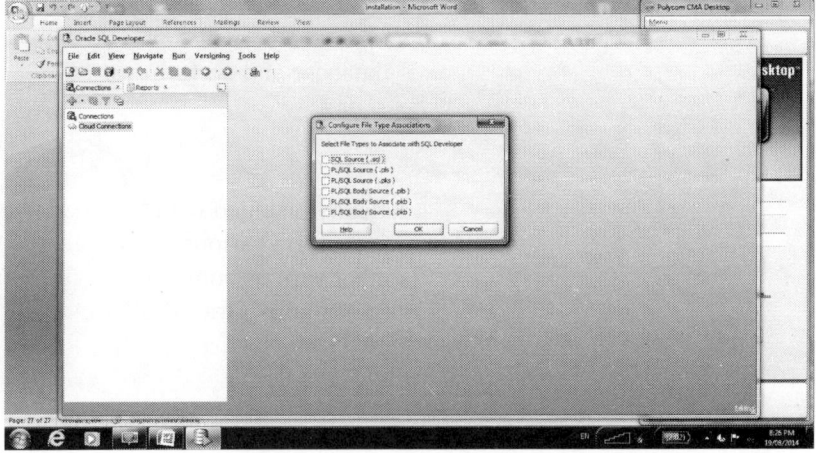

Figure 31.32   SQL Developer startup screen.

Tick all the check boxes and press OK.

Right Click Connections in the left pane and Select New Connection and Enter following details as shown in Figure 31.33.

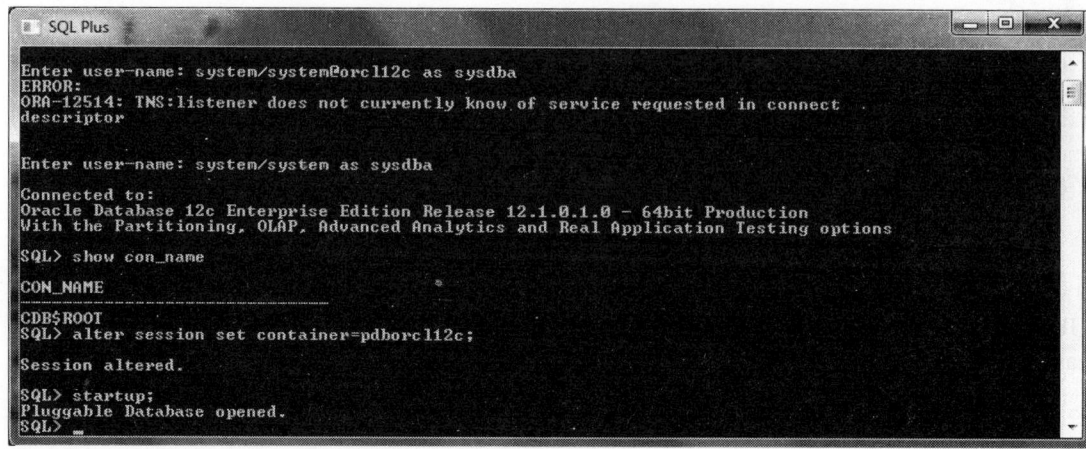

Figure 31.33 New database connection.

Click the "Test" button.

Make sure that you have started the Container database ORCL12C as well as Plugged database PDBORCL12C before testing the connection.

Start the Container database through Services within the Control Panel -> Administrative tools. Do not forget to start both OracleServiceORCL12c database and listener OracleOraDB12Home1TNSListener.

Connect through SQL Plus as sysdba and start the plugged database as shown in Figure 31.34.

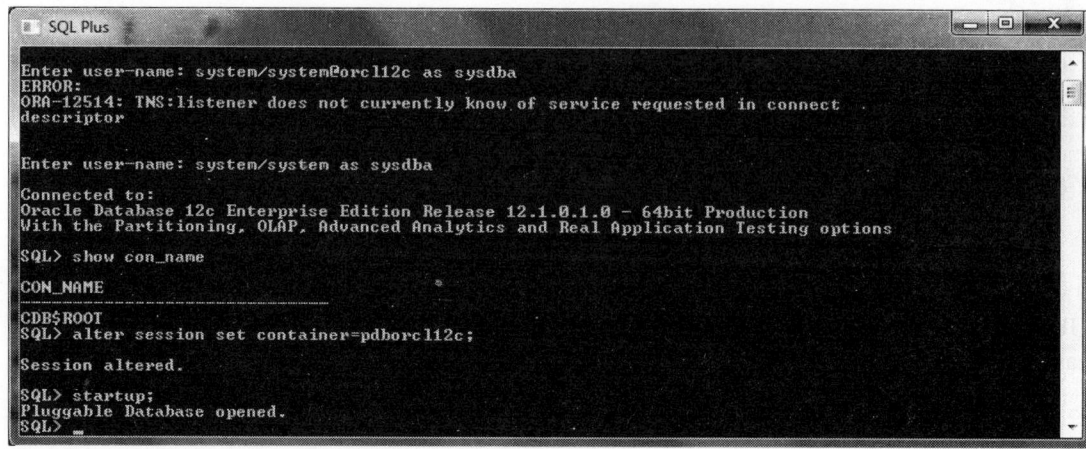

Figure 31.34 Starting the PDB.

For clarity, here are the commands:

Connect as system/system as sysdba

SQL> show con_name

CDB$ROOT

SQL> alter session set container=pdborcl12c;

SQL> startup;

Pluggable Database Opened.

By default the user account 'scott' is locked. We need to unlock the same by following command:

SQL> alter user scott account unlock;

You may face an error saying that password has expired. In that case, specify a new password for the "scott' user by following command:

SQL> alter user scott identified by tiger;

Now, Click Test on the SQL developer screen, and the status should appear as SUCCESS.

Note: If you receive an ERROR message "Status : Failure – Test Failed : ORA-01033: Oracle initialization or shutdown in progress." it means that the plugged database is not running.

Click CONNECT and you will see the screenshot as shown in Figure 31.35.

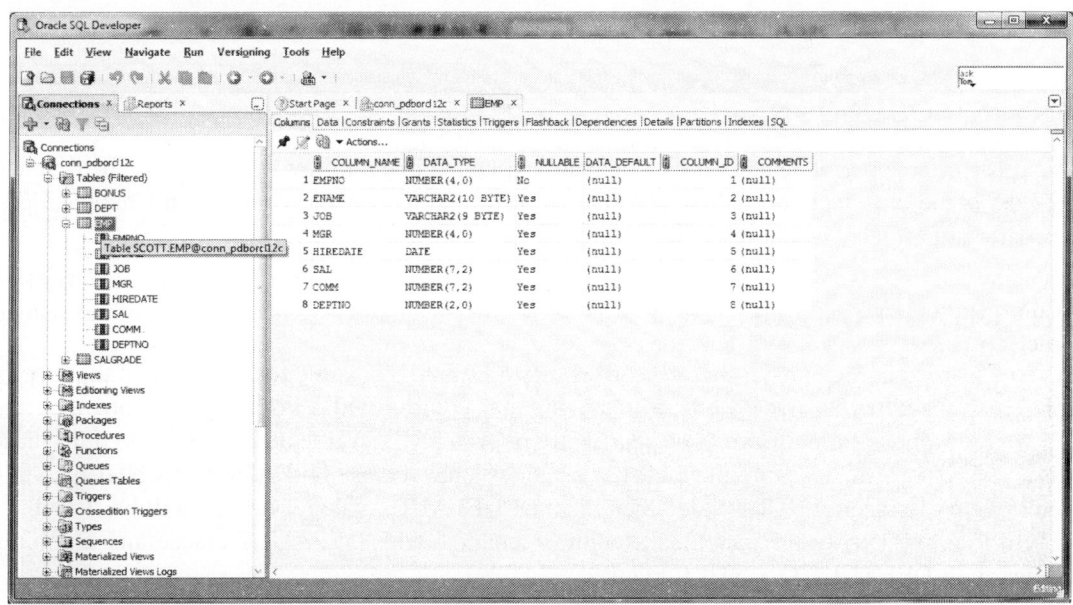

Figure 31.35   SQL developer screen after CONNECTION is successful.

In this book, we will perform tasks using commands rather than through SQL Developer GUI tool. I gave a brief introduction to SQL Developer so that one should be aware of such an easy to use tool.

New Features in Oracle 12*c*

32.1 INTRODUCTION

Oracle 12c offers several new features which are explained in the following sections. The first and foremost is the introduction of Pluggable Database which has been elaborated in Chapter 31 on Installation of Oracle Database 12c.

32.2 DEFAULT ON NULL

We have learned in Section 6.7 that we can specify a DEFAULT value for a column at the time of table creation. If we do not specify a value for that column while inserting a record then the DEFAULT value is stored. But if we specifically insert a NULL value then the DEFAULT clause fails and a NULL value is stored. Oracle12c provides a new clause DEFAULT ON NULL so that even if we try to insert a NULL value then also the DEFAULT value specified will be stored.

In Figure 32.1, we have created a column "marks" with DEFAULT clause and a column "grade" with DEFAULT ON NULL clause.

```
SQL> create table test (rollno number, marks number default 0, grade char(1) default on null 'x');
Table created.
SQL> insert into test(rollno) values (1);
1 row created.
SQL> insert into test(rollno,marks) values (2,20);
1 row created.
SQL> insert into test values (3,40,'A');
1 row created.
SQL> insert into test values (4,null,null);
```

```
1 row created.
SQL> select * from test;
```

ROLL NO	MARKS	GRADE
1	0	x
2	20	x
3	40	A
4		x

Figure 32.1 DEFAULT ON NULL clause.

In the first INSERT statement, we have not specified any value for both MARKS and GRADE. Therefore, zero was taken for MARKS and 'x' for GRADE.

In second INSERT statement, 20 was specified for MARKS and no value for GRADE. The value 'x' was taken for GRADE.

Third statement has supplied values for both.

Fourth statement specified NULL for both MARKS and GRADE. As MARKS has DEFAULT clause, therefore, NULL was taken and GRADE has DEFAULT ON NULL clause, therefore 'x' is taken for GRADE.

32.3 VISIBLE AND INVISIBLE COLUMNS

This new feature enables us to define certain columns in a table as invisible so that they do not appear in DESCRIBE and SELECT command. In Figure 32.2, we have created a column named "salary" with invisible clause.

```
SQL> create table employees (emp_id number,name varchar2(20),salary number(8) invisible);
Table created.
SQL> desc employees
Name                    Null?   Type
EMP_ID                          NUMBER
NAME                            VARCHAR2(20)
SQL> insert into employees values (1,"satish",2000);
insert into employees values (1,"satish",2000)
*
ERROR at line 1:
ORA-00913: too many values
SQL> insert into employees(emp_id,name,salary) values (1,"satish",2000);
1 row created.
SQL> select * from employees;
EMP_ID     NAME

1          satish
SQL>select emp_id,name,salary from employees;
EMP_ID     NAME           SALARY

1          satish         2000
```

Figure 32.2 INVISIBLE column.

When we tried to insert record without specifying the columns then it failed with ERROR – too many values. This happened because as salary column is invisible, the database assumes that the EMPLOYEES table has only two columns and not three. To supply value for INVISIBLE column SALARY, we need to mention the column name in the INSERT command as has been done in the second INSERT statement. When we SELECT records from the table, note that the invisible column has not been displayed. To display the INVISIBLE column also, we need to mention the column name explicitly in the SELECT statement.

We can change the status of a column VISIBLE/INVISIBLE by ALTER TABLE command as shown in Figure 32.3.

```
SQL> alter table employees  modify salary visible;

Table altered.

SQL> select * from employees;

  EMP_ID   NAME       SALARY
  _____   ____       _____
     1     satish      2000
```

Figure 32.3 Modifying visible/invisible attribute.

32.4 POPULATE A PRIMARY KEY USING SEQUENCE

In Oracle 11g in order to generate a primary, we have to first create a sequence and then create a BEFORE INSERT trigger to insert the value from sequence into the primary key column. Oracle 12c allows us to specify a DEFAULT clause with sequence name to achieve the same result without the extra effort of writing the trigger. In Figure 32.4, while creating the table, we have mentioned sequence name SEQ_EMPID.NEXTVAL in the DEFAULT clause of EMPID column.

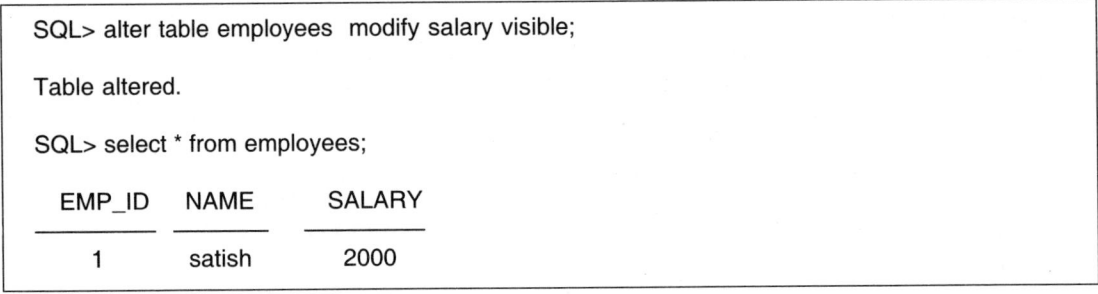

```
SQL> create sequence seq_empid;
SQL> create table employees ( empid number default seq_empid.nextval, name varchar2(10),
salary number);
Table created.
SQL> insert into employees(name,salary) values ('satish',2000);
1 row created.
SQL> insert into employees(name,salary) values ('mishkin',3000);
1 row created.
SQL> select * from employees;
    EMPID        NAME       SALARY
    _____        ____       _____
      1          satish      2000
      2          mishkin     3000
```

Figure 32.4 Specifying sequence in the DEFAULT clause.

Note that while adding new records we have not used the sequence.nextval option.

32.5 IDENTITY COLUMNS

In order to populate a primary key column using sequence, we had to first create the sequence and then specify the sequence name with the DEFAULT clause while creating the table. If the user mistakenly drops the sequence then all the INSERT statements will fail. Oracle 12c has a provision of specifying IDENTITY column which will generate primary key value based on a sequence defined while creating the table. The sequence will not exist as a separate object. Figure 32.5 displays how to create a column with identity clause.

```
SQL> drop table employees;
Table dropped.
SQL> create table employees (emp_id number generated by default as identity
(start with 1 increment by 1),
name varchar2(10), salary number);
Table created.
SQL> insert into employees(name,salary) values ('rishi',5000);
1 row created.
SQL> insert into employees(name,salary) values ('anjali',3000);
1 row created.
SQL> select * from employees;
            EMP_ID              NAME              SALARY
            _____            _____          _____
               1                rishi              5000
               2                anjali             3000
```

Figure 32.5 Identity column.

32.6 CROSS APPLY

In Chapter 11 on Joins (Section 11.2), we learned about inner and outer joins. CROSS APPLY returns the matching rows from two SELECT statements in the form of one result set. It displays the rows from outer SELECT that matches with the rows in INNER SELECT as a merged result set.

Assuming that the table DEPARTMENT and EMPLOYEES contain records as shown in Figure 32.6.

```
SQL> select * from department;
            DEPTNO              DNAME              LOCATION
            _____            _____   _____
               10               SALES              BHOPAL
               20               MANUFACTURING      INDORE
               30               FINANCE            JABALPUR
               99               SERVICE            GWALIOR
```

```
SQL> select * from employees;
```

EMPNO	ENAME	COMM	SAL	DEPTNO
1111	satish	2000	6000	10
2222	mishkin	1000	4000	20
3333	ronak	1500	5000	30
4444	rishi	3000	8000	40

Figure 32.6　Sample records to understand CROSS join.

Note that DEPTNO 99 exists in DEPARTMENT table, but no employee belongs to this department.

EMPNO 4444 belongs to deptno 40 which is non-existent in DEPARTMENT table.

We will use CROSS JOIN to display the merged result set from DEPARTMENT table with matching records from EMPLOYEES table as shown in Figure 32.7.

```
SQL> select * from department a
     CROSS APPLY
     ( select * from employees b
     where a.deptno=b.deptno ) ;
```

DEPTNO	DNAME	LOCATION	EMPNO	ENAME	COMM	SAL	DEPTNO
10	SALES	BHOPAL	1111	satish	2000	6000	10
20	MANUFACTURING	INDORE	2222	mishkin	1000	4000	20
30	FINANCE	JABALPUR	3333	ronak	1500	5000	30

Figure 32.7　Cross apply.

32.7　OUTER APPLY JOIN

Outer Apply will show the merged result set of the two SELECT statements such that the matching as well as non-matching records of the OUTER SELECT are displayed (Figure 32.8).

```
SQL> select * from department a
     OUTER APPLY
     ( select * from employees b
     where a.deptno=b.deptno ) ;
```

DEPTNO	DNAME	LOCATION	EMPNO	ENAME	COMM	SAL	DEPTNO
10	SALES	BHOPAL	1111	satish	2000	6000	10
20	MANUFACTURING	INDORE	2222	mishkin	1000	4000	20
30	FINANCE	JABALPUR	3333	ronak	1500	5000	30
99	SERVICE	GWALIOR					

Figure 32.8　Outer apply.

Note that department 99 has also appeared although no employee belongs to it.

32.8   EXTENDED DATATYPES

In Chapter 4, we learned that the maximum size of VARCHAR2 and RAW is 4000 bytes. Oracle 12c enables us to increase the maximum size to 32767 bytes by using extended data types. There is a new Oracle parameter MAX_STRING_SIZE which can take two values: STANDARD and EXTENDED. The STANDARD is by default which supports maximum size of 4000 bytes. In order to enable 32767 sizes, we need to change the parameter MAX_STRING_SIZE to EXTENDED.

Note that we need to Upgrade the Oracle database before we apply this parameter value. This is because all data dictionary needs to be upgraded to support the new extended size. Moreover once we have changed the parameter to EXTENDED, we cannot revert to STANDARD.

In Figure 32.9, we are changing the MAX_STRING_SIZE parameter on PDB named PDBORCL12C. The same procedure can also be applied to CDB. We can have separate values of this parameter in container and pluggable databases as well as between different PDBs.

```
SQL> connect system/system as sysdba
SQL> alter session set container  = pdborcl12c;
NOTE: Database must be shutdown before UPGRADE
SQL> shutdown immediate;
Pluggable Database closed.
We need to start the database in UPGRADE mode before applying the new parameter value
SQL> startup upgrade;
Pluggable Database opened.
SQL> ALTER SYSTEM SET max_string_size=extended scope=spfile;
System altered.
Now the data dictionary needs to be upgraded so as to enable 32767 bytes of extended data
types. Oracle provides a SQL script utl32k.sql for this purpose which is located in the folder
D:\app\oracle\product\12.1.0\dbhome_1\RDBMS\ADMIN\
Run the utl32k.sql script as follows
SQL> @D:\app\oracle\product\12.1.0\dbhome_1\RDBMS\ADMIN\utl32k.sql
Now we can start the database in normal mode
SQL> shutdown immediate;
Pluggable Database closed.
SQL> startup;
Pluggable Database opened.
```

Figure 32.9   Changing MAX_STRING_SIZE parameter.

Now, we will create a table with extended data type as shown in Figure 32.10.

```
SQL> create table tbl_extended(name varchar2(32767), image raw(32767));
Table created.
SQL> desc tbl_extended
Name              Null?   Type

NAME                      VARCHAR2(32767)
IMAGE                     RAW(32767)
```

Figure 32.10   Creating table with EXTENDED data types.

32.9   PRIVILEGE ANALYSIS

In Chapters 14 and 15, we learnt about privileges and roles. Till Oracle 11g we do not have any feature whereby we can analyze the various privileges and roles being actually used by other users. Oracle 12c has a feature by which we can analyze or monitor the usage pattern of the various privileges and roles granted to other users. We can even find out which granted privileges are not being used.

To understand the concept practically, we are assuming that there is a schema "HR" having a table named "EMPLOYEE". The "HR" user has given SELECT, INSERT, UPDATE and DELETE privilege to user "HR_MANAGER" and SELECT privilege on the same table to two more users namely "SALES_MANAGER" and "FINANCE_MANAGER".

To learn practically we will use the pluggable database PDB1 within CDB1.

Here we will use the DBA SYSTEM user to capture privilege usage. If we desire that the "HR" user should also be able to define privilege capture then the user must be granted execute privilege on package DBMS_PRIVILEGE_CAPTURE.

In Figure 32.11 HR user grants SELECT, INSERT, UPDATE privilege to HR_MANAGER user and SELECT privilege to FINANCE_MANAGER and SALES_MANAGER user.

```
SQL> conn system_pdb1/system_pdb1@localhost:1521/pdb1 as sysdba
SQL> grant execute on dbms_privilege_capture to hr;
Grant succeeded.
SQL> conn hr/hr@localhost:1521/pdb1
Connected.
SQL> grant select,insert,update,delete on employee to hr_manager;
Grant succeeded.
SQL> grant select on employee to sales_manager;
Grant succeeded.
SQL> grant select on employee to finance_manager;
Grant succeeded.
```

Figure 32.11   Granting privileges.

First we need to define the privilege capture and then start the analysis at three levels

1. Privileges used by all users
2. Privileges used through roles
3. Privileges used through contexts

32.9.1   Capture of Privileges used by all Users

To capture privilege used by all users, we need to use the SYS.DBMS_PRIVILEGE_CAPTURE.CREATE_CAPTURE package as shown in Figure 32.12.

```
SQL> conn system/system@localhost:1521/pdb1 as sysdba
SQL> exec SYS.DBMS_PRIVILEGE_CAPTURE.CREATE_CAPTURE ( name =>
'All_privs', description => 'All privs used', type => dbms_privilege_capture.g_database);
PL/SQL procedure successfully completed.
Now we have to start analysis of the defined capture
SQL> exec SYS.DBMS_PRIVILEGE_CAPTURE.ENABLE_CAPTURE (name => 'All_privs');
PL/SQL procedure successfully completed.
SQL>exit;
```

Figure 32.12   Capture privilege of all users.

Note that in the 'TYPE' parameter of the package we have specified 'g_database' which implies all users to be analyzed.

Make sure that you exit the SQL plus session as the privilege capture analysis will come into action at the start of new sessions.

Now users 'HR_MANAGER' will issue SELECT and INSERT operation on HR.EMPLOYEES table and user 'SALES_MANAGER' will run SELECT on the same table as shown in Figure 32.13.

```
SQL> conn hr_manager/hr_manager@localhost:1521/pdb1
Connected.
SQL> select * from hr.employee;

        EMPNO           NAME            DESIGNATION
        _____          _____          _____

          1             Satish          Senior Manager
          2             Mishkin         Engineer

SQL> insert into hr.employee values (3,'Nishit');
1 row created.
SQL> commit;
Commit complete.
SQL> conn sales_manager/sales_manager@localhost:1521/pdb1
Connected.
SQL> select * from hr.employees;

        EMPNO           NAME
        _____          _____

          1             Satish
          2             Mishkin
          3             Nishit
```

Figure 32.13 Operations based on privilege.

Now, as DBA, we will stop the capture of privilege access (Figure 32.14).

```
SQL> conn system_pdb1/system_pdb1@localhost:1521/pdb1 as sysdba
SQL> exec SYS.DBMS_PRIVILEGE_CAPTURE.DISABLE_CAPTURE (name => 'All_privs');
PL/SQL procedure successfully completed.
```

Figure 32.14 Stop capture.

Now, we will generate the results of capture by using GENERATE_RESULT procedure of DBMS_PRIVILEGE_CAPTURE package (see Figure 32.15).

```
SQL> exec SYS.DBMS_PRIVILEGE_CAPTURE.GENERATE_RESULT (name => 'All_privs')
PL/SQL procedure successfully completed.
```

Figure 32.15 Generate result.

To see the capture results we need to query the DBA_USED_OBJPRIVS view as shown in Figure 32.16.

```
SQL>  COL username FORMAT A15
SQL>  COL object_owner FORMAT A12
SQL>  COL object_name FORMAT A30
SQL>  COL obj_priv FORMAT A25
SQL>  select username, object_owner, object_name, obj_priv
      from   dba_used_objprivs
      where  username in ('HR_MANAGER', 'SALES_MANAGER', 'FINANCE_MANAGER')
      and    object_name in ('EMPLOYEE');
```

USERNAME	OBJECT_OWNER	OBJECT_NAME	OBJ_PRIV
HR_MANAGER	HR	EMPLOYEE	SELECT
HR_MANAGER	HR	EMPLOYEE	INSERT
SALES_MANAGER	HR	EMPLOYEE	SELECT

Figure 32.16   View capture results

To drop the capture, we need to use the DROP_CAPTURE procedure of
SYS.DBMS_PRIVILEGE_CAPTURE package (see Figure 32.17).

```
SQL> exec SYS.DBMS_PRIVILEGE_CAPTURE.DROP_CAPTURE (name => 'All_privs');
```

Figure 32.17   Drop capture.

32.9.2   Capture of Privileges through Roles

Just as we captured privilege usage for all users, we can analyze the usage of privileges granted through roles to users. As DBA of PDB1, we have created two roles ROLE_HR and ROLE_FINANCE as shown in Figure 32.18.

```
SQL> conn system_pdb1/system_pdb1@localhost:1521/pdb1 as sysdba
SQL> Create role role_hr;
SQL> Grant select,insert,update,delete on hr.employee to role_hr;
SQL> Create role role_finance;
SQL> Grant select on hr.employee to role_finance;
SQL> Grant role_hr to hr_manager;
SQL> Grant role_finance to finance_manager;
```

Figure 32.18   Creating roles.

Now, we will define and enable capture for roles as shown in Figure 32.19.

```
SQL>   exec   SYS.DBMS_PRIVILEGE_CAPTURE.CREATE_CAPTURE   (name=>
'Role_privs',description=>'Privs used by HR_MANAGER, FINANCE_MANAGER',type =>
dbms_privilege_capture.g_role,roles =>   role_name_list('ROLE_HR', 'ROLE_FINANCE'));
SQL> select name, type, enabled, roles, context from   dba_priv_captures;
```

NAME	TYPE	E	ROLES	CONTEXT
Role_privs	ROLE	N	ROLE_ID_LIST(107, 108)	

```
SQL> exec SYS.DBMS_PRIVILEGE_CAPTURE.ENABLE_CAPTURE (name => 'Role_privs') ;
PL/SQL procedure successfully completed.
```

Figure 32.19   Create capture based on role.

We will now connect as HR_MANAGER and perform SELECT, INSERT operations on HR.EMPLOYEE table as shown in Figure 32.20. Then we will connect as FINANCE_MANAGER and perform a SELECT operation on HR.EMPLOYEE table.

```
SQL> conn hr_manager/hr_manager@localhost:1521/pdb1
Connected.
SQL> select * from hr.employee;

        EMPNO          NAME
        _____          ____

          1            Satish
          2            Mishkin

SQL> insert into hr.employee values (3,'Nishit');
1 row created.
SQL> commit;
Commit complete.
SQL> conn finance_manager/finance_manager@localhost:1521/pdb1
Connected.
SQL>
SQL>
SQL> select * from hr.employee;
        EMPNO          NAME
        _____          ____

          1            Satish
          2            Mishkin
          3            Nishit
```

Figure 32.20 Operations based on roles.

As DBA of PDB1 we will disable capture and generate results of capture as shown in Figure 32.21.

```
SQL> conn system_pdb1/system_pdb1@localhost:1521/pdb1 as sysdba
Connected.
SQL> exec SYS.DBMS_PRIVILEGE_CAPTURE.DISABLE_CAPTURE (name => 'Role_privs')
PL/SQL procedure successfully completed.
SQL> exec SYS.DBMS_PRIVILEGE_CAPTURE.GENERATE_RESULT (name =>'Role_privs')
PL/SQL procedure successfully completed.
SQL> select   username, object_owner, object_name, obj_priv, used_role from
dba_used_objprivs where   used_role in ('HR_MGR', 'SALES_CLERK');
```

USERNAME	OBJECT_OWN	OBJECT_NAM	OBJ_PRIV	USED_ROLE
HR_MANAGER	HR	EMPLOYEE	SELECT	ROLE_HR
HR_MANAGER	HR	EMPLOYEE	INSERT	ROLE_HR
FINANCE_MANAGER	HR	EMPLOYEE	SELECT	ROLE_FINANCE

Figure 32.21 Disable capture and generate result.

32.9.3 Capture of Privileges through Context

Context is a very important parameter we can use to analyze privileges based on CLIENT_INFO, HOST, IP_ADDRESS, OS_USER, USERENV, etc. The information about these can be obtained from the Oracle Docs website. Here we will define capture based on USERNAME which is actually defined as SESSION_USER in CONTEXT.

Let us first delete all the captures defined earlier. Figure 32.22 shows how to find the defined captures and delete them.

```
SQL> select name, type, enabled, roles, context
from   dba_priv_captures;

     NAME        TYPE        E             ROLES              CONTEXT
   _____   _____   _____   _____   _____

   Role_privs    ROLE        N       ROLE_ID_LIST(105, 111)

SQL> exec SYS.DBMS_PRIVILEGE_CAPTURE.DROP_CAPTURE (name => 'Role_privs');

PL/SQL procedure successfully completed.
```

Figure 32.22   Drop captures.

We have defined and enabled a CAPTURE based on SYS_CONTEXT in Figure 32.23.

```
SQL> exec SYS.DBMS_PRIVILEGE_CAPTURE.CREATE_CAPTURE
(name =>'Context_Capture',description =>'ContextCapture',
type =>dbms_privilege_capture.g_role_and_context,
roles =>role_name_list('ROLE_HR','ROLE_FINANCE'),
condition =>'SYS_CONTEXT("USERENV","SESSION_USER")="HR_MANAGER"');
SQL> exec SYS.DBMS_PRIVILEGE_CAPTURE.ENABLE_CAPTURE (name =>
'Context_Capture')
PL/SQL procedure successfully completed.
```

Figure 32.23   Capture on SYS_CONTEXT.

As the capture is defined and enabled, we will connect as HR_MANAGER user and perform SELECT, INSERT operations on HR.EMPLOYEE table as shown in Figure 32.24.

```
SQL> conn hr_manager/hr_manager@localhost:1521/pdb1
Connected.
SQL> select * from hr.employee;

     EMPNO        NAME
   _____   _____

       1        Satish
       2        Mishkin
       3        Nishit

SQL> insert into hr.employee values (4,'Deepa');
1 row created.
SQL> commit;
Commit complete.
```

Figure 32.24   Operations by users.

In Figure 32.25, we have generated the capture result and displayed the same.

```
SQL> conn system_pdb1/system_pdb1@localhost:1521/pdb1 as sysdba
Connected.
SQL> exec SYS.DBMS_PRIVILEGE_CAPTURE.DISABLE_CAPTURE (name
=>'Context_Capture');

PL/SQL procedure successfully completed.

SQL> exec SYS.DBMS_PRIVILEGE_CAPTURE.GENERATE_RESULT (name =>
'Context_Capture');

PL/SQL procedure successfully completed.

SQL> select  username, object_owner, object_name, obj_priv, used_role
    from   dba_used_objprivs
    where  username ='HR_MANAGER';
```

USERNAME	OBJECT_OWN	OBJECT_NAM	OBJ_PRIV	USED_ROLE
HR_MANAGER	HR	EMPLOYEE	SELECT	ROLE_HR
HR_MANAGER	HR	EMPLOYEE	INSERT	ROLE_HR

Figure 32.25   Generate capture result.

32.10   REDACTION

Redaction is a security feature which allows a user to hide data of a column from other users.

We will create two users "sales_manager" and "sales_rep" and a table named "tbl_sales" owned by "sales_manager" schema (see Figure 32.26). The table "tbl_sales" will have a column named "margin" which should be visible to "sales_manager" only. Although both users will have access to all the table columns, but "sales_rep" will not be able to view the value in "margin" column.

```
SQL> conn system_pdb1/system_pdb1@localhost:1522/pdb1 as sysdba
Connected.
SQL> startup;
Pluggable Database opened.
SQL>create user sales_manager identified by sales_manager;
SQL>grant connect,resource to sales_manager;
SQL> alter user sales_manager quota 100M on users;
SQL> create user sales_rep identified by sales_rep;
User created.
SQL> grant connect,resource to sales_rep;
Grant succeeded.
SQL> alter user sales_rep quota 100M on users;
User altered.
SQL> grant execute on dbms_redact to sales_manager;
```

Figure 32.26   Creating environment.

We have given execute privilege on package "dbms_redact" to sales_manager so that he can apply policy to hide value in column "margin" from sales_rep user. In Figure 32.27, SALES_MANAGER user is creating TBL_SALES table.

```
SQL> conn sales_manager/sales_manager@localhost:1522/pdb1orcl12c;
Connected.
SQL> create table tbl_sales (product_id number,product_desc varchar2(25),
      price number, margin number);
SQL> insert into tbl_sales values (1,'Samsung LED TV 24 inch',20000,2000);
1 row created.
SQL> insert into tbl_sales values (2,'Samsung LED TV 32 inch',30000,5000);
1 row created.
SQL> select * from tbl_sales;
```

PRODUCT_ID	PRODUCT_DESC	PRICE	MARGIN
1	Samsung LED TV 24 inch	20000	2000
2	Samsung LED TV 32 inch	30000	5000

```
SQL>grant select on tbl_sales to sales_rep;
Grant succeeded.
```

Figure 32.27 Creating tables.

As "sales_manager", we will create a Redaction Policy to hide the values in MARGIN column (see Figure 32.28).

```
BEGIN
DBMS_REDACT.add_policy(object_schema => "SALES_MANAGER",
object_name => "TBL_SALES",
policy_name => "SALES MARGIN INFO",
expression => 'SYS_CONTEXT("USERENV", "SESSION_USER") = "SALES_REP"',
column_name => "MARGIN",
function_type => dbms_redact.FULL
);
END;
/
```

Figure 32.28 Add redaction policy.

The policy says that if the user is SALES_REP, then hide the value in MARGIN column. Let us now connect as sales_rep and see the data in MARGIN column as shown in Figure 32.29.

```
SQL> conn sales_rep/sales_rep@localhost:1522/pdb1orcl12c;
Connected.
SQL> select * from sales_manager.tbl_sales;
```

PRODUCT_ID	PRODUCT_DESC	PRICE	MARGIN
1	Samsung LED TV 24 inch	20000	0
2	Samsung LED TV 32 inch	30000	0

Figure 32.29 SALES_REP accessing SALES_MANAGER.TBL_SALES.

If we want to add another column (say MAX_DISCOUNT) into redaction policy then we have to use the ALTER_POLICY procedure of DBMS_REDACT package as in Figure 32.30.

```
BEGIN
DBMS_REDACT.alter_policy(object_schema => 'SALES_MANAGER',
object_name => 'TBL_SALES',
policy_name => 'SALES MARGIN INFO',
action => dbms_redact.ADD_COLUMN,
column_name => 'MAX_DISCOUNT',
function_type => dbms_redact.FULL
);
END;
/
```

Figure 32.30   ALTER_POLICY.

We can remove the policy by using DROP_POLICY procedure as shown in Figure 32.31.

```
BEGIN
DBMS_REDACT.drop_policy(object_schema => 'SALES_MANAGER',
object_name => 'TBL_SALES',
policy_name => 'SALES MARGIN INFO'
);
END;
/
```

Figure 32.31   Drop policy.

Working More with CDB and PDBs

33.1 INTRODUCTION

In this chapter, we will learn more about working with CDB and PDB. We will cover various aspects like

- Start and Stop CDB
- Start and Stop PDB
- Start All PDBs
- Stop All PDBs
- Start All PDBs automatically on CDB startup
- Connecting to a PDB
- Creating tablespace in CDB
- Creating tablespace and data file in PDB
- Common and local users

33.1.1 Start and Stop CDB

When we create a Container database in windows, Oracle automatically creates a service named "OracleService{instance name}". Suppose we created a CDB named CDB1 then a service named "OracleServiceCDB1" will be automatically created. Go to "Control Panel" → "Administrative Tools" and double click "Services" as shown in Figure 33.1.

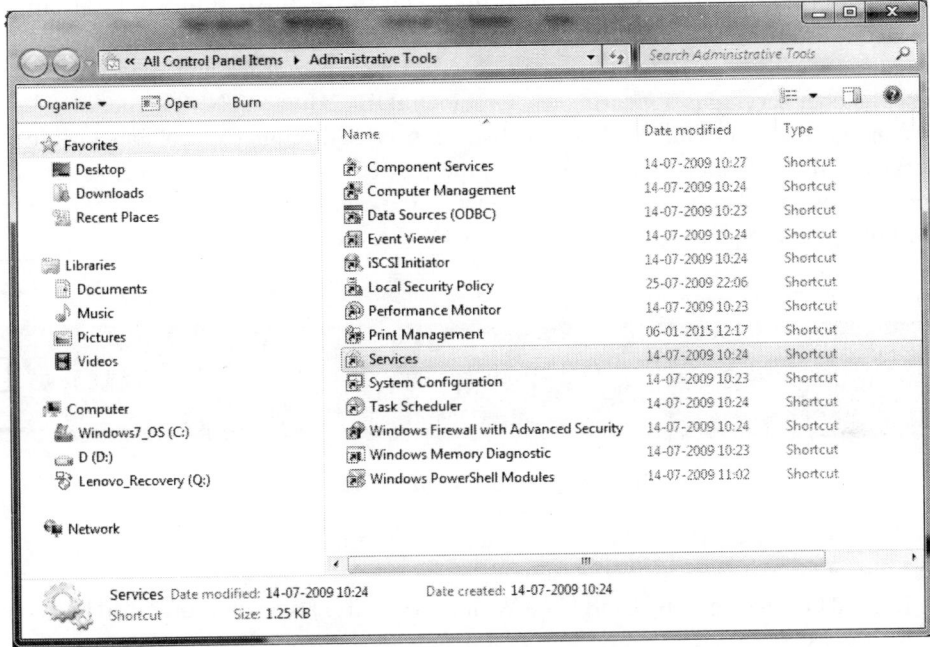

Figure 33.1 Services in control panel.

On running "Services" a window, as shown in Figure 33.2, will appear.

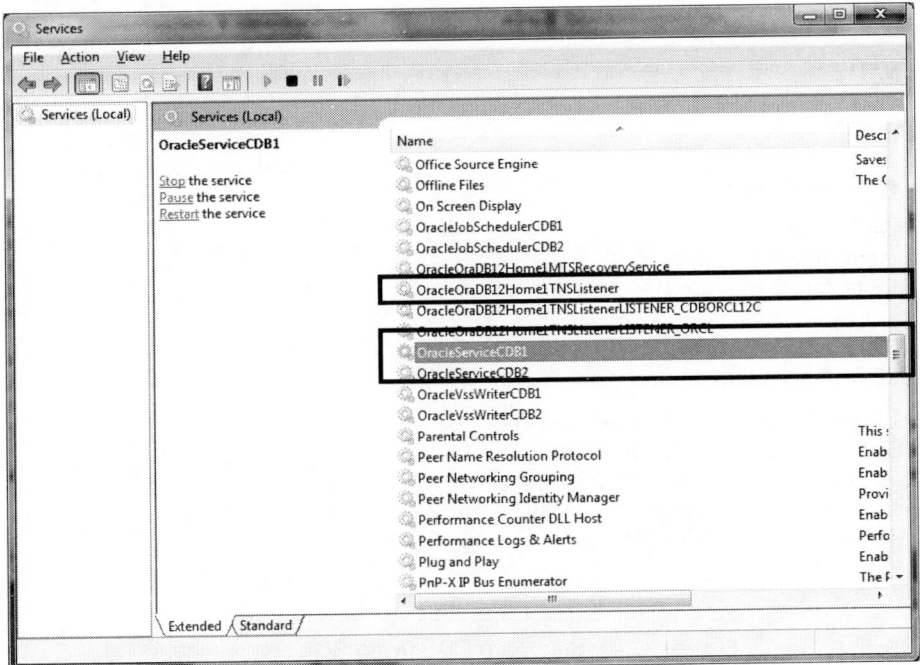

Figure 33.2 Oracle service.

Note that the installation of Container Database with name CDB1 appears as OracleServiceCDB1 in Services window. Moreover, whenever Oracle database is installed, a listener service is automatically created which actually listens on port 1521 for new database connections. In our case, listener service is appearing as "OracleOraDB12Home1TNSListener".

We can Start/Stop both the database and listener service through Control Panel. Right click the OracleServiceCDB1 and click "Start". Similarly the service can be stopped by using "Stop" option.

The services can also be started and stopped using command line interface. Go to windows command prompt and type the command as shown in Figure 33.3.

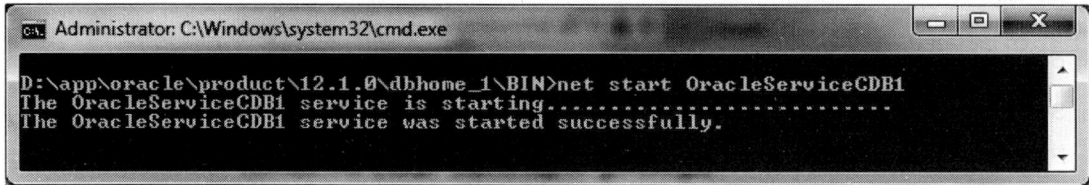

Figure 33.3   Start Oracle service.

Similarly, we can start/stop the Listener service by running "net start OracleOraDB12Home1TNSListener".

We learned how to start/stop CDB from Windows Control Panel and command line commands. We can also start/stop the CDB using SQL commands as shown in Figure 33.4.

```
SQL> conn system/system@localhost:1521/cdb1 as sysdba

Connected.

SQL> show con_name

CON_NAME
------------------------------
CDB$ROOT

SQL> shutdown immediate;

Database closed.
Database dismounted.
ORACLE instance shut down.

SQL> startup;

ORACLE instance started.

Total System Global Area 1653518336 bytes
Fixed Size                 2403304 bytes
Variable Size            989856792 bytes
Database Buffers         654311424 bytes
Redo Buffers               6946816 bytes
Database mounted.
Database opened.
```

Figure 33.4   Start/Stop CDB using SQL commands.

33.1.2 Start and Stop PDB

Start PDB

We will create a new PDB named "PDB3" in container database "CDB1". If the pluggable database is not existing already then create the same using commands as shown in Figure 33.5.

```
SQL> conn system/system@localhost:1521/cdb1 as sysdba

SQL> create pluggable database pdb3 admin user system_pdb3
identified by system_pdb3
roles=(DBA);

Pluggable Database Created.

SQL>select pdb_name, status from cdb_pdbs;

PDB_NAME   STATUS
----------  -------------
PDB$SEED    NORMAL
PDB3        NEW

The status of newly created PDB appears as NEW

SQL> select con_id, name, open_mode from v$pdbs;

   CON_ID     NAME              OPEN_MODE
--------------  --------------------  -----------------------
      2       PDB$SEED          READ ONLY
      3       PDBORCL           MOUNTED
      4       PDB3              MOUNTED

The mode is shown as "MOUNTED" which means the PDB is created but no operation can be
performed. When database is started the mode changes to "READ WRITE".

We can view the physical location of data files by querying v$datafile data dictionary
SQL> select name from v$datafile where con_id=4;
NAME
-------------------------------------------------------------
D:\APP\ORACLE\ORADATA\CDB1\F5C02A8A66624C5886BDA1BFF452F890\DATAFILE\
O1_MF_SYSTM_BV8SQJ0S_.DBF

D:\APP\ORACLE\ORADATA\CDB1\F5C02A8A66624C5886BDA1BFF452F890\DATAFILE\
O1_MF_SYSAUX_BV8SQJ1R_.DBF

Now we will change the session from CDB1 to PDB3.

SQL> alter session set container=pdb3;

Session altered.
SQL> show con_name

CON_NAME
------------------------------
PDB3
```

Contd...

```
"STARTUP" command starts the database in "READ WRITE" mode.

SQL> startup;
Pluggable Database opened.

SQL> select con_id, name, open_mode from v$pdbs;

   CON_ID NAME                    OPEN_MODE
---------- ------------------------------ ----------
      4   PDB3                    READ WRITE
```

Figure 33.5   Creating PDB.

Stopping PDB

To stop PDB we can use the "SHUTDOWN IMMEDIATE" command if already connected to the PDB as shown in Figure 33.6.

```
SQL> show con_name

CON_NAME
------------------------------
PDB3

SQL> shutdown immediate;
Pluggable Database closed.
```

Figure 33.6   Stop PDB.

Alternatively, if we are connected as DBA of Container Database, we can use the "ALTER PLUGGABLE DATABASE" command as shown in Figure 33.7.

```
SQL> conn system/system@localhost:1521/cdb1 as sysdba
Connected.

SQL> alter pluggable database pdb3 close immediate;

Pluggable database altered.

SQL> select con_id,name,open_mode from v$pdbs;

   CON_ID NAME                    OPEN_MODE
---------- ------------------------------ ----------------------
      2 PDB$SEED                  READ ONLY
      3 PDBORCL                   MOUNTED
      4 PDB3                      MOUNTED
```

Figure 33.7   Stop PDB as DBA of container database.

Start All PDBs with single command

When we start a Container Database all the PDBs within that CDB do not start automatically. We need to start each PDB individually. But oracle provides an "ALL OPEN" option with "ALTER PLUGGABLE DATABASE" command to start all the PDBs as shown in Figure 33.8.

```
SQL> conn system/system@localhost:1521/cdb1 as sysdba
Connected.

SQL> alter pluggable database all open;
Pluggable database altered.

SQL> select con_id,name,open_mode from v$pdbs;

     CON_ID            NAME                 OPEN_MODE
  -------------     ------------------    --------------------
        2            PDB$SEED             READ ONLY
        3            PDB1                 READ WRITE
        4            PDB3                 READ WRITE
```

Figure 33.8 Starting all PDBs.

Stop All PDBs

Just as we started all PDBs within a CDB, similarly, we can stop all PDBs by using "ALTER PLUGGABLE DATABASE" command as shown in Figure 33.9.

```
SQL> alter pluggable database all close immediate;

Pluggable database altered.

SQL> select con_id,name,open_mode from v$pdbs;
     CON_ID     NAME                 OPEN_MODE
  -------------  ------------------    --------------------
        2        PDB$SEED             READ ONLY
        3        PDB1                 MOUNTED
        4        PDB3                 MOUNTED
```

Figure 33.9 Stopping all PDBs.

33.1.3   Start All PDBs Automatically on Starting CDB

When we shutdown a CDB then all the PDBs are automatically closed. But when we start the CDB none of the PDBs are automatically started. We want to start all the PDBs automatically when we start the CDB. To do so we need to create a trigger named "Sys.After_Startup" as shown in Figure 33.10.

```
SQL> create or replace trigger Sys.After_Startup after startup on database
   begin
     execute immediate 'alter pluggable database all open';
   end After_Startup;
   /

Trigger created.
```

Figure 33.10 Trigger to start all PDBs automatically.

Once the trigger is created let us first shutdown CDB1 and start it again to see the impact of trigger and check whether all PDBs started automatically or not. Refer Figure 33.11.

```
SQL>show con_name

CON_NAME
-------------------------------
CDB$ROOT

SQL> startup;
ORACLE instance started.

Total System Global Area 1653518336 bytes
Fixed Size                2403304 bytes
Variable Size             989856792 bytes
Database Buffers          654311424 bytes
Redo Buffers              6946816 bytes
Database mounted
Database opened

SQL> select con_id,name,open_mode from v$pdbs;
   CON_ID    NAME         OPEN_MODE
-------------- --------------- ---------------------
      2       PDB$SEED     READ ONLY
      3       PDB1         READ WRITE
      4       PDB3         READ WRITE
```

Figure 33.11 Status of PDBs.

All the PDBs are automatically started in "READ WRITE" mode because of the trigger.

33.1.4 Connecting to a PDB

We can connect to the PDB using "ALTER SESSION" command as shown in Figure 33.12.

```
SQL> conn system/system@localhost:1521/cdb1 as sysdba
Connected.
SQL> alter session set container=pdb3;
Session altered.
SQL> show con_name
CON_NAME
------------------------------
PDB3
```

Figure 33.12   Connect to PDB using ALTER SESSION.

We can directly connect to the PDB using EZCONNECT command as shown in Figure 33.13

```
SQL> conn pdb1_system/pdb1_system@localhost:1521/pdb1;
Connected.
```

Figure 33.13   EZCONNECT command.

33.1.5   Creating Teblespace in CDB

CDBs and PDBs store data in their respective data files which reside on hard disk. Oracle organizes space allocated to a database using logical structure called tablespaces which in turn refer to the physically stored data files.

Let us see the already existing tablespaces and the corresponding data files. Refer Figure 33.14.

```
SQL> conn system/system@localhost:1521/cdb1 as sysdba
Connected.

SQL> select tablespace_name, con_id from cdb_tablespaces where con_id=1;

TABLESPACE_NAME                CON_ID
------------------------------ --------------
SYSTEM                              1
SYSAUX                              1
UNDOTBS1                            1
TEMP                                1
USERS                               1
SQL> select file_name from cdb_data_files where con_id=1;
FILE_NAME
-----------------------------------------------------------------
D:\APP\ORACLE\ORADATA\CDB1\DATAFILE\O1_MF_SYSTEM_BTHQO2PF_.DBF
D:\APP\ORACLE\ORADATA\CDB1\DATAFILE\O1_MF_SYSAUX_BTHQLPT6_.DBF
D:\APP\ORACLE\ORADATA\CDB1\DATAFILE\O1_MF_UNDOTBS1_BTHQQT3D_.DBF
D:\APP\ORACLE\ORADATA\CDB1\DATAFILE\O1_MF_USERS_BTHQQRCR_.DBF
```

Figure 33.14   Tablespaces and data files of CDB.

In Figure 33.15 we have created a new tablespace and associated it to the physical files on hard disk for the CDB.

```
SQL> conn system/system@localhost:1521/cdb1 as sysdba
Connected.

create tablespace cdb1_tbsp_new datafile
'D:\app\oracle\oradata\cdb1\datafile\cdb1_datafile_new.dbf' size 10M;
Tablespace created.

SQL> select tablespace_name, con_id from cdb_tablespaces where con_id=1;

TABLESPACE_NAME                  CON_ID
-------------------------------  -----------
SYSTEM                              1
SYSAUX                              1
UNDOTBS1                            1
TEMP                                1
USERS                               1
CDB1_TBSP_NEW                       1

6 rows selected.
```

Figure 33.15   Creating tablespace and associating it to a datafile.

We can verify the creation of new data file in the folder 'D:\app\oracle\oradata\cdb1\datafile\' as shown in Figure 33.16.

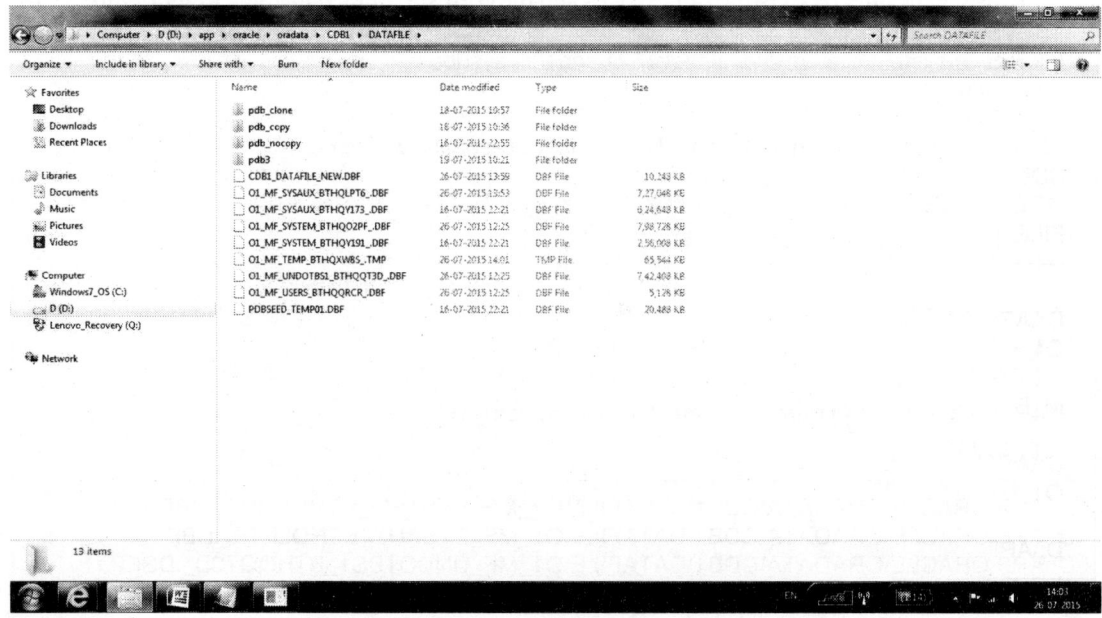

Figure 33.16   Location of datafile on windows folder.

33.1.6   Creating Tablespace and Data File in PDB

The procedure is same as that for CDB and is listed in Figure 33.17.

```
SQL> alter session set container=pdb3;

Session altered.

SQL>
SQL> create tablespace pdb3_tbsp_new datafile
'D:\app\oracle\oradata\CDB1\DATAFILE\pdb3\pdb3_datafile_new.dbf' size 10M;

Tablespace created.

SQL> conn system/system@localhost:1521/cdb1 as sysdba
Connected.

SQL> select con_id,name from v$pdbs;

   CON_ID        NAME
-------------   ----------------------
     2          PDB$SEED
     3          PDB1
     6          PDB3

SQL> select tablespace_name, con_id from cdb_tablespaces where con_id=6;

   TABLESPACE_NAME              CON_ID
--------------------------------   --------------
     SYSTEM                         6
     SYSAUX                         6
     TEMP                           6
     PDB3_TBSP_NEW                  6

SQL> select file_name from cdb_data_files where con_id=6;

FILE_NAME
--------------------------------------------------------------------------------

D:\APP\ORACLE\ORADATA\CDB1\F5C02A8A66624C5886BDA1BFF452F890\DATAFILE\
O1_MF_SYSTE

M_BV8SQJ0S_.DBF

D:\APP\ORACLE\ORADATA\CDB1\F5C02A8A66624C5886BDA1BFF452F890\DATAFILE\
O1_MF_SYSAUX_BV8SQJ1R_.DBF

D:\APP\ORACLE\ORADATA\CDB1\DATAFILE\PDB3\PDB3_DATAFILE_NEW.DBF
```

Figure 33.17   Creating tablespace and datafile for PDB.

We can verify the addition of new data file in the folder
D:\app\oracle\oradata\CDB1\DATAFILE\pdb3 as shown in Figure 33.18.

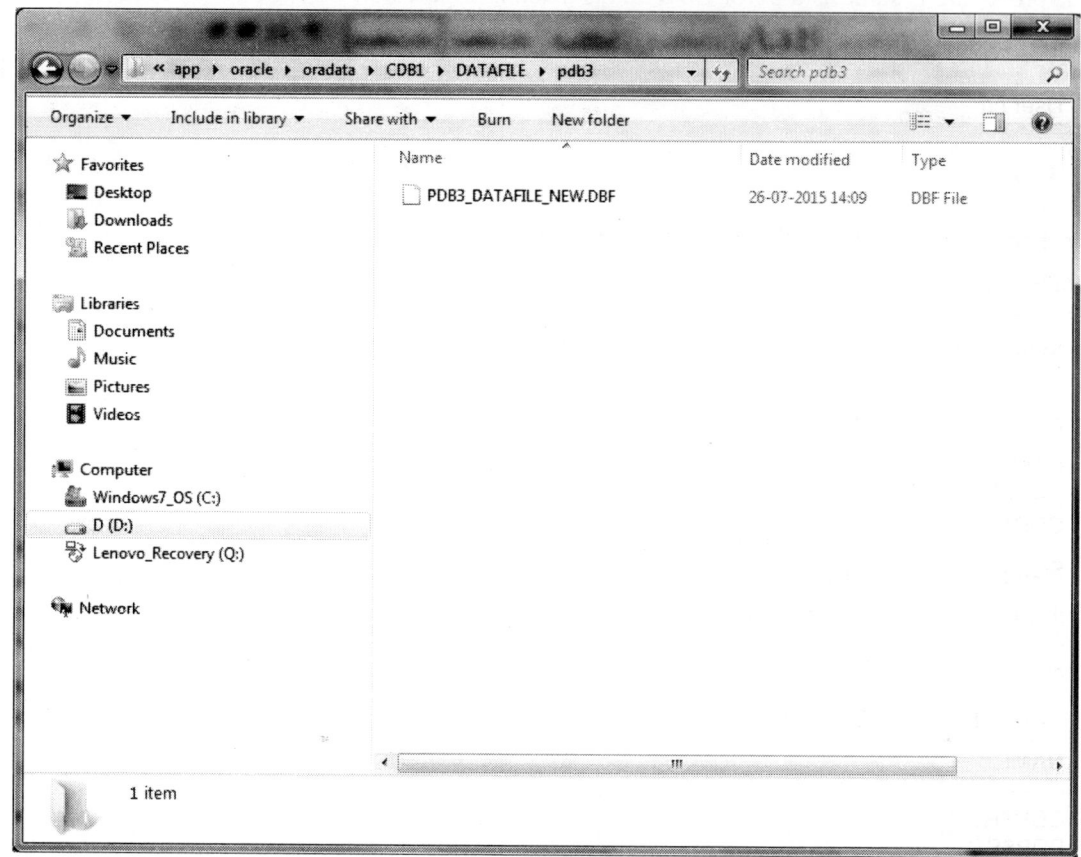

Figure 33.18   Physical location of datafiles.

33.1.7 Common and Local Users

Prior to Oracle 12c database there was no concept of common and local users. But due to multi-tenant architecture (Container and Pluggable databases) of Oracle 12c, the concept of common and local users has been introduced.

Common user: A common user is created in CDB and is automatically replicated to all PDBs (except SEED PDB). The common user name must start with C##.

Local user: A local user is created in a PDB and has access to that specific PDB only.
     Now, we will create a COMMON user "satish" in CDB1 (see Figure 33.19).

```
SQL> SQL> conn system/system@localhost:1521/cdb1 as sysdba
Connected.

SQL> create user c##satish identified by asnani container=all;

User created.
```

Figure 33.19   Create COMMON user.

Finding Container ID for CDB and PDBs

Oracle12c assigns a zero ID to the Global Database Name and the corresponding instance is also assigned the same ID. We can find the container ID from the dynamic data dictionary view v$containers as in Figure 33.20.

```
SQL> select name, cdb, con_id from v$database;

NAME          CDB       CON_ID
---------     -------   --------------
CDB1          YES       0

SQL> select instance_name, con_id from v$instance;

INSTANCE_NAME        CON_ID
-----------------------   ------------
cdb1                     0

SQL> select name, con_id from v$containers;

NAME                      CON_ID
-------------------------   ------------
CDB$ROOT                  1
PDB$SEED                  2
PDB1                      3
PDB3                      6

4 rows selected.
```

Figure 33.20   Finding Container ID.

Figure 33.21 shows the method to find out whether the common user c##satish has been created in the CDB and all PDBs.

```
SQL> select username, common, con_id from cdb_users where username like 'C##%';

USERNAME       COM    CON_ID
-----------------   --------   --------------
C##SATISH       YES    1
C##SATISH       YES    3
C##SATISH       YES    6
```

Figure 33.21   COMMON user.

Note that the common user has been created in the CDB$ROOT, PDB1, PDB3, but not the seed PDB PDB$SEED.

Now, before the common user c##satish can connect to the CDB$ROOT he must be granted CONNECT and RESOURCE privilege. Figure 33.22 shows the connection string for COMMON user in CDB.

```
SQL> conn system/system@localhost:1521/cdb1 as sysdba
Connected.

SQL> grant connect, resource to c##satish;

Grant succeeded.

SQL> conn c##satish/asnani@localhost:1521/cdb1

Connected.
SQL> create table temp(a number);

Table created.
```

Figure 33.22   COMMON user connecting to CDB.

Now, since "c##satish" user is a COMMON user, therefore, he can connect to all the PDBs within the CDB. Common user "c##satish" can connect to the PDB only, if he has been granted the CONNECT and RESOURCE role by the DBA of CDB. CONNECT role is required so that the user can connect to the database. RESOURCE role is assigned so that the user can create objects like tables, views, etc. Figure 33.23 shows how to grant privileges and syntax to connect to PDB.

```
SQL> conn system_pdb1/system_pdb1@localhost:1521/pdb1 as sysdba

Connected.

SQL> grant connect, resource to c##satish;

Grant succeeded.

SQL> conn c##satish/asnani@localhost:1521/pdb1

Connected.
```

Figure 33.23   COMMON user connecting to PDB.

Let us now create a local user named "mishkin" in pluggable database PDB1. The local user has access to the specific PDB in which it has been created and cannot connect to CDB or other PDBs as shown in Figure 33.24.

```
SQL> conn system_pdb1/system_pdb1@localhost:1521/pdb1 as sysdba
Connected.
SQL> create user mishkin identified by gudu;

User created.

SQL> grant connect, resource to mishkin;

Grant succeeded.

SQL> conn mishkin/gudu@localhost:1521/pdb1
Connected.
SQL> conn mishkin/gudu@localhost:1521/cdb1
ERROR:
ORA-01017: invalid username/password; logon denied

Warning: You are no longer connected to ORACLE.
```

Figure 33.24   LOCAL user.

"mishkin" user can connect to PDB1, but cannot connect to CDB1.

Plugging and Unplugging PDBs

34.1 INTRODUCTION

Oracle 12c offers a facility wherein we can unplug a PDB from its Container DB and plug it into another container DB. We will create two container databases named CDB1 and CDB2 and three pluggable databases named PDB_COPY, PDB_NOCOPY and PDB_CLONE within CDB1. There are three methods to plug a PDB into a CDB, and therefore, we will create three PDBs. Later in this chapter we will unplug these PDBs from CDB1 and plug then into CDB2.

34.2 CREATING CDB

Oracle database comes with a utility called "DBCA" (database configuration assistant) which can be used to create new database—container/pluggable or remove any existing database. To invoke DBCA, browse to D:\app\oracle\product\12.1.0\dbhome_1\BIN and run dbca.exe as shown in Figure 34.1.

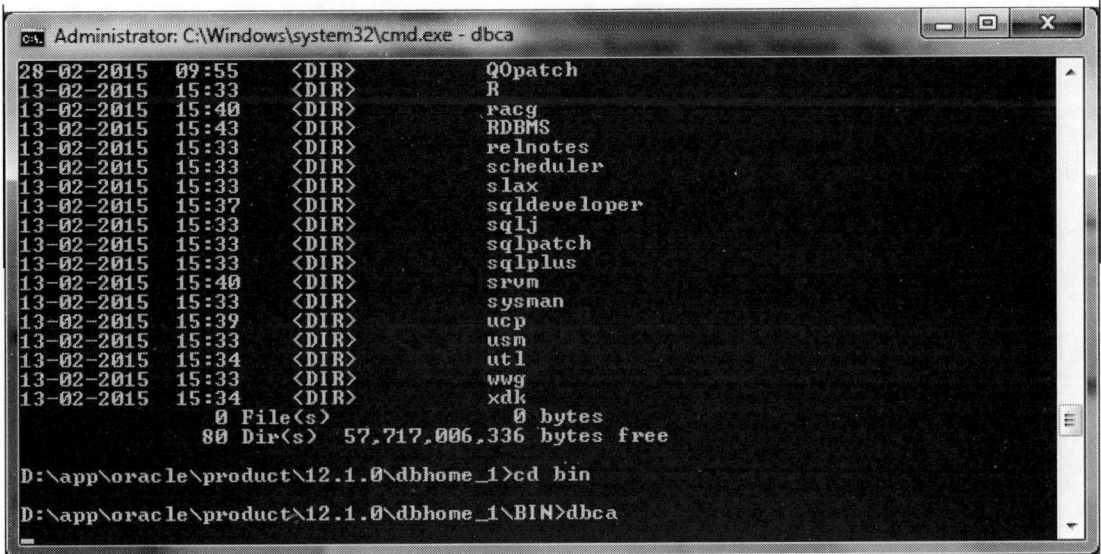

Figure 34.1   Running DBCA utility.

A screen will appear as shown in Figure 34.2.

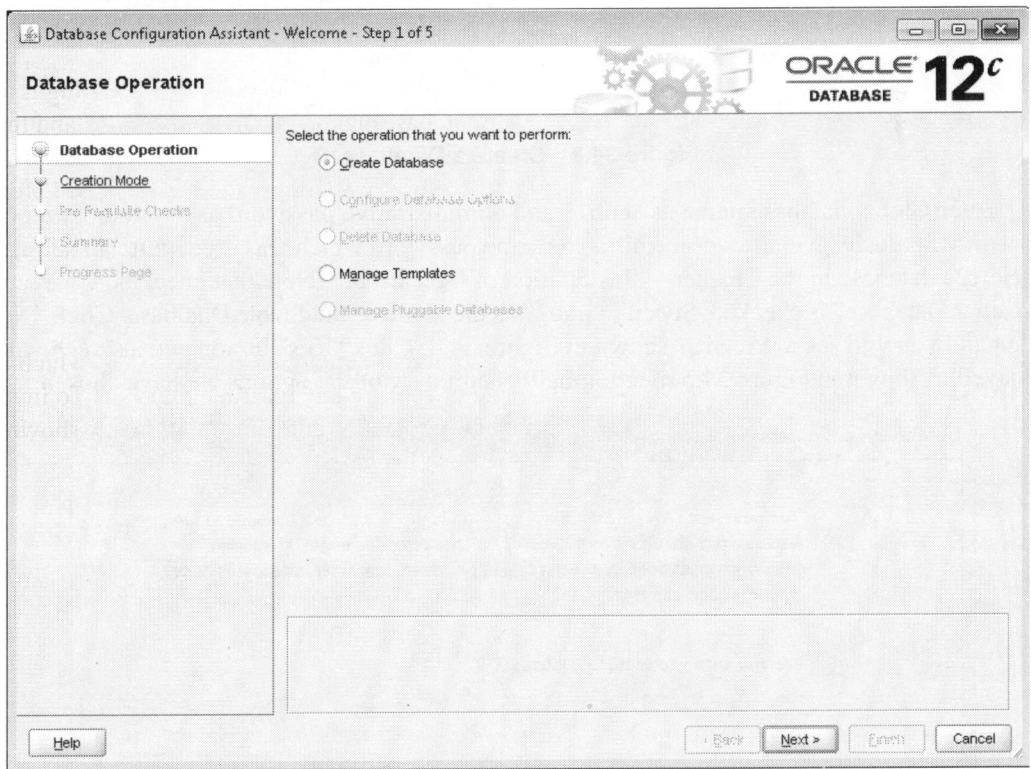

Figure 34.2   DBCA first screen.

Select "Create Database" and click "Next" button and you will see screen as shown in Figure 34.3.

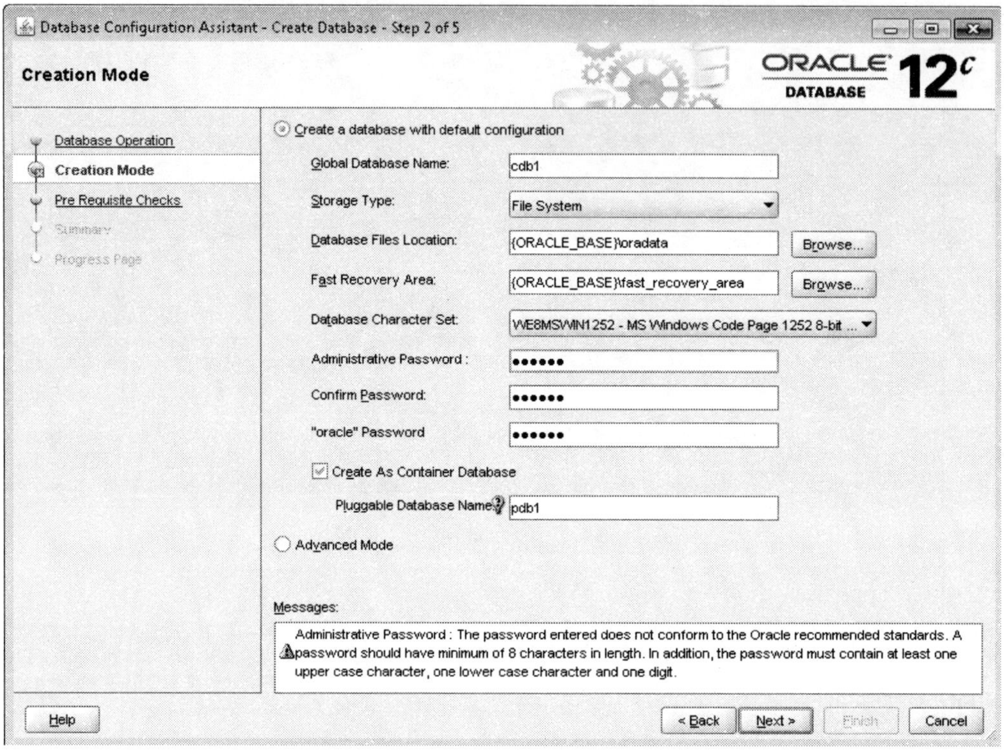

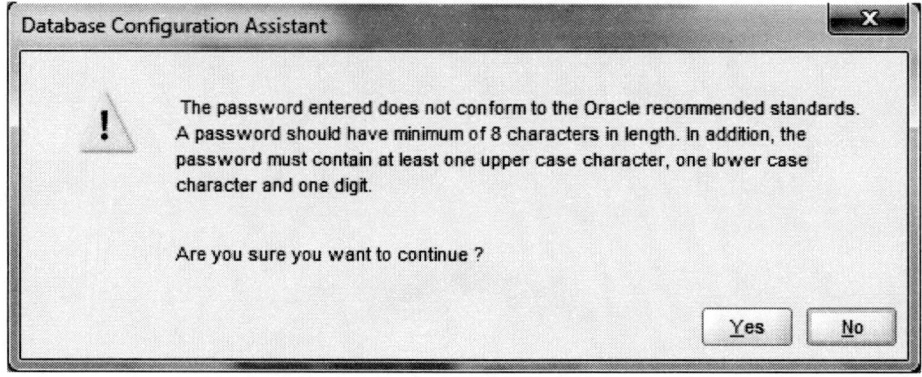

Figure 34.3   Create a Database.

Enter Global database name as "cdb1" and administrative password as "system". Enter the password of "oracle" windows user (this is the same password which was used while installing the Oracle 12c database in the Chapter – "Installation of Oracle 12c". Note that check box "Create as Container Database" is checked. Specify "pdb1" as the name of Pluggable Database. Click "Next" button and you will see a screen as shown in Figure 34.4. Click "Yes" button and a screen will be displayed as shown in Figure 34.5 mentioning the summary of the options we have chosen.

Figure 34.4   Password confirmation.

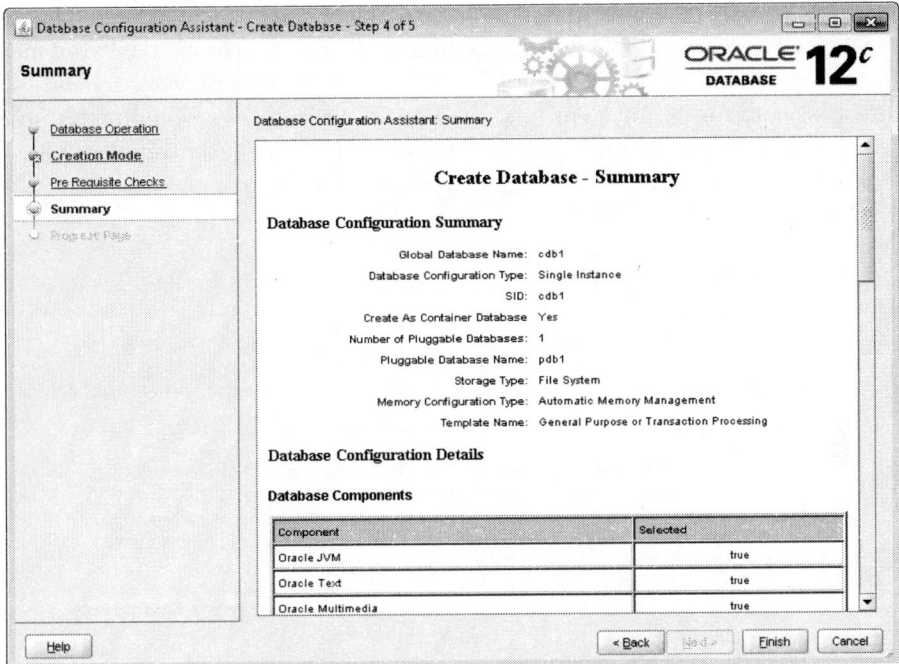

Figure 34.5   Create database summary.

Click "Finish" and you can view the progress of the Oracle installation as shown in Figure 34.6.

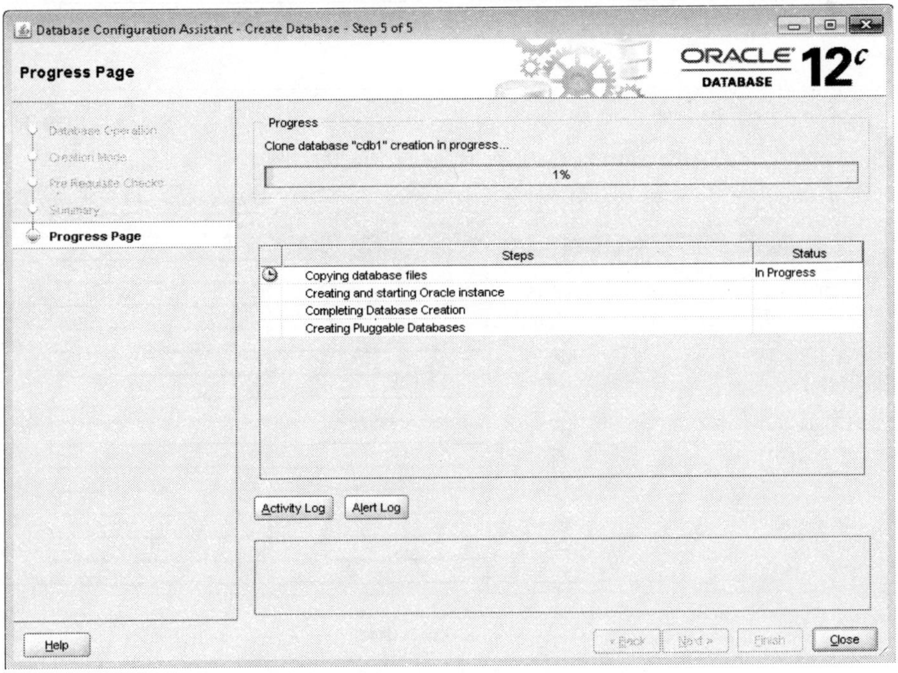

Figure 34.6   Installation progress.

The installation may take several minutes depending on the PC configuration. Installation on Intel Core i5 2.67 GHz PC with 4 GB RAM took around 10 minutes. Now, a password management screen will be displayed as shown in Figure 34.7. Click on "Password Management" screen and specify some password for the "system" and "sys" user. As learners I would prefer you keep the "system" password for "system" user and "sys" password for "sys" user (Figure 34.8).

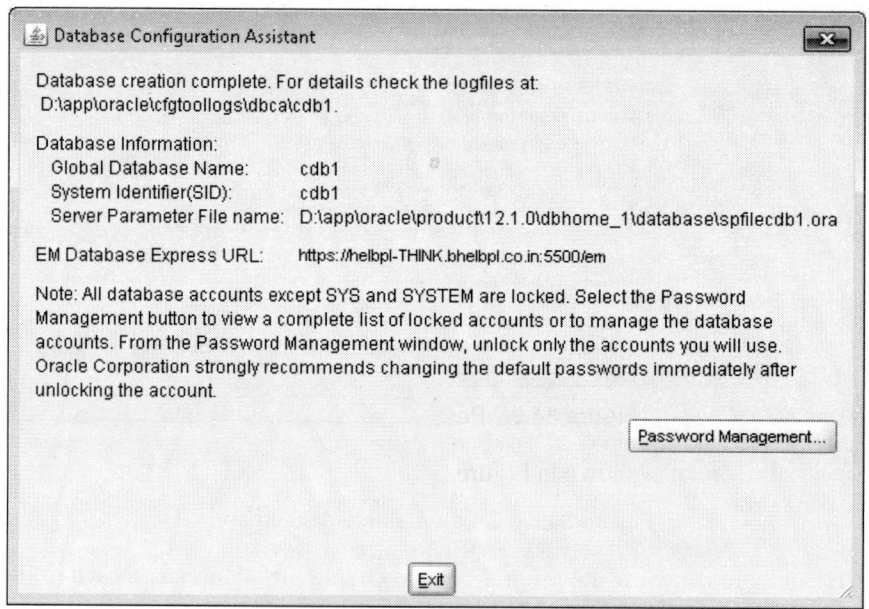

Figure 34.7   Password management.

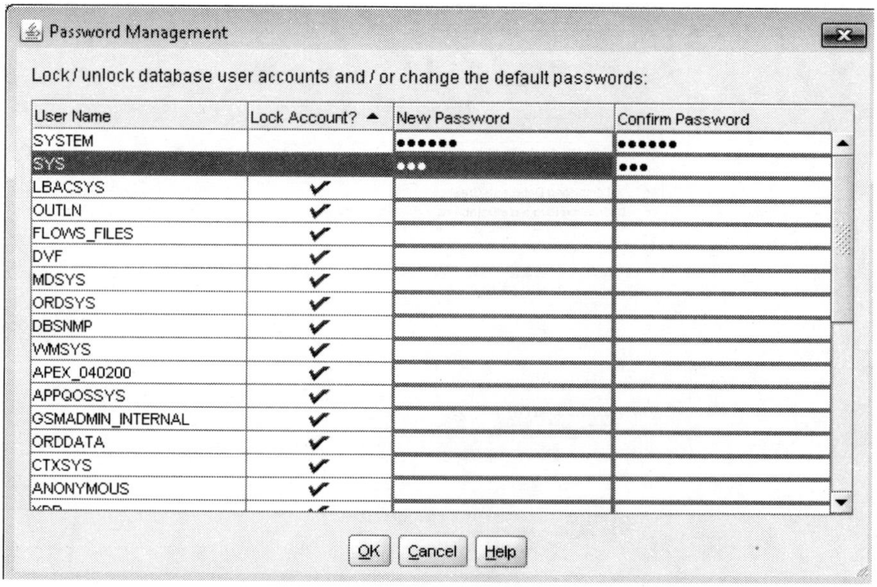

Figure 34.8   Password for "system" and "sys" user.

Click "OK" button and Oracle will ask confirmation for keeping too simple password as in Figure 34.9.

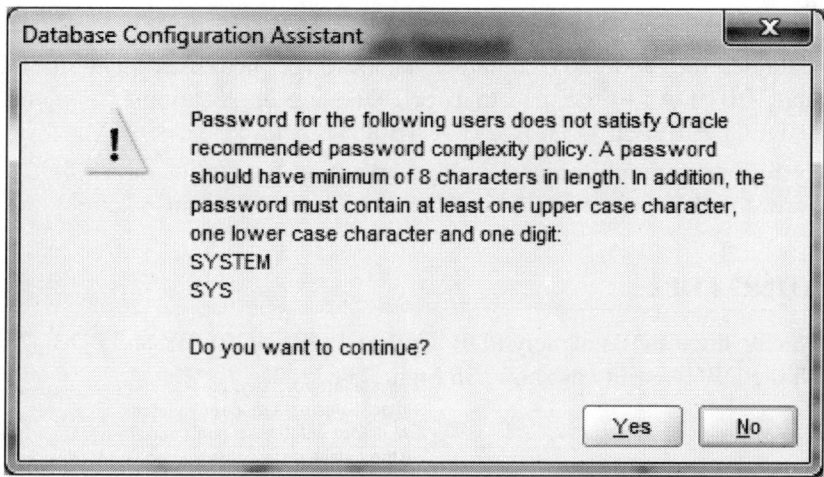

Figure 34.9 Password complexity.

Click "Yes" and screen as shown in Figure 34.10 will appear. Click "Close" and the software installation is complete.

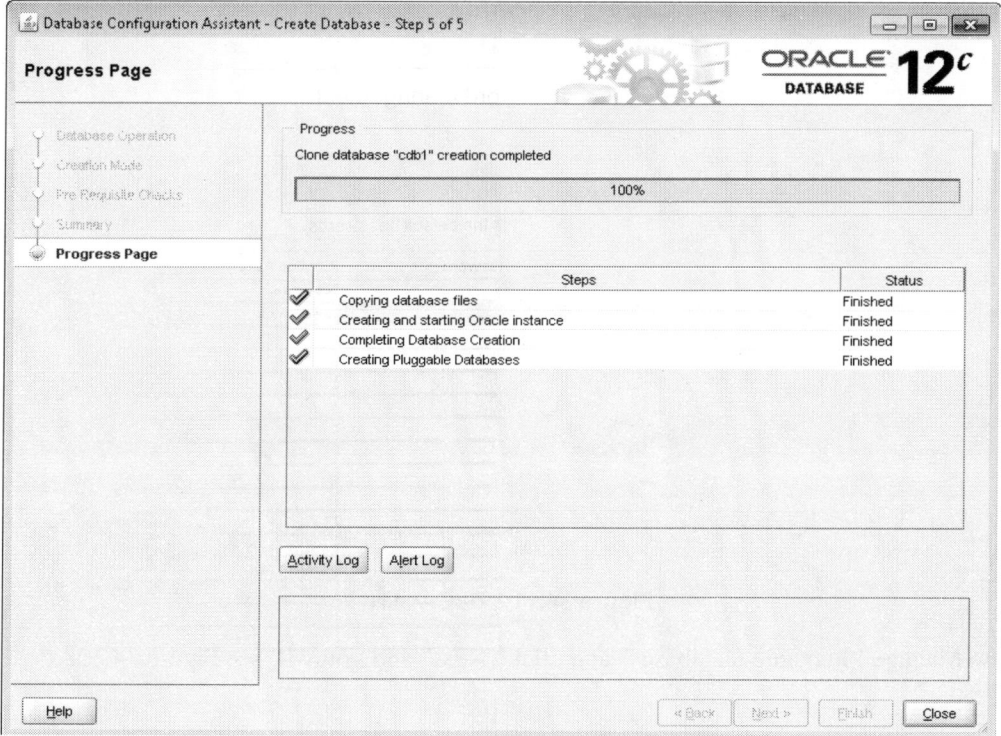

Figure 34.10 Installation completion.

Click "Close" to end the installation.

Again launch DBCA utility and create a container database named "CDB2" with a pluggable database "PDB1".

> **Note:** The datafiles for the CDB1 container database are located at location D:\app\oracle\oradata\CDB1\DATAFILE and that for PDB1 are at location D:\app\oracle\oradata\CDB1\DECE70B9F2C3453FB637F96AB6C542A0.
>
> Oracle follows internal folder naming convention for the location where datafiles for PDB are stored. This name will be different in case of your installation.

34.3 CREATING PDBs

Now, we will create three PDBs namely PDB_COPY, PDB_NOCOPY and PDB_CLONE within CDB1. Launch the DBCA utility as shown in Figure 34.11.

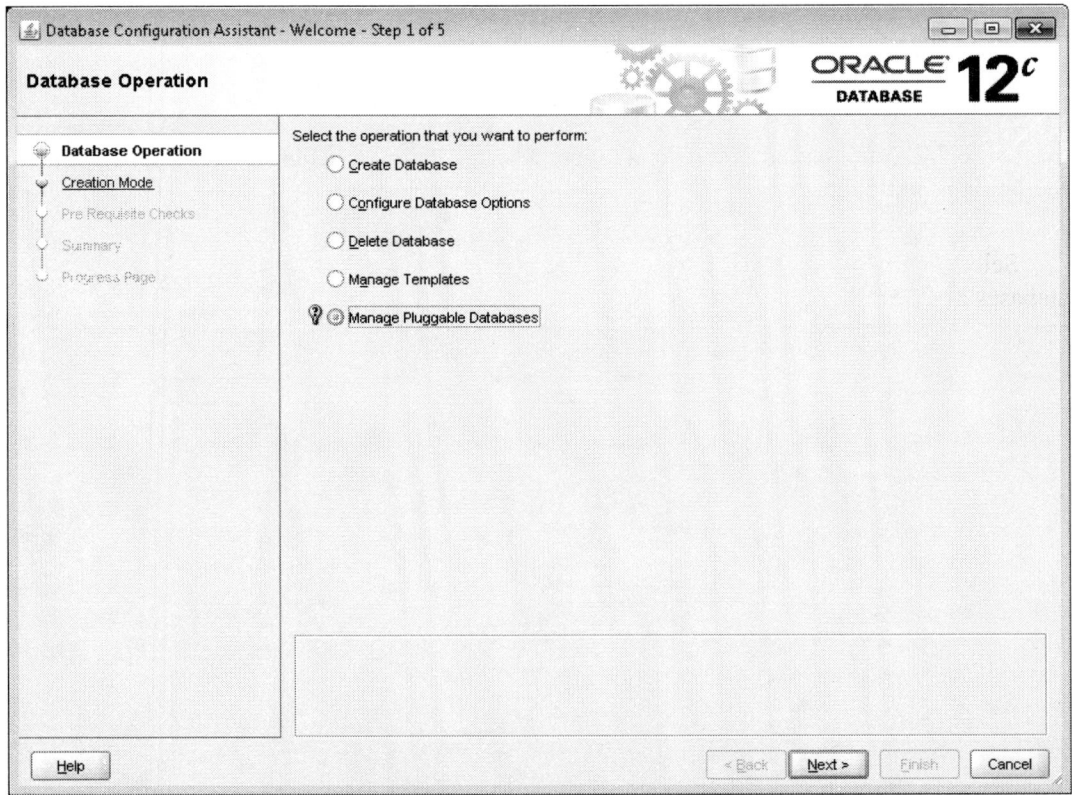

Figure 34.11 DBCA utility.

Select "Manage Pluggable Databases" and click "Next" and you will see Figure 34.12.

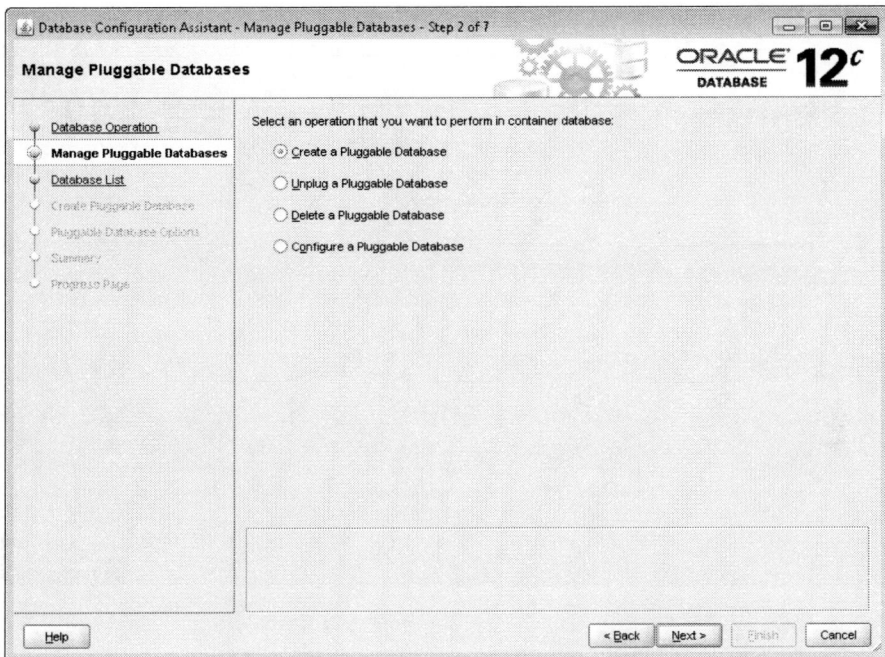

Figure 34.12   Manage pluggable database.

Select "Create a Pluggable Database" and click "Next". You will see a list of container databases as shown in Figure 34.13.

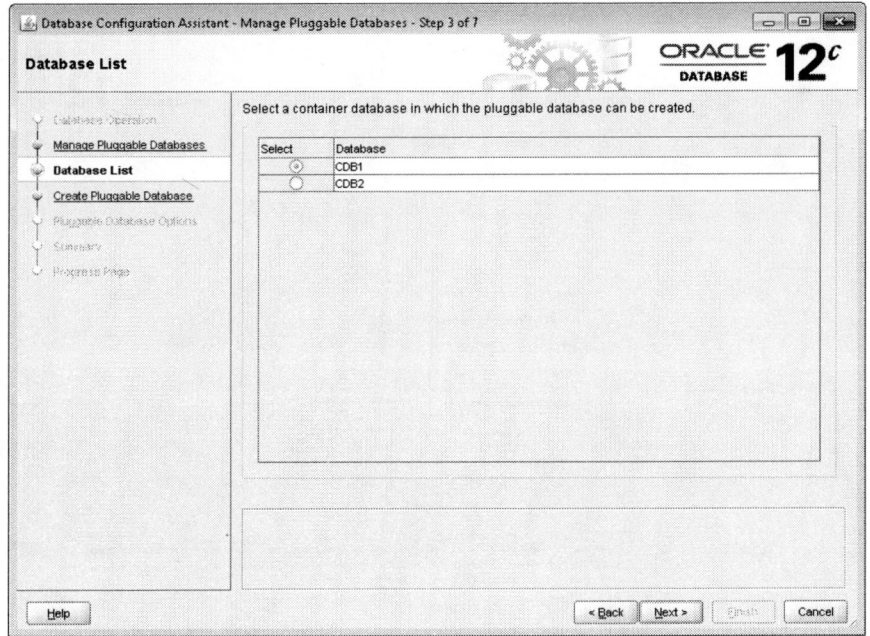

Figure 34.13   List of container databases.

Select "CDB1" and click "Next". A screen will appear as shown in Figure 34.14.

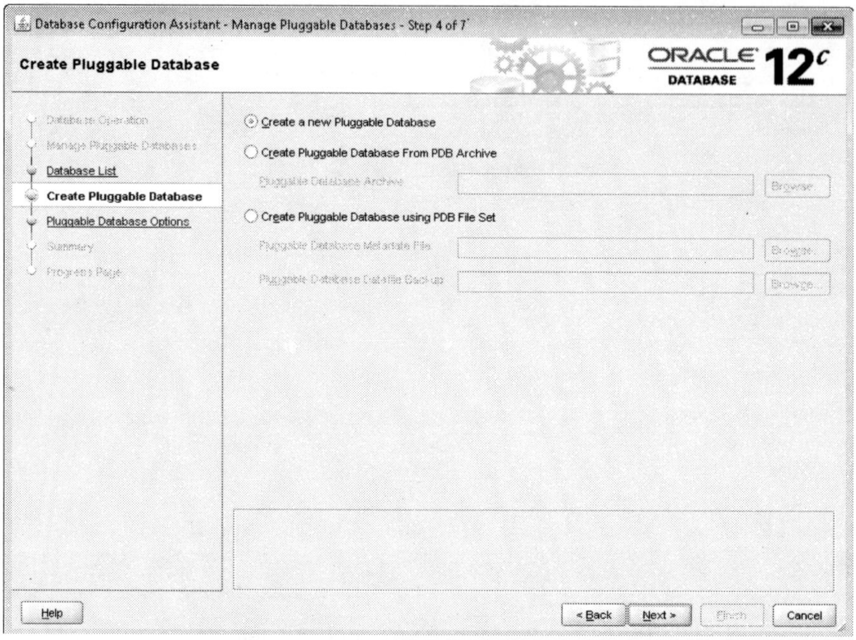

Figure 34.14 Create a pluggable database.

Select "Create a new Pluggable Database" and click "Next". You will see a list of options for creating pluggable database as shown in Figure 34.15.

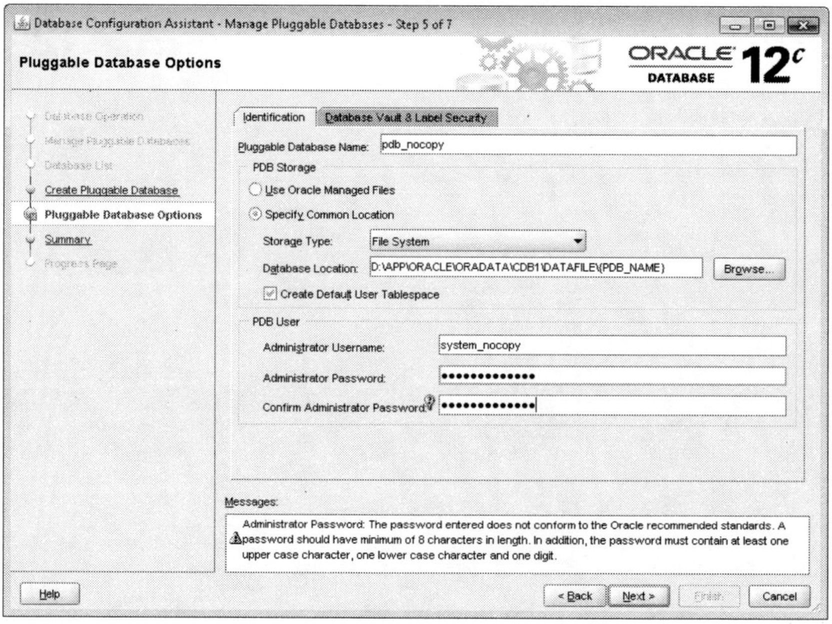

Figure 34.15 Pluggable database options.

Select "Specify Common Location" instead of "Use Oracle Managed Files". We have chosen this option so that we can specify the location of datafiles for the new PDB. On choosing "Use Oracle Managed Files", the oracle creates a folder for the PDB data files with its own internal naming convention which is not very intuitive. Specify "Administrative Username and password" as "system_nocopy". You can choose password of your choice. Click "Next" to view the summary of pluggable database to be created (Figure 34.16).

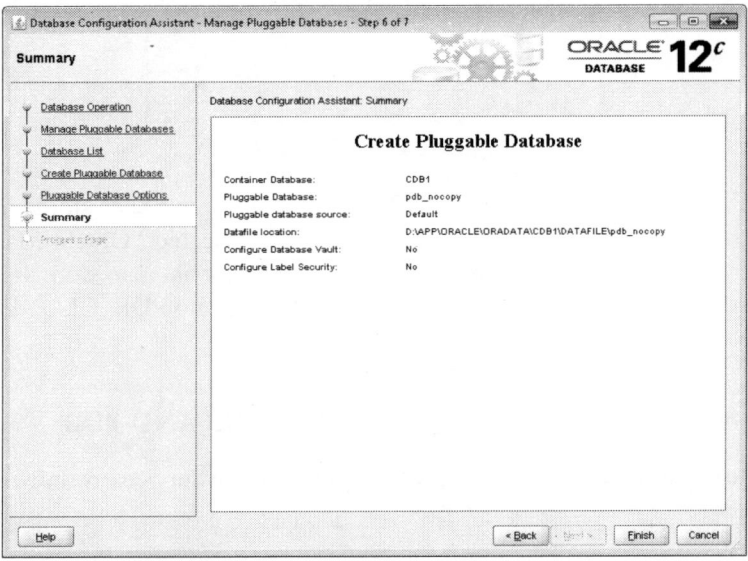

Figure 34.16   Pluggable database summary.

Click "Finish" and you will see the progress of pluggable database installation as shown in Figure 34.17.

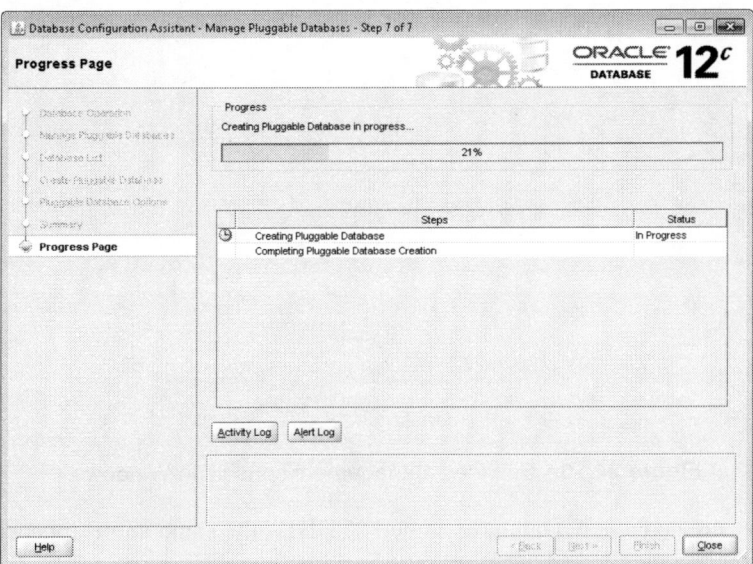

Figure 34.17   Pluggable database progress.

Finally you will see a popup windows showing successful creation of pluggable database as shown in Figure 34.18.

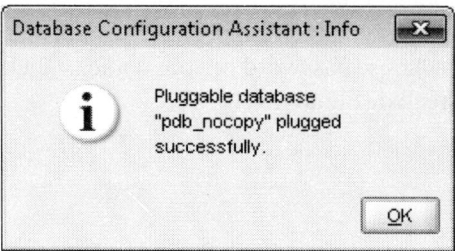

Figure 34.18 Success.

Note that all the datafiles for the new PDB "pdb_nocopy" have been stored in D:\app\oracle\ oradata\CDB1\DATAFILE\pdb_nocopy folder. If we had selected "Oracle Managed Files" in Figure 34.15 then oracle would have used its own unique folder name to store the data files.

Now, create two more pluggable databases PDB_COPY and PDB_CLONE in CDB1 using the DBCA utility.

34.4 STARTING ORACLE DATABASE SERVICE—CDB AND PDB

In Windows Go to Control Panel → Administrative Tools and run Services as shown in Figure 34.19.

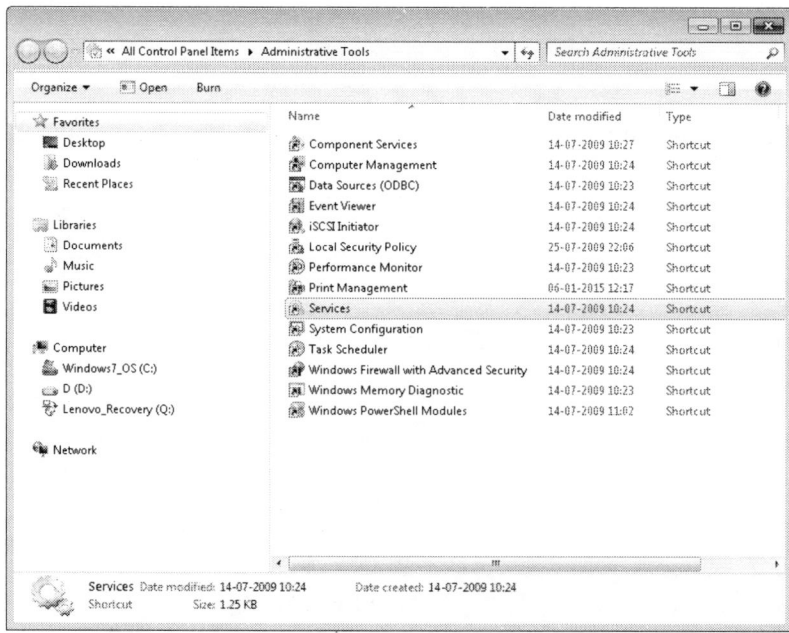

Figure 34.19 Services management console in Windows.

As we have created a new Database named "CDB1", the same name appears with the word "OracleServices" pre-appended in the Windows Services panel (Figure 34.20).

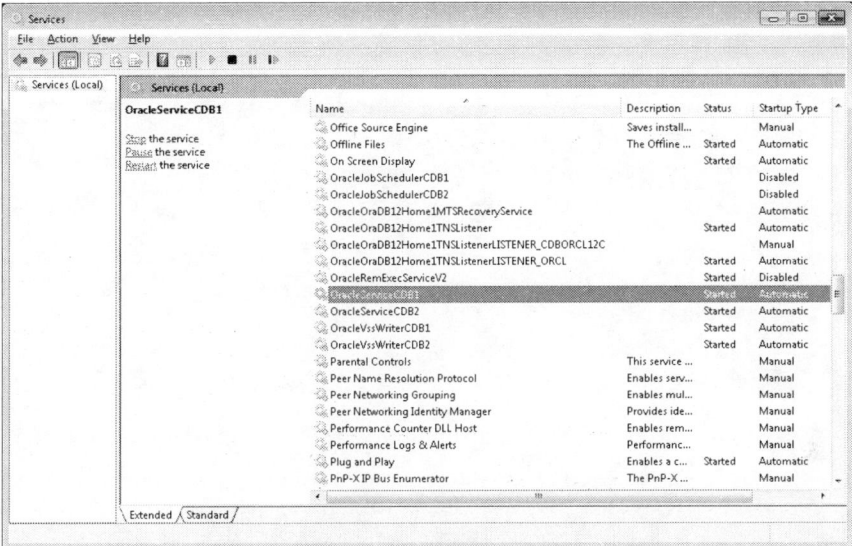

Figure 34.20   Starting Oracle service.

Right click the service name as shown in Figure 34.21 and click "Start".

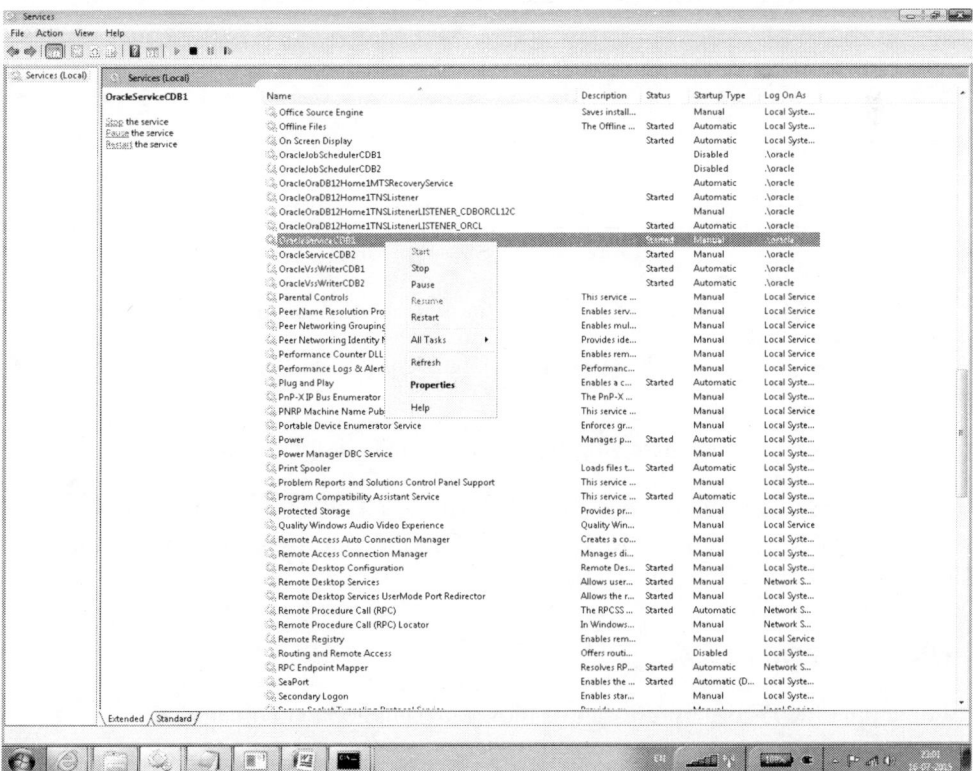

Figure 34.21   Starting Oracle service.

Now invoke SQL*Plus and login with SYSTEM user as shown in Figure 34.22.

Figure 34.22 Connecting to the new CDB.

Let us now start the PDB1 which is within the CDB1 container database (Figure 34.23).

```
SQL> alter session set container=pdb1;

Session altered.

SQL> startup;
Pluggable Database opened.
```

Figure 34.23 Starting PDB1.

The SYSTEM user of CDB1 can also login into the PDB1 as shown in Figure 34.24.

```
SQL> conn system/system@localhost:1521/pdb1 as sysdba
Connected.
```

Figure 34.24 System user logging to PDB1.

Now, we have two container databases CDB1 and CDB2. In CDB1 we have a pluggable database PDB_NOCOPY. Similar to PDB_NOCOPY, create two more pluggable databases PDB_COPY and PDB_CLONE in CDB1.

34.5 UNPLUG PDB

We need to unplug the PDB before it can be moved or plugged to another CDB.

Let us know unplug PDB_NOCOPY from CDB1.

It is necessary that we close the pluggable database before it is unplugged. We also need to generate an XML file for the PDB which will contain information about the tablespaces and data files. Figure 34.25 contains the commands to close the PDB and generate an XML file.

```
SQL> conn system/system@localhost:1521/cdb1 as sysdba
Connected.

SQL> alter pluggable database pdb_nocopy close immediate;

Pluggable database altered.

SQL> select name,open_mode from v$pdbs;

        NAME                    OPEN_MODE
------------------------    ----------------------
    PDB$SEED                    READ ONLY
    PDB_NOCOPY                  MOUNTED

SQL> alter pluggable database pdb_nocopy unplug into
'D:\app\oracle\oradata\pdb_nocopy.xml';

Pluggable database altered.
```

Figure 34.25   Close PDB and generate XML.

Open the XML file D:\app\oracle\oradata\pdb_nocopy.xml and see that it contains the location of physical datafiles - D:\APP\ORACLE\ORADATA\CDB1\DATAFILE\PDB_NOCOPY\

34.6   DROPPING PDB

Now we will DROP the PDB keeping the datafiles so that when we plug it into another CDB we can associate the same datafiles. In Figure 34.26 we are dropping the PDB without losing the datafiles.

```
SQL> drop pluggable database pdb_nocopy keep datafiles;

Pluggable database dropped.
```

Figure 34.26   Dropping PDB.

While dropping the PDB, we specified the clause KEEP DATAFILES because of which the data files exist in the specified folder.

34.7   CHECKING COMPATIBILITY OF THE PDB TO BE PLUGGED INTO ANOTHER CDB

Let us now check whether the PDB_NOCOPY is compatible with the container database CDB2 where we intend to plug it. We need to create a PL/SQL code as shown in Figure 34.27 to find the compatibility.

```
SQL> conn system/system@localhost:1521/cdb2 as sysdba
Connected.

Note that we are connecting to the CDB2 as sysdba where we want to plug in the PDB_NOCOPY

set serveroutput on

DECLARE
  compatible BOOLEAN := FALSE;
BEGIN
  compatible := DBMS_PDB.CHECK_PLUG_COMPATIBILITY(pdb_descr_file => D:\app\oracle\
oradata\ pdb_nocopy.xml');
  if compatible then
    DBMS_OUTPUT.PUT_LINE('Pluggable PDB_NOCOPY is compatible');
  else
    DBMS_OUTPUT.PUT_LINE('Pluggable PDB_NOCOPY is not compatible');
  end if;
END;
/

Pluggable PDB_NOCOPY is compatible

PL/SQL procedure successfully completed.
```

Figure 34.27   PDB compatibility.

34.8   PLUGGING THE PDB

There are three methods of plugging a PDB into another CDB.

1. Using NOCOPY method
2. Using COPY method
3. Using CLONE MOVE method

NOCOPY— In this method the PDB moves to the new CDB but the physical location of the datafiles remain the same as earlier.

COPY—We can specify a new physical location for the datafiles. The earlier datafiles will be copied to the new location.

CLONE MOVE—As the name suggests a new PDB will be created in another CDB while original PDB will also exist in its own parental CDB.

34.8.1   Plugging the PDB using NOCOPY Method

Now, we will create a new PDB 'PDB_NOCOPY_PLUG' in the CDB2 container database using NOCOPY method as shown in Figure 34.28.

```
SQL> conn system/system@localhost:1521/cdb2 as sysdba
Connected.

SQL> create pluggable database PDB_NOCOPY_PLUG using
   'D:\app\oracle\oradata\pdb_nocopy.xml'NOCOPY TEMPFILE REUSE;

Pluggable database created.

SQL> SQL> select NAME,OPEN_MODE from v$pdbs;

NAME                         OPEN_MODE
---------------------------- --------------------
PDB$SEED                      READ ONLY
PDB1                          MOUNTED
PDB_NOCOPY_PLUG               MOUNTED
```

Figure 34.28   Create PDB using NOCOPY.

Note that since we have used NOCOPY method, therefore, the location of datafiles remains the same D:\app\oracle\oradata\CDB1\DATAFILE\pdb_nocopy although the PDB_NOCOPY has moved to CDB2 as PDB_NOCOPY_PLUG.

34.8.2   Plugging the PDB using COPY Method

We will now move the PDB_COPY from CDB1 to CDB2. First we need to generate the XML file for unplugging PDB_COPY from CDB1 as shown in Figure 34.29.

```
SQL> conn system/system@localhost:1521/cdb1 as sysdba
Connected.
SQL> alter pluggable database pdb_copy close immediate;
Pluggable database altered.

SQL> select name,open_mode from v$pdbs;

NAME                         OPEN_MODE
---------------------------- ----------
PDB$SEED                      READ ONLY
PDB_COPY                      MOUNTED

SQL> alter pluggable database pdb_copy unplug into
'D:\app\oracle\oradata\pdb_copy.xml';
Pluggable database altered.
```

Figure 34.29   Closing and unplugging PDB.

Now, create a folder named PDB_COPY_PLUG within D:\app\oracle\oradata\CDB2\ where the copy of the files of the pluggable database PDB_COPY will be placed. Figure 34.30 shows the steps to plug a PDB using COPY option.

```
SQL> conn system/system@localhost:1521/cdb2 as sysdba
Connected.

SQL>create pluggable database pdb_copy_plug using 'D:\app\oracle\oradata\pdb_copy.xml'
COPY FILE_NAME_CONVERT=
(
'D:\app\oracle\oradata\CDB1\DATAFILE\pdb_copy',
'D:\app\oracle\oradata\CDB2\PDB_COPY_PLUG'
);
Pluggable database created.

SQL> select pdb_name, status from cdb_pdbs where pdb_name='PDB_COPY_PLUG';
PDB_NAME                       STATUS
----------------------------   -------------
PDB_COPY_PLUG                  NEW

SQL> select open_mode from v$pdbs where name='PDB_COPY_PLUG';

OPEN_MODE
-------------------
MOUNTED
```

Figure 34.30   Create PDB with COPY option.

As we have used the COPY method, therefore, all datafiles get copied into D:\app\oracle\ oradata\CDB2\PDB_COPY_PLUG folder.

34.8.3   Plugging the PDB using CLONE Method

We will now move the PDB_CLONE from CDB1 to CDB2. First we need to generate the XML file for unplugging PDB_CLONE from CDB1 as shown in Figure 34.31.

```
SQL> conn system/system@localhost:1521/cdb1 as sysdba
Connected.

SQL> alter pluggable database pdb_clone close immediate;

Pluggable database altered.

SQL> select name,open_mode from v$pdbs;

SQL> select name,open_mode from v$pdbs;

NAME                   OPEN_MODE
------------------     --------------------
PDB$SEED               READ ONLY
PDB1                   MOUNTED
PDB_COPY               MOUNTED
PDB_CLONE              MOUNTED

SQL> alter pluggable database pdb_clone unplug into 'D:\app\oracle\oradata\pdb_clone.xml';

Pluggable database altered.
```

Figure 34.31   Close PDB and generate XML.

Now, create a folder named PDB_CLONE_PLUG within D:\app\oracle\oradata\CDB2\ where the copy of the files of the pluggable database PDB_CLONE will be placed. Figure 34.32 shows commands to plug PDB using CLONE method.

```
SQL> conn system/system@localhost:1521/cdb2 as sysdba
Connected.

SQL> create pluggable database pdb_clone_plug
 AS CLONE using 'D:\app\oracle\oradata\pdb_clone.xml'
 MOVE
 FILE_NAME_CONVERT=
 (
 'D:\app\oracle\oradata\CDB1\DATAFILE\pdb_clone',
 'D:\app\oracle\oradata\CDB2\PDB_CLONE_PLUG'
 );
Pluggable database created.

SQL> select pdb_name, status from cdb_pdbs where pdb_name='PDB_CLONE_PLUG';
PDB_NAME             STATUS
--------------------    -------------

PDB_CLONE_PLUG      NEW

SQL> select open_mode from v$pdbs where name='PDB_CLONE_PLUG';

OPEN_MODE
----------
MOUNTED
```

Figure 34.32   Create PDB using CLONE method.

As we have used the CLONE method, therefore, all datafiles exist in both D:\app\oracle\oradata\CDB2\PDB_CLONE_PLUG and D:\app\oracle\oradata\CDB1\DATAFILE\pdb_clone folder.

Transaction Handling

35.1 INTRODUCTION

In today's environment, we are dealing with multi-user applications like Railway Reservation, Banking, etc. where several concurrent transactions are happening without any interference between them and maintaining the consistency of transactions. In case of Railway reservation, several individuals may be contesting for the same seat, but it never happens that the same seat gets allotted to two individuals. In banking system, when we transfer some amount from one account to another, the amount is first debited from the first account and then credited to the second account. Imagine a situation where the amount gets debited from the first account, but the second account is not credited. The database management system should be capable of identifying the failed step 2 and revert step 1 also.

Two terminologies namely Session and Transaction need to be understood before we proceed further.

Session

Whenever a user connects to the database through SQL Plus or SQL Developer, a unique session is created. Each session is allocated some space in RAM on Server defined by the configuration of the Oracle Database. A user say "scott" may create multiple sessions.

Transaction

A transaction is a logical unit of work which must be completed in entirety or may be failed in completeness. It is basically a group of related SQL commands which must be committed or rolled back as one unit of work. In the banking example, both the steps must happen or neither should happen to maintain the consistency of the database.

A session may comprise several transactions.

Beginning of a Transaction

In Oracle, a transaction begins when:

- Any DML (or a SET of DML) command(s) followed by commit or rollback
- A set of commands within BEGIN and END;

End of a Transaction

In Oracle, a transaction ends when:

- COMMIT or ROLLBACK is done
- Any DDL command is executed. Every DDL command executes auto COMMIT
- Any DCL command like GRANT is executed which also implies auto commit
- Disconnect from database (DISCONNECT, EXIT, QUIT)

35.2 UNDERSTANDING COMMIT AND ROLLBACK IN MULTI-USER ENVIRONMENT

To understand handling of concurrent transactions, the impact of COMMIT and ROLLBACK must be clear. In oracle, by default, one transaction can see the impact of DML operations of another transaction only when it is COMMITTED. If session 1 has performed a DML statement, but has not committed, the impact of that DML will not be visible to another session 2. The moment session 1 issues COMMIT, the same change becomes visible to the other session.

Assume a table "tbl_student" with 3 columns—ROLLNO, NAME, MARKS—and sequence of various SQL commands as shown in Figure 35.1.

Time	Transaction T1	Transaction T2
1	SQL> create table tbl_student (rollno number,name char(10), marks number); Table created. SQL> insert into tbl_student values (1, 'Satish',23); 1 row created. SQL> insert into tbl_student values (2, 'Mishkin',41); 1 row created. SQL> update tbl_student set name = 'Ronak' where rollno=1; 1 row updated.	
2	SQL> select * from tbl_student; ROLLNO NAME MARKS 1 Ronak 23 2 Mishkin 41 The effect of DML statements within the same transaction is visible immediately to that transaction.	Select * from tbl_student; *no rows selected*. The effect of DML statements of T1 is not visible to T2 as COMMIT has not been done in T1. Oracle does not allow uncommitted DMLs to be read by other transactions.

3	COMMIT:	
4	SQL> select * from tbl_student;	SQL> select * from tbl_student;

	ROLLNO	NAME	MARKS
	1	Ronak	23
	2	Mishkin	41

	ROLLNO	NAME	MARKS
	1	Ronak	23
	2	Mishkin	41

Figure 35.1 Impact of DML operation on transactions.

If one transaction performs a DML operation and does a ROLLBACK, then that change is never visible to the other session transaction as shown in Figure 35.2.

Time	Transaction T1	Transaction T2
1	SQL> select * from tbl_student;	

ROLLNO   NAME   MARKS

1   Satish   23
2   Mishkin   41

SQL> update tbl_student set name=
'Ronak' where rollno=1;
1 row updated.
SQL> commit;
Commit complete.
SQL> delete from tbl_student where
rollno=2;
1 row deleted. | |
| 2 | SQL> select * from tbl_student;

ROLLNO   NAME   MARKS

1   Ronak   23

Impact of DML operations within same
session are immediately visible. | SQL> select * from tbl_student;

ROLLNO   NAME   MARKS

1   Ronak   23
2   Mishkin   41

Only committed transactions of T1 are visible to
T2. As DELETE is not followed by COMMIT
therefore it is no reflected in T2. |
| 3 | ROLLBACK; | |
| 4 | SQL> select * from tbl_student;

ROLLNO   NAME   MARKS

1   Ronak   23
2   Mishkin   41

The ROLLBACK has undone the
DELETE command. Actually
ROLLBACK undoes all DML
operations until the last COMMIT. | SQL> select * from tbl_student;

ROLLNO   NAME   MARKS

1   Ronak   23
2   Mishkin   41 |

Figure 35.2 Impact of ROLLBACK on transactions.

35.3   PURPOSE OF TRANSACTION HANDLING

Transaction handling comes into play only when there are multiple concurrent users trying to modify the same record. The objective of transaction handling is to support highest concurrency and still maintaining the consistency of the database.

35.4   PROBLEMS DUE TO CONCURRENT TRANSACTIONS

Various data related problems may arise when multiple concurrent transactions are allowed to happen. Whenever we connect to the database user say "scott", a unique session is created. If we make one more connection to the database with same user "scott", then another unique session is created. A session may comprise one or more transactions. Here we will make separate transaction T1 through session 1 and transaction T2 through session 2.

35.4.1   Lost Update Problem

Transaction 1 updates a record and Commits. Transaction 2 then updates the same record with different values and Commits. Now, when session 1 reads the record, the changes made by session 2 are found, and the changes made by session 1 are lost.

Let us assume a table "tbl_rail" which has 3 columns – Boogie, Seat and Name of traveller. It has two records one each for seat 1 and 2 in S1 boogie. Initially both seats 1 and 2 are not assigned to any person, therefore, value in the name column is NULL as shown in Figure 35.3.

```
SQL> select * from tbl_rail;

BOOGIE     SEAT     NAME
_____   _____   _____

  S1         1
  S1         2
```

Figure 35.3   Vacant seats.

Transaction 1 now will allot seat 1 to traveller named "satish" and after sometime transaction T2 will allot the same seat to person named "mishkin" as shown in Figure 35.4.

Time	Transaction T1	Transaction T2
1	Update tbl_rail set name='satish' where boogie='S1' and seat=1;	
2	SQL> select * from tbl_rail; BO SEAT NAME ___ _____ _____ S1 1 Satish S1 2	SQL> select * from tbl_rail; BO SEAT NAME ___ _____ _____ S1 1 S1 2 As the UPDATE of T1 has not been committed therefore to T2 it appears that seat 1 is not allotted to anyone.

Contd...

3		Let us assume that T2 tries to allocate seat 1 to person named "Mishkin". SQL> update tbl_rail set name='Mishkin' where boogie='S1' and seat=1; WAITS ..... T1 updated the same record earlier but has not committed the same. Now T2 is updating the same record. By default Oracle does not allow two transactions to simultaneously update the same record. Therefore UPDATE statement of T2 waits for the T1 to complete the transaction by issuing COMMIT or ROLLBACK.
4	COMMIT;	1 row updated. The UPDATE of T2 automatically executes when T1 does a COMMIT.
5	SQL> select * from tbl_rail; BO SEAT NAME ―― ―― ―― S1 1 Satish S1 2 According to T1 seat 1 is allotted to Satish	SQL > select* from tbl_rail BO SEAT NAME ―― ―― ―― S1 1 Mishkin S1 2 According to T2 seat is allotted to Mishkin
6		COMMIT;
7	SQL> select * from tbl_rail; BO SEAT NAME ―― ―― ―― S1 1 Mishkin S1 2 As soon as T2 performs COMMIT, the seat 1 gets allotted to "Mishkin". But earlier as per T1 the seat was allotted to Satish. This is known as *the lost update problem*. The transaction which updates the same record last overrides the updates done by previous transactions	SQL> select * from tbl_rail; BO SEAT NAME ―― ―― ―― S1 1 Mishkin S1 2

Figure 35.4 Allotting seats.

It may appear from the earlier discussion that database is not able to maintain integrity in case of concurrent transactions. All DBMS provide various mechanisms to deal with such situations which will be discussed later in this chapter. The agenda here is just to highlight the data updating problem which may arise, if multiple transactions try to update the same record.

35.4.2   Phantom Reads

T1 reads a set of records with specified WHERE clause. T2 then adds a new record satisfying the same WHERE condition and COMMITs. Now when T1 executes the same SELECT command, it sees an additional record which seems to have appeared magically.

Figure 35.5 demonstrates the concept of Phantom Reads. Transaction T1 sees two records initially. Transaction T2 adds a new record and COMMITs the same. Now, when T1 fires the same query, it sees a new record. This is known as Phantom Read.

Time	Transaction T1	Transaction T2
1	SQL> select * from tbl_student where college='UIT'; COLL ROLLNO NAME UIT 1 Satish UIT 2 Mishkin	
2		SQL> insert into tbl_student values ('UIT',3,'Ronak'); 1 row created. SQL> commit; Commit complete.
3	SQL> select * from tbl_student where college='UIT'; COLL ROLLNO NAME UIT 1 Satish UIT 2 Mishkin UIT 3 Ronak T1 sees an additional record for roll no 3 which did not exist earlier.	

Figure 35.5 Phantom reads.

35.4.3 Non-repeatable READ

T1 reads a record. T2 modifies the same record and COMMITs. Now, when T1 reads the same record again, it sees the modified record. The first READ of T1 cannot be repeated with the same result. This concept has been explained in Figure 35.6.

Time	Transaction T1	Transaction T2
1	SQL> select * from tbl_student where college='UIT'; COLL ROLLNO NAME UIT 1 Satish UIT 2 Mishkin	
2		SQL> update tbl_student set name='Rishi' where rollno=2; 1 row updated. SQL> commit; Commit complete. Name for rollno 2 has been modified from "Mishkin" to "Rishi".

3	SQL> select * from tbl_student where college='UIT';	

COLL	ROLLNO	NAME
UIT	1	Satish
UIT	2	Rishi

T2 now sees the modified values for rollno 2.

Figure. 35.6   Non-repeatable read.

35.4.4   Dirty Reads (Uncommitted Dependency Problem)

This problem occurs when a transaction is allowed to read uncommitted data of another transaction. T1 modifies a record, but does not COMMIT. T2 reads the uncommitted row. Now, T1 rolls back the modification. The row now read by T2 is DIRTY as the change has been undone.

Oracle database does not allow DIRTY READS meaning that an uncommitted change by one transaction cannot be read by another transaction. This means that we cannot demonstrate the DIRTY READ problem in Oracle Database.

Figure 35.7 theoretically explains the DIRTY READ problem.

Time	Transaction T1	Transaction T2
1	ROLLNO — NAME 1 — Satish 2 — Mishkin	
2		ROLLNO — NAME 1 — Satish 2 — Mishkin
3	Update tbl_student set name='Ronak' where roll no=2;	
4		ROLLNO — NAME 1 — Satish 2 — Ronak Assuming that T2 is allowed to read uncommitted changes of T1.
5	ROLLBACK;	
6		ROLLNO — NAME 1 — Satish 2 — Mishkin

Figure 35.7   Dirty read.

35.4.5 Inconsistent Analysis Problem

Let us assume that at the end of the day a Bank is reconciling the net debit and credit for the day. If the number of accounts in the bank is huge then it will take some time for database to calculate the sum of debit and credit columns. While our program is calculating the SUM, it may happen that an individual performs a withdrawal/deposit transaction. Now, question arises whether this transaction should be considered for determining the net debit/credit for the day or not. If we do not consider this transaction then we will lend into Inconsistent Analysis Problem.

To demonstrate this we will create a program t1.sql which will calculate the net debit and credit for all the accounts using CURSOR. As our bank table is having very few records we will introduce time lapse for summing by using Oracle built-in package named DBMS_LOCK. By default a user cannot access this package, therefore, we will login as SYSDBA and grant EXECUTE privilege on DBMS_LOCK to SCOTT user. Till the time our program t1.sql is running, we will INSERT a new record from Transaction 2.

Assuming that tbl_bank has following records:

SQL> select * from tbl_bank;

ACCTID	TRANS_ID	TRANS_DATE	DEBIT	CREDIT
1	1	24-SEP-14	0	10000
2	2	24-SEP-14	0	8000
1	3	24-SEP-14	500	0
2	4	25-SEP-14	300	0
1	5	27-SEP-14	0	900

In Figure 35.8, transaction T1 is running the program to summarise net debit and credit. Meanwhile the program is executing, transaction T2 is adding a new record.

Time	Transaction T1	Transaction T2
1	SQL>connect system/system as SYSDBA	
2	SQL> grant execute on dbms_lock to scott; Grant succeeded.	
3	SQL>**connect scott/tiger**	SQL>**connect scott/tiger**

4	Contents of t1.sql
	 set serveroutput on
	 declare
	     v_total_debit number:=0;
	     v_total_credit number:=0;
	 begin
	 for c in
	 (select * from tbl_bank_transactions) loop
	     dbms_lock.sleep(5);
	     v_total_debit:=v_total_debit+c.debit;
	     v_total_credit:=v_total_credit+c.credit;
	 end loop;
		Contents of t2.sql
		 SQL> insert into tbl_bank_transactions
		 values (1,'TXN06',sysdate,200,0);
		
		 SQL> Commit;

Contd...

	dbms_output.put_line('TOTAL DEBIT: '||v_total_debit); dbms_output.put_line('TOTAL CREDIT: '||v_total_credit); end; /	
5	SQL> @t1.sql ..... takes some time to display result TOTAL DEBIT: 800 TOTAL CREDIT: 18900 PL/SQL procedure successfully completed. NOTE: **dbms_lock.sleep(5); introduces a delay of 5 seconds at each record**	
6	SQL> @t1.sql ..... takes some time to display result TOTAL DEBIT: 800 TOTAL CREDIT: 18900 PL/SQL procedure successfully completed. NOTE: Total debit is still shown as ₹ 800 even though t2.sql added a debit of 200 while t1.sql was calculating the sum of debit and credit. This is known as the Inconsistent Analysis Problem because as of time the TOTAL DEBIT in BANK is ₹ 1000 and not ₹ 800.	Soon after executing t1.sql from Transaction 1 we will execute t2.sql from Transaction 2. t2.sql should be executed before t1.sql completes. SQL> t2.sql

Figure 35.8 Inconsistent analysis problem.

This inconsistency happens because Oracle Database takes a kind of snapshot of the database whenever a transaction occurs. When t1.sql was started, the database did not contain the transaction made through t2.sql, therefore, the impact of t2.sql is not visible in t1.sql. In order to get a consistent analysis, the transactions must be stopped from occurring, while t1.sql is running. This can be achieved by stopping all the applications and SQL*Plus connections to the database, while a consistent analysis is being done. This is the reason why banks shut down the operations for few hours at the end of the day.

35.5 ACID PROPERTIES OF A DATABASE

A database management system must possess four basic properties to ensure the consistency of data:

35.5.1 Atomicity

All the SQL statements within a transaction must execute, and if any one of the statements fails then all the statements should fail. It is like "DO or DIE". DO implies every statement must be executed successfully and DIE implies, if any one statement fails then all other statements must fail.

Suppose a person X transfers an amount M from his bank account to another account of person Y, then this involves two steps:

(a) An amount M will be deducted from account X.

(b) An amount M will be added to account Y.

If both the steps execute successfully then there is no problem. But what if step 1 executes successfully but step 2 fails. Now, this is a dangerous situation wherein an amount has been deducted from one account, but the same has not been added to the other account. The atomicity principle says that both the transactions must be executed successfully or if any of the transaction fails then all the transactions must fail. This would mean that if step 2 fails then, step 1 must also fail. In technical terms step 1 should be rolled back, if step 2 fails. Moreover if step 1 fails, then step 2 should not be executed.

We will create a table tbl_bank with 3 columns namely acctid, name and balance. The data size of balance column will be kept as NUMBER(4).

Assume following two records:

SQL> select * from tbl_bank;		
ACCTID	NAME	BALANCE
1	Satish	5000
2	Mishkin	9000

We have intentionally taken data size of BALANCE column as NUMBER(4) and a balance of ₹ 9000 in account id 2. Now, we will transfer an amount of ₹ 2000 from account 1 to account 2. First step of deduction of amount ₹ 2000 from account 1 will be success and addition of same amount to account id 2 will fail because the net balance would become $9000 + 2000 = 11,000$ which cannot be accommodated by NUMBER(4) data type.

As per atomicity principle when step 2 fails then step 1 should be rolled back automatically. Let us a create a small PL/SQL program for transferring amount from one account to another as shown in Figure 35.9.

Line No	
1	Begin
2	
3	update tbl_bank set balance=balance - 2000 where acctid=1;
4	
5	update tbl_bank set balance=balance + 2000 where acctid=2;
6	
7	commit;
8	
9	end;
10	/

Figure 35.9 T3.sql.

Note that we have specified COMMIT as the last statement. This ensures that both step 1 and step 2 are part of the same transaction. If we specify COMMIT just after step 1 statement also then it will become a separate transaction from step 2 statement.

Let us now execute the t3.sql as shown in Figure 35.10.

```
SQL> @t3
ORA-01438: value larger than specified precision allowed for this column
ORA-06512: at line 5
```

Figure 35.10 Running t3.sql.

The program has ended with an ERROR at line 5 which implies that second UPDATE has failed. Let us check whether first UPDATE has been successful or not.

```
SQL> select * from tbl_bank;

ACCTID          NAME          BALANCE
_____          _____        _____
   1            Satish           5000
   2            Mishkin          9000
```

Figure 35.11 Status of UPDATE statements.

Figure 35.11 indicates that both the UPDATEs have failed and is perfectly in accordance with the ATOMICITY principle which states that either all transactions should execute or all should fail, if any one fails. As the second UPDATE has failed, therefore, Oracle database has rolled back the first UPDATE also.

We can improve the t3.sql program by using proper exception handling as shown in Figure 35.12.

```
set serveroutput on
begin
  update tbl_bank set balance=balance - 2000 where acctid=1;
  update tbl_bank set balance=balance + 2000 where acctid=2;
    commit;
exception
when others then
if SQLERRM like 'ORA-01438%' then
    dbms_output.put_line('Transaction Failed');
  else
    dbms_output.put_line(SQLERRM);
  end if;
end;
/
```

Figure 35.12 Using exception handling in t3.sql.

Oracle database always maintains the ATOMICITY principle for all transactions.

35.5.2 Consistency

The consistency ensures that the database is in a consistent state before the start of the transaction and remains in a consistent state after the transaction is done. The consistency has to be maintained whether the transaction is successful or not.

Example: Account X is having an initial balance of ₹ 5000 and account Y having an initial balance of ₹ 7000 of the same Bank. At this situation the net account balance of the bank is ₹ 12000. Now when an amount of ₹ 1000 is successfully debited from account X and successfully credited to account Y then the net value with bank should still be ₹ 12000. Although the amount in X will become ₹ 4000 and amount in Y would become ₹ 8000. If any of the credit or debit fails then the entire transaction must FAIL so as to retain the original consistent state of ₹ 12000 with X having ₹ 5000 and Y having ₹ 7000.

We learnt about applying various constraints like Primary Key, CHECK, DEFAULT, and FOREIGN KEY, etc. in Chapter 6. **Consistency also dictates that no data manipulation can bypass or override these constraints.** Suppose we create an EMPLOYEE table with a CHECK constraint that sum of SAL and COMM cannot be more than ₹ 10,000. Assuming that we already have a record wherein the SAL is ₹ 6000 and COMM is ₹ 3000. Now, if we try to update the same record setting SAL to ₹ 8000 then the statement/transaction must FAIL so as to preserve the consistency applied through CHECK constraint. **These constraints cannot be bypassed through any of the sources like SQL client, Web applications, Console applications or any other technology.** Figure 35.13 demonstrates this principle.

```
SQL> drop table employee;
SQL> create table employee (empno number,ename varchar2(10),sal number,comm number,
constraint cons_chk_sal_comm check ( sal + comm < 10000));
SQL> insert into employee values (1, 'satish',6000,3000);
commit;
SQL> update employee set sal=8000 where empno=1;
ERROR at line 1:
ORA-02290: check constraint (SCOTT.CONS_CHK_SAL_COMM) violated
SQL> select * from employee;
```

EMPNO	ENAME	SAL	COMM
1	Satish	6000	3000

Figure 35.13   Consistency for CHECK constraint.

Note that the Oracle database has not updated the record as it would have violated the Integrity CHECK Constraint.

35.5.3 Isolation

The isolation property ensures that the concurrent execution of transactions results in a system state that would be obtained, if transactions were executed serially, i.e., one after the other.

Concurrent transactions should not interfere with each other.

Depending on concurrency control method, the effects of an incomplete transaction might not even be visible to another transaction.

We assume two transactions execute at the same time, each attempting to modify the same data. One of the two must wait until the other completes in order to maintain isolation.

To understand isolation concept, let us assume that account A is having ₹ 1000, and account B is having ₹ 2000. Transaction T1 transfers an amount of ₹ 500 from account A to account B. At the same time transaction T2 transfers ₹ 200 from account B to account A.

Figure 35.14 shows the sequence of transactions T1 and T2.

Time Stamp	T1	T2
1	Balance in A = ₹ 1000	Balance in B = ₹ 2000
2	(x) A = A − 500	(p) B = B − 200
3	(y) B = B + 500	(q) A = A + 200

Figure 35.14   Concurrent transactions.

In no circumstance statement (y) executes before statement (x), and similarly statement (q) cannot execute before statement (p). This is the fundamental principle of any database transaction that all statements should be executed in a sequence. The database cannot pick statements at random within a transaction and execute them.

But we are also aware that databases use time slots to execute transactions. It may happen that first statement (x) is executed, followed by statement (p) then by (q) followed by (y). Following six sequences (Figure 35.15) of statements may execute which are called schedules:

Schedule 1	x → y → p → q
Schedule 2	x → p → q → y
Schedule 3	x → p → y → q
Schedule 4	p → q → x → y
Schedule 5	p → x → y → q
Schedule 6	p → x → q → y

Figure 35.15   Schedules.

Isolation principle simply states that the two concurrent transactions execute in isolation irrespective of each other. In strict isolation mode even after T1 and T2 has been run at the same time, but still they will execute one after the other only as both of them are interfering with each other. Interference means both are updating each others records.

The sequence of statements being executed is very crucial from the point of recovering from statement failures. In Schedule 1, if statement (y) fails then T1 is rolled back, and T2 will execute successfully. Similarly, if statement (q) fails then T1 will execute successfully, and T2 will be rolled back. Same logic applies to Schedule 4.

Let us now assume that Schedule 2 is followed and all statements are success as shown in Figure 35.16.

Time	T1	T2
Initially	A = 1000	B = 2000
1	(x) A = A − 500 A = 500	
2		(p) B = B − 200 B = 1800
3		(q) A = A + 200 A = 700
4	(y) B = B + 500 B = 2300	
5	A = 700	B = 2300

Figure 35.16   Schedule 2.

After the successful execution of T1 and T2, the net balance of A is ₹ 700 and that of B is ₹ 2300.

Let us assume that statement x, p, q are success and y fails. A statement may fail due to power failure, database service down, hard disk corruption, file system corruption, etc. Figure 35.17 shows the result of successful execution of statements (x),(p),(q) and failure of (y).

Time	T1	T2
Initially	A = 1000	B = 2000
1	(x) A = A − 500 **SUCCESS** A = 500	B = 2000
2		(p) B = B − 200 **SUCCESS** A = 500, B = 1800
3		(q) A = A + 200 **SUCCESS** A = 700, B = 1800
4	(y) B = B + 500 **FAILS** A = 500, B = 1800	

Figure 35.17 Schedule x,p,q,y and y failing.

This is landing into a highly inconsistent state. Account A net balance is ₹ 500 and that of account B is ₹ 1800. The above scenario violates the atomicity principle also. In order to deal with such concurrent updating situation databases like Oracle use record locking mechanism.

Figure 35.18 contains the code to create the table, and Figure 35.19 contains the statements executed on Oracle database for concurrent access to same accounts in different transactions.

```
SQL> drop table tbl_bank;
SQL> create table tbl_bank(acctid char(1), name varchar2(10), balance number);
SQL> insert into tbl_bank values ('A','Satish',1000);
SQL> insert into tbl_bank values ('B','Mishkin',2000);
SQL> commit;
```

Figure 35.18 Create table tbl_bank for concurrent transactions.

Whenever a record id being updated in a transaction, it is first locked exclusively before the actual update happens. Now, if another transaction tries to update the same record then the lock placed by first transaction must be released before new lock is acquired by the second transaction. The lock is released by a transaction only when COMMIT or ROLLBACK is fired in that transaction.

Time	Transaction T1	Transaction T2
1	(x) Update tbl_bank set balance = balance – 500 where acctid='A'; *The account A record is locked till COMMIT or ROLLBACK*	
2		(p) Update tbl_bank set balance = balance – 200 where acctid='B'; *The account B record is locked till COMMITT or ROLLBACK*
3		(q) Update tbl_bank set balance = balance + 200 where acctid='A'; **WAITS...** **This waits because T1 has locked the A record**
4	(y) Update tbl_bank set balance = balance + 500 where acctid='B'; **WAITS...** **This waits because T2 has locked the A record**	
5		*T2 waiting for T1 to release lock on A account and T1 is waiting for T2 to release lock on B account. This is called deadlock.* *Oracle database automatically detects deadlocks and returns the following message automatically* **ORA-00060: deadlock detected while waiting for resource**
6		**As ERROR has occurred in T2 then it must be ROLLED BACK** ROLLBACK;
7	***Update of time 4, statement (y) succeeds....***	
8		SQL> select * from tbl_bank; A NAME BALANCE ―――――――― ―――――――― A Satish 1000 B Mishkin 2000 **As T2 rolled back both statements (p) & (q) reverted. Moreover as T1 has not been committed therefore its impact is also not visible.**

9	*As T1 has succeeded it should be committed* COMMIT;	

10	SQL> select * from tbl_bank;
	
	  A NAME BALANCE
	  ——— ———
	  A Satish 500
	  B Mishkin 2500
		SQL> select * from tbl_bank;
		
		  A NAME BALANCE
		  ——— ———
		  A Satish 500
		  B Mishkin 2500

Figure 35.19 Statements for concurrent updating.

Finally by record locking mechanism, Oracle has successfully performed transaction T1 and rolled back the impact of transaction T2.

A better approach to deal with record locking and thereby allowing concurrent conflicting transactions is to use explicit row locking programmatically. Now, we will create a PL/SQL program (Figure 35.20) to replace the transactions T1 and T2.

Line No	Program Code
1	set serveroutput on
2	declare
3	v_acctid char(1);
4	begin
5	—statement (x)
6	select acctid into v_acctid from tbl_bank where acctid='A' for update nowait;
7	update tbl_bank set balance=balance - 500 where acctid='A';
8	**dbms_lock.sleep(10);**
9	—statement (y)
10	select acctid into v_acctid from tbl_bank where acctid='B' for update nowait;
11	update tbl_bank set balance=balance + 500 where acctid='B';
12	commit;
13	exception
14	when others then
15	if SQLERRM like 'ORA-00054%' then —*Resource Busy*
16	rollback;
17	dbms_output.put_line('Transaction Failed....Please try later');
18	end if;
19	end;
20	/

Figure 35.20 T1.sql.

Line No	Program Code
1	set serveroutput on
2	declare
3	v_acctid char(1);
4	begin
5	**—statement (p)**
6	select acctid into v_acctid from tbl_bank where acctid='B' for update nowait;
7	update tbl_bank set balance=balance - 200 where acctid='B';
8	**—statement (q)**
9	select acctid into v_acctid from tbl_bank where acctid='A' for update nowait;
10	update tbl_bank set balance=balance + 200 where acctid='A';
11	commit;
12	exception
13	when others then
14	if SQLERRM like 'ORA-00054%' then **—resource busy**
15	rollback;
16	dbms_output.put_line('Transaction Failed....Please try later');
17	end if;
18	
19	end;
20	/

Figure 35.21 T2.sql.

We have designed the t1.sql and t2.sql in such a way that statement (x) is executed first followed by a sleep time of 10 seconds so that statement (p) of t2.sql gets executed next, followed by statement (q) which is then followed by statement (y) of t1.sql.

Run t1.sql in one session and soon after run t2.sql in another session as shown in Figure 35.22.

Time	Transaction T1.sql	Transaction T2.sql
1	SQL>@t1.sql	
2	Statement (x) will be executed followed by a sleep time of 10 seconds	SQL>@t2.sql
3		Statement (p) will be executed successfully.
4		Statement (q) will be executed and will FAIL as account A record is already locked by statement (x) and EXCEPTION section code will be executed.
5		
6		
7		
8		

Contd...

9		
10	PL/SQL procedure successfully completed.	Transaction Failed....Please try later PL/SQL procedure successfully completed.
11	SQL> select * from tbl_bank; A NAME BALANCE ——— ——— A Satish 500 B Mishkin 2500	SQL> select * from tbl_bank; A NAME BALANCE ——— ——— A Satish 500 B Mishkin 2500

Figure 35.22   Programmatic record locking to handle concurrency.

This simply means that T1 has executed successfully, whereas T2 has been rolled back.

35.6 ISOLATION LEVELS

To deal with various issues associated with concurrent transactions, databases support different levels of isolation so that concurrent transactions do not interfere with each other. Some of the following isolation modes allow for maximum concurrency with least consistency, whereas others allow for least concurrency, but highest consistency.

- Read uncommitted
- Read committed
- Repeatable read
- Serializable

The classification between these isolation levels depends on whether or not they allow Phantom Reads, Non-repeatable Reads and Dirty Reads. Figure 35.23 shows the detailed support for the problems related to concurrent transactions in various isolation levels.

	Phantom Reads	**Non-repeatable Reads**	**Dirty Read**
Read uncommitted	Yes	Yes	Yes
Read committed	Yes	Yes	No
Repeatable read	Yes	No	No
Serializable	No	No	No

Figure 35.23 Isolation levels.

When dealing with concurrent transactions, we have to consider two different scenarios:

1. *When different transactions are accessing different records.* This does not need any special treatment as transactions are manipulating different records/resources which may occur at the same time without any interference. By access we are referring to DML operations.

2. *When different transactions are accessing same record.* This needs special consideration as the different transactions may manipulate the same record with different values. This is where the isolation levels and record locking comes into play so as to maintain the consistency of database.

35.6.1 Read Uncommitted

Read Uncommitted implies that if a record has been modified by one transaction, but not committed still that modification will be visible to the other transactions. Because of this mode of operation, it will allow Phantom Reads, Non-repeatable Reads and Dirty Reads. This allows for highest concurrency, but least consistency.

The above table (Figure 35.23) simply implies that Read uncommitted isolation level allows Phantom Reads, Non-repeatable Reads and Dirty Reads. As such this can cause serious consistency problems, but can allow maximum concurrent transactions modifying different records. This mode should be used in applications wherein possibility of concurrent transactions accessing same resource does not exist. Concurrency can be in two possible situations. One situation is when different transactions are accessing different records, and the second is when different transactions are accessing same record. Consistency issues arise in later situation.

35.6.2 Read Committed

In this level, one transaction can see the changes of another transaction only when it is committed. This mode allows for Phantom Reads and Non-repeatable reads, but does not allow Dirty Reads. Databases generally allow READ COMMITTED level which when used in conjunction with programmatically locking of records to preserve consistency with maximum concurrency.

35.6.3 Repeatable Read

This level allows Phantom Reads, but does not allow Non-repeatable reads and Dirty Reads. This is more restrictive level from Read Committed. Restrictive in the sense that it will support lesser number of concurrent transactions with greater consistency.

35.6.4 Serializable

This is the most restrictive level in which no Phantom Reads, Non-repeatable Reads and Dirty Reads are allowed. It assumes that no two concurrent transactions occur, and each is executed in isolation with the other. The transactions occur one after the other only in a serial fashion. This allows for greatest consistency, but brings in least concurrency.

35.7 ORACLE ISOLATION LEVELS

Oracle database supports two isolation levels, namely.

35.7.1 Serializable

Schedule 1 and 4 of Figure 35.15 are said to be running in **Strict Isolation mode technically called SERIALIZABLE**. Serializability means all statements of one transaction are executed followed by all statements of another interfering transaction. No interleaving of statements across transactions is allowed and as such it is the isolation level which provides highest consistency. But Serializability reduces the parallel execution of concurrent transactions and hence is not the preferred choice as it cannot support a large number of transactions in a given period of time. Let us know understand the behaviour of Serializable isolation level in Oracle. Figure 35.24 shows two transactions running in Serializable isolation level.

Time	Transaction T1	Transaction T2
1	set transaction isolation level serializable;	set transaction isolation level serializable;
2	(x) Update tbl_bank set balance=balance - 500 where acctid='A';	
3		(p) Update tbl_bank set balance=balance - 200 where acctid='B';
4		(q) Update tbl_bank set balance=balance + 200 where acctid='A'; **WAITS....** **ERROR: ORA-08177: can't serialize access for this transaction**
5		As the ERROR has occurred we should rollback the transaction ROLLBACK;
6	(y) Update tbl_bank set balance=balance + 500 where acctid='B'; 1 row updated	
7	COMMIT;	
8	T1 successful	T2 failed and Rolled Back

Figure 35.24   Isolation level—Serializable.

35.7.2   Read Committed

This is the default isolation level supported by Oracle database. In this level, Non-repeatable reads and Phantom reads are allowed, but Dirty reads are not allowed. As such this level may lead to inconsistencies during interleaving concurrent transactions. Therefore, to attain highest concurrency with interleaving transactions, manual record locking is used to maintain the consistency also. Figure 35.25 represents the programmatic approach used in Read Committed isolation level to provide consistency in overlapping concurrent transactions. The command to change to the Read Committed Isolation level is

SQL> set transaction isolation level read committed;

Before executing an UPDATE the session can lock the record for exclusive changes using SELECT... FOR UPDATE statement as shown in Figure 35.25 time slot 2. Once a record is locked by a session then that record becomes unavailable to other sessions for update. If any other session tries to update the same record then Oracle displays an error message as shown in time slot 3. After locking the record session 1 can peform actual UPDATE operation thereby releasing the lock. Now when session 2 executes SELECT .... FOR UPDATE for the same record it is not displayed

Time	Transaction T1	Transaction T2
1	SQL> set transaction read committed;	SQL> set transaction read committed;
2	SQL> select * from tbl_rail where name is null and boogie='S1' and seat=1 for update nowait; BO SEAT NAME ___ _____ S1 1	
3		SQL> select * from tbl_rail where name is null and boogie='S1' and seat=1 for update nowait; ERROR at line 1: ORA-00054: resource busy and acquire with NOWAIT specified or timeout expired
4	SQL> update tbl_rail set name='Satish' where name is null and boogie='S1' and seat=1; 1 row updated.	
5	SQL> commit; Commit complete.	
6		SQL> select * from tbl_rail where name is null and boogie='S1' and seat=1 for up date; no rows selected

Figure 35.25   Read Committed

35.7.3   Read Only

Oracle supports one more isolation level called Read Only which is similar to Serializable except that no DML operations can be performed during this mode.

Figure 35.26 contains the code to set the Read Only isolation level and perform a DML operation.

T1
SQL> set transaction read only; Transaction set. SQL> update tbl_bank set balance = balance -200 where acctid='A'; update tbl_bank set balance = balance -200 where acctid='A' * ERROR at line 1: ORA-01456: may not perform insert/delete/update operation inside a READ ONLY transaction

Figure 35.26   Read only isolation level.

35.8 DURABILITY

After a transaction is committed, the changes are preserved irrespective of any failure like HD, Server H/W, DB crashes, Power Failure. If we book a ticket online and get a success message then that will remain permanent even if the system crashes. To maintain the durability Oracle database flushes the transaction logs into hard disk before acknowledging commit. In SQL command prompt when after performing a DML operation we execute COMMIT and the system displays "Commit complete. ..." then that transaction must persist even after Database, OS or application crash.

Index